Accounting for
Non-Accounting Students

Accounting for Non-Accounting Students

THIRD EDITION

J R Dyson

Department of Accounting and Law, Napier University, Edinburgh

PITMAN PUBLISHING

PITMAN PUBLISHING
128 Long Acre, London WC2E 9AN

A Division of Longman Group Limited

First published in 1987
Second edition 1991
Third edition 1994

© J R Dyson 1987, 1991, 1994

A CIP catalogue record for this book can be obtained from the British Library.

ISBN 0 273 60435 X

Typeset by PanTek Arts, Maidstone, Kent.
Printed and bound at the Bath Press.

The Publishers' policy is to use paper manufactured from sustainable forests.

To Auntie Clarice

CONTENTS

Preface   xi

Acknowledgements   xvii

Part 1 INTRODUCTION TO ACCOUNTING

1 **The accounting world**   3

Learning objectives • The nature and purpose of accounting • Accounting
and the non-accountant • Branches of accounting • The accountancy profession •
Types of entity • Conclusion • Key points • Check your learning • Answers •
Questions

2 **Accounting rules**   22

Learning objectives • Boundary rules • Measurement rules • Ethical rules •
The basic accounting rules restated • A conceptual framework • Conclusion •
Key points • Check your learning • Answers • Questions

Part 2 FINANCIAL ACCOUNTING

3 **Recording accounting information**   41

Learning objectives • The dual aspect rule • Recording information • A ledger
account example • Balancing the accounts • The trial balance • Conclusion •
Key points • Check your learning • Answers • Questions

4 **Basic financial statements**   71

Learning objectives • The measurement of profit • Preparation of the basic
financial statements • An illustrative example • Format of accounts • Post-trial
balance adjustments • A comprehensive example • Estimating accounting
profit • Conclusion • Key points • Check your learning • Answers • Questions

5 **Manufacturing accounts**   110

Learning objectives • Contents • Construction • A comprehensive example •
Conclusion • Key points • Check your learning • Answers • Questions

6 **Partnership and company accounts**   130

Learning objectives • Partnerships • Limited liability companies • Structure
and operation • The profit and loss account • The balance sheet •
A comprehensive example • Conclusion • Key points • Check your
learning • Answers • Questions

7 **Cash flow statements**   157

Learning objectives • Accounting profit and cash flow • Format and contents •
A comprehensive example • Cash and cash equivalents • Direct and indirect
methods • Conclusion • Key points • Check your learning • Answers •
Questions

8 **Interpretation of accounts**   180

Learning objectives • Background to interpretation • Ratio analysis •
Profitability ratios • Liquidity ratios • Efficiency ratios • Investment ratios •
An illustrative example • Interpretation • Conclusion • Key points • Check
your learning • Answers • Summary of the main ratios • Questions

Part 3 COST AND MANAGEMENT ACCOUNTING

9 **Basic cost accounting procedures**   219

Learning objectives • Nature and purpose • Historical review • Planning and
control • The implementation procedure • Conclusion • Key points • Check
your learning • Answers • Questions

10 **Direct costs**   237

Learning objectives • Direct material costs • Choice of pricing method •
Direct labour • Other direct costs • Conclusion • Key points • Check your
learning • Answers • Questions

11 **Indirect costs**   256

Learning objectives • Production overhead • A comprehensive example •
Non-production overhead • Predetermined rates • Conclusion • Key points •
Check your learning • Answers • Questions

12 **Marginal costing**   280

Learning objectives • The problem of fixed costs • The marginal costing
system • The application of marginal costing • Criticisms of marginal costing •
Marginal costing formulae • An illustrative example • Limiting factors •
Conclusion • Key points • Check your learning • Answers • Questions

13 **Product costing systems and recent developments**   301

Learning objectives • Costing methods • Some recent developments
Conclusion • Key points • Check your learning • Answers • Questions

14 **Budgetary control**   319

Learning objectives • Budgeting and budgetary control • Budget procedure
Functional budgets • An illustrative example of functional budgets • Fixed
and flexible budgets • Conclusion • Key points • Check your learning •
Answers • Questions

15 **Standard costing**   342

Learning objectives • Background and administration • Variance analysis •
An illustrative example • Sales variances • Operating statements •
Conclusion • Key points • Check your learning • Answers • Questions

16 **Capital investment appraisal**   372

Learning objectives • The background • The selection of projects •
Sources of funds • Conclusion • Key points • Check your learning •
Answers • Questions

Part 4 ANNUAL REPORTS

17 **Disclosure of information**   399

Learning objectives • Minimum disclosure requirements • Contents of an
annual report • Conclusion • Key points • Check your learning • Answers •
Questions

18 **The principal reports**   406

Learning objectives • The chairman's report • The directors' report • The
auditors' report • Conclusion • Key points • Check your learning •
Answers

19 **The main financial statements**   413

Learning objectives • The background to published accounts • Additional
features • The group profit and loss account • The group balance sheet •
Group cash flow statements • Conclusion • Key points • Check your
learning • Answers

20 **Supplementary financial reports and other issues**   428

Learning objectives • Common supplementary reports • Less common
supplementary reports • Current financial reporting issues • Conclusion •
Key points • Check your learning • Answers • Assignment on company
reporting

Part 5 CASE STUDIES   457

1 The realization concept
2 Interpretation of accounts
3 The usefulness of financial reports
4 Cost and management accounting systems
5 Product pricing
6 Budgetary control

Appendix 1: Further reading   483

Appendix 2: Discount table   484

Appendix 3: Answers to end-of-chapter questions   485

Index   569

PREFACE

This is a book for non-accountants. It is intended primarily for students who are required to study accounting as part of a non-accounting degree or professional studies course. It should also be of value to those working in commerce, government or industry who find that their work involves them in dealing with accounting information. It is hoped that the book will help to explain why there is need for such information.

Non-accounting students (such as engineers, personnel managers, purchasing officers, and sales managers) are sometimes unable to understand why they are required to study accounting. This is often found to be the case when they have to take an examination in the subject, and they are then presented with a paper of some considerable technical rigour.

Accounting books written specifically for the non-accountant are also often extremely demanding. The subject needs to be covered in such a way that non-accounting students do not become confused by too much technical information. They do not require the same detailed analysis that is only of relevance to the professional accountant. Some accounting books specially written for the non-accountant go to the opposite extreme. They outline the subject so superficially that they are of no real practical help either to examination candidates or to those non-specialists requiring some guidance on practical accounting problems.

The aim of this book is to serve as a good introduction to the study of accounting. The subject is not covered superficially. In parts, the book goes into considerable detail, but only where it is necessary for a real understanding of the subject. It is appreciated that non-accountants are unlikely to be involved in the *detailed* preparation of accounting information such as, for example, in the compilation of a company's annual accounts. However, if such accounts are to provide the maximum possible benefit to their users, it is desirable that users should have a good knowledge of how they are prepared and how to extract the maximum possible information from them.

This concept is analogous to that of driving a car. It is perfectly possible to drive a car without knowing anything about how it works. However, to get the best possible performance from the car, it is useful to know something about the engine. It is not necessary to know as much about the car as a motor mechanic. All that is required is just sufficient knowledge to be able to drive the car so that is operates at its maximum efficiency. Similarly, it is not absolutely necessary to know how to prepare accounts to be able to use them, but they will mean a great deal more if the user knows something about their construction.

THE BACKGROUND TO THE BOOK

Many colleges and universities now run a number of degree and diploma courses which include accounting as a compulsory subject. Whilst the syllabuses for such courses have sometimes to be approved by external bodies, the detailed contents of the syllabuses are often left to the individual lecturer to decide. This book has been written with that type of course especially in mind.

The material contained in the book has been designed so that it can be covered in about 90 class contact hours. If more time is available, there will be an opportunity for students to tackle additional exercises in the classroom under the general supervision of their lecturer, but if less class contact time is available, it will probably be necessary for students to work largely unsupervised.

The book is divided into four main parts. Part 1 puts the subject of accounting into context. Part 2 deals with financial accounting, and Part 3 with cost and management accounting. It is possible that most students will more readily identify with Part 3 of this book, since cost and management accounting probably relates more directly to their current day-to-day responsibilities. It might seem more logical, therefore, to begin by studying that branch of accounting, but experience suggests that students find it very difficult to understand cost and management accounting if they have not first studied financial accounting. Part 4 of the book outlines the contents of a limited liability company's annual report. Some lecturers may prefer to cover this part of the book before moving on to cost and management accounting. It would then be possible to link directly and immediately the material covered in Chapter 8 on the interpretation of accounts with the information contained in a company's annual report.

However, the section on annual reports has been placed at the end of the book for two main reasons:

1 The contents may not be of immediate interest to most non-accounting students until they become senior officers in their respective companies; and
2 this subject requires an almost unlimited amount of class contact hours, so that is is perhaps best left to the end of the course when lecturers will know how much spare time they have available.

THE THIRD EDITION

The response from both lecturers and students to the earlier editions of this book has been most encouraging, so that it is with very great pleasure that both the author and the publisher present the third edition.

This new edition has been completely revised and re-written, but for convenience the main changes are summarized below:

1 The learning objectives have been made more positive.
2 Each chapter is preceded with a topical news item relating broadly to the contents of that chapter.
3 Additional diagrams have been added to most chapters.
4 'Key points' have been added at the end of each chapter.
5 All chapters now conclude with 'Check your learning' questions (with answers), and these link up with the learning objectives summarized at the beginning of each chapter.
6 Chapter 7 on source and application of funds has been replaced by a new chapter on cash flow statements.
7 Chapter 12 now becomes the marginal costing chapter.
8 Chapter 13 deals with product costing systems, but it also covers recent developments in management accounting. Cost book-keeping is no longer included.
9 Chapter 20 has been extended so that it includes more types of financial reports, as well as a brief outline of some current issues in financial reporting.
10 A fifth part containing six case studies has been added to the book. Three of the cases deal with financial accounting problems, and three with management accounting issues. These case studies complement the text. Their aim is to encourage students to find out more for themselves, e.g. by using the library, and by investigating what is happening in the real world. There are no specific solutions to these case studies, but some guidelines will be found in the *Lecturer's Guide*.

Prior to the preparation of this edition, many lecturers and students gave me some extremely helpful suggestions for improving the book. I have tried to incorporate all of these (at least in part if not in whole). For example, some lecturers wanted more on partnership accounts, or on process costing. I appreciate that the demands of certain courses may require these topics to be covered in come detail, but I would still question whether *non-accounting* students really do need to be able to deal with (say) partnership dissolution, or with the intricacies of equivalent units.

I was also encouraged to include some material on current issues and developments in accounting, and the list of suggestions became somewhat formidable! I hope lecturers will appreciate that in a book of this nature, it is not possible to include everything; I have had to be both selective and brief. Thus, I have not been able to give much space to topics such as ABC, strategic management accounting, corporate governance, or 'green' accounting. None the less, in this edition, there is now some reference to many such issues, and so lecturers should at least be able to refer their students to them.

Even so, I would urge some caution. This is a book mainly for *non-accountants* at about *first-year degree level*. I would recommend lecturers not to try to do too much too quickly. I think that at the beginning of their course, it is important to get across to students what accountants do, how they do it, and why. This can then be followed by a critical review of the procedures, and a search for better ways of doing things. I believe that the basic principles of accounting can best be established by using quantitative examples, and I think this applies just as much to non-accounting students as it does to accounting ones. That is why the book contains a great many calculative exhibits and exercises. Lecturers should, however, aim to go beyond getting a mere arithmetic solution. They should encourage students to question what and why something has been done, and what use it is likely to be.

I know that such an approach is not easy. There can be severe time constraints on running classes in such a way, and lecturers are often under pressure 'to get through the syllabus'. Indeed, as long as 'the' answer agrees with the back of the book, there is a tendency to rush on to the next chapter.

HOW TO USE THE BOOK

Lecturers will have their own way of introducing the various subjects. It is to be hoped, however, that they will still use the various exhibits in the book to demonstrate particular accounting procedures. It is believed that lecturers spend far too much time photocopying questions for use in lectures. The students then spend their time in lectures trying to take down what the lecturer is writing on the blackboard without really listening to what he is saying.

If this book is used as it is intended, it is not necessary for lecturers to photocopy additional exhibits and answers. The book contains sufficient exhibits for most one-year courses, and every exhibit is followed by a detailed solution. Thus there is no need for students to copy answers that have been written on the blackboard: they should be able to listen to the lecturer as each point is demonstrated step by step.

Most chapters are also followed by a number of tutorial exercises. Since detailed solutions for these questions are contained in Appendix 3, lecturers will also be spared having to provide solutions of their own.

There are, however, some additional questions at the end of most chapters. The answers to these questions are included in a separate *Lecturer's Guide* which is available at no cost to *bona fide* lecturers on application to the publishers.

A WORD TO STUDENTS

If you are using this book as part of a formal course, your lecturer will provide you with a work scheme which will outline just how much of the book you are expected to cover each week. In addition to the work done in your lecture, you will probably have to read each chapter two or three times. As you read a chapter work through each exhibit, and then have a go at doing it without reference to the solution.

You are also recommended to attempt as many of the questions that follow each chapter as you can, but avoid looking at the solutions until you are absolutely certain that you do not know how to answer the question. The more questions that you attempt, the more confident you will be that you really do understand the subject matter. However, you must not spend all your time studying accounting, so make sure that you put enough time into your other subjects

Many students study accounting without having the benefit of attending lectures. If you fall into this category, it is suggested that you adopt the following study plan:

1 Organize your private study so that you have covered every topic in your syllabus by the time of your examination. You will probably need to allow for extra time to be spent on Chapters 3, 4, 8, 12 and 15.
2 Read each chapter slowly, being careful to work through each exhibit. Do not worry if you do not immediately understand each point: read on to the end of the chapter.
3 Read the chapter again, this time making sure that you do understand each point. Try doing each exhibit without looking at the solution.
4 Attempt as many questions at the end of the chapter as you can, but do not look at the solutions until you have finished or you are certain that you cannot do the question.
5 If you have time, re-read the chapter.

One word of caution. Accounting is not simply a matter of elementary arithmetic. The solution to many accounting problems often calls for a considerable amount of personal judgement, and hence there is bound to be some degree of subjectivity attached to the solution.

The problems demonstrated in this book are not readily solved in the real world, and the suggested answers ought to be subject to a great deal of argument and discussion. It follows that non-accountants ought to be severely critical of any accounting information that is supplied to them, although it is difficult to be constructive in your criticism unless you have some knowledge of the subject matter.

By the end of this book, you should have a sufficient knowledge of accounting to be able to examine critically and constructively much of the accounting information that you are likely to meet. In addition, if you have to take an examination in accounting, you should be able to pass it with flying colours!

A REQUEST

As on previous occasions, I hope that both lecturers and students will write to me about how they have found the book. I am well aware that there are bound to be improvements that can still be made to it, but I have tried (following total quality management principles) to get it right (even if it is the *third* time!). Please let me know whether or not I have succeeded.

ACKNOWLEDGEMENTS

This book could not have been written without the help of a considerable number of people. Many of them have contributed directly to the ideas that have gone into the writing of it, while in other cases I am aware that I have absorbed their views without always being fully conscious of doing so.

I am indebted to far too many colleagues, friends and relatives to name them all individually, but I would like to place on record my thanks to all of my colleagues in the Business School and the Department of Mathematics at Napier University. Without their ready assistance and tolerant benevolence, this book would be all the poorer. I would also like to thank all those lecturers and students elsewhere who have made various suggestions of improving the third edition. As mentioned in the Preface, all their ideas have been carefully considered, and most of them have been incorporated.

My thanks are also due to the Chartered Institute of Management Accountants, and to the Editors of the *Financial Times*, the *Guardian, The Press Association* and *The Scotsman* for permission to reproduce copyright material. This material may not be reproduced, copied or transmitted unless written permission is obtained from the original owner or publisher. I hope that the inclusion of some actual news stories will enliven the introduction to each chapter, and I also hope that it will encourage students to read regularly the financial pages of some high-quality newspapers!

An explanation
To avoid tedious repetition and tortuous circumlocution, the masculine pronoun has been adopted in this book. No offence is intended to anyone, most of all my female readers, and I hope none will be taken.

PART 1

Introduction to accounting

CHAPTER 1

The accounting world

£50m experts criticised in Maxwell funds hunt

SARAH WHITEBLOOM

MPs yesterday severely criticised top City firms which have already run up £50 million fees in the search for the missing Maxwell millions – while only recovering a fraction of the pension funds.

The all-party Commons social security select committee voiced serious concerns over the length of time that highly paid accountants and lawyers were taking to recover assets.

The committee estimates that the six firms of City professionals will have scooped £100 mllion by the time they have finished. This level of fees, they say, cannot be justified.

Only £20 million of the £460 million "illegally removed" from pension funds has been recovered. Liquidators and administrators are charging fees of up to £191 per hour with principal partners commanding far more.

The MPs recommend that Mirror Group Newspapers provide financial support to the Maxwell pensioners, who have been particularly hard-hit by the collapse.

With the recovery procedure likely to take another three or four years, the MPs argue: "Unless the authorities take drastic action soon it will take several more to complete the tidying up of the whole Maxwell process."

The report calls for a review of procedures for monitoring insolvencies, and suggests that independent monitors be appointed to all high-value cases.

The accountants Robson Rhodes, liquidators of Bishopsgate Investment Management – the Maxwell firm managing pension assets through which the missing millions disappeared – come in for particular criticism over the time it is taking to recover funds. Its fees amount to more than £2.6 million. Its legal adviser, Stephenson Harwood, has netted £2.9 million.

MPs were impressed at progress of the Maxwell private companies' administrator Arthur Andersen – which has charged £12.4 million so far.

However, for Price Waterhouse, administrator of Maxwell Communication Corporation, and its lawyer Norton Rose, the committee notes it is unfortunate that their fees are the highest, given they are the prime professionals with the longest job to do.

The Guardian, 27 July 1993

Exhibit 1.0 Accounting has for a long time been considered a well-paid profession, as perhaps this article from the *Guardian* confirms.

This chapter is an introduction to the world of accounting. It begins with an explanation of the nature and purpose of accounting. This is followed by a section outlining the reasons why it is important for non-accountants to study the subject. The next section describes briefly the main branches of accounting. A further section summarizes the basic structure of the accountancy profession. The final section describes the major types of organization or entity that we will be covering in the book.

LEARNING OBJECTIVES

By the end of this chapter, you will be able to:
● define the nature and purpose of accounting;
● explain why non-accountants need to know something about accounting;
● identify eight main branches of accounting;
● list six United Kingdom professional accountancy bodies;
● describe three different types of business organizations.

THE NATURE AND PUPOSE OF ACCOUNTING

The word *account* in everyday language is often used as a substitute for an *explanation* or a *report* of certain actions or events. If you are an employee, for example, you may have to explain to your employer just how you have been spending your time, or if you are a manager, you may have to report to the owner on how the business is doing. In order to explain or to report, you will, of course, have to remember what you were doing or what happened. As it is not always easy to remember, you may need to keep some written record. In effect, such records can be said to form the basis of a rudimentary accounting (or reporting) system.

In a primitive sense, man has always been involved in some form of accounting. It may have gone no further than a farmer (say) measuring his worth simply by *counting* the number of cows or sheep that he owned. However, the growth of a monetary system enabled a more sophisticated method to be developed. It then became possible to calculate the increase or decrease in individual wealth over a period of time, and to assess whether (say) a farmer with ten cows and fifty sheep was wealthier than one who had sixty pigs. Exhibit 1.1 illustrates just how difficult it would be to assess the wealth of a farmer in a non-monetary system.

Even with the growth of a monetary system, it took a very long time for formal documentary systems to become common, although it is possible to trace the origins of modern book-keeping at least as far back as the twelfth century. We know that from about that time, traders began to adopt a system of recording information that we now refer to as *double-entry book-keeping*. By the end of the fifteenth century, double-entry book-keeping was widely used in Venice and the surrounding areas. Indeed, the first-known book on the subject was published in 1494 by an Italian mathematician called Pacioli. Modern book-keeping systems are still based on principles established in the fifteenth century, although they have had to be adapted to suit modern conditions.

Why has a recording system devised in medieval times lasted for so long? There are two main reasons:

1 it provides an accurate record of what has happened to a business over a specified period of time;

Exhibit 1.1 Accounting for a farmer's wealth

His possessions	A year ago	Now	Change
Cows	● ● ● ● ● ● ● ● ● ●	● ● ● ● ● ● ● ● ● ● ● ● ● ● ● ●	+5
Hens [● = 10]	● ● ● ● ● ● ● ● ● ●	● ● ● ● ● ● ●	−30
Pigs	● ● ● ● ● ●	● ● ● ●	−2
Sheep [● = 10]	● ● ● ● ●	● ● ● ● ● ● ●	+20
Land [● = 1 acre]	● ● ● ●	● ● ● ●	no change
Cottage	●	●	no change
Carts	● ● ●	●	−2
Ploughs	●	● ●	+1

2 information extracted from the system can help the owner or the manager operate the business much more effectively.

In essence, the system provides the answers to three basic questions which owners want to know. These questions are depicted in Exhibit 1.2, and they can be summarized as follows:

1 What profit has the business made?
2 How much does the business owe?
3 How much is owed to it?

The medieval system dealt largely with simple agricultural and trading entities (an entity is simply the jargon accountants use to describe any type of organization). Modern systems have to cope with complex industrial operations and sophisticated financial arrangements. Furthermore, a business may be so big or so complex nowadays that the owners have to employ managers to run it for them. Indeed, the senior managers themselves may be largely dependent upon being told what is happening by their juniors. A traditional book-keeping system was not designed to cope with situations where owners were separated from managers. It was designed largely to supply summarized information only to the owner-managers of a business who knew in detail from their own experience what was going on. The system was not intended to cope with frequent day-to-day reporting to managers remote from production or trading operations.

As a result, Pacioli's system has had to be adapted so that it can satisfy the demand for information from two main sources:

Exhibit 1.2 An owner's vital questions

State	Now	A year ago	Better or worse off?
Stock	2 Cows	1 Cow	Worse
Owed to Jim	100 Kilos of barley	50 Kilos of barley	Better
Due from Hetty	3 Gross eggs	4 Gross eggs	Better
Overall			?

1 from owners who want to know from time to time how the business is doing;
2 from the managers of a business who need information in order to help them plan and control the business.

We shall be meeting the terms 'plan' and 'control' frequently in this book. Both terms can have several different meanings, but we shall adopt the following definitions:

> **to plan:** to determine what and how something should be done;
> **to control:** to ensure that the planned results are achieved.

Owners and managers do not necessarily require the same information, so this has meant that accounting has developed into two main specialisms:

1 financial accounting, which is concerned with the supply of information to the owners of an entity;

Exhibit 1.3 The main users of accounting information
Source: The Corporate Report, ASSC, 1975

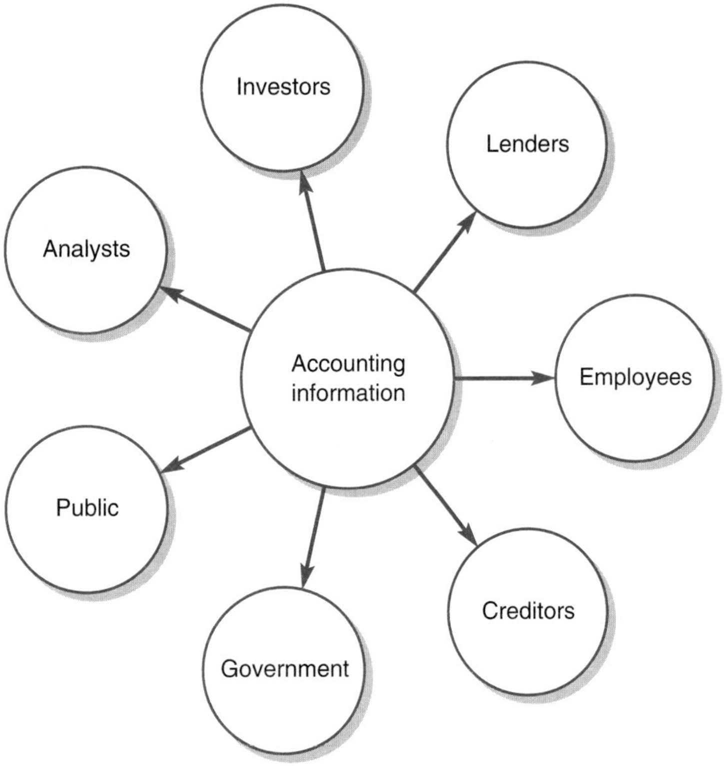

2 management accounting, which is concerned with the supply of information to the managers of an entity.

We shall be spending a great deal of time in subsequent chapters dealing with both financial and management accounting.

While it is useful to classify accounting into these two broad categories, Exhibit 1.3 shows that accountants are now involved in supplying information to a wide range of other interested parties, such as analysts, creditors, employees, the government, investors, lenders, and the public.

In this book, we are going to be mainly concerned with the supply of information to owners and managers, but first, we need to examine why non-accountants need to study accounting. We do this in the next section.

ACCOUNTING AND THE NON-ACCOUNTANT

Whatever your job, whether you repair machines in a factory, teach children in a school, or nurse sick patients in a hospital, you probably feel that you seem to spend all your time filling in forms and reading reports. Why?

Why can you not just get on with repairing machines, teaching children, or nursing the sick?

It is true that in many organizations there is now an awful lot of paperwork. It can get out of hand, but usually there is a reason behind it all. A great deal of information that is collected may, for example, be required by law. Some entities (such as companies like ICI or Marks and Spencer) have a statutory obligation to publish (that is, to make available for public inspection) a minimum amount of information about their affairs. This process requires a considerable amount of material to be collected about the company's activities before it can be summarized in a form suitable for publication. In the previous section, we referred to this process as *financial accounting*. It may be somewhat tiresome for you to become involved in it, but if the company is to comply with the law, the information has to be obtained.

Even so, unless you are at a very senior level in the entity, it is unlikely that as a non-accountant you will be directly involved in the detailed preparation of the financial accounts. You may have to supply *some* information, but you will probably not be involved to any great extent. Until you become a senior manager, the type of information that you have to provide is more likely to be needed for *management* accounting purposes.

As you have probably experienced, besides having to *supply* a great deal of information to senior management, you almost certainly *receive* an enormous amount as well. You know the feeling: your in-tray is constantly being topped up with scores of urgent memos and reports. Why?

The idea behind it all is very simple, although it may not appear so when you are constantly being harassed. The belief is that if you *know* what is going on, you will be much better placed to run your department much more efficiently and effectively. 'Efficient' and 'effective' are another two terms that we shall be using quite a lot in this book, so what do they mean? We will define them as follows:

> **Efficient:** the maximum output obtained from any given input;
> **Effective:** the success achieved in arriving at a desired outcome.

As your department gets bigger and more complex, you will not always know what is going on simply by casual observation. You need to be given information so that you can plan the direction you want to go in over (say) the next few weeks or months, and then ensure that you do indeed go in that direction.

Do you feel that all of this is unnecessary? It can be if the information you receive is irrelevant for your purposes. To be useful, it *has* to be what you want, and you have to be able to rely on it. This will not be the case if you have not been consulted about it, and the system has been imposed upon you by senior management. Furthermore, the information is likely to be inaccurate if it is prepared by employees who are unaware of its importance.

Perhaps you are thinking, 'This is all very well. It might possibly be of some benefit, but I still don't see why I have to study such a boring subject as accounting.' This is a fair point, so we will try and summarize the main reasons why you should study accounting:

1 **To make sure that you follow legal requirements**
   As we have seen, some organizations are required by law to disclose publicly information about their activities. The required information is inevitably complex, it is normally written in a strange technical financial language, and it is often presented in a highly prescribed format. The responsibility for complying with the law rests ultimately with the senior management of the organization. While the accountants may help with the detailed preparation of the accounts (as they are called), the overall responsibility cannot be delegated to them. It follows that any non-accountant who aspires to being a senior manager cannot avoid having to know something about this process.

2 **To help you do a better job**
   Larger organizations almost certainly have some form of detailed internal information supply. You may be involved in both supplying and receiving it. Its purpose is to help you and other managers do your respective jobs much more efficiently and effectively. It is supposed to help you plan your department's activities, to monitor and to control them, and to provide additional information about decisions you have to take about your department's affairs. This will often be translated and reported to you in financial terms (although you will also receive non-financial information). It will not mean anything and you will not be able to use it, if you do not understand it. Furthermore, you certainly will not have been able to contribute to the development of the information system so that it is of particular benefit to you.

We believe that these arguments fully justify the time that you will be giving to the study of accounting. By the time that you have worked your way through this book, we hope you will find, despite your initial fears, that you agree accounting can be both interesting and useful!

Accounting has now developed into a considerable number of specialisms and, as you are likely to come across at least some of them in your career, it might be helpful if we provide a brief description of the main ones for you. We do so in the next section.

BRANCHES OF ACCOUNTING

The work that accountants now undertake ranges far beyond that of simply summarizing information in order to calculate how much profit a business has made, how much it owes, and much is owed to it. Although this work is still very important, accountants have gradually got involved in other types of work. Of course, other information specialists (such as market researchers and operational analysts) have also been drawn into the preparation of management information and, at one time, some observers expected accounting to be taken over by these newer and more scientifically based disciplines. However, this has not happened. There are three main reasons: (a) financial information supply to external users still has a dominant influence on internal management information; (b) other information specialists have been reluctant to become involved in detailed accounting matters; and (c) accountants have been quick to absorb new methods and techniques into their work.

The main branches of accounting are shown in Exhibit 1.4, and a brief description of them is given below:

Exhibit 1.4 Branches of accounting

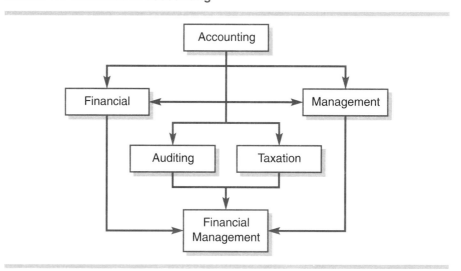

Accountancy and accounting

Accountancy is a profession whose members are engaged in the collection of financial data, the summary of that data, and then the presentation of it in a form which helps recipients take effective decisions. Many writers use accountancy and accounting as synonymous terms, but in this book we shall use the term *accountancy* to describe the profession, and the term *accounting* to refer to the subject.

Auditing

Auditing forms a most important branch of accountancy. Once accounts have been prepared, they may have to be checked in order to ensure that they do not present a distorted picture. The checking of accounts and the reporting on them is known as *auditing*. Not all businesses have their accounts audited, but for some organizations (such as limited liability companies) it is a legal requirement.

Auditors are usually trained accountants who specialize in checking accounts rather than preparing them. If they are appointed from outside the organization, they are usually referred to as *external* auditors. A limited company's auditors are appointed by the shareholders, and not by the management. The auditors' job is to protect the interests of the shareholders. They answer to them, and not to anyone in the company. By contrast, *internal* auditors are employees of the company. They are appointed by, and answer to, the company's management.

Internal auditors perform routine tasks and undertake detailed checking of the company's accounting procedures, whereas external auditors are likely to go in for much more selective testing. None the less, they usually work very closely together, although the distinction made between them still remains important.

It might occur to you that as internal auditors are employees of the company, they must have much less independence than external auditors. In practice, however, even external auditors have limited independence. This is because the directors of a company usually recommend the appointment of a particular firm of auditors to the shareholders. It is rare for shareholders to object to the directors' recommendation so, if the directors are in dispute with the auditors, they can always hint that they are thinking of appointing another firm. The auditors can always appeal directly to the shareholders, but they are not usually successful.

Book-keeping

Book-keeping is a mechanical task involving the collection of basic financial data. The data are first entered in special records known as *books of account*, and then extracted and summarized in the form of what is known as a *profit and loss account*, and a *balance sheet*. This process normally takes place once a year, but it may occur more frequently. We shall be going into some detail in later chapters about profit and loss accounts and balance sheets. For the moment, all you need to remember is the following summary:

1 a profit and loss account shows whether the business has made a profit or loss during the year, i.e. it measures how well the business has done);

2 a balance sheet lists what the entity owns (its assets), and what it owes (its liabilities) as at the end of the year.

The book-keeping procedures usually end when the basic data have been entered in the books of account and the accuracy of such entry has been tested. At that stage, the *accounting* function takes over. Accounting tends to be used as a generic term covering almost anything to do with the collection and use of basic financial data. It should, however, be more properly applied to the use that the data are put once they have been extracted from the books of account. Book-keeping is a routine operation, while accounting requires the ability to examine a problem using both financial *and* non-financial data.

Cost book-keeping, costing, and cost accounting

You may come across these terms used somewhat loosely. They form part of a branch of accounting that deals with the collection of detailed financial data for *internal* management purposes. The information is used in planning and controlling the entity.

Cost book-keeping is the process that involves the recording of cost data in books of account. It is, therefore, similar to book-keeping as described above, except that data are recorded in very much greater detail. Cost accounting makes use of that data once they have been extracted from the cost books in providing information for managerial planning and control. Accountants are now discouraged from using the term 'costing' unless it is qualified in some way, i.e. by referring to some branch of costing such as standard costing, but you will still find the term in general use.

The difference between a book-keeping/accounting system and a cost book-keeping/cost accounting system is largely one of degree. A cost accounting system contains a great deal more data, and thus once they are summarized, there is much more information available to the management of the company.

Financial accounting

Financial accounting is the more specific term applied to the preparation and subsequent publication of highly summarized financial information. The information is usually presented for the benefit of the owners of an entity, but it can also be used by management for planning and control purposes. The information will also be of interest to others, e.g. employees and creditors (as depicted in Exhibit 1.3).

Financial management

Financial management is a relatively new branch of accounting that has developed over the last 20 years. Financial managers are responsible for setting financial objectives, making plans based on those objectives, obtaining the finance needed to achieve the plans, and generally safeguarding all the financial resources of the entity. Financial managers are much more heavily involved in the *management* of the entity than is generally the case with either financial or management accountants. It should also be noted that the financial manager draws on a much wider range of disciplines (such as economics and mathematics), and relies more extensively on non-financial data than does the more traditional accountant.

Management accounting

Management accounting is another all-embracing term. We suggested earlier that cost book-keeping deals with the routine collection and summary of data for internal management purposes, while cost accounting is more involved in planning and control. Management accounting covers *any* type of information provided for management, for whatever purpose. It incorporates cost accounting data and adapts them for specific decisions which management may be called upon to make. Indeed, a management accounting system can incorporate *all* types of financial and non-financial information, and it may be obtained from a wide range of sources far beyond those used in traditional financial accounting.

Taxation

Taxation is a highly complex technical branch of accounting. Accountants involved in tax work are responsible for computing the amount of tax payable by both business entities and individuals. It is not necessary for either companies or individuals to pay more tax than is lawfully due, so it is quite in order for them to minimize the amount of tax payable. If tax experts attempt to reduce their clients' tax bills strictly in accordance with the law, this is known as tax *avoidance*. Tax avoidance is a perfectly legitimate exercise, but tax *evasion* (the non-declaration of sources of income on which tax might be due) is a very serious offence. In practice, the border line between tax avoidance and tax evasion is a fairly narrow one.

The main branches of accounting described above cannot always be put into such neat categories. Accountants in practice (that is, those who work from an office and offer their services to the public, like a solicitor) usually specialize in auditing, financial accounting or taxation. Most accountants working in industry or the public sector will be employed as management accountants, although some may deal specifically with auditing, financial accounting, or taxation matters within a particular entity.

One other highly specialist branch of accounting that you may sometimes read about is that connected with *insolvency*, i.e. with bankruptcy or liquidation. *Bankruptcy* is a formal legal procedure. The term is applied to an individual when his financial affairs are so serious that he has to be given some form of legal protection from his creditors. The term *liquidation* is usually applied to a company when it also gets into serious financial difficulties, and its affairs have to be wound up (that is, for it to go out of existence).

Companies do not necessarily go immediately into liquidation if they get into financial difficulties. An attempt will usually be made either to rescue them, or at least to protect certain types of creditors. In these situations, accountants sometimes act as *administrators*. Their appointment freezes creditors' rights and prevents the company from being put into liquidation during a period when the administrators are attempting to manage the company. By contrast, *receivers* may be appointed on behalf of loan creditors. The creditors' loans may be secured on certain property, and the receivers will try to obtain the income from that property, or they may even attempt to sell it.

We hope that you never come into contact with insolvency practitioners, so we will move on to have a look at another topic, the structure of the accountancy profession.

THE ACCOUNTANCY PROFESSION

Within the UK, there is nothing to stop anyone calling himself an accountant, and setting up in business offering accountancy services. However, some accounting work is restricted (such as the audit of limited liability companies) unless the accountant holds a recognized qualification. Indeed, some accountants are sometimes described as being *qualified* accountants. This term is usually applied to someone who is a member of one of the major accountancy bodies (although many 'non-qualified' accountants would strongly dispute that they were not 'qualified' to offer a highly professional service). There are six major accountancy bodies operating in the British Isles, and they are as follows:

1 Institute of Chartered Accountants in England and Wales (ICAEW);
2 Institute of Chartered Accountants in Ireland (ICAI);
3 Institute of Chartered Accountants of Scotland (ICAS);
4 Chartered Association of Certified Accountants (ACCA);
5 Chartered Institute of Management Accountants (CIMA);
6 Chartered Institute of Public Finance and Accountancy (CIPFA).

The organization of the accountancy profession is also shown in Exhibit 1.5.

The Irish Institute (number 2) is included in the above list because it has a strong influence in Northern Ireland.

Exhibit 1.5 Organization of the accountancy profession
Note: The Association of Accounting Technicians is sponsored by all the bodies except the Irish Institute.

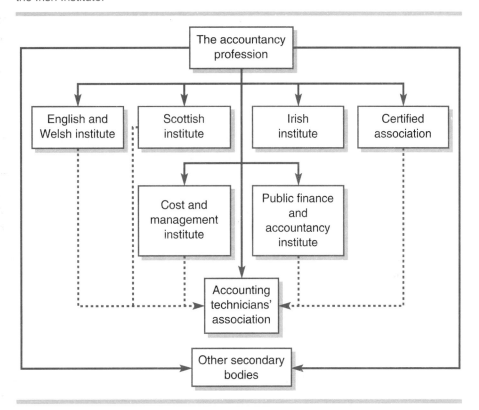

As can be seen from the list, all these bodies now have a Royal Charter, but only ICAEW, ICAI, and ICAS members are referred to as *chartered accountants*. Chartered accountants have usually had to undergo a period of training in a practising office, i.e. one that offers accounting services to the public, like a solicitor. Much practice work is involved in auditing and taxation but, after qualifying, many chartered accountants go to work in commerce or industry. ACCA members may also obtain their training in practice, but relevant experience elsewhere counts towards their qualification. CIMA members usually train and work in industry, while CIPFA members specialize almost exclusively in central and local government.

Apart from the six major bodies, there are a number of important (although far less well known) smaller accountancy associations and societies, e.g. the Association of International Accountants, the Society of Company and Commercial Accountants, the Association of Authorized Public Accountants, and the Association of Cost and Executive Accountants. All of these bodies offer some form of accountancy qualification, but they have not yet managed to achieve the status or prestige that is attached to being a member of one of the six major bodies. They are referred to as *secondary* bodies.

There is also another very important accountancy body known as the *Association of Accounting Technicians*. The Association was formed in 1980 as a professional organization especially for those accountants who *assist* qualified accountants in dealing with accounting information. Although it is an independent body, it is sponsored by five of the six major professional bodies (the exception being the Irish Institute). In order to become an accounting technician, it is necessary to take (or be exempt from) the Association's examinations. The examinations are not easy, although they tend to be less technically demanding and more practical than those of the six major bodies.

You can see that the accountancy profession is extremely diverse, and if you meet someone who calls himself an accountant, you may not be able to tell what that means. Nonetheless, whatever their qualifications, all accountants will have one thing in common: their job is to help *you* do your job more effectively. Accountants offer a service. They can do a lot to help you, but you do not necessarily have to do what they say. You should listen to their advice, but as accountants are largely specialists in financial matters, you also should obtain advice from other sources. Then make up your own mind what you should do. If things go wrong: never, never blame the accountant (or the computer!). As a manager, it is *your* decision, right or wrong.

You may be thinking 'This is all very well, but I am not really in a position to disregard the accountant's advice.' Exactly! That is what this book is about. By the end of it you will be in an excellent position to judge the quality of his advice. We shall be examining the detailed material in later chapters, but before we end this chapter we need to look at the main types of entity with which we shall be dealing.

TYPES OF ENTITY

Entities can be categorized into two broad groups: manufacturing and servicing. Manufacturing entities *make* things (e.g. furniture, or chemicals), while service entities provide advice or assistance (e.g. a garage, or a hospital). In recent years, manufacturing industry in the UK has appeared to be on the decline, while the service sector has become much more important. For example, think of all the new supermarkets that have opened recently in your part of the country. Even within the manufacturing sector, however, there can be a servicing element, e.g. an oil company can provide a canteen for its employees. Similarly, a local authority may be involved in some form of manufacturing, such as designing and printing its own stationery.

In this book we shall be concentrating almost exclusively on manufacturing entities. This might appear a bit odd in view of the growing importance of the service sector, but there two good reasons:

1 The manufacturing sector enables us to use a much wider range of accounting techniques than is the case with the service sector.
2 The accounting techniques used in manufacturing industry can be easily and readily adapted to suit the service sector and, by the end of the book, you will be able to do this for yourself.

If you are involved in the service sector, don't worry! We shall only be covering the basic principles of accounting, and you will find them of use, irrespective of where you work!

In fact, it is not possible or necessary in a book of this nature to deal with every type of entity (Exhibit 1.6 depicts some of the main ones). We shall be concentrating on just *three*: sole traders, partnerships and limited liability companies. A brief description of each is outlined below.

Exhibit 1.6 Types of entity

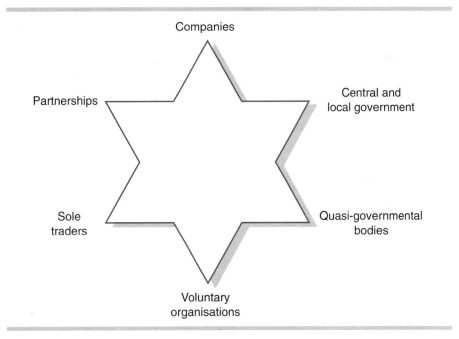

Sole traders

Like much else in accounting, the term 'sole trader' is rather misleading. There are two main reasons why this is the case:

1 'sole' does not necessarily mean that only one person *works* for the entity;
2 it may not 'trade' in the sense of just selling a product, since it could be involved in manufacturing, or it may provide a service (like a plumber).

The term really refers to how the entity is owned and financed, the main requirement being that only one individual should own it.

Sole traders usually work on a very informal basis, and some private matters relating to the owner are often indistinguishable from those of the entity. Chapters 3, 4, and 5 of this book are concerned primarily with sole traders. In these chapters we shall be introducing you to how financial data are recorded and summarized. You will find that it is much easier to understand the procedures if we restrict ourselves to examples of sole trader entities.

Partnerships

A partnership is very similar to a sole trader entity, except that two or more people are involved in the ownership of the business. Sometimes partnerships grow out of a sole trader entity, the sole trader perhaps realizing that he needs to put more money into the business, or that he wants someone to share the responsibility. In other cases, a new business may start out as a partnership, e.g. when two friends get together to start a home-decorating service.

The partners should arrange between themselves how much money they will each put into the business, what jobs they will do, how many hours they will work, and how the profits and losses will be shared. In the absence of any agreement (whether formal or informal), the provisions laid down in the Partnership Act 1890 are deemed to apply. Otherwise, partnerships are not covered by any specific legislation.

As the accounting procedures involved in dealing with partnerships are very similar to those that apply to sole traders, we shall not be going into too much detail about partnership accounting in this book.

Limited liability companies

A limited liability company is a formal type of business entity, so much so that, in law, it is regarded as having a quite separate existence from its owners. There are some extremely severe legal requirements, therefore, surrounding the creation and operation of such an entity, and its owners are restricted in what they can do with it (unlike sole traders or partnerships who have much more freedom). The restrictions are now contained within a consolidating Act of Parliament (the Companies Act 1985 as amended by the Companies Act 1989).

At this stage, we will not say any more about limited liability companies because we shall be examining them in some detail in Chapter 6. Thereafter we shall be dealing almost exclusively with limited liability companies.

CONCLUSION

The main aim of this chapter has been to introduce the non-accountant to the world of accounting. We have emphasized that the main purpose of accounting is to provide financial information to anyone who wants it.

Of course, information must be useful if it is to have any purpose but, as a non-accountant, you may feel reluctant to question any accounting information that lands on your desk, even though you have no idea what it means! Equally, you may not understand why the accountant is always asking you what you might think are irrelevant questions, so you feed him any old nonsense. You then perhaps feel a bit guilty and a little frustrated. You would like to know more, but you dare not ask. We hope that by the time you have worked your way through this book, you will have the confidence to ask and, furthermore, that you will understand the answer. Good luck!

Now that the world of accounting has been outlined, we can turn to more detailed subject matter. The first task is to learn the basic rules of accounting. These are covered in the next chapter, but it might be as well if you first read through this chapter again before you move on to the next one. It might also be a good idea to attempt some of the questions that end this chapter.

KEY POINTS

1 To account for something means to explain about it, or report on it.

2 An entity is any type of organization, and it can be in either the profit-making or the not-for-profit sector.

3 Owners of an entity want to know (a) how well it is doing; (b) what it owes; and (c) how much is owed to it.

4 Accounting is important for non-accountants because (a) they must make sure their own entity complies with any legal requirements; and (b) an accounting system can provide them with information that will help them do their jobs more effectively and efficiently.

5 The main branches of accounting are: auditing, book-keeping, cost accounting, financial accounting, financial management, management accounting, and taxation.

6 There are six main accountancy bodies: the Institute of Chartered Accountants in England and Wales, the Institue of Chartered Accountants in Ireland, the Institute of Chartered Accountants of Scotland, the Chartered Association of Certified Accountants, the Chartered Institute of Management Accountants, and the Chartered Institute of Public Finance and Accountancy.

7 There are two main economic sectors within the British economy: manufacturing and servicing. There are different forms of ownership and control in both sectors. Profit-making entities fall into three main types: sole traders, partnerships and limited liability companies.

CHECK YOUR LEARNING

1 Insert the missing words in each of the following sentences:
   (a) The word _____ in everyday language means an explanation or a report.
   (b) The owner of a business wants to know how much _____ it has made.

2 What are the two main branches of accounting?

3 State whether each of the following assertions is either true or false:
   (a) Auditors are responsible for preparing accounts   True/False
   (b) Management accounts are required by law   True/False

4 Which of the following activities is not an accounting function?
   (a) auditing   (b) book-keeping   (c) management consultancy   (d) taxation

5 How many major professional accountancy bodies are there in the British Isles?
   (a) three   (b) six   (c) nine   (d) ten or more

6 Fill in the blanks:
   (a) _____ trader   (b) Partnership _____ 1890   (c) limited liability _____

ANSWERS

1 (a) account   (b) profit
2 (a) financial accounting   (b) management accounting
3 (a) false   (b) false
4 (c) management consultancy
5 (b) six
6 (a) sole   (b) Act   (c) company

QUESTIONS

1.1 State briefly the main reasons why a company may employ a team of accountants.

1.2 Why does a limited liability company have to engage a firm of external auditors, and for what purpose?

1.3 Why should a non-accountant study accounting?

1.4 What statutory obligations require the preparation of management accounts in any kind of entity?

1.5 What statutory obligations support the publication of financial accounts in respect of limited liability companies?

1.6 Describe briefly the nature and purpose of accounts.

ADDITIONAL QUESTIONS (WITHOUT ANSWERS)

1.7 Assume that you were a personnal officer in a manufacturing company, and that one of your employees was a young engineering manager called Joseph Sykes. Joseph has been chosen to attend the local University's Business School to study for a diploma in management. Joseph is reluctant to attend the course because it will include a subject called 'financial management'. As an engineer, he thinks that it will be a waste of time for him to study such a subject.

Required:
Draft an internal memorandum addressed to Joseph Sykes explaining why it would be of benefit to him to study financial management.

1.8 Clare Wong spends a lot of her time working for a large local charity. The charity has grown enormously in recent years, and the trustees have been advised to overhaul their accounting procedures. This would involve its workers (most of whom are voluntary) in more book-keeping, and there is a great deal of resistance to this move. The staff have said that they are there to help the needy, and not to get involved in book-keeping

Required:
As the financial consultant to the charity, prepare some notes that you could use in speaking to the voluntary workers in order to try and persuade them to accept the new proposals.

CHAPTER 2

Accounting rules

Prudence pays dividends for M&S

By Neil Buckley

"IT doesn't worry me if I'm not described as entre-preneurial and all those other business-school adjectives," says Sir Richard Greenbury, Marks and Spencer's chairman and chief executive. "I'm quite prepared to be a tortoise provided we get there."

Sir Richard's cautious prudence has paid off. M&S yesterday snatched back the crown of the UK's most profitable retailer.

The Stock Market's downbeat reaction sur-prised some analysts, who suggested the city was concerned about a wage settlement that will add 6 per cent to M&S's wage bills, and was disap-pointed that sales growth was not greater.

But, as one analyst put it, "Marks and Spencer has never been a top-line story". The company makes money by being a superbly-run operation, and that was perhaps more true this year than ever, with pre-tax profits up 10 per cent even stripping out last year's exceptional items, on turnover up only 3.4 per cent overall.

Improvements in information technology helped M&S keep firmer control of its stock, avoiding the need to discount to get rid of surpluses as many other retailers do.

That technology has also improved distribution, enabling M&S to respond quickly to changes in fashions, and keep operating costs down. The result was a 6.8 per cent rise in UK operating prof-its, on turnover up only 1.8 per cent.

The improvements in efficiency also enabled M&S to freeze prices for 75 per cent of its cloth-ing, and reduce prices for 25 per cent by cutting its buying margins.

Profits were also boosted by improved perfor-mances abroad. Sales in continental Europe increased 22 per cent, while operating profits were up 15 per cent to £27m. In North America, there was evidence that the company's homegrown expertise was bearing fruit. The Canadian opera-tions climbed out of the red for the first time, with an operating profit of £0.1m, after the closure of 30 stores and a 55 per cent reduction in staffing in the past two years.

Brooks Brothers in the US increased operating profits by 20 per cent – the third successive rise – while Kings Super Markets also saw operating profits grow 20 per cent. In the Far East, improved merchandise values, cataloguing and distribution lifted sales 64 per cent, and operating profits 68 per cent to £10.6m.

As UK consumers start spending again, and the company steps up its overseas expansion, M&S looks likely to remain a tortoise to watch.

The Financial Times, 19 May 1993

Exhibit 2.0 Judging from this article, accountants are not alone in believing that prudence pays!

> By the end of this chapter, you will be able to:
> ● identify fourteen accounting rules;
> ● classify them into three broad groupings;
> ● describe each accounting rule;
> ● explain why each is important.

We suggested in Chapter 1 that accountancy is a profession engaged in the supply of financial information to a number of interested parties. In fact, the amount of information that is available is so enormous that it is necessary to place some limit on the type of data dealt with.

Modern accounting systems have evolved over a long period of time. They have not developed from any sort of theoretical model, but have grown out of practical necessity. As a result, a number of basic procedures have developed. These procedures may perhaps best be described as the *basic rules of accounting*. Some authors refer to them under a variety of other names, such as assumptions, axioms, concepts, conventions, postulates, principles, or procedures.

In preparing and presenting information, accountants have considerable freedom over which rules to adopt and how they should be interpreted. Since 1971, the accountancy profession has tried to restrict the room for manoeuvre by issuing a series of accounting guides. The guides issued prior to 1990 are known as Statements of Standard Accounting Practice (SSAPs). The ones issued since then are called Financial Reporting Standards (FRSs). When preparing accounting statements, qualified accountants are supposed to follow the letter and not just the spirit of the recommendations contained in SSAPS and FRSs. However, it is impracticable to lay down totally rigid rules for each and every situation, so accountants are still able to employ a great deal of individual discretion.

It would be possible, of course, to ignore all of the generally recognized accounting rules and to prepare accounts in an entirely novel way. This would be like trying to play football under different rules than the ones laid down by the Football Association. If the accepted rules were disregarded, any match played under entirely new rules would result in a game that would be almost incomprehensible to most of the spectators.

A similar situation would apply in accounting if the conventional rules were abandoned. Such rules include, for example, the amount and type of information to be collected, and the length of the accounting period. These are practical rules, like those in football covering the size of the pitch and the length of the match. Other accounting rules are more of an ethical nature, for example, one rule states that the accepted rules must be applied consistently, while another one says that information should not be presented in a deliberately distorted fashion. These rules may again be compared with those in football that cover misconduct: for example, the ball must not be handled, or an opponent should not be kicked.

The basic accounting rules will be outlined in subsequent sections. For convenience, they have been classified as follows:

1 boundary rules;
2 measurement rules;
3 ethical rules.

A diagrammatic summary of the main accounting rules that we are going to examine is shown in Exhibit 2.1.

Exhibit 2.1 The basic accounting rules

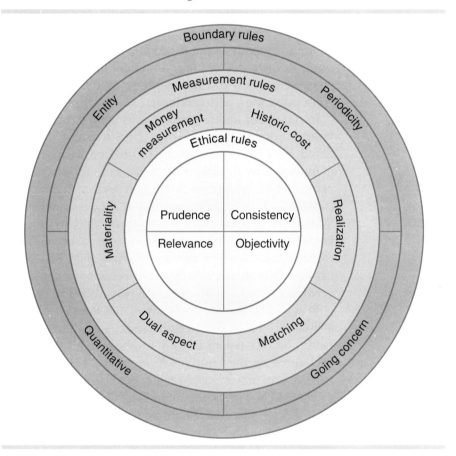

This classification is largely arbitrary. It has been chosen to help you examine more clearly some of the most important accounting rules. There are something like 150 identifiable accounting rules, but we are only going to look at the 14 that are of particular relevance to non-accountants.

BOUNDARY RULES

In small entities, the owners can probably obtain all the information that they want to know by finding out for themselves. In larger entities, this is often impracticable, so a more formal way of reporting back to the owners has to be devised. However, it would be difficult to inform the owners about literally *everything* that had happened to the entity. A start has be made, therefore, by determining what should and should not be reported. Hence, accountants have devised a number of what we will call *boundary* rules. The boundary rules attempt to place a limit on the amount and type of data collected and stored within the entity.

There are four main boundary rules, and they will be examined in the following sub-sections.

Entity

There is so much information available about any organization that accountants start by drawing a boundary around what we have referred to as an *entity*. As we outlined in the last chapter, an entity could be a profit-making business, such as a shop buying and selling goods, or a firm of solicitors offering a service. Such businesses are usually referred to as *profit-making* entities. A profit-making entity may be organized in the form of a sole trader, a partnership, or of a limited liability company. However, an entity might well be a *non-profit making* (some accountants prefer the term *not-for-profit making*) entity, such as a charity or a local authority. The primary purpose of such organizations is to provide a service to the public, the profit motive being either irrelevant or of secondary importance.

The accountant tries to restrict the amount of data collected to that of the entity itself. This is sometimes very difficult, especially in small entities where there is often no clear distinction between the public affairs of the entity and the private affairs of the owner. In a profit-making business, for example, the owners sometimes charge their household expenditure to the business, and they might also use their private bank account to pay for goods and services meant for the business. In such a situation, the accountant has to decide where the business ends and the private affairs of the owners begin. He has then to establish exactly what the business owes the owner and the owner owes the business. The accountant will, however, only be interested in recording in the books of the business the effect of these various transactions on the *business*. He is not interested in the effect on they have on the owner's private affairs. Indeed, it would be an entirely different exercise if the accountant did deal with his private affairs. This would mean that he was accounting for a different entity altogether, i.e. the private entity, instead of the public one, although the two entities may be almost indistinguishable.

Periodicity

Most entities have an unlimited life. They are usually started in the expectation that they will operate for an indeterminate period of time, but it is clearly unhelpful for the owner to have to wait years before any report is prepared on how it is doing. He almost certainly wishes to receive fairly regular reports at frequent, short intervals.

If an entity has an unlimited life, any report must be prepared at the end of what must inevitably be an arbitrary period of time. In practice, *financial* accounting statements are usually prepared annually. Such a time period has developed largely as a matter of custom. It does, however, reflect the agricultural cycle in Western Europe, and there does seem to be a natural human tendency to compare what has happened this year with what happened last year. None the less, where entities have an unlimited life (as is usually the case with manufacturing organizations), the preparation of annual accounts presents considerable problems in relating specific events to appropriate accounting periods. We shall be having a look at this problem in Chapter 4.

Apart from custom, there is no reason why an accounting period could not be shorter or longer than twelve months. Management accounts are usually prepared for very short periods, but sometimes this applies even to financial accounts. For example, in the fashion industry, where the product designs may change very quickly, managers may want (say) quarterly reports. By contrast, the construction industry faced with very long-term contract work may find it more appropriate to have (say) a five-year reporting period. In fact, irrespective of the length of the main accounting period (i.e. whether it is quarterly or five yearly), managers usually need regular reports covering a very short period. Cash reports, for example, could be prepared on a weekly, or even on a daily basis.

It must also not be forgotten that some entities (e.g. limited liability companies), are required by law to produce annual accounts, and as tax demands are also based on a calendar year, it would not be possible for most entities to ignore the conventional twelve-months period. In any case, given the unlimited life of most entities, you will appreciate that *any* period must be somewhat arbitrary, no matter how carefully a particular entity has tried to relate its accounting period to the nature of its business.

Going concern

The periodicity rule requires a regular period of account to be established, regardless either of the life of the entity or of the arbitrary nature of such a period. The going concern rule arises out of the periodicity rule. This rule requires us to assume that an entity will continue in existence for the foreseeable future unless we have some strong evidence to suggest that this not the case. It is important to make absolutely certain that this assumption is correct, because a different set of accounting rules would be adopted if its immediate future is altogether uncertain.

Quantitative

Accountants usually restrict the data that are collected to those which are easily quantifiable. For example, it is possible to count the number of vans that an entity owns, or the number of people that it employs, but it is difficult to calculate the benefit that the vans provide, or the skill of the employees. Such concepts are almost impossible to quantify, and they are, therefore, not included in a conventional accounting system.

MEASUREMENT RULES

The boundary rules determine *what* data should be included in an accounting system, whereas the measurement rules explain *how* that data should be recorded. There are six main measurement rules, and we outline them briefly in the following sub-sections.

Money measurement

It would be very cumbersome to record information simply in terms of quantifiable amounts. It would also be impossible to make any fair comparisons between various types of assets (such as livestock and farm machinery), or different types of transactions (such as the sale of eggs and the purchase of corn). In order to make a meaningful comparison, we need to convert the data into a common and recognizable measure.

As we suggested in Chapter 1, the monetary unit serves such a purpose. It is a useful way of converting accounting data into a common unit, and since most quantifiable information is capable of being translated into monetary terms, there is usually no difficulty in adopting the monetary measurement rule.

Historic cost

The historic cost rule is an extension of the money meaurement rule. It requires transactions to be recorded at their *original* (i.e. their historic) cost. Subsequent changes in prices or values, therefore, are usually ignored. Increased costs may arise because of a combination of an improved product, or through changes in the purchasing power of the monetary unit, i.e. through inflation.

As we shall see in Chapter 20, inflation tends to overstate the level of accounting profit as it is traditionally calculated. Over the last 20 years or so, there have been several attempts in the UK to change the method of accounting in order to allow for the effects of inflation. There has been so much disagreement on what should replace what we now call *historic cost accounting* (HCA), that no other method has been acceptable. Throughout most of this book, we shall be adopting the historic cost rule.

Realization

One of the problems of putting the periodicity rule into practice is that it is often difficult to relate a specific transaction to a particular period. For example, assume that a business arranges to sell some goods in 1994, it delivers them in 1995, and it is paid for them in 1996. In which year were the goods *sold*: 1994, 1995, or 1996? In conventional accounting, it would be most unusual to include them in the sales for 1994, because the business has still got a legal title to them. They could be included in the accounts for

1996 when the goods have been paid for. Indeed, this method of accounting is not uncommon. It is known as cash flow accounting (CFA). In CFA, transactions are only entered in the books of account when a cash exchange has taken place. By contrast, in HCA, it is customary to enter most transactions in the books of account when the legal title to the goods has been transferred from one party to another and when there is an obligation for the recipient to pay for them. This means that in the above example, the goods would normally be considered to have been sold in 1995.

The realization rule covers this point. It requires transactions relating to the sale of goods to be entered in the accounts for that period in which the legal title for them has been transferred from one party to another. In the jargon of accounting, they are then said to be *realized*. It is important to appreciate that for goods and services to be treated as realized, they do not need to have been paid for: the cash for them may be received during a later period (or for that matter, may have been received in an earlier period).

The realization rule is normally regarded as applying to sales, but *purchases* (meaning goods that are intended for resale) may be treated similarly. Thus, they would not be included in an entity's accounts until it had a legal title to them (i.e. in law, it would be regarded as owning them).

The realization rule can produce some rather misleading results. For example, the company may treat the goods as having been sold in 1995. In 1996, it then finds out that the purchaser cannot pay for them. What can it do? Its accounts for 1995 have already been approved. They cannot be taken back, but obviously the sales for that year were overstated (and hence, almost certainly, the profit). The customer defaults in 1996, so how can the *bad debt* (as it is known) be dealt with in *that* year? We shall be explaining how in Chapter 4.

Matching

The realization rule relates mainly to the purchase and sale of goods, in other words, to what are known as *trading* items. However, a similar rule known as the *matching* rule applies to other incomes (such as dividends and rents received), and expenditure (such as electricity and wages).

A misleading impression would be given if the cash received during a particular period was simply compared with the cash paid out during the same period. The exact period in which the cash is either received or paid may bear no relationship to the period in which the business was transacted. Thus, accountants normally adjust cash received and cash paid on what is known as an *accruals and prepayments* basis. An accrual is an amount that is *owed* by the entity at the end of an accounting period in respect of services *received* during that period. A prepayment is an amount that is *owing* to the entity at the end of the accounting period as a result of it paying in advance for services to be rendered in respect of a future period.

The conversion of cash received and cash paid on to an accruals and pre-payments basis at the end of an accounting period often involves a considerable amount of arithmetical adjustment. Account has to be taken for accruals and prepayments at the end of the previous period (i.e *opening* accruals and prepayments), as well as for accruals and prepayments at the end of the current period (i.e. *closing* accruals and prepayments). We shall be dealing with accruals and prepayments in more detail in Chapter 4.

An accruals and prepayments system of accounting enables the incomes of one period to be matched much more fairly against the costs of the same period. The comparison is not distorted by the accidental timing of cash receipts and cash payments. However, as the matching rule requires the accountant to estimate the level of both accruals and prepayments as at the end of each accounting period, a degree of subjectivity is automatically built into the estimate.

Dual aspect

The dual aspect rule is a useful practical rule, although it really only reflects what is obvious. It is built round the fact that every time something is given, someone (or something) else receives it. In other words, every time a trans-action take place, there is always a twofold effect. For example, if the amount of cash in a business goes up, someone must have given it, or if the business buys some goods, then someone else must be selling them.

We explained in Chapter 1 that this twofold effect was recognized many centuries ago. It gave rise to the system of recording information known as *double-entry book-keeping*. This system of book-keeping is still widely used. Although the concept is somewhat obvious, it has proved extremely useful, so much so that even modern computerized recording systems are based on it. From long experience, it has been found that the system is a most convenient way of recording all sorts of useful information about the entity, and of ensuring some form of control over its affairs.

There is no real need to adopt the dual aspect rule in recording informa-tion: it is entirely a practical rule that has proved itself over many centuries. Voluntary organizations (such as a drama club, or a stamp col-lecting society) may not think that it is worth while to adopt the dual aspect rule, but you are strongly recommended to incorporate it into your book-keeping system in any entity with which you are concerned.

We examine double-entry book-keeping in more detail in the next chapter.

Materiality

Strict application of the various accounting rules may not always be practi-cal. It could involve a considerable amount of work that may be out of all proportion to the information that is eventually obtained. The materiality rule permits other rules to be ignored if the effects are not considered to be *material*, that is, if they are not significant.

Hence, the materiality rule avoids the necessity to follow other account-ing rules to the point of absurdity. For example, it would normally be considered unnecessary to value the closing stock of small amounts of stationery, or to maintain detailed records of inexpensive items of office equipment. However, it should also be borne in mind that what is immaterial for a large organization may not be so for a small one.

If you decide that a certain item is immaterial, then it does not matter how you deal with it in the accounts, because it cannot possibly have any significant effect on the results. When dealing with insignificant items, therefore, the materiality rule permits the other accounting rules to be ignored.

ETHICAL RULES

There is an old story in accounting about the company chairman who asked his chief accountant how much profit the company had made. The chief accountant replied by asking how much profit the chairman would like to make. Accountants recognize that there is some truth in this story, since it is quite possible for different accountants to use the same basic data in preparing accounting statements, and yet still arrive at a different level of profit!

You might think that by faithfully following all of the accounting rules, *all* accountants should be able to calculate exactly the same amount of profit. Unfortunately, this is not the case since, as we have seen, most of the main accounting rules are capable of wide interpretation. The matching rule, for example, requires an estimate to be made of amounts owing and owed at the end of an accounting period, while the materiality rule allows the accountant to decide just what is material. Both rules involve an element of subjective judgement, and so no two accountants are likely to agree precisely on how they should be applied.

In order to limit the room for individual manoeuvre, a number of other rules have evolved. These rules are somewhat ethical in nature, and indeed some authors refer to them as accounting *principles* (thereby suggesting that there is a moral dimension to them). Other authors, however, refer to *all* of the basic accounting rules as principles, but it really does not matter what you call them as long as you are aware of them. Basically, the ethical rules require accountants to follow not just the letter, but the spirit of the other rules.

There are four main ethical accounting rules, and we will review them individually in the following sub-sections.

Prudence

The prudence rule (which is sometimes known as *conservatism*) arises out of the need to make a number of estimates in preparing periodic accounts. Managers and owners are often naturally over-optimistic about future events. As a result, there is a tendency to be too confident about the future, and not to be altogether realistic about the entity's prospects. There may be, for example, undue optimism over the credit-worthiness of a particular customer. Insufficient allowance may, therefore, be made for the possibility of a bad debt. This might have the effect of overstating profit in one period, and understating it in a future period. We shall come across this problem again in Chapter 4.

The prudence rule is sometimes expressed in the form of a simple maxim:

If in doubt, overstate losses and understate profits

Consistency

As we have seen, the preparation of traditional accounting statements requires a considerable amount of individual judgement to be made in the application of the basic accounting rules. To compensate for this flexibility, the *consistency* rule states that once specific accounting policies have been adopted, they should be followed in all subsequent accounting periods.

It would be considered quite unethical to change those rules just because they were unfashionable, or because alternative ones gave better results. Thus, once adopted, the various rules must be applied faithfully and *consistently*. Of course, if the circumstance of the entity change radically, it may be necessary to adopt different policies, but this should only be done in exceptional circumstances. If different policies are adopted, then the effect of any change should be clearly highlighted and any comparative figure adjusted accordingly.

The application of this rule gives confidence to the users of accounting statements. If the accounts have been prepared on a consistent basis the users can be assured that they are comparable with previous sets of accounts.

Objectivity

Accounts should be prepared with the minimum amount of bias. This is not an easy task, since individual judgement is required in interpreting the rules and adapting them to suit particular circumstances. Owners may want, for example, to adopt policies which would result in higher profit figures, or in disguising poor results.

If optional policy decisions are possible within the existing rules, it is advisable to fall back on the prudence rule. Indeed, it tends to be an overriding one. If you are in any doubt about which rule to adopt (or how it should be interpreted), the prudence rule tends to take precedence.

It must be recognized, however, that if it is always adopted as the easy way out of a difficult problem, you could be accused of lacking objectivity. In other words, you must not use this rule to avoid making difficult decisions. Indeed, it is just as unfair to be as excessively cautious as it is to be widely optimistic. Extremism of any kind suggests a lack of objectivity, so you should avoid being either over-cautious or over-optimistic.

Relevance

The amount of information that could be supplied to any interested party is practically unlimited. If too much information is disclosed, it becomes very difficult to absorb, so it should only be included if it is it going to help the user.

The selection of relevant information requires much experience and judgement, as well as calling for a great understanding of the user's requirements. The information needs to be designed in such a way that it meets the *objectives* of the specific user group. If too much information is given, the user might think that it is an attempt to mislead him, and as a result, all of the information may be totally rejected.

In this context, accountants try to present accounts in such a way that they represent 'a true and fair view'. The Companies Act 1985, for example, requires company accounts to reflect this particular criterion, and it is advisable to apply it to all entities. Unfortunately, the Act does not define what is meant by 'true and fair', but it is assumed that accounts will be so if an entity has followed the rules laid down in appropriate accounting and financial reporting standards.

Financial reporting standards are formulated by an Accounting Standards Board (ASB), and professionally qualified accountants are required to follow its recommendations. As we mentioned earlier, these are contained in Financial Reporting Standards (FRSs) and in any Statements of Accounting Standards (SSAPs) issued by the former Accounting Standards Committee (ASC), and not yet withdrawn by the ASB. FRSs are not statutory requirements, although some recognition in law in given to them, and the ASB has much greater power to enforce its recommendations than did the old ASC.

By the time that the ASC had been disbanded in 1990, it had issued 25 SSAPs, although three of them had been withdrawn. By the end of 1993, the ASB had issued three FRSs, withdrawn one SSAP, and substantially amended a number of others.

Such standards are considered to represent the most authoritative view of how certain matters should be dealt with in 'financial statements whose purpose is to give a true and fair view of the financial position and of the profit or loss for the period' (as the SSAP's explanatory foreword put it). This is perhaps rather a strange way of requiring compliance with the standards, because it suggests that some accounts are not meant to give a true and fair view!

The standards cover such diverse subjects as the accounting policies adopted by an entity, and the treatment of depreciation, taxation and stock valuations. Although professionally qualified accountants are supposed to follow the recommendations contained within the standards, they still leave room for considerable individual interpretation, and no real disciplinary action has yet been taken against any accountants for not following either the letter or the spirit of them.

We shall be returning to the work of the ASB in Part 4 of the book.

THE BASIC ACCOUNTING RULES RESTATED

It would be convenient at this stage if we summarized the basic accounting rules outlined in the previous section, so that it will be easy for you to refer back to when studying later chapters. In summary, therefore, the basic accounting rules are as follows:

Boundary rules

1 **Entity**. Accounting data must be restricted to the entity itself. They should exclude the private affairs of those individuals who either own or manage the entity, except insofar as there is a direct impact on it.
2 **Periodicity**. Accounts should be prepared at the end of a defined period of time, and this period should be adopted as the regular period of account.
3 **Going concern**. The accounts should be prepared on the assumption that the entity will continue in existence for the foreseeable future.
4 **Quantitative**. Only data that are capable of being easily quantified should be included in an accounting system.

Measurement rules

1 **Money measurement**. Data must be translated into monetary terms before they are included in an accounting system.
2 **Historic cost**. Financial data should be recorded in the books of account at their historic cost, that is, at their original purchase cost, or at their original selling price.
3 **Realization**. Transactions that reflect financial data should be entered in the books of account when the legal title to them has been transferred from one party to another party, irrespective of when a cash settlement takes place.
4 **Matching**. Cash received and cash paid during a particular accounting period should be adjusted in order to reflect the economic activity that has actually taken place during that period.
5 **Dual aspect**. All transactions should be recorded in such a way that they capture the giving and the receiving effect of each transaction.
6 **Materiality**. The basic accounting rules must not be rigidly applied to insignificant items.

Ethical rules

1 **Prudence**. If there is some doubt over the treatment of a particular transaction, income should be under-estimated and expenditure over-estimated, so that profits are more likely to be understated and losses overstated.

2 **Consistency**. Accounting rules and policies should not be amended unless there is a fundamental change in circumstances that necessitates a reconsideration of the original rules and policies.

3 **Objectivity**. Personal prejudice must be avoided in the interpretation of the basic accounting rules.

4 **Relevance**. Accounting statements should not include information that prevents users from obtaining a true and fair view of the information being communicated to them.

Before we finish this chapter, we ought to have a brief look at some accounting theory. No! Don't close the book just yet. It won't be as bad as you think!

A CONCEPTUAL FRAMEWORK

As we explained at the beginning of this chapter, the basic accounting rules have evolved over a period of time: nobody worked them out on paper before they were applied in practice. This means that when some new accounting problem arises, we do not know how to deal with it. Some accountants (especially university lecturers), therefore, argue that what is needed is a *conceptual framework*. In other words, we ought to devise a theoretical model of accounting, and then any new accounting problem could be solved merely by running it through the model.

It all sounds very sensible, but it is not easy to devise such a model. Several attempts have been made, and none of them have been successful. Basically, there are two approaches that can be adopted. We summarize them below.

1 We can list all the accounting rules that have ever been used, and then extract the ones that are the most widely used. There are two main problems in adopting this approach:

   (a) To be meaningful, we would have to conduct an extremely wide survey of existing practice. As yet, the sheer scale required by this exercise has defeated most researchers.

   (b) Such an exercise would simply freeze existing practice: it would not improve it.

2 Alternatively, we could determine (a) who uses accounting statements; (b) what they want them for (i.e. we would need to establish user *objectives*); and (c) what rules we need to adopt to meet those objectives. Again, the scale of the exercise has defeated most researchers, but even if some agreement could be reached on who are the users of accounting statements and what are their objectives, the selection of appropriate rules becomes much more debatable.

It follows that the ASB (whose job would presumably be easier if it could solve new accounting problems by referring them to some sort of model) may still have to deal with new issues on a fire-fighting basis. As new problems arise, it puts forward a solution which it hopes will be acceptable. If not, then it has to try again. And so, at the present time, the accountancy profession lurches on from one crisis to another. Exhibit 2.2 expresses this point of view in strong journalistic terms.

Exhibit 2.2

Yeltsin of accounting ready to take the flak

OUTLOOK

Roger Cowe

• •

IT MAY not be quite as dramatic, or as dangerous, as tanks on the streets of Moscow, but a crucial battle is also taking place in the supposedly staid world of accounting. It will determine whether company accounts become more meaningful and more reliable, or whether we slide back into the bad old 1980s days of "pick your own" profits.

This gentle battle could determine whether the government has to step in to exert more state control over this quintessentially capitalist profession.

Just as in Moscow, it isn't always easy to tell who are the good guys. But the mantle of Boris Yeltsin is worn by a Scots academic, Professor David Tweedie, who is in charge of the Accounting Standards Board (ASB).

He has the unwavering support of the armed forces, in the shape of the Financial Reporting Review Panel, which can force companies to toe the line. But the position of the secret police – in this context, the auditing profession – seems to be a little ambivalent.

Professor Tweedie came to power three years ago. As with most new leaders, intially he received substantial popular support. But in the last few months there has been a growing amount of sniping and complaint: the forces of reaction have been massing to slow down or reverse the reforms.

In Professor Tweedie's own words: "It will be make or break time in the next 12 months. It will get rough."

He is not surprised, having forecast that it would go like this. "We are making massive changes to accounting thinking, we're not just tinkering at the edges," professor Tweedie said. "Now we are really getting into some tough issues. It was inevitable that we would see the flak fly."

That flak is coming from a number of different directions. Some auditors are worried that the new standards are too prescriptive, but without really settling the key difficulties of the past. Others feel that Professor Tweedie's academic background has got the better of his practical experience. And there is the usual group who argue that he is simply trying to do too much too quickly.

Top finance directors fall into that category, but they are not just concerned with accounting standards. They have also been showered with new requirements stemming from the Cadbury Code on corporate governance, and the audit profession's own attempts to sharpen up its act.

Auditing is actually the nub of the problem.

Accounting is an art, not a science. Crucial judgements are involved in preparing a set of accounts, resulting in a range of possible outcomes. That is why auditors are needed: to take their own view of all those judgements.

Because so much judgement is involved, it is impossible for auditors simply to declare "Yes" or "No". But that is what the law requires of an audit opinion.

Of course, auditors could go further than the minimalist "true and fair view" required by law.

They could give shareholders the benefit of the huge amount of work done in arriving at that opinion, in an extended audit report. Privately, auditors will tell directors how optimistic or pessimistic the figures are.

Despite their supposed role as guardians of shareholders' interest, however, auditors are rightly terrified of publicising such views, except possibly to non-executive auditor committees. The reason is that they are sued at the drop of a profit statement, and are presently prevented from limiting their joint and several liability.

Limiting the amount for which auditors can be sued could open the way to fuller auditor reporting, and make Professor Tweedie's job easier. In the absence of sensible audit reports, the ASB must act as remote auditor, laying down the law with Stalinist fierceness.

And those who complain about the avalanche of new regulations would do well to remember that they were brought in to counter the decadence of the past.

The Guardian, 5 October 1993.

That is all the theory with which we shall be dealing (it wasn't too bad, was it?), and we shall be referring back to some of these problems in later chapters.

CONCLUSION

In this chapter we have identified 14 basic accounting rules that accountants usually adopt in the preparation of accounting statements. We have described four of these rules as boundary rules, six as measurement rules and four as ethical rules. We have argued that the boundary rules limit the amount and type of information that is traditionally collected and stored in an accounting system. The measurement rules provide some guidance on how that information should be recorded, and the ethical rules lay down a code of conduct on how all the other rules should be interpreted.

The exact number, classification and description of these various accounting rules is subject to much debate amongst accountants. Most entities can, in fact, adopt what rules they like, although it would be most unusual if they did not accept the going concern, matching, prudence and consistency rules.

In the next chapter, we shall examine the dual aspect rule in a little more detail. This rule is at the heart of double-entry book-keeping and most modern accounting systems are based upon it.

KEY POINTS

1 In preparing accounting statements, accountants adopt a number of rules that have evolved over a number of centuries.

2 There are four main boundary rules: entity, periodicity, going concern, and quantitative.

3 The six main measurement rules are: money measurement, historic cost, realization, matching, dual aspect, and materiality.

4 Ethical rules include: prudence, consistency, objectivity, and relevance.

5 No satisfactory conceptual framework of accounting has yet been developed by the accountancy profession (although the ASB is attempting to do so). Thus, new accounting problems have to be dealt with on a fire-fighting basis.

CHECK YOUR LEARNING

1 State whether each of the following comments is true or false:
  (a) Accounting is based on a theoretical framework. True/False
  (b) All of the basic accounting rules are codified in law. True/False
  (c) Accountants can adapt accounting rules to suit particular circumstances. True/False

2 Fill in the missing blanks in the following statement:
If in doubt, _____ losses, and _____ profits.

3 Indicate the category of the following six accounting rules:

	Boundary	Measurement	Ethical
(a) going concern	☐	☐	☐
(b) matching	☐	☐	☐
(c) money measurement	☐	☐	☐
(d) objectivity	☐	☐	☐
(e) periodicity	☐	☐	☐
(f) prudence	☐	☐	☐

ANSWERS

1 (a) false (b) false (c) true
2 over-state; under-state
3 (a) boundary (b) measurement (c) measurement (d) ethical
  (e) boundary (f) ethical

QUESTIONS

In questions 2.1, 2.2 and 2.3 you are required to state which accounting rule the accountant would most probably adopt in dealing with the problem.

2.1 (1) Electricity consumed in period 1 and paid for in period 2.
(2) Equipment originally purchased for £20 000 which would now cost £30 000.
(3) The company's good industrial relations record.
(4) A five year construction contract.
(5) A customer who might go bankrupt owing the company £5000.
(6) The company's vehicles which would only have a small scrap value if the company goes into liquidation.

2.2 (1) A demand by the company's chairman to include every detailed transaction in the presentation of the annual accounts.
(2) A sole-trader business which has paid the proprietor's income tax based on the business profits for the year.
(3) A proposed change in the methods of valuing stock.
(4) The valuation of a gallon of petrol in one vehicle at the end of accounting period 1.
(5) A vehicle which could be sold for more than its purchase price.
(6) Goods which were sold to a customer in period 1, but for which the cash was only received in period 2.

2.3 (1) The proprietor who has supplied the business capital out of his own private bank account.
(2) The sales manager who is always very optimistic about the credit-worthiness of prospective customers.
(3) The managing director who does not want annual accounts prepared as the company operates a continuous 24 hours a day, 365 days a year process.
(4) At the end of period 1, it is difficult to be certain whether the company will have to pay legal fees of £1000 or £3000.
(5) The proprietor who argues that the accountant has got a motor vehicle entered twice in the books of account.
(6) Some goods were purchased and entered into stock at the end of period 1, but they were not paid for until period 2.

2.4 The following is a list of problems which an accountant may well meet in practice:
(1) The transfer fee of a footballer.
(2) Goods sold in one period, but the cash for them is received in a later period.
(3) The proprietor's personal dwelling house has been used as security for a loan which the bank has granted to the company.
(4) What profit to take in the third year of a five-year construction contract.
(5) Small stocks of stationery held at the accounting year end.
(6) Expenditure incurred in working on the improvement of a new drug.

Required:
State:
(a) which accounting rule the accountant would most probably adopt in dealing with each of the above problems; and
(b) the reasons for your choice.

ADDITIONAL QUESTIONS (WITHOUT ANSWERS)

2.5 The Companies Act 1985 lists five prescribed accounting principles, while SSAP 2 (Disclosure of accounting policies) refers to four fundamental accounting concepts.

Required:
Write a report for your managing director comparing and contrasting the five accounting principles laid down in the Companies Act 1985 with the four fundamental accounting concepts outlined in SSAP 2. (*Note:* before preparing your report, you are advised to consult both the Act and the Standard.)

2.6 The adoption of the realization and matching rules in preparing financial accounts requires a great deal of subjective judgement.

Required:
Write an essay examining whether it would be fairer, easier, and more meaningful to prepare financial accounts on a cash flow basis.

PART 2

Financial accounting

CHAPTER 3

Recording accounting information

Siebe cost-cutting puts profits up by 9%

By Andrew Bolger

A drive to cut costs enabled Siebe, the UK-based international engineering systems and controls group, to increase profits in spite of continuing recession in nearly all of its main markets.

Pre-tax profits rose 9 per cent to £185.1m for the year to April 3, although sales were nearly 1 per cent lower at £1.62bn. Net cash flow increased by £15.2m to £95.2m and gearing, excluding finance leases, fell from 78.8 to 60.4 per cent.

Mr Barrie Stephens, chairman, said the group was well on course to reduce the gearing percentage to the mid-50s by the autumn – a commitment made to shareholders when the group bought Foxboro, the US controls business, in 1990.

Mr. Stephens said: "Market shares have increased in all four core businesses. Each division launched a signifcant number of successful new products during the year.

"These excellent results also reflect our rigorous management of working capital and cash flow and emphasise the powerful position from which we shall grow and enhance our shareholders' value as economic conditions surely improve."

The group said the final quarter of the period confirmed indications of an improvement in the US and UK. It also believed that Japanese markets would recover within the next 18 months.

Mr Stephens said: "These encouraging indications, together with Siebe's significantly stronger order book and strong balance sheet, with cash of £205m, leads the group to look forward with confidence to the future."

Siebe increased its net trading margins across the group from 10.4 to 11.4 per cent, with all segments showing improvement. Productivity increased, with manning reduced by 6.1 per cent, or 1,932 employees.

Sales volumes were down 4.3 per cent in constant currency terms. Overseas business accounted for 91.5 per cent or group sales and 89.2 per cent of group profits.

Group spending on research and development was £65.5m, or 4 per cent of turnover, which was taken through the profit and loss account.

A further £23m of spending on software was capitalised as intangible assets, although that was less than the equivalent depreciation charge of £31m.

Earnings per share rose by 14 per cent to 27.2p from 23.8p. A final dividend of 6.6725p gives a total for the year of 10p, against 9.075p, a rise of 10.2 per cent, which is covered 2.7 times.

The Financial Times, 3 June 1993

Exhibit 3.0 Before you can control your costs, you have to know what they are . . .

In the last chapter, we outlined a number of basic accounting rules, including the dual aspect rule. In this chapter, we are going to examine this rule in much more detail.

Most modern book-keeping systems adopt the dual aspect rule, irrespective of whether they are hand written, mechanized or computer based. While it is unlikely that as a non-accountant you will be involved in the recording of accounting data, you may well be presented with information based on that data. In presenting it to you, it is sometimes assumed that you have some knowledge of double-entry book-keeping.

This chapter has been specially designed to introduce the *non-accountant* to the subject of double-entry book-keeping. The chapter contains a number of book-keeping examples, and while it might seem unnecessary for you to work through them, you are recommended to do so for two main reasons:

1 it will help you to become familiar with accounting terminology;
2 a knowledge of the methods used in preparing accounting information will help you to assess its *usefulness* in doing your job much more effectively and efficiently.

We had better warn you that this will not be an easy chapter for you to work through. And we mean *work*, rather than just read through. Most sections contain an exhibit which illustrates a particular book-keeping procedure. These exhibits must be studied most carefully.

To help you get the most out of this chapter, you are recommended to adopt the following procedure:

1 read the descriptive material in each section very carefully;
2 make sure that you understand the requirements of each exhibit;
3 examine the answer to each exhibit, paying particular attention to the following points:
   (a) the way in which it has been presented, i.e. its format;
   (b) how the data in the exhibit have been converted in response to the requirements of the question;
4 once you have worked through the answer, try to do the question on your own without reference to the solution;
5 if you go wrong, or you find that you do not know how to do the question, re-read the earlier parts of the chapter, and then have another go at it.

We begin our study of the dual aspect rule by examining its basic fundamental concept. We do so in the next section.

LEARNING OBJECTIVES

By the end of this chapter, you will be able to:
● describe what is meant by the terms 'debit' and 'credit';
● write up some simple ledger accounts;
● extract a trial balance;
● identify six accounting errors not revealed in a trial balance.

THE DUAL ASPECT RULE

The dual aspect rule arises from a recognition that every time a transaction takes place, there must always be a two-sided effect *within* the entity (a transaction is simply the doing or performing of any business). A few examples should help to make point clear:

1 If an owner of an entity pays £10 000 into his business bank account out of his private bank account, the business bank account will go *up* by £10,000, but the amount owed by the business to the owner will also go *up* by £10 000.
2 If the business owes Jones £3000 and it sends him a cheque for £2000, the amount that it owes Jones will go *down* by £2000, but its bank account will also go *down* by £2000.
3 If Smith owes a business some money, and it receives £1000 from him, the business's cash will go *up* by £1000, but the amount owed by Smith will go *down* by £1000.
4 If a business pays £5,000 in cash for a car, the the total value of the cars it owns will go *up* by £5000, but its cash balance will go *down* by £5000.

These examples are illustrated in diagrammatic form in Exhibit 3.1

Transaction 1 results in an up/up effect; transaction 2 results in a down/down effect; and transactions 3 and 4 have an up/down effect. Thus, although some transactions move in the same direction, other transactions can move in opposite directions. None the less, there is *always* a twofold effect: there are no exceptions. Note that this twofold effect takes place *within* the entity. We are not interested in the effect that it may have on outside parties: that is their own affair, and not ours, except insofar as it has an impact on our business.

The recognition of the twofold effect of all transactions gave rise to the system of recording accounting data that we now refer to as *double-entry book-keeping*. Its main objective is very simple: it is to record the dual

Exhibit 3.1 Examples of the twofold effect when a transaction takes place

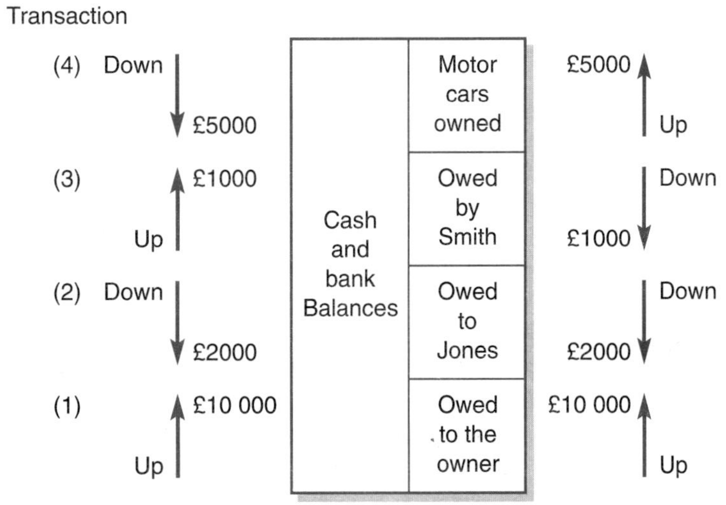

effect of all transactions. But why should we want to record everything twice over? There are two main reasons:

1 it provides valuable information about the effect of each transaction in respect of the business;
2 as every transaction is recorded twice, it provides a check on the accuracy of each recording; in other words, it is a form of control.

The recording of accounting data is achieved by classifying all transactions into appropriate groupings. These are then stored separately in what are known as *accounts*. An account is simply a history or a record of a particular type of transaction. In a manual system all of the accounts are usually kept in bound books known as *ledgers*. Nowadays, however, many entities store information in computer-based systems, although hand-written recording systems are still quite common in smaller businesses.

The effect of a particular transaction on an account is to cause the balance on the account either to go up or to go down. Remember that all transactions are recorded in monetary terms, so a particular transaction could either *increase* the total amount held within an account, or it could have the opposite effect, and *decrease* it. We can put it another way, and suggest that the account either *receives* an additional amount, or it *gives* (or releases) it. It is this receiving and giving effect that has given rise to two Latin terms commonly used in accounting, and with which you must become familiar. The two terms are as follows:

> **Debit:** meaning to receive, or value received;
> **Credit:** meaning to give, or value given.

Accountants judge the twofold effect of all transactions on particular accounts from a receiving and giving point of view, and each transaction is recorded on that basis. Thus, when a transaction takes place, it is necessary to ask the following questions:

1 which account should *receive* this transaction (i.e. which account should be *debited*?);
2 which account has *given* this amount (i.e. which account should be *credited*?).

Accounts have been designed to keep the debit entries separate from the credit entries. This helps to emphasize the opposite, albeit *equal* effect each transaction has within the recording system. The separation is achieved by recording the debit entries on the left-hand side of the page, and the credit entries on the right-hand side. In a hand-written system, each account is normally kept on a separate page (known as a folio) in a *book of account* (although if there are a lot of accounts, it may be neces-

Exhibit 3.2 Example of a ledger account

Date	Description	Folio	Amount £	Date	Description	Folio	Amount £
	Debit side				Credit side		

Tutorial notes
1 The columnar headings would normally be omitted.
2 The description of each entry is usually limited to the *title* of the corresponding account in which the equal and opposite entry may be found.
3 The folio column is used to refer to the folio (or page) number of the corresponding account.
4 This example of a ledger account may nowadays only be found in a fairly basic handwritten book-keeping system. Computerized and mechanized systems of recording information usually necessitate an alternative format.

sary to keep several books of account). A book of account is also sometimes known as a *ledger*, and hence accounts are often referred to as *ledger accounts*. The format of a typical hand-written ledger account is illustrated in Exhibit 3.2.

There is no logical reason why debits should be entered on the left-hand side of an account, and credits on the right-hand side. It is purely a matter of custom, like driving on the left-hand or right-hand side of the road.

In the next section we will show you how particular transactions are recorded in appropriate ledger accounts.

RECORDING INFORMATION

It would not be helpful to either the owners or the managers of a business if the information was not recorded systematically. What has evolved, therefore, is a practical method of capturing the twofold nature of all transactions in separate accounts. Normally, each transaction is recorded in two quite separate accounts, so the book-keeper has to decide in which two accounts to enter a particular transactions. The following sub-sections illustrate the procedure that he will adopt.

Choice of accounts

Most transactions can be easily assigned to an appropriate account. The total number and type will depend partly upon the amount of information that the owner wants (for example, he might keep salaries and wages in separate accounts), and partly upon the nature of the business (a manufacturing entity will probably need more accounts than a service entity). In practice, there are a number of accounts that are common to most entities, but if you do not know which account to use, you should adopt the following rule:

> **If in doubt, open another account.**

If an account does prove superfluous, it can always be closed down. While some accounts are common to most entities, it will not always be clear what they should be used for. An idea of the overall system is shown in Exhibit 3.3, and we also list a brief summary of the main types of accounts:

Capital

The **Capital Account** records what the owner has contributed (or given) to the entity out of his private resources in order to start the business and keep it going. In other words, it shows what the business owes him.

Exhibit 3.3 The inter-linking of different types of accounts

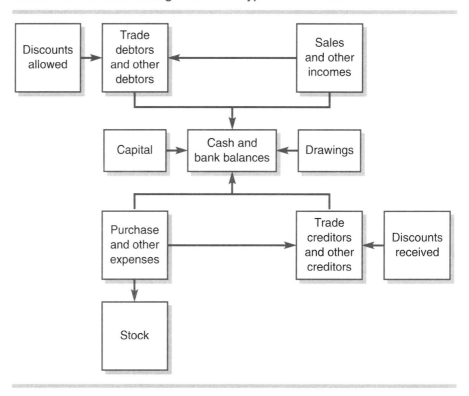

| Cash at bank | The **Bank Account** records what money the entity keeps at the bank. It shows what has been put in (usually in the form of cash and cheques) and what has been taken out (usually by cheque payments). |

Cash in hand · The **Cash Account** works on similar lines to that of the Bank Account, except that it records the physical cash received (such as notes, coins and cheques) before they are paid into the bank. The cash may be used to purchase goods and services, or it may be paid straight into the bank. From a control point of view, it is best not to pay for purchases directly out of cash receipts, but to draw an amount out of the bank specifically for sundry cash purchases. Any large amount should be paid by cheque.

Creditors · **Creditors Accounts** record what the entity owes its suppliers for goods or services purchased or supplied on credit (see also trade creditors).

Debtors · **Debtors Accounts** record what is owed to the entity by its customers for goods or services sold to them on credit (see also trade debtors).

Discounts allowed · **Discounts allowed** are cash discounts granted to the entity's customers for the prompt settlement of any debts due to the entity. The amount of cash received from debtors who claim a cash discount will then be less than the total amount for which they have been invoiced.

Discounts received · **Discounts received** relate to cash discounts given by the entity's suppliers for the prompt payment of any amounts due to them. Thus, the amount paid to the entity's creditors will be less than the invoiced amount.

Drawings · The term *drawings* has a special meaning in accounting. The **Drawings Account** is used to record what cash (or goods) the owner has withdrawn from the business for his own personal use.

Petty cash · The **Petty Cash Account** is similar to both the Bank Account and the Cash Account. It is usually limited to the recording of minor cash transactions, such as bus fares, or tea and coffee for the office. The cash used to finance this account will normally be transferred from the Bank Account.

Purchases · The term *purchases* has a restricted meaning in accounting. It relates to those goods that are bought primarily with the intention of selling them (normally at a profit). The purchase of some motor cars, for example would not usually be recorded in the **Purchases Account** unless they have been bought with the intention of selling them to customers. Goods not intended for resale are usually recorded in separate accounts. Some purchases may also require further work to be done on them before they are eventually sold.

Trade creditors

Trade Creditor Accounts are similar to Creditors Accounts except that they relate specifically to trading items, i.e. purchases.

Trade debtors

Trade Debtor Accounts are similar to Debtor Accounts except that they also relate specifically to trading items, i.e. sales.

Trade discounts

Trade discounts are a form of special discount. They may be given for placing a large order, for example, or for being a loyal customer. Trade discounts are deducted from the normal purchase or price or selling price. They are not recorded in the books of account, and they will not appear on any invoice.

Sales

The **Sales Account** records the value of goods sold to customers during a particular accounting period. The account includes both cash and credit sales. It does not include receipts from (say) the sale of a motor car purchased for use within the business.

Stock

Stock includes the value of goods which had not been sold at the end of an accounting period. In accounting terminology, this would be referred to as **closing stock**. The closing stock at the end of one period becomes the **opening stock** at the beginning of the next period.

Once the book-keeper has chosen the accounts in which to record all the transactions for a particular accounting period, he has then to decide which account should be debited and which account should be credited. We examine this problem in the next sub-section.

Entering transactions in accounts

There is one simple rule to adopt in follow in entering transactions in their respective accounts:

> **Debit the account which receives**
> and
> **Credit the account which gives.**

This rule is illustrated in Exhibit 3.4 which contains some common ledger account entries.

Exhibit 3.4 Example of some common ledger account entries

Example 1

The proprietor contributes some cash to the business.

Debit: Cash Account   *Credit:* Capital Account

Reason: The Cash Account receives some cash given to the business by the owner. His Capital Account is the giving account and the Cash Account is the receiving account.

Example 2

Some cash in the till is paid into the business bank account.

Debit: Bank Account   *Credit:* Cash Account

Reason: The Cash Account is the giving account because it is releasing some cash to the Bank Account.

Example 3

A van is purchased for use in the business; it is paid for by cheque.

Debit: Van Account   *Credit:* Bank Account

Reason: The Bank Account is giving some money in order to pay for a van, so the Bank Account must be credited as it is the giving account.

Example 4

Some goods are purchased for cash.

Debit: Purchases Account   *Credit:* Cash Account

Reason: The Cash Account is giving up an amount of cash in order to pay for some purchases. The Cash Account is the giving account, and so it must be credited.

Example 5

Some goods are purchased on credit terms from Fred.

Debit: Purchases Account   *Credit:* Fred's Account.

Reason: Fred is supplying the goods on credit terms to the business. He is, therefore, the giver and his account must be credited.

Example 6

Some goods are sold for cash.

Debit: Cash Account   *Credit:* Sales Account

Reason: The Cash Account receives the cash from the sale of goods, the Sales Account being the giving account.

Example 7
Some goods are sold on credit terms to Sarah.

> *Debit:* Sarah's Account   *Credit:* Sales Account

> *Reason***:** Sarah's Account is debited because she is receiving the goods, and the Sales Account is credited, because it is supplying (or giving) them.

It is not easy for beginners to think of the receiving and of the giving effect of each transaction. You will find that it is very easy to get them mixed up and to then reverse the entries. If we look at Examples 6 and 7 in Exhibit 3.4, for example, it is difficult to understand why the Sales Account should be credited. Why is the Sales Account the giving account? Surely it is *receiving* an amount and not giving anything? In one sense, it is receiving something, but that applies to any entry in any account. So in the case of the sales account, regard it as a *supplying* account, because it gives (or releases) something to another account.

If you find this concept difficult to understand, think of the effect on the *opposite* account. A cash sale, for example, results in cash being increased (not decreased). The cash account must, therefore, be the receiving account, and it must be debited. Somebody (say Jones) must have given the cash, but as it is a cash sale, we credit it straight to the sales account. If you find it easier, think of the Sales Department having supplied, given or *sold* the goods to Jones.

Most students find it easier, in fact, to work out the double-entry effect of respective transactions by relating them to the movement of cash. You might find it useful,therefore, to remember the following procedure:

Either   **Debit:** the Cash (or Bank) Account and
       Credit: the corresponding account,
       if the entity **receives** some cash.
Or   **Debit:** the corresponding account and
       Credit: the Cash (or Bank) Account,
       if the entity **gives** some cash.

If a movement of cash is not involved in a particular transaction, work out the effect on the corresponding account on the assumption that one account *is* affected by a cash transaction. In the case of a credit sale, for example, the account that benefits from the *receipt* of the goods must be that of an individual, so that individual's account must be debited (instead of the cash account, as it would be in the case of a cash sale). The corresponding entry must, therefore, be *credited* to some account. In this case it will be to the sales account.

You might also find it useful to remember another general rule used in double-entry book-keeping:

> **For every debit there must be a credit**
> and
> **For every credit there must be a debit.**

There are no exceptions to this rule. As this chapter develops, more practice will be obtained in deciding which account to debit and which account to credit. After some time, it becomes largely a routine exercise, and you will find yourself making the correct entries automatically.

It would now be helpful to illustrate the entry of a number of transactions in specific ledger accounts. We do so in the next section.

A LEDGER ACCOUNT EXAMPLE

This section illustrates the procedure adopted in entering various transactions in ledger accounts. The section brings together the basic material covered in the earlier part of this chapter. It demonstrates the use of various types, and the debiting and crediting effect of different type of transactions.

The example relates to a sole trader commencing business on his own account. As we explained in earlier chapters, while most non-accountants will not be involved in sole-trader entities, this type of entity is useful in illustrating the basic principles of double-entry book-keeping. Indeed, a more complex form of entity would only obscure those principles.

The example is also confined to a business that purchases and sells goods on cash terms. Businesses that buy and sell goods on credit terms will be a feature of later examples. The example is shown in Exhibit 3.5.

It is unnecessary for you as a non-accountant to spend too much time on detailed ledger account work, but before moving on to the next section, you are recommended to work through Exhibit 3.5 without reference to the answer. This exercise will help you to familiarize yourself with the dual aspect concept, and therefore enable you to understand much more clearly the basis on which accounting information is recorded.

After entering all the transactions for a particular period in appropriate ledger accounts, the next stage in the exercise is to calculate the balance on each account as at the end of each accounting period. This procedure is outlined in the next section.

Exhibit 3.5 Joe Simple: A sole trader

The following information relates to Joe Simple who started a new business on 1 January 19X1:

1 1.01.X1 Joe started the business with £5000 in cash.
2 3.01.X1 He paid £3000 of the cash into a business bank account.
3 5.01.X1 Joe bought a van for £2000 paying by cheque.
4 7.01.X1 He brought some goods, paying £1000 in cash.
5 9.01.X1 Joe sold some of the goods, receiving £1500 in cash.

Required:
Enter the above transaction in Joe's ledger accounts.

Answer to Exhibit 3.5
Joe Simple's books of account:

Cash Account

	£		£
1.01.X1 Capital (1)	5000	3.01.X1 Bank (2)	3000
9.01.X1 Sales (5)	1500	7.01.X1 Purchases (4)	1000

Capital Account

	£		£
		1.01.X1 Cash (1)	5000

Bank Account

	£		£
3.01.X1 Cash (2)	3000	5.01.X1 Van (3)	2000

Van Account

	£		£
5.01.X1 Bank (3)	2000		

Purchases Account

	£		£
7.01.X1 Cash (4)	1000		

Sales Account

	£		£
		9.01.X1 Cash (5)	1500

Tutorial notes
1 The numbers in brackets after each entry refer to the exhibit notes; they have been inserted for tutorial guidance only.
2 The narration relates to that account in which the equal and opposite entry may be found.

BALANCING THE ACCOUNTS

During a particular accounting period, some accounts (such as the bank and cash accounts) will contain a great many debit and credit entries. Some accounts may contain either mainly debit entries (e.g. the purchases account), or largely credit entries (e.g. the sales account). It would be somewhat inconvenient to allow the entries (whether mainly debits, credits, or a mixture of both) to build up without occasionally striking a balance. Indeed, the owner will almost certainly want to know not just what is in each account, but also what its overall or *net* balance is (i.e the total of all the debit entries less the total of all the credit entries). Thus, at frequent intervals, it will be necessary to calculate the balance on each account.

Balancing an account requires the book-keeper to add up all the respective debit and credit entries, take one total away from the other, and arrive at the net balance.

Accounts may be balanced fairly frequently, e.g. once a week or once a month, but some entities only balance their books when they prepare their annual accounts. However, in order to keep a tight control on the management of the business, it is advisable to balance the books at reasonably short intervals. The frequency will depend upon the nature and the size of the entity, but once a month is probably sufficient for most entities.

The balancing of the accounts is part of the double-entry procedure, and the method is quite formal. In Exhibit 3.6 we show how to balance an account with a *debit* balance on it (i.e., when its total debit entries exceed its total credit entries).

Exhibit 3.6 Balancing an account with a debit balance

Cash Account

	£			£
1.01.X1 Sales (1)	2 000	10.01.X1 Jones (1)		3 000
15.01.X1 Rent received (1)	1 000	25.01.X1 Davies (1)		5 000
20.01.X1 Smith (1)	4 000			
31.01.X1 Sales (1)	8 000	31.01.X1 Balance c/d (2)		7 000
(3)	£15 000		(3)	£15 000
1.02.X1 Balance b/d (4)	7 000			

Note: The number shown after each narration relates to the tutorial notes below.

Tutorial notes

1 The total debit enties equal £15 000 (2000 + 1000 + 4000 + 8000). The total credit entries equal £8000 (3000 + 5000). The net balance on this account, therefore, at 31 January 19X1 is a *debit* balance of £7000 (15 000 – 8000). Until both the debit entries and the credit entries have been totalled, of course, it will

not usually be apparent whether the balance is a debit one or a credit one. However, it should be noted that there can never be a credit balance in a *cash* account, because it is impossible to pay out more cash than has been received.

2 The debit balance of £7000 is inserted on the *credit* side of the account at the time that the account is balanced (in the case of Exhibit 3.6, at 31 January 19X1). This then enables the total of the credit column to be balanced so that it agrees with the total of the debit column. The abbreviation 'c/d' means carried down. In this exhibit the debit balance is carried down in the account in order to start the new period on 1 February 19X1.

3 The £15 000 shown as a total in both the debit and the credit columns demonstrates that the columns balance (they do so, of course, because £7000 has been inserted in the credit column to make them balance). The totals are double-underlined with the currency sign placed in front of them in order to signify that they are a final total.

4 The balancing figure of £7000 is brought down ('b/d') in the account to start the new period on 1 February 19X1. The double-entry has been completed because £7000 has been debited *below* the line (i.e. below the £15 000 debit total), and the £7000 balancing figure credited *above* the line (i.e. above the £15 000 total).

Exhibit 3.6 demonstrates how an account with a debit entry is balanced. In Exhibit 3.7, we illustrate a similar procedure, but his time the account has a *credit* balance.

Exhibit 3.7 Balancing an account with a credit balance

Scott's Account

	£			£
31.01.X1 Bank (1)	20 000	15.01.X1 Purchases (1)		10 000
31.01.X1 Balance c/d (2)	5 000	20.01.X1 Purchases (1)		15 000
(3)	£25 000		(3)	£25 000
		1.02.X1 Balance b/d (4)		5 000

Note: The number shown after each narration relates to the tutorial notes below.

Tutorial notes

1 Apart from the balance, there is only one debit entry in Scott's account: the bank entry of £20 000. The total credit entries amount to £25 000 (10 000 + 15 000). Scott has a *credit* balance, therefore, in his account as at 31 January 19X1 of £5000 (10 000 + 15 000 − 20 000). With many more entries in the account it would not always be possible to tell immediately whether the balance was a debit one or a credit one.

2 The credit balance of £5000 at 31 January 19X1 is inserted on the *debit* side of the account in order to enable the account to be balanced. The balance is then carried down (c/d) to the next period.

3 The £25 000 shown as the total for both the debit and the credit columns identifies the balancing of the account. This has been made possible because of the insertion of the £5000 balancing figure on the debit side of the account.

4 The balancing figure of £5000 is brought down (b/d) in the account in order to start the account in the new period beginning on 1 February 19X1. The double-entry has been completed because the debit entry of £5000 *above* the £25 000 line on the debit side equals the credit entry *below* the £25 000 line on the credit side.

Exhibits 3.6 and 3.7 demonstrate the importance of always obeying the cardinal rule of double-entry book-keeping:

> **For every debit there must be a credit**
> and
> **For every credit there must be a debit.**

This rule must still be followed even if the two entries are made in the same account (as is the case when an account is balanced). If this rule is not obeyed, the accounts will not balance. This could mean that a lot of time is spent looking for an apparent error, or it could even mean that some incorrect information is given to the owner or managers of the business, since there is bound to be a mistake in at least one account.

The next stage after balancing each account is to check that the double-entry has been completed throughout the entire system. This is done by compiling what is known as a *trial balance*. We examine this procedure in the next section.

THE TRIAL BALANCE

A trial balance is a statement compiled at the end of a specific accounting period. It lists all the ledger account debit balances and all the ledger account credit balances. A trial balance is a convenient method of checking that all the transactions and all the balances have been entered correctly in the ledger accounts.

Once all the debit balances and credit balances have been listed in the trial balance, the total of all the debit balances is then compared with the total of all the credit balances. If the two totals agree, we can be reasonably confident that the book-keeping procedures have been carried out accurately.

It should be noted that a trial balance is a working paper: it does not form part of the double-entry process.

We illustrate the preparation of a trial balance in Exhibit 3.8. We also take the opportunity of giving some more examples of how transactions are entered in ledger accounts. You are recommended to work through part (a) of the Exhibit before moving on to part (b). When you are confident that you understand the procedures involved, have a go at doing the question without looking at the solution.

Exhibit 3.8 Edward – Compilation of a trial balance

Edward started a new business on 1 January 19X1. The following transactions took place during his first month in business:

19X1
1.01 Edward commenced business with £10 000 in cash
3.01 He paid £8000 of the cash into a business bank account.
6.01 He bought a van on credit from Perkin's garage for £3000.
9.01 Edward rented shop premises for £1000 per quarter; he paid for the first quarter immediately by cheque.
12.01 He bought goods on credit from Roy Limited for £4000.
15.01 He paid shop expenses amounting to £1500 by cheque.
18.01 Edward sold goods on credit to Scott and Company for £3000.
21.01 He settled Perkin's account by cheque.
24.01 Edward received a cheque from Scott and Company for £2000; this cheque was paid immediately into the bank.
27.01 Edward sent a cheque to Roy Limited for £500.
31.01 Goods costing £3000 were purchased from Roy Limited on credit.
31.01 Cash sales for the month amounted to £2000.

Required:
(a) Enter the above transactions in appropriate ledger accounts, balance off each account as at 31 January 19X1, and bring down the balances as at that date; and
(b) extract a trial balance as at 31 January 19X1.

Cash Account

	£		£
1.01.X1 Capital (1)	10 000	3.01.X1 Bank (2)	8 000
31.01.X1 Sales (12)	2 000	31.01.X1 Balance c/d	4 000
	£12 000		£12 000
1.02.X1 Balance b/d	4 000		

Capital Account

	£		£
		1.01.X1 Cash (1)	10 000

Bank account

	£		£
3.01.X1 Cash (2)	8 000	9.01.X1 Rent payable (4)	1 000
24.01.X1 Scott and		15.01.X1 Shop expenses (6)	1 500
Company (9)	2 000	21.01.X1 Perkin's garage (8)	3 000
		27.01.X1 Roy Limited (10)	500
		31.01.X1 Balance c/d	4 000
	£10 000		£10 000
1.02.X1 Balance b/d	4 000		

Van Account

		£		£
6.01.X1	Perkin's Garage (3)	3 000		

Perkin's Garage Account

		£			£
21.01.X1	Bank (8)	3 000	6.01.X1	Van (3)	3 000

Rent Payable Account

		£		£
9.01.X1	Bank (4)	1 000		

Purchases Account

		£			£
12.01.X1	Roy Limited (5)	4 000			
31.01.X1	Roy Limited (11)	3 000	31.01.X1	Balance c/d	7 000
		£7 000			£7 000
1.02.X1	Balance b/d	7 000			

Roy Limited Account

		£			£
27.01.X1	Bank (10)	500	12.01.X1	Purchases (5)	4 000
31.01.X1	Balance c/d	6 500	31.01.X1	Purchases (11)	3 000
		£7 000			£7 000
			1.02.X1	Balance b/d	6 500

Shop Expenses Account

		£		£
15.01.X1	Bank (6)	1 500		

Sales Account

		£			£
			18.01.X1	Scott & Company (7)	3 000
31.01.X1	Balance c/d	5 000	31.01.X1	Cash (12)	2 000
		£5 000			£5 000
			1.02.X1	Balance b/d	5 000

Scott and Company Account

		£			£
18.01.X1	Sales (7)	3 000	24.01.X1	Bank (9)	2 000
			31.01.X1	Balance c/d	1 000
		£3 000			£3 000
1.02.X1	Balance b/d	1 000			

Tutorial notes

1 The number shown after each narration has been inserted for tutorial guidance only in order to illustrate the insertion of each entry in the appropriate account.
2 There is no need to balance an account and carry down the balance when there is only a single entry in one account (for example, Edward's Capital Account).
3 Note that some accounts have no balance in them at all as at 31 January 19X1 (for example, Perkin's Garage Account).

Answer to Exhibit 3.8 (b)

Trial Balance at 31 January 19X1

	Dr £	Cr £
Cash	4 000	
Capital		10 000
Bank	4 000	
Van	3 000	
Rent payable	1 000	
Purchases	7 000	
Roy Limited		6 500
Shop expenses	1 500	
Sales		5 000
Scott and Company	1 000	
	£21 500	£21 500

Tutorial notes

1 The total debit balance agrees with the total credit balance, and therefore the trial balance balances. This confirms that the transactions appear to have been entered in the books of account correctly.
2 The total amount of £21 500 shown in both the debit and credit columns of the trial balance does not have any significance, except to prove that the trial balance balances.

Did you manage to get your trial balance to balance? If not, re-read the earlier parts of this chapter, and then have another attempt at the Exhibit.

Once a trial balance has been balanced, we can be reasonably confident that we have carried out the double-entry procedures accurately. However, there are some errors that do not affect the balancing of the trial balance. These errors may be summarized as follows:

1 **Omission:** a transaction could have been completely omitted from the books of account.
2 **Complete reversal of entry:** a transaction could have been entered in (say) Account A as a debit and in Account B as a credit, when it should have been entered as a credit in Account A and as a debit in Account B.

3 **Principle:** a transaction may have been entered in the wrong *type* of account, e.g. the purchase of a new delivery van may have been debited to the purchases account, instead of the delivery vans account.

4 **Commission:** a transaction may have been entered in the correct type of account, but in the wrong *personal* account, e.g. in Bill's Account instead of in Ben's Account.

5 **Compensating:** an error may have been made in (say) adding the debit side of one account, and a identical error in adding the credit side of another account; the two errors would then cancel each other out.

6 **Original entry:** a transaction may be entered incorrectly in both accounts, e.g. as £291 instead of as £921.

Even allowing for the types of errors listed above, the trial balance still serves three useful purposes. These are as follows:

1 to check the accuracy of the transactions entered in the accounts;
2 to obtain a summary of the balance on each account;
3 to provide the information needed in preparing the annual accounts.

We shall be dealing with the third purpose in some detail in the next chapter.

CONCLUSION

As a non-accountant, it is most unlikely that you will become involved in having to write up ledger accounts. In this chapter, we have avoided going into unnecessary detail about double-entry book-keeping that is irrelevant for your purposes. As part of your managerial role, you will almost certainly be supplied with information which has been extracted from a ledger system. In order to assess its real benefit to you, we believe that it is most important that you should know something about where it has come from, what it means, and what reliability can be placed on it. Before leaving this chapter, therefore, we recommend that you make absolutely sure that you are familiar with the following features of a double-entry book-keeping system:

- the type of accounts generally used in practice;
- the meaning of the terms *debit* and *credit*;
- the definition of the terms *debtor* and *creditor*;
- the method of entering transactions in ledger accounts;
- the balancing of ledger accounts;
- the importance of the trial balance.

This chapter has provided you with the basic information necessary to become familiar with the six features listed above. If you are reasonably confident that you now have a basic grasp of double-entry book-keeping, you can move on to an examination of how financial accounts are prepared. Before before doing so, however, you are recommended to test your understanding of the contents of this chapter by attempting some of the chapter questions.

CHECK YOUR LEARNING

1 Fill in the missing blanks in the following sentence:
A debit entry goes on the _____-hand side of a ledger account, and a _____ entry goes on the right-hand side.

2 Which two ledger accounts would you use in recording each of the following transactions?
(a) cash sales
(b) rent paid by cheque
(c) wages paid in cash
(d) a supplier of goods paid by cheque
(e) goods sold on credit to Ford

3 State which account would be debited, and which account would be credited in respect of each of the following items:
(a) cash paid to a supplier
(b) office rent paid by cheque
(c) cash sales
(d) dividend received by cheque

4 Is there anything wrong with the following abbreviated bank account?

Debit	£000	Credit	£000
10.3.X6 Wages paid	1000	6.6.X6 Interest received	500

5 State whether each of the following errors would be discovered as as result of preparing a trial balance:

(a) £342 has been entered in both ledger accounts instead of £432   Yes/No
(b) The debit column in Prim's account has been overstated by £50   Yes/No
(c) £910 has been put in Anne's account instead of in Agnes'   Yes/No

ANSWERS

1 (a) left; credit
2 (a) cash; sales   (b) rent paid; bank   (c) wages; cash (d) supplier's; bank
  (c) Ford; sales
3   Debit   Credit
  (a) Supplier   Cash
  (b) Office rent   Bank
  (c) Cash   Sales
  (d) Bank   Dividends received
4 The entries are on the wrong side.
5 (a) no   (b) yes   (c) no

QUESTIONS

3.1 Adam has just gone into business. The following is a list of his transactions for the month of January 19X1:
1 Cash paid into the business by Adam.
2 Goods for resale purchased on cash terms.
3 Van bought for cash.
4 One quarter's rent for premises paid in cash.
5 Some goods sold on cash terms.
6 Adam buys some office machinery for cash.

Required:
State which account in Adam's books of account should be debited and which account should be credited for each transaction.

3.2 The following is a list of Brown's transactions for February 19X2:
1 Transfer of cash to a bank account.
2 Cash received from sale of goods.
3 Purchase of goods paid for by cheque.
4 Office expenses paid in cash.
5 Cheques received from customers from sale of goods on cash terms.
6 A motor car for use in the business paid for by cheque.

Required:
State which account in Brown's books of account should be debited and which account should be credited for each transaction.

3.3 Corby is in business as a retail distributor. The following is a list of his transactions for March 19X3:
1 Goods purchased from Smith on credit.
2 Corby introduces further capital in cash into the business.

3 Goods sold for cash.
4 Goods purchased for cash.
5 Cash transferred to the bank.
6 Machinery purchased, paid for in cash.

Required:
State which account in Corby's books of account should be debited and which account should be credited for each transaction.

3.4 Davies buys and sells goods on cash and credit terms. The following is a list of his transactions for April 19X4:
1 Capital introduced by Davies paid into the bank.
2 Goods purchased on credit terms from Swallow.
3 Goods sold to Hill for cash.
4 Cash paid for purchase of goods.
5 Dale buys goods from Davies on credit.
6 Motoring expenses paid by cheque.

Required:
State which account in Davies' books of account should be debited and which account credited for each transaction.

3.5 The following is a list of Edgar's transactions for May 19X5:
1 Goods purchased on credit from Gill.
2 Goods sold on credit to Ash.
3 Goods sold for cash to Crosby.
4 Goods purchased in cash from Lowe.
5 Cheque sent to Gill.
6 Cash received from Ash.

Required:
State which account in Edgar's books should be debited and which account should be credited for each transaction.

3.6 Ford buys and sells goods on cash and credit terms. The following is a list of his transactions for June 19X6.
1 Goods sold on cash terms to Orange.
2 Goods purchased from Carter on credit.
3 Goods sold to Holly on credit.
4 Goods bought on cash terms from Apple.
5 Holly returns some of the goods.
6 Goods returned to Carter.

Required:
State which account in Ford's books should be debited and which account should be credited for each transaction.

3.7 The following transactions relate to Gordon's business for the month of July 19X7:
1 Bought goods on credit from Watson

2 Sold some goods for cash.
3 Sold some goods on credit to Moon.
4 Sent a cheque for half the amount owing to Watson.
5 Watson grants Gordon a cash discount.
6 Moon settles most of his account in cash.
7 Gordon allows Moon a cash discount that covers the small amount owed by Moon.
8 Gordon purchases some goods for cash.

Required:
State which accounts in Gordon's books of accounts should be debited and which account should be credited for each information.

3.8 Harry started a new business on 1 January 19X8. The following transactions cover his first three months in business:
1 Harry contributed an amount in cash to start the business.
2 He transferred some of the cash to a business bank account.
3 He paid an amount in advance by cheque for rental of business premises.
4 Bought goods on credit from Paul.
5 Purchased a van paying by cheque.
6 Sold some goods for cash to James.
7 Bought goods on credit from Nancy.
8 Paid motoring expenses in cash.
9 Returned some goods to Nancy.
10 Sold goods on credit to Mavis.
11 Harry withdrew some cash for personal use.
12 Bought goods from David paying in cash.
13 Mavis returns some goods.
14 Sent a cheque to Nancy.
15 Cash received from Mavis
16 Harry receives a cash discount from Nancy.
17 Harry allows Mavis a cash discount.
18 Cheque withdrawn at the bank in order to open a petty cash account.

Required:
State which accounts in Harry's books of account should be debited and which account should be credited for each transaction.

3.9 The following is a list of transactions which relate to Ivan for the first month that he is in business:
1.9.X9 Started the business with £10 000 in cash.
2.9.X9 Paid £8000 into a business bank account.
3.9.X9 Purchased £1000 of goods in cash.
10.9.X9 Bought goods costing £6000 on credit from Roy.
12.9.X9 Cash sales of £3000.
15.9.X9 Goods sold on credit terms to Norman for £4000.
20.9.X9 Ivan settles Roy's account by cheque.
30.9.X9 Cheque for £2000 received from Norman.

Required:
Enter the above transactions in Ivan's ledger accounts.

3.10 Jones has been in business since 1 October 19X1. The following is a list of his transactions for October 19X1:

1.10.X1 Capital of £20 000 paid into a business bank account.
2.10.X1 Van purchased on credit from Lang for £5000.
6.10.X1 Goods purchased on credit from Green for £15 000.
10.10.X1 Cheque drawn on the bank for £1000 in order to open a petty cash account.
14.10.X1 Goods sold on credit for £6000 to Haddock.
18.10.X1 Cash sales of £5000.
20.10.X1 Cash purchases of £3000.
22.10.X1 Miscellaneous expenses of £500 paid out of petty cash.
25.10.X1 Lang's account settled by cheque.
28.10.X1 Green allows Jones a cash discount of £500.
29.10.X1 Green is sent a cheque for £10 000.
30.10.X1 Haddock is allowed a cash discount of £600.
31.10.X1 Haddock settles his account in cash.

Required:
Enter the above transactions in Jones' ledger accounts.

3.11 The transactions listed below relate to Ken's business for the month of November 19X2:

1.11.X2 Started the business with £15 000 in cash.
2.11.X2 Transferred £14 000 of the cash to a business bank account.
3.11.X2 Paid rent of £1000 by cheque.
4.11.X2 Bought goods on credit from the following suppliers:
   Ace   £5000
   Mace   £6000
   Pace   £7000
10.11.X2 Sold goods on credit to the following customers:
   Main   £2000
   Pain   £3000
   Vain   £4000
15.11.X2 Returned goods costing £1000 to Pace.
22.11.X2 Pain returned goods sold to him for £2000.
25.11.X2 Additional goods purchased from the following suppliers:
   Ace   £3000
   Mace   £4000
   Pace   £5000
26.11.X2 Office expenses of £2000 paid by cheque.
27.11.X2 Cash sales for the month amounted to £5000.
28.11.X2 Purchases paid for in cash during the month amounted to £4000.
29.11.X2 Cheques sent to the following suppliers:
   Ace   £4000
   Mace   £5000
   Pace   £6000
30.11.X2 Cheques received from the following customers:
   Main   £1000
   Pain   £2000
   Vain   £3000

30.11.X2 The following cash discounts were claimed by Ken:

      Ace   £200

      Mace   £250

      Pace   £300

30.11.X2 The following cash discounts were allowed by Ken:

      Main   £100

      Pain   £200

      Vain   £400

30.11.X2 Cash transfer to the bank of £1000.

Required:

Enter the above transactions in Ken's ledger accounts.

3.12 The following transactions relate to Pat's business for the month of December 19X3:

  1.12.X3 Started the business with £10 000 in cash.

  2.12.X3 Bought goods on credit from the following suppliers:

      Grass   £6000

      Seed   £7000

10.12.X3 Sold goods on credit to the following customers:

      Fog   £3000

      Mist   £4000

12.12.X3 Returned goods to the following suppliers:

      Grass   £1000

      Seed   £2000

15.12.X3 Bought additional goods on credit from Grass for £3000 and from Seed for £4000.

20.12.X3 Sold more goods on credit to Fog for £2000 and to Mist for £3000.

24.12.X3 Paid office expenses of £5000 in cash.

29.12.X3 Received £4000 in cash from Fog and £6000 in cash from Mist.

31.12.X3 Pat paid Grass and Seed £6000 and £8000 respectively in cash.

Required:

(a) Enter the above transactions in Pat's ledger accounts.

(b) Balance off the accounts as at 31 December 19X3.

(c) Bring down the balances as at I January 19X4.

(d) Compile a trial balance as at 31 December 19X3.

3.13 Vale has been in business for some years. The following balances were brought forward in his books of account as at 31 December 19X2:

	£	£
	Dr	Cr
Bank	5 000	
Capital		20 000
Cash	1 000	
Dodd		2 000
Fish	6 000	
Furniture	10 000	
	£22 000	£22 000

During the year to 31 December 19X3 the following transactions took place.
1　Goods bought from Dodd on credit for £30 000.
2　Cash sales of £20 000.
3　Cash purchases ot £15 000.
4　Goods sold to Fish on credit for £50 000.
5　Cheques sent to Dodd totalling £29 000.
6　Cheques received from Fish totalling £45 000.
7　Cash received from Fish amounting to £7000
8　Office expenses paid in cash totalling £9000.
9　Purchase of delivery van costing £12 000 paid by cheque.
10　Cash transfers to bank totalling £3000.

Required:
(a)　Compile Vale's ledger accounts for the year 31 December 19X3, balance off the accounts and bring down the balances as at 1 January 19X4.
(b)　Extract a trial balance as at 31 December 19X3.

3.14　Brian started in business on 1 January 19X4. The following is a list of his transactions for his first month of trading:
1.1.X4　Opened a business bank account with £25 000 obtained from private resources.
2.1.X4　Paid one month's rent of £2000 by cheque.
3.1.X4　Bought goods costing £5000 on credit from Linda.
4.1.X4　Purchased motor car from Savoy Motors for £4000 on credit.
5.1.X4　Purchased goods costing £3000 on credit from Sydney.
10.1.X4　Cash sales of £6000.
15.1.X4　More goods costing £10 000 purchased from Linda on credit.
20.1.X4　Sold goods on credit to Ann for £8000.
22.1.X4　Returned £2000 of goods to Linda.
23.1.X4　Paid £6000 in cash into the bank.
24.1.X4　Ann returned £1000 of goods.
25.1.X4　Withdrew £500 in cash from the bank to open a petty cash account.
26.1.X4　Cheque received from Ann for £5500; Ann also claimed a cash discount of £500.
28.1.X4　Office expenses of £250 paid out of petty cash.
29.1.X4　Sent a cheque to Savoy Motors for £4000.
30.1.X4　Cheques sent to Linda and Sydney for £8000 and £2000 respectively. Cash discounts were also claimed from Linda and Sydney of £700 and £l00 respectively.
31.1.X4　Paid by cheque another month's rent of £2000.
31.1.X4　Brian introduced £5000 additional capital into the business by cheque.

Required:
(a)　Enter the above transactions in Brian's ledger accounts for January 19X4, balance off the accounts and bring down the balances as at 1 February 19X4.
(b)　Compile a trial balance as at 31 January 19X4.

3.15 The following balances have been extracted from Field's ledger accounts as at 28 February 19X5:

	£
Bank	13 000
Cash	2 000
Capital	15 000
Creditors	4 000
Debtors	10 000
Drawings	5 000
Electricity	4 000
Furniture	7 000
Office expenses	3 000
Purchases	50 000
Sales	100 000
Wages	25 000

Required:
Compile Field's trial balance as at 28 February 19X5.

3.16 An accounts clerk has compiled Trent's trial balance as at 31 March 19X6 as follows:

	Dr	Cr
	£	£
Bank (overdrawn)	2 000	
Capital	50 000	
Discounts allowed		5 000
Discounts received	3 000	
Dividends received	2 000	
Drawings		23 000
Investments		14 000
Land and buildings	60 000	
Office expenses	18 000	
Purchases	75 000	
Sales		250 000
Suspense (unexplained balance)		6 000
Rates		7 000
Vans	20 000	
Van expenses		5 000
Wages and salaries	80 000	
	£310 000	£310 000

Required: Compile Trent's corrected trial balance as at 31 March 19X6.

3.17 The following balances have been extracted from Severn's books of account as at 30 April 19X7:

	£000
Purchases	300
Cash	8
Discounts received	2
Rents received	5
Wages	44
Discounts allowed	5
Creditors	12
Telephone	3
Sales	500
Capital	100
Sales returns	20
Bank interest received	1
Furniture and fittings	18
Bank (deposit)	50
Advertising	14
Motor cars	22
Bank (current)	5
Purchases returns	15
Land and buildings	40
Debtors	30
Plant and equipment	37
Drawings	45
Fees received	10
Motor car expenses	4

Required:
Compile Severn's trial balance at 30 April 19X7.

ADDITIONAL QUESTIONS (WITHOUT ANSWERS)

3.18 Donald's transactions for the month of March 19X9 are as follows:

	£
Cash receipts	
Capital contributed	6 000
Sales to customers	3 000
Cash payments	
Goods for sale	4 000
Stationery	500
Postage	300
Travelling	600
Wages	2 900
Transfers to bank	500

	£
Bank receipts	
Receipts from trade debtors:	
Smelt	3 000
Tait	9 000
Ure	5 000
Bank payments	
Payments to trade creditors:	
Craig	2 800
Dobie	5 000
Elgin	6 400
Rent and rates	3 200
Electricity	200
Telephone	100
Salaries	2 000
Miscellaneous expenses	600
Other transactions	
Goods purchased from:	
Craig	3 500
Dobie	7 500
Elgin	7 500
Goods returned to Dobie	400
Goods sold to:	
Smelt	4 000
Tait	10 000
Ure	8 000
Goods returned by Ure	900
Discounts allowed:	
Smelt	200
Tait	500
Ure	400
Discounts received:	
Craig	50
Dobie	100
Elgin	200

Required:
(a) Enter the above transactions in appropriate ledger accounts;
(b) balance each account as at 31 March 19X9; and
(c) extract a trial balance as at that date.

3.19 The following trial balance was extracted from Ryan's books of account as at 30 June 19X2:

	£ Dr	£ Cr
Bank		1 500
Capital		61 500
Cash	100	
Trade creditors:		
Arnot		2 000
Bain		3 000
Croft		4 000
Trade debtors:		
Xram	11 200	
Yousif	12 300	
Zlot	13 400	
Vehicles	35 000	
	£72 000	£72 000

During July 19X2, the following transactions took place:

(1) Cash and bank

	Receipts			Payments	
	Cash	Bank		Cash	Bank
	£	£		£	£
Watt (sales)	2 000	4 000	Arnot		1 800
Xram		9 000	Bain		3 000
Yousif		10 000	Croft		2 500
Zlot		12 000	Ducat (purchases)		6 000
Sales		1 500	Drawings	1 200	
			Heat and light		750
			Wages and salaries		3 400
			Office expenses		550
			Purchases	1 000	

(2) Other transactions

	Purchases	Purchases Returns	Sales	Sales Returns	Discounts
	£	£	£	£	£
Arnot	3 000	500			150
Bain	4 500	1 500			250
Croft	6 000	700			200
Ducat	7 000	600			100
Watt			9 000	300	450
Xram			8 000	400	50
Yousif			22 000	2 000	350
Zlot			26 000	1 000	650

Required:
(a) Enter the above transactions in appropriate ledger accounts;
(b) balance each account as at 31 July 19X2; and
(c) extract a trial balance as at that date.

CHAPTER 4

Basic financial statements

Pru helped by accruals accounting

By Norma Cohen
Investments Correspondent

PRUDENTIAL Corporation, Britain's largest life assurance company, yesterday reported that under the new proposed "accruals" basis of accounting for profits, its 1992 earnings rose 9 per cent to £807m.

The Pru had earlier reported profits for the same period using the so-called embedded value method of accounting, which is currently the industry standard.

The method however, has been criitcised by securities analysts as flawed because it does not recognise profits or losses from insurance policies until they mature. Under accruals accounting, profits are much more closely related to ongoing activities.

So far, the Pru is the only big UK insurer to have reported results on an accruals basis.

The Association of British Insurers, after a two-year study, had asked the industry to begin experimenting with the method. Earnings were somewhat lower than analysts had anticipated, reflecting somewhat worse than expected continuous disability business in its M&G reinsurance arm. However, analysts noted that the effects of a reorganisation in Prudential's UK life assurance businesses, which has absorbed £180m in costs, has produced unexpected cost savings which will be reflected in the 1993 statutory profits.

Profits on new business rose 30 per cent to £226m, largely on sales of single premium products and the so-called prudence bond in particular. But profits on business in force fell sharply from £52m to £36m, partly reflecting reduced investment returns in Australia and Canada.

Meanwhile, it emerged that a leading shareholders group, Pensions Investment Research Council, has sharply criticised the Pru for failing to follow best practice in corporate governance. The Pru is one of the UK's largest shareholders and its chief executive, Mr. Mick Newmarch, has been outspoken on matters of board behaviour.

The Financial Times, 21 May 1993.

Exhibit 4.0 Accruals accounting is widely applied in manufacturing industry, but according to this article it is not common in the insurance industry.

We suggested in Chapter 1 that the owners of a business want to know the answers to three fundamental questions:

1 What profit has the business made?
2 How much does the business owe?
3 How much is owed to it?

We finished the last chapter with an illustration of how to construct a trial balance. The trial balance not only enables us to check how accurate the book-keeping has been, but it also enables us to prepare what we might call the *basic financial statements*. As can be seen from Exhibit 4.1, these normally include a trading account, a profit and loss account, and a balance sheet.

Exhibit 4.1 The basic financial statements

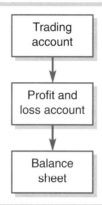

The information contained in the basic financial statements will then enable us to answer the three questions asked by the owners of a business. In this chapter, we are going to show you how to prepare some basic financial statements.

In the last chapter, we concentrated on sole-trader accounts. We shall be doing the same in this chapter, because a more complicated form of business organization would obscure the main points that we want to make. In the first section, we will have a look at what accountants mean by profit, before we move on to have a look at how financial statements are constructed.

LEARNING OBJECTIVES

By the end of this chapter, you will be able to:
● describe what accountants mean by profit;
● make four post-trial balance adjustments;
● prepare a basic set of financial statements;
● list five main defects of conventional financial statements.

THE MEASUREMENT OF PROFIT

The owners of a business often try to measure the profit that a business has made (i.e. how well it has done) by deducting the cash held at the end of a period from cash held at the beginning (after allowing for capital introduced or withdrawn during the period). It is then assumed that the difference represents profit (if the cash has increased) or loss (if the cash has decreased). This is *not* what accountants mean by profit.

As we outlined in Chapter 2, accounts are normally prepared by adopting a certain number of accounting rules. You will remember that the realization rule requires us to match the sales revenue for a particular period against the cost of selling those goods during the same period. The matching rule requires a similar procedure to be adopted for other types of incomes and expenses. It is unlikely that the difference between cash received and cash paid will be the same as the difference between *income* and *expenditure*. Cash transactions may relate to earlier or later periods, whereas incomes and expenditure (as defined in accounting) measure the *actual* economic activity which has taken place during a clearly defined period of time. By income we mean something that the entity has *gained* during a particular period, and expenditure as something the entity has *lost* during the same period.

There are great many problems, of course, in trying to measure income and expenditure in this way, rather than on a cash receipts and cash payments basis. In calculating profit, expenditure is especially difficult to determine. If the entity purchases a machine, for example, that has an estimated life of 20 years, how much of the cost should be charged against the income for (say) Year 1 compared with Year 20?

Accountants deal with this problem by attempting to classify *expenditure* into capital and revenue. Capital expenditure is expenditure that is likely to provide a benefit to the entity for more than one accounting period, and revenue expenditure is expenditure that is likely to provide a benefit for only one period. As the basic financial statements are normally prepared on an annual basis, we can regard revenue expenditure as being virtually the same as annual expenditure. If a similar benefit is required the next year, then the service will have to be re-ordered and another payment made.

Examples of revenue expenditure include goods purchased for resale, electricity charges, rates paid to the local authority, and wages and salaries. Examples of capital expenditure include land and buildings, plant and machinery, motor vehicles, and furniture and fittings. Such items are described as *fixed assets*, because they are owned by the entity and they are intended for long-term use within it.

It is also possible to classify *income* into capital and revenue, although the terms capital income and capital revenue are not normally adopted. Income of a revenue nature would include the revenue from the sale of goods to customers, dividends and rents received. Income of a capital nature would include the resources invested by the owner in the business, and loans made to it (such as bank loans).

In practice, it is not always easy to distinguish between capital and revenue items, and the distinction is often an arbitrary one. Some items of expenditure are particularly difficult to determine, although fortunately most transactions fall into recognizable categories.

The distinction between capital and revenue items is very important because, essentially, accounting profit is the difference between revenue income and revenue expenditure (see Exhibit 4.2). If capital and revenue

Exhibit 4.2 Accounting profit

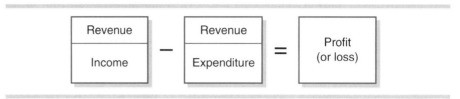

items are not classified accurately, the accounting profit will be incorrectly calculated. This could be disastrous, especially if the amount was over-stated, because the owner might then draw too much out of the business, or he might have to pay more tax. Bearing in mind the prudence rule, it would be much less serious if the profit was under-stated, because it is likely that more cash would be retained within the business.

In the next section we will show you how to calculate accounting profit.

PREPARATION OF THE BASIC FINANCIAL STATEMENTS

We are now in a position to examine how the basic financial statements are prepared, and hence how to calculate the amount of profit a business has made. We will assume that a trial balance has been prepared and that the books balance. Assuming that this is the case, there are then two main stages we have to take in order to prepare the statements. We will deal with each stage separately.

The profit and loss account stage

Following the compilation of the trial balance, the first step we need to take in compiling the basic financial statements is to prepare a profit and loss account (although a trading entity would first require a trading account). In this chapter, we are going to use trading entities as examples, because we want to show you how to deal with the sale and purchase of goods, and the accounting problems that these can cause.

In order to compile a trading and profit and loss account, we need to extract from the trial balance all the revenue income and expenditure items. These are then matched against each other in the form of a statement called (as you would expect) a *trading and a profit and loss account*. By deducting the total of the revenue balances from the total of the revenue expenditure balances, we can determine the level of the profit (or loss) for the period. There are two important points to note. These are as follows:

1 The **trading account** comes before the profit and loss account. It matches the sales revenue for a certain period against the cost of goods sold (i.e. purchases) for the same period. The difference between the sales revenue

and the cost of goods sold is known as *gross profit*. The gross profit is then transferred to the profit and loss account where it is added to the other revenue incomes of the business. That total is then matched against all the other expenses of the business (such as heat and light, and wages and salaries). The difference between the gross profit plus other non-trading incomes, less the other expenses is known as *net profit* (or net loss). This all sounds very complicated, but we can express it in the form of two equations:
(a) Sales revenue – cost of goods sold = gross profit;
(b) (Gross profit + other revenue incomes) – revenue expenditure = net profit (or net loss).

2 Both the trading account and the profit and loss account are accounts in their own right. This means that any transfer to or from them forms part of the double-entry procedure, and so a corresponding and equal entry has to be made in some other account.

The balance sheet stage

The second stage in the preparation of the basic financial statements is to summarize all the balances left in the trial balance once the trading account and profit and loss account balances have been extracted. Those balances that are still there are then summarized in the form of a statement called a *balance sheet*. A balance sheet is simply a listing of all the remaining balances left in the ledger account system once a trading and profit and loss account has been prepared. Unlike a trading and profit and loss account, a balance sheet does not form part of the double-entry: it is merely a listing of the balances that remain in a ledger system at the end of an accounting period. We could also describe it another way, and suggest that it is a listing of all the capital revenue and capital expenditure balances.

We are now in a position to show you how to prepare a set of basic financial statements. We will do so in the next section.

AN ILLUSTRATIVE EXAMPLE

In this section, we explain how to prepare a trading account and a profit and loss account, and a balance sheet. This is illustrated in Exhibit 4.3.

You are now recommended to work through Exhibit 4.3 again, but this time without reference to the answer.

Exhibit 4.3

The following trial balance has been extracted from Bush's books of account as at 30 June 19X7:

Name of account		Dr £	Cr £
Bank (1)		5 000	
Capital (at 1 July 19X6) (2)			11 000
Cash (3)		I 000	
Drawings (4)		8 000	
Motor vehicle at cost (5)		6 000	
Motor vehicle expenses (6)	(R)	2 000	
Office expenses (7)	(R)	3 000	
Purchases (8)	(R)	30 000	
Trade creditors (9)			4 000
Trade debtors (10)		10 000	
Sales (11)	(R)		50 000
		£65 000	£65 000

Notes: (1) There were no opening or closing stocks.
(2) R = revenue items.

Required:
(a) Prepare Bush's trading and profit and loss account for the year to 30 June 19X7; and
(b) a balance sheet as at that date.

Answer to Exhibit 4.3 (a)

BUSH
Trading, profit and loss account for the year to 30 June 19X7

	£		£
Purchases (8)	30 000	Sales (11)	50 000
Gross profit c/d	20 000		
	£50 000		£50 000
Motor vehicle expenses (6)	2 000	Gross profit b/d	20 000
Office expenses (7)	3 000		
Net profit c/d	15 000		
	£20 000		£20 000
		Net profit b/d	15 000

Tutorial notes
1 The number shown in brackets after each narration refers to the account number of each balance extracted from the trial balance.
2 Both the trading account and the profit and loss account cover a period of time. In this exhibit it is for the year *to* (or alternatively, *ending*) 30 June 19X7.
3 It is not customary to keep the trading account totally separate from the profit and loss account. The usual format is the one shown above whereby the trading account balance (that is, the gross profit) is carried down straight into the profit and loss account.

4 Note that the proprietor's drawings [account (4)], are not an expense of the business. They are treated as an *appropriation*, i.e. an amount withdrawn by the proprietor in advance of any profit that the business might have made.

Answer to Exhibit 4.3 (b)

BUSH
Balance sheet at 30 June 19X7

	£	£		£	£
Capital			*Fixed assets*		
Balance at 1 July			Motor vehicle at		
19X6 (2)		11 000	cost (5)		6 000
Add: Net profit					
for the year*	15 000		*Current assets*		
Less: Drawings (4)					
	8 000	7 000	Trade debtors (10)	10 000	
			Bank (1)	5 000	
			Cash (3)	1 000	16 000
Current liabilities					
Trade creditors (9)		4 000			
		£22 000			£22 000

*This balance has been obtained from the profit and loss account.
Note: The number in brackets shown after each narration refers to the account number of each balance listed in the trial balance on page 76.

Tutorial notes
1 The balance sheet is prepared at a particular moment in time. It depicts the balances as they were at a specific date. In this example, the balances are shown as at 30 June 19X7.
2 The format of this balance sheet shows the capital and liability balances on the left-hand side of the page, and the asset balances on the right-hand side.
3 The left-hand side of the balance sheet is divided into two main sections:
    (a) the capital section shows how the business has been financed (usually from a combination of the original capital contributed by the proprietor and the profit that has been left in the business); and
    (b) the current liabilities section shows the amounts owed to various parties outside the entity and due for payment within 12 months.
4 As far as the capital section is concerned, the net profit obtained from the profit and loss account must be added to it, because it is a remaining balance within the ledger system. In effect, it is a summary balance: it is merely a *net* balance obtained after matching the revenue income and expenditure balances. It is preferable to deduct any drawings that the proprietor may have made from the net profit for the year in order to show how much profit has been left in the business out of that year's profits.
5 The current liabilities should be listed in the order of those that are going to be paid last being placed before those that are going to be paid first, e.g. creditors should come before a bank overdraft.

6 The right-hand side of the balance sheet is also divided into two main sections:
   (a) the fixed assets section includes those assets that are intended for long-term use within the business; and
   (b) the current assets section includes assets that are constantly being turned over, for example, stocks, debtors and cash.

7 Fixed assets are usually shown at their original, i.e. at their *historic* cost. The fact that they are stated at cost should be noted on the balance sheet.

8 Both fixed assets and current assets should be listed with the least liquid (or realizable) asset being placed first, e.g. property should come before machinery, and stocks before debtors.

9 The total of fixed assets and current assets is known as *total assets*.

FORMAT OF ACCOUNTS

In preparing the answer to Exhibit 4.3, we adopted what is known as the *horizontal* format. In the UK, it is now much more fashionable to prepare such statements in a *vertical* format so that the information can be read down the page on a line-by-line basis. There are three good reasons for adopting this method:

1 it does not presuppose any knowledge of double-entry book-keeping, since the information is not presented in the style of a ledger folio;
2 it highlights the various sections more clearly;
3 it is easier to read down a page than across it.

As you are probably more likely to meet financial statements prepared in the vertical format, we shall be adopting it throughout the rest of this book.

The vertical format is ilustrated in Exhibit 4.4 using the data obtained from Exhibit 4.3.

Exhibit 4.4

BUSH
Trading and profit and loss account for the year to 30 June 19X7

	£	£
Sales		50 000
Less: Cost of goods sold:		
Purchases		30 000
Gross profit		20 000
Less: Expenses:		
Motor vehicle expenses	2 000	
Office expenses	3 000	5 000
Net profit for the year		£15 000

BUSH
Balance sheet at 30 June 19X7

	£	£
Fixed assets		
Motor vehicle at cost		6 000
Current assets		
Trade debtors	10 000	
Bank	5 000	
Cash	1 000	
	16 000	
Less: Current liabilities:		
Trade creditors	4 000	12 000
		£18 000
Financed by:		
Capital		
Balance at 1 July 19X6		11 000
Add: Net profit for the year	15 000	
Less: Drawings	8 000	7 000
		£18 000

You are recommended to study Exhibit 4.4 carefully, noting how the information shown in Exhibit 4.3 has been re-arranged. There are, in fact, very few changes, except that the information now reads down the page instead of across it.

We have now examined the preparation and format of the basic financial statements. The exhibits that we have used, of course, have been deliberately simple. We must now examine some major complications that arise in the preparation of these statements. We do so in the next section, but be warned: we have to cover quite a lot of difficult material, so take your time over it.

POST-TRIAL BALANCE ADJUSTMENTS

Once a trial balance has been prepared, additional information usually comes to light, so it is necessary to make a number of last minute adjustments to the accounts. The normal procedure is to calculate a provisional balance for each account and then to prepare the trial balance. Any errors should be located at this stage. When the books have been balanced, it is then possible to build in any recent information without too much difficulty.

When this has been done, the final accounts can be prepared. It is only when the accounts have been finalized that the further adjustments are normally entered into the ledgers. The ledger accounts will then be balanced, and any balances that remain at the end of the period will be carried down to the next period.

There are four main types of year-end adjustments that are normally required after a provisional trial balance has been extracted. These are shown in Exhibit 4.5, and they may be summarized as follows:

1 closing stock adjustments;
2 depreciation adjustments;
3 accruals and prepayment adjustments;
4 adjustments for bad and doubtful debts.

Exhibit 4.5 Main adjustments made to the trading and profit and loss account after the compilation of the trial balance.

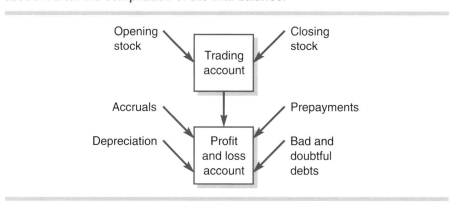

We examine each of these adjustments in the following sub-sections.

Stock adjustments

It is most unlikely that all of the purchases that have been made during a particular period will have been sold by the end of it, so some stock will almost certainly still be in the stores at the period end. In accounting terminology, purchases still on hand at the period end are also referred to as stock.

In calculating the gross profit for the period, therefore, it is necessary to make some allowance for closing stock, since we want to match the cost of goods sold (and not the cost of all of those goods actually purchased during the period) with the sales revenue earned for the period. Consequently, we have to check the quantity of stock we have on hand at the end of the accounting period, and then put some value on it. In practice, this is an extremely difficult exercise, and we shall be examining it in more detail in Chapter 10. Most examples used in this part of the book assume that the value of the closing stock is readily available.

We also have another problem in dealing with stock. Closing stock at the end of one period becomes the opening stock at the beginning of the next period. In calculating the cost of goods sold, therefore, we have to allow for opening stock. In fact, the cost of goods sold can be quite easily calculated by adopting the following formula:

> **Cost of goods sold = (Opening stock + Purchases) – Closing stock**

The book-keeping entries are not quite as easy to understand, but they may be summarized as follows:

1 Enter the opening stock in the trading account. To do so, make the following entries in the books of account: DEBIT trading account; CREDIT stock account; with the value of the opening stock as estimated at the end of the previous period (this should have been brought as a debit balance in the stock account at the beginning of the current period).
2 Estimate the value of the closing stock (using one of the methods described in Chapter 10).
3 Enter the closing stock in the trading account. To do so, make the following entries in the books of account: DEBIT stock account; CREDIT trading account; with the value of the closing stock as estimated in stage 2 above.

By making these adjustments the trading account should now appear as in Exhibit 4.6.

Exhibit 4.6 Example of a trading account with stock adjustments

	£		£
Opening stock	1 000	Sales	4 000
Purchases	2 000	Closing stock	1 500
Gross profit c/d	2 500		
	£5 500		£5 500

Note: This format does not show clearly the cost of goods sold, so it is customary to *deduct* the closing stock from the total of opening stock and purchases. Thus, the information will be presented as follows:

	£		£
Opening stock	1 000	Sales	4 000
Purchases	2 000		
	3 000		
Less: Closing stock	1 500		
	1 500		
Gross profit c/d	2 500		
	£4 000		£4 000

Study this amended format very carefully, because it will be encountered frequently in subsequent examples.

Depreciation adjustments

As we have already explained, expenditure which covers more than one accounting period is known as *capital expenditure*. Capital expenditure as such is not normally included in either the trading account or the profit and loss account, but it would be misleading to exclude it altogether from the calculation of profit.

Expenditure on fixed assets (such as plant and machinery, motor vehicles and furniture) is presumably necessary in order to help provide a general service to the business. The benefit received from the purchase of fixed assets must (by definition) extend beyond at least one accounting period. The cost of the benefit provided by fixed assets ought, therefore, to be charged to those accounting periods that benefit from such expenditure. The problem is in determining what charge to make. In accounting terminology, such a charge is known as *depreciation*.

There is also another reason why fixed assets should be depreciated. By *not* charging each accounting period with some of the cost of fixed assets, the level of profit will be correspondingly higher. Thus, the owner will be able to withdraw a higher level of profit from the business. If this is the case, insufficient cash or funds may be left in the business, and he may then find it difficult to buy new fixed assets or replenish his stocks.

In practice, it is not easy to measure the benefit provided to each accounting period by many groups of fixed assets. Most depreciation methods tend to be somewhat simplistic. The one method most commonly adopted is known as *straight-line depreciation*. This method charges an equal amount of depreciation to each accounting period that benefits from the purchase of a fixed asset. The annual depreciation charge is calculated as follows:

$$\text{Annual depreciation charge} = \frac{\text{Original cost of the asset} - \text{estimated residual value}}{\text{Estimated life of the asset}}$$

You can see that in order to calculate the annual depreciation charge, it is necessary to work out (a) how long the asset is likely to last, and (b) what it can be sold for when its useful life is ended.

Although it is customary to include fixed assets at their historical (i.e. original) cost in the balance sheet, some fixed assets (such as property) may be revalued at regular intervals. If this is the case, then the depreciation charge will be based on the revalued amount, and not on the historic cost. It should also be noted that even if the asset is depreciated on the basis of its revalued amount, there is still no guarantee that it can be replaced at that amount. A combination of inflation and obsolescence may mean that the eventual replacement cost is far in excess of either the historic cost or the revalued amount. It follows that when the fixed asset eventually comes to be replaced, the entity may still not have sufficient funds available to replace it.

Besides straight-line depreciation, there are other methods that may be adopted. One such method that is sometimes used (although it is far less common than the straight-line method) is known as the *reducing balance method*. This method is similar to the straight-line one in that it is based on the historic cost of the asset. It also requires an estimate to be made of the life of the asset and of its estimated residual value. The depreciation rate is usually expressed as a percentage, and the rate is then applied to the *reducing* balance of the asset, i.e. after the depreciation charge in previous years has been deducted. The procedure is illustrated in Exhibit 4.7.

Exhibit 4.7 An illustration of the reducing balance method of depreciating fixed assets

Assume that an asset costs £1000, and that the depreciation rate is 50% of the reduced balance. The depreciation charge per year would then be as follows:

Year		£
1. 1. X1	Historic cost	1000
31.12.X1	Depreciation charge for the year (50%)	500
	Reduced balance	500
31.12.X2	Depreciation charge for the year (50%)	250
	Reduced balance	250
31.12.X3	Depreciation charge for the year (50%)	125
	Reduced balance	125

. . . and so on, until the asset has been written down to its estimated residual value.

The reducing balance depreciation rate can be calculated by using the following formula:

$$r = 1 - \sqrt[n]{\frac{R}{C}}$$

Where: r = the depreciation rate to be applied;
n = the estimated life of the asset;
R = its estimated scrap value; and
C = its historic cost.

The reducing balance method results in a much higher level of depreciation in the first few years of the life of an asset, and a much lower charge in later years. It is a suitable method to adopt when calculating the depreciation rate for vehicles, for example, because vehicles tend to have a high depreciation rate in their early years, and a low rate towards the end of their life. In addition, maintenance costs tend to be low initially, and become greater as the vehicles become older. Consequently, the combined depreciation charge plus the maintenance costs produce a more even pattern of total vehicle costs than does the straight-line method.

There are other methods of depreciating fixed assets, but since these are rarely used, we do not think that it is necessary for us to go in to them in this book.

The ledger account entries for depreciation are quite straightforward. The annual charge for depreciation will be entered in to the books of account as follows:

DEBIT Profit and loss account;
CREDIT Accumulated depreciation account
with the depreciation charge for the year.
(*Note:* Each group of fixed assets will normally have its own accumulated depreciation account.)

As far as the balance sheet is concerned, it is customary to disclose the following details for each group of fixed assets:

1 historic cost (or revalued amount), i.e. the gross book value (GBV);
2 accumulated depreciation;
3 net book value (NBV).

(In other words, line 1 less line 2 = line 3.)

We illustrate how this is normally shown in a balance sheet in Exhibit 4.8. Exhibit 4.8 shows how the accumulated depreciation is deducted from the original cost for each group of assets, thereby arriving at the respective net book value for each group. The total net book value (£88 000 in Exhibit 4.8)

Exhibit 4.8 Balance sheet disclosure of fixed assets

Fixed assets	Historic cost £	Accumulated depreciation £	Net book value £
Buildings	100 000	30 000	70 000
Equipment	40 000	25 000	15 000
Furniture	10 000	7 000	3 000
	£150 000	£62 000	88 000
Current assets			
Stocks		10 000	
Debtors		8 000	
Cash		2 000	
			20 000
			£108 000

forms part of the balancing of the balance sheet. The total cost of the fixed assets and the total accumulated depreciation are shown purely for information. Such totals do not form part of the balancing process.

Accruals and prepayments adjustment

We explained in Chapter 2 why, at the end of a particular accounting period, it is sometimes necessary to make an adjustment for accruals and prepayments. We will now examine this procedure in a little more detail.

Accruals

An accrual is an amount outstanding for a service provided during a particular accounting period which is still to be paid for at the end of it. It is expected that the amount due will normally be settled in cash in a subsequent accounting period. The entity may, for example, have paid the last quarter's electricity bill one week before the year end. In its accounts for that year, therefore, it needs to allow for (or *accrue*) the amount that it will owe for the electricity consumed during the last week of the year.

The accrual will be based on an estimate of either the likely cost of one week's supply of electricity, or if it has received the invoice, as a proportion of the amount payable.

The ledger account entries are reasonably straightforward. It is not normal practice to open a separate account for accruals, the double-entry being completed within the account that relates to the particular service. Exhibit 4.9 illustrates the procedure.

Exhibit 4.9 Accounting for accruals

Electricity Account

		£			£
1.04.X1	Bank	400	1.04.X1	Balance b/d*	400
1.07.X1	Bank	300			
1.09.X1	Bank	100			
1.01.X2	Bank	500			
31.03.X2	Balance c/d**	600	31.03.X2	Profit and loss account	1500
		£1900			£1900
			1.04.X2	Balance b/d	600

* This balance is assumed to be an accrual made in the year to 31 March 19X1.
** This amount is an accrual for the year to 31 March 19X2.

You will note that in Exhibit 4.9, the balance on the electricity account at 31 March 19X2 is transferred to the profit and loss account. The ledger account entries are as follows:

DEBIT Profit and loss account;
CREDIT Electricity account
with the electricity charge for the year.

The double-entry has been completed for the accrual by debiting it in the accounts for the year to 31 March 19X2 (i.e. above the line), and crediting it in the following year's account (i.e. below the line). The accrual of £600 will be shown on the balance sheet at 31 March 19X2 in the current liabilities section under the sub-heading 'accruals'.

Prepayments

A prepayment is an amount paid in cash during an accounting period for a service that has not yet been provided. For example, if a company's year end is 31 December, and it buys a van half-way through (say) 1994 and licences it for 12 months, half of the fee paid will relate to 1994 and half to 1995. It is necessary, therefore, to adjust the 1994's accounts so that only half of the fee is charged in that year. The other half will eventually be charged to the 1995 accounts. The book-keeping procedure is illustrated in Exhibit 4.10.

Exhibit 4.10 Accounting for prepayments

Van Tax Account

		£			£
1.01.X1	Balance b/d*	40	31.12.X1	Profit and	
1.07.X1	Bank	100		loss account	90
			31.12.X1	Balance c/d**	50
		£140			£140
1.01.X2	Balance b/d	50			

*   This balance is assumed to be a prepayment arising in the previous period.
** This amount is assumed to be a prepayment for the year to 31 December 19X1.

You will note from Exhibit 4.10 that the balance on the van tax account is transferred to the profit and loss account. The double-entry procedure is as follows:

DEBIT Profit and loss account;
CREDIT Van tax account
with the annual cost of the tax on the van.

The double-entry has been completed by debiting the prepayment in next year's accounts (i.e. below the line) and crediting it to this year's accounts (i.e. above the line).

The prepayment of £50 made at 31 December 19X1 will be shown in the balance sheet at that date in the current assets section under the sub-heading 'prepayments'.

Adjustments for bad debts and provisions for doubtful debts

The fourth main adjustment made in preparing basic financial statements relates to bad debts and provisions for bad debts.

We explained in Chapter 2 that the realization rule allows us to claim profit for any goods that have been sold, even if the cash for them is not received until a later accounting period. This means that we are taking a risk in claiming the profit on those goods in the earlier period, even if the legal title has been passed to the customer. If the goods are not eventually paid for, we will have over-estimated the profit for the period when we thought that we had sold them. The owner might already have taken the profit out of the business (e.g. by increasing his cash drawings), and it then might be too late to do anything about it.

Fortunately, there is a technique whereby we can build in an allowance for any possible *bad* debts (as they are called). This is quite a tricky operation, so we will need to explain in two stages: (a) how to account for bad debts; and (b) how to allow for the possibility that some debts may be *doubtful*. We do so below.

Bad debts

Once it is clear that a debt is bad (in other words, if it highly unlikely that it will ever be paid), then it must be written off immediately. This means that we have to charge it to the current year's profit and loss account, even though it may relate to an earlier period. We have to deal with it this way, because it is usually impractical to change accounts once they have been finalized (it is a bit like trying to put spilt milk back into a bottle). As we mentioned earlier, based on that earlier estimate of profit the owner may have long since drawn his share out of the business.

The double-entry procedure for writing off bad debts is quite straightforward. The entries are as follows:

DEBIT Profit and loss account;
CREDIT Trade debtor's account
with the amount of the bad debt to be written off.

Trade debtors will be shown in the balance sheet *after* deducting any bad debts that have been written off to the profit and loss account.

The provision for doubtful debts account

The profit in future accounting periods would be severely distorted if the entity suffered a whole series of bad debts. It seems prudent, therefore, to allow for the possibility that some debts may become bad. In order to ensure that we do not overstate profit, we can set up a provision for doubtful debts (a provision is simply an amount set aside for something that is highly likely to happen). This means that we have to open what we call a 'provision for doubtful debts' account.

This involves estimating the likely level of bad debts. The estimate will be normally be based on the experience that the entity has had in dealing with specific bad debts. In simple book-keeping exercises, the provision is usually expressed as a percentage of the outstanding trade debtors. The double-entry procedure is as follows:

DEBIT Profit and loss account;
CREDIT Provision for doubtful debts account
with the amount of the provision needed to meet the expected level of bad debts.

The procedure is illustrated in Exhibit 4.11.

Exhibit 4.11 Accounting for doubtful debts

You are presented with the following information for the year to 31 March 19X3:

	£
Trade debtors at 1 April 19X2	20 000
Trade debtors at 31 March 19X3 (including £3 000 of specific bad debts)	33 000
Provision for doubtful debts at 1 April 19X2	1 000

Note: A provision for doubtful debts is maintained equivalent to 5% of the trade debtors as at the end of the year.

Required:
(a) Calculate the increase required in the doubtful debts provision account for the year to 31 March 19X3; and
(b) show how both the trade debtors and the provision for doubtful debts account would be featured in the balance sheet at 31 March 19X3.

Answer to Exhibit 4.11

	£
(a)	
Trade debtors as at 31 March 19X3	33 000
Less: Specific bad debts to be written off to the profit and loss account for the year to 31 March 19X3	3 000
	30 000
Provision required: 5% thereof	1 500
Less: Provision at 1 April 19X2	1 000
Increase in the doubtful debts provision account to be charged to the profit and loss account for the year to 31 March 19X3	500

Tutorial note

The balance on the provision for doubtful debts account will be higher at 31 March 19X3 than it was at 1 April 19X2. This arises because the level of trade debtors is higher at the end of 19X3 than it was at the end of 19X2. The required increase in the provision of £500 will be *debited* to the profit and loss account. If it had been possible to reduce the provision (because of a lower level of trade debtors at the end of 19X3 compared with 19X2), the decrease would have been *credited* to the profit and loss account.

(b) Balance sheet extract at 31 March 19X3

	£	£
Current assets		
Trade debtors	30 000	
Less: Provision for doubtful debts	1 500	
		28 500

The treatment of bad debts and doubtful debts in ledger accounts is a fairly complicated and technical exercise, However, as a non-accountant it is important for you to grasp just two essential points:

1 A debt should never be written off until it is absolutely certain that it is bad (because once written off, no further attempt will probably ever be made to recover it).
2 It is prudent to allow for the possibility of some doubtful debts, although as sometimes happens, it is rather a questionable decision to reduce profit by an arbitrary amount, e.g. by guessing whether it should be 3% or 5% of outstanding debtors. Obviously, the level that you choose can make a big difference to profit!

We have covered a great deal of technical matter in this chapter, so it would now be helpful to bring all the material together in the form of a comprehensive example. We do so in the next section.

A COMPREHENSIVE EXAMPLE

In this section, we use a comprehensive example to cover all the basic procedures that we have outlined so far in the chapter. The example used in Exhibit 4.12 is a fairly detailed one, so take your time in working through it.

Exhibit 4.12

Wayne has been in business for many years. His accountant has extracted the following trial balance from his books of account as at 31 March I9X5:

	£	£
Bank	1 200	
Capital		33 000
Cash	300	
Drawings	6 000	
Insurance	2 000	
Office expenses	15 000	
Office furniture at cost	5 000	
Office furniture: accumulated depreciation at 1 April 19X4		2 000
c/f	29 500	35 000

		£	£
	b/f	29 500	35 000
Provision for doubtful debts at 1 April 19X4			500
Purchases		55 000	
Salaries		25 000	
Sales			100 000
Stock at 1 April 19X4		10 000	
Trade creditors			4 000
Trade debtors		20 000	
		£139 500	£139 500

Notes: The following additional information is to be taken into account:

1 Stock at 31 March 19X5 was valued at £15 000.
2 The insurance included £500 worth of cover which related to the year to 31 March 19X6
3 Depreciation is charged on office furniture at 10% per annum of its original cost (it is assumed not to have any residual value).
4 A bad debt of £1000 included in the trade debtors balance of £20 000 is to be written off.
5 The provision for doubtful debts is to be maintained at a level of 5% of outstanding trade debtors as at 31 March 19X5, i.e. after excluding the bad debt referred to in note 4 above.
6 At 31 March 19X5, there was an amount owing for salaries of £1000.

Required:
(a) Prepare Wayne's trading, and profit and loss account for the year to 31 March 19X5; and
(b) a balance sheet as at that date.

Answer to Exhibit 4.12

(a)
WAYNE

Trading and profit and loss account for the year to 31 March 19X5

	£	£	(Source of entry)
		100 000	(TB)
Sales			
Less: Cost of goods sold:			
Opening stock	10 000		(TB)
Purchases	55 000		(TB)
	65 000		
Less: Closing stock	15 000		(QN 1)
		50 000	
	c/f	50 000	

		£	£	
			b/f	50 000	
Gross profit				
Less: Expenses:				
Insurance (2000 – 500)		1 500		(Wkg 1)
Office expenses		15 000		(TB)
Depreciation: office furniture		500		(Wkg 2)
Bad debt		1 000		(QN 4)
Increase in provision for doubtful debt		450		(Wkg 3)
Salaries (25 000 + 1000)		26 000		(Wkg 4)
			44 450	
Net profit for the year			£5 550	

(b)

WAYNE

Balance sheet at 31 March 19X5

Fixed assets	£ Cost	£ Accumulated depreciation	£ Net book value	(Source of entry)
Office furniture	5 000	2 500	2 500	(TB & Wkg 5)
Current assets				
Stock		15 000		(QN 1)
Trade debtors				
(20 000 – 1000)	19 000			(Wkg/3)
Less: Povision for				
doubtful debts	950	18 050		(Wkg 3)
Prepayment		500		(QN 2)
Cash at bank		1 200		(TB)
Cash in hand		300		(TB)
		35 050		
Less: Current liabilities				
Trade creditors	4 000			(TB)
Accrual	1 000			(QN 6)
	5 000	30 050		
		£32 550		
Financed by:				
Capital				
Balance at 31 March 19X4		33 000		(TB)
Add: Net profit for the year	5 550			(P&L A/c)
Less: Drawings	6 000	(450)		
		£32 550		

Key:
TB = from trial balance.
QN = extracted straight from the question and related notes.
Wkg = workings (see below).
P&L A/c = balance obtained from the profit and loss account.

Workings

1 Insurance:

As per the trial balance	2 000
Less: Prepayment (QN 2)	500
Charge to the profit and loss account	1 500

2 Depreciation:

Office furniture at cost	5 000
Depreciation: 10% of the original cost	500

3   Increase in provision for doubtful debts:

Trade debtors at 31 March 19X5	20 000
Less: Bad debt (QN 4)	1 000
	19 000
Provision required: 5% thereof	950
Less: Provision at 1 April 19X4	500
Increase in provision: charge to profit and loss	450

4 Salaries:

As per the question	25 000
Add: Accrual (QN 6)	1 000
	26 000

5 Accumulated depreciation:

Balance at 1 April 19X4 (as per TB)	2 000
Add: Depreciation for the year (Wkg 2)	500
Accumulated depreciation at 31 March 19X5	2 500

After you have worked through Exhibit 4.12 as carefully as you can, try to do the question without referring to the answer.

We are nearly at the end of a long chapter, but before we move on to other matters, we ought to examine fairly critically what we have done. We do so in the next section.

ESTIMATING ACCOUNTING PROFIT

As we have worked through the book, we have tried to point out that the calculation of accounting profit calls for a great deal of subjective judgement. Accounting requires much more than merely being very good at mastering some advanced arithmetical exercises, so we think that it will be helpful (indeed essential) for us to summarize the major defects inherent in the traditional method of calculating accounting profit.

As a non-accountant, it is most important that you appreciate one vital fact: the method that we have outlined results in an *estimate* of what the accountant thinks the profit should be. You must not place too much reliance on the *absolute* level of accounting profit. It can only be as accurate and as reliable as the assumptions upon which it is based. If you accept that a profit figure is based on reasonable assumptions, then you can be fairly confident that it is reliable. That way, you will not go too far wrong in using the information for decision-making purposes. But you must know what the assumptions are, and you must accept them. The message can, therefore, be put as follows:

> **Always question accounting information before accepting it.**

A summary of the main reasons why you should not place too much reliance on the actual level of accounting profit (especially if you are unsure about the assumptions upon which it is based) is outlined below:

1 Goods are treated as being sold when the legal title to them changes hands, and not when the customer has paid for them. In some cases, the cash for some sales may never be received.
2 Goods are regarded as having been purchased when the legal title to them is transferred to the purchaser, although there are occasions when they may not be received or paid for (e.g. if a supplier goes into receivership).
3 Goods that have not been sold at the period end have to be quantified and valued. This procedure involves a considerable amount of subjective judgement.
4 There is no clear distinction between so-called capital and revenue items.
5 Estimates have to be made to allow for accruals and prepayments.
6 The cost of fixed assets is apportioned between different accounting periods using methods that are fairly simplistic and highly questionable.
7 Arbitrary reductions in profit are made to allow for doubtful debts.
8 Historic cost accounting makes no allowance for inflation. In a period of inflation, for example, the value of £100 at 1 January 19X1 is not the same as £100 at 31 December 19X1. Hence, profit tends to be overstated (partly because of low closing stock values, and partly because depreciation charges will be based on the historic cost).

The above disadvantages of historical cost accounting are extremely serious (and you may even be able to think of some more). As yet, however, accountants have not been able to suggest anything better. If at this stage you are feeling pretty disillusioned, therefore, and you do not feel to have much confidence in accounting information, then take comfort in the old adage that 'it is better to be vaguely right than precisely wrong'!

CONCLUSION

In this chapter, we have examined in some detail the construction of the basic financial statements. You should now be in a far better position to assess the relevance and reliability of any accounting information that is presented to you.

The material that we have covered has provided a broad foundation for all the remaining chapters. It is essential that before moving on to the other chapters, you satisfy yourself that you really do understand the mechanics behind the preparation of the basic financial statements. To test your understanding of this subject, you are recommended to work through all of the Exhibits once again, and then to attempt some of the chapter exercises.

KEY POINTS

1 **Basic financial statements are made up of a trading account (if it is a trading entity), a profit and loss account, and a balance sheet.**

2 **A trial balance provides the basic information for the preparation of the main financial statements: revenue items are transferred to the profit and loss account (or to the trading account), and capital items to the balance sheet.**

3 **The trading and profit and loss accounts all form part of the double-entry system. The balance sheet is merely a listing of balances.**

4 **Following the completion of the trial balance, some last minute adjustments have usually to be made to the accounts: the main ones are closing stock, depreciation, accruals and prepayments, and bad and doubtful debts.**

5 **Accounting profit is merely an estimate. The method used to calculate it is highly questionable, and it is subject to very many criticisms. Undue reliance should not be placed on the actual level of profit shown in the accounts. The assumptions upon which profit is based should be carefully examined, and it should be viewed merely as a guide to decision making.**

CHECK YOUR LEARNING

1 Are the following statements true or false?
  (a) Accounting profit is normally the difference between
      cash received and cash paid.   True/False

    (b) A provision for bad debts results in cash leaving the
        business.   True/False
    (c) An amount owing for rent at the year end is an accrual.   True/False
    (d) There is no such thing as the correct level of accounting
        profit.   True/False

2 Fill in the missing word(s) in each of the following statements:
    (a) opening stock + _____ – closing stock = gross profit.
    (b) gross profit + other incomes – total expenditure = _____ _____.
    (c) _____ – liabilities = capital.

3 A company buys a machine for £12 000. It is expected to have a life of ten years, and an estimated residual value of £2000. If the company uses the straight-line method of depreciation what is the annual charge to the profit and loss account?
    (a) £12 000
    (b) £1000
    (c) £2000
    (d) none of these

4 List five basic defects of conventional accounting statements.

ANSWERS

1 (a) false (b) false (c) true (d) true
2 (a) purchases (b) net profit (c) assets
3 £1000 (12 000 – 1000 ÷10)
4 (a) distinction between capital and revenue; (b) revenue recognition; (c) stock valuation problems; (d) depreciation calculations; (e) estimates for outstanding creditors and debtors

QUESTIONS

4.1 The following trial balance has been extracted from Ethel's books of account as at 31 January 19X1:

	Dr £	Cr £
Capital		10 000
Cash	3 000	
Creditors		3 000
Debtors	6 000	
Office expenses	11 000	
Premises	8 000	
Purchases	20 000	
Sales		35 000
	£48 000	£48 000

Required: Prepare Ethel's trading, and profit and loss account for the year to 31 January 19XI, and a balance sheet as at that date.

4.2   Marion has been in business for some years. The following trial balance has been extracted from her books of account as at 28 February 19X2.

	Dr £000	Cr £000
Bank	4	
Buildings	50	
Capital		50
Cash	2	
Creditors		24
Debtors	30	
Drawings	55	
Heat and light	10	
Miscellaneous expenses	25	
Purchases	200	
Sales		400
Wages and salaries	98	
	£474	£474

Required:
Prepare Marion's trading and profit and loss account for the year to 28 February 19X2 and a balance sheet as at that date.

4.3   The following trial balance has been extracted from the books of Garswood as at 31 March 19X3.

	Dr £	Cr £
Advertising	2 300	
Bank	300	
Capital		55 700
Cash	100	
Discounts allowed	100	
Discounts received		600
Drawings	17 000	
Electricity	1 300	
Investments	4 000	
Investment income received		400
Office equipment	10 000	
Other creditors		800
Other debtors	1 500	
Machinery	20 000	
Purchases	21 400	
Purchases returns		1 400
Sales		63 000
Sales returns	3 000	
Stationery	900	
Trade creditors		5 200
Trade debtors	6 500	
Wages	38 700	
	£127 100	£127 100

Required:

Prepare Garswood's trading, and profit and loss account for the year to 31 March 19X3, and a balance sheet as at that date.

4.4 The following information has been extracted from Lathom's books of account for the year to 30 April 19X4:

	£
Purchases	45 000
Sales	60 000
Stock (at 1 May 19X3)	3 000
Stock (at 30 April 19X4)	4 000

Required:

(a) Prepare Lathom's trading account for the year to 30 April 19X4; and
(b) state where the stock at 30 April 19X4 would be shown on the balance sheet as at that date.

4.5 Rufford presents you with the following information for the year to 31 March 19X5:

	£
Purchases	48 000
Purchases returns	3 000
Sales	82 000
Sales returns	4 000
Stock at 1 April 19X4	4 000

He is not sure how to value the stock as at 31 March 19X5. Three methods have been suggested. They all result in different closing stock values, viz.:

Method 1	£8 000
Method 2	£16 000
Method 3	£4 000

Required:

(a) Calculate the effect on gross profit for the year to 31 March 19X5 by using each of the three methods of stock valuation; and
(b) state the effect on gross profit for the year to 31 March 19X6 if method 1 is used instead of method 2.

4.6 Standish has been trading for some years. The following trial balance has been extracted from his books of account as at 31 May 19X6:

	Dr £	Cr £
Capital		22 400
Cash	1 200	
Creditors		4 300
Debtors	6 000	
Drawings	5 500	
Furniture and fittings	8 000	
Heating and lighting	1 500	
c/f	22 200	26 700

	b/f	22 200	26 700
Miscellaneous expenses		6 700	
Purchases		52 000	
Sales			79 000
Stock (at 1 June 19X5)		7 000	
Wages and salaries		17 800	
		£105 700	£105 700

Note: Stock at 31 May 19X6: £12 000.

Required:
Prepare Standish's trading, and profit and loss account for the year to 31 May 19X6, and a balance sheet as at that date.

4.7 Witton commenced business on 1 July 19X6. The following trial balance was extracted from his books of account as at 30 June 19X7:

	Dr	Cr
	£	£
Capital		3 000
Cash	500	
Drawings	4 000	
Creditors		1 500
Debtors	3 000	
Motor car at cost	5 000	
Office expenses	8 000	
Purchases	14 000	
Sales		30 000
	£34 500	£34 500

Additional information:
1 Stocks at 30 June 19X7: £2000.
2 The motor car is to be depreciated at a rate of 20% per annum on cost; it was purchased on 1 July 19X6.

Required:
Prepare Witton's trading, and profit and loss account for the year to 30 June 19X7, and a balance sheet as at that date.

4.8 Croxteth has been in the retail trade for many years. The following is his trial balance as at 31 July 19X8:

		Dr	Cr
		£	£
Bank		2 000	
Capital			35 000
Creditors			4 800
Delivery vans at cost		40 000	
Depreciation:			
Delivery vans (at 1 August 19X7)			12 000
	c/f	42 000	51 800

		b/f	42 000	51 800
Shop equipment (at 1 August 19X7)				2 400
Drawings			8 000	
Purchases			70 000	
Sales				85 000
Shop equipment at cost			8 000	
Shop expenses			7 200	
Stock (at 1 August 19X7)			4 000	
			£139 200	£139 200

Additional Information:

1 Stock at 31 July 19X8: £14 000.
2 Depreciation on delivery vans at a rate of 30% per annum on cost, and on shop equipment at a rate of 10% per annum on cost.

Required:

Prepare Croxteth's trading, and profit and loss account for the year to 31 July 19X8, and a balance sheet as at that date.

4.9 The following is an extract from Barrow's balance sheet at 31 August 19X8:

Fixed assets	*Cost*	*Accumulated depreciation*	*Net book value*
	£	£	£
Land	200 000	–	200 000
Buildings	150 000	60 000	90 000
Plant	55 000	37 500	17 500
Vehicles	45 000	28 800	16 200
Furniture	21 000	12 600	7 400
	£470 000	£138 900	£331 100

Barrow's depreciation policy is as follows:

1 a full year's depreciation is charged in the year of acquisition, but none in the year of disposal;
2 no depreciation is charged on land;
3 buildings are depreciated at an annual rate of 2% on cost;
4 plant is depreciated at an annual rate of 5% on cost after allowing for an estimated residual value of £5000;
5 vehicles are depreciated on a reduced balance basis at an annual rate of 40% on the reduced balance;
6 furniture is depreciated on a straight-line basis at an annual rate of 10% on cost after allowing for an estimated residual value of £2000.

Additional information:

1 During the year to 31 August 19X9, new furniture was purchased for the office. It cost £3000 and it is to be depreciated on the same basis as the old furniture. Its estimated residual value is £300.

2 There were no additions to or disposals of any other fixed assets during the year to 31 August 19X9.

Required:
(a) Calculate the depreciation charge for each of the fixed asset groupings for the year to 31 August 19X9; and
(b) show how the fixed assets would appear in Barrow's balance sheet as at 31 August 19X9.

4.10 Pine started business on 1 October 19X1. The following is his trial balance at 30 September 19X2:

	£	£
Capital		6 000
Cash	400	
Creditors		5 900
Debtors	5 000	
Furniture at cost	8 000	
General expenses	14 000	
Insurance	2 000	
Purchases	21 000	
Sales		40 000
Telephone	1 500	
	£51 900	£51 900

The following information was obtained after the trial balance had been prepared:

1 Stock at 30 September 19X2: £3000.
2 Furniture is to be depreciated at a rate of 15% on cost.
3 At 30 September 19X2, Pine owed £500 for telephone expenses, and insurance had been prepaid by £200.

Required:
Prepare Pine's trading, and profit and loss account for the year to 30 September 19X2, and a balance sheet as at that date.

4.11 Dale has been in business for some years. The following is his trial balance at 31 October 19X3:

	Dr	Cr
	£	£
Bank	700	
Capital		85 000
Depreciation (at 1 November 19X2):		
Office equipment		14 000
Vehicles		4 000
Drawings	12 300	
Heating and lighting	3 000	
Office expenses	27 000	
Office equipment, at cost	35 000	
c/f	78 000	103 000

	b/f	78 000	103 000
Rates		12 000	
Purchases		240 000	
Sales			350 000
Stock (at 1 November 19X2)		20 000	
Trade creditors			21 000
Trade debtors		61 000	
Vehicles at cost		16 000	
Wages and salaries		47 000	
		£474 000	£474 000

Additional information (not taken into account when compiling the above trial balance) is as follows:

1 Stock at 31 October 19X3: £26 000.
2 Amount owing for electricity at 31 October 19X3: £1500.
3 At 31 October 19X3, £2000 had been paid in advance for rates.
4 Depreciation is to be charged on the office equipment for the year to 31 October 19X3 at a rate of 20% on cost and on the vehicles at a rate of 25% on cost.

Required:
Prepare Dale's trading, and profit and loss account for the year to 31 October 19X3, and a balance sheet as at that date.

4.12 The following information relates to Astley for the year to 30 November 19X4:

Item	Cash paid during the year to 30 November 19X4	As at 1 December 19X3 Accruals/ Prepayments		As at 30 November 19X4 Accruals/ Prepayments	
	£	£	£	£	£
Electricity	26 400	5 200	–	8 300	–
Gas	40 100	–	–	–	4 900
Insurance	25 000	–	12 000	–	14 000
Rates	16 000	–	4 000	6 000	–
Telephone	3 000	1 500	–	–	200
Wages	66 800	1 800	–	–	–

Required:
(a) Calculate the charge to the profit and loss account for the year to 30 November 19X4 for each of the above items.
(b) Demonstrate what amounts for accruals and prepayments would be shown in the balance sheet as at 30 November 19X4.

4.13 Duxbury started in business on 1 January 19X3. The following is his trial balance as at 31 December 19X3:

	Dr £	Cr £
Capital		40 000
Cash	300	
Delivery van, at cost	20 000	
Drawings	10 600	
Office expenses	12 100	
Purchases	65 000	
Sales		95 000
Trade creditors		5 000
Trade debtors	32 000	
	£140 000	£140 000

Additional information:
1 Stock at 31 December 19X3 was valued at £10 000.
2 At 31 December 19X3, an amount of £400 was outstanding for telephone expenses, and the rates had been prepaid by £500.
3 The delivery van is to be depreciated at a rate of 20% per annum on cost.
4 Duxbury decides to set aside a provision for doubtful debts equal to 5% of trade debtors as at the end of the year.

Required:
Prepare Duxbury's trading, and profit and loss account for the year to 31 December 19X3, and a balance sheet as at that date.

4.14 Beech is a retailer. Most of his sales are made on credit terms. The following information relates to the first four years that he has been in business:

	19X4	19X5	19X6	19X7
Trade debtors as at 31 January:	£60 000	£55 000	£65 000	£70 000

The trade is one which experiences a high level of bad debts. Accordingly, Beech decides to set aside a provision for doubtful debts equivalent to 10% of trade debtors as at the end of the year.

Required:
(a) Show how the provision for doubtful debts would be disclosed in the respective balance sheets as at 31 January 19X4, 19X5, 19X6 and 19X7; and
(b) calculate the increase/decrease in provision for doubtful debts transferred to the respective profit and loss accounts for each of the four years.

4.15 The following is Ash's trial balance as at 31 March 19X5:

	Dr £	Cr £
Bank		4 000
Capital		20 500
Depreciation (at 1 April 19X4): furniture		3 600
Drawings	10 000	
Electricity	2 000	
Furniture, at cost	9 000	
Insurance	1 500	
Miscellaneous expenses	65 800	
Provision for doubtful debts		
(at 1 April 19X4)		1 200
Purchases	80 000	
Sales		150 000
Stock (at 1 April 19X4)	10 000	
Trade creditors		20 000
Trade debtors	21 000	
	£199 300	£199 300

Additional information:
1 Stock at 31 March 19X5: £15 000.
2 At 31 March 19X5 there was a specific bad debt of £6000. This was to be written off.
3 Furniture is to be depreciated at a rate of 10% per annum on cost.
4 At 31 March 19X5, Ash owes the electricity board £600, and £100 had been paid in advance for insurance.
5 The provision for doubtful debts is to be made equal to 10% of trade debtors as at the end of the year.

Required:
Prepare Ash's trading, and profit and loss account for the year to 31 March 19X5, and a balance sheet as at that date.

4.16 Elm is a wholesaler. The following is his trial balance at 30 June 19X6:

	Dr £	Cr £
Advertising	3 000	
Bank	400	
Capital		73 500
Cash	100	
Depreciation (at 1 July 19X5):		
furniture		1 800
vehicles		7 000
Discounts allowed	400	
Discounts received		500
Drawings	10 000	
Electricity	3 200	
c/f	17 100	82 800

	b/f	17 100	82 800
Furniture, at cost		12 000	
General expenses		28 900	
Interest on investments			800
Investments, at cost		5 000	
Provision for doubtful debts			
(at 1 July 19X5)			2 300
Purchases		645 000	
Purchases returns			2 000
Rates		6 000	
Sales			820 000
Sales returns		4 000	
Stock (at 1 July 19X5)		47 000	
Telephone		1 300	
Trade creditors			13 000
Trade debtors		42 000	
Vehicles, at cost		35 000	
Wages and salaries		77 600	
		£920 900	£920 900

Additional information:
1 Stock at 30 June 19X6: £50 000.
2 The provision for doubtful debts is to be made equal to 5% of trade debtors as at 30 June 19X6.
3 Furniture is to be deprecated at a rate of 15% on cost, and the vehicles at a rate of 20% on a reducing balance basis.
4 At 30 June 19X6 amount owing for electricity, £300, rates paid in advance £1000.

Required:
Prepare Elm's trading, profit and loss account for year to 30 June 19X6, and a balance sheet as as that date.

4.17 Lime's business has had liquidity problems for some months. The following trial balance was extracted from his books of account as at 30 September 19X7:

		Dr	Cr
		£	£
Bank			15 200
Capital			19 300
Cash from sale of office equipment			500
Depreciation (at 1 October 19X6):			
office equipment			22 000
Drawings		16 000	
Insurance		1 800	
Loan (long-term from Cedar)			50 000
Loan interest		7 500	
Miscellaneous expenses		57 700	
	c/f	83 000	107 000

		b/f	83 000	107 000
Office equipment, at cost			44 000	
Provision for doubtful debts				
(at 1 October 19X6)				2 000
Purchases			320 000	
Rates			10 000	
Sales				372 000
Stock (at 1 October 19X6)			36 000	
Trade creditors				105 000
Trade debtors			93 000	
			£586 000	£586 000

Additional information:
1 Stock at 30 September 19X7: £68 000.
2 At 30 September 19X7, accrual for rates of £2000 and insurance prepaid of £200.
3 Depreciation on office equipment is charged at a rate of 25% on cost. During the year, office equipment costing £4000 had been sold for £500. Accumulated depreciation on this equipment amounted to £3000. Lime's depreciation policy is to charge a full year's depreciation in the year of acquisition, and none in the year of disposal.
4 Specific bad debts of £13 000 are to be written off.
5 The provision for doubtful debts is to be made equal to 10% of outstanding trade debtors as at 30 September 19X7.

Required:
Prepare Lime's trading, and profit and loss account for the year to 30 September 19X7, and a balance sheet as at that date.

4.18 Teak has extracted the following trial balance from his books of account as at 31 December 19X8:

	Dr	Cr
	£	£
Building society deposit	20 000	
Capital		66 500
Cash at bank and in hand	400	
Depreciation:		
Plant and equipment		
(at 1 January 19X8)		30 000
vehicles (at 1 January 19X8)		16 000
Dividends received (interim)		100
Interest received from building society		700
Interest received from Gray		500
Investments at cost	5 000	
Loan to Gray (repayable 1 October 19X9)	10 000	
Office expenses	39 000	
Plant and equipment at cost	50 000	
Purchases	83 000	
c/f	207 400	113 800

		Dr	Cr
	b/f	207 400	113 800
Sales			164 000
Stock (at 1 January 19X8)		2 800	
Trade debtors/trade creditors		13 200	22 200
Vehicles at cost		64 000	
Vehicle expenses		12 600	
		£300 000	£300 000

Additional information:
1 Stock at 31 December 19X8: £15 800.
2 During the year to 31 December 19X8, Teak had used some goods (purchased through the business) for his own personal consumption. At cost price these were estimated to be worth £6000. No entries had been made in the books of account to record this transaction.
3 At 31 December 19X8 there was an amount owing for office expenses of £1200. At the same date Teak was due to receive interest from the building society of £800, and a final dividend of £600 from a company in which he had some investments.
4 Depreciation is to be charged on plant and equipment at a rate of 30% per annum on cost, and on vehicles at a rate of 25% on the reduced balance
5 Office expenses include Teak's drawings for the year of £9000.

Required:
Prepare Teak's trading, and profit and loss account for the year to 31 December 19X8, and a balance sheet as at that date.

ADDITIONAL QUESTIONS (WITHOUT ANSWERS)

4.19 Daly's book-keeper has extracted the following trial balance as at 31 January 19X1:

	Dr	Cr
	£000	£000
Administrative expenses	63	
Capital		252
Cash at bank and in hand	9	
Creditors		8
Debtors	1	
Drawings	18	
Furniture and fittings at cost:	200	
accumulated depreciation		
(at 1 February 19X0)		90
Motor vehicles at cost:	800	
accumulated depreciation		
(at 1 February 19X0)		480
Purchases	500	
Rent, rates, heat and light	9	
Sales		760
Stock (at 1 February 19X0)	35	
c/f	1635	1590

	b/f	1635	1590
Trade creditors			170
Trade debtors		70	
Wages and salaries		55	
		£1760	£1760

Additional information:
1 Stock at 31 January 19X1: £40 000.
2 Depreciation is charged on the fixed assets as follows:
      Furniture and fittings: 15% on cost;
      Motor vehicles: 60% on the reduced balance.
3 A trade debt of £10 000 is to be written off.
4 A provision for bad and doubtful debts is to be established equivalent to 5% of outstanding trade debtors as at the end of the year.

Required:
Prepare Daly's trading and profit and loss account for the year to 31 January 19X1, and a balance sheet as at that date.

4.20 Patsy Chan has been in business for several years. The following trial balance was extracted from her books of account as at 30 September 19X9:

	Dr	Cr
	£000	£000
Bad debt	15	
Capital		653
Carriage inwards	10	
Carriage outwards	34	
Cash at bank and in hand	7	
Discounts allowed	18	
Discounts received		27
Dividends received		2
Drawings	12	
Investments at cost	20	
Motor vehicles at cost:	600	
accumulated depreciation		
(at 1 October 19X8)		300
Office expenses	35	
Plant and equipment at cost:	240	
accumulated depreciation		
(at 1 October 19X8)		144
Provision for bad and doubtful debts		
(at 1 October 19X8)		3
Purchases	570	
Salaries	105	
Sales		900
c/f	1666	2029

	b/f	1 666	2 029
Stock (at 1 October 19X8)		200	
Trade creditors			71
Trade debtors		160	
Wages		74	
		£2100	£2100

Additional information:

1 Stock at 30 September 19X9: £180 000.
2 Depreciation is charged as follows:
    Motor vehicles: 25% on cost;
    Plant and equipment: 30% on cost.
3 Wages owing at 30 September 19X9: £2000.
4 Business rates paid in advance at 30 September 19X9: £5000.
5 A provision for bad and doubtful debts is maintained equivalent to $2\frac{1}{2}$% of outstanding trade debtors as at the end of the year.

Required: Prepare Patsy Chan's trading and profit and loss account for the year to 30 September 19X9, and a balance sheet as at that date.

CHAPTER 5

Manufacturing accounts

Daimlar loss poses accounts question

Roger Cowe

A loss of almost DM1 billion reported by Daimler Benz for the first half of the year raised furore in Germany, and has thrown up worries about real profitability of other main industrial groups in Germany.

Driven by the need to gain a quotation on the New York stock exchange to raise capital, Daimler for the first time used American accounting codes. While analysts predict that the number of German firms seeking US quotations will be in double figures by the turn of the century, the question in Germany this week has been a simple one: what other German giants, like Volkswagen and Siemens, subjects themselves to the same rigours?

The extent of the Daimler loss is emphasised in that the first half of the last year the motor, engineering and aerospace company made a profit of a similar figure. The turnround is not all about different accounting conventions. It also reflects the impact of recession and the crisis at Daimler as it struggles to adapt its 1980s strategy of agglomoration to the tough 1990s.

But it is the switch in accounting rules that is under the microscope, not surprisingly.

Under German rules, Daimler Benz made a profit of DM168 million – the difference has raised fears that German companies in general have been overstanding their financial difficulties.

The furore has left US accounting with a glowing reputation, and US companies appearing to be at the conservative end of the accounting spectrum. UK practice – more closely allied to the US than the Continent – has also been basking in a reflected saintly glow.

This is hardly fair on the Germans, and overstates the purity of the US generally accepted accounting principles.

German accounting, as is generally true across the Continent, is in fact highly conservative by US-UK standards. A fundamentally cautious approach is supplemented by the fact that tax liability is based largely on financial accounts, unlike in the UK and US where tax rules are quite separate. This naturally encourages German companies to understate profits, contrary to the impression given by the Daimler Benz affair. Likewise, stock and other assets values are generally lower than they would be in Britain – revaluation of buildings, almost derigueur in Britain, is not allowed.

But these are details compared to the issue that has caused such a fuss this week: a general approach in Germany of smoothing profits from one year to the next through the use of provision. There is a tradition of taking the peak off profits in good years then releasing provision to reduce the dip when the economic cycle turns down.

The inclusion of all nasty charges, provisions and write-offs that arise in the US accounting makes Daimler's results look much worse than under German rules. But in good times the US approach will give higher profits than the German approach.

The clash reflects a different approach to financial reporting. Basically, there is also a different philosophy about the role of public companies and the capital market. Investors on the Continent, especially in Germany, are less concerned with quarter-by-quarter earnings performance of their companies. They are more interested in long-term stability.

For companies like Daimler, VW and Siemens though, submitting themselves to more detailed and more frequent reporting is likely to be seen as a price worth paying to tap an important source of funding.

The Guardian, 25 September 1993

Exhibit 5.0 A change in accounting rules can have an adverse effect on profit, but as Daimler has found, a recession can be equally devastating on manufacturing industry.

In the two previous chapters, we have been dealing almost entirely with trading entities. This means that we have assumed that when goods have been purchased, no further work needed to be done on them before they were sold.

There are, of course, many businesses whose main purpose is simply to buy and sell goods. We have referred to such businesses as *trading* entities. There are, however, many other businesses who *manufacture* their own products, and so they may buy materials that require further work to be done on them before they are sold. Such materials are known as *raw materials*.

A manufacturing entity will not normally have a purchases account within its ledger system, since by definition it does not buy goods for immediate resale: it does some work on them first before they are sold. Before we can begin to compile the trading account, therefore, we have to calculate what it has cost the entity to put the goods or materials it has bought into a *finished goods* state. This cost is called the *manufacturing cost*, and it is the equivalent of a trading entity's purchases. In order to calculate the manufacturing cost, we need an additional account, and this account is called a *manufacturing account*.

In this chapter, we are going to examine what a manufacturing account contains, and how it is constructed. Manufacturing accounts are, in fact, similar to trading and profit and loss accounts in three respects:

1 they form part of the double-entry system;
2 they are used as periodic financial summary statements;
3 they can be presented in either the horizontal or the vertical format.

The chapter falls into two main parts. Thee first part examines the contents of a manufacturing account, and the second part explains how it is constructed.

LEARNING OBJECTIVES

By the end of this chapter, you will be able to:
● describe the nature and purpose of manufacturing account;
● prepare a basic manufacturing account;
● incorporate one into a basic set of financial statements.

CONTENTS

A manufacturing account mainly records manufacturing costs, and it rarely includes any incomes. The costs which are debited to the account can be divided into two important categories. These are as follows:

1 direct costs, i.e. costs that can be traced directly to the product, such as materials and labour;

2 indirect costs, i.e. costs that are difficult to trace to individual products, e.g. canteen expenses and factory management.

Direct and indirect costs may be more formally defined as follows:

A **direct cost** is a cost which can be economically identified with a particular department, section, product or unit.
An **indirect cost** is a cost which cannot be economically identified with a particular department, section, product or unit.

The manufacturing account is usually broken down into three main categories, viz.:

1 materials;
2 labour;
3 indirect costs.

These categories are sometimes known as the *elements of cost*, and they are illustrated in a fairly simple example in Exhibit 5.1. The manufacturing account in Exhibit 5.1 is shown in the vertical format. As explained in the last chapter, this format is considered easier to follow for non-specialists unused to double-entry procedures, and we shall continue to adopt it this chapter. A detailed explanation of the items in the account follows the exhibit.

Exhibit 5.1 Format of a basic manufacturing account

	£000	£000
Direct costs (1)		
Direct material (2)	20	
Direct labour (3)	70	
Other direct expenses (4)	5	
Prime cost (5)	—	95
Manufacturing overhead (6)		
Indirect material cost (7)	3	
Indirect labour cost (7)	7	
Other indirect expenses (7)	10	
Total manufcturing overhead incurred (8)	—	20
Total manufacturing costs incurred (9)		115
Work-in-progress (10)		
Opening work-in-progress	10	
Closing work-in-progress	(15)	(5)
Manufacturing cost of goods produced (11)		110
Manufacturing profit (12)		11
Market values of goods produced transferred to the trading account (13)		£121

Notes:

1 The number shown after each item refers to the tutorial notes (see below). The amounts have been inserted purely for illustrative purposes.
2 The term 'factory' or 'work' is sometimes substituted for the term *manufacturing.*

Tutorial notes

1 *Direct costs.* The exhibit relates to a *company's* manufacturing account. It is assumed that the direct costs listed for materials, labour and other expenses relate to those expenses which have been easy to identify with the specific products that the company manufactures.
2 *Direct materials.* The charge for direct materials will be calculated as follows:

Direct material cost = (Opening stock of raw materials +
purchases of raw materials) – Closing stock of raw materials

The total of direct material cost is sometimes referred to as *materials consumed.* Direct materials will include all the raw material costs and component parts which have been easy to identify with particular products.
3 *Direct labour.* Direct labour will include all those employment costs that have been easy to identify with particular products.
4 *Other direct expenses.* Besides direct material and direct labour costs, there are sometimes other direct expenses that are easy to identify with particular products, for example. the cost of hiring a specific machine. Such expenses are relatively rare.
5 *Prime cost.* The total of direct material costs, direct labour costs and other direct expenses is known as prime cost.
6 *Manufacturing overhead.* Overhead is the collective term given to represent the total of all indirect costs, so any manufacturing costs that are not easy to identify with specific products will be classified separately under this heading.
7 *Indirect material cost, indirect labour cost and* other *indirect expenses.* Manufacturing overhead will probably be shown separately under these three headings,
8 *Total manufacturing overhead incurred.* This item represents the total of indirect material cost, indirect labour cost and other indirect expenses.
9 *Total manufacturing costs incurred.* The total of prime cost and the total of total manufacturing overhead incurred equals the total manufacturing costs incurred.
10 *Work-in-progress.* Work-in-progress represents the estimated cost of incomplete work that is not yet ready to be transferred to finished stock. There will usually be some opening and closing work-in-progress.
11 *Manufacturing cost of goods produced.* The manufacturing cost of goods produced equals the total manufacturing costs incurred plus (or minus) the difference between the opening and closing work-in-progress.
12 *Manufacturing profit.* The manufacturing cost of goods produced is sometimes transferred to the finished goods stock account without any addition for manufacturing profit. If this is the case the double-entry effect is as follows:

Debit finished goods stock account, *Credit* manufacturing account
with the manufacturing cost of goods produced.

The finished goods stock account is the equivalent of the purchases account in a trading organization.

Sometimes, however, a manufacturing profit is added to the manufacturing cost of goods produced before it is transferred to the trading account. The main purpose of this adjustment is to enable management to compare more fairly the company's total manufacturing cost inclusive of profit with outside prices (since such prices will also be normally inclusive of profit). The profit added to the manufacturing cost of goods produced may simply be an appropriate percentage, or it may represent the level of profit that the industry generally expects to earn. Any profit element added to the manufacturing cost (irrespective of how it is calculated) is an internal book-keeping arrangement, as the profit has not been *realized* or earned outside the business. The double-entry is affected as follows:

Debit manufacturing account, *Credit* profit and loss account with the manufacturing profit.

13 *Market value of goods produced.* As explained in 12 above, the market value of goods produced is the amount which will be transferred (that is, debited) to the trading account.

You are now recommended to study Exhibit 5.1 most carefully. If you are not sure about a particular item, then refer to the accompanying tutorial notes. Once you are clear about the basic structure of a manufacturing account, you can move on to the next section.

CONSTRUCTION

In this section, we are going to explain how to construct a manufacturing account. This can best be understood by reference to an example. We use one in Exhibit 5.2.

Exhibit 5.2

The following balances, *inter alia*, have been extracted from the Wren Manufacturing company as at 31 March 19X5:

	Dr £
Carriage inwards (on raw materials)	6 000
Direct expenses	3 000
Direct wages	25 000
Factory administration	6 000
Factory heat and light	500
Factory power	1 500
Factory rent and rates	2 000

Factory supervisory costs	5 000
Purchase of raw materials	56 000
Raw materials stock (at 1 April 19X4)	4 000
Work-in-progress (at 1 April 19X4)	5 000

Additional information:

1 The stock of raw materials at 31 March 19X5 was valued at £6000.
2 The work-in-progress at 31 March 19X5 was valued at £8000.
3 A profit loading of 50% is added to the total cost of manufacture.

Required:
Prepare Wren's manufacturing account for the year to 31 March 19X5.

Answer to Exhibit 5.2

Wren Manufacturing Company
Manufacturing account for the year to 31 March 19X5

	£	£	£
Direct materials			
Raw material stock at 1 April 19X4		4 000	
Purchases	56 000		
Carriage inwards (1)	6 000	62 000	
		66 000	
Less: Raw material stock at 31 March 19X5		6 000	
Cost of materials consumed			60 000
Direct wages			25 000
Direct expenses			3 000
Prime cost			88 000
Other manufacturing costs (2)			
Administration		6 000	
Heat and light		500	
Power		1 500	
Rent and rates		2 000	
Supervisory		5 000	
Total manufacturing overhead expenses			15 000
Total manufacturing costs incurred			103 000
Work-in-progress			
Add: Work-in-progress at 1 April 19X4		5 000	
Less: work-in-progress at 31 March 19X5		(8 000)	(3 000)
Manufacturing cost of goods produced			100 000
Manufacturing profit (50%) (3)			50 000
Market value of goods produced (4)			£150 000

Tutorial notes

1 Carriage inwards (i.e. the cost of transporting goods to the factory) is normally regarded as being part of the cost of purchases.
2 Other manufacturing costs include production overhead expenses. In practice, there would be a considerable number of other manufacturing costs.
3 A profit loading of 50% has been added to the manufacturing cost (see Note 3 of the question). The manufacturing profit is a debit entry in the manufacturing account. The corresponding credit entry will eventually be made in the profit and loss account.
4 The market value of goods produced will be transferred to the finished goods stock account.

You are now recommended to work through Exhibit 5.2 again, but this time without reference to the answer.

A COMPREHENSIVE EXAMPLE

Exhibit 5.2 deals with the manufacturing account in isolation. In order to understand how the manufacturing account complements the trading account, the profit and loss account and the balance sheet, it is necessary for us to work through a comprehensive example. The relationship is also shown in Exhibit 5.3.

Exhibit 5.3 The relationship between a manufacturing, trading and a profit and loss account and a balance sheet.

We will do so using Exhibit 5.4. It looks to be a formidable question, but remember that you have dealt with most of the items in the previous chapter: only the manufacturing account details are new. There are also some detailed tutorial notes, so you should not get stuck.

Exhibit 5.4

The following trial balance has been extracted from the books of account of the Knight Manufacturing Company as at 31 December 19X3:

	Dr £	Cr £
Bank overdraft		2 500
Capital		24 000
Direct wages	75 000	
Discounts allowed	3 000	
Discounts received		1 000
Drawings	8 000	
Finished goods stock (at 1 January 19X3)	15 000	
Long-term loan		5 000
Long-term loan interest	500	
Manufacturing expenses (administration and supervisory)	35 000	
Motor van at cost	5 000	
Motor van: depreciation (at 1 January 19X3)		2 000
Motor van expenses	850	
Office expenses	1 650	
Plant and equipment at cost	28 000	
Plant and equipment: depreciation (at 1 January 19X3)		14 000
Purchases of raw materials	50 000	
Raw material stock (at 1 January 19X3)	6 000	
Sales		250 000
Salaries (administration)	29 000	
Salaries (selling and distribution)	14 000	
Trade creditors		12 500
Trade debtors	30 000	
Work-in-progress (at 1 January 19X3)	10 000	
	£311 000	£311 000

Additional information:
1 Stocks at 31 December 19X3 were valued as follows:

	£
Raw materials	7 000
Work-in-progress	12 000
Finished goods	18 000

2 Depreciation is to be charged on the motor van at a rate of 20% on cost and on the plant and equipment at a rate of 25% on cost.
3 There were no accruals or prepayments at the end of the year.
4 A manufacturing profit of 20% should be added to the manufacturing cost of goods produced.
5 The motor van is used entirely for the delivery of goods to customers.

Required:
(a) Prepare Knight's manufacturing trading and profit and loss account for the year to 31 December 19X3; and (b) a balance sheet as at that date.

Answer to Exhibit 5.4

(a)

Knight Manufacturing Company
Manufacturing trading and profit and loss account for the year to 31 December 19X3

	£	£	£	£
Sales (1)				250 000
Less: Cost of goods sold:				
Finished stock at				
1 January 19X3			15 000	
Market value of finished				
goods produced (2):				
Direct materials				
Raw materials stock at				
1 January 19X3		6 000		
Purchases or raw materials		50 000		
		56 000		
Less: Raw material stock				
at 31 December 19X3		7 000		
Cost of materials consumed		49 000		
Direct wages		75 000		
		124 000		
Prime cost				
Other manufacturing costs:				
administration and supervisory	35 000			
Plant and equipment				
depreciation	7 000			
		42 000		
Total manufacturing costs incurred		166 000		
Work-in-progress:				
Add: Work-in-progress at				
1 January 19X3	10 000			
Less: Work-in-progess at				
31 December 19X3	(12 000)	(2 000)		
	c/f	164 000	15 000	250 000

		c/f	164 000	15 000	250 000
Manufacturing costs of goods produced			164 000		
Manufacturing			32 800	196 800	
				211 800	
Less: Finished stock at 31 December 19X3				18 000	193 800
Gross profit (3)					56 200
Add: Other incomes (4):					
Manufacturing profit				32 800	
Discounts received				1 000	33 800
					90 000
Less: Other expenses (4):					
Administration					
Office expenses			1 650		
Salaries			29 000	30 650	
Selling and distribution:					
Motor van depreciation			1 000		
Motor van expenses			850		
Salaries			14 000	15 850	
Finance					
Discounts allowed			3 000		
Loan interest			500	3 500	50 000
Net profit for the year					£40 000

(b)

Knight Manufacturing Company
Balance sheet at 31 December 19X3

	£	£	£
Fixed assets (5)	*Cost*	*Accumlated depreciation*	*Net book value*
Plant and equipment (6)	28 000	21 000	7 000
Motor van (7)	5 000	3 000	2 000
(8)	33 000	24 000	9 000
Current assets			
Stocks: Raw materials (9)	7 000		
Work-in-progress (9)	12 000		
Finished goods (9)	18 000		
Trade debtors		37 000	
		30 000	
		67 000	
Less: Current liabilities:			
Trade creditors	12 500		
Bank overdraft	2 500	15 000	52 000
			£61 000

Financed by:		£
Capital		
Balance at 1 January 19X3		24 000
Add: Net profit for the year	40 000	
Less: Drawings	8 000	32 000
Proprietor's capital (10)		56 000
Loan (11)		5 000
		£61 000

Tutorial notes

1 Notice that with the vertical format the account begins wlth sales.

2 A detailed explanation is then given of how the manufacturing cost of goods produced has been arrived at. This part of the manufacturing account is similar to the one used in Exhibit 5.2.

3 At the gross profit stage both the manufacturing account and the trading account have been effectively completed.

4 If the information permits, it is customary to sectionalize other incomes and expenses into appropriate categories. Thus in this example the other expenses have been classified into administration, selling and distribution, and finance expenses.

5 As explained in the last chapter, the fixed assets should be analyzed into different classes of assets. The cost, accumulated depreciation, and the net book value for each group of fixed asset should also be shown.

6 The accumulated depreciation of £21 000 for plant and equipment has been obtained from the trial balance by taking the accumulated depreciation of £14 000 as at 1 January 19X3 and adding the £7 000 depreciation charge for the year to 31 December 19X3 to it. The question states that depreciation is to be charged for that year at a rate of 25% on the cost of the machinery (i.e. 25% x £28 000).

7 The accumulated depreciation charge on the motor van has been calculated by taking the accumulated depreciation balance of £2 000 as at 1 January 19X3 from the trial balance, and adding it to the £1 000 depreciation charge for the year. The question states that depreciation is to be charged on the motor van at a rate of 20% of its cost (i.e. 20% x £5 000).

8 The total net book value for all classes of fixed assets is required for balancing purposes.

9 Details for the different categories of stock should be disclosed.

10 It is useful to disclose separately the total amount of capital invested by the proprietor in the business.

11 The question states that the loan is a long-term loan. It should be shown separately as part of the capital section, and not as part of the proprietor's capital.

Exhibit 5.4 appears to be quite a complicated example, so we think that you should now work through it again without reference to the solution.

CONCLUSION

A manufacturing account is required for those businesses that undertake further work on goods purchased before they are sold to customers. Manufacturing accounts are normally prepared annually along with all of the other basic financial statements.

Some entities may prepare a manufacturing account more frequently than once a year, but the traditional double-entry book-keeping system is not really designed to cope with short-term reporting requirements. As we explained in Chapter 1, many manufacturing entities now incorporate a cost and management accounting system into their reporting procedures. Such a system then gives them a lot more detailed information about their manufacturing costs than does one based on the procedures outlined in this chapter. Thus those entities that have a cost and management accounting system will not normally find it necessary to prepare a manufacturing account.

We shall be dealing with cost and management accounting in Part 3 of this book. In the meantime, we still have to cover some more important aspects of financial accounting. We shall be doing so in the remaining three chapters of this part of the book.

KEY POINTS

1 Those entities that undertake further work on any goods purchased before offering them for resale may wish to prepare a manufacturing account.

2 A manufacturing account is part of the double-entry system. It will usually be prepared annually along with the other basic financial statements. It may be presented in either the horizontal or the vertical format, and it comes before the trading account.

3 Its main elements include: direct materials, direct labour and various indirect manufacturing expenses.

4 Direct cost means a cost that can be economically identified with a specific unit (or department, or some other section).

5 A separate manufacturing account will not always be needed, as many manufacturing entities now operate a cost and management accounting system. This system provides better and more frequent information than does a simple manufacturing account.

CHECK YOUR LEARNING

1 State whether each of the following assertions is either true or false:
   (a) A manufacturing account will normally be required if an entity makes a product.   True/False

    (b) An indirect cost is a cost that can be economically identified
       with a specific department.   True/False
    (c) Opening work-in-progress has to be added to the total of
       manufacturing costs incurred.   True/False

2 Put the following items in the order that you would expect to find them in a
manufacturing account:
Closing work-in-progress
Direct labour
Direct materials
Indirect labour
Indirect materials
Opening work-in-progress

3 To which element of cost does the following definition refer?
'Goods purchased for incorporation into products for sale'

ANSWERS

1 (a) true   (b) false   (c) true
2 Direct materials; Direct labour; Indirect materials; Indirect labour; Opening work-in-progress; Closing work-in-progress
3 Raw material

QUESTIONS

5.1 The following information relates to Megg for the year to 31 January 19X1:

	£000
Stocks at I February 19X0:	
Raw material	10
Work-in progress	17
Direct wages	65
Factory: Administration	27
Heat and light	9
Indirect wages	13
Purchases of raw materials	34
Stocks at 31 January 19X1:	
Raw material	12
Work-in-progress	14

Required:
Prepare Megg's manufacturing account for the year to 31 January 19XI.

5.2 The following balances have been extracted from the books of account of
Moor for the year to 28 February 19X2:

	£
Administration expenses	33 000
Direct wages	50 000
Factory indirect wages	27 700

Purchase of raw materials	127 500
Sales	250 000
Selling and distribution expenses	10 200
Stocks at 1 March 19XI:	
Raw materials	13 000
Work-in-progress	8 400
Finished goods	24 000
Stocks at 28 February 19X2:	
Raw materials	15 500
Work-in-progress	6 300
Finished goods	30 000

Required:
Prepare Moor's manufacturing, trading, and profit and loss account for the year to 28 February 19X2.

5.3 The following balances have been extracted from the books of Stuart for the year to 31 March 19X3:

	Dr	Cr
	£000	£000
Administration: Factory	230	
General	112	
Bank	7	
Capital at 1 April I9X2		264
Creditors		335
Debtors	184	
Direct wages	330	
Miscellaneous expenses	16	
Plant and machinery: At cost	594	
Accumulated depreciation at 31 March 19X3		199
Purchases of raw materials	1123	
Sales		1932
Stock at 1 April 19X2:		
Raw material	38	
Work-in-progress	29	
Finished goods	67	
	£2730	£2730

Additional information:
Stocks at 31 March 19X3: £000

Raw material	44
Work-in-progress	42
Finished goods	65

Required:
Prepare Stuart's manufacturing, trading, and profit and loss account for the year to 31 March 19X3, and a balance sheet as at that date.

5.4 The following balances have been extracted from the books of the David and Peter Manufacturing company as at 30 April 19X4.

	Dr £000	Cr £000
Administration salaries	76	
Capital at 1 May 19X3		218
Cash	18	
Creditors		102
Debtors	116	
Direct wages	70	
Drawings	26	
Factory equipment: At cost	360	
Accumulated depreciation at 1 May 19X3		180
General factory expenses	13	
General office expenses	9	
Heat and light (factory 3/4; general 1/4)	52	
Purchase of raw material	100	
Sales		420
Stocks at 1 May 19X3:		
Raw material	12	
Work-in-progress	18	
Finished goods	8	
Rent and rates (factory 2/3; general 1/3)	42	
	£920	£920

Additional information:

1 Stocks at 30 April 19X4:

	£000
Raw material	14
Work-in-progress	16
Finished goods	22

2 The factory equipment is to be depreciated at a rate of 15% per annum on cost.

Required:
Prepare the David and Peter Manufacturing company's manufacturing, trading, and profit and loss account for the year to 30 April 19X4, and a balance sheet as at that date.

5.5 Jeffrey is in business as a manufacturer. He has extracted the following trial balance from his books of account as at 31 May 19X5:

	Dr £000	Cr £000
Bank	6	
Capital		58
Creditors		156
Debtors	89	
Drawings	15	
c/f	110	214

		b/f	110	214
Factory expenses:				
Direct wages			200	
General expenses			60	
Office equipment:				
At cost			30	
Accumulated depreciation at 1 June 19X4				9
Office expenses			127	
Plant:				
At cost			160	
Accumulated depreciation at 1 June 19X4				70
Purchases of finished goods			55	
Purchases of raw materials			180	
Sales				693
Stocks at 1 June 19X4:				
Raw material			17	
Work-in-progress			21	
Finished goods			26	
			£986	£986

Additional information:

1 Stocks at 31 May 19X5: £000
   Raw materials 20
   Work-in-progress 30
   Finished goods 29

2 Goods manufactured by Jeffrey are transferred to finished stock at the cost of manufacture plus 20%.

3 Office equipment is to be depreciated at a rates of 10% per annum on cost, and plant at a rate of 20% per annum on cost.

Required:

Prepares Jeffrey's manufacturing, trading, and profit and loss account for the year to 31 May 19X5, and a balance sheet as at that date.

5.6 Clarico is a small manufacturing company. The following trial balance has been extracted from the books of account as at 30 June 19X6:

		Dr	Cr
		£000	£000
Administration		39	
Capital			252
Carriage inwards		22	
Cash		7	
Delivery vans:			
At cost		36	
Accumulated depreciation at 1 July 19X5			18
Delivery vans expenses		12	
Drawings		110	
	c/f	226	270

		b/f	226	270
Electricity			16	
Plant:				
At cost:			110	
Accumulated depreciation at 1 July 19X5				40
Provision for doubtful debts (at 1 July 19X5)				55
Purchases:				
Raw materials			450	
Finished goods			30	
Rent and rates			70	
Sales				1570
Sales expenses			56	
Stocks at 1 July 19X5:				
Raw materials			120	
Work-in-progress			40	
Finished goods			48	
Trade creditors				265
Trade debtors			800	
Wages:				
Factory direct			142	
Factory indirect			48	
Administration			26	
Sales			18	
			£2200	£2200

Additional information:

1 Stocks at 30 June 19X6   £000

Raw materials	102
Work-in-progress	74
Finished goods	76

2 Manufactured goods are transferred to finished goods stock at cost plus 10%.

3 Provision is to be made for the following amounts owing at 30 June 19X6:

    £000

Electicity	4
Rent	15
Delivery van expenses	3

4 The following expenses had been paid in advance at 30 June 19X6:

    £000

Rates	25
Delivery van licences	2

5 The bad debts provision is to be made equal to 10% of outstanding trade debtors as at 30 June 19X6.

6 Depreciation for the year is to be charged as follows:

Plant:	20% on cost
Delivery vans:	25% on cost

7 Expenses are to be apportioned as follows:

	Factory	Administration
	%	%
Electricity	80	20
Rent and rates	60	40

Required:
Prepare Clarico's manufacturing, trading, and profit and loss account for the year to 30 June 19X6, and balance sheet as at that date.

ADDITIONAL QUESTIONS (WITHOUT ANSWERS)

5.7   Joan Petrie owns a small manufacturing company. The following trial balance has been extracted from her books of account as at 30 September 19X9:

	Dr	Cr
	£000	£000
Advertising	40	
Capital		3 500
Cash at bank and in hand	16	
Discounts allowed	25	
Discounts received		15
Drawings	32	
Factory: Direct expenses	13	
Indirect expenses	262	
Wages and slaries	2 900	
Fixed assets at cost	5 000	
Accumulated depreciation		
(at 1 October 19X8)		1 500
Office expenses	1 552	
Purchases of raw materials	729	
Rent, rates, heat and light	40	
Sales		8 087
Stocks at 1 October 19X8:		
Raw materials	80	
Work-in-progress	70	
Finished goods	50	
Trade creditors		121
Trade debtors	820	
Wages and salaries (administration 50%,		
distribution 50%)	1 594	
	£13 223	£13 223

Additional information:
1 Stocks at 30 September 19X9:

	£000
Raw materials	95
Work-in-progress	54
Finished goods	65

2 Depreciation is charged on fixed assets at a rate of 10% per annum on cost. It is apportioned as follows:

	%
Factory	75
Administration and distribution	25
	100

3 Rent, rates, heat and light apportioned 50% to the factory and 50% to the office.

4 A profit loading of 30% is added to the manufactured cost of goods.

Required:

Prepares Joan Petrie's manufacturing, trading and profit and loss account for the year to 30 September 19X9, and a balance sheet as at that date.

5.8 Dunk's accountant has extracted the following trial balance as at 31 October 19X1:

	Dr £000	Cr £000
Advertising	9	
Bank overdraft		17
Capital		418
Carriage inwards	5	
Carriage outwards	37	
Delivery vans at cost	200	
Accumulated depreciation (at 1 November 19X0)		100
Direct factory expenses:		
General	7	
Raw materials	198	
Wages and salaries	530	
Discounts allowed	50	
Discounts received		11
Distribution costs	60	
Drawings	42	
Indirect factory expenses:		
General	4	
Material	10	
Wages and salaries	13	
Office: General expenses	8	
Lighting and heating	6	
Rent and rates	23	
Wages and salaries	46	
Plant and equipment at cost	600	
Accumulated depreciation (at 1 November 19X0)		360
c/f	1848	906

		b/f	1 848	906
Provision for bad and doubtful debts				
(at 1 November 19X0)				3
Sales				1300
Salespersons' salaries and expenses			76	
Stocks at 1 November 19X0:				
Raw materials			22	
Work-in-progress			70	
Finished goods			130	
Trade creditors				33
Trade debtors			96	
			£2242	£2242

Additional information:

1 Stocks at 31 October 19X1:

	£000
Raw materials	10
Work-in-progress	91
Finished goods	70

2 Depreciation:

Delivery vans:	25% on cost
Plant and machinery (all factory):	20% on cost.

3 Accruals at 31 October 19X1:

	£000
Indirect factory expenses	2
Office rent	7

4 Prepayments at 31 October 19X1:

	£000
Telephone	1
Salespersons' expenses	4

5 A profit loading of 10% is added to the cost of manufactured goods.

6 A bad debt of £16 000 is to be written off.

7 A provision for bad and doubtful debts is maintained equivalent to 5% of out-standing trade debtors as at the end of each year.

Required:

Prepare Dunk's manufacturing, trading and profit and loss account for the year to 31 October 19X1, and a balance sheet as at that date.

CHAPTER 6

Partnership and company accounts

Royal Bank advances 91% to £92m despite bad debt provisions

By John Gapper,
Banking Correspondant

A return to profit in its core branch banking business and trebled profits in its Direct Line telephone insurance operation helped Royal Bank of Scotland raise interim pre-tax profits by 91 per cent, from £48m to £91.6m.

The bank, which increased loans to customers in the six months to March 31 helped by a £650m rise in personal mortgages, said it was confident that full-year provisions for bad and doubtful debts would be below last year.

Lord Younger, chairman, said he was confident of further progress in the second half, helped by renewed economic growth.

"The upturn in performance at the full year is not only being sustained, but is gathering momentum," he said.

Although profit before provisions rose 32 per cent to £285m (£216m), the rise at the pre-tax level was obtained by bad debt provsions. These stood at £183m (£163m), but were substantialy lower than the figure of £238m for last year's second half.

These latest accounts were prepared under the FRS 3 accounting standard, and the comparatives have been restated accordingly.

The interim dividend has been raised to 3p (2.8p) on earnings per share of 5p (2.9p).

The core ratio of tier 1 capital to risk-weighed assets rose to 7 per cent (6.6 per cent) after the bank retained £15.7m (£1m).

Branch banking returned to profit with £6m (£8.4m profit), after a poor second half pushed it into a £16.1m loss in 1991–92. The Columbus restructuring project was estimated to have raised profits by £5m.

The corporate and institutional banking division raised profits by 39 per cent to £57.1m. "Very considerable progress" had been made in selling treasury and capital markets services to existing corporate customers.

Citizens Financial Group, the US retail banking subsidiary which is to boost its assets by nearly 50 per cent by acquiring Boston Five Bancorp, lifted profits by £12m to £20.9m.

Mr George Mathewson, chief executive, said Royal Bank had been approached by a large US bank which hoped to link with its Ibos service, offering cross-border banking services to companies in Britain, Spain, Portugal and France.

The proposed disposal of 90.1 per cent of Charterhouse, Royal Bank's merchant bank, is expected to lead to a book loss of £35m, The net reduction to reserves will be £12m, after writing back £23m of goodwill on disposal.

Net interest income rose to £421m (384m) as the spread between the interest earned on assets and paid on liabilities rose to 2.2 percentage points (1.9 percentage points) and interest bearing assets rose 12 per cent.

Other operating income rose to £313m (240m) and now constitutes 42 per cent of total income (38 per cent). Expenses rose by 10 per cent, but the cost to income ratio fell to 61.4 per cent (65.6 per cent)

The shares closed unchanged at 267p.

The Financial Times, 6 May 1993

Exhibit 6.0 The terms used in writing about a company's performance pre-suppose a good knowledge of accounting, as can be seen in this article.

In the last three chapters, we have been dealing mainly with the sole trader type of entity. However, as we argued in Chapter 1, this term is not to be taken too literally. The term *sole trader* means that the entity is *owned* by one individual, although hundreds of employees may work for it. The owner can also be engaged in any kind of business, and not just one that relates to trading.

Sole-trader entities are quite common, especially among very small businesses (e.g. those employing less than perhaps 20 people), but there are two other main types of entities which are perhaps just as common. These are partnerships and limited liability companies, and we examine each of them in this chapter.

In order to form a partnership, at least two people are required. Almost any type of entity can be operated as a partnership. A partnership may simply involve two or more people getting together to form a business. A company may be formed by one person but the formation of a *limited liability company* is bound by some fairly severe legal restrictions.

As a result of its unique legal position, the accounts of limited liability companies present particular difficulties, but before examining them in detail, we will deal first with partnerships. We do so in the next section.

LEARNING OBJECTIVES

By the end of this chapter, you will be able to:
- prepare some simple partnership accounts;
- describe the nature of limited liability;
- distinguish between private and public limited companies;
- prepare a basic set of company accounts.

PARTNERSHIPS

A partnership is similar to a sole trader. It is presumed to exist when two or more people get together in business with the objective of making a profit. We will look in a little more detail at this common form of business entity in the following sub-sections.

Management

The law limits the total number of people who may get together to form a partnership. Apart from a few exceptions (such as firms of accountants and solicitors), a partnership may not consist of more than 20 partners. In order to be considered a partner, it is not necessary to contribute any capital. If an individual is regarded as being a partner, then it is assumed that he *is* a partner.

The partnership will be managed by general agreement among the partners, but if there is no apparent agreement (either formal or informal), then it is presumed that the partnership will operate in accordance with the Partnership Act 1890. This Act lays down arrangements for dealing with such matters as the amount of capital to be contributed, the management of the business, and the division of the profits or losses among the partners.

If the partners have come to an agreement among themselves, then partnerships (like sole traders) can operate without the detailed intervention of the law.

Accounts

Partnership accounts are very similar to those of sole traders (see Exhibit 6.1). There are just three essential differences. These are as follows:

1 The net profit for the year is shown as a balancing figure in the profit and loss account. It is then transferred to what is called the profit and loss *appropriation* account. This account shows how the profit is divided among the partners.
2 Details concerning the partners' share of profits and of their drawings are usually kept in current accounts. Current accounts enable such details to be kept separate from the partners capital accounts, thereby ensuring that amounts contributed as capital are not obscured by day-to-day transactions.
3 The capital section on the balance sheet shows the respective partners' capital and current accounts balances.

Exhibit 6.1 Accounting for partnerships

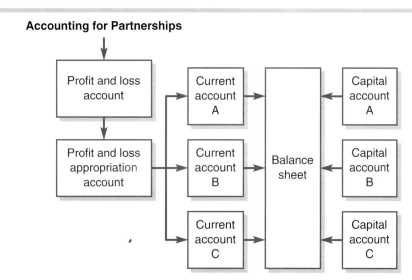

A calculative example of partnership accounting is shown in Exhibit 6.2.

Exhibit 6.2 Illustration of partnership accounts

Duke & Luke
Profit and loss appropriation account for the year to 31 March 19X9

	£	£
Net profit (1)		20 000
Appropriation (2):		
Duke (70%)	14 000	
Luke (30%)	6 000	
		20 000

Duke & Luke
Balance sheet (extract) at 31 March 19X9

	£	£
Net assets (3)		24 500
Financed by:		
Capital accounts (4)		
Duke		10 000
Luke		5 000
		15 000
Current accounts (5)		
Duke	6 000	
Luke	3 500	9 500
		£24 500

Tutorial notes

1 Profit is calculated in exactly the same way as that for sole trader entities.
2 The exhibit assumes that the partners have agreed to share out the profit in the ratio 70 : 30, the double-entry effect being as follows:
   Dr Profit and loss appropriation account
      with £20 000
   Cr Duke's current account
      with £14 000
   Cr Luke's current account
      with £6 000
   By making these transfers to the partners' current accounts, no balance remains in the profit and loss appropriation account.
3 It is assumed that the net assets of the partnership are £24 500.
4 The partners have contributed £15 000 in capital (Duke £10 000 and Luke £5 000). It should be noted that profit may not necessarily be apportioned in the capital sharing ratios; this is a matter for the partners to agree among themselves.
5 The partners' current accounts represent their respective net balances as at the end of the year (after allowing for the balance brought forward, the partner's share of the profit and any drawings that may have been made during the year).

6 The total of the capital account and the current account balances represent the total amount of capital invested in the business by the partners. The current account balances are, however, usually just a short-term source of finance, since the partnership agreement would probably allow the partners to withdraw from their current accounts at any time. By using current accounts the balances on the capital accounts will remain at their original levels, unless more capital is contributed or some withdrawn.

With only one exception, details showing the share of profit among the partners are *always* recorded in the profit and loss appropriation account, irrespective of their description. Thus, such matters as the payment of partnership salaries, the payment of interest on capital and current accounts, and the charging of interest on their drawings are all shown in the appropriation account. The one exception applies when a partner makes a specific identifiable loan to the partnership, and that loan lies outside the partnership agreement. The interest on it is then charged to the profit and loss account.

The preparation of partnership accounts is a fairly routine accounting exercise. As a non-accountant, you almost certainly will not be involved in the exercise, so in this book we do not need to go into any further detail.

We can now turn to the other important type of business entity: the *limited liability company*.

LIMITED LIABILITY COMPANIES

There is a great personal risk in operating a business as a sole trader or as a partnership. If the business runs short of funds, the owners may be called upon to settle the businesss debts out of their own private resources. This type of risk can have an inhibiting effect on the development of new businesses. Hence the need for a different type of entity which will neither make the owners bankrupt nor inhibit new developments. This need became apparent in the nineteenth century as a result of the industrial revolution when in order to finance the new and rapidly expanding industries (such as the railways, iron, and steel) enormous amounts of capital were required.

These sorts of ventures were undertaken at great personal risk. By agreeing to become involved in them, investors often faced bankruptcy if the ventures were unsuccessful (as they often were). It became apparent that the development of industry would be severely restricted unless some means could be devised of restricting the personal liability of prospective investors.

Hence the need for a form of *limited liability*. In fact, the concept of limited liability was not entirely an innovation of the nineteenth century, although it did not receive legal recognition until the Limited Liability Act was passed in 1855. The Act only remained in force for a few months before it was repealed and incorporated into the Joint Stock Companies Act 1856.

By accepting the principle of limited liability, the 1855 Act also recognized the *entity* concept. By distinguishing between the private and public affairs of business proprietors, it effectively created a new form of entity. Since the 1850s, Parliament has passed a number of other Companies Acts, all of which have continued to give legal recognition to the concept of limited liability.

The important point about a limited liability company is that no matter what financial difficulties a company may get into, its members cannot be required to contribute more than an agreed amount of capital. Thus, there is no risk of members being forced into bankruptcy.

The concept of limited liability is often very difficult for business owners to understand, especially if they have formed a limited liability company out of what was perhaps a sole-trader or a partnership entity. Unlike such entities, companies are bound by some fairly severe legal restrictions that affect their operations.

The legal restrictions can be somewhat burdensome, but they are necessary for the protection of all those parties who might have dealings with the company, such as creditors and employees. If a limited liability company runs short of funds, the creditors and employees might not get paid. It is only fair, therefore, to warn all those people who might have dealings with it they run a risk in dealing with it. Consequently, such a company has to be more open about its affairs than would otherwise be the case.

STRUCTURE AND OPERATION

In this section, we are going to examine briefly the structure and operation of limited liability companies. In order to make it easier to follow, we have broken down our examination into a number of sub-sections.

Share capital

Although the law recognizes that limited liability companies are separate beings with a life of their own (i.e. separate from those individuals who collectively own and manage them), it also accepts that someone has to take responsibility for promoting, the company, i.e. bringing it into being. In fact, only one person is now required to form a company, and that person (or persons, if there is more than one), agrees to make a capital contribution by buying a number of shares. The capital of a company is known as its *share capital*. The share capital will be made up of a number of shares of a certain denomination, such as 10p, 50p, and £1. A member may hold only one share, or many hundreds or thousands, depending upon the total share capital of the company, the denomination of the shares, and the amount that he wishes to contribute.

The maximum amount of capital that the company envisages ever raising has to be stated. This is known as its *authorized share capital*, although this does not necessarily mean that it will ever issue shares up to that amount. In practice, it will probably only issue sufficient capital to meet its immediate and foreseeable requirements. The amount of share capital that it has actually issued is known as the *issued share capital*. Sometimes when shares are issued, prospective shareholders are only required to contribute to them in instalments. Once all of the issued share capital has been received in cash, it is described as being *fully paid*.

There are two main types of shares: *ordinary* shares and *preference* shares. Ordinary shares do not usually entitle the shareholder to any specific level of dividend (see page 139), and the rights of other types of shareholders always take precedence over the rights of the ordinary shareholders, e.g. if the company goes into liquidation. Preference shareholders are normally entitled to a fixed level of dividend, and they usually have priority over the ordinary shareholders if the company is liquidated. Sometimes, the preference shares are classed as *cumulative*. This means that if the company cannot pay its preference dividend in one year, the amount due accrues until such time as the company has the profits to pay all of the accumulated dividends.

There are many other different types of shares, but in this book, we need only concern ourselves with ordinary shares and preference shares.

| Types of companies | A prospective shareholder may invest in either a public company or a private company. A public company must have an authorized share capital of at least £50,000, and it becomes a public company merely by stating that it *is* a public company. In fact, most public limited companies have their shares listed on the Stock Exchange, and hence they are often referred to as *listed* companies. |

As a warning to those parties who might have dealings with them, public companies have to include the term 'public limited liability company' after their name (or its abbreviation 'plc').

Any company that does not make its shares available to the public is regarded as being a *private* company. Like public companies, private companies must also have an authorized share capital, although no minimum amount is prescribed. Otherwise, they are very similar to public companies in respect of their share capital requirements.

Private companies also have to warn the public that their liability is limited. They must do so by describing themselves as 'limited liability companies', and attaching the term 'limited' after their name (or the abbreviation 'ltd').

Loans

Besides obtaining the necessary capital from their shareholders, companies often borrow money in the form of *debentures*. A company may invite the public to loan it some money for a certain period of time (although the period can be unspecified) at a certain rate of interest. A debenture loan may be secured on specific assets of the company, on its assets generally, or it might not be secured at all. If it is secured and the company cannot repay it on its due repayment date, the debenture holders may sell the secured assets, and use the amount to settle the amount owing to them.

Debentures, like shares, may be bought and sold freely on the Stock Exchange. The nearer the redemption date for the repayment for the debentures, the closer the market price will be to their nominal (i.e. their face, or stated paper) value, but sometimes if they are to be redeemed at a premium (i.e. in excess of their nominal value), the market price may exceed the nominal value.

Debenture holders are not shareholders of the company, and they do not have voting rights. However, for tax purposes, debenture interest can be charged as a business expense against the profit for the year (unlike dividends paid to shareholders).

Disclosure of information	It is necessary for both public and private companies to supply a *minimum* amount of information to their members. We shall be examining the detailed requirements in Part 4 of this book. You might find it surprising to learn that shareholders have neither a right of access to the company's premises, nor a right to receive any information that they demand. This might not seem fair, but it would clearly be difficult for a company's managers to cope with thousands of shareholders, all of whom suddenly all turned up one day demanding to be let into the buildings in order to inspect the company's books of account!

Instead, shareholders in both private and public companies have to be supplied with an annual report containing at least the minimum amount of information required by the Companies Act 1985. The company also has to file (as it is called) a copy of the report with the Registrar of Companies at Companies House (either in Cardiff or in Edinburgh). This means that on payment of a small fee, the report is open for inspection by any member of the public who wants to consult it. Some companies (defined as small or medium-sized) are permitted to file an abbreviated version of their annual report with the Registrar, although the full report must still be sent to their shareholders.

Company accounts	Company accounts are very similar to those of sole traders and partnerships (Exhibit 6.3 shows the basic stucture).

They do, however, tend to be more detailed, and some modifications have to be made in order to comply with various legal requirements. We shall be looking at company accounts in more detail a little later on in the chapter.

Exhibit 6.3 A company's basic financial statements

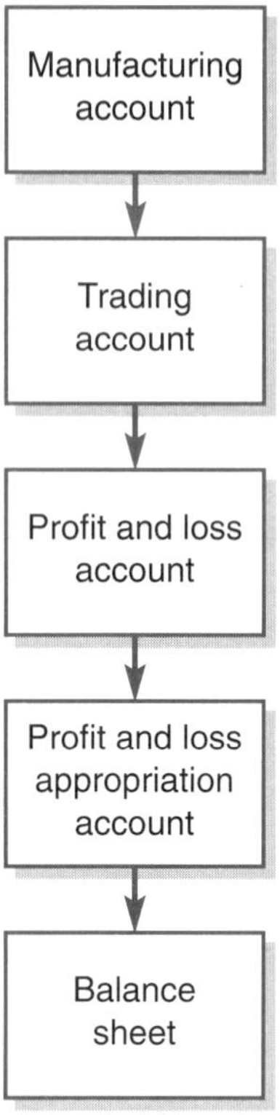

```
┌─────────────────┐
│  Manufacturing  │
│     account     │
└─────────────────┘
         │
         ▼
┌─────────────────┐
│     Trading     │
│     account     │
└─────────────────┘
         │
         ▼
┌─────────────────┐
│  Profit and loss│
│     account     │
└─────────────────┘
         │
         ▼
┌─────────────────┐
│  Profit and loss│
│  appropriation  │
│     account     │
└─────────────────┘
         │
         ▼
┌─────────────────┐
│     Balance     │
│      sheet      │
└─────────────────┘
```

Directors   It must be clearly understood that any limited liability company is regarded as being a separate entity, i.e. separate from those shareholders who own it collectively, and separate from anyone who works for it. This means that all those who are employed by it (no matter how senior) are its employees. None the less, someone has to take responsibility for the management of the company, of course, so the shareholders usually delegate that responsibility to directors.

Directors are the most senior level of management. They are responsible for the day-to-day running of the company, and they answer to the shareholders. Directors are officers of the company, and any remuneration paid to them as directors is charged as an expense of the business. Directors may also be shareholders, but any payment that they receive as such is regarded as being a private matter, and it must not be confused with any income that they receive as directors.

The distinction between employees and shareholder-employees is an important one, although it is one that is not always understood. This is especially the case in very small companies where both employees and shareholders may be one and the same. As we have tried to emphasize, in law, the company is regarded as being a separate entity. Even if there are just two shareholders who both work full-time for the company, the company is still treated as distinct from that of the two individuals who happen to own it. They may take decisions which appear to affect no one else except themselves, but because they operate the company under the protection of limited liability, they have certain obligations as well as rights. Consequently, they are not as free to operate the company as they might if they ran it as a partnership.

Dividends

Profits are usually distributed to shareholders in the form of a dividend. A dividend is usually calculated on the basis of so many pence per share. The actual dividend will be recommended by the directors to the shareholders. It will depend upon the amount of net profit earned during the year, and how much profit the directors want to retain in the business.

A dividend may have been paid during the year as an interim dividend. In effect, an interim dividend is a payment on account. In preparing the annual accounts, the directors recommend a proposed dividend (sometimes referred to as the *final* dividend). The proposed dividend has to be approved by the shareholders at a general meeting.

Taxation

Taxation is another feature which clearly distinguishes a limited liability company from that of a sole-trader or partnership entity.

Sole-trader and partnership entities do not have tax levied on them as entities. Instead, tax is levied on the amount of profit the owner or partners have made during the year. The tax that is then due for payment is a private matter (although the tax demand may be addressed to the partnership), and in accordance with the entity rule, it lies outside the boundary of the entity. Any tax that appears to have been paid by the entity on the owner's or partners' behalf is treated as part of their drawings (i.e. an amount paid to them as part of their share of the profits).

Companies are treated quite differently. Companies are taxed in their own right, like individuals. They have their own form of taxation, known as *corporation tax*. Corporation tax was introduced in 1965, and all companies are eligible to pay it. It is based on the company's accounting profits for a particular financial year. The accounting profit has to be adjusted, however, because some items are treated differently for tax purposes, e.g. the depreciation of fixed assets. The corporation tax based on a company's profits is then due for payment nine months after the company's year end.

The corporation tax due will normally be shown in the company's balance sheet at the year end under current liabilities as a creditor, and it should normally have all been paid by the time that the next balance sheet is prepared.

Corporation tax has sometimes be paid in advance. This is known as *advance corporation tax* (ACT). ACT is due for payment each time that the company pays a dividend. The amount due is based on the dividend. Any ACT paid is eventually deducted from the total corporation charge payable for the year. The net amount due (i.e. the total amount of corporation tax payable for the year less any ACT paid) is known as *mainstream corporation tax*. The book-keeping entries are extremely complex but, fortunately, we do not need to go into them in this book.

Now that we have outlined the basic structure and operation of limited liability companies, we can begin to examine company accounts in some detail. We start with the profit and loss account.

THE PROFIT AND LOSS ACCOUNT

As we suggested earlier, the preparation of a company's manufacturing, trading and profit and loss account is basically no different from those of sole-trader entities. Almost an identical format may be adopted, and it is only after the net profit stage that some differences become apparent.

Like partnership accounts, company accounts also include a profit and loss appropriation account (although no clear dividing line is usually drawn between where the profit and loss account ends and the appropriation account begins). We illustrate a company's profit and loss appropriation account in Exhibit 6.4.

Exhibit 6.4 Example of a company's profit and loss appropriation account

	£000
Net profit for the year before taxation	1000
Taxation	(300)
Net profit for the year after taxation	700
Dividends	(500)
Retained profit for the year	200
Retained profits brought forward	400
Retained profits carried forward	£600

As can be seen from Exhibit 6.4, the company's net profit for the year is used (or appropriated) in three ways:

1 to pay tax;
2 to pay dividends;
3 for retention within the business.

THE BALANCE SHEET

The structure of a limited liability company's balance sheet is also very similar to that of a sole trader or of a partnership. The main differences arise because of the company's share capital structure. There are, however, some other features that are not usually found in non-company balance sheets.

We illustrate the main features of a company's balance sheet in Exhibit 6.5. Study this exhibit carefully, but please note that the information has been kept to a minimum. We have not given the full details where there are insignificant differences between a company's balance sheet and those of other entities.

Exhibit 6.5 Example of a company 's balance sheet

Exhibitor Limited
Balance sheet at 31 March 19X1

	£000	£000	£000
Fixed assets			600
Investments (1)			100
Current assets		6000	
Less: Current liabilities			
Trade creditors	2950		
Accruals	50		
Corporation tax (2)	300		
Proposed dividend (3)	500	3800	2200
			£2900

	Authorized	Issued and fully paid
Financed by:		
Capital and reserves (4)		
	£000	£000
Ordinary shares of £X each (5)	2000	1500
Preference shares of £X each (5)	500	500
	£2500	2000
Capital reserves (6)		200
Revenue reserves (7)		600
Shareholders' funds (8)		2800
Loans (9)		100
		£2900

Note: The number shown after each narration refers to the tutorial notes below.

Tutorial notes

1 *Investments.* This item usually represents long-term investments in the shares of other companies. Short-term investments (such as money invested in bank deposit accounts) would he included in current assets. The shares may be either in public limited liability companies or in private limited companies.

   It is obviously more difficult to buy shares in private companies and to obtain current market prices for them. The market price of the investments should be stated, or where this is not available, a directors' valuation should be obtained.

2 *Corporation tax.* Corporation tax represents the tax due on the company's profits for the year. It is due for payment nine months after the company's year end, that is, in Exhibitor's case, on 1 January 19X2.

3 *Proposed dividend.* A proposed dividend will probably be due for payment very shortly after the year end, so it will usually be shown as a current liability.

4 *Capital and reserves.* Details of the authorized, issued and fully paid-up share capital should be shown.

5 *Ordinary shares and preference shares.* Details about the different types of shares that the company has issued should be shown.

6 This section may include several different reserve accounts of a capital nature, that is, amounts that are not available for distribuion to the shareholders as dividend. It might include, for example, a share premium account, i.e. the extra amount paid by shareholders in excess of the nominal value of the shares. This extra amount does not rank for dividend, but sometimes shareholders are willing to pay a premium if they think that the shares are particularly attractive. Another asset may have been revalued, and the difference between the original cost and the revalued amount will be credited to this account.

7 *Revenue reserves.* Revenue reserve accounts are amounts which are available for distribution to the shareholders. Sometimes profits which could be distributed to shareholders are put into general reserve accounts, although no real purpose is served in classifying them in this way.

8 *Shareholders' funds.* The total amount available to shareholders at the balance sheet date is equal to the share capital originally subscribed, plus all the capital, reserve and revenue reserve account balances.

9 *Loans.* The loans section of the balance sheet will include all the long-term loans obtained by the company, i.e. those loans which do not have to be repaid for at least twelve months, such as debentures and long-term bank loans.

A COMPREHENSIVE EXAMPLE

In this section, we are going to examine the structure of a company's accounts in a little more detail. We use Exhibit 6.6 as an example. The example assumes that the accounts are being prepared for internal management purposes (we deal with accounts for external purposes in Part 4 of the book). Work through the answer to Exhibit 6.6 making sure that you understand each step in its construction.

Exhibit 6.6

The following information has been extracted from the books of Handy Limited as at 31 March 19X5:

	Dr £	Cr £
Bank	2 000	
Capital: 100 000 issued and fully paid ordinary shares of £1 each		100 000
50 000 issued and fully paid 8% preference shares of £1 each		50 000
Debenture loan stock (10%: repayable 19X9)		30 000
Debenture loan stock interest	3 000	
Discounts alowed	2 000	
Discounts received		5 000
Dividends received		700
Dividends paid: Ordinary interim	5 000	
Preference	4 000	
Freehold land at cost	200 000	
Investments (listed: market value at 31 March 19X5 was £11 000	10 000	
Office expenses	15 000	
Office salaries	35 000	
Motor van at cost	15 000	
Motor van: accumulated depreciation at 1 April 19X4		6 000
Motor van expenses	2 700	
Purchases	220 000	
Retained profits at 1 April 19X4		9 000
Sales		300 000
Share premium account		10 000
Stocks at cost (at 1 April 19X4)	20 000	
Trade creditors		50 000
Trade debtors	27 000	
	£560 700	£560 700

Additional information:
1 The stocks at 31 March 19X5 were valued at cost at £40 000.
2 Depreciation is to be charged on the motor van at a rate of 20% per annum on cost. No depreciation is to be charged on the freehold land.
3 Corporation tax (based on profits for the year at a rate 35%) has been estimated at £10 000.
4 The directors propose a final ordinary dividend of 10p per share.
5 The authorized share capital of the company is as follows:
   (a) 150 000 ordinary shares of £1 each; and
   (b) 75 000 preference shares of £1 each.

Required:

(a) Prepare Handy Limited's trading, profit and loss account for the year to 31 March 19X5; and

(b) a balance sheet as at that date.

Answer to Exhibit 6.6

(a)   Handy Limited
          Trading, profit and loss account for the year to 31 March 19X5

	£	£	£
Sales			300 000
Less: Cost of goods sold:			
Opening stocks		20 000	
Purchases		220 000	
		240 000	
Less: Closing stocks		40 000	200 000
Gross profit			100 000
Add: Incomes:			
Discounts received		5 000	
Dividends received		700	5 700
Less: Expenditure:			105 700
Debenture loan shock interest		3 000	
Discounts allowed		2 000	
Motor van depreciation (1)	3 000		
Motor van expenses	2 700	5 700	
Office expenses		15 000	
Office salaries		35 000	60 700
Net profit for the year future taxation			45 000
Less: Corporation tax (based on the profits for the year at a rate of 35%) (2)			10 000
Net profit future year after taxation			35 000
Less: Dividends (3):			
Preference dividend paid (8%)		4 000	
Interim ordinary paid (5p per share)		5 000	
Proposed final ordinary dividend (10p per share)		10 000	19 000
Retained profit for the year			16 000
Retained profits brought forward			9 000
Retained profits carried forward (4)			£25 000

(b)

Handy Limited
Balance sheet at 31 March 19X5

Fixed assets	£ Cost	£ *Accumulated depreciation*	£ *Net book value*
Freehold land (5)	200 000	–	200 000
Motor van (6)	15 000	9 000	6 000
	£215 000	£9 000	206 000

Investments			
At cost (market value at 31 March 19X5: £11 000) (7)			10 000
Current assets			
Stocks at cost		40 000	
Trade debtors		27 000	
Bank		2 000	
		69 000	
Less: Current liabilities			
Trade creditors	50 000		
Corporation tax (due for payment on 1 January 19X6) (8)	10 000		
Proposed ordinary dividend (9)	10 000	70 000	
Net current assets			(1 000)
			£215 000

Financed by:		
Capital and reserves	*Authorized*	*Issued and fully paid*
Ordinary shares of £1 each (10)	150 000	100 000
Preference shares of £1 each (10)	75 000	50 000
	£225 000	150 000
Share premium account (11)		10 000
Retained profits (12)		25 000
Shareholders' funds (13)		185 000
Loans (14)		
10% debenture stock (repayable 19X9)		30 000
		£215 000

Note: The number shown after each narration refers to the tutorial notes.

Tutorial notes

1 Depreciation has been charged on the motor van at a rate of 20% per annum, on cost as instructed in question note 2.

2 Question note 3 requires £10 000 to be charged as corporation tax. Note that the corporation tax rate of 35% is applied to the taxable profit, and not to the accounting profit of £45 000. The taxable profit has not been given in the question.

3 A proposed ordinary dividend of 10p has been included as instructed in question note 4.

4 The total retained profit of £25 000 is carried forward to the balance sheet (see tutorial note 12 below).

5 Question note 2 states that no depreciation is to be charged on the freehold land.

6 The accumulated depreciation for the motor van of £9 000 is the total of the accumulated depreciation brought forward at 1 April 19X4 of £6 000 plus the £3 000 written off to the profit and loss account for the current year (see tutorial note I above).

7 Note that the market value of the investments has been disclosed on the face of the balance sheet.

8 The corporation tax charged against profit (question note 3, will be due for payment on 1 January 19X6 (to be precise, nine months plus one day after the year end). It is, therefore, a current liability.

9 The proposed ordinary dividend will be due for payment shortly after the year end, so it is also a current liability. The interim dividend and the preference dividend have already been paid, so they are not current liabilities

10 Details of the authorized, issued and fully paid share capital should be disclosed.

11 The share premium is a capital account: it cannot be used for the payment of dividends. This account will tend to remain unchanged in successive balance sheets, although there are a few highly restricted purchases for which it may be used.

12 The retained profits become part of a revenue account balance that the company could use for the payment of dividends. The total retained profits of £25 000 is the amount brought in to the balance sheet from the profit and loss account.

13 The total amount of shareholders' funds should always be shown.

14 The loans are long-term loans. Loans are not part of shareholders' funds, and they should be shown in the balance sheet as a separate item.

You are now recommended to work through Exhibit 6.6 again without reference to the answer.

CONCLUSION

This chapter began with an outline of a partnership entity. We then briefly examined the background to the legislation affecting limited liability companies. This was followed by some examples of how company accounts are prepared for *internal* purposes.

Although a great deal of information can be obtained from studying the annual accounts of a company, it is difficult to extract the most relevant and significant features. You need some further guidance, therefore, in how to make the best use of the financial accounting information presented to you. That guidance is provided in the next two chapters.

KEY POINTS

1 Partnership accounts are very similar to sole-trader accounts, except that: (a) partners often incorporate separate capital and current accounts into the partnership records; (b) details of the partners' share of profits and losses are shown in a profit and loss appropriation account; and (c) the capital section on the balance sheet will show the total amount of capital supplied by each partner, as well as the balances on the respective current accounts.

2 Company accounts have to be adapted in order to meet certain legal requirements. Basically, the structure of the annual accounts is similar to that of sole traders and partnerships.

3 The profits of a company are taxed separately (like an individual). The tax is based on the accounting profit for the year, and any tax due at the year end will be shown in the balance sheet as a creditor.

4 The net profit after tax may be paid to shareholders in the form of a dividend (although some profit may still be retained within the business). Any proposed dividend (i.e. one recommended but not yet paid) should be shown in the balance sheet as a creditor.

5 As a result of paying a dividend, some corporation tax may be due for payment in advance. This is known as advance corporation tax (ACT).

CHECK YOUR LEARNING

1 Fill in the blank spaces in each of the following statements:
(a) A partnership is presumed to exist when _____ _____ _____ people get together in business with the objective of making a _____.
(b) A partnership may not normally consist of more than _____ partners
(c) Limited liability is a _____ _____ concept.
(d) The shares in a _____ _____ _____ company can be bought and sold on the Stock Exchange.
(e) There are two main types of shares, _____ and _____
(f) Debentures are a form of _____

2 Complete the following equations:
(a) Sales – cost of goods sold = _____
(b) Profit for the year after taxation – _____ = retained profit for the year

(c) _____ – current liabilities = net current assets

(d) Ordinary shares + share premium account + retained profits = _____

(e) Retained profits brought forward + _____ = retained profits carried forward

3 State in which section of the balance sheet you are likely to find the following items:

(a) amount owing for taxation

(b) debenture stock

(c) plant and machinery

(d) preference shares

(e) trade debtors

ANSWERS

1 (a) two or more; profit (b) 20 (c) nineteeth–century (d) public limited liability
(e) ordinary; preference (f) loan

2 (a) gross profit (b) dividends (c) current assets (d) shareholders' funds
(e) retained profits for the year

3 (a) current liabilities (b) loans (c) fixed assets (d) share capital
(e) current assets

QUESTIONS

6.1 The following balances have been extracted from the books of Margo Limited for the year to 31 January 19X1:

	Dr £000	Cr £000
Cash at bank and in hand	5	
Plant and equipment:		
At cost	70	
Accumulated depreciation (at 31.1.X1)		25
Profit and loss account (at 1.2.X0)		15
Profit for the financial year (to 31.1.X1)		10
Share capital (issued and fully paid)		50
Stocks (at 31.1.X1)	17	
Trade creditors		12
Trade debtors	20	
	£112	£112

Additional information:

1 Corporation tax based on the profits for the year is estimated at £3 000.

2 Margo Limited's authorized share capital is £75 000 of £1 ordinary shares.

3 A dividend of 10p per share is proposed (ignore advance corporation tax).

Required:

Prepare Margo Limited's profit and loss account for the year to 31 January 19X1 (insofar as the information permits), and a balance sheet as at that date.

6.2 Harry Limited was formed in 1980. The following balances as at 28 February 19X1 have been extracted from the books of account after the trading account has been complied:

	Dr £000	Cr £000
Administration expenses	65	
Cash at bank and in hand	10	
Distribution costs	15	
Dividend paid (on preference shares)	6	
Furniture and equipment:		
At cost	60	
Accumulated depreciation at 1.3.X1		36
Gross profit for the year		150
Ordinary share capital (shares of £1 each)		100
Preference shares (cumulative 15% of £1 shares)		40
Profit and loss account (at 1.3.X1)		50
Share premium account		20
Stocks (at 28.2.X2)	130	
Trade creditors		25
Trade debtors	135	
	£421	£421

Additional information:
1 Corporation tax based on the profits for the year is estimated at £24 000.
2 Furniture and equipment is depreciated at an annual rate of 10% of cost and it is all charged against administrative expenses.
3 A dividend of 20p per ordinary share is proposed (ignore advance corporation tax).
4 All of the authorized share capital has been issued and is fully paid.

Required:
Prepare Harry Limited's profit and loss account for the year to 28 February 19X2, and a balance sheet as at that date.

6.2 The following balances have been extracted from the books of Jim Limited as at 31 March 19X3:

	Dr £000	Cr £000
Advertising	3	
Bank	11	
Creditors		12
Debtors	118	
Furniture and fittings:		
At cost	20	
Accumulated depreciation (at 1.4.X2)		9
Directors' fees	6	
Profit and loss account (at 1.4.X2)		8
c/f	158	29

	b/f	158	29
Purchases		124	
Rent and rates		10	
Sales			270
Share capital (issued and fully paid)			70
Stock (at 1.4.X2)		16	
Telephone and stationery		5	
Travelling expenses		2	
Vehicles:			
At cost		40	
Accumulated depreciation (at 1.4.X2)			10
Wages and salaries		24	
		£379	£379

Additional information:
1. Stock at 31 March 19X2 was valued at £14 000.
2. Furniture and fittings and the vehicles are depreciated at a rate of 15% and 25% respectively on cost.
3. Corporation tax based on the year's profits is estimated at £25 000.
4. A dividend of 40p per share is proposed (ignore advance corporation tax).
5. The company's authorized share capital is £100 000 of £1 ordinary shares.

Required:
Prepare Jim Limited's trading, and profit and loss account for the year to 31 March 19X3, and a balance sheet as at that date.

6.4 The following trial balance has been extracted from Cyril Limited as at 30 April 19X4:

		Dr	Cr
		£000	£000
Advertising		2	
Bank overdraft			20
Bank interest paid		4	
Creditors			80
Debtors		143	
Directors' remuneration		30	
Freehold land and buildings:			
At cost		800	
Accumulated depreciation at 1.5.X3			102
General expenses		15	
Investments at cost		30	
Investment income			5
Motor vehicles:			
At cost		36	
Accumulated depreciation (at 1.5.X3)			18
Preference dividend paid		15	
	c/f	1075	225

	b/f	1075	225
Preference shares (cumulative 10% shares of £1 each)			150
Profit and loss account (at 1.5.X3)			100
Purchases		480	
Repairs and renewals		4	
Sales			900
Share capital (authorized, issued and fully paid ordinary shares of £1 each)			500
Share premium account			25
Stock (at 1.5.X3)		120	
Wages and salaries		221	
		£1900	£1900

Additional information:
1 Stock at 30 Aprili 19X4 was valued at £140 000.
2 Depreciation for the year of £28 000 is to be provided on buildings and £9000 for motor vehicles.
3 A provision of £6000 is required for the auditors' remuneration.
4 £2000 had been paid in advance for renewals.
5 Corporation tax based on the year's profits is estimated at £60 000.
6 The directors propose an ordinary dividend of 10p per share.
7 The market value of the investments at 30 April 19X4 was £35 000.
8 Ignore advance corporation tax.

Required:
Prepare Cyril Limited's trading, and profit and loss account for the year to 30 April 19X4, and a balance sheet as at that date.

6.5 Nelson Limited was incorporated in 1980 with an authorized share capital of 500 000 £1 ordinary shares, and 200 000 5% cumulative preference shares of £1 each. The following trial balance was extracted as at 31 May 19X5:

	Dr	Cr
	£000	£000
Administrative expenses	257	
Auditor's fees	10	
Cash at bank and in hand	5	
Creditors		85
Debentures (12%)		100
Debenture interest paid	6	
Debtors	225	
Directors' renumeration	60	
Dividends paid:		
Ordinary interim	20	
Preference	5	
c/f	588	185

	b/f	588	185
Furniture, fittings and equipment:			
At cost		200	
Accumulated depreciation at 1.6.X4			48
Investments at cost (market value at 31.5.X5:			
£340 000)		335	
Investment income			22
Ordinary share capital (issued and fully paid)			400
Preference share capital			200
Profit and loss account (at 1.6.X4)			17
Purchases		400	
Sales			800
Share premium account			50
Stock at 1.6.X4		155	
Wages and salaries		44	
		£1722	£1722

Additional information:
1 Stock at 31 May 19X5 was valued at £195 000.
2 Administrative expenses owing at 31 May 19X5 amounted to £13 000.
3 Depreciation is to be charged on the furniture and fittings at a rate of $12\frac{1}{2}\%$ on cost.
4 Salaries paid in advance amounted to £4000.
5 Corporation tax based on the profit for the year is estimated at £8000.
6 Provision is to be made for a final ordinary dividend of 1.25p per share.
7 Ignore advance corporation tax.

Required:
Prepare Nelson Limited's trading, profit and loss account for the year to 31 May 19X5, and a balance sheet as at that date.

6.6 The following trial balance has been extracted from the books of Keith Limited as at 30 June 19X6:

	Dr	Cr
	£000	£000
Advertising	30	
Bank	7	
Creditors		69
Debentures (10%)		70
Debtors (all trade)	300	
Directors' renumeration	55	
Electricity	28	
Insurance	17	
Investments (quoted)	28	
Investment income		4
c/f	465	143

	b/f	465	143
Machinery:			
At cost		420	
Accumulated depreciation at 1.7.X5			152
Office expenses		49	
Ordinary share capital (issued and fully paid)			200
Preference shares			50
Preference share dividend		4	
Profit and loss account (at 1 July 19X5)			132
Provision for doubtful debts			8
Purchases		1240	
Rent and rates		75	
Sales			2100
Stock (at 1.7.X5)		134	
Vehicles:			
At cost		80	
Accumulated depreciation (at 1.7.X5)			40
Wages and salaries		358	
		£2825	£2825

Additional information:

1 Stock at 30 June 19X6 valued at cost amounted to £155 000.
2 Depreciation is to be provided on machinery and vehicles at a rate of 20% and 25% respecively on cost.
3 Provision is to be made for auditors' renumeration of £12 000.
4 Insurance paid in advance at 30 June 19X6 amounted to £3 000.
5 The provision for doubtful debts is to be made equal to 5% of outstanding trade debtors as at 30 June 19X6.
6 Corporation tax based on the profits for the year of £60 000 is to be provided.
7 An ordinary dividend of 10p per share is proposed.
8 The investments had a market value of £30 000 at 30 June 19X6.
9 The company has an authorized share capital of 600 000 ordinary shares of £0.50 each of 50 000 8% cumulative preference shares of £1 each.
10 Ignore advance corporation tax.

Required:
Prepare Keith Limited's trading and profit and loss account for the year to 30 June 19X6, and a balance sheet as at that date.

ADDITIONAL QUESTIONS (WITHOUT ANSWERS)

6.7 Hanna and Western are in partnership sharing profits and losses in the ratio 3 to 2. According to the partnership agreement, Hanna is allowed a salary of £7 000 per annum, and both partners are entitled to receive interest of 10% per annum on their capital account balances as at the beginning of each financial year.

The following trial balance has been extracted from their books of account as at 31 August 19X8:

	Dr £000	Cr £000
Administrative expenses	84	
Capital at 1 September 19X7:		
Hanna		120
Weston		80
Cash at bank and in hand	3	
Creditors		21
Debtors	70	
Delivery vans at cost	160	
Accumulated depreciation		
(at 1 September 19X7)		80
Distribution costs	34	
Drawings: Hanna	40	
Weston	30	
Plant and equipment at cost	100	
Accumulated depreciation		
(at 1 September 19X7)		60
Purchases	200	
Sales		400
Stock (at 1 September 19X7)	40	
	£761	£761

Additional information:
1 Stock at 31 August 19X8: £50 000.
2 Depreciation is to be charged as follows:
    Delivery vans: 25% on cost.
    Plant and equipment: 15% on cost.

Required:
Prepare Hanna and Weston's trading, profit and loss appropriation account for the year to 31 August 19X8, and a balance sheet as at that date.

6.8 Muir Limited's trial balance for the year to 30 November 19X1 is shown below:

	Dr £000	Cr £000
Administrative expenses	210	
Called up share capital (£1 ordinary shares)		720
Cash at bank and in hand	40	
Distribution costs	580	
Dividends received		4
Fixed asset investments (at cost)	20	
Land and property at cost	200	
Accumulated depreciation (at 1 December 19X0)		16
Profit and loss account (at 1 December 19X0)		160
Purchases	1360	
c/f	2410	900

		b/f	2410	900
Sales				2480
Stock (at 1 December 19X0)			260	
Trade creditors				120
Trade debtors			430	
Vans at cost:			700	
Accumulated deppreciation (at 1 December 19X0)				300
			£3800	£3800

Additional information:
1 Stock at 30 November 19X1: £250 000.
2 Depreciation is to be charged as follows:
    Property: 4% on cost (land at cost = £100 000)
    Vans: 25% on cost.
3 At 30 November 19X1:
    £10 000 was owing for office salaries
    £5000 had been paid in advance for van licenses.
4 Corporation tax based on the profit for the year at a rate of 35% is estimated to be £55 000.
5 The directors propose to pay an ordinary dividend of 10p per share.
6 Advance corporation tax may be ignored.

Required:
Prepare Muir's profit and loss account for the year to 30 November 19X1, and a balance sheet as at that date.

6.9 The following trial balance has been extracted from the books of account of McAdam Limited as at 31 December 19X2:

	Dr	Cr
	£000	£000
Administrative expenses	2 370	
Bank overdraft		130
Called up share capital:		
Ordinary shares of 31 each		800
10% cumulative preference shares		200
Creditors		600
Debtors	570	
Deferred taxation		500
Distribution costs	900	
Fixed asset investments:		
Dividends received		120
Investments at cost	700	
Furniture and fittings at cost	100	
Accumulated depreciation (at 1 January 19X2)		40
Interim dividend paid (10p per ordinary share)	80	
Plant and equipment at cost	7 000	
c/f	11 720	2 390

	b/f	11 720	23 90
Accumulated depreciation (at 1 January 19X2)			4 000
Preference dividend paid		10	
Profit and loss account			3 000
Purchases		8 000	
Sales			13 200
Share premium account			380
Stock at 1 January 19X2		2 000	
Trade creditors			980
Trade debtors		2 220	
		£23 950	£23 950

Additional information:

1 Stock at 31 December 19X2: £2 400 000.
2 Depreciation is to be charged as follows:
    Furniture and fittings: 10% on cost
    Plant and equipment (all relating to distribution activities): 50% on the reduced balance.
3 Corporation tax based on the profit for the year at a rate of 35%: £530 000.
4 The directors propose to pay a final ordinary dividend of 20p per ordinary share.
5 Advance corporation tax may be ignored.

Required:
Prepare McAdam's profit and loss account for the year to 31 Dcember 19X2, and a balance sheet as at that date.

CHAPTER 7

Cash flow statements

Control Techniques restates cash flow

By Andrew Jack

Control Techniques, the Powys-based electronic drives group, has been required to restate the cash flow figures in its 1992 annual report after discussions with the Financial Reporting Review Panel, the UK accounts watchdog.

In an unusual move following an examination of its accounts by the panel, the company has circulated amended numbers in a statement on Topic, the Stock Exchange news service, to correct what it calls a "classification error".

The accounts for the year to September 30 1992 wrongly showed the cash impact of the disposal of two subsidiaries under FRS 1, the accounting standard on the format of the cash flow statement.

This had the effect of incorrectly showing the company with net inflow before financing of £100,000, while the amended version shows it with a net outflow of £1.14m for the year. Control said the change had no impact on the 1992 profit and loss account or balance sheet figures.

The error was not picked up by the Birmingham office of Coopers & Lybrand which approved the 1992 accounts without qualification. It charged £199,000 for its audit during the year and a further £117,000 for other services.

Coopers, the UK's largest accountancy firm, said: "It was a complex standard being applied for the first time. A technical error was made but it wasn't material and it has been corrected. There was a mistake. Everybody accepts that."

The original cash flow statement showed £1.39m in proceeds from the sale of Control Techniques Process Instruments and the Thermosensors, segment of Control Techniques Process Systems.

But it failed to exclude the elements of working capital of the businesses sold in the reconcilation from operating profit to net cash flow from operating activities in a note required by FRS 1.

The Financial Times, 27 September 1993

Exhibit 7.0 The importance of cash flow accounting is clearly illustrated in this article.

When we have been dealing with manufacturing, trading, profit and loss accounts, and balance sheets in previous chapters, we have operated within the accounting rules laid down in Chapter 2. The accounts that we have prepared have provided us with some basic information about the profitability of a particular entity (i.e. how well it has performed), but we have been much less concerned about its *liquidity* (i.e. how much cash it has got). In fact, the type of basic accounts with which we have been dealing tell us very little about an entity's *cash* position.

This is rather curious, because such information is vital. An entity is technically insolvent (i.e. it is unlawful for it to carry on in business) if it cannot pay its creditors. We can, of course, always check the cash position by having a look at the balance sheet, but it tells us very little. What we really need is a statement that gives us some detail about the movement in the entity's cash position during a particular period. Since 1993, such a statement has been a professional requirement. It is known as a *cash flow statement*, and it forms the subject of this chapter.

The chapter falls into two main sections. In the first section, we will have a closer look at the relationship between accounting profit and cash flow, and, in the second section, we will examine the construction of a cash flow statement in some detail.

LEARNING OBJECTIVES

By the end of this chapter, you will be able to:
- make a distinction between profitability and liquidity;
- prepare a basic cash flow statement.

ACCOUNTING PROFIT AND CASH FLOW

Experience has taught accountants that it is unwise to rely entirely upon the profit and loss account and the balance sheet to monitor an entity's liquidity (i.e. cash) position. The opening and closing cash and bank balances can be obtained from the balance sheet, but this does not provide us with any information about where the cash has come from and where it has gone to. Such information is vital if we are to know how successful the entity has been in monitoring its cash position, and whether it has got enough cash to cover its future activities.

It is also important to provide some additional evidence about the cash position to those owners of a business in those cases where they think that any profit is calculated by taking cash receipts away from cash payments. If the owners think this way, then as long as the profit appears acceptable, they might pay very little attention to how much cash they have got. If sales are expanding rapidly, for example, the owners or managers may be entirely misled into believing that the entity is doing very well. No wonder that they are completely mystified when suddenly the entity goes into liquidation!

This rather paradoxical situation is known as *over-trading*, and it arises because credit sales get out of step with cash receipts and cash payments. In order to avoid over-trading, it is importance to ensure that the entity's daily cash receipts and payments are closely monitored.

You will recall that in an earlier chapter we suggested that owners want to know the answers to three important questions, i.e.:

1 What profit has the business made?
2 How much does the business owe?

3 How much is owed to it?

In view of the importance of keeping a tight control over cash, there ought perhaps to be a fourth question:

4 What is the cash position?

The answer might be provided by looking at the balance sheet, but that does not tell us very much.

We have stressed throughout the book that accounting profit does not necessarily lead to an automatic increase in cash. This is because accounting statements are normally prepared on the basis of the realization and matching rules. These rules require us to adjust the cash received and the cash paid to reflect the operational activity for a particular accounting period. Thus, neither the sales (or other incomes), nor purchases (or other expenses) will necessarily cause an immediate change in the cash position. Furthermore, capital items (such as the purchase of fixed assets and the issue of shares and debentures) are, of course, not included in the profit and loss account.

For these reasons it is very difficult to assess an entity's liquidity position from the information normally disclosed in traditional financial accounting statements. We need another type of statement that will give us a lot more information about what has happened to the cash position during a particular accounting period. This is what a cash flow statement is all about.

In the next section, we examine what one looks like, and how it is constructed.

FORMAT AND CONTENTS

It might occur to you that we are making an awful lot of fuss over something that is very simple. Surely, if we want to know more about the cash position, all we need do is look in the cash book. If we have access to it, of course, there is no reason why this could not be done, but you must remember that even in the smallest of businesses, the cash book is likely to contain a great many entries. A summary could be prepared under appropriate headings, of course, and a cash flow statement is often structured in this way. However, it makes it a lot easier for users of financial statements if different entities use a similar format, and that is why the accountancy profession has come up with some examples.

The basic structure of a cash flow statement is illustrated in Exhibit 7.1.

Exhibit 7.1 Example of a basic cash flow statement

Example of a basic cash flow statement

	£000
Operating activities [1]	2000
Investments and the servicing of finance [2]	
Dividends paid	(200)
Taxation [3]	
Tax paid	(300)
Investing activities [4]	
Purchase of fixed assets	(400)
Financing [5]	
Issue of ordinary shares	100
Increase in cash [6]	1200

Tutorial notes

1 This item is taken from the profit and loss account. Operating activities are those that relate to the trading activities of the entity. The operating profit does, however, require to be converted onto a cash flow basis, and it will need to be reconciled with the amount shown in the profit and loss account. We shall come back to this point later in the chapter.

2 Besides dividends paid, this item will also include interest received, and interest paid.

3 Taxes include the amount of corporation tax and other taxes paid during the year.

4 This heading includes cash paid for the purchase of intangible fixed assets (e.g. patents and trade marks), and tangible fixed assets, as well as the cash received from the sale of fixed assets.

5 Financing activities include the cash received from the issue of shares and debentures, and the cash paid on the redemption of debentures.

6 The increase in cash during the year (it might be a decrease) will be reconciled with the opening and closing cash balance shown in the balance sheet.

Exhibit 7.1 shows only the basic outline of the recommended format, but you may still wonder why it is so complex. Why not use a couple of main heading like 'cash received' and 'cash paid', and then list the items under a number of appropriate headings? It would be possible to do it this way, but remember the cash flow statement should be presented along with the profit and loss account and the balance sheet. It makes sense, therefore, if all three statements are closely interconnected. The close relationship among the three statements is shown in Exhibit 7.2.

Exhibit 7.2 The inter-relationship between the basic financial statements and a cash flow statement

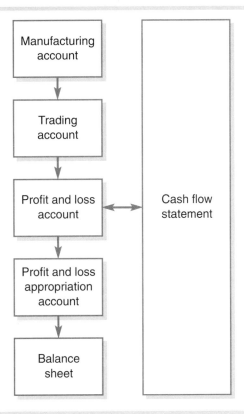

The format used in Exhibit 7.1 enables a close link to be demonstrated between the cash flow statement and the profit and loss account, since the first item shown in the cash flow statement is the operating profit which is extracted from the profit and loss account. In a more advanced example, you will see that the last item ('increase in cash') is also reconciled with the opening and closing cash balances.

We must now return to the adjustment required to the operating profit. We referred to this in Exhibit 7.1 (Tutorial note 1). The amount shown in the profit and loss account will, of course, have been calculated on an accruals and prepayments basis. It will also have included such non-cash items as depreciation, profits and losses on the sale of fixed assets, bad debts written off, and provisions for bad debts. We need to adjust the operating profit, therefore, onto a cash basis. The way that you can do this is shown in Exhibit 7.3.

Exhibit 7.3 The reconciliation of operating profit to net cash from operating activities

The reconciliation of operating profit to net cash from operating activities

	£	£
Take the operating profit		X
Add the following items:		
Depreciation charges	X	
Losses on the sale of fixed assets	X	
Bad debts written off	X	
Increases in provisions for doubtful debts	X	
Any other non-cash items that have been debited to the profit and loss account	X	
Decreases in stocks	X	
Decreases in trade debtors	X	
Decreases in other debtors	X	
Decreases in prepayments	X	
Increases in trade creditors	X	
Increases in creditors	X	
Increases in accruals (apart from items relating to taxation and proposed dividends)	X	X
		X
Deduct the following items:		
Profits on the sale of fixed assets	X	
Increases in stocks	X	
Increases in trade debtors	X	
Increases in other debtors	X	
Increases in prepayments	X	
Decreases in trade creditors	X	
Decreases in other creditors,	X	
Decreases in accruals (apart from items relating to taxation and proposed dividends)	X	X
Balance = Net cash flow (or outflow)		X

Exhibit 7.3 looks somewhat complicated, but you will be able to refer back to it whenever you are not sure whether a specific item should be added to or subtracted from the operating profit. The Exhibit shows that you need to make some adjustments for increases (or decreases) in stocks, trade and other debtors, prepayments, trade and other creditors, and accruals. The increase or decrease is obtained by taking the closing balance sheet amounts away from similar amounts shown in last year's balance sheet.

You may wonder why you have to adjust for them at all. The answer is quite simple. The changes in these items (accountants would normally refer to the net total as *working capital*) have an effect on the cash position. For example, if there is an increase in the stocks, there is a presumption that more stocks will have been purchased, so they will have to have been be paid for. That means a reduction in cash. By contrast, if the creditors have gone up, then the cash position will have improved, because less cash will have been paid out. This is rather a difficult concept to understand, so we have summarized the effect of it for you in Exhibit 7.4.

Exhibit 7.4 The effect of working capital movements on cash flow

Item		Movement (Closing balance – opening balance)		Effect on cash
Stocks	(i)	Increase	(i)	Down (more cash has been spent on stock)
	(ii)	Decrease	(ii)	Up (less cash has been spent on stock)
Debtors and prepayments	(i)	Increase	(i)	Down (less cash has been received)
	(ii)	Decrease	(ii)	Up (more cash has been received)
Creditors and accruals	(i)	Increase	(i)	Up (less cash has been spent)
	(ii)	Decrease	(ii)	Down (more creditors have been paid)

Note that we do not include in our definition of working capital, the movement in either the taxation balances or for proposed dividends. The reason for this is that we take the operating profit *before* taxation, and before we deduct anything for dividends. Movements in the taxation and dividend balances have not, therefore, had any effect on the operating profit, and they can be ignored when calculating the net cash flow from operating activities. Tax and dividends paid are, however, taken into account under separate headings elsewhere in the cash flow statement (taxation under 'Taxation', and dividends under 'Returns on investments and servicing of finance').

We have now covered a lot of difficult ground. It is unlikely, of course, that as a non-accountant you will ever be expected to construct a cash flow statement, but you may well find that you have to use one. You will find that it will mean much more to you if you know where the figures have come from, so in the next section we are going to show you how to construct a cash flow statement.

A COMPREHENSIVE EXAMPLE

The best way of understanding how a cash flow statement is constructed is to work through a fairly simple example. The one that we have chosen does not involve a complicated *group* structure, i.e. when a company owns a substantial proportion of shares in other companies (we will be looking at group cash flow statements in Chapter 19).

You should note that the requirements relating to cash flow statements are contained in Financial Reporting Standard No 1: Cash Flow Statements (FRS 1). This standard has to be followed by most companies (the main exceptions being those that come under the category of small companies). Small companies are those that meet two out of the three laid-down criteria, viz:

1 an annual turnover of £2.8 million or less;
2 a balance sheet total of not more than £1.4 million;
3 employing not more than 50 employees.

Notwithstanding the exceptions built into FRS 1, however, *all* entities are recommended to prepare a cash flow statement.

We will use the single company structure format as illustrated in FRS 1, but as Exhibit 7.5 is not a complicated one, we will not need to include all of the items that it covers.

Exhibit 7.5

You are presented with the following summarized information for Martin Limited for the year to 31 March 19X8:

MARTIN LIMITED
Profit and loss account (extract) for the year to 31 March 19X8

	19X8
	£000
Net profit for the year before taxation	85
Taxation	(35)
Net profit after taxation	50
Proposed dividend	(30)
	20
Retained profits brought forward	(25)
Retained profits carried forward	£45

MARTIN LIMITED
Balance sheet (extracts) at 31 March 19X8

	19X7 £000	19X7 £000	19X8 £000	19X8 £000
Fixed assets				
Plant at cost		45		95
Less: accumulated depreciation		18		25
		27		70
Current assets				
Stocks	51		67	
Debtors	110		170	
Bank	2		1	
	163		238	
Less: Current liabilities				
Creditors	15		28	
Taxation	30		35	
Dividends	20		30	
	65		93	
		98		145
		£125		£215
Financed by:				
Capital and reserves				
Ordinary shares of £1 each		100		150
Retained profits		25		45
Shareholders' funds		125		195
Loans				
Debenture stock		–		20
		£125		£215

Additional information:

1 There were no sales of fixed assets during the year.

2 During the year to 31 March 19X8, 50 000 ordinary shares of £1 each and £20 000 of debenture stock were issued for cash.

3 The debenture interest paid during the year to 31 March 19X8 amounted to £2000.

4 The taxation refers to corporation tax, and advance corporation tax may be ignored.

Required:

Prepare a cash flow statement for the year ended 31 March 19X8.

Answer to Exhibit 7.5

MARTIN LIMITED

Cash flow statement for the year ended 31 March 19X8

	£000	£000
Net cash inflow from operating activites [1]		31
Returns on investments andservicing of finance		
Interest paid [7]	(2)	
Dividends paid [8]	(20)	
Net cash outflow from returns on investments and servicing of finance		(22)
Taxation		
Corporation tax paid [9]		(30)
Investing activities		
Payments to acquire tangible fixed assets [10]	(50)	
Net cash outflow from investing activities		(50)
Net cash outflow before financing		(71)
Financing		
Issue of ordinary share capital [11]	50	
Issue of debenture stock [12]	20	
Net cash inflow from financing		70
Increase in cash and cash equivalents [13]		£(1)

Notes to the cash flow statement:

1 Reconciliation of operating profit to net cash inflow from operating activites

	£000
Operating profit [2]	87
Depreciation charges [3]	7
Increase in stocks [4]	(16)
Increase in debtors [5]	(60)
Increase in creditors [6]	13
Net cash inflow from operating activities	£31

2 Analysis of changes in cash and cash equivalents during the year

	£000
Balance at 1 April 19X7 [14]	2
Net cash outflow [15]	(1)
Balance at 31 March 19X8 [16]	£1

3 Analysis of the balances of cash and cash equivlents as shown in the balance sheet [17]

	19X8	19X7	Change in year
	£000	£000	£000
Cash at bank and in hand	£1	£2	£1

4 Analysis of changes in financing during the year

	Share capital £000	Debenture loan £000
Balance at 1 April 19X7[18]	100	–
Cash inflow from financing[19]	50	20
Balance at 31 March 19X8[20]	£150	£20

Tutorial notes

1 The composition of the net cash inflow from operating activities is detailed in question note 1. This note forms part of the answer. It is also required by FRS 1.

2 In this example, the operating profit of £87 000 is the £85 000 shown as net profit before taxation in the profit and loss account, plus the £2000 debenture interest paid (as per question note 3).

3 Depreciation for the year has been calculated as follows:

	£000
Accumulated depreciation a 31 March 19X8 (as per the balance sheet)	25
Less: Accumulated depreciation at 31 March 19X7 (as per the balance sheet)	18
∴ Depreciation for the year =	£7

It is possible to calculate the depreciation in this way, because there were no sales of fixed assets during the year. The depreciation charge for the year would normally be obtained from the profit and loss account.

4 Increase in stocks, 5 debtors, and 6 creditors

	stocks £000	debtors £000	creditors £000
As per the balance sheets:			
Balances at 31.03.X8	67	170	28
Less: Balances at 1.04.X7	51	110	15
∴ Increase =	£16*	£60*	£13#

* = less cash; # = more cash

7 As per question note 3.

8 Dividends paid and 9 Tax paid

	Dividends £000	Tax £000
Balances at 1.04.X7 (as per the balance sheet)	20	30
Add: As per the profit and loss account for the year to 31.03X8	30	35
	50	65
Less: Balances at 31.03.X8 (as per the balance sheet)	30	35
∴ Amount paid during the year to 31.03.X8	£20	£30

10 Fixed assets:

The question states that there were no sales of fixed assets during the year. However, there were obviously some purchases of fixed assets, because the plant at cost has increased from £45 000 in 19X7 to £95 000 in 19X8, an increase of £50 000.

11 and 12 Financing:

See question note 4 (FRS 1 also requires this note).

13 See question note 2 (FRS 1 also requires this note). Note that the solution refers to cash and 'cash equivalents'. Cash equivalents do not come into this question, but we will return to them later.

14 From the balance sheet at 1.04.X7.

15 From the cash flow statement.

16 As per the balance sheet at 31.03.X8.

17 This note is required by FRS 1, but in this example, it is hardly necessary. In more complicated examples, there would be some additional information to disclose.

18, 19 and 20

Another note required by FRS 1. All the information comes from the capital section of the balance sheet. The amounts are obtained by deducting the closing balance sheets figures from the opening balances. Note that the increases in share capital and debenture stock are shown in the cash flow statement, because these amounts have been received in cash.

You are now recommended to work through Exhibit 7.5 without reference to the solution.

CASH AND CASH EQUIVALENTS

In this chapter so far, we have used the term 'cash' rather loosely, and we must now examine what it means in a little more detail. In fact, FRS 1 refers to 'cash and cash equivalents'. They are defined as follows:

Cash: Cash in hand and deposits repayable on demand with any bank or other financial institution. Cash includes cash-in-hand and deposits denominated in foreign currency.

Cash equivalents: Short-term, highly liquid investments which are readily convertible into known amounts of cash without notice and which were within three months of maturity when acquired; less advances from banks repayable within three months from the date of the advance. Cash equivalents include investments and advances denominated in foreign currencies provided that they fulfil the above criteria.

You might find that the above definition of 'cash' is acceptable: apart from notes and coins, it also includes amounts held at the bank (in your private life you probably think of your own bank account as being cash). Cash equivalents are, however, somewhat different. FRS 1 argues that *some* investments can so easily and quickly be turned into cash that they can be counted as cash. You may not agree with this definition, e.g. you could quarrel with the time limit of three months (why three months: why not four?). However, as long as you bear this definition in mind when assessing an entity's cash position, it is a reasonably useful working definition.

DIRECT AND INDIRECT METHODS

In preparing our cash flow statement so far, we have adopted what FRS 1 refers to as the 'indirect method'. This method enables us to link directly the profit and loss account to the cash flow statement. However, FRS 1 also permits a 'direct method' approach.

If we adopted the direct method, we would not take the operating profit and adjust it for movements in stocks, debtors, and creditors. Instead, we would include the cash received from debtors, and the cash paid to creditors, along with other cash payments. Thereafter, the statement is identical to the indirect method. We give an example of it in Exhibit 7.6.

Exhibit 7.6 The format of the direct method of constructing cash flow statements

MURRAY LTD
Cash flow statement for the year ended 31 December 19X6

	£000
Operating activities	
Cash received from customers	200
Cash payments to suppliers	(100)
Cash paid to and on behalf on employees	(50)
Other cash payments	(10)
Net cash inflow from continuing operating activities	40

Returns on investments and servicing of finance*
* Thereafter, the statement is identical to the indirect method

The direct method, therefore, might be more like your idea of what a cash flow statement should look like. We have some sympathy with this view. However, the ASB thought that there were some extra costs involved in adopting the direct method, so it does not insist on its use. In any case, in question note 1 to the statement, a reconciliation has still to be made between operating profit and the movement in working capital. We have decided to adopt the indirect method in this book, because our experience to date suggests that it likely to become the most popular method, and the one, therefore, that you are most likely to meet.

CONCLUSION

The preparation of a cash flow statement is a complex operation. As a non-accountant, it is most unlikely that you will ever have to prepare one for yourself. It is our view, however, that in order to make the best possible use of such a statement, it is necessary for you to know something about its construction. In this chapter we have attempted to give you sufficient information so that you can construct your own cash flow statement, and in the process learn more about it.

A cash flow statement (especially one constructed using the indirect method) links directly with the profit and loss account and the balance sheet. It contains some extremely useful information, since unlike the traditional financial statements, it gives a lot more detail about the movement in the cash position. This is vital, because it is possible for an entity to be profitable without necesssarily having the cash resources to keep it going. Strict control over cash resources is absolutely essential, and a cash flow statement can help in this respect.

This chapter is closely linked with the next one which deals with the interpretation of accounts. Before moving on, however, you are recommended to test your understanding of cash flow statements by attempting some of the chapter questions.

KEY POINTS

1 Entities may have a long-term profitable future, but in the short term they may be short of cash. This may curb their activities, and in extreme cases, they may be forced out of business.

2 To avoid this happening, owners and managers should be supplied with information about the cash movement and resources of the entity, i.e. about its liquidity. This can be done by preparing a cash flow statement.

3 A cash flow statement can be presented in any format, but most companies are required to adopt the recommendations contained in FRS 1.

4 FRS 1 permits the cash flow statement to be presented in either (a) a direct method format, or (b) an indirect method format. The indirect method is preferred, because it can be linked directly to the profit and loss account and the balance sheet.

5 The definition of 'cash' includes 'cash equivalents'. Cash equivalents are basically highly liquid short-term investments, i.e. investments that can be turned very quickly into physical cash.

CHECK YOUR LEARNING

1 State whether each of the following assertions is either true or false:
   (a) Accounting profit is the difference between cash received
       and cash paid.   True/False
   (b) Depreciation reduces the cash position.   True/False
   (c) Tax paid decreases the cash position.   True/False
   (d) A proposed dividend increases the cash position.   True/False
   (e) A decrease in debtors increases the cash position.   True/False
   (f) An increase in creditors decreases the cash position.   True/False

2 Fill in the missing blanks in each of the following statements:
   (a) There are _____ main sections in a cash flow statement.
   (b) If stocks go up, cash goes _____.
   (c) If accruals go up, cash goes _____
   (d) If the opening cash was £15 000, and the closing cash was £20 000, there
       was a _____ _____ _____ of £5000.

3 How close to maturity should an investment be before it can be classed as a
   cash equivalent?

ANSWERS

1 (a) false (b) false (c) true (d) false (e) true (f) false
2 (a) five (b) down (c) up (d) net cash inflow
3 three months.

QUESTIONS

7.1 You are presented with the following information:

DENNIS LIMITED
Balance sheet at 31 January 19X2

	31 January 19X1		31 January 19X2	
	£000	£000	£000	£000
Fixed assets:				
Land at cost		600		700
Current assets:				
Stock	100		120	
Debtors	200		250	
Cash	6		10	
	306		380	
Less: Current liabilities:				
Creditors	180	126	220	160
		£726		£860

Capital and reserves:		
Ordinary share capital	700	800
Profit and loss account	26	60
	£726	£860

Required:
Prepare Dennis Limited's cash flow statement for the year ended 31 January 19X2.

7.2 The following balance sheets have been prepared for Frank Limited:

Balance sheets at:	28.2.X1		28.2.X2	
	£000	£000	£000	£000
Fixed assets:				
Plant and machinery at cost		300		300
Less: Depreciation		80		100
		220		200
Investments at cost		–		100
Current assets:				
Stocks	160		190	
Debtors	220		110	
Bank	–		10	
Less: Current liabilities:	380		310	
Creditors	200		160	
Bank overdraft	20		–	
	220	160	160	150
		£380		£450
Capital and reserves:				
Ordinary share capital		300		300
Share premium account		50		50
Profit and loss account		30		40
		380		390
Shareholders' funds				
Loans:				
Debentures		–		60
		£380		£450

Additional information:
There were no purchases or sales of plant and machinery during the year.

Required:
Prepare Frank Limited's cash flow statement for the year ended 28 February 19X2.

7.3 You are presented with the following information:

STARTER

Profit and loss account for the year to 31 March 19X3

	£	£
Sales		10 000
Less: Cost of goods sold:		
Purchases	5 000	
Less: Closing stock	1 000	4 000
Gross profit		6 000
Less: Depreciation		2 000
Net profit for the year		£4 000

Balance sheet at 31 March I9X3

	£	£
Van		10 000
Less: Depreciation		2 000
		8 000
Stock	1 000	
Trade debtors	5 000	
Bank	12 500	
	18 500	
Less: Trade creditors	2 500	16 000
		£24 000
Capital		20 000
Add: Net profit for the year		4 000
		£24 000

Note: Starter commenced business on 1 April 19X2.

Required :
Using the indirect method, compile Starter's cash flow statement for the year ended 31 March 19X3.

7.4 The following is a summary of Gregory Limited's accounts for the year ended 30 April 19X4.

Profit and loss account for the year ended 30 April 19X4

	£000
Net profit before tax	75
Taxation	25
	50
Dividend (proposed)	40
Retained profit for the year	£10

Balance sheet at 30 April 19X4

	30.04.X9		30.04.X4	
Fixed assets:	£000	£000	£000	£000
Plant at cost		400		550
Less: Depreciation		100		180
		300		370
Current assets:				
Stocks	50		90	
Debtors	70		50	
Bank	10		2	
	130		142	
Less: Current liabilities:				
Creditors	45		55	
Taxation	18		25	
Proposed dividend	35		40	
	98	32	120	22
		£332		£392
Capital and reserves:				
Ordinary share capital		200		200
Profit and loss account		132		142
		332		342
Loans		–		50
		£332		£392

Additional information:
There were no sales of fixed assets during the year ended 30 April 19X4.

Required:
Prepare Gregory Limited's cash flow statement for the year ended 30 April 19X4.

7.5 The following summarized accounts have been prepared for Pill Limited:

Profit and loss account for the year ended 31 May 19X5

	19X4	19X5
	£000	£000
Sales	2 400	3 000
Less: Cost of goods sold	1 600	2 000
Gross profit	800	1 000
Less: Expenses:		
Administrative expenses	310	320
Depreciation: Vehicles	55	60
Furniture	35	40
	400	420

		400	580
Net profit		400	580
Taxation		120	150
		280	430
Dividends		200	250
Retained profits for the year		£80	£180

Balance sheet at 31 May 19X5

	31.5.X4		31.5.X5	
	£000	£000	£000	£000
Fixed assets:				
Vehicles at cost	600		800	
Less: Depreciation	200	400	260	540
Furniture	200		250	
Less: Depreciation	100	100	140	110
Current assets:				
Stocks	400		540	
Debtors	180		200	
Cash	320		120	
	900		860	
Less: Current liabilities:				
Creditors	270		300	
Corporation tax	170		220	
Proposed dividends	150		100	
	590	310	620	240
		£810		£890
Capital and reserves:				
Ordinary share capital		500		550
Profit and loss account		120		300
Shareholders' funds		620		850
Loans:				
Debentures (10%)		190		40
		£810		£890

Additional information :
There were no sales of fixed assets during the year ended 31 May 19X5.

Required :
Compile Pill Limited's cash flow statement for the year ended 31 May 19X5.

7.2 The following information relates to Brian Limited for the year ended 30 June 19X6:

Profit and loss account for the year to 30 June 19X6

	£000	£000
Gross profit		230
Administrative expenses	76	
Loss on sale of vehicle	3	
Increase in provision for doubtful debts	1	
Depreciation on vehicles	35	115
Net profit		115
Taxation		65
		50
Dividends		25
Retained profit for the year		£25

Balance sheet at 30 June 19X6

	19X5		19X6	
	£000	£000	£000	£000
Fixed assets:				
Vehicle at cost		150		200
Less: Deprecition		75		100
		75		100
Current assets:				
Stocks		60		50
Trade debtors	80		100	
Less: Provision for doubtful debts	4	76	5	95
Cash		6		8
		142		153
Less: Current Liabilities:				
Trade creditors	60		53	
Taxation	52		65	
Proposed dividend	20	132	25	143
Net current assets		10		10
		£85		£110
Capital and reserves:				
Ordinary share capital		75		75
Profit and loss account		10		35
		£85		£110

Additional information :

1 The company purchased some new vehicles during the year for £75 000.

2 During the year the company sold a vehicle for £12 000 in cash. The vehicle had originally cost £25 000, and £10 000 had been set aside for depreciation.

Required :

Prepare a cash flow statement for Brian Limited for the year ended 30 June 19X6.

ADDITIONAL QUESTIONS (WITHOUT ANSWERS)

7.7 The following summarized information relates to Weir Limited for the year ended 30 September 19X9:

Profit and loss account

	£000
Profit before taxation	320
Taxation	100
Profit after taxation	220
Dividends	80
Retained profit for the year	£140

Balance sheets at 30 September

	19X8 £000	19X9 £000
Fixed assets:		
At cost	2 130	2 560
Less: Accumulated depreciation	740	930
	1 390	1 630
Current assets:		
Stocks	470	535
Trade debtors	540	620
Prepayments	45	40
	1 055	1 195
Current liabilities:		
Bank overdraft	(95)	(110)
Trade creditors	(145)	(180)
Accruals	(50)	(30)
Taxation	(200)	(50)
Dividends	(60)	(70)
	(550)	(440)
Debenture loans	(580)	(630)
	£1 315	£1 755
Capital and reserves:		
Called up share capital	350	615
Share premium account	15	30
Revaluation reserve	130	150
Profit and loss account	820	960
	£1 315	£1 755

Additional information :

1 A provision for bad and doubtful debts is maintained. At 1 October 19X8, the balance was £30 000, and at 30 September 19X9 it was £40 000.
2 During the year to 30 September 19X9, fixed assets originally costing £65 000 (and on which depreciation of £40 000 had been charged) were sold for £30 000 in cash.

Required :

Prepare Weir's cash flow statement for the year ended 30 September 19X9.

7.8 The following summarized information relates to Conway Limited:

Profit and loss account for the year ended 31 October 19X9

	£000
Gross profit	2 400
Distribution costs	(190)
Administration expenses	(900)
Profit before taxation	1 310
Taxation	(200)
Profit after taxation	1 110
Dividends	(170)
Retained profit for the year	£940

Balance sheets at 31 October 19X9

	19X8 £000	19X9 £000
Fixed assets:		
At cost	3 400	5 800
Less: Accumulated depreciation	1 400	2 100
	2 000	3 700
Current assets:		
Stocks	700	100
Trade debtors (net of provision)	2 000	6 000
Other debtors	200	250
Bank and cash	950	–
	3 850	6 350
Current liabilities:		
Bank overdraft	–	(400)
Trade creditors	(300)	(1 200)
Other creditors	(400)	(210)
Taxation	(350)	(450)
Dividend	(100)	(150)
	(1 150)	(2 410)
Long-term loans (15% debenture stock):	–	(2 000)
	£4 700	£5 640

Capital and reserves:		
Called up share capital	2 500	3 500
Share premium account	500	500
Profit and loss account	1700	1 640
	£4 700	£5 640

Additional information :

1 During the year to 31 October 19X9, fixed assets originally costing £650 000 were sold for £300 000 in cash. The accumulated depreciation on these fixed assets was £400 000.

2 The company maintains a provision for bad and doubtful trade debtors. The provision at 1 November 19X8 was £100 000 and at 31 October 19X9 it was £500 000.

3 During the year to 31 October 19X9, a bonus issue of two shares for every five shares held was made to the company's shareholders.

Required :

Prepare Conway's cash flow statement for the year ended 31 October 19X9.

CHAPTER 8

Interpretation of accounts

Young & Co slips 7.5% to £5.17m as operating margins decline

By Catherine Milton

Higher interest costs helped depress pre-tax profits at Young & Co's Brewery, the south London-based real ale brewer, by 7.5 per cent from £5.59m to £5.17m for the year to March 27.

Stripping out last time's exceptional profit of £244,223 on the sale of assets, the decline was 3 per cent.

Turnover was £72.9m (£68.1m). Operating profits rose to £8.19m (£8.03m).

Interest charges rose to £3.02m (£2.68m) mainly because of increased borrowings for the August 1991 acquisition of HH Finch, the owner of 22 pubs and six wine bars, and fluctuations in interest rates.

The company said gearing at the year-end was unchanged at about 30 per cent. In April, Young raised £15m from a debenture issue partly to repay bank loans.

Operating margins slipped to 11.23 per cent (11.79 per cent). Mr John Young, chairman, said: "We offer lower prices. In the light of events we probably should have put them up but we try to offer better prices than our competitors.

"Recovery is slow and gradual. In the south and south-east, the recession is still biting quite hard."

He said the company's four hotels, opened on existing pub sites, were repaying their investment.

The company is opening another on Monday in south London and has planning permission for two more. Mr Young said he thought the company would ultimately run seven or eight hotels.

The board proposes a same-again final dividend of 7.5p giving a maintained total for the year of 14.5p. Earnings per share fell to 26.4p (27.51p).

The Financial Times, 20 May 1993

Exhibit 8.0 The use of ratios in reporting on the financial results of a company is demonstrated in this article.

In previous chapters, we have shown that a set of basic accounting statements can tell you a great deal about an entity's performance. In this chapter, we are going to explain how you can use those statements to an even greater effect, i.e. how to squeeze out the maximum possible amount of information. Accountants call this process interpreting the accounts, and it forms the subject of this chapter.

In order to understand the importance of this topic, we need to review some of the material covered in the earlier part of the book. We do so in the next section.

By the end of this chapter, you will be able to:
- explain the usefulness and importance of ratio analysis;
- calculate at least nine basic accounting ratios;
- apply those ratios in interpreting a set of accounts.

BACKGROUND TO INTERPRETATION

You will recall that in Chapter 1, we suggested that owners want to know the answers to three basic questions. We keep coming back to these questions, and as they are so important we will repeat them once again. They are as follows:

1 How much profit has the business made?
2 How much does the business owe?
3 How much is owed to the business?

In Chapters 3 to 6 we described how an accountant would go about trying to answer these questions, but as we have seen, the method is far from satisfactory. We have only been able to *estimate* the profit, and as far as the balance sheet is concerned we show only the total amount of what is owed and owing. Furthermore, in trying to answer the owner's questions, we have used some highly arguable assumptions.

If such results are used in isolation, the owner could be misled by the apparent long-term trend of his profits, and by his current liquidity (i.e. cash) position. For example, his debtor and creditor balances do not tell him very much: are they too high or too low? We do not really know until we have put them into context. A debtor's balance of £200 000 would appear be a very large amount for a small business, but it would be insignificant for a large international company.

The results, therefore, need to be put into context, and we need to go into them in much greater detail.

It might also be necessary to do this to satisfy the demand for information from other groups of interested parties, e.g. analysts, creditors, employees, the general public, the government, investors, journalists, management, shareholders, and the trade unions. All of these groups will have some interest in how an entity performs (especially if it is a public company), and the information contained within the basic statements may not tell them what they want to know.

If you are asked to interpret a set of accounts, therefore, the amount of work you will have to undertake will depend upon the reasons for your investigation. For example, if you are asked to examine a company's accounts because your own company is considering making a take-over bid, you will probably need all the information that you can get. However, if you are a creditor, your main interest will be in finding out whether the company is in a position to pay what it owes you.

It might be helpful if we give you some general guidance that you can follow in carrying out your investigation, but obviously you will need to adapt it to suit the circumstances. We summarize the procedure in the following sub-sections.

Obtaining information

You are recommended to look at the economic environment in which the company operates. In which countries is it based? What is the state of their economies? What are the prospects for the economic sector in which the company is placed? How does it compare with other companies in the same sector?

Then try to obtain as much information about the company as you can. It is not usually difficult to obtain information if you search for it. You can start with the company's annual report and accounts. The company's own public relations department may be willing to supply you with additional information about the company. There are also a number of commercial agencies that specialize in obtaining company information, and you may be able to find some information in newspaper and journal articles.

You will find that by assimilating information about the company from such a wide range of sources, you will already have got some idea of what you think of it.

Calculating trends and ratios

It is desirable to look at the company's performance over a number of years. As suggested previously, you can do this by obtaining copies of the company's annual report and accounts. As a general rule, we suggest that you obtain copies covering a period of some three to five years. Too short a period will not enable you to plot much of a trend, and too long a period could mean that the information has become out-of-date.

Once you have collected a set of reports, you can use them to establish some trends, and to calculate some statistics. The exact number and type will depend upon the purpose of your investigation, and some of them may need to be fairly specialist. For example, if you were dealing with a hotel's accounts, you might want to calculate the rooms occupied as a proportion of the total number of rooms in the hotel, or in the case of a retailing organization, the sales staff salaries as a proportion of sales revenue.

You can begin to assess the trends and calculate the ratios by using a number of different techniques, but they all have one overriding purpose: they attempt to put the accounting information into context. The four main techniques are shown in Exhibit 8.1, and we summarize them as follows:

1 **Horizontal analysis.** This technique involves making a line-by-line comparison of the company's accounts for each accounting period that you have chosen to investigate. You might observe, for example, that the sales were £100m in 1993, £110m in 1994, and £137.5m in 1995. Thus, they have increased by 10% in 1994, and by 25% in 1995. This type of comparison is something that we tend to do naturally when we look at a set of accounts, although if you are going to calculate the percentage changes, you will probably need a calculator.

2 **Trend analysis.** Trend analysis is similar to horizontal analysis, except that the first set of accounts in the series is given a weighting of 100. Subsequent accounts are then related to the base of 100. In the example used above, the 1993 sales would be expressed as 100, the 1994 sales as 110, and the 1995 sales as 137.5. This method enables us to see what changes have taken place much more easily than by inspecting the absolute amounts. For example, it is much easier to grasp the significance of say 159, than it is £323 739392.

3 **Vertical analysis.** This technique requires all of the profit and loss account, and all of the balance sheet items to be expressed as a percentage of their respective totals. For example, if trade debtors in 1995 were £20m and the balance sheet total was £50m, trade debtors would be expressed as 40%, compared (say) with 35% in 1994, and 30% in 1993. Again, the reason for adopting this method is that it is much easier to grasp the significance of the figures.

4 **Ratio analysis.** We are shortly going to deal with ratio analysis in some detail, but for the moment, all you need note is that a ratio attempts to relate one item to another item, e.g. 20 to 40, and then perhaps express the relationship as a percentage, i.e. 50%.

If you had adopted all of the above techniques in your analysis, you would already have a great deal of information about the company, so you could now begin a detailed assessment of it. It is unlikely, however, that you would use all four analytical techniques, and you might only use parts of others. For example, in trend analysis, you probably would not need to calculate a trend for literally every line in the accounts: you could be much more selective and choose the most significant items.

There is one further point that we need to make before to move on to the next section. It is unlikely that the annual accounts have been adjusted for inflation, so to make a fairer comparison between different accounting periods, you should make some allowance for inflation. We return to this subject in Chapter 20, but we suggest that for the moment, you could use the Retail Price Index (RPI) as a rough guide.

In the next section, we take a closer look at ratio analysis.

Exhibit 8.1 Main analytical techniques used in interpreting accounts

Type of analysis	19X1	19X2	19X3
(1) Horizontal	£100 M ⟷	£110 M ⟷	£137.5 M
(2) Trend	100 ⟷	110 ⟷	137.5
(3) Vertical	%	%	%
	60	55	50
	30	33	35
	10	12	15
	100	100	100
(4) Ratio	6	7	8
	60	55	50
	10%	13%	16%

RATIO ANALYSIS

In this section we are going to deal with ratio analysis in some detail. We need to go into detail, partly because it is so useful, and partly because unless we do, you will not understand it! But don't be put off! You will find that the time spent studying this topic will be well worth while: you will find it useful in both your business and your private life, e.g. if you ever want to buy some shares.

We will start our study by examining what is meant by a *ratio*. Data may be extracted from accounting statements and converted into statistics.

These statistics can then be used to examine an entity's performance over a given period of time. They may also be used to compare the current year's performance with previous years, or with similar entities. Such comparisons may be done on a percentage basis or by using simple factors. For example, we might report that the net profit is 7% of the annual sales, or that the dividend for the year represents three times the profit for that year. In order to make such statistics easier to understand, we will refer to them all as *ratios*.

Ratios are not usually very helpful when viewed in isolation, but they can be invaluable when they are used to plot a trend, or in interpreting accounts, i.e. to tell us more about the entity than we can possibly know by trying to 'read' the accounts. Students often believe that by calculating a great many ratios, they have then 'interpreted' the accounts. In fact, the calculation of a number of ratios is only a beginning. What must follow is a detailed investigation into the entity's performance, including a comparison with previous periods, and with other similar entities.

However, let us return to ratios. In order to establish clearly the concept underpinning a ratio, we will assume that you have put £1000 in a building society account on 1 January 1994. During the year to 31 December 1994, you leave the £1000 in your account. You do not withdraw any of it, and you do not add to it. At the end of the year, the building society credits you with £100 of interest. If we express the interest as a *ratio*, the calculation will be as follows:

$$\frac{£100}{1000} \times 100 = \underline{\underline{10\%}}$$

This might all seem quite obvious, but it is worth labouring the point. The £100 received represents 10% of the £1000 invested. In other words, there is a clear relationship between the interest earned and what it took to earn it.

You will find that as we go through this chapter we are going to express many other accounting relationships in the form of percentages. Make sure, therefore, that you always establish a clear, meaningful relationship between the numerator (the £100 in the above example), and the denominator (the £1000 in the example). This is not always easy, so be careful, and make sure that you do not try to link some quite spurious relationships, such as dividends received to the cost of goods sold.

It would be possible to produce hundreds of recognized accounting ratios, but for the purposes of this book, we will limit ourselves to just a small number of key ones. We do so for three main reasons:

1 we do not need to use very many in demonstrating the *principles* of ratio analysis;
2 a select number of ratios will give sufficient information;

3 experience suggests that in any subsequent analysis, it is difficult to handle scores of ratios.

We will examine the main ratios under four main headings: (a) profitabililty ratios; (b) liquidity ratios; (c) efficiency ratios; and (d) investment ratios. This classification is, however, somewhat arbitrary, and some could be included in several classifications. A diagrammatic version of this classification is shown in Exhibit 8.2. We begin with profitability ratios.

Exhibit 8.2 Classification of accounting ratios

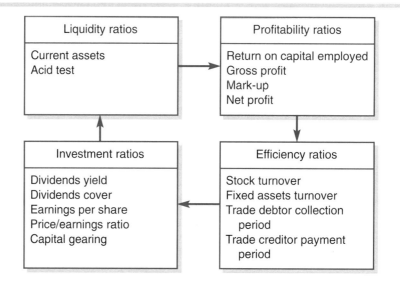

PROFITABILITY RATIOS

Users of accounts will want to know how much profit a business has made, and then to compare it with previous periods or with other entities. The absolute level of accounting profit will not be of much help, because it needs to be related to to the size of the entity, and how much capital it has got invested in it. There are four main profitability ratios, and we consider each of them in the following sub-sections.

Return on capital employed ratio

The best way of assessing profitability is to calculate a ratio known as the *return on capital employed* (ROCE) ratio. It can be expressed quite simply as follows:

$$\frac{\text{Profit}}{\text{Capital}} \times 100 = X\%$$

This ratio (like most other ratios) is usually expressed as a percentage, and it is one of the most important. Even so, there is no common agreement about how it should be calculated. The problem is that both 'profit' and 'capital' can be defined in several different ways. As a result, a variety of ROCE ratios can be produced by merely by changing the definitions of either profit or capital. The main ingredients that could be included are summarized as follows:

Profit	*Capital*
1. Operating profit	1. Total assets
2. Net profit before interest and taxation	2. Total assets less intangible assets
3. Net profit before taxation	3. Total assets less current liabilities
4. Net profit after taxation	4. Shareholders' funds
5. Net profit after taxation and preference dividend	5. Shareholders' funds less preference shares
	6. Shareholders' funds plus long-term loans
	7. Shareholders' funds plus total liabilities (this could be the same as total assets)

Which definitions should you adopt? Provided that the numerator and denominator are compatible, that really depends upon your purpose. If you are looking at profit from the point of view of the entity as a whole, we would suggest that profit should mean the *net profit before interest and taxation*. That profit must then be related to the total amount of capital needed to generate it, i.e. shareholders' funds plus long-term loans (we include long-term loans in capital because we have taken the profit *before* interest). However, if we were looking at profit from only an ordinary shareholder's point of view, we might define profit as being the *net profit after taxation and preference dividends* (i.e. the amount available for distribution to ordinary shareholders), and capital as *shareholders' funds less preference shares* (i.e. the total amount of capital that the ordinary shareholders have invested in the business).

Does this relationship make sense to you? Net profit after taxation and preference dividends reflects what *could* be distributed to ordinary shareholders. Shareholders' funds less preference shares gives the total amount of capital contributed (or financed) by the ordinary shareholders (ordinary shares + capital reserves + revenue reserves + other reserves + retained profits).

Irrespective of the definitions, ROCE is usually calculated using the capital as at the year end. However, as profit builds up during the year, we really ought to take the *average* capital invested in the entity during the year. It is customary to take a simple average, i.e. $\frac{1}{2}$(opening capital + closing capital).

You may need to calculate ROCE for different purposes, so it would be useful if we summarize the main methods used in calculating this most important ratio. Here they are:

$$1 \quad \frac{\text{Net profit before taxation}}{\text{Average shareholders' funds}} \times 100 = X\%$$

$$2 \quad \frac{\text{Net profit after taxation}}{\text{Average shareholders' funds}} \times 100 = X\%$$

$$3 \quad \frac{\text{Net profit after taxation and preference dividends}}{\text{Average shareholders's funds less preference shares}} \times 100 = X\%$$

$$4 \quad \frac{\text{Profit before taxation and interest}}{\text{Average shareholders' funds plus long-term loans}} \times 100 = X\%$$

By calculating the return on capital employed, we can get a far better idea of the entity's profitability than we can by merely looking at the absolute level of profit. ROCE means that we can avoid making sweeping assertions about (say) a profit of £500 million being high (it might be thought rather poor if the capital employed was £10 billion), or a profit of £500 being low (it might be acceptable if the capital invested was £2000). High and low in this context can only be viewed in a relative sense.

There are a number of other important profitability ratios which we ought to consider. One is the *gross profit ratio*.

Gross profit ratio

This ratio enables us to judge how successful the entity has been at trading. It is calculated as follows:

$$\frac{\text{Gross profit}}{\text{Total sales revenue}} \times 100 = X\%$$

The gross profit ratio measures how much profit the entity has earned in relation to the amount of sales that it has made. The definition of gross profit does not usually cause any problems. Most entities adopt the definition which we have used in this book, viz. sales less the cost of goods sold, so meaningful comparisons can usually be made between different entities. However, when we look at *published* accounts in Part 4, you will find that since there is no statutory definition of cost of sales, companies may use different definitions for even the gross profit ratio.

Mark-up ratio

The gross profit ratio complements another main trading ratio: for convenience, we will refer to it as the *mark-up ratio*. The mark-up ratio is calculated as follows:

$$\frac{\text{Gross profit}}{\text{Cost of goods sold}} \times 100 = X\%$$

Mark-up ratios measure the amount of profit added to the cost of goods sold, [i.e. cost of goods sold = (opening stock + purchases) − closing stock], and the cost of good sold plus profit equals the sales revenue. The mark up may be reduced to stimulate extra sales activity, but this will have the effect of reducing the gross profit. However, if extra goods are sold, there may be a greater volume of sales. This will help to compensate for the reduction in the mark up on each unit.

Net profit ratio Owners sometimes like to compare their net profit with the sales revenue. This can be expressed in the form of the *net profit ratio*. The net profit ratio is calculated as follows:

$$\frac{\text{Net profit before taxation}}{\text{Total sales revenue}} \times 100 = X\%$$

It is difficult to make a fair comparison between net profit ratios calculated for different entities. Individual operating and financing arrangements vary so much that entities are bound to have different levels of expenditure, no matter how efficient one entity is compared with another. Thus it may only be realistic to use the net profit ratio in making *internal* comparisons. Over a period of time, a pattern may emerge, and it might then be possible to establish a trend. If you do use the net profit ratio to make inter-company comparisons, make sure you allow for different circumstances.

We can now turn to our second main category of accounting ratios: liquidity ratios. We do so in the next section.

LIQUIDITY RATIOS

Liquidity ratios measure the extent to which assets can be quickly turned into cash. In other words, they try to assess how much cash the entity has available in the short term (this usually means within the next twelve months). For example, it is easy to extract the total amount of trade debtors and trade creditors from the balance sheet, but are they at an acceptable level? We cannot really tell until we put them into context. We can do this by calculating two liquidity ratios known as the *current assets ratio* and the *acid test ratio*. We deal with both of them in the following sub-sections.

Current assets ratio

The current assets ratio is calculated as follows:

$$\frac{\text{Current assets}}{\text{Current liabilities}}$$

It is usually expressed as a factor, e.g. 3 to 1, or 3 : 1, although you will sometimes see it expressed as a percentage.

In most circumstances we can expect that current assets will be in excess of current liabilities. The current assets ratio will then be at least 1 : 1. If this is not the case, the entity may not have sufficient liquid resources available (i.e. current assets that can be quickly turned into cash) to meet its immediate financial commitments. Some textbooks argue that the current ratio must be at least 2 : 1, but there is no evidence to support this assertion. You are not, therefore, advised to accept that a 2 . 1 relationship is required.

The term 'current' means receivable or payable within the next twelve months, so the entity may not always have to settle all of its current debts within the next week or even the next month. Be careful then, before you assume that a factor of (say) 1 : 2 suggests that the company will be going into immediate liquidation! For example, corporation tax may not have to be paid for at least nine months, and it may be several months before a proposed dividend is actually paid.

In the meantime, the company may receive regular receipts of cash from its debtors, and it may be able to balance these against what it has to pay to its creditors. In other instances, some entities (such as supermarkets), do not do much trade on credit terms, so it is not uncommon for them to have a current assets ratio of less than 2 : 1. This is not likely to be a problem for them, because cash is flowing in daily through the check-outs.

In some cases, however, a current assets ratio of less than 2 : 1 may signify a serious financial position, especially if the current assets consist of a very high proportion of stocks. This leads us on to the second liquidity ratio: the acid test ratio.

Acid test ratio

It may not be easy to dispose of stocks in the short term (i.e. they cannot be readily turned into cash), but in any case, the entity would then be depriving itself of those very assets that enable it to make a trading profit. It seems sensible, therefore, to see what would happen to the current ratio if stocks were not included in the definition of current assets. This ratio is called the acid test (or quick) ratio. It is calculated as follows:

$$\frac{\text{Current assets} - \text{stocks}}{\text{Current liabilities}}$$

Like the current ratio, the acid test ratio is usually expressed as a factor (or occasionally as a percentage). It is probably a better measure of the entity's immediate liquidity position than the current assets ratio because it excludes stocks, as they are not always easily sold. Do not assume, however that if current assets less stocks are less than the current liabilities, then the entity's cash position is vulnerable. As we explained above, some of the current liabilities may be not due for payment for some months. As with the current assets ratio, some textbooks suggest that the acid test ratio must be at least $1:1$, but there is no evidence to support this view, so you are advised not to suggest it. We can now move on to our third main category of accounting ratios: efficiency ratios.

EFFICIENCY RATIOS

Traditional accounting statements do not tell us how *efficiently* an entity has been managed, that is, how well its resources have been looked after. Profit may, to some extent, be used as a measure of efficiency, but as we have explained in earlier chapters, accounting profit is subject to too many arbitrary adjustments to be entirely reliable. What we need to do, therefore, is put what evidence we do have into context, and then to compare it with earlier accounting periods and with other similar entities.

There are very many different types of ratios that we can use to measure the efficiency of an entity, but in this book we will cover only the more common ones. These are examined below.

Stock turnover ratio

$$\frac{\text{Cost of goods sold}}{\text{Average stock}} = \text{X times}$$

The average stock is usually calculated as follows:

$$\frac{\text{Opening stock} + \text{closing stock}}{2} = \text{X}$$

This ratio is normally expressed as a number (e.g. 5 or 10) and not as a percentage. Note that there are also various other ways in which the stock turnover can be calculated.

Sometimes the sales revenue is substituted for the cost of goods sold, but it should not be used if it can be avoided because the sales contain a profit loading which can cause the ratio to become distorted. Many accountants also prefer to substitute a more accurate average stock level than the simple average shown above (particularly if goods are purchased at irregular intervals).

In other instances they may compare the closing stock with the cost of sales in order to gain a clearer idea of the stock position at the end of the year. This may be misleading, however, if the company's trade is seasonal, and the year end falls during a quiet period.

The greater the turnover of stock, the more efficient the entity would appear to be in purchasing and selling goods. A stock turnover of 2, for example, would suggest that the entity has about six months of sales in stock. In most circumstances, this would appear to be high, whereas a stock turnover of (say) 12 would mean that the entity had only a month's normal sales in stock.

Fixed assets turnover ratio

Another important area to examine from the point of view of efficiency, relates to fixed assets. Fixed assets (such as plant and machinery) enable the business to function more efficiently, so a high level of fixed assets ought to generate more sales. We can check this by calculating a ratio known as the *fixed assets turnover ratio*. It is calculated as follows:

$$\frac{\text{Total sales revenue}}{\text{Fixed assets at net book value}} = X$$

The fixed assets turnover ratio may also be expressed as a percentage. The more times that the fixed assets are covered by the sales revenue, the greater the recovery of the investment in fixed assets.

This ratio is really only useful if it is compared with previous periods or with other entities. In isolation, it does not mean very much. For example, is a turnover of 5 good, and 4 poor? All we can suggest is that if the trend is upwards, then the investment in fixed assets is beginning to pay off, at least in terms of increased sales. Note also that the ratio can be strongly affected by the entity's depreciation policies. There is an argument, therefore, for taking the gross book value of the fixed assets, and not their net book value.

Trade debtor collection period

Investing in fixed assets is all very well, but there is not much point in generating extra sales if the customers do not pay for them. Customers might be encouraged to buy more by a combination of lower selling prices and generous credit terms. If the debtors are slow at paying, the entity might find that it has run into cash flow problems. It is important, therefore, for it to watch its trade debtor position very carefully. We can check how successful it has been by calculating the *average trade debtor collection period*. The ratio is calculated as follows:

$$\frac{\text{Average trade debtors}}{\text{Total credit sales}} \times 365 = \text{X days}$$

The average trade debtors are usually calculated by using a simple average [i.e. $\frac{1}{2}$(opening trade debtors + closing trade debtors)]. The closing trade debtor figure is sometimes substituted for average trade debtors. This is acceptable, provided that the figure is representative of the overall period.

It is important to relate trade debtors to credit sales if possible: cash sales must be excluded from the calculation. The method shown above for calculating the ratio would relate the average trade debtors to X days' sales, but it would be possible to substitute weeks or months for days. It is not customary to express the ratio as a percentage.

An acceptable debtor collection period cannot be suggested, as much depends upon the type of trade in which the entity is engaged. Some entities expect settlement within 28 days of delivery of the goods, or on immediate receipt of the invoice. Other entities might expect settlement within 28 days following the end of the month in which the goods were delivered. On average, this adds another 14 days (half a month) to the overall period of 28 days. If this is the case, a company would appear to be highly efficient in collecting its debts if the average debtor collection period was about 42 days (in the United Kingdom, the average debtor collection period is 78 days).

Like most of the other ratios, however, it is important to establish a trend, and if the trend is upwards, then it might suggest that the company's credit control was beginning to weaken.

Trade creditor payment period

A similar ratio can be calculated for the average trade creditor payment period. The formula is as follows:

$$\frac{\text{Average trade creditors}}{\text{Total credit purchases}} \times 365 = \text{X days}$$

The average trade creditors would again be a simple average of the opening and closing balances, although it is quite common to use the closing trade creditors. The trade creditors must be related to credit purchases, and weeks or months may be substituted for the number of days. Like the trade debtor collection period, it is not usual to express it as a percentage.

An upward trend in the average level of trade creditors would suggest that the entity is having some difficulty in finding the cash to pay its creditors. Indeed, it might be a sign that it is running into financial difficulties.

We move on now to our fourth main category of accounting ratios: *investment ratios*.

INVESTMENT RATIOS

The various ratios examined in the previous sections are probably of interest to all users of accounts, such as creditors, employees, and managers, as well as shareholders. There are, however, some other ratios which are primarily (although not exclusively) of interest to prospective investors. These ratios are known as *investment* ratios, and the main ones are outlined below.

Dividend yield

The first investment ratio which you might find useful is the dividend yield. It usually applies to *ordinary* shareholders, and it may be calculated as follows:

$$\frac{\text{Dividend per share}}{\text{Market price per share}} \times 100 = X\%$$

The dividend yield measures the rate of return an investor gets by comparing the cost of his shares with the dividend receivable (or paid). For example, if an investor buys 100 £1 ordinary shares at a market rate of £2 per share (200p), and the dividend was 10p, his yield would be 5% (10/200 × 100). As far as the company is concerned, while he may have invested £200 (100 × £2 per share), he will be registered as holding 100 shares at a a nominal value of £1 each (100 shares × £1). He would be entitled, therefore, to a dividend of £10 (10p × 100 shares), but from his point of view, he will be getting a return of £10 on £200, i.e. 5%.

Dividend cover

Another useful investment ratio is called dividend cover. It is calculated as follows:

$$\text{Dividend cover} = \frac{\text{Net profit after taxation and preference dividend}}{\text{Paid and proposed ordinary dividends}} = X \text{ times}$$

This ratio shows the number of times that ordinary dividend could be paid out of current earnings. The dividend is usually described as being X times covered by the earnings. Thus, if the dividend is covered twice, the company would be paying out half of its earnings as an ordinary dividend.

Earnings per share

Another important investment ratio is that known as earnings per share (EPS). This ratio enables us to put the profit into context, and to avoid looking at it in simple absolute terms. It usually is looked at from the ordinary shareholder's point of view, and it may be calculated as follows:

$$\frac{\text{Net profit after taxation and preference dividend}}{\text{Number of ordinary shares in issue during the year}} = \text{Xp}$$

It is customary to calculate this ratio by taking the net profit after taxation (although there is no reason why it could not be taken before taxation). Preference dividends are deducted because they are usually paid before ordinary shareholders receive a dividend.

EPS enables a fair comparison to be made between one year's earnings and another by relating the earnings to something tangible, i.e. the number of shares in issue.

Price/earnings ratio

Another common investment ratio is the price earnings ratio (or P/E ratio). It is calculated as follows:

$$\frac{\text{Market price per share}}{\text{Earnings per share}} = \text{X}$$

The P/E ratio enables a comparison to be made between the earnings per share (as defined above) and the market price. It tells us that the market price is X times the earnings. It means that it would take X years before we recovered the market price paid for the shares out of the earnings (assuming that they remained at that level, and that they were all distributed). Thus the P/E ratio is a multiple of earnings, and a high or low ratio can only be judged in relation to other companies in the same sector of the market.

Capital gearing ratio

We come finally to our last investment ratio: the *capital gearing ratio*. This is usually a most difficult one for students to understand, possibly because (like ROCE) there are so many ways of calculating it.

As we outlined in an Chapter 6, companies are financed out of a mixture of share capital, retained profits and borrowings. Borrowings may be long term (such as debentures), or short term (such as credit given by trade creditors). In addition, the company may have set aside all sorts of provisions (e.g. for taxation) which it expects to meet sometime in the future. These may also be regarded as 'borrowings'. From an ordinary shareholder's point of view, even preference share capital can be classed as 'borrowings', because the preference shareholders may have priority over ordinary shareholders, both in respect of dividends, and upon liquidation.

If a company, therefore, finances itself from a high level of borrowings, there is obviously a higher risk in investing in it. This arises for two main reasons:

1 the higher the borrowings, the more interest that the company will have to pay, and that may affect the company's ability to pay an ordinary dividend;
2 if the company cannot find the cash to repay its borrowings, the ordinary shareholders may not get any money back in any subsequent liquidation.

As far as item (1) is concerned, there will be no real problem if income is rising, because the interest on borrowings will become a smaller and smaller proportion of the total income. But it could become a problem if income is falling, because the interest will have to be paid first before any ordinary dividend can be paid.

There are many different ways of calculating capital gearing, so the first point we need to establish is: what is our objective? The objective can be expressed as follows:

To calculate the proportion of the entity financed out of borrowings.

But how should it be calculated? There are three factors involved in the relationship: (a) the amount financed by the ordinary shareholders; (b) the amount financed out of borrowings; and (c) the total amount of financing. Or put in the form of an equation:

Shareholders' funds + borrowings = total amount financed

Thus, if we want to express this equation as a ratio, we can do so in at least two ways, viz.:

1 $$\frac{\text{Borrowings}}{\text{Shareholders' funds + borrowings}}$$

2 $$\frac{\text{Borrowings}}{\text{Shareholders' funds}}$$

We prefer the first method, since if we express it as a percentage, it appears clearer, i.e. 'X% of the company has been financed by borrowings'. The second method tells us the borrowings represent a certain proportion of the shareholders' funds (including preference shares). You might not agree with our reasoning, and if you prefer the second method, there is no reason why you should not use it.

Irrespective of which method we adopt, we now have to decide what we mean by 'shareholders' funds' and 'borrowings'. It is not too difficult to define shareholders' funds. They include the following items:

- Ordinary share capital
- Preference share capital (see below)
- Share premium account
- Capital reserves
- Revenue reserves
- Other reserves
- Profit and loss account.

Borrowings may (but will not necessarily) include the following items:

- Preference share capital (see above)
- Debentures
- Loans
- Overdrafts
- Provisions
- Accruals
- Current liabilities
- Other amounts due for payment.

Note that in a complex group structure, you might also come across other items that could be classed as 'borrowings', but the above analysis is sufficient for our purposes.

There is not much doubt about what to include in shareholders' funds. Some accountants might exclude preference share capital because that is a form of borrowing, in which case it will be classed as such. Borrowings are a little trickier to determine, but we are not going to complicate the calculation of the ratio by getting involved in too much technical detail. We recommend, therefore, that you go for a fairly straightforward approach and adopt the following definition of capital gearing:

$$\frac{\text{Preference shares} + \text{long-term loans}}{\text{Shareholders' funds} + \text{long-term loans}} \times 100 = \text{X\%}$$

A company that has financed itself out of a high proportion of borrowings (e.g. in the form of a combination of preference shares and long-term loans) is known as a high geared company. Conversely, a company with a low level of borrowing is regarded as being low geared. Note that high and low in this context are relative terms. As we outlined above, a high geared company is potentially a higher risk investment, as it has to earn sufficient profit to cover even the interest payments and the preference dividend before it can pay out any ordinary dividend. This should not be a problem when profits are rising, but if they are falling, then they may not be sufficient to cover even the preference dividend.

We have now covered 18 common accounting ratios, and this is only a *small* sample of the number of ratios that could be used! These are summarized at the end of this chapter. However, these 18 are enough for you to be able to interpret a set of accounts. If the ratios are used in isolation, many of them are not particularly helpful, but you will find that as part of a detailed analysis they are invaluable. We will show you what we mean in the next section.

AN ILLUSTRATIVE EXAMPLE

In this section, we use the ratios outlined above to interpret a set of accounts. In order to establish a reasonable trend, we really need to adopt something like a five-year period. It would also be useful to compare our results with the ratios obtained from similar entities (there are some commercial organizations that provide such comparative data). However, for our purposes, such a long period would be impractical, and it would also obscure the basic procedures that we want to illustrate. Consequently, we shall limit our data to a single company for a two-year period. We do so in Exhibit 8.3.

Exhibit 8.3

You are provided with the following summarized information relating to Gill Limited for the year to 31 March 19X3:

Gill Limited
Trading, profit and loss account for the year to 31 March 19X3

		19X2		19X3	
		£000	£000	£000	£000
Sales			160		180
Less: Cost of goods sold:					
Opening stock		10		14	
Purchases		110		130	
	c/f	110	160	144	180

	b/f	110		160		144		180
Less: Closing stock		14		96		24		120
Gross profit				64				60
Less: Expenses:								
Administration		18				24		
Loan interest		1				1		
Selling and distribution		12		31		16		41
Net profit before taxation				33				19
Taxation				15				6
Net profit after taxation				18				13
Dividends: preference (paid)		2				2		
ordinary (proposed)		8		10		5		7
Retained profit for the year				8				6
Retained profit brought forward				4				12
Retained profit for the year				£12				£18

GILL LIMITED
Balance sheet at 31 March 19X3

	19X2			19X3		
	£000 Cost	£000 Depreci- ation	£000 Net book value	£000 Cost	£000 Depreci- ation	£000 Net book value
Fixed assets						
Freehold property	60	–	60	60	–	60
Vehicles	42	14	28	48	22	26
	£102	£14	88	£108	£22	86
Current assets						
Stocks		14			24	
Trade debtors		20			60	
Bank		3			1	
		37			85	
Less: current liabilities						
Trade creditors	10			62		
Taxation	15			6		
Proposed dividend	8	33	4	5	73	12
			£92			£98
Capital and reserves						
Authorized, issued and fully paid ordinary shares of £1 each			40			40
Preference shares (10%)			20			20
Profit and loss account			12			18
Shareholders' funds		c/f	72			78

Shareholders' funds	b/f	72	78
Loans			
Debenture stock (5%)		20	20
		£92	£98

Additional information :

1 Purchases and sales are made evenly throughout the year.
2 All purchases and all sales are made on credit terms.
3 You may assume that price levels are stable.
4 The company only sell one product: in 19X2 it sold 40 000 units and in 19X3 60 000 units.
5 There were no sales of fixed assets during the year.
6 The market value of the ordinary shares was estimated to be worth £2.30 per share at 31 March 19X2 and £1.80 per share at 31 March 19X3.

Required :

(a) Compute significant ratios for the two years to 31 March 19X2 and 19X3 respectively and
(b) using the ratios which you have calculated in part (a) of the question, comment upon the results for the year to 31 March 19X3.

Answer to Exhibit 8.3

(a) Significant ratios   GILL LIMITED

	19X2	19X3
Profitability ratios:		

Return on capital employed (ROCE):

$$\frac{\text{Net profit before taxation}}{\text{Shareholders' funds*}} \times 100 \quad = \frac{33\,000}{72\,000} \times 100 \quad = \frac{19\,000}{78\,000} \times 100$$

$$= 45.83\% \qquad\qquad = 24.36\%$$

* The opening balance for shareholders' funds for 19X2 has not been given, so the closing balance has been used.

Gross profit:

$$\frac{\text{Gross profit}}{\text{Total sales revenue}} \times 100 \quad = \frac{64\,000}{160\,000} \times 100 \quad = \frac{60\,000}{180\,000} \times 100$$

$$= 40.00\% \qquad\qquad = 33.33\%$$

Mark up:

$$\frac{\text{Gross profit}}{\text{Cost of goods sold}} \times 100 \quad = \frac{64\,000}{96\,000} \times 100 \quad = \frac{60\,000}{120\,000} \times 100$$

$$= 66.67\% \qquad\qquad = 50.00\%$$

Net profit:

$$\frac{\text{Net profit before taxation}}{\text{Total sales revenue}} \times 100 \quad = \frac{33\,000}{160\,000} \times 100 \quad = \frac{19\,000}{180\,000} \times 100$$

$$= 20.63\% \qquad\qquad = 10.56\%$$

Liquidity ratios:

Current assets:

$$\frac{\text{Current assets}}{\text{Current liabilities}} = \frac{37\,000}{33\,000} \qquad = \frac{85\,000}{73\,000}$$

$$= 1.12 \text{ to } 1 \qquad = 1.16 \text{ to } 1$$

Acid test:

$$\frac{\text{Current assets} - \text{stocks}}{\text{Current liabilities}} = \frac{37\,000 - 14\,000}{33\,000} = \frac{85\,000 - 24\,000}{73\,000}$$

$$= 0.70 \text{ to } 1 \qquad = 0.84 \text{ to } 1$$

Efficiency ratios:

Stock turnover:

$$\frac{\text{Cost of goods sold}}{\text{Average stock*}} = \frac{96\,000}{\frac{1}{2}(10\,000 + 14\,000)} = \frac{120\,000}{\frac{1}{2}(14\,000 + 24\,000)}$$

$$= 8.0 \text{ times} \qquad = 6.3 \text{ times}$$

* $\frac{1}{2}$(Opening stocks + closing stocks)

Fixed assets turnover:

$$\frac{\text{Total sales revenue}}{\text{Fixed assets at net book value}} = \frac{160\,000}{88\,000} = \frac{180\,000}{86\,000}$$

$$= 1.82 \text{ times} \qquad = 2.09 \text{ times}$$

Trade debtor collection period:

$$\frac{\text{Closing trade debtors*}}{\text{Total credit sales}} = \frac{20\,000}{160\,000} \times 365 = \frac{60\,000}{180\,000} \times 365$$

$$= 46 \text{ days} \qquad = 122 \text{ days}$$

*Opening trade debtors have not been given for 19X2, so closing trade debtors have been used.

Trade creditor collection period:

$$\frac{\text{Closing trade creditors*}}{\text{Total credit purchases}} \times 365 = \frac{10\,000}{100\,000} \times 365 = \frac{62\,000}{130\,000} \times 365$$

$$= 37 \text{ days} \qquad = 175 \text{ days}$$

*Opening trade creditors have not been given for 19X2, so closing trade creditors have been used.

Investment ratios:

Dividend yield:

$$\frac{\text{Dividend per share}}{\text{Market price per share}} \times 100 = \frac{20}{230} \times 100^* = \frac{12.5}{180} \times 100^{**}$$

$$= 8.70\% \qquad = 6.94\%$$

$$= \frac{8000}{40\,000} \times 100 = \frac{5000}{40\,000} \times 100$$

$$= 20\text{p} \qquad = 12.5\text{p}$$

Dividend cover:

Net profit after taxation and
$$\frac{\text{preference dividend}}{\text{Paid and proposed}} = \frac{18\,000 - 2000}{8000} = \frac{13\,000 - 2000}{5000}$$
ordinary dividends

$$= 2.00 \text{ times} \qquad = 2.20 \text{ times}$$

Earnings per shares (EPS):

Net profit after taxation and
$$\frac{\text{preference dividend}}{\text{Number of ordinary shares}} = \frac{18\,000 - 2000}{40\,000} = \frac{13\,000 - 2000}{40\,000}$$
in issue during the year

$$= 40.00\text{p} \qquad = 27.50\text{p}$$

Price/earnings (P/E) ratio:

$$\frac{\text{Market price per share}}{\text{Earnings per share}} = \frac{2.30}{0.40} = \frac{1.80}{0.275}$$

$$= 5.75 \qquad = 6.55$$

Capital gearing:

Preference shares +
$$\frac{\text{Long-term loans}}{\text{Shareholders' funds +}} \times 100 = \frac{20\,000 + 20\,000}{72\,000 + 20\,000} \times 100 = \frac{20\,000 + 20\,000}{78\,000 + 20\,000} \times 100$$
Long-term loans

$$= 43.48\% \qquad = 40.82\%$$

(b) Comments on the ratios

Profitability

1 The selling price of the product in 19X2 must have been £4.00 per unit since the company sold 40 000 units and its total sales revenue was £160 000 (£160 000 ÷ 40 000). In 19X3 the company sold 60 000 units and its total sales revenue was £180 000. The selling price per unit must, therefore, have been £3.00. It would appear that Gill Limited deliberately reduced its selling price per unit by 25% (1 x 100/4 = 25%). There was thus a 50% increase in sales volume (from 40 000 units to 60 000), but its total sales revenue only increased by £20 000 (or 12.5%).

2 The relatively modest increase in sales revenue did not help to increase the gross profit (down from £64 000 to £60 000), largely because the reduction in mark up (down from 66.67% to 50%) did not generate sufficient extra sales.

3 The large increase in sales volume also affected overall profitability. The net profit on sales was reduced from 20.63% to 10.56%, partly because of the reduction in gross profit and partly because other expenses increased by £10 000. Consequently, the return on capital employed was much reduced: from 45.83% to 24.36%. This is still a favourable rate of return when compared with alternative forms of investment, but the company's management must view the downward trend with some concern.

Liquidity

1 Gill's current assets position does not appear to have been greatly affected by the overall decline in profitability. In fact the current assets ratio has increased slightly,

from 1.12 to 1 to 1.16 to 1. The current assets are in excess of current liabilities in both years, so provided that receipts from trade debtors can be kept in step with payments to trade creditors, the company would appear not to have an immediate liquidity problem.

2 If stocks are excluded from current assets, however, the position is a little more worrying. The acid test ratio was 0.71 to 1 in 19X2, and 0.84 to 1 in 19X3, so there has been an improvement in Gill's immediate liquidity position. Even so, by the end of 19X3 the company did not have sufficient cash to pay its proposed dividend, so it was dependent on either being able to obtain overdraft facilities from the bank, or on cash receipts from its trade debtors (note that there was a similar situation in 19X2). Fortunately, the tax would probably not have to be paid until 1 January 19X4 (i.e. nine months after the year end).

Efficiency

1 Gill was not as efficient in trading in 19X3 as it had been in 19X2. Its stock turnover was down from 8.0 to 6.3, which means that it was not turning over its stocks as quickly in 19X3 as it did in 19X2.

2 The company's investment in fixed assets (as measured by its sales activity) has improved from 1.82 times in 19X2 to 2.09 times in 19X3. This arose largely because the purchase of new assets only increased the gross book value of its fixed assets by £6000, whereas the depreciation charge for the year reduced the total net book value by £8000, a net difference of £2000.

3 The extra sales generated during 19X3 were made at some cost to its potential liquidity position. At the end of 19X3 its outstanding trade debtors represented 46 days' sales, but at the end of 19X3, they represented 122 days' sales. This suggests that Gill encouraged a greater sales volume by reducing both its selling prices and by offering more generous credit terms. It is also possible that the company was so busy coping with the increased operational activity that it did not have time to control its debtor position.

4 Gill appears to have been fortunate in 19X3 in not having to pay its trade creditors as promptly as it did in 19X2. At the end of the 19X2, its trade creditors represented about 23 days' purchases (or nearly six months' purchases). If Gill had to pay its creditors as quickly in 19X3 as it had done in 19X2, its total trade creditors at the end of 19X3 would have amounted to about £13 000 (130 000 x 37/365), instead of the £62 000 actually owing at that date. By paying its trade creditors more quickly, Gill would probably have had a bank overdraft of some £48 000 (62 000 – 13 000) = 49 000 – 1 000, instead of the favourable balance of £1000.

Investment

1 Gill Limited is a private company, so its shares would not be freely available on a recognized stock exchange. The market price of the shares given in the question is bound to be rather a questionable one, and it probably does not reflect the earnings potential of the company.

2 The dividend yield has fallen from 8.7% in 19x2 to 6.94% in 19X3. Compared with the yield currently available from other investments, these yields are about averge, although the reduction in the dividend for 19X3 could be the start of a downwards trend.

3 Whilst the reduction in the dividend from 20% in 19X2 to 12.5% in 19X3 is worrying, the dividend is well covered by the earnings. Indeed, the company could have paid the same dividend in19X3 as it did in 19X2, and the dividend would still have been

covered 1.38 times (13 000 – 2000/8000). It would appear that the company's policy is to pay less than half of its earnings as dividend, even if it means reducing the dividend. This would not matter as much to a private company as it would to a public one. In a public company a reduction in dividend can result in a fall in the market value of its shares, thus reflecting the reduction in confidence that the market has in the company.

4   No new shares were issued during the year. Thus, as a result of the reduction in profits, the earnings per share declined from 40.00p to 27.50p.

5   The increase in the price earnings ratio (up from 5.75 to 6.55) is surprising. It was probably caused by the market's view (albeit a rather restricted one) that the company's future is a reasonably good one, notwithstanding the reduction in the comapny's profit. However, this company is a private one, so we cannot be certain how the market price of its shares has been determined.

6   Gill Limited is a fairly high geared company. In 19X2, nearly 44% of its financing had been raised in the form of fixed interest stock, but in 19X3 this was reduced to just under 41%. By financing itself in this way, the company is committed to making annual payments of £3000 (2000 of preference dividend + 1000 of debenture interest). In absolute terms, this amount is not large, and so although it is a relatively high geared company, its earnings should be sufficient to cover its interest commitments.

Summary

1   In 19X3 Gill Limited achieved its presumed objective of increasing its sales. It did this partly by reducing its unit selling price, and partly by offering extended credit terms to its customers. The effect of this policy has been to reduce gross profit by £4000 and its net profit by £14 000,

2   The new policy did not affect its liquidity position, largely because the extended credit terms (leading to delays in the settlement of its trade debts) were offset by similar delays in paying its trade creditors.

3   As a result of the reduction in its profits for 19X3, the company reduced its dividend, although its earnings were still sufficient for it to maintain the same dividend as in 19X2.

4   The market (such as it is) does not seem to agree that the reduction in the profit or of the dividend is serious. Indeed, it can be argued the company's future is healthy provided that it can persuade its trade debtors to pay their debts more promptly.

You are now recommended to study Exhibit 8.3 most carefully. Make sure that you know how to calculate the ratios, and that you know what they mean. Then try and list your own views on Gill Limited's progress during 19X3. The comments listed above are only brief ones, and much more could have been written about the company. However, we hope that we have been able to demonstrate that ratio analysis enables us to extract a great deal more information about the company than could be obtained merely by attempting to 'read' the profit and loss account and the balance sheet.

Although ratios help us to put the information into context, they must then be used as part of a detailed overall analysis. Think of ratios as signposts. They point us in the right direction, but they are not a substitute for the journey itself. We now need to undertake that journey. In other words, we must look a little closer at what we mean by 'interpretation'. We do so in the next section.

INTERPRETATION

Once you have collected all the data that you need about a company, and you have established a considerable number of trends and calculated innumerable ratios, you have to write a story. This means that you have to *interpret* what has happened, i.e. you need to explain what has happened, and possibly predict what *will* happen. What can you do to make some sense out of all the information that you have got? Much depends, of course, upon the reason for your investigation, but the following questions might help help you to come to some provisional conclusions:

1 **The market for the company's products.** Has this expanded or contracted in recent years? How has the company coped with the changes in market conditions? What is the market likely to be like over (say) the next five years? How will it be affected by general demographic, economic, political, and social factors? Does the company seem attuned to these possible changes?
2 **Sales and profits.** Have these increased or decreased over the period? If there has been any growth, has it been because of internal expansion or because of acquisition? Does the management seem keen enough to pursue growth, or is the company stagnating?
3 **Capital investment.** What capital investment has there been and what is planned? How would future investments be financed? What retained reserves has the company built up?
4 **Management.** What is the record of the management? Are the senior managers near retirement? Are they young enough to want change? Are they ambitious? How well do they seem to have managed the company's resources? Is its liquidity position secure? How good are they at portraying a favourable public image for the company?
5 **Employees and industrial relations.** Does the company appear to have a stable workforce? Has it had any industrial disputes? What is its attitude and relationship as far as the trade unions are concerned? How does the output and profit record per employee compare with other companies?
6 **Generally.** The 'feel good' factor. Having found out a great deal about the company, does it inspire you with some confidence about its future? Is it likely to expand in the short term, and survive in the long term ? Overall, do you feel good about the company?

The above questions are not exhaustive, but they should be a help to you in your analysis. There is no doubt that having extensively researched a company's history and examined its future, you will already have formed a provisional view before you come to make your recommendations. All that remains for you to do is to set them down on paper. At that stage you may well find that you are expected to produce a *brief* report, so you then have the difficult task of summarizing all that you have learned about the company in just a few pages. You may well find that this is almost as difficult as carrying out the investigation!

CONCLUSION

This chapter concludes one of the main parts of the book. By now, you should know something about the nature of accounting information, where it comes from, and how it can be of help to both owners and managers.

As has been argued throughout this book, the techniques adopted by accountants are open to some fairly serious criticisms, so it is only right that we should have expressed some reservations about the reliability of accounting information. None the less, no one has yet devised a better method of accounting, and, until they do, we have to make the best of the present one. We would argue that by being fully aware of the deficiences of financial accounting, the non-accountant can make allowances for them when faced with such information.

The next part of the book deals with cost and management accounting. This is a most important branch of accounting for non-accountants working in both the manufacturing and service sectors of the economy. In fact, until you are in a senior position, you are more likely to come across management accounting information than financial accounting. You may think it odd, therefore, that we have begun our study of accounting with financial accounting, but it is our experience that management accounting can only be fully appreciated when it has been preceded by a study of financial accounting. Thus, if you are in any doubt about what we have covered so far, you are recommended to re-read some of the earlier chapters and have another go at the exercises.

KEY POINTS

1 The interpretation of accounts involves examining accounts in some detail so as to be able to explain what has happened and to predict what is likely to happen.

2 The examination can be undertaken by using a number of techniques such as horizontal analysis, trend analysis, vertical analysis, and ratio analysis.

3 Ratio analysis, in particular, is a popular method of interpreting accounts. It involves comparing one item in the accounts with another closely related item. Ratios are normally expressed in the form of a percentage or a

factor. There are literally hundreds of recognized accounting ratios (the main ones are summarized at the very end of the chapter), as well as those that relate only to specific industries.

4 When relating one item with another, and expressing it in the form of a ratio, be careful to make sure that there is a close and logical correlation between the two items.

5 Remember that in the case of some ratios, different definitions can be adopted. This applies particularly to ROCE and capital gearing. In other cases, remember that sometimes only year-end balances are used, and not an annual average. This applies especially to ratios relating to stocks, debtors, and creditors.

CHECK YOUR LEARNING

1 State whether the following assertions are true or false:
   (a) Ratio analyis aims to put the financial results of an entity into perspective.   True/False
   (b) Ratio analysis is only one form of analysis that can be used in interpreting accounts.   True/False
   (c) Ratio analysis helps establish whether or not an entity is a going concern.   True/False

2 Fill in the missing blanks in the following equations:
   (a) $\dfrac{\text{gross profit (50)}}{\text{sales (200)}} \times \underline{\hspace{1cm}} \% = 25\%.$

   (b) $\dfrac{\text{Profit}}{\text{Capital}} \times 100 = \underline{\hspace{2cm}}.$

   (c) trade debtors $\times$ 365 = trade debtor collection period $\underline{\hspace{2cm}}$.

   (d) $\dfrac{\underline{\hspace{2cm}}}{\text{average stock}} = $ stock turnover ratio.

   (e) $\dfrac{\text{net profit after taxation and preference dividend}}{\underline{\hspace{3cm}}} = $ dividend cover.

   (f) $\dfrac{\text{preference shares} + \underline{\hspace{2cm}}}{\text{shareholders' funds} + \text{long term loans}} \times 100 = $ capital gearing

3 State how each of the following ratios would normally be classed:
   (a) gross profit ratio: 70%   High/Low/Neither
   (b) net profit ratio: 3%   High/Low/Neither
   (c) return on capital employed: 30%   High/Low/Neither
   (d) trade debtors collection period: 125 days   High/Low/Neither
   (e) capital gearing: 40%   High/Low/Neither

ANSWERS

1 (a) true (b) true (c) true
2 (a) 100 (b) return on capital employed (c) credit sales (d) cost of goods sold
  (e) ordinary dividends (f) long-term loans
3 (a) high (b) low (c) high (d) high (e) neither

SUMMARY OF THE MAIN RATIOS

Profitability ratios

$$\text{ROCE} = \frac{\text{Net profit before taxation}}{\text{Average shareholders' funds}} \times 100$$

$$\text{ROCE} = \frac{\text{Net profit after taxation}}{\text{Average shareholders' funds}} \times 100$$

$$\text{ROCE} = \frac{\text{Net profit after taxation and preference dividends}}{\text{Average shareholders' funds less preference shares}} \times 100$$

$$\text{ROCE} = \frac{\text{Profit before taxation and interest}}{\text{Average shareholders' funds} + \text{long-term loans}} \times 100$$

$$\text{Gross profit ratio} = \frac{\text{Gross profit}}{\text{Total sales revenue}} \times 100$$

$$\text{Mark up} = \frac{\text{Gross profit}}{\text{Cost of goods sold}} \times 100$$

$$\text{Net profit ratio} = \frac{\text{Net profit before taxation}}{\text{Total sales revenue}} \times 100$$

Liquidity ratios

$$\text{Current assets ratio} = \frac{\text{Current assets}}{\text{Current liabilities}}$$

$$\text{Acid test ratio} = \frac{\text{Current assets} - \text{stocks}}{\text{Current liabilities}}$$

Efficiency ratios

$$\text{Stock turnover} = \frac{\text{Cost of goods sold}}{\text{Average stock}}$$

$$\text{Fixed assets turnover} = \frac{\text{Total sales revenue}}{\text{Fixed assets at net book value}}$$

$$\text{Trade debtor collection period} = \frac{\text{Average trade debtors}}{\text{Total credit sales}} \times 365$$

$$\text{Trade creditor payment period} = \frac{\text{Average trade creditors}}{\text{Total credit purchases}} \times 365$$

Investment ratios

$$\text{Dividend yield} = \frac{\text{Dividend per share}}{\text{Market price per share}} \times 100$$

$$\text{Dividend cover} = \frac{\text{Net profit after taxation and preference dividend}}{\text{Paid and proposed ordinary dividends}}$$

$$\text{Earnings per share} = \frac{\text{Net profit after taxation and preference dividend}}{\text{Number of ordinary shares in issue during the year}}$$

$$\text{Price/earnings ratio} = \frac{\text{Market price per share}}{\text{Earnings per share}}$$

$$\text{Capital gearing} = \frac{\text{Preference shares} + \text{long-term loans}}{\text{Shareholders' funds} + \text{long-term loans}} \times 100$$

QUESTIONS

8.1 The following information has been extracted from the books of account of Betty for the year to 31 January 19X1.

Trading and profit and loss account for the year to 31 January 19X2.

	£000	£000
Sales (all credit)		100
Less: Cost of goods sold:		
Opening stock	15	
Purchases	65	
	80	
Less: Closing stock	10	70
Gross profit		30
Administrative expenses		16
Net profit		£14

Balance sheet at 31 January 19X1

	£000	£000
Fixed assets (net book value)		29
Current assets:		
Stock	10	
Trade debtors	12	
Cash	3	
	25	
Less: current liabilities		
Trade creditors	6	19
		£48
Financed by:		
Capital at 1 February 19X0		40
Add: Net profit	14	
Less: Drawings	6	8
		£48

Required:

Calculate the following accounting ratios:

1 gross profit;
2 net profit;
3 return on capital employed;
4 current ratio;
5 acid test;
6 stock turnover; and
7 debtor collection period.

8.2 You are presented with the following summarized accounts:

JAMES LIMITED

Profit and loss account for the year to 28 February 19X2

	£000
Sales (all credit)	1200
Cost of sales	600
Gross profit	600
Administrative expenses	(500)
Debenture interest payable	(10)
Profit on ordinary activities	90
Taxation	(30)
	60
Dividends	(40)
Retained profit for the year	£20

JAMES LIMITED
Balance sheet at 28 February 19X2

	£000	£000	£000
Fixed assets (net book value)			685
Current assets			
Stock		75	
Trade debtors		200	
		275	
Less: Current liabilities			
Trade creditors	160		
Bank overdraft	10		
Taxation	30		
Proposed dividend	40	240	35
			£720
Capital and reserves			
Ordinary share capital			600
Profit and loss account			20
Shareholders' funds			620
Loans:			
10% debentures			100
			£720

Required :
Calculate the following accounting ratios:
1 return on capital employed;
2 gross profit;
3 mark up;
4 net profit;
5 acid test;
6 fixed asset turnover;
7 debtor collection period; and
8 capital gearing.

8.3 You are presented with the following information for each of three companies:

Profit and loss accounts for the year to 31 March 19X3

	Mark Limited	*Luke Limited*	*John Limited*
	£000	£000	£000
Profit before tax	£64	£22	£55

Balance sheet (extracts) at 31 March 19X3

	Mark Limited £000	Luke Limited £000	John Limited £000
Capital and reserves			
Ordinary share capital of £1 each	100	177	60
Cumulative 15% preference shares of £1 each	–	20	10
Share premium account	–	70	20
Profit and loss account	150	60	200
Shareholders's funds	250	327	290
Loans			
10% debentures	–	–	100
	£250	£327	£390

Required :
Calculate the following accounting ratios·
1 return on capital employed; and
2 capital gearing.

8.4 The following information relates to Helena Limited:

Trading account year to 30 April

	19X1 £000	19X2 £000	19X3 £000	19X4 £000	19X5 £000	19X6 £000
Sales (all credit)	–	130	150	190	210	320
Less: Cost of goods sold:						
Opening stock	–	20	30	30	35	40
Purchases (all in credit terms)	–	110	110	135	145	305
	–	130	140	165	180	345
Less: Closing stock	–	30	30	35	40	100
	–	100	110	130	140	245
Gross profit	–	£30	£40	£60	£70	£75
Trade debtors at 30 April	£40	£45	£40	£70	£100	£150
Trade creditors at 30 April	£20	£20	£25	£25	£30	£60

Required :
Calculate the following account ratios for each of the five years to 30 April 19X2
to 19X6 inclusive;
1 gross profit;
2 mark up;
3 stock turnover;
4 trade debtor collection period; and
5 trade creditor payment period.

8.5 You are presented with the following information relating to Hedge public limited company for the year to 31 May 19X5;

(a) The company has an issued and fully paid share capital of £500 000 ordinary shares of £1 each. There are no preference shares.
(b) The market price of the shares at 31 May 19X5 was £3.50.
(c) The net profit after taxation for the year to 31 May 19X5 was £70 000.
(d) The directors are proposing a dividend of 7p per share for the year to 31 May 19X5.

Required :
Calculate the following accounting ratios;
1 dividend yield;
2 dividend cover;
3 earnings per share; and
4 price/earnings ratio.

8.6 The following information relates to Style Limited for the two years to 30 June 19X5 and 19X6 respectively:

Trading, profit and loss accounts for the years

	19X5		19X6	
	£000	£000	£000	£000
Sales (all credit)		1500		1900
Less: Cost of goods sold:				
Opening stock	80		100	
Purchases (all on credit terms)	995		1400	
	1075		1500	
	100	975	200	1300
Gross profit		525		600
Less: Expenses		250		350
Net profit		£275		£250

Balance sheet at 30 June

	19X5		19X6	
	£000	£000	£000	£000
Fixed assets (net book value)		580		460
Current assets:				
Stock	100		200	
Trade debtors	375		800	
Bank	25		–	
	500		1000	
Less: Current liabilities:				
Bank overdraft	–		10	
Trade creditors	80		200	
	80	420	210	790
		£1000		£1250

Capital and reserves:		
Ordinary share capital	900	900
Profit and loss account	100	350
Shareholders's funds	£1000	£1250

Required :
(a) Calculate the following accounting ratios for the two years 19X5 and 19X6 respectively;

1 gross profit;	5 stock turnover;
2 mark up;	6 current ratio;
3 net profit;	7 acid test;
4 return on capital employed;	8 trade debtor collection period; and
	9 trade creditor payment period.

(b) Comment upon the company's performance for the year to 30 June 19X6.

ADDITIONAL QUESTIONS (WITHOUT ANSWERS)

8.7 The following summarized information relates to Turnbull public limited company.

Year to 31 October	19X2	19X3	19X4	19X5	19X6
	£000	£000	£000	£000	£000
Profit and loss accounts:					
Sales (all credit)	5500	5600	5700	6000	9300
Cost of sales	(3030)	(3050)	(3000)	(3250)	(5400)
Gross profit	2470	2550	2700	2750	3900
Distribution costs	(520)	(550)	(600)	(600)	(900)
Administration expenses	(1500)	(1500)	(1500)	(1500)	(2000)
Profit before taxation	450	500	600	650	1000
Taxation	(60)	(90)	(120)	(150)	(200)
Profit after taxation	390	410	480	500	800
Dividends	(90)	(90)	(100)	(150)	(150)
Transferred to reserves	300	320	380	350	650
Balance sheets at 31 October					
Fixed assets at cost	3100	3200	3900	4600	6000
Less: Accumulated depreciation	200	300	400	500	600
	2900	2900	3500	4100	5400
Current assets:					
Stocks	600	700	750	750	2400
Trade debtors	800	800	900	900	1600
Cash and bank	100	100	100	150	260
	1500	1600	1750	1800	4260

Current liabilities:

Trade creditors	(2390)	(2140)	(2470)	(2690)	(5750)
Taxation	(60)	(90)	(120)	(150)	(200)
Dividend	(90)	(90)	(100)	(150)	(150)
	(2540)	(2320)	(2690)	(2990)	(6100)
	£1860	£2180	£2560	£2910	£3560

Capital and reserves:

Called up share capital					
(ordinary shares of £1 each)	500	500	500	500	500
Profit and loss account	1360	1680	2060	2410	3060
	£1860	£2180	£2560	£2910	£3560

Notes :

(1) Stock at 1 November 19X1: £550 000

(2) All purchases are obtained on credit terms.

Required :

Prepare a report for the Board of Directors of Turnbull plc examining the financial performance of the company during the five-year period 1 November 19X1 to 31 October 19X6.

8.8 The following information relates to three companies all operating in the same industry.

	Begg plc £000	Chow plc £000	Doyle plc £000
Profit and loss accounts for the year to 30 November 19X1			
Turnover	11 200	11 500	13 000
Cost of sales	(5 600)	(4 800)	(7 100)
Gross profit	5 600	6 700	5 900
Operating expenses	(4 000)	(3 300)	(4 700)
Profit before taxation	1 600	3 400	1 200
Taxation	(600)	(1 100)	(550)
Profit after taxation	1 000	2 300	650
Dividends	(600)	(200)	(300)
Retained profit	400	2 100	350
Balance sheets at 30 November 19X1			
Fixed assets at cost	2 600	2 700	2 800
Less: Accumulated depreciation	1 000	700	1 400
	1 600	2 000	1 400

Current assets:			
Stocks	1 700	1 300	1 300
Trade debtors	2 900	5 200	2 000
Debtors	300	1 800	300
Cash and bank	400	50	2 200
	5 300	8 350	5 800
Current liabilities:			
Trade creditors	(1 300)	(1 200)	(1 500)
Other creditors	(1 000)	(1 400)	(1 450)
Taxation	(600)	(1 100)	(550)
Dividends	(600)	(200)	(300)
	(3 500)	(3 900)	(3 800)
	£3 400	£6 450	£3 400
Capital and reserves:			
Called up share capital			
(ordinary shares of £1 each)	500	2 000	750
Profit and loss account	2 900	4 450	2 650
	£3 400	£6 450	£3 400
Market price of shares at			
30 November 19X1	£22.20	£1.90	£7.40

Required :

Assume that you are a trainee investment analyst in a firm of stockbrokers.

Prepare a report for your section manager comparing and contrasting the financial performance of the three companies.

PART 3

Cost and management accounting

CHAPTER 9

Basic cost accounting procedures

Cost reductions point way forward for Pilkington

By Maggie Urry

Mr Roger Leverton, who joined Pilkington as chief executive last summer, said there were some positive signs within the glass group's annual results despite the fall in pre-tax profits from £95.7m – restated from £77m to comply with FRS 3 – to £40.7m and the reduced dividend.

He said for the first time cost reductions had more than offset inflation. During the year costs of £70m had been taken out while inflation had increased costs by £66m. Over the last three years annual costs of £170m had been cut, largely through job reductions.

Cash flow excluding disposals, but before dividends, was positive in the second half of the year for the first time since 1990, he said.

Capital expenditure had been reduced to £125m in the year, below the depreciation charge for the first time since the mid 1980s Mr Leverton said it would stay at about the £120m level for the next couple of years. Working capital had also been cut, by £30m in the year and by £200m since 1990.

However, trading results from each of the group's divisions were lower, except for the rest of the world group which includes Argentina, Brazil and Australasia.

Operating profits from continuing businesses in European glass fell 29 per cent to £37.5m, while North American profits dropped 68 per cent to £3.5m. In both areas excess glass-making capacity had put pressure on prices. The rest of the world increased profits 80 per cent to £39m with Argentina making a record profit and the Australian business benefiting from cost cutting.

Visioncare, the spectacle and contact lens business, saw profits down from £20.9m to £18.8m, although within that the Sola spectacle side, which is soon to be sold, increased profits; contact lens profits fell from £5m to £2m.

Gearing at the year end was 78 per cent with net debt, including finance leases, of £932m (£760m). The Heywood Williams acquisition would take gearing to about 88 per cent, Mr Andrew Robb, finance director, said.

However, the sale of Sola was expected to be agreed soon, he said, and would be for a "good premium over book value of £130m". That would "make a substantial dent in gearing". More disposals over the next two years would bring gearing down further.

Pilkington is expected to reduce its stake in the Australian operations to 80 per cent and is likely to sell the contact lens business once profits there recover.

The Financial Times, 11 June 1993.

Exhibit 9.0 This article shows that the control of costs is an important factor in improving a company's performance.

In Part 2 of this book, we have been mainly concerned with *financial accounting*, but in Part 3 we are going to deal with the other main branch of accounting: *management accounting*. In this chapter, we examine the background to cost and management accounting. The chapter falls into four main sections. The first section outlines the nature and purpose of management accounting. The second section reviews the historical development of the subject. The third section examines what is meant by planning and control. The fourth section explains how accountants go about implementing a cost and management accounting system. We start by describing what is meant by cost and management accounting.

<table>
<tr>
<td>

LEARNING OBJECTIVES

</td>
<td>

By the end of this chapter, you will be able to:
- describe the nature and purpose of cost and management accounting;
- outline the five main procedures involved in implementing a cost and management accounting system.

</td>
</tr>
</table>

NATURE AND PURPOSE

For convenience, we have called this part of the book 'cost and management accounting', but these terms should really be separated into 'management accounting' and 'cost accounting', because cost accounting is really a sub-branch of management accounting. For guidance, the Chartered Institute of Management Accounting (CIMA) has issued a booklet called *Management Accounting Official Terminolgy of the CIMA*, and we are going to make extensive use of the recommended definitions.

The definition of cost accounting is given as follows:

Cost accounting: the establishment of budgets, standard costs and actual costs of operations, processes, activities or products; and the analysis of variances, profitability or the social use of funds.

It should be noted that CIMA does not recommend the term 'costing' unless it is accompanied by what it describes as a qualifying adjective, e.g. 'standard costing'.

The term 'management accounting' is defined as follows:

Management accounting: an integral part of management concerned with identifying, presenting and interpreting information used for:

formulating strategy;
planning and controlling activities;
decision taking;
optimizing the use of resources;
disclosure to shareholders and others external to the entity;
disclosure to employees;
safeguarding assets.

This definition is followed by a long explanation stating that management accounting involves participation in management to ensure that there is effective action in six major functional areas. These are as follows:

1 formulation of plans to meet objectives (strategic planning);
2 formulation of short-term operation plans (budgeting/profit; planning);
3 acquisition and use of finance (financial management) and recording of transactions (financial accounting and cost accounting);
4 communication of financial and operating information;
5 corrective action to bring plans and results into line (financial control);
6 reviewing and reporting on systems and operations (internal audit, management audit).

This functional analysis is shown in Exhibit 9.1.

Exhibit 9.1 Elements of management accounting

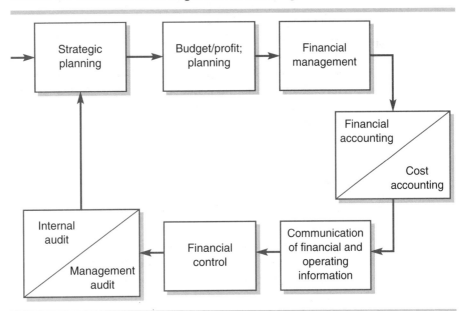

The recording of transactions (function 3) includes both financial accounting and cost accounting, so CIMA is clearly of the view that *management accounting* is an all-embracing term. In the earlier part of the book, we have argued that the two main branches of accounting are financial and management, and we have not suggested that financial accounting is a branch of management accounting. However, CIMA is correct in the sense that information of a financial accounting nature can form part of a management accounting system. Also, note that as we mentioned above, there is no doubt that that cost accounting is regarded as being a sub-branch of management accounting.

You will be relieved to know that we are not going to deal with all of the above-listed functions, as some are more advanced than we can cover in this book. For example, even on a professional accountancy course, financial management is usually taught only at the final level. Instead, we shall be spending quite a lot of time looking at cost accounting, along with some wider aspects of management accounting, such as budgeting and financial control.

We are adopting this approach because, in order to explain where a great deal of management accounting comes from and how it is prepared, we need to examine cost accounting in some detail. Like financial accounting, management accounting is also riddled with some quite arbitrary procedures. As a non-accountant, therefore, it is essential that you are familiar with them, so that you can question the validity of any management accounting information put before you. Otherwise, you might be taking some very questionable decisions!

In essence, the basic cost accounting procedures are very similar to those covered in the financial accounting section of this book, i.e. certain data are collected, recorded, stored, and eventually extracted in a form suitable for presentation to management. However, it will not be necessary for us to go into too much detail about the collection and storage of cost accounting data. We shall be much more concerned with the way that it is presented to management, and the reliance that can be placed on it. But, first, it would be helpful to explain something about the development of the subject. We do so in the next section.

HISTORICAL REVIEW

As we explained in the earlier chapters of this book, accounting evolved out of a need for information on how well a business was doing, how much it owed, and how much was owing to it. As businesses became more complex, and as ownership gradually became separated from managerial control, it became necessary to supply owners with some documentary information. Indeed, so much so, that over the last 150 years, the law has increasingly protected the rights of company shareholders by insisting that they should be supplied with a certain amount of information.

The information supplied is usually extracted from company records kept specially for that purpose, but these records may also be used to supply the management of the company (or any other entity) with information in order to run it. Sometimes the records are kept mainly for external reporting purposes, and these may be the only major documentary source of information for internal purposes.

If such a situation applies, management's only source of information will be the annual accounts. The management may only be aware when these are prepared that urgent action needed to be taken several months ago, e.g. perhaps to avoid a cash crisis. By then, of course, it may be too late. In theory, the management ought to know that some problems were beginning to build up, but, in practice, they may not be aware of just how serious these had become. This is because managers can sometimes become so involved in dealing with day-to-day matters that unless they are advised otherwise, they assume there are no problems. By the time they are warned, it may be too late to do anything. It should also be remembered that the annual accounting procedure is not designed for internal reporting purposes, so the records may not reflect the type of information the management needs.

You will not be surprised to learn that with increasing industrialization and specialization, managers began to demand information that was designed specially for *them*. In responding to this demand, accountants sometimes set up quite different recording systems from those required for financial reporting purposes (even though much of the data were common to both systems). These are known as *interlocking* systems, but nowadays it is much more common to find that only one single system is kept. This is known as an *integral* system.

The separation of management accounting information from financial accounting information (even on an integral basis) evolved gradually over a long period of time. Indeed, cost accounting is a relatively new branch of accounting. It was hardly known in the UK before 1914, but the increased industrial activity caused by the First and Second World Wars created a greater demand for management information. It was not until about 1960 that cost accounting systems became common, but even in the 1990s, there are still very many entities (including some large ones) who do not have even a rudimentary system. Hence, the management of such companies have to rely on some highly unsatisfactory data for decision-making purposes. We would argue very strongly for better information to be supplied to managers so that they can direct the company's activities more effectively. We turn to this subject in more detail in the next section.

PLANNING AND CONTROL

If an entity is to be run effectively and efficiently, managers must know what it is that they are trying to do. It is important, therefore, that the entity lays down some basic objectives. These might be quite straightforward. For example, a company might aim to achieve a return of (say) 20% on its capital employed, or a hospital may lay down maximum waiting periods for different types of operations.

Once the objectives have been established, the managers have then to work out the best way of achieving them. In other words, they have to prepare some plans, and then put them into action. From time to time, the managers will want to check what is actually happening against what they planned to happen. If there is a divergence between planned and actual results, then they will want to take some action that will bring future activities back into line with the plans. This is known as taking corrective action. In other words, they will want to *control* what is happening. Control is a word that you will come across frequently in management accounting, so we had better give the CIMA's definition. CIMA actually calls the sort of procedure that we have described as *operational control*. The definition is as follows:

> **Operational control:** the management of daily activities in accordance with strategic and tactical plans.

In order to understand this definition, you need to know what is meant by strategic planning and tactical planning. CIMA defines them as follows:

> **Strategic planning**: the formulation, evaluation and selection of strategies for the purpose of preparing a long-term plan of action to attain objectives.
> **Tactical planning**: planning the utilization of resources to achieve specific objectives in the most effective and efficient way.

Cost accounting information can play a most important part in this process. Unlike a financial accounting system, it is specially designed to help management in planning and controlling the company's activities. It has, therefore, the following advantages over a financial accounting system:

1 information can be produced regularly and frequently;
2 it is very detailed;
3 it is as up to date as it possibly can be;
4 it does not depend exclusively on historical data;
5 it encourages a forward-looking approach.

These are substantial claims, but we hope to convince you of them in subsequent chapters. In the meantime, we will outline the stages involved in implementing a cost accounting system. We do so in the next section.

THE IMPLEMENTATION PROCEDURE

The implementation of a cost accounting system involves five basic stages, which can be summarized as follows:

1 the creation of an organizational structure;
2 the adoption of a documentary coding system;
3 the selection of a suitable product costing system;
4 the treatment of fixed production overheads;
5 the choice of a suitable cost control method.

An outline of the basic procedure is also shown in Exhibit 9.2.

Exhibit 9.2 Stages in implementing a product costing system

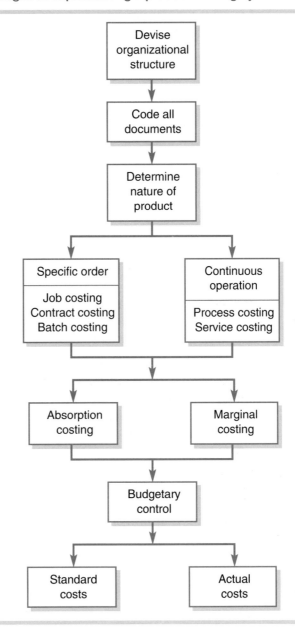

We provide a basic outline each of these stages in the following sub-sections.

Stage 1: Create an organizational structure

Organizational planning and control can best be achieved by establishing clear lines of managerial responsibility. This may require a careful examination of the way in which the company is structured, and what specific responsibility is given to individuals within it.

In large organizations this may involve setting up a considerable number of interrelated departments and sub-departments. These may range from various production departments at the factory level through to a number of selling departments located in the head office. This might be described as the pyramid format and it is shown in diagrammatic form in Exhibit 9.3.

Exhibit 9.3 The organizational structure of a company: the pyramid format

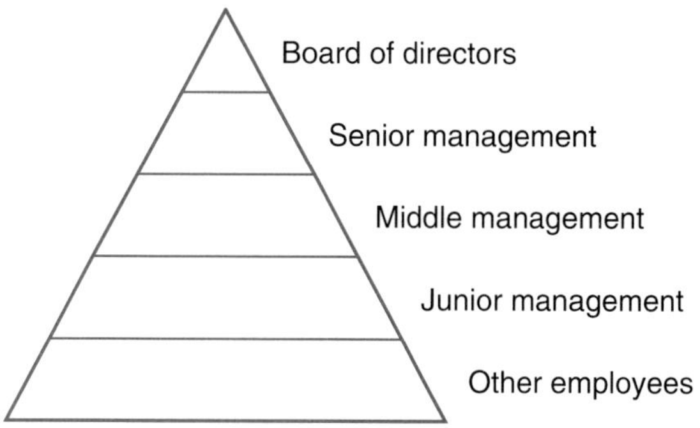

In large companies, it is not uncommon for the organizational structure to be of a *divisional* nature, perhaps based on the products it makes, or on the geographical areas in which it operates. Within each division there may be a number of factories (or works). Each factory may be divided into functions (e.g. administration, distribution, and production), and each function into departments (e.g. machine shop, stores control, and wages). The organization structure of a typical manufacturing company is shown in Exhibit 9.4.

The organizational structure within a manufacturing company can be quite complex. It is likely, for example, that there will be hundreds of departments within each function, and even in small companies there could well be several dozens.

Exhibit 9.4 The organizational structure of a manufacturing company

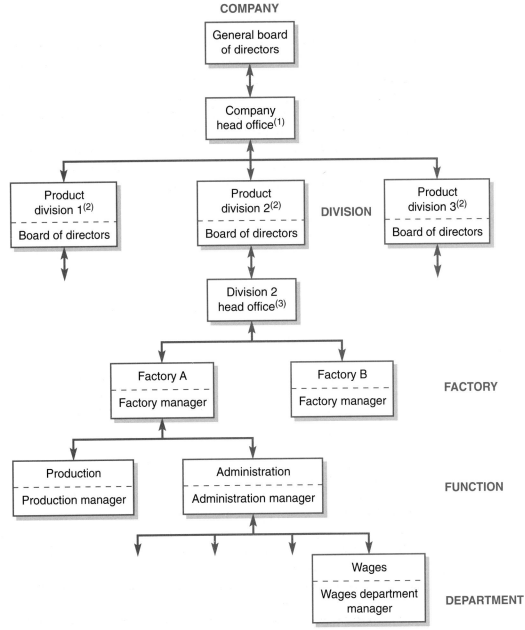

Notes:
1) The company's head office co-ordinates overall company policy. It also provides assistance and guidance generally throughout the company. The head office itself will be divided into a number of functions, such as accounting, marketing and personnel. Within each function there will probably be a number of departments, such as cash, taxation and salaries.
2) Divisions will usually be managed by a divisional board of directors, the board being answerable to the general board. Divisions often operate as separate limited liability companies in their own right (although all their shares may be owned by the main company).
3) Divisional head offices provide services for their respective divisions, similar to those provided by the company head office for the company as a whole. Divisional head offices will also be divided into a number of functions, and each function into departments.

Accountants use the term *cost centre* to describe what is often referred to as a department. The CIMA definition of a cost centre is as follows:

> **Cost centre**: a production or service location, function, activity or item of equipment whose costs may be attributed to cost units.

Hence, a cost centre need not necessarily be just a department. Before one can be delineated, two main criteria must be met. These are as follows:

1 a cost centre must represent a clearly defined area of activity;
2 one individual must have specific responsibility for managing it.

The number of cost centres actually designated will depend upon the degree of control which the company wants to achieve (this also applies to other types of entities). The smaller the area for which an individual has responsibility, the more cost centres there will be.

Apart from cost centres, accountants sometimes speak of *responsibility centres*, and *profit centres*. The CIMA definitions are as follows:

> **Responsibility centre**: a unit or function of an organization headed by a manager having direct responsibilty for its performance.
> **Profit centre**: a part of a business accountable for costs and revenues. It may be called a business centre, *business unit, or strategic business unit*.

Thus, responsibility centres may, therefore, cover a much wider area of managerial responsibility than cost centres. Accountants describe these procedures as *responsibilty accounting*. Responsibility accounting as such is not defined by CIMA, but it may be considered a system whereby an individual is given responsibility for all revenues and costs that can be traced to clearly defined areas of activity.

Managers can only be expected to answer for what goes on in such centres if they are clearly responsible for them. For example, if decisions made by the manager of a cost centre were constantly being over-ruled by a more senior manager, then the cost centre manager can always disclaim responsibility for whatever happens in it. It is essential, therefore, for this system of responsibility accounting to work, cost centre managers be given guidance on what they are expected to do, and then be left to get on with it.

The theory behind responsibility accounting suggests that the autonomous management of individual units results in greater efficiency, because individuals work more effectively if they are left alone. Thus, if each individual unit is well managed, the entity as a whole will also be well managed. No doubt you will be able to judge from your own experience whether there is any truth in this argument.

In practice, it is not always easy to decide where one manager's responsibility ends and another manager's responsibility begins. Similarly, it is sometimes difficult to know which manager should take responsibility for certain types of costs. In order to illustrate this point, we will use business rates as an example of the problems involved,

Business rates are a form of local authority taxation. They are levied on property located in a particular local authority area. They cannot easily be identified with specific departments within a particular entity. Thus, no one cost centre manager will have obvious responsibility for business rates. So which cost centre manager should it be?

It might be tempting to charge the rates to a sundry cost centre, but accountants do not recommend the use of such centres, because they tend to attract more and more costs that are difficult to identify with a particular cost centre. The use of sundry cost centres then tends to defeat one of the main objectives of responsibility accounting, i.e. to ensure that all costs (as well as incomes) do become the responsibility of one specific manager.

In the case of business rates, therefore, the best advice that we can give is to suggest that they are charged to the legal department cost centre, since that department is likely to be involved in dealing with any dispute that may arise. However, it must be clearly recognized that the legal department manager does not have any control over the rates, and this must be taken into account when he has to answer for his departmental costs.

Stage 2: Adopt a documentary coding system

Clearly, the type of organizational structure described above is highly complex. There are formidable problems in directing an entity as a whole if it consists of a considerable number of largely autonomous units. For example, a great deal of administrative effort is involved in ensuring that each cost centre is charged with its fair share of the entity's total costs.

It is necessary, therefore, to ensure that all the relevant accounting data are carefully documented, and that the cost of each transaction is charged to the correct cost centre. If this is not done, it is possible that a cost centre manager could take a decision based on some quite misleading data. In order to ensure that mistakes are minimized, it is recommended that the following procedure be adopted (although modern communication and computer systems of transmitting data may not always make the entire procedure necessary):

1 all transactions should be documented;
2 verbal instructions should be discouraged; telephone messages should be confirmed later in writing;
3 all documents should be specially designed to suit the particular transactions;
4 there should be a separate document for each type of transaction;
5 designated documents should only be supplied to authorized users;
6 all transactions should be approved and signed only by authorized personnel.

A cost accounting system normally involves a great deal of documentation so, in order to make sure that cost centres are charged correctly, it is usually necessary to adopt some formal coding system (this will almost certainly be unavoidable if the company uses computers). Unfortunately, codes can become very cumbersome, and it is very easy to make a mistake when coding a document (just as it is when dialling a telephone number). Furthermore, coding may be done by relatively junior members of staff who often do not understand why it is important to code the document correctly.

In a large organization, it may be necessary to adopt quite a complicated code consisting of a considerable number of digits. Such a code, for example, may be built up as follows:

Responsibility centre	*Number of digits required*
Division	000
Factory	000
Cost centre	000
Type of expense	0000
Total digits required	13

For example, let us assume that the Glasgow factory (code 123) is part of the fibres' division (code 015), and it has a maintenance department (code 666). During a particular period, it purchases some raw materials (code 5432). When the invoice is eventually received from the supplier, it will be coded as follows: 015/123/666/5432.

It would be possible, of course, to reduce the number of digits if there were only a small number of responsibility centres, and a detailed analysis was not required. If possible, codes of just a few digits should be introduced, as mistakes can very easily be made even when a code has less than six digits.

We must emphasize that a cost accounting system will not work properly unless its purpose has been explained to *all* staff, and they understand its importance. This applies particularly to those who are coding the documents, since in our experience they do not always appreciate the importance of what they are doing. Operating a cost accounting system is expensive. There is no point having one if the information cannot be relied on, or for that matter, if it is not wanted. A cost accounting system should never be imposed on staff: it should only be introduced after there has been considerable consultation, and when it is generally agreed that there will be some obvious benefits.

Stage 3: Select an appropriate product costing system

The third stage in implementing a cost accounting system is to choose a method that is suitable for the type of goods produced or services administered by the entity. The CIMA definition of a product cost is as follows:

> **Product cost**: the cost of a finished product built up from its cost elements.

Do not be mislead by the term 'product': it also applies to service industries. However, the system will vary in some detail depending upon the nature of the product. For example, the costing system required for a glass manufacturing company will not be the same as that for a hospital. Different product costing systems will be examined in Chapter 13.

The CIMA definition of a product cost quoted above included the term 'cost elements'. CIMA again provides a helpful definition. It is as follows:

> **Elements of cost**: the constituent parts of costs according to the factors upon which expenditure is incurred, namely, materials, labour and expenses.

The elements of cost are shown in diagrammatic form in Exhibit 9.5. However, the diagram may be somewhat misleading. For example, the selling price appears to be derived by adding a profit element to the total cost of sales. It is rare for selling prices to be derived in this way. They are usually determined by the market, i.e. prices charged by the entity's competitors. However, the diagram does help to establish the point about controlling costs. If the entity cannot fix its own selling prices, then in order to make a profit it has to ensure its total costs are less than its total sales revenue.

Another point about Exhibit 9.5. is the way that it depicts the treatment of overheads. This is another problem an entity faces when installing a cost accounting system. We outline the problem in the next sub-section, and we will also be returning to it in subsequent chapters.

Stage 4: Determine the treatment of fixed production overheads

The fourth main stage in implementing a cost accounting system concerns the treatment of fixed production overheads. Overheads refer to those costs that cannot be economically identified with specific units, and fixed means that they are unlikely to increase (or decrease) irrespective of how many units are produced. The entity can deal with such overheads in one of two ways:

1 it can share them out among specific units, using some agreed apportionment method; or
2 it can just deal with them in total.

Exhibit 9.5 Unit cost structure: The elements of cost

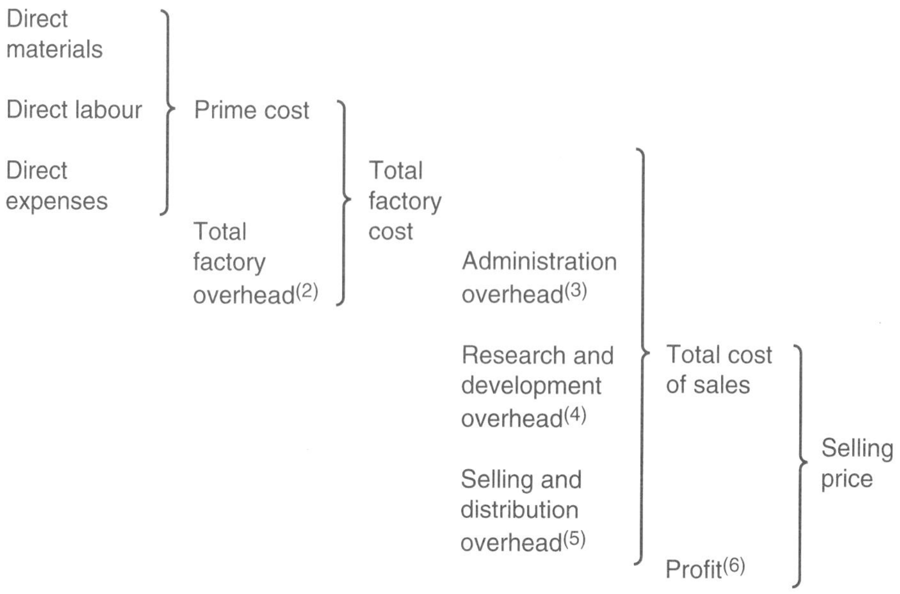

Notes:

1 The structure of the elements of cost is very similar to the structure used in Chapter 5 for manufacturing accounts. The chart assumes that the cost accounting system is based on absorption costing.

2 Factory overhead includes indirect production costs and other factory costs that are not easy to identify with production.

3 Administration overhead will include the non-factory cost of operating the company.

4 Research expenditure includes the cost of working on new products and processes. Development costs relate to costs incurred in developing existing products and processes.

5 Selling and distribution overhead includes the cost of promoting the company's product and the cost of distributing them to its customers.

6 A profit loading may be added to the total cost of sales in order to arrive at the unit's selling price.

The method of dealing with overheads is important, because it will determine what type of accounts will need to be kept within the ledger system, and the nature of the information that can be extracted from it.

The first method is known as *absorption costing*, and we shall be dealing with it in Chapter 11. The second method is known as *marginal costing*, and it will be examined in Chapter 12. The two techniques are shown in diagrammatic format in Exhibit 9.6.

Exhibit 9.6 Absorption costing versus marginal costing

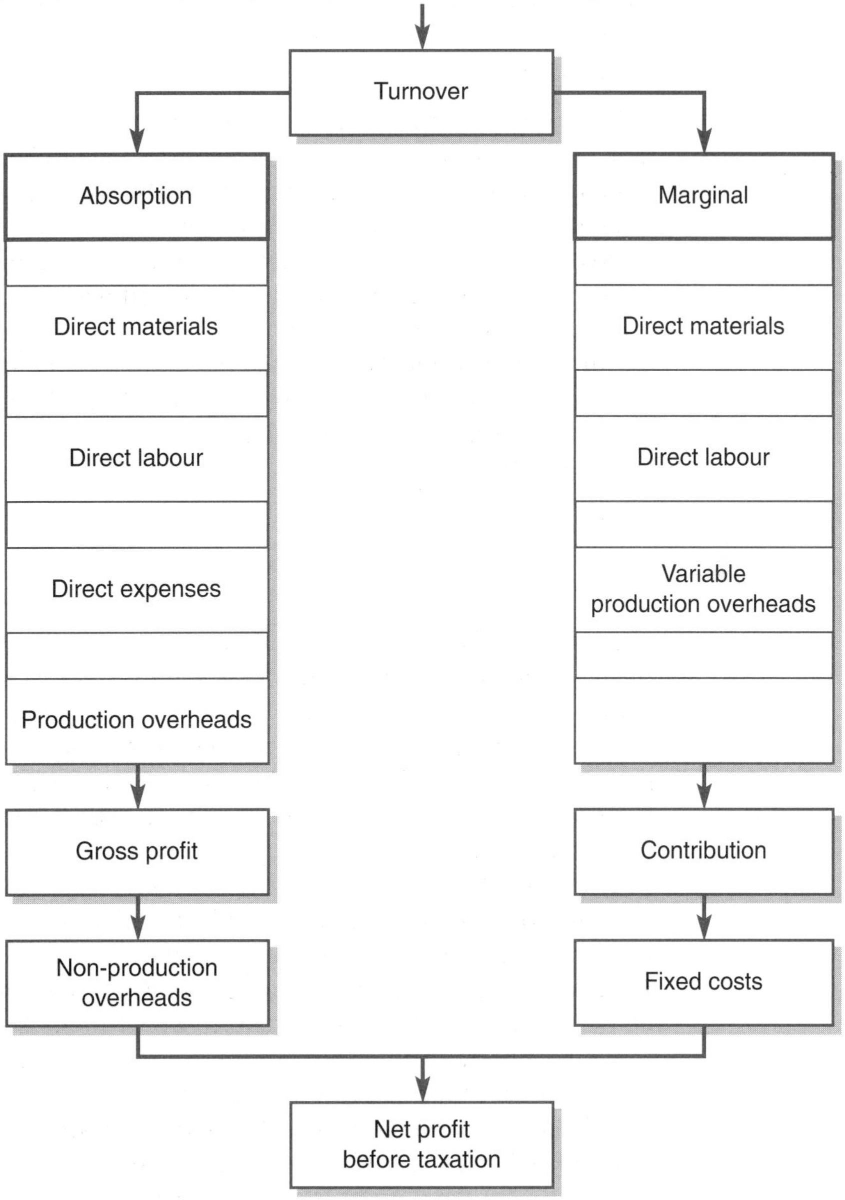

```
                              ┌──────────────┐
                              │   Turnover   │
                              └──────────────┘
         ┌──────────────────────────┴──────────────────────────┐
         ▼                                                      ▼
┌──────────────────────┐                        ┌──────────────────────┐
│     Absorption       │                        │      Marginal        │
├──────────────────────┤                        ├──────────────────────┤
│                      │                        │                      │
│   Direct materials   │                        │   Direct materials   │
│                      │                        │                      │
│   Direct labour      │                        │   Direct labour      │
│                      │                        │      Variable        │
│   Direct expenses    │                        │ production overheads │
│                      │                        │                      │
│ Production overheads │                        │                      │
└──────────────────────┘                        └──────────────────────┘
         ▼                                                      ▼
┌──────────────────────┐                        ┌──────────────────────┐
│     Gross profit     │                        │     Contribution     │
└──────────────────────┘                        └──────────────────────┘
         ▼                                                      ▼
┌──────────────────────┐                        ┌──────────────────────┐
│    Non-production    │                        │     Fixed costs      │
│      overheads       │                        │                      │
└──────────────────────┘                        └──────────────────────┘
         └──────────────────────────┬──────────────────────────┘
                                     ▼
                          ┌──────────────────────┐
                          │      Net profit      │
                          │   before taxation    │
                          └──────────────────────┘
```

Irrespective of whether an entity adopts an absorption or a marginal cost approach to keeping its cost accounting records, it should be noted that *non-production overheads* are not normally apportioned to production units. We will return briefly to non-production overheads in Chapter 11.

Stage 5: Choose a cost control method

The fifth main stage in implementing a costing system is to decide on the method of control. There are two basic choices, and they may be summarized as follows:

1 **Budgetary control**. To obtain the maximum benefit from a cost accounting system, an entity is recommended to incorporate a system of budgetary control. Basically, this involves working out what the entity intends to do (i.e. planning), and what it will cost. The control element involves comparing the actual results against the plans, and then taking any corrective action if this is considered necessary. We deal with budgetary control in Chapter 14.

2 **Standard costing**. This method of control is similar to budgeting except that it involves setting plans and controlling the results for individual units or processes. Standard costing is discussed in further detail in Chapter 15.

CONCLUSION

This chapter has given a brief outline of the nature and purpose of cost and management accounting, and how such a system would be installed in an entity. Management accounting is now a very important branch of accounting. Its main purpose is to assist management in planning and controlling the entity. Cost accounting is a sub-branch of management accounting. Its main purpose is to provide record information and extract it in a format suitable for use in managerial decision making.

There are five main steps involved in installing a cost accounting system: (a) the creation of an organizational structure; (b) the installation of a documentary coding system; (c) the selection of a product costing system; (d) a decision about the treatment of fixed production overheads; and (e) the choice of an appropriate cost control method.

We will be returning to many of the ideas outlined in this chapter in greater detail in subsequent chapters. Chapter 10 deals with direct costs, and Chapter 11 with indirect costs. Marginal costing is explored in Chapter 12, while Chapter 13 outlines various product costing systems along with a summary of some current issues in management accounting. Cost control methods are covered in Chapter 14 on budgeting and in Chapter 15 on standard costing. Chapter 16, the final chapter in this part of the book, examines some capital investment appraisal techniques.

KEY POINTS

1 Management accounting is one of the main branches of accounting.
2 Its main purpose is to assist management in planning and controlling an entity.
3 Important elements involved in this work involve devising plans, and monitoring their progress.
4 Cost accounting is an important sub-branch of management accounting.
5 Its main aim is to record data, and to summarize them in a form that will assist in managerial decision making.
6 Cost accounting requires an organizational structure, coded documents, a suitable product costing system, a decision about the treatment of overheads, and the selection of a cost control method.

CHECK YOUR LEARNING

1 Fill in the missing blanks in each of the following statements:
   (a) Financial accounting is more concerned with reporting to parties _____ to the business.
   (b) _____ accounting is more concerned with internal reporting.
   (c) Planning and controlling is essential in an entity in order to ensure that it is run _____ and _____.

2 How many main stages are there in implementing a cost accounting system?

3 List three main elements of cost.

4 Which two main methods of cost accounting methods may be chosen in order to deal with fixed production overheads?

5 What are the two main cost control techniques?

ANSWERS

1 (a) external/outside   (b) management   (c) effectively; efficiently
2 five
3 materials; labour; overheads
4 absorption costing; marginal costing
5 budgetary control; standard costing

QUESTIONS

9.1 Briefly describe the differences between financial accounting and management accounting.

9.2 List at least five categories of cost.

9.3 List the five main categories into which the organizational structure of a manufacturing entity might be classified?

9.4 What is a cost centre?

9.5 Distinguish between absorption costing and marginal costing.

ADDITIONAL QUESTIONS (WITHOUT ANSWERS)

9.6 Write a report for your managing director examining the main types of information that may be obtained from a cost and management accounting system.

9.7 Business organizations are usually based on some form of authoritative organizational structure.

Required:
(a) Outline the main principles to be adopted in developing a business organizational structure; and
(b) explain why such a structure is necessary for the successful implementation of a cost and management accounting system.

CHAPTER 10

Direct costs

Accounting change leaves BR over £100m better off

By Richard Tomkins,
Transport Correspondent

British Rail is braced for a hostile reaction to an accounting move that will benefit its profit-and-loss account by more than £100m when it publishes its annual results tomorrow.

Critics are likely to claim the figures have been massaged in an effort to stimulate private sector interest in railway privatisation, due to start next year.

BR will defend itself by saying the move is a delayed response to long-standing government directive requiring its accounts to conform with normal commercial practice.

The move will boost operating profits by nearly £90m for InterCity, one of the most attractive parts of the railway to private-sector train operators.

In the year to March 1992, InterCity originally reported a profit of just £2m. That is now understood to have been restated to show a profit of £91m.

In the latest year, ending March 1993, InterCity was expected to have suffered heavily from recession. Now it is expected to be substantially in profit.

Overall, BR has been left £120m better off by the move, reducing last year's pre-tax losses of £145m to a loss of just £25m. In the year just ended, the effect is expected to reduce losses of £250m-£300m to a loss of about £170m.

BR says the change was ordered by the Department of Transport in December 1989 to give a more accurate picture of business performance, and has taken until now to introduce.

The main effect is to alter the way BR accounts for infrastructure renewals such as track replacement or resignalling. Previously, these were counted as costs in the year in which they were incurred, and were charged to the profit-and-loss account.

Under the new policy, infrastructure spending will be counted as capital investment and charged to the balance sheet. The only cost charged against the profit-and-loss account will be an annual one for depreciation calculated over the asset's lifetime.

A further boost will come from a change in the treatment of grants for capital investment. Instead of being written off in the year in which they are received, they will be released to the profit-and-loss account over the lifetime of the investment, partly offsetting the depreciation charge.

BR said InterCity was a particularly big beneficiary of the accounting change because it was the division that had invested most.

The Financial Times, 29 June 1993

Exhibit 10.0 Controlling costs is not the only way of improving profits, but it helps!

We suggested in the last chapter that the principal aims of cost accounting are to help management (a) plan and (b) control an entity's activities. This may be achieved by establishing a number of clear objectives, creating an organizational structure based on responsibility accounting, laying down plans in accordance with the overall objectives, and then leaving individual managers to get on with working towards achievement of those plans. The control element is achieved by a constant comparison of the actual results against the plans. If the actual results are unfavourable, then action will be taken to bring them into line with the plans. This process requires managers to be fed regular and frequent information about the progress of their respective cost centres.

In the case of a production unit cost centre, this procedure will almost certainly require a comparison to be made of the actual cost of each unit against the planned cost. As we suggested in Chapter 9, unit costs are comprised of two main elements: direct costs and indirect costs. The formal definition of these terms as given by CIMA is as follows:

> **Direct cost**: expenditure which can be economically identified with a specific saleable cost unit.
> **Indirect cost**: expenditure on labour, materials or services which cannot be economically identified with a specific saleable cost unit.

These definitions are fairly imprecise. For example, what is meant by 'economically identified'? All we can suggest is that it depends on the circumstances (like much else in accounting): what is economic in one case may not be economic in another. Ultimately, it becomes a matter of judgement. This means that it is possible to calculate a wide range of different costs for a specific unit (or a process or a service) depending upon the definition adopted of 'economically identifiable'. In practice, it is usually possible (from an economic point of view) to identity some material and labour costs with specific units of production, but it is not usually possible for other types of expenses to be similarly identified.

You will appreciate, therefore, that a great deal of subjective judgement is involved in identifying direct costs, although, as we shall see in the next chapter, there is even more subjectivity in dealing with indirect costs! As a result, the entire process of building up the total cost of a particular unit is based on a number of arguable assumptions. This means that it is very rare to be able to calculate the exact cost of any one unit, because the cost of that unit will depend upon the assumptions adopted in calculating it.

In this chapter, we examine the problems involved in dealing with *direct* costs. We will assume that we are dealing with a manufacturing company that makes a specific units. We recognize that not all manufacturing companies produce such units, and that not all entities are manufacturing. However, we shall come back to this point in Chapter 13. We begin our examination of direct costs by having a look at *materials*.

By the end of this chapter, you will be able to:
- identify costs that can be traced to particular activities;
- describe four main methods of charging direct materials costs to production;
- recognize direct labour costs and other direct expenses.

DIRECT MATERIAL COSTS

Materials consist of raw materials and component parts. CIMA defines raw materials as 'goods purchased for incorporation into products for sale'. The CIMA terminology does not define component parts, but we can assume that they include those miscellaneous items of ready-made parts purchased for the assembly of a finished unit. Before we examine the treatment of 'direct' material cost we must offer some explanation of what is perhaps meant by 'economically identifiable'.

As an example, let us assume that we are making a table. We can observe that it is made of wood. It might be relatively easy to quantify the amount of wood used, simply because it is substantial enough to be recognized. However, the screws needed to hold this table together may be so insignificant that it is not worth while identifying them separately from screws used in making other tables. In other words, it is just not worth the expense involved in trying to work out the cost of (say) six screws. Thus, the wood would probably be treated as a direct material cost, while the screws would be classed as indirect.

In practice, it is often relatively easy to identify the physical quantity of goods used in manufacturing a particular unit (as we could do with the screws in the above example), but it is not always easy to determine what they cost. For example, this is often the case with liquids, because they are usually stored in containers. The containers will be topped up from time to time with additional purchases, but all of the contents of the container will become mixed. As the price paid for the various batches of liquid will almost certainly vary, what then is the cost of issuing (say) one litre of liquid to production? There is no way of knowing. Hence, although it may be relatively easy to identify the actual quantity of material issued to production, it may be difficult to cost it.

If the amount of material used in production is significant enough, the accountant would estimate the cost. Of course, if he can work out the actual cost of materials, he would use that cost. Not surprisingly, this is known as the *specific identification method*. If it cannot be used, then he will have to choose one of a number of other recognized accounting methods. We outline some of them in the following sub-sections.

First-in, first-out (FIFO)

It is sensible to issue the oldest stock to production first, followed by the next oldest and so on, and this should be done wherever possible. This method of storekeeping means that old stock is not kept in store for very long, thus avoiding the possibility of deterioration or obsolescence. However, some materials (such as grains and liquids) may be stored in such a way that they become a mixture of old and new stock, and it is then not possible to identify each separate purchase. None the less, in pricing the issue of stock to production, it would still seem logical to follow the first-in, first-out procedure, and charge production with the oldest price first, followed by the next oldest price, and so on.

FIFO is a very common method used in charging out materials to production. The procedure is as follows:

1 Start with the price paid for the oldest material in stock, and charge any issues to production at that price.
2 Once all of the goods originally purchased at that price have been issued, use the next oldest price until all of that stock has been issued.
3 The third oldest price will be next used, then the fourth, and so on.

The prices attached to the issue of goods to production are not, of course, necessarily the same as those that were paid for the actual purchases of those goods. Indeed, they cannot be, for if had been possible to identify *specific* receipts with *specific* issues, the specific identification method would have been used.

We illustrate the use of the the FIFO pricing method in Exhibit 10.1.

Exhibit 10.1 The FIFO method of charging direct materials to production

The following information relates to the receipts and issue of material X into stock during January 19X1:

Date	Receipts into stores			Issue to production
	Quantity	Price	Value	Quantity
	Units	£	£	Units
1.01X1	100	10	1000	
10.01.X1	150	11	1650	
15.01.X1				125
20.01.X1	50	12	600	
31.01.X1				150

Required :
Using FIFO (first in, first out) method of pricing the issue of goods to production, calculate the following:
(a) the issue prices at which goods will be charged to production; and
(b) the closing stock value at 31 January 19X1.

Answer to Exhibit 10.1

(a) The issue price of goods to production:

Date of issue	Tutorial note	Calculation		£
5.01.X1	(1)	100	units × £10=	1000
	(2)	25	units × £11=	275
		125		£1275
31.01.X1	(3)	125	units × £11=	1375
	(4)	25	units × £12=	300
		150		£1675

(b) Closing stock:

25 units × £12=	£300

Check:

Total receipts (1000 + 1650 + 600)	3250
Total issues (1275 + 1675)	2950
Closing stock	£300

Tutorial notes

1 The goods received on 1 January 19X1 are now assumed to have all been issued.
2 This leaves 125 units in stock out of the goods received on 10 January 19X1.
3 All the goods purchased on 10 January 19X1 are assumed to have been issued.
4 There are now 25 units left in stock out of the goods purchsed on 20 January 19X1.

Although Exhibit 10.1 is a simple example, it can be seen that if the amount of material issued to production includes a number of batches purchased at different prices, the FIFO method involves using a considerable number of different prices.

Last-in, first-out (LIFO)

Instead of FIFO, we could use LIFO. LIFO adopts the *latest* prices, and these are then used to charge the issue of goods to production. Once the physical quantity of the issue has been identified, the goods are priced to production at the price paid for the last receipt of goods. If more goods are being issued than had been purchased at that price, the next oldest price will be used, and so on. This means that if there has been a large number of issues of goods to production, the total value of the issue could be comprised of a considerable number of prices.

The LIFO method is illustrated in Exhibit 10.2.

Exhibit 10.2 The LIFO pricing method of charging direct materials to production

The same data are used as in Exhibit 10.1

Required :
Using LIFO (last in, first out) method of pricing the issue of goods to production, calculate the following:
(a) the issue prices at which goods will be issued to production; and
(b) the value of closing stock at 31 January 19X1.

Answer to Exhibit 10.2

(a) The issue price of goods to production:

Date of issue	Tutorial note	Calculation	£
15.01.X1	(1)	125 units × £11=	1375
31.01.X1	(2)	50 units × £12=	600
		25 units × £11=	275
		75 units × £10=	750
		150	£1625

(b) Closing stock value:
25 units × £10=   £250

Check:

Total receipts (1000 + 1650 + 600)	3250
Total issues (1375 + 1625)	3000
Closing stock	£250

Tutorial notes

1 This was the latest price at 15 January 19X1.
2 The latest price at 31 January 19X1 was £12, but only 50 units were purchased. The next oldest price, therefore, is used, but only 25 units are left at £11, because 125 units were priced out at £11 on 15 January 19X1. The balance is made up of goods purchased for £10 per unit, which also leaves 25 units in stock at that price.

Like the FIFO method, LIFO can involve a great deal of tedious arithmetic, but there is a certain logic to it. By using the latest prices, production is being charged with current economic prices. Thus the closing stock will be be valued at much older prices, and this means that by using LIFO in times of rising prices, the gross profit tends to be lower than it does under FIFO (thereby allowing, to some extent, for inflation).

The lower profit arises because of a combination of a higher charge to production, and a lower value placed on closing stock (a lower closing stock figure reduces the cost of goods sold, because a smaller amount is being deducted from the total of opening stock plus purchases). The reverse applies, of course, when prices are falling.

In the UK, FIFO is an acceptable method of valuing stock for taxation purposes, but LIFO is not permitted. A company could still use LIFO for internal purposes if it wanted, but a different method would then have to be adopted in computing its tax charge. As this would involve more work, LIFO tends not to be used (although this is not the case in the United States of America).

Weighted average

In order to avoid the detailed arithmetical calculations which are involved in using both the FIFO and LIFO methods, it is possible to substitute an *average* pricing method. There are two main types, and they are as follows:

1 periodic weighted average;
2 continuous weighted average method.

The *periodic* weighted average method involves calculating an average issue price based on all the prices paid for materials purchased during a particular period. The goods issued to production during that period are all then charged out at that average price. By using this method, it is not possible to charge out goods to production until after the end of the period, because the issue price cannot be calculated until all the purchase prices for the period are known. This method is illustrated in Exhibit 10.3.

Exhibit 10.3 The periodic weighted average pricing method of charging direct materials to production

The same data are used as in Exhibit 10.1.

Required:
Using the periodic weighted average method of pricing the issue of goods to production, you are required to calculate the following:
(a) the issue price for January 19X1; and
(b) the closing stock value as at 31 January 19X1.

Answer to Exhibit 10.3

(a) The issue price of goods to production:

Total value of receipts (1000 + 1650 + 600) =	£3250
Total number of units received (100 + 150 + 50) =	300
∴ Periodic weighted average price =	£10.83

∴ Issue on 15.01.X1: 125 units x £10.83 =   £1354

∴ Issue on 31.01.X1: 150 units x £10.83 =   £1625

(b) Value of closing stock:

	£	£
Total receipts		3250
Less: Issues – 15.01.X1	1354	
– 25.01.X1	1625	2979
∴ Closing stock value =		£271

The *continuous* weighted average method necessitates frequent changes to be made in calculating issues prices. Although it appears a very complicated method, it is the easiest one to use provided that the receipts and issues of goods are recorded in a stores ledger account. An example of a stores ledger account in shown in Exhibit 10.4.

Exhibit 10.4 Example of a stores ledger account

Stores ledger account										
Material: Maximum:						Code: Minimum:				
Date	Receipts				Issues				Stock		
	GRN No.	Quantity	Unit price	Amount	Stores Req. No.	Quantity	Unit price	Amount	Quantity	Unit price	Amount
			£	£			£	£		£	£

Notes
GRN = goods received note
Stores Req. No = Stores requisition number

You will note that the stores ledger account shows both the quantity and the value of the stock in store at any one time. The *continuous weighted average price* is obtained by dividing the total value of the stock by the total quantity. A new price will be struck each time new purchases are taken into stock. Unlike the periodic weighted average price, it is not necessary to wait until the end of the period before calculating a new price.

The continuous weighted average price method is illustrated in Exhibit 10.5. We use the same data that we have used in the earlier exhibits, but we have taken the opportunity to present a little more information, so that we can explain more clearly how to to calculate a continuous weighted average price.

Exhibit 10.5 The continuous weighted average price method of charging direct materials to production

You are presented with the following information relating to the receipt and issue of material X into stock during January 19X1:

Date	Receipts into stores			Issues to production			Stock balance	
	Quantity	Price	Value	Quantity	Price	Value	Quantity	Value
	Units	£	£	Units	£	£	Units	£
1.01.X1	100	10	1000				100	1000
10.01.X1	150	11	1650				250	2650
15.01.X1				125	10.60	1325	125	1325
20.01.X1	50	12	600				175	1925
25.01.X1				150	11.00	1650	25	275
31.01.X1							25	275

Note:
The company uses the continous weighted average method of pricing the issue of goods to production.

Required :
Check that the prices of goods issued to production during January 19X1 have been calculated correctly.

Answer to Exhibit 10.5

The issue prices of goods to production during January 19X1 using the continuous weighted average method have been calculated as follows:

15.01.X1 $\dfrac{\text{Total stock value at 10.01.X1}}{\text{Total quantity in stock at 10.01.X1}} = \dfrac{2650}{250} = £10.60$

25.01.X1 $\dfrac{\text{Total stock value at 20.01.X1}}{\text{Total quantity in stock at 20.01.X1}} = \dfrac{1925}{175} = £11.00$

Other methods

There are a considerable number of other methods that may be considered suitable for determining the pricing of material issues to production. Many of them are are examined in some detail in accounting textbooks, but they have little practical importance. However, there is one other method which we ought to mention. This is the *standard cost method* (which we will be meeting again in Chapter 15).

The standard cost method involves estimating what materials are likely to cost in the future. Instead of the actual price, the estimated cost (or *planned* cost, as it is known) would then be used to charge out the cost of materials. Of course, any substantial difference between actual and planned costs would have to be investigated, and it might mean there had been a considerable under- (or over-) charging of materials to production. Any difference would be written off in total to the profit and loss account for the period in which the difference occurred.

The standard cost method is usually adopted as part of a standard costing system. Such a system adopts standard costs for all elements of cost. Frequent comparisons have to be made with actual costs and immediate action taken if there are any discrepancies between them.

CHOICE OF PRICING METHOD

It would be helpful at this stage if we summarized the advantages and disadvantages of each of the pricing methods outlined in the previous section in order to make it easier for your to decide which one you prefer. The summary is shown in Exhibit 10.6.

Exhibit 10.6 A summary of the advantages and disadvantages of different material pricing methods

Method	Advantages	Disadvantages
1 FIFO	(a) it is logical (b) it may match the physical issue of goods (c) the closing stock is closer to the current economic value (d) the stores ledger account is self-balancing: there are no balancing adjustments to be written off to the profit and loss account (e) it is acceptable for tax purposes	(a) it is arithmetically cumbersome (b) the cost of production relates to out-of-date prices

Method	Advantages	Disadvantages
2 LIFO	(a) production is charged with costs that are close to current economic values (b) the stores ledger account is self-balancing: there are no balancing adjustments to be written off to the profit and loss account	(a) it is arithmetically cumbersome (b) the closing stock is valued at much older prices that may bear little relationship to current economic prices (c) this method is not acceptable for tax purposes
3 Periodic weighted average	(a) it is simple to calculate (b) the issue price relates both to quantities purchased and to changing prices (c) it is highly accurate because the price is not calculated until the period has ended (d) it achieves a compromise between the lowest and highest prices (e) it is not distorted by the quantities purchased	(a) the price cannot be calculated until the period has ended (b) prices in previous periods are ignored (c) it lags behind current economic prices (d) it may not relate to any price actually paid (e) it may be necessary to write off balancing to the profit and loss account adjustments
4 Continuous weighted average	(a) previous period prices are taken into account (b) it is easy to calculate (c) it relates the prices of goods purchased to quantities purchased (d) it produces a price that is not distorted either by low or high prices paid, or by small or large quantities purchased (e) a new price is calculated on new receipts of goods, so the price is constantly being updated	(a) it lags behind current economic prices (b) it may not relate to prices actually paid (c) it may be necessary to write off balancing adjustments to the profit and loss adjustments to the profit and loss account

Precise rules cannot be laid down for the choice of a pricing method. LIFO is largely unsuitable for use in the UK because of its tax disadvantages. The periodic weighted average method is somewhat impracticable since it can only be used *after* the period has ended. FIFO attempts to match the physical issue the goods by using the oldest prices first. In the case of some purchases (such as liquids and grains), this may largely be a theoretical advantage, because there can be no certainty that the goods being issued necessarily relate to the order in which they were purchased. On balance, the continuous weighted average method would appear to be the one that is most suitable: it is easy to calculate, and it does not result in the use of an extreme range of prices. None of these methods would be adopted if the company operates a standard costing system, but even standard costs can lead to some considerable problems. We will be looking at these in Chapter 15.

As we have seen, the charging of material costs to production in not a straightforward exercise. It is usually clear what *quantity* of material has been transferred to production (if not, then it would be treated as an indirect cost), but it may be much more difficult to price it. This problem arises because it is often not possible to distinguish between different purchases of goods, and hence to isolate each individual price.

In future, as modern production techniques become more sophisticated, direct material pricing may become less of a problem. Many companies are now installing what are called 'just-in-time' (JIT) production methods, and these methods may also be applied to purchasing. We will come back to JIT in Chapter 13.

The need to use an estimated price (irrespective of the method adopted), means that the total cost of the unit must also be an estimate. In turn, this also means that the value of any closing stock must also be any estimate, and that will the affect the the entity's financial accounts. However, as we shall see in the next chapter, the problems become more acute, because we also have to estimate how much *indirect* cost we are going to charge each unit. It follows that it is normally impossible to talk about the true cost of anything. Costs can only be true in an arithmetical sense. This point will be developed in greater detail in the next chapter.

We can now move on to have a look at the other main type of direct cost: labour. We do so in the next section.

LABOUR

Labour costs include the cost of employees' salaries, wages, bonuses, and employer's national insurance and pension fund contributions. Wherever it is economically viable to do so, we will want to charge labour costs to each specific unit, otherwise they will have to be treated as part of indirect costs.

The identification and pricing of direct labour is much easier than is the case with direct material. Basically, the procedure is as follows:

1 Employees working on specific units will be required to keep a record of how many hours they spend on each unit.
2 The total hours worked on each unit will then be multiplied by their hourly rate.
3 A percentage amount will added to the total to allow for the the employer's labour costs (e.g. national insurance, pension fund contributions and holiday pay).
4 The total amount then is then charged directly to that unit.

We illustrate the procedure in Exhibit 10.7

Exhibit 10.7 The charging of direct labour cost to production

Alex and Will are working on Unit X. Alex is paid £10 an hour, and Will £5. Both men are required to keep an accurate record of how much time they have spent on Unit X. Alex spends 10 hours and Will 20. The employer has estimated that it costs him an extra 20% on top of what he pays them to meet his contributions towards national insurance, pension contributions and holiday pay.

Required:
Calculate the direct labour cost of producing Unit X.

Answer to Exhibit 10.7

Calculation of the direct labour cost

	Hours	Rate per hour	Total
		£	£
Alex	10	10	100
Will	20	5	100
			200
Employer's costs (20%)			40
Total direct labour cost			£240

We should make it clear that in practice it is by no means easy to obtain an accurate estimate of the direct labour cost of one unit. We start from an assumption that if it is very difficult to do so, then probably it will be costly, and therefore not worth while. But even in those cases where there is no doubt that employees are working on one unit (as in Exhibit 10.7), we are dependent upon them keeping an accurate record. If you have ever had it do this in your own job, you will know that this is not easy, especially if you are frequently being switched from one job to another. It is also difficult to account for all those five minutes spent chatting in the corridor!

Notwithstanding the difficulties, however, it is important that management should emphasise to the employees just how important it is that they do keep an accurate record of their time. Labour costs may form a high proportion of total cost (especially in service industries), so tight control is important. This is particularly so, of course, if tender prices are based on total unit cost. A high cost could mean that the company fails to get a contract, whereas too low a cost diminishes profit.

OTHER DIRECT COSTS

Apart from material and labour costs, there may be other types of costs that can be economically identified with specific units. These are, however, relatively rare, because unlike material and labour, it is usually difficult to trace a physical link with specific units. It only occurs, therefore, in some very special cases. For example, the company may hire specialist plant for work on a specific unit. It is then easy to identify the physical link between the unit and the plant, and to identify the hire charge with the unit.

Notwithstanding the difficulties of identifying other expenses with production, it is important to do so wherever possible. Otherwise, the indirect charge becomes bigger and bigger, and that causes even more problems in building up the cost of a specific unit.

CONCLUSION

This chapter has dealt specifically with *direct* costs, i.e. those costs that can be economically identified with specific cost units. We have emphasized that even where such an exercise is viable, there are still considerable problems. In identifying direct material cost, for example, it is usually necessary to estimate its cost. This may be done by adopting a well-established pricing method, such as FIFO, LIFO, periodic weighted average, continuous weighted average, or a standard cost, but this still does not disguise the fact that, whichever method is used, they all lead to an *estimated* charge. This means, of course, that the value of any closing stock must also be an estimate. Thus, it is not possible to argue that there is any one true cost. Indeed, a cost may only be accurate in the arithmetical sense, because it is usually based on a whole series of assumptions.

It is not usually too difficult to estimate direct labour costs, provided that accurate time records are kept by employees working on specific units. However, where employees switch from one job to another in quick succession (as with supervisory time) it may be difficult to keep an accurate record. Thus, supervisory time, for example may have to be treated as an indirect cost.

There are occasionally some other costs that can be charged directly to production. These are comparatively rare, and are usually so obvious that no great difficulty arises in treating them as direct costs.

KEY POINTS

1 Unit costing serves three main purposes: (a) in valuing closing stock; (b) in estimating selling prices; and (c) in planning and controlling overall costs.

2 The procedure involves identifying those costs that are economically identifiable with a specific unit: it may be impossible to identify some costs with a specific unit, while with other costs it may be possible, but it either becomes very expensive or the results may be immaterial.

3 Some materials can be readily identified with specific units, but their purchase price is not always known. If these are to be charged to specific units, an estimated price has to be determined. The most common methods are FIFO. LIFO, periodic weighted average, continuous weighted average, and standard cost.

4 Wherever possible, labour costs should also be charged directly to specific units. This is not usually as difficult as it is with materials.

5 Some other services may also be identifiable with a specific unit, and if their costs can be economically determined, they should be charged directly to production.

CHECK YOUR LEARNING

1 Fill in the missing blanks in each of the following statements:
   (a) Expenditure which can be economically identified with a specific saleable unit is known as a _____ _____.
   (b) Overhead is comprised of _____ material cost, _____ labour cost, and _____ expenses.
   (c) Goods purchased for incorporation into products for sale are known as _____ _____.
   (d) Labour costs include employees' _____ and _____, bonuses, employer's national insurance and pension fund contributions.

2 List three methods of charging the cost of direct materials to production.

3 What is the term used to describe a planned or an estimated cost?

4 Is the following statement true or false?
   When prices are rising, using current economic prices to charge materials to production results in a lower level of profit.   True/False

ANSWERS

1 (a) direct cost   (b) indirect; indirect; indirect;   (c) raw materials   (d) salaries; wages
2 FIFO; LIFO; weighted average (periodic or continuous)
3 standard costing
4 True

QUESTIONS

10.1 The following stocks were taken into stores as follows:

1.1.X1 1000 units @ £20 per unit.
15.1.X1   500 units @ £25 per unit.

There were no opening stocks.
On 31.1.X1 1250 units were issued to production.

Required:
Calculate the amount which would be charged to production on 31 January 19XI for the issue of material on that date using each of the following methods of material pricing:

1 FIFO (first in, first out);
2 LIFO (last in, first out); and
3 periodic weighted average.

10.2 The following information relates to material ST 2:

		Units	Unit price £	Value £
1.2.X2	Opening stock	500	1.00	500
10.2.X2	Receipts	200	1.10	220
12.2.X2	Receipts	100	1.12	112
17.2.X2	Issues	400	–	–
25.2.X2	Receipts	300	1. I5	345
27.2.X2	Issues	250	–	–

Required:
Calculate the value of closing stock at 28 February 19X2 assuming that the continuous weighted average method of pricing materials to production has been adopted.

10.3 You are presented with the following information for Trusty Limited:

19X3	Purchases (units)	Unit cost £	Issues to production (units)
1 January	2 000	10	
31 January			1 600
1 February	2 400	11	
28 February			2 600
1 March	1 600	12	
31 March			1 000

Note: There was no opening stock.

Required:
Calculate the value of closing stock at 31 March 19X3 using each of the following methods of pricing the issue of materials to production.

1 FIFO (first in, first out);
2 LIFO (last in, first out); and
3 continous weighted average.

10.4 The following information relates to a certain raw material taken into stock:

	Receipts		Issues to production
	Units	Value	Units
		£	
1.4.X4	50	350	
3.4.X4	30	213	
5.4.X4			60
9.4.X4	20	139	
11.4.X4			25
14.4.X4			10
18.4.X4	35	252	
23.4.X4	60	423	
26.4.X4			100
30.4.X4	45	315	

The opening stock was 20 units at a value of £120.

Required:
Using the periodic weighted average method of pricing the issue of materials to production, calculate the value of the closing stock as at 30 April 19X4.

10.5 The following information relates to Steed Limited for the year to 31 May 19X5:

	£
Sales	500 000
Purchases	440 000
Opening stock	40 000
Closing stock value using the following pricing methods:	
1 FIFO (first in, first out)	90 000
2 LIFO (last in, first out)	65 000
3 Periodic weighted average	67 500
4 Continous weighted average	79 950

Required:
Prepare Steed Limited's gross profit for the year to 31 May 19X5 using each of the above closing stock values.

10.6 Iron Limited is a small manufacturing company. During the year to 31 December 19X2 it has taken into stock and issued to production the following items of raw material, known as XY1:

Date 19X2	Receipts into stock			Issues to production
	Quantity (litres)	Price per unit £	Total value £	Quantity (litres)
January	200	2.00	400	
February				100
April	500	3.00	1 500	
May				300
June	800	4.00	3 200	
July				400
October	900	5.00	4 500	
December				1 400

Notes:
1 There were no opening stocks of raw materials XY1.
2 There other costs involved in converting raw material XY1 into the finished product (marketed as *Carcleen*) amounted to £7000.
3 Sales of *Carcleen* for the year to 31 December 19X2 amounted to £20 000.
4 For the purpose of this question, an accounting period is defined as the calendar year.

Required:
(a) Illustrate the following methods of pricing the issue of materials to production:
   1 first in, first out (FIFO);
   2 last in, first out (LIFO);
   3 periodic weighted average;
   4 continous weighted average.
(b) Calculate the gross profit for the year using each of the above methods of pricing the issue of materials to production.

ADDITIONAL QUESTIONS (WITHOUT ANSWERS)

10.7 The folowing information relates to one of Osprey's stores ledger accounts:

Date 19X8	Receipts Quantity (kilos)	Price per kilo £	Issues Quantity (kilos)
January	145	10	100
February	180	9	170
March	240	11	150
April	110	11	250
May	220	12	200
June	150	15	165

Stock at 1 January 19X8: 20 kilos at £11.50 per kilo.

Required:
Calculate the cost of the closing stock of the above materialas at 30 June 19X8 using each of the following stock valuation methods:

(a) FIFO (first in, first out);
(b) LIFO (last in, first out); and
(c) continuous weighted average.

10.8 Waters has recorded the following information in one of its stores ledger accounts:

19X9	*Receipts*		*Sales*
	Quantity	*Cost per unit*	
	Units	*£*	*Units*
January	290	6	200
February	580	9	700
March	410	12	300
April	730	15	600
May	290	5	200
June	410	7	600
July	720	11	700
August	600	9	500
September	580	11	600
October	590	7	700
November	840	11	750
December	280	4	300

At 1 January 19X9 there were 60 units in stock at a total estimated value of £300. The selling price was £10 per unit.

Required:
(a) Compare and contrast the gross profit for the year to 31 December 19X9 using each of the following stock valuation methods:
   (i)   FIFO (first in, first out);
   (ii) LIFO (last in, first out); and
   (iii) continuous weighted average; and
(b) prepare a report for the Board of Directors outlining which stock valuation method you would recommend.

CHAPTER 11

Indirect costs

Costs-hit Mozolowski & Murray calls in receiver

One of Scotland's largest manufacturers of conservatories has been forced to call in the receivers – despite high sales and a full order book.

The board of Mozolowski & Murray instructed its bankers to call in Price Waterhouse as receiver yesterday, after a refinancing attempt failed at the eleventh hour.

The Kinross-based firm, which employs about 60 people, was the subject of a management buy-out in the second half of 1991.

Since then, turnover has held up well at around £5 million a year, and with order books standing at the £1 million mark.

However, costs have escalated out of control since the MBO, according to Iain Bennet of Price Waterhouse.

With the new board placing a great deal of emphasis on sales growth, soaring advertising costs appear to have been a major factor contributing to the firm's troubles.

Mozolowski & Murray's directors have been locked in discussion with its bankers in an ultimately unsuccessful attempt to refinance the company.

The final straw was when last month's tradng performance proved poorer than anticipated to the tune of £50,000.

Mr Bennet said: "The board are clearly disappointed that the refinancing effort failed, but I take comfort from the fact that a number of people were willing to invest more in the company."

He was unable at this stage to rule out redundancies among the workforce. "The first thing we have to do is look at the cost base. Unfortunately, that might mean job losses," he said.

The Scotsman, 6 August 1993

Exhibit 11.0 The lack of control over advertising almost forced this company into liquidation. It was fortunate in being rescued by its original founder within a few days of the receivers being called in.

In the last chapter, we dealt with the treatment of direct costs. Direct costs were defined as those costs that can be economically identified with a specific unit. In this chapter, we will examine the treatment of indirect costs, i.e. those costs that cannot be economically identified with a specific unit. The total of such costs is known as *overhead*. Overhead includes material costs, labour costs, and other types of cost.

If the recommendations outlined in Chapter 9 are accepted, and all costs are first allocated (i.e. charged to) a specific cost centre, then as far as specific units are concerned, indirect costs will arise from two main sources:

1 from production cost centres: those costs that cannot be economically identified with specific units (even though it may have been possible to identify them initially with a specific production cost centre);

2 from service cost centres: those costs that are not directly identifiable with production cost centres, and so they must all be indirect costs as far as specific units are concerned.

There is no obvious way of identifying indirect costs with specific units (otherwise, there would not be indirect costs), so if we want to calculate the total cost of producing a particular unit, the indirect costs have to be shared out.

We explain how this is done in subsequent sections. The procedure is also outlined in diagrammatic form in Exhibit 11.1.

Exhibit 11.1 Flow of costs in an absorption costing system

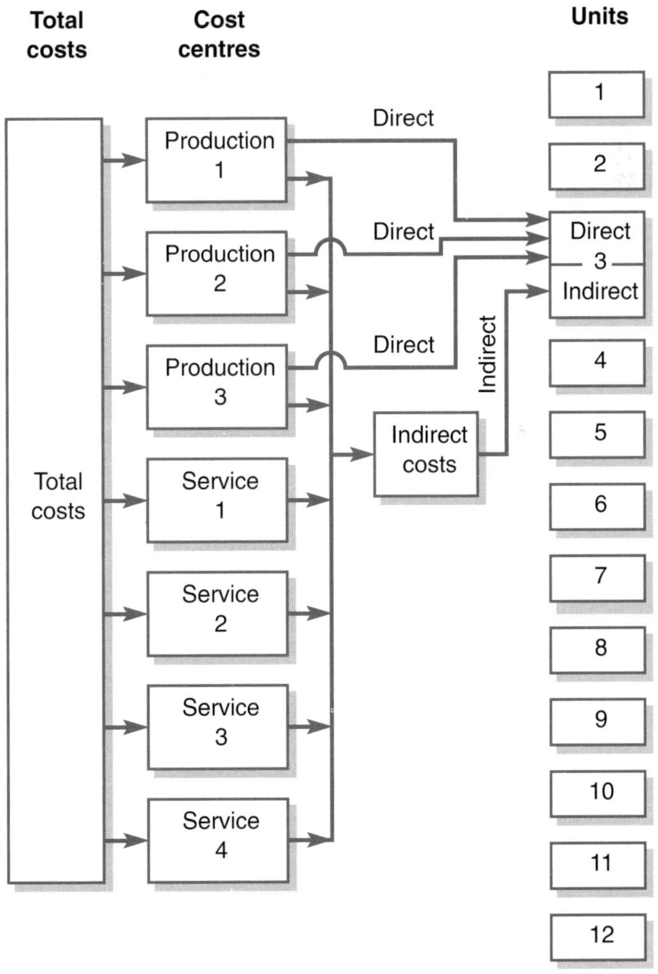

By the end of this chapter, you will be able to:
- describe the nature of indirect production costs;
- apportion service costs to production cost centres;
- absorb indirect costs into cost units;
- identify non-production costs;
- assess the usefulness of absorption costing.

PRODUCTION OVERHEAD

We suggested in Chapter 9 that if cost accounting is going to be used as part of a control system, it is necessary for all costs within an entity to become the direct responsibility of a designated cost centre manager. In this section, we will examine how the total production overhead eventually gets charged to specific units. It is quite a complicated procedure, so we will take you through it in stages.

Stage 1: Allocate all costs to specific cost centres

We cannot emphasize too strongly the importance of allocating all costs to specific cost centres. Allocation is the process of charging whole items of cost either to cost centres (or to cost units), i.e. they can be easily identified with the cost centre (or cost unit) so there is no need to apportion the cost. It is not always easy to allocate every type of cost to an easily identifiable cost centres, and sometimes it is necessary to select a particular cost centre, even though its manager may only be remotely responsible for the expenditure.

For control purposes, however, it will still be necessary to charge such costs to a particular cost centre, and then, at some later stage, to *apportion* (i.e. share) them among those cost centres that have benefited from the service provided. For example, most cost centres could be expected to be charged with their share of factory rates, and so they would probably be apportioned on the basis of floor space. Thus, if the rates for the factory amounted to £5000, and it had just two cost centres, one occupying 60% of the total floor space, and the other the remaining 40%, the first cost centre would be charged with £3000 of the rates and the second cost centre with £2000.

Stage 2: Share out the production service cost-centre costs

Production service cost-centre costs will contain mainly allocated costs, but they could also include some apportioned costs (e.g. rates). By definition, service cost-centre costs are not directly related to the production of specific units, so in relation to production units, they must all be indirect costs.

The next stage in unit costing, therefore, is to share out the total service cost-centre costs among the production cost centres. This is usually done by apportioning the total cost for each service cost centre among those production cost centres that benefit from the service. The method used to apportion the service cost-centre costs may be very simple. A few of the more common methods are as follows:

1 **Numbers of employees**. This method would be used for those service cost centres that provide a service to individual employees, e.g. the canteen, the personnel department, and the wages office. Costs will then be apportioned on the basis of the number of employees working in a particular production department as a proportion of the total number of employees working in all production cost centres.
2 **Floor area**. This method would be used for such cost centres as cleaning and building maintenance.
3 **Activity**. Examples of where this method might be used include the drawings office (on the basis of drawings made), materials handling (based on the number of requisitions processed), and the transport department (on the basis of vehicle operating hours).

A problem arises in dealing with the apportionment of service cost centre costs when service cost centres provide a service for each other. For example, the wages office will probably provide a service for the canteen staff, and in turn, the canteen staff may provide a service for the wages staff. Before the service cost-centre costs can be apportioned among the production cost-centres, therefore, it is necessary to make sure that service cost-centre costs are charged out to each other.

The problem becomes a circular one, however, because it is not possible to charge (say) some of the canteen costs to the wages office until the canteen has been charged with some of the costs of the wages office. Similarly, it is not possible to charge out the wages office costs until part of the canteen costs have been charged to the wages office. The treatment of *reciprocal* service costs (as they are called) can become an involved and time-consuming process unless a clear policy decision is taken about their treatment. There are three main ways of dealing with this problem:

1 **Ignore interdepartmental service costs**. If this method is adopted, the respective service cost-centre costs are only apportioned among the production cost-centres. Any servicing that the service cost-centres provide for each other is ignored.
2 **Specified order of closure**. This method requires the service cost centre-costs to be closed off in some specified order and apportioned among the production cost centres and the remaining service cost centres. As the service cost centres are gradually closed off, there will eventually be only one service cost centre left. Its costs will then be apportioned among the production cost centres. Some order of closure

has to be specified, and this may be quite arbitrary. It may be based, for example, on those centres which provide a service for the largest number of other service cost centres, or it could be based on the cost centres with the highest or the lowest cost in them prior to any interdepartmental servicing. It could also be based on an estimate of the benefit received by other centres.

3 **Mathematical apportionment.** Each service cost centre's total cost is apportioned among production cost centres and other service cost centres on the basis of the estimated benefit provided. The effect is that additional amounts keep being charged back to a particular service cost centre as further apportionment takes place. It can take a very long time before there is no more cost to charge out to any of the service cost-centres, but when it is reached, all the service cost centre costs will then have been charged to the production cost centres. This method involves a great deal of exhaustive arithmetical apportionment, and it is also very time consuming, especially where there are a great many service cost centres. Although it is possible to carry out the calculations manually, it is more easily done by computer programme.

In choosing one of the above methods, it should be remembered that they all depend upon an *estimate* of how much benefit one department receives from another. Such an estimate amounts to no more than an informed guess. It seems unnecessary, therefore, to build an involved arithmetical exercise on the basis of some highly questionable assumptions. We would suggest that, in most circumstances, interdepartmental servicing charging may be ignored.

We have covered some fairly complicated procedures in dealing with Stage 1 and 2, so before moving on to Stage 3 we will illustrate the procedure in Exhibit 11.2.

Exhibit 11.2

You are provided with the following indirect cost information relating to the New Manufacturing Company Limited for the year to 31 March 19X5:

	£
Cost centre	
Production 1: indirect expenses (to units)	24 000
Production 2: indirect expenses (to units)	15 000
Service cost centre A: allocated expenses	20 000
Service cost centre B: allocated expenses	8 000
Service cost centre C: allocated expenses	3 000

Additional information:

The estimated benefit provided by the three service cost centres to other cost centres is as follows:

Service cost centre A: Production 1 50%; Production 2 30%; Service cost centre
B 10%; Service cost centre C 10%.

Service cost centre B: Production 1 70%; Production 2 20%; Service cost centre
C 10%.

Service cost centre C: Production 1 50%; Production 2 50%.

Required:
Calculate the total amount of overhead to be charged to cost centre units for both
Production cost centre 1 and Production cost centre 2 for the year to 31 March 19X5.

Answer to Exhibit 11.2

New Manufacturing Company Limited
Overhead distribution schedule for the year to 31 March 19X5

Cost centre	*Production*		*Service*		
	1	2	A	B	C
	£	£	£	£	£
Allocated indirect expenses	24 000	15 000	20 000	8 000	3 000
Apportion service cost centre costs:					
A (50 : 30 : 10 : 10)	10 000	6 000	(20 000)	2 000	2 000
B (70 : 20 : 0 : 10)	7 000	2 000	–	(10 000)	1 000
C (50 : 50 : 0 : 0)	3 000	3 000	–	–	(6 000)
Total overhead to be absorbed by specific units	£44 000	£26 000	–	–	–

Tutorial notes

1 Units passing through Production cost centre 1 will have to share total overhead expenditure amounting to £44 000. Units passing through Production cost
centre 2 will have to share total overhead expenditure amounting to £26 000.
Units passing through both departments may be identical: for example, they
might be assembled in cost centre 1 and packed in cost centre 2.

2 The total amount of overhead to be shared amongst the units is £70 000
(44 000 + 26 000 or 24 000 + 15 000 + 20 000 + 8000 + 3000). The total
amount of overhead originally collected in each of the five cost centres does
not change.

3 This exhibit does involve some interdepartmental re-apportionment of service
cost centre costs. However, no problem arises because of the basis upon
which the question requires the respective service cost centre costs to be
apportioned.

4 The objective of apportioning service centre costs is to charge them out to the
production cost centres so that they can be charged to specific units.

Stage 3: Absorption of production overhead

Once all the indirect costs has been collected in the production cost centres, the next step is to charge the total amount to specific units. This procedure is known as *absorption*.

The method of absorbing overhead into units is normally a simple one. Accountants recommend a single factor, preferably one that is related as closely as possible to the movement of overhead. In other words, an attempt is made to choose a factor which directly correlates with the amount of overhead expenditure incurred. Needless to say (like so much else in accounting) there is no obvious factor to choose! Indeed, if there was an obvious close relationship, it is doubtful whether it would be necessary to distinguish betweeen direct and indirect costs.

There are six main methods that can be used for absorbing production overhead. All six methods adopt the same basic equation:

$$\text{Cost centre overhead absorption rate} = \frac{\text{Total cost centre overhead}}{\text{Total cost centre activity}}$$

A different absorption rate will be calculated for each production cost centre, so by the time that a unit has passed through a number of production cost centres, it will have been charged with a share of overhead from a number of production cost centres.

The six main absorption methods are as follows.

Specific units   This method is the simplest to operate. It is calculated as follows:

$$\text{Absorption rate} = \frac{\text{Total cost centre overhead}}{\text{Number of units processed in the cost centre}}$$

The same rate would be applied to each unit, thus it is only a suitable method if the units are identical.

Direct material cost

$$\text{Absorption rate} = \frac{\text{Total cost centre overhead}}{\text{Cost centre total direct material cost}} \times 100$$

The direct material cost of each unit is then multiplied by the absorption rate.

It is unlikely that there will normally be a strong relationship between the direct material cost and the level of overheads. There might be some special cases, but they are probably quite unusual, e.g. where a company uses a high level of precious metals and its overheads strongly reflect the cost of protecting those materials.

Direct labour costs

$$\text{Absorption rate} = \frac{\text{Total cost centre overhead}}{\text{Cost centre total direct labour cost}} \times 100$$

The direct labour cost of each unit is then multiplied by the absorption rate.

Overheads tend to relate to the amount of time that a unit spends in production, so this method may be particularly suitable, since the direct labour cost is a combination of hours worked and rates paid. It may not be suitable, however, where the total direct labour cost consists of a relatively low level of hours worked and of a high labour rate per hour, because the cost will not then relate very closely to time spent in production.

Prime cost

$$\text{Absorption rate} = \frac{\text{Total cost centre overhead}}{\text{Prime cost}} \times 100$$

The prime cost of each unit is then multiplied by the absorption rate. This method assumes that there is a close relationship between prime cost and overheads. In most cases, this is unlikely to be true.

As there is probably no close relationship between either direct materials or direct labour and overheads, then it is unlikely that there will be much of a correlation between prime cost and overheads. Hence, the prime cost method tends to combine the disadvantages of both the direct materials and the direct labour cost methods without having any real advantages of its own.

Direct labour hours

$$\text{Absorption rate} = \frac{\text{Total cost centre overhead}}{\text{Cost centre total direct labour hours}}$$

The direct labour hours of each unit are then multiplied by the absorption rate.

This method is highly acceptable, especially in those cost centres that are labour intensive, because time spent in production is related to the cost of overhead incurred.

Machine hours

$$\text{Absorption rate} = \frac{\text{Total cost centre overhead}}{\text{Cost centre total machine hours}}$$

The total machine hours used by each unit is then multiplied by the absorption rate.

This is a most appropriate method to use in those departments that are machine intensive. There is probably quite a strong correlation between the amount of machine time that a unit takes to produce and the amount of overhead incurred.

We illustrate these absorption methods in Exhibit 11.3.

Exhibit 11.3

Old Limited is a manufacturing company. The following information relates to the assembling department for the year to 30 June 19X8:

	Assembling department
	Total
	£000
Direct material cost incurred	400
Direct labour incurred	200
Total factory overhead incurred	100
Number of units produced	10 000
Direct labour hours worked	50 000
Machine hours used	80 000

Required:
Calculate the overhead absorption rates for the assembling department using each of the following methods:
1 specific units;
2 direct material cost;
3 direct labour cost;
4 prime cost;
5 direct labour hours; and
6 machine hours.

Answer to Exhibit 11.3

1 Specific units:

$$\text{OAR} = \frac{\text{TCCO}}{\text{Number of units}} = \frac{100\,000}{10\,000} = £10.00 \text{ per unit}$$

2 Direct material costs:

$$\text{OAR} = \frac{\text{TCCO}}{\text{Direct material cost}} \times 100 = \frac{100\,000}{400\,000} \times 100 = 25\%$$

3 Direct labour cost:

$$\text{OAR} = \frac{\text{TCCO}}{\text{Direct labour cost}} \times 100 = \frac{100\,000}{200\,000} \times 100 = 50\%$$

4 Prime cost:

$$\text{OAR} = \frac{\text{TCCO}}{\text{Prime cost}} \times 100 = \frac{100\,000}{400\,000 + 200\,000} \times 100 = 16.67\%$$

5 Direct labour hours:

$$\text{OAR} = \frac{\text{TCCO}}{\text{Direct labour hours}} = \frac{100\,000}{50\,000} = £2.00 \text{ per direct labour hour}$$

6 Machine hours:

$$OAR = \frac{TCCO}{\text{Machine hours}} = \frac{100\ 000}{80\ 000} = £1.25 \text{ per machine hour}$$

Exhibit 11.3 illustrates the six absorption methods outlined in the text. You will appreciate, of course, that in practice, only one absorption method would be chosen for each production cost centre, although different production cost centres may adopt different methods, e.g. one may choose a direct labour hour rate, and another may adopt a machine hour rate.

The most appropriate absorption rate method will depend upon individual circumstances. A careful study would have to be made of the correlation between (a) direct materials, direct labour, other direct expenses, direct labour hours, and machine hours; and (b) total overhead expenditure. However, it is generally accepted that overhead tends to move with time, so the longer a unit spends in production, the more overhead that particular unit will generate. Thus, each individual unit ought to be charged with its share of overhead based on the *time* that it spends in production.

This argument suggests that labour intensive cost centres should use the direct labour hour method, while machine intensive departments should use the machine hour rate.

A COMPREHENSIVE EXAMPLE

At this stage it would be useful to illustrate overhead absorption in the form of a comprehensive example, although it would clearly be impracticable to use one that involved hundreds of cost centres. In any case, we are trying to demonstrate the principles of absorption costing, and too much data would obscure those principles. Thus, the example contains only the most essential information.

Exhibit 11.4

Oldham Limited is a small manufacturing company producing a variety of pumps for the oil industry. It operates from one factory that is geographically separated from its head office. The components for the pumps are assembled in the assembling department; they are then passed through to the finishing department where they are painted and packed. There are three service cost centres: administration, stores and work study.

The following costs were collected for the year to 30 June 19X6:

Allocated cost centre overhead costs:	£000
Administration	70
Assembling	25
Finishing	9
Stores	8
Work study	18

Additional information:

1 The allocated cost centre costs are all considered to be indirect costs as far as specific units are concerned.

2 During the year to 30 June 19X6, 35 000 machine hours were worked in the assembling department, and 60 000 direct labour hours in the finishing department.

3 The number of employees working in each department was as follows:

Administration	15
Assembling	25
Finishing	40
Stores	2
Work study	3
	85

4 During the year to 30 June 19X6, the stores received 15 000 requisitions from the assembling department, and 10 000 requisitions from the finishing department. The stores department did not provide a service for any other department.

5 The work study department carried out 2000 chargeable hours for the assembling department, and 1000 chargeable hours for the finishing department.

6 One special pump (code named MEA 6) was produced during the year to 30 June 19X6. It took 10 machine hours of assembling time, and 15 direct labour hours were worked on it in the finishing department. Its total direct costs (material and labour) amounted to £100.

Required:

(a) Calculate an appropriate absorption rate for:
  (i)   the assembling department; and
  (ii) the finishing department.
(b) Calculate the total factory cost of the special pump.

Answer to Exhibit 11.4

(a)   OLDHAM LIMITED
        Overhead distribution schedule for the year to 30 June 19X6

| Cost centre | Production | | Service | | |
	Assembling	Finishing	Adminis-tration	Stores	Work study
	£000	£000	£000	£000	£000
Allocated costs (1)	25	9	70	8	18
Apportion administration (2):					
25 : 40 : 3 : 2	25	40	(70)	2	3

Apportion stores (3):					
3 : 2	6	4	–	(10)	–
Apportion work study:					
2 : 1	14	7	–	–	(21)
Total overhead to be absorbed	£70	£60	–	–	–

Tutorial notes

1 The allocated costs were given in the question.
2 Administration costs have been apportioned on the basis of employees. Details were given in the question. There were 85 employees in the factory, but 15 of them were employed in the administration department. Administration costs have, therefore, been apportioned on a total of 70 employees, or £1000 per employee. The administration department is the only service department to provide a service for the other service departments, so no problem of interdepar-tmental servicing arises.
3 The stores costs have been apportioned on the number of requisitions made by the two production cost centres, that is 15 000 + 10 000 = 25 000, or 3 to 2.
4 The work study costs have been apportioned on the basis of chargeable hours i.e. 2000 + 1000 = 3000, or 2 to 1.

Calculation of chargeable rates:
1 Assembling department:
$$\frac{TCCO}{Total\ machine\ hours} = \frac{70\ 000}{35\ 000} = £2.00\ per\ machine\ hour$$

2 Finishing department:
$$\frac{TCCO}{Total\ direct\ labour\ hours} = \frac{60\ 000}{60\ 000} = £1.00\ per\ direct\ labour\ hour$$

It would seem appropriate to absorb the assembling department's overhead on the basis of machine hours because it appears to be a machine intensive department. The finishing department appears more labour intensive, so its overhead will be absorbed on that basis.

(b) MEA 6: Calculation of total factory cost

	£	£
Direct costs (as given)		100
Add: factory overhead:		
Assembling department (10 machine hours × £2.00 per MH)	20	
Finishing department (15 direct labour hours × £1.00 per DLH)	15	35
Total factory cost		£135

You are now recommended to work through Exhibit 11.4 without reference to the answer.

NON-PRODUCTION OVERHEAD

In this chapter so far, we have concentrated on the apportionment and absorption of production overheads. Most companies will, however, incur expenditure on activities that are not directly connected with production activities. For example, there could be selling and distribution costs, research and development costs, and head office administrative expenses. How should all of these costs be absorbed into unit cost?

Before this question can be answered, it is necessary to find out why we should want to apportion them. There are basically three main reasons:

1 **Control**. The more that an entity's costs are broken down, the easier it is to monitor them. It follows that just as there is an argument for having a detailed system of responsibility accounting at cost centre level, so there is an argument for having a similar system at unit cost level. However, in the case of non-production expenses, this argument is not a very strong one. We have seen that in order to calculate the production cost of a unit it is necessary to apportion a whole range of costs, and then to select a number of appropriate absorption methods. The practice of absorbing fixed production overhead into specific units is a highly questionable procedure, but for control purposes, the absorption of non-production fixed overheads is even more questionable.

The relationship between units produced and non-production overhead is usually so remote, that no meaningful estimate of the benefit received can be made. Consequently, the apportionment of non-production overhead is merely an arithmetical exercise, and no manager could be expected to take responsibility for such costs that have been charged to his cost centre, still less for any that have then been built into unit cost. From a control point of view, therefore, the exercise is not very helpful.

2 **Selling price**. In some cases, it might be necessary to add to the production cost of a specific unit, a proportion of non-production overhead in order to determine a selling price that covers all costs and allows a margin for profit. This system of fixing selling prices can apply in some industries, e.g. in tendering for long-term contracts, or in estimating decorating costs. In most cases, however, selling prices are determined by the market, and companies are not usually in a position to fix their selling prices, based on cost with a percentage added on for profit (this is known as cost-plus pricing).

Even when selling prices cannot be based on total cost, however, it may be useful to have an idea of the company's total unit costs in relation to its selling prices, but it must be clearly recognized that the calculation of such total units costs can only provide a general guide.

3 **Stock valuation**. You might think that a total unit cost will be required for stock valuation purposes, since it will be necessary to include the

cost of closing stocks in the annual financial accounts. However, there is an accounting standard that deals with the valuation of stocks (SSAP 9), and it does not permit the inclusion of non-production overhead in stock valuation. Thus, a company is unlikely to apportion non-production overhead for internal stock valuation purposes if a different method has to be adopted for financial reporting purposes.

It is obvious from the above summary that there are few benefits to be gained by charging a proportion of non-production overhead to specific cost units. In theory, the exercise is attractive, because it would be both interesting and useful to know the *actual* (or true) cost of each unit produced. In practice, however, it is impossible to arrive at any such cost, so it seems pointless to become engaged in spurious arithmetical exercises just for the sake of neatness.

The only real case for apportioning non-production overhead applies where selling prices can be based on cost. What can be done in those situations? There is still no magic formula, and an arbitrary estimate has still to be made. Sometimes a percentage is applied to the total production cost. This is bound to be somewhat questionable, since there can be no close relationship between production and non-production activities. It follows that the company's tendering or selling price policy will not be rigid if it is based on this type of cost-plus pricing.

It is with some reservation, therefore, that (just in case you do come across the apportionment of non-production overhead in your own company) we introduce you to several ways in which non-production overhead could be apportioned to specific units. Remember though, that this is largely an arithmetical exercise, and does not achieve any further degree of control. If your company does adopt this procedure, you should put your accountants through a fairly severe cross-examination before you accept it. The three methods of apportioning non-production overhead to specific units are as follows:

1 **Administrative overhead**
Administrative overheads could be absorbed by relating the total cost of the overhead to the total cost of production. The formula is as follows:

$$\text{Absorption rate} = \frac{\text{Total administrative overhead}}{\text{Total production cost}} \times 100$$

The absorption rate is then applied to the total production cost of each unit.

It is also possible that in some circumstances the following formula could be adopted:

$$\text{Absorption rate} = \frac{\text{Total administrative overhead}}{\text{Total sales revenue}} \times 100$$

The formula is then applied to the selling price of each particular unit.

2 **Research and development overhead**

As with administrative overhead, a research and development overhead absorption rate may be calculated on the basis of total production cost, i.e:

$$\text{Absorption rate} = \frac{\text{Total research and development overhead}}{\text{Total production cost}} \times 100$$

The rate is then applied to the total production cost of each unit.

3 **Selling and distribution overhead**

The absorption rate for selling and distribution overhead can again be calculated by reference to the total cost of production, i.e.:

$$\text{Absorption rate} = \frac{\text{Total selling and distribution overhead}}{\text{Total cost of production}} \times 100$$

The rate is then applied the total production cost of each unit. Alternatively, it might be related to the sales revenue. The formula would then be:

$$\text{Absorption rate} = \frac{\text{Total selling and distribution overhead}}{\text{Total sales revenue}} \times 100$$

The absorption rate would then be applied to the selling price of each unit.

It must be emphasized once again that the absorption of non-production overhead among specific units does not help in *controlling* costs. It is largely an arithmetical exercise, and it may only be of some use when selling prices are fixed on a cost-plus basis. Before leaving this chapter, there is one further problem in absorbing fixed production overhead that we need to deal with. We do so in the next section.

PREDETERMINED RATES

An absorption rate can, of course, be calculated on a historical basis (i.e. after the event), or it can be predetermined (i.e. calculated in advance).

As we have tried to emphasize all the way through this chapter, there is no close correlation between fixed overhead and any particular measure of activity: we can only apportion it on what seems to be a reasonable basis. However, if we know the total actual overhead incurred, we can make sure that it is all charged to specific units, even if we are not sure of the relationship it has with any particular unit.

To do so, of course, we cannot calculate an absorption rate until we know (a) the *actual* cost of overheads, and (b) the *actual* activity level (whether this is measured in machine hours, direct labour hours, or on some other basis). In other words, we can only make the calculation when we know what has happened.

The adoption of historical absorption rates is not usually very practicable. We have to wait until the actual period is over before we can calculate an absorption rate, cost our products and invoice our customers. We would, therefore, normally wish to calculate an absorption rate in advance. This is known as a *predetermined* rate.

In order to calculate a predetermined absorption rate, we have to estimate both the overhead which we think the company will incur, and the direct labour hours or machine hours that we expect to work (if we are using hours as the method of absorbing overhead). If one or other of these estimates turns out to be inaccurate, then we would have either under-charged our customers (if the rate was too low), or over-charged them (if the rate was too high).

This situation could be very serious for the company. Low selling prices caused by using a low absorption rate could have made the company's products very competitive, but there is not much point in selling a lot of units if they are being sold at a loss. Similarly, a high absorption rate may result in a high selling price. Thus, each unit may make a large profit, but not enough units may be sold to enable the company to make an overall profit.

Exhibit 11.5 The under- and over-recovery of overheads by using pre-determined rates

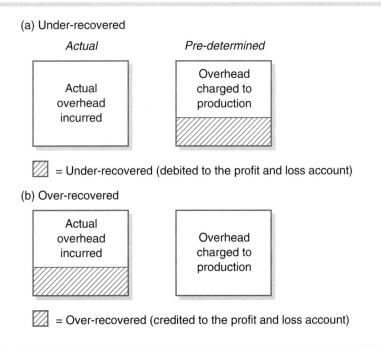

(a) Under-recovered

Actual   *Pre-determined*

Actual overhead incurred

Overhead charged to production

= Under-recovered (debited to the profit and loss account)

(b) Over-recovered

Actual overhead incurred

Overhead charged to production

= Over-recovered (credited to the profit and loss account)

The use of predetermined absorption rates may, therefore, result in an under- or an over-recovery of overhead. Overhead may be under- or over-absorbed if the company has under- or over-estimated the actual cost of the overhead or the actual level of activity (irrespective of how it is measured). The difference between the actual overhead incurred and the total overhead charged to production (calculated on a predetermined basis) gives rise to what is known as a *variance*. If the actual overhead incurred is in excess of the amount charged out, the variance will be *adverse*, i.e. the profit will less than expected. However, if the total overhead charged to production was less than was estimated, then the variance will be *favourable*. (The effect of this procedure is shown in diagrammatic form in Exhibit 11.5.) Other things being equal, a favourable variance gives rise to a higher profit, and an adverse variance results in a lower profit.

It is a cardinal rule in costing that variances should be written off to the profit and loss account at the end of the costing period in which they were incurred. It is not considered fair to burden the next period's accounts with the previous period's mistakes. In other words, it is as well to start off a new accounting period unburdened by the past.

Throughout this chapter we have clearly expressed many reservations about the way in which accountants have traditionally dealt with overheads. In recent years, dissatisfaction about overhead absorption has become widespread, and now a different technique called *activity based costing* (ABC) is being advocated. We will have a look at ABC in Chapter 13.

CONCLUSION

Absorption costing aims to help management plan and control a company's operations more effectively and efficiently, it is necessary for stock valuation purposes, and in some industries it may be used in determining selling prices.

The technique is a highly questionable one. It depends initially on being able to determine those costs that can be economically identified with specific unit (direct costs), and those that cannot (indirect costs). This distinction is not always easy to make in practice, and there is a danger that more and more costs will be then identified as indirect.

The technique is carried out in a number of stages. The first stage is to allocate all costs to appropriate cost centres. The second stage is to apportion those costs that provide a benefit to other cost centres. The third stage is to apportion service cost-centre costs among relevant production cost centres. The fourth stage is to absorb the total overhead collected in each production cost centre into specific units.

The apportionment and the absorption stages both depend upon a relationship being established between the overhead cost and an appropriate measure of activity, even though such relationships are likely to be somewhat distant. Non-production overhead is also sometimes absorbed into unit costs, but the relationship between this type of expenditure and production activity is even more remote than it is for production overhead. For control purposes, therefore, it is not recommended, although it is sometimes done if selling prices are fixed on a cost-plus pricing basis.

Overhead absorption rates have usually to be predetermined, because it is impracticable to wait until the period has ended before production is charged with a share of overheads. If this were the case, then it would take some time before goods were eventually invoiced to customers. The use of predetermined rates means that some overhead may be over- or under-absorbed at the period end, and, as a result, a favourable or an adverse variance will arise. The variance will be favourable or adverse depending upon whether the cost and/ or the level of activity has been over- or under-estimated. Variances should be written off to the profit and loss account for the period in which they were incurred. They should not be carried forward, and hence become a charge in the next period's accounts.

Any variances that do arise may have a very serious long-term effect, as it could mean that the company could be either under- or over-pricing its products. Under-pricing may lead to an under recovery of total cost, whilst over-pricing could result in a reduction in sales volume. Ultimately, this could lead to a lower level of profit.

Absorption costing is a technique which must be used with caution. It is necessary for stock valuation purposes, but as long as managers are aware of its limitations, it can also be useful in helping to control the company's production costs.

KEY POINTS

1 Indirect costs are those that are not economic to identify with specific units. Indirect costs are collectively referred to as overheads.

2 In order to charge unit costs with a share of fixed production overheads, all costs should first be allocated to specific cost centres.

3 The cost of those services that provide a benefit for other cost centres should then be apportioned to those cost centres that have benefited from the service.

4 Costs collected in those service cost centres that provide a direct service to production cost centres should be apportioned to those production cost centres.

5 An absorption rate for each production cost centre should then be calculated by using the direct labour hour or machine hour methods.

6 The absorption rate calculated for each production cost centre is used to charge each production unit passing though it with a share of the overheads.

7 The total production cost of each unit can be calculated as follows: direct material + direct labour + direct expenses + apportioned production overheads.

8 The absorption of non-production overhead is not recommended, except where it necessary for pricing purposes.

9 Normally, absorption rates will be predetermined.

10 Under- or over-absorbed overhead should not be carried forward to the next period's accounts.

CHECK YOUR LEARNING

1 State whether each of the following assertions is either true or false:
(a) Some costs can be both a direct departmental cost and at the same time be an indirect unit cost.   True/False
(b) All service costs are indirect as far as units are concerned.   True/False
(c) Prime cost is the best method to use in absorbing overheads in a machine department.   True/False
(d) Some service costs are included in unit costs.   True/False
(e) The absorption of non-production overheads into production units helps control the cost.   True/False

2 List three methods of absorbing production overheads into specific units.

3 In general, how could non-production overheads be absorbed into product costs?

ANSWERS

1 (a) true (b) true (c) false (d) true (e) false
2 (1) direct material cost; direct labour hour; machine hour
3 as a proportion of total production cost

QUESTIONS

11.1 Scar Limited has two production departments and one service department. The following information relates to January 19X1:

	£
Allocated expenses	
Production department: A	65 000
B	35 000
Service department	50 000

The allocated expenses shown above are all indirect expenses as far as individual units are concerned.
The benefit provided by the service department is shared amongst the production departments A and B in the proportion 60:40.

Required:
Calculate the amount of overhead to be charged to specific units for both production department A and production department B.

11.2 Bank Limited has several production departments. In the assembly department it has been estimated that £250 000 of overhead should be charged to that particular department. It now wants to charge a customer for a specific order. The data relevent are:

	Assembly department	Specific unit
Number of units	50 000	–
Direct material cost (£)	500 000	8.00
Direct labour cost (£)	1 000 000	30.00
Prime cost (£)	1 530 000	40.00
Direct labour hours	100 000	3.5
Machine hours	25 000	0.75

The accountant is not sure which overhead absorption rate to adopt.

Required:
Calculate the overhead to be absorbed by a specific unit passing through the assembly department using each of the following overhead absorption rate methods:
1 specific units;
2 percentage of direct material cost;
3 percentage of direct labour cost;
4 percentage of prime cost;
5 direct labour hours; and
6 machine hours.

11.3 The following information relates to the activities of the production department of Clough Limited for the month of March 19X3:

	Production department	Order number 123
Direct materials consumed (£)	120 000	20
Direct wages (£)	180 000	25
Overhead chargeable (£)	150 000	
Direct labour hours worked	30 000	5
Machine hours operated	10 000	2

The company adds a margin of 50% to the total production cost of specific units in order to cover administration expenses and to provide a profit.

Required:
(a) Calculate the total selling price of order number 123 if overhead is absorbed using the following methods of overhead absorption:
   1 direct labour hours;
   2 machine hours.
(b) State which of the two methods you would recommend for the production department.

11.4 Burns Limited has three production departments (processing, assembly and finishing) and two service departments (administration and work study). The following information relates to April 19X4.

	£
Direct material:	
Processing	100 000
Assembling	30 000
Finishing	20 000
Direct labour:	
Processing (£4 × 100 000 hours)	400 000
Assembling (£5 × 30 000 hours)	150 000
Finishing (£7 × 10 000 hours) + (£5 × 10 000 hours)	120 000
Administration	65 000
Work study	33 000
Other allocated costs:	
Processing	15 000
Assembling	20 000
Finishing	10 000
Administration	35 000
Work study	12 000

Apportionment of costs:

	Process	*Assembling*	*Finishing*	*Work study*
	%	%	%	%
Administration	50	30	15	5
Work study	70	20	10	–

Total machine hours: Processing 25 000

All units produced in the factory pass through the three production departments before they are put into stock. Overhead is absorbed in the processing department on the basis of machine hours, on the basis of direct labour hours in the assembling department, and on the basis of the direct labour cost in the finishing department.

The following details relate to unit XP6:

	£	£
Direct materials:		
Processing	15	
Assembling	6	
Finishing	1	22
Direct labour:		
Processing (2 hours)	8	
Assembling (1 hour)	5	
Finishing (1 hour × £7 + 1 hour × £5)	12	25
Prime cost		£47

XP6: Number of machine hours in the processing department = 6

Required:
Calculate the total cost of producing unit XP6.

11.5 Outlane Limited's overhead budget for a certain period is as follows:

	£000
Administration	100
Depreciation of machinery	80
Employer's national insurance	10
Heating and lighting	15
Holiday pay	20
Indirect labour cost	10
Insurance: machinery	40
property	11
Machine maintenance	42
Power	230
Rent and rates	55
Supervision	50
	£663

The company has four production departments: L, M, N and O. The following information relates to each department.

Department	L	M	N	O
Total number of employees	400	300	200	100
Number of indirect workers	20	15	10	5
Floor space (square metres)	2 000	1 500	1 000	1 000
Kilowatt hours	30 000	50 000	90 000	60 000
Machine maintenance hours	500	400	300	200
Machine running hours	92 000	38 000	165 000	27 000
Capital cost of machines (£)	110 000	40 000	50 000	200 000
Depreciation rate of machines (on cost)	20%	20%	20%	20%
Cubic capacity	60 000	30 000	10 000	50 000

Previously the company has absorbed overhead on the basis of 100% of the direct labour cost. It has now decided to change to a separate machine hour rate for each department.

The company has been involved in two main contracts during the period, the details of which are as follows:

Department	Contract 1: Direct labour hours and machine hours	Contract 2: Direct labour hours and machine hours
L	60	20
M	30	10
N	10	10
O	–	60
	100	100

Direct labour cost per hour in both departments was £3.00.

Required:

(a) Calculate the overhead to be absorbed by both contract 1 and 2 using the direct labour cost method; and

(b) calculate the overhead to be absorbed using a machine hour rate for each department.

11.6 Sarah Limited has two production cost centres (D and P) and three service cost centres (1, 2, and 3). The following information relates to June 19X6.

Allocated costs	£000
Production cost centres:	
D	45
P	35
Service cost centres:	
1	160
2	71
3	34

All of the above costs are indirect as far as individual production units are concerned.

The service cost centres provide a service both for the production cost centres and for each other. The estimated benefit provided by each service cost to the other cost centre is as follows:

		Production		*Service*		
		D	P	1	2	3
		%	%	%	%	%
Service:	1	55	20	–	15	10
	2	45	40	5	–	10
	3	50	10	20	20	–

Required:

Calculate the total amount of overhead to be absorbed by production cost centre D and production centre P.

ADDITIONAL QUESTIONS (WITHOUT ANSWERS)

11.7 Doyle Limited makes a special type of floor covering. The process involves three production cost centres L, M, and N, and two service cost centres, I and O.

The budgeted overhead expenditure for the year to 31 December 19X7 is as follows:

	Total
	£000
Canteen expenses	200
Depreciation	300
Heating and lighting	90
Indirect labour production costs	500
Rent, rates, and insurance	100
Repairs and maintenance	60
	£1250

Other information:

	L	M	N	I	O
			Cost centre		
Budgeted direct labour hours (000s)	50	50	25	–	–
Budgeted machine hours (000s)	100	50	20	–	
Capital value of plant and machinery (£000)	1 500	1 000	250	200	50
Cubic capacity (metres)	30 000	30 000	20 000	5 000	5 000
Direct allocation: repairs and maintenance (£000)	20	20	10	5	5
Floor areas (sq. metres)	4 000	3 000	1 000	1 000	1 000
Number employed	40	30	15	10	5

Required:

(a) Prepare a statement showing the total overhead cost budgeted for each cost centre; and

(b) calculate an appropriate budgeted overhead absorption rate for each of the three production cost centres.

11.8 Greaves Limited has prepared the following budget for the year to 31 March 19X8:

	Production cost centres	
	F	G
Costs:	£000	£000
Direct materials	100	30
Direct labour	300	250
Other direct expenses	40	10
Allocated overheads	30	20
Apportioned overheads	50	30

Other information:

Total budgeted direct labour hours	30 000	25 000
Total budgeted machine hours	40 000	5 000

All units manufactured by Greaves flow through cost centre F and cost centre G.

During the year to 31 March 19X8, the company manufactured a special new unit called 'tacko'. Tacko's actual direct costs per unit were as follows:

	£
Direct materials	90
Direct labour	200
Direct expenses	10

One unit of tacko required 10 direct labour hours and 15 machine hours in cost centre F, and 30 direct labour hours and 5 machine hours in cost centre G.

Required:

(a) Calculate for *each* cost centre five different methods of absorbing production overheads; and

(b) by adopting the most appropriate absorption rates, calculate the total cost of producing one unit of tacko.

CHAPTER 12

Marginal costing

Volkswagan says its car operations are close to break-even

By Kevin Done and Christopher
Parkes in Wolfsburg.

Volkswagen, the troubled German carmaker, is close
to staunching the losses in its core VW car division.

The VW brand operations accounted for around
two-thirds of group turnover and were already
operating close to break-even in April and May,
Mr Ferdinand Piëch, chairman of the VW group
management board said yesterday.

The Volkswagen parent company made a loss
of DM578m (£230m) in January, when the VW
division was forced to implement extensive short-
time working and make provisions for significant
job cuts.

Mr Piëch said VW parent company losses had
been reduced to an estimated DM325m in
February and trimed to DM40m in March.

The VW division had cut 31 days of production
in the first half of this year, but was reducing vehicle stocks. Mr Piëch said he was hopful of
resuming full production after the summer.

He saw no reason to change his earlier forecast
that the group would achieve a small profit for the
full year despite its DM1.25bn first-quarter loss.

Mr Piëch said the first signs were appearing of
a fragile recovery in demand in the German new
car market. Prices were improving in the used car
market and new orders had risen over the past
three weeks.

Mr Piëch said Volkswagen had failed "to prepare for the bad times" in the previous eight years
of rising car sales in Europe.

"We came into the crisis needing to produce at
100 per cent of capacity just to break even,
depending on the plant," he said.

He added the company's goal was to reduce the
break-even level to "70 per cent of capacity or
better," but it could take six years to achieve this
target.

The "drastic measures" taken since January
had reduced the break-even level to 85-90 per
cent, but the company was still using 78 per cent
of capacity.

"My first task is to get into the black by the end
of the year even with this level of capacity utilisa-
tion, to bring the break-even down from 100 per
cent to under 80 per cent," he said.

The Financial Times, 26 May 1993

Exhibit 12.0 This article uses the term 'break-even'. The term is covered in this chapter.

As we suggested in Chapter 9, once a company has decided to install a
cost accounting system and it has chosen an appropriate product costing system, it has to decide how it should deal with fixed production
overhead. It has two choices: it can either absorb fixed overheads into
product costs, or it can ignore them. The first approach is known as
absorption costing, and the second approach is known as *marginal* costing.
We examined absorption costing in the last chapter, while in this one we
are going to look at marginal costing.

You will recall that absorption costing may provide some misleading
information, especially if it is used for short-term decision making. The
main problem arises because it requires all costs to be shared out among

specific units, irrespective of whether those costs change as a result of greater or lesser activity. This procedure lends weight to the argument that those costs that do not change with activity (i.e. fixed costs) should not be charged to specific units.

This argument is a very attractive one, especially when it is related to short-term problems. As the chapter develops, we hope to convince you about usefulness of marginal costing, but first we must have another look at what we mean by fixed costs.

LEARNING OBJECTIVES

> By the end of this chapter, you will be able to:
> ● describe the difference between a fixed cost and a variable cost;
> ● use marginal costing in managerial decision making;
> ● analyse its importance when taking decisions.

THE PROBLEM OF FIXED COSTS

In absorption costing, we do not recognize the distinction between fixed costs and variable costs. Those costs were referred to in Chapter 9, and here are the formal CIMA definitions:

> **Fixed cost:** the cost which is incurred for a period, and which, within certain output and turnover limits, tends to be unaffected by fluctuations in the levels of activity (output or turnover). Examples are rent, rates, insurance, and executive salaries.
> **Variable cost:** cost which tends to vary with the level of activity.

In absorption costing we disregard the fact that fixed costs will not be affected by changes in levels of activity, and yet we charge some of those costs to that unit as though they had been affected by it! This questionable procedure can best be illustrated by an example.

Suppose that we are costing a particular car journey by someone who already owns a car, and that the car is fully taxed and insured. The the main cost of the journey will be that spent on petrol (although the car may depreciate more quickly, and it might require more servicing). The tax and insurance costs will not be affected by one particular journey: they are fixed costs, no matter how many extra journeys are undertaken. Thus, as far as a specific journey is concerned, we are only interested in the extra cost, i.e. the cost of the petrol. The decision to estimate only the *extra* cost of the journey (or for that matter, the extra cost of producing one more unit) gives rise to the system known as marginal costing.

The formal CIMA definition is as follows:

> **Marginal costing:** the accounting system in which variable costs are charged to cost units and fixed costs of the period are written off in full against the aggregate contribution. Its special value is in decision making.

In the above example, if we used absorption costing in estimating the cost of the journey, we would add up all the costs of running the car over (say) a year and divide the total cost by its annual mileage. The average (or absorbed cost) per mile would then be applied to the mileage expected to be incurred on that particular journey. It would clearly be absurd to cost it in this way: the total cost of running the car will not be affected by the journey. What we need to calculate is the marginal (or the extra) cost of the journey. This would then be contrasted with the cost of other forms of transport, such as rail or air. Even then, the cost may not be the sole criterion in deciding whether to use the car, the train, or the 'plane, because we would also need to take into account non-quantifiable factors, such as comfort and convenience. This latter point illustrates that in managerial decision making, *non-financial* factors have also to be taken into account.

In costing the extra cost of a car journey, we are effectively ignoring the *fixed* costs of owning a car. They do form part of the overall cost of car ownership, of course, and they do have to be taken into account when deciding how much it costs to run a car. Once the car has been purchased, however, the fixed costs can be ignored as far as a specific journey is concerned.

Managers in industry face similar decisions. These decisions can also best be solved by using marginal costing. An absorbed cost is not very helpful in deciding upon the outcome of a specific event, e.g. in reducing selling prices or in contracting for new work. In taking such specific decisions, the company's fixed costs may not be immediately affected. In the long run, of course, even the fixed costs may change, e.g. if the company expands (or contracts) on any scale.

None the less, marginal costing is extremely useful in decision-making generally, although it is especially useful in dealing with short-term decisions. We explain how it works in the next section.

THE MARGINAL COSTING SYSTEM

Cost accounting records are usually kept on the basis of absorption costing, even if marginal costing is used in many decision-making situations. One of the main reasons for adopting absorption costing is that for financial accounting purposes, SSAP 9 states that production overheads should be included in the value of the closing stocks.

It would be possible to keep the cost books on a marginal costing basis, but this would mean that extra work would be involved in converting it into a format suitable for financial reporting requirements. In practice, it is much easier to keep the books on an absorption basis, and then adapt it for decision making. None the less, the management should be made fully aware of the danger of ignoring fixed costs in any kind of decision making situation. In the long run, the company must recover all of its costs if it is to survive, even if it may be perfectly legitimate to ignore fixed costs in the short term.

In theory, marginal costing is a very simple system to adopt, although in practice, there are some considerable problems to overcome. These problems arise largely because of the assumptions that have been built into the system. We may summarize these assumptions as follows:

1 it is possible to analyse total costs into fixed costs and variable costs;
2 fixed costs remain constant in the short term irrespective of the level of activity;
3 fixed costs do not bear any relationshlp to specific units produced;
4 variable costs tend to vary in *direct* proportion to activity;
5 some costs are semi-variable, i.e. they contain an element of both fixed and variable costs (e.g. electricity costs and telephone charges both contain a fixed rental element, with a variable charge depending upon the use made of the service).

While these assumptions are somewhat simplistic, they are useful in helping to arrive at decisions where it is safe to ignore fixed costs.

The marginal costing procedure is basically very simple. All that is required is to classify total cost into its fixed and variable elements (instead of into its direct and indirect elements, as in absorption costing).

An example of a marginal cost statement is shown in Exhibit 12.1.

Exhibit 12.1 A typical marginal cost statement

	Product			
	A	B	C	Total
	£000	£000	£000	£000
Sales revenue (1)	100	70	20	190
Less: Variable cost of sales (2)	30	40	10	80
Contribution (3)	70	30	10	110
Less: Fixed costs (4)				60
Profit/(Loss) (5)				£50

Tutorial notes

1 The total sales revenue would be analysed into different product groupings (in this example for products A, B, and C).
2 The variable costs include direct materials, direct labour costs, other direct expenses and variable overhead. In most cases, direct costs are the same as variable costs, but there can be some instances of where they are not the same, for example, a machine operator's salary that is fixed under a guaranteed annual wage agreement.

3 The term *contribution* is used to describe the difference between the sales revenue and the variable cost of those sales. A positive contribution helps to pay for the fixed costs.

4 The fixed cost include all the other costs that do not vary in direct proportion to the sales revenue. Fixed costs are assumed to remain constant over a period of time. They do not bear any relationship to the units produced or the sales achieved, and therefore it is not possible to apportion them amongst the individual products. The total of the fixed costs can *only* be deducted from the total contribution.

5 Total contribution less the fixed costs gives the profit (if the balance is positive) or a loss (if the balance is negative).

We can see from Exhibit 12.1 that it is possible to express the information in equation form, i.e.:

$$
\begin{aligned}
\text{Let} \quad S &= \text{sales revenue} \\
V &= \text{variable costs} \\
C &= \text{contribution} \\
P &= \text{fixed costs} \\
P &= \text{profit} \\
\text{Therefore:} \quad S - V &= C \\
C - F &= P \\
\text{or} \quad C &= F + P \\
\therefore \quad S - V &= F + P
\end{aligned}
$$

The equation $S - V = F + P$ is known as the *marginal cost equation*, and it captures the essence of marginal costing. We will explain how it is applied in the next section.

THE APPLICATION OF MARGINAL COSTING

By using the marginal cost equation, we can cost rapidly any specific decision that the management is thinking of taking. Indeed, even if a decision might require a change in the basic marginal costing assumptions, e.g. if a decision might affect the level of fixed costs, the data can be amended relatively easily. This applies for two main reasons. These are as follows:

1 we can normally assume that fixed costs will remain constant, and they will not normally be affected by a particular decision;

2 we can calculate the contribution at any level of sales activity (since the variable costs are assumed to vary in direct proportion to the sales revenue), and then deduct the fixed costs in total (adjusted if necessary).

These points are illustrated in Exhibit 12.2.

Exhibit 12.2 Examples of changes in variable cost and contribution

	One unit	100 units	1000 units	%
	Product			
	£	£	£	
Selling price	10	1 000	10 000	100
Less: Variable costs	6	600	6 000	60
Contribution	£4	£400	£4 000	40%

Tutorial notes

1 The variable cost per unit is 60%, and the contribution 40% of the sales revenue.
2 The relationship is assumed to hold good no matter how many units are sold.
3 For every unit sold, the company makes a contribution of £4.
4 The fixed costs are ignored, because they are assumed not to change with the level of activity.

Once all the fixed costs have been covered by the total contribution, each extra unit sold results in an additional amount of profit equal to the contribution earned by that unit. Note, however, that profit is not necessarily the same as contribution. This will only be the case once the total contribution has covered the fixed costs. The point is illustrated in Exhibit 12.3.

Exhibit 12.3 Effect on profit at varying levels of activity

Activity in units	1000	2000	3000	4000	5000
	£	£	£	£	£
Sales	10 000	20 000	30 000	40 000	50 000
Less: Variable costs	5 000	10 000	15 000	20 000	25 000
Contribution	5 000	10 000	15 000	20 000	25 000
Less: Fixed costs	10 000	10 000	10 000	10 000	10 000
Profit/(loss)	£(5 000)	–	£5 000	£10 000	£15 000

Tutorial notes

1 The exhibit illustrates five levels of activity: from 1000 units to 5000 units.
2 At each level of activity, the fixed costs remain constant.
3 At each level of activity, the variable costs remain in direct proportion to the sales revenue, i.e. 50%. This means that the relationship of contribution to sales is also 50%.

We can see from Exhibit 12.3 that only when the fixed costs have been covered by the contribution (at an activity level of 2000 units), does any further increase in contribution equal the increase in profit. At an activity level of 2000 units, the company's sales revenue is just sufficient to cover its total costs: at this level it makes neither a profit nor a loss. This is referred to as its *break-even point*: CIMA defines this as 'the level of activity at which there is neither a profit nor a loss'.

The relationship of contribution to sales is known (rather confusingly) as the *profit/volume* (or P/V) *ratio*. Note that it does not mean profit in relationship to sales, but the contribution in relation to sales.

The P/V ratio is extremely useful. Once it has been calculated, we can apply it to any level of sales, deduct the fixed costs, and hence arrive at the new profit on the amended level of sales. Sometimes, of course, the fixed costs will be affected by a change in activity, but if they do change, only a minor adjustment needs to be made to the marginal equation in order to allow for the movement in the level of fixed costs.

The relationships that we have described above are sometimes presented in the form of a chart known as a *break-even chart*. The formal CIMA definition of such a chart is 'a chart which indicates approximate profit or loss at different levels of sales volume within a limited range'.

Accountants believe that it is sometimes much easier to make the point about the relationship between sales, variable costs and fixed costs if it is presented diagrammatically. A break-even chart is illustrated in Exhibit 12.4. The Exhibit is based on the same data as used in Exhibit 12.3.

Exhibit 12.4 shows quite clearly the relationships that are assumed to exist when marginal costing is adopted. Thus, the sales revenue, the variable costs and the fixed costs are all assumed to be linear, i.e. they are all represented by straight lines from a point where there is no activity right through to infinity. In practice, these relationships are not likely to remain linear over such a wide range of activity, and the basic marginal costing assumptions may only be valid over a narrow range.

While this point may appear to create some difficulty in using marginal costing, it should be appreciated that wide fluctuations in activity are not normally experienced, and so it is usually possible to assume that the relatlonship will be linear.

You must remember that the information presented in the format described above is only a *guide* to management. It must not be taken too literally, and, in any case, there are many other factors that must also be taken into account.

Another major problem associated with a break-even chart is that it does not show clearly the actual *amount* of profit/loss (a ruler has to be applied to the chart). In order to avoid this problem, the data can be displayed in the form of a *profit/volume chart*. This is defined by CIMA as a 'chart showing the impact on profit of changes in turnover'. The construction of such a chart is illustrated in Exhibit 12.5 using the same data as in Exhibit 12.3.

Exhibit 12.4 A break-even chart

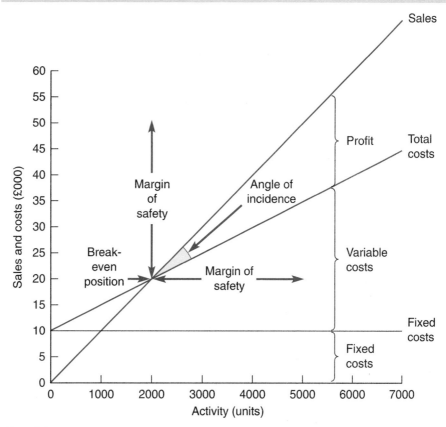

Tutorial notes

1 The total cost line is a combination of the fixed costs and the variable costs. It thus ranges from a total cost of £10 000 (fixed costs only) at a nil level of activity, to £35 000 when the activity level is 5000 units (fixed costs of £10 000 + variable costs of £25 000).

2 The angle of incidence is the angle formed between the sales line and the total cost line. The wider the angle, the greater the amount of profit. A wide angle of incidence plus a wide margin of safety (see 3 below) indicates a highly profitable position.

3 The margin of safety is the distance between the sales achieved and the sales level needed to breakeven. It can be measured either in units (along the x axis) or in sales revenue terms (along the y axis).

4 Activity (measured along the x axis) may be measured either in units, or as a percentage of the theoretical maximum level of activity, or in terms of sales revenue.

We must not give the impression that marginal costing has no problems, so it would be useful if we summarize some of the major criticisms that can be levied at it. We do so in the next section.

Exhibit 12.5 Profit/volume chart

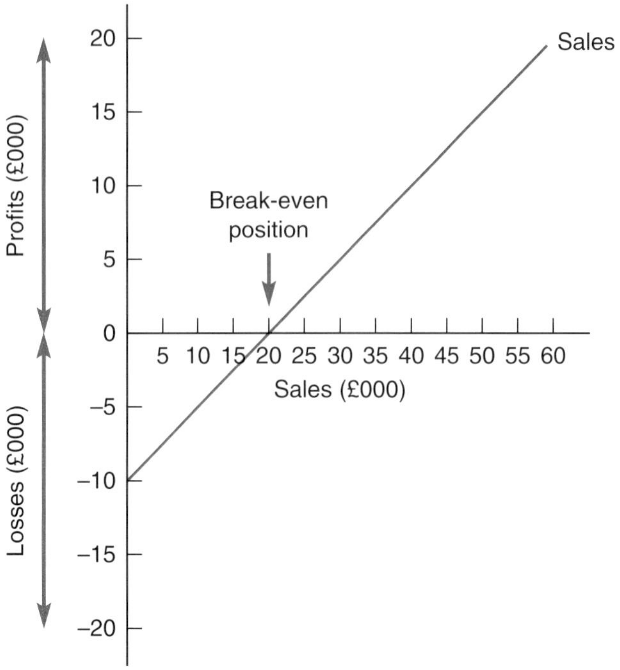

Tutorial notes

1 The *x* axis can be represented either in terms of units, as a percentage of the theoretical maximum level of activity, or in terms of sales revenue.
2 The *y* axis represents profits (positive amounts) or losses (negative amounts).
3 With sales at a level of £50 000, the profit is £15 000. The sales line cuts the *x* axis at the break-even position, and if there are no sales, the loss equals the fixed costs of £10 000.

CRITICISMS OF MARGINAL COSTING

The assumptions adopted in preparing marginal cost statements lead to a number of important reservations about the technique. These are as follows:

1 Costs cannot be easily divided into fixed and variable categories.
2 Variable costs do not vary in direct proportion to activity at all levels of activity, e.g. the cost of direct materials may change as a result of shortages of supply, or through bulk buying, while direct labour costs may be fixed in the short run, since the company may need to give a minimum period of notice to employees before they can be dismissed.
3 The fixed costs will change to some extent as activity increases or decreases.
4 It is difficult to decide over what period of time costs do remain fixed:

in the long run all costs become variable in the sense that the company can avoid them altogether, e.g. by going into liquidation!

5 A specific decision affecting one product may in turn affect other products, especially if they are complementary, e.g. a garage sells both oil and petrol.

6 Fixed costs cannot be entirely ignored, because if the company is to survive it must recover all of its costs.

7 The break-even and profit/volume charts are too simplistic: they do not look at individual products, and they assume that any change in one product will have an identically proportionate effect on all the other products.

8 Non-cost factors (such as the security of supplies and the availability of finance) cannot be ignored in arriving at a specific decision.

These are all very severe criticisms of marginal costing. None the less, provided that (a) it is used with some caution, (b) the information is only treated as a *guide* to decision making, and (c) other non-cost factors are taken into account, it is can still be of great benefit in managerial decision making.

MARGINAL COSTING FORMULAE

We have seen that the marginal costing requires total cost to be classified into fixed and variable categories, and that the respective relationships can be put in the form of an equation. It is possible to extract a number of other equations from the basic marginal cost equation, and these can be quite useful in examining specific problems.

For convenience, we summarize the main ones below:

1 Sales – variable cost of sales = contribution $\quad S - V = C$

2 Contribution – fixed costs = profit/(loss) $\quad C - F = P$

3 Break-even (B/E) point = contribution – fixed costs $\quad C - F$

4 B/E in sales value terms $= \dfrac{\text{Fixed costs} \times \text{sales}}{\text{Contribution}} \qquad \dfrac{F \times S}{C}$

5 B/E in units $= \dfrac{\text{Fixed costs}}{\text{Contribution per unit}} \qquad \dfrac{F}{C \text{ per unit}}$

6 Margin of safety (M/S) in sales value terms $= \dfrac{\text{Profit} \times \text{sales}}{\text{Contribution}} \qquad \dfrac{P \times S}{C}$

7 M/S in units $= \dfrac{\text{Profit}}{\text{Contribution per unit}} \qquad \dfrac{P}{C \text{ per unit}}$

We examine the application of some of these formula in Exhibit 12.6 .

Exhibit 12.6 Example showing the use of the marginal cost formulae

The following information relates to Happy Limited for the year to 30 June 19X8:

Number of units sold   10 000

	Per unit £	Total £000
Sales	30	300
Less: Variable costs	18	180
Contribution	12	120
Less: Fixed costs		24
Profit		£96

Required:

In value and unit terms calculate the following:

1 the break-even position; and
2 the margin of safety.

Answer to Exhibit 12.6

1 Break-even position in value terms:

$$\frac{F \times C}{C} = \frac{24\ 000 \times 300\ 000}{120\ 000} = \underline{\underline{£60\ 000}}$$

Break-even in units:

$$\frac{F}{C\ per\ unit} = \frac{24\ 000}{12} = \underline{\underline{2000\ units}}$$

2 Margin of safety in value terms:

$$\frac{P \times S}{C} = \frac{96\ 000 \times 300\ 000}{120\ 000} = \underline{\underline{£240\ 000}}$$

Margin of safety in units:

$$\frac{P}{C\ per\ unit} = \frac{96\ 000}{12} = \underline{\underline{8000\ units}}$$

Check that you understand the signifance of the answer to Exhibit 12.6. You might also use the data to prepare both a break-even chart, and a profit-volume chart.

AN ILLUSTRATIVE EXAMPLE

It would now be helpful to incorporate the principles behind marginal costing into a simple example. Exhibit 12.7 outlines a typical problem which a board of directors might well face.

Exhibit 12.7

Looking ahead to the financial year ending 31 March 19X5, the directors of Problems Limited are faced with a budgeted loss of £10 000. This is based on the following data:

Budgeted number of units	10 000
	£000
Sales revenue	100
Less: Variable costs	80
Contribution	20
Less: Fixed costs	30
Budgeted loss	£(10)

The directors would like to aim for a profit of £20 000 for the year to 31 March 19X5. Various proposals have been put forward, none of which require a change in the budgeted level of fixed costs. These proposals are as follows:
1 Reduce the selling price of each unit by 10%
2 Increase the selling price of each unit by 10%
3 Stimulate sales by improving the quality of the product; this would increase the variable cost of the unit by £1.50 per unit.

Required:
(a) For each proposal calculate:
(i) the break-even position in units in value terms;
(ii) the number of units required to be sold in order to meet the profit target.
(b) State which proposal you think should be adopted.

Answer to Exhibit 12.7

Problems Limited
(a) (i) and (ii)

Workings:	£
Profit target	20 000
Fixed costs	30 000
Total contribution required	£50 000

The budgeted selling price per unit is £10 (100 000/10 000).

The budgeted outlook compared with each proposal may be summarized as follows:

Per unit:	Budgeted position	Proposal 1	Proposal 2	Proposal 3
	£	£	£	£
Selling price	10	9	11	10.00
Less: Variable costs	8	8	8	9.50
(a) Unit contribution	£2	£1	£3	£0.50
(b) Total contribution required to break even (= fixed costs) (£)	30 000	30 000	30 000	30 000
(c) Total contribution required to meet the profit target (£)	50 000	50 000	50 000	50 000
∴ no. of units to break even [(b)/(a)]	15 000	30 000	10 000	60 000
∴ no. of units to meet the profit target [(c)/(a)]	25 000	50 000	16 667	100 000

(b)
Comments:
1 By continuing with the present budget proposals, the company would need to sell 15 000 units to break even, or 25 000 units to meet the profit target. This in order to break even the company needs to increase its sales by 50%, or by 250% to meet the profit target.
2 A reduction in selling price of 10% per unit would require sales to increase by 300% in order to break even, or by 500% to meet the profit target.
3 By increasing the selling price of each unit by 10%, the company would only have to sell at the budgeted level to break even, but its unit sales would have to increase by two-thirds to meet the profit target.
4 By improving the product at an increased variable cost of £1.50 per unit, the company would require a sixfold increase to break even, or tenfold to meet the profit target.

Conclusion:
It would appear that increasing the selling price by 10% would be a more practical solution for the company to adopt. In the short run, at least it will break even, and there is the possibility that sales could be sufficient to make a small profit. In the long run it has much better chance of meeting the profit target than do the other proposals. Some extra stimulus would be needed, however, to lift sales to this level over such a relatively short period of time. In any case, it is not clear why an increase in price should increase sales, unless the product is one which only sells at a comparatively high price, such as cosmetics and patent medicines. It must also be questioned whether the cost relationships will remain as indicated in the exhibit over such a large increase in activity. In particular, it is unlikely that the fixed costs will remain entirely fixed if there is such a large increase in sales.

LIMITING FACTORS

We saw in Exhibit 12.7 that when optional decisions are considered, the aim will always be to maximize contribution, because the greater the contribution, the more chance there is of covering the fixed costs and hence of making a profit. When managers are faced with a choice, therefore, between (say) producing product A at a contribution of £10 per unit, or of producing product B at a contribution of £20 per unit, they would normally choose product B. Sometimes, however, it may not be possible to produce unlimited quantities of product B because there could be a limit on how many units could either be sold or produced.

Such limits are known as limiting factors (or key factors). CIMA defines these as 'anything which limits the activity of an entity. An entity seeks to optimize the benefit it obtains from the limiting factor'

Limiting factors may arise for a number of reasons, e.g. it may not be possible to sell more than a certain number of units; there may be production restraints (such as shortages of raw materials, skilled labour, or factory space); or the company may not be able to finance the anticipated rate of expansion.

If there is a product that cannot be produced and sold in unlimited quantities, then it is necessary to follow a simple rule in order to decide which product to concentrate on producing. The rule can be summarized as follows:

> **Choose that work which provides the maximum contribution per unit of limiting factor employed**

This sounds very complicated, but it is, in fact, quite simple to use. The procedure we adopt is illustrated below:

1 Assumption: direct labour is in short supply.
2 Calculate the contribution made by each product.
3 Divide the contribution each product makes by the number of direct labour hours used in making each product.
4 The solution = the contribution per direct labour hour employed (i.e. the limiting factor).

Thus, if we had to choose between two jobs (say), A and B, we would convert A's contribution and B's contribution into the amount of contribution earned for every direct labour hour worked on A and on B respectively. We would then opt for that job which earned the most contribution per direct labour hour. We illustrate the application of key factors in Exhibit 12.8.

In Exhibit 12.8 we assumed that there was only one limiting factor, but there could, of course, be many more. This situation is illustrated in Exhibit 12.9.

Exhibit 12.8

Quays Limited manufactures a product for which there is a shortage of raw materials known as PX. During the year to 31 March 19X7, only 1000 kilograms of PX will be available. PX is used in manufacturing both product 8 and product 9. The following information is relevent:

Per unit	Product 8	Product 9
	£	£
Selling price	300	150
Less: Variable costs	200	100
Contribution	£100	£50
P/V ratio	$33\frac{1}{3}$	$33\frac{1}{3}$
Kilograms required	5	2

Required:
State which product Quays Limited should concentrate on producing.

Answer to Exhibit 12.8

	Product 8	Product 9
	£	£
Contribution per unit	100	50
Limiting factor per unit	5	2
∴ contribution per kilogram	£20	£25

Choice:
Product 9 because it gives the highest contribution per unit of limiting factor.

Check:
Maximum contribution of product 8:
200 units (1000/5) × contribution per unit = 200 × 100 = £20 000

Maximum contribution of product 9:
500 units (1000/2) × contribution per unit = 500 × 50 = £25 000

Exhibit 12.9 An example of marginal costing using two key factors

Information:

1 Assume that it is not possible for Company XL to sell more than 400 units of product 9.

2 The company aims to sell all of the 400 units. If it did the total contribution would be £20 000 (400 × 25).

3 The 400 units would consume 800 units of raw materials (400 × 2 kilograms), leaving 200 kilograms for use in producing product 8.

4 Product 8 requires 5 kilograms per unit of raw materials, so 40 units could be completed at a total contribution of £4000 (40 × 100).

Summary of the position:

	Product 8	Product 9	Total
Units sold	40	400	
Raw materials (kilograms used)	200	800	1 000
Contribution per unit (£)	100	50	
Total contribution (£)	4 000	20 000	24 000

Note: The £24 000 total contribution compares with the contribution of £25 000 which the company could have made if there were no limiting factors affecting the sales of product 9.

CONCLUSION

Marginal costing is particularly useful in short-term decision making, but it is of less value when decisions have to be viewed over the long term. The system revolves around two main assumptions:

1 some costs remain fixed, irrespective of the level of activity;
2 other costs vary in direct proportion to sales.

These assumptions are not valia over the long term, but, provided that they are used with caution, they can be usefully adopted in the short term.

It should also be remembered that marginal costing is only a *guide* to decision making, and that other non-cost factors have to be taken into account.

So far, in this part of the book, we have assumed that we have been dealing largely with manufacturing companies who produce a specific unit. There are, of course, many other types of organizations, and we now need to see what type of cost accounting systems may be useful to them. We do so in the next chapter.

KEY POINTS

1 In marginal costing, total cost is analysed into fixed costs and variable costs.

2 As fixed costs are assumed to be unrelated to activity, they are ignored in making short-term managerial decisions. Fixed costs are also ignored in stock valuations.

3 A company will aim to maximize the *contribution* that each unit makes to profit.

4 The marginal cost relationships can be expressed in the form of an equation: S – V = C + P, where S = sales, V = variable costs, C = contribution, and P = profit.

5 It may not always be possible to maximize unit contribution, because materials, labour, or finance may be in short supply.

6 In the long run, fixed cost cannot be ignored.

CHECK YOUR LEARNING

1 Fill in the missing blanks in each of the following sentences:
   (a) A _____ _____ is a cost which is incurred for a period, and which, within certain outputs and turnover limits, tends to be unaffected by fluctuations in the levels of activity.
   (b) Costs which tend to vary with the level of activity are known as _____ _____.

2 Complete the following equations:
   (a) Sales revenue – _____ = contribution
   (b) Contribution – fixed costs = _____
   (c) Break-even point = _____ – _____
   (d) Break-even point in units = $\dfrac{\text{fixed costs}}{}$
   (e) $\dfrac{\text{Profit} \times \text{sales}}{\text{contibution}}$ = _____

3 What term is used to describe anything that restricts the level of activity of an entity?

ANSWERS

1 (a) fixed cost   (b) variable costs
2 (a) variable cost of sales   (b) profit/(loss)   (c) contribution – fixed costs
   (d) contribution per unit   (e) margin of safety (in sales value terms)
3 limiting (or key) factor

QUESTIONS

12.1 The following information relates to Pole Limited for the year to 31 January 19X2.

	£000
Administration expenses:	
Fixed	30
Variable	7
Semi-variable (fixed 80%, variable 20%)	20

Materials:

Direct	60
Indirect	5
Production overhead (all fixed)	40

Research and development expenditure:

Fixed	60
Variable	15
Semi-variable (fixed 50%, variable 50%)	10
Sales	450

Selling and distribution expenditure:

Fixed	80
Variable	4
Semi-variable (fixed 70%, variable 30%)	30

Wages:

Direct	26
Indirect	13

Required:
Using the above information, compile a marginal cost statement for Pole Limited for the year to 31 January 19X2.

12.2 You are presented with the following information for Giles Limited for the year to 28 February 19X2.

	£000
Fixed costs	150
Variable costs	300
Sales (50,000 units)	500

Required:
(a) Calculate the following:
   (i) the break-even point in value terms and in units; and
   (ii) the margin of safety in value terms and in units.
(b) Prepare a break-even chart.

12.3 The following information applies to Ayre Limited for the two years to 31 March 19X2 and 19X3 respectively:

Year	Sales	Profits
	£000	*£000*
31.3.19X2	750	100
31.3.19X3	1000	250

Required:
Assuming that the cost relationships had remained as given in the question, calculate the company's profit if the sales for the year to 31 March 19X3 had reached the budgeted level of £1 200 000.

12.4 The following information relates to Carter Limited for the year to 30 April 19X3:

Units sold	50 000
Selling price per unit	£40
Net profit per unit	£9
Profit/volume ratio	40%

During 19X4 the company would like to increase its sales substantially, but to do so it would have to reduce the selling price per unit by 20%. The variable cost per unit will not change, but because of the increased activity, the company will have to invest in new machinery which will increase the fixed costs by £30 000 per annum.

Required:
Given the new conditions, calculate how many units the company will need to sell in 19X4 in order to make the same amount of profit as it did in 19X3.

12.5 Puzzled Limited would like to increase its sales during the year to 31 May 19X5. To do so, it has several mutually exclusive options open to it:

1 reduce the selling price per unit by 15%;
2 improve the product resulting in an increase in the variable cost per unit of £1.30;
3 spend £15 000 on an advertising campaign;
4 improve factory efficiency by purchasing more machinery at a fixed extra annual cost of £22 500.

During the year to 31 May 19X4, the company sold 20 000 units. The cost details were as follows:

	£000
Sales	200
Variable costs	150
Contribution	50
Fixed costs	40
Profit	£10

These cost relationships are expected to hold in 19X5.

Required:
State which option you would recommend and why.

12.6 Micro Limited has some surplus capacity. It is now considering whether it should accept a special contract to use some of its spare capacity. However, this contract will use some specialist direct labour which is in short supply.
   The following details relate to the proposed contract:

	£
Contract price	50 000
Variable costs:	
Direct materials	10 000
Direct labour	30 000

4000 direct labour hours would be required in order to complete the contract. The company's budget for the year during which the contract would be undertaken is as follows:

	£000
Sales	750
Less: Variable costs	500
Contribution	250
Less: Fixed costs	230
Profit	£20

Direct labour hours: 50 000 maximum available during the year.

Required:
State, giving your reasons, whether the special contract should be accepted.

ADDITIONAL QUESTIONS (WITHOUT ANSWERS)

12.7 The following information relates to Mere's budget for the year to 31 December 19X7:

Product	K	L	M	Total
	£000	£000	£000	£000
Sales	700	400	250	1350
Direct materials	210	60	30	300
Direct labour	100	200	200	500
Variable overhead	90	60	50	200
Fixed overhead	20	40	40	100
	420	360	320	1100
Profit/(loss)	280	40	(70)	250
Budgeted sales (units)	140	20	25	

Note:
Fixed overheads are apportioned on the basis of direct labour hours.

The directors are worried about the loss that product M is budgeted to make, and various suggestions have been made to counteract the loss, viz.:
1 stop selling product M;
2 increase its selling price by 20%;
3 reduce its selling price by 10%;
4 reduce its costs by purchasing a new machine costing £350 000, thereby decreasing the direct labour cost by £100 000 (the machine would have a life of five years; its residual value would be nil).

Required:
Evaluate each of these proposals.

12.8 Temple Limited has been offered two new contracts, the details of which are as follows:

Contract	1	2
	£000	£000
Contract price	1 000	1 500
Direct materials	300	300
Direct labour	300	600
Variable overhead	100	100
Fixed overhead	100	200
	800	1 200
Profit	200	300
Direct materials required (kilos)	50 000	100 000
Direct labour hours required	10 000	25 000

Note:
The flxed overhead has been apportioned on the basis of direct labour cost.

Temple is a one product firm. Its budgeted cost per unit for the year to 31 December 19X8 is summarized below:

	£
Sales	6000
Direct materials (100 kilos)	700
Direct labour (200 hours)	3000
Variable overhead	300
Fixed overhead	1000
	5000
Profit	1000

The company would only have the capacity to accept one of the new contracts. Unfortunately, materials suitable for use in all of its work are in short supply, and the company has estimated that only 200 000 kilos would be available during the year to 31 December 19X8.

Even more worrying is the shortage of skilled labour, and only 100 000 direct labour hours are expected to be available during the year.

The good news is that there may be an upturn in the market for its normal contract work.

Required:
Advise management which contract to accept.

CHAPTER 13

Product costing systems and recent developments

Shanks & McEwan to make £19.3m provision

Shanks & McEwan, the waste disposal company, is to set up a £19.3m provision to cover a reorganisation of its construction division encompassing late payments and sums relating to variations in contracts that it is not certain it will collect.

The provisions will be taken in the year ended March 27 1993, results for which will be announced later this month.

Mr Roger Hewitt, chief executive, said Shanks's waste divisions traded "satisfactorily" during the year. Pre-tax profits would be no less than £29m before the provision announced yesterday.

The group intended to recommend a final dividend of 3.44p, unchanged from 1992.

After a sharp early fall, Shank's share price settled down 7p at 162p.

Mr Hewitt said the group had traditionally been involved in long-term contracts, building roads, tunnels and bridges. Due to government pressure, payment on many of these contracts was often only being made after protracted negotiations with central government and local government clients.

It was no longer clear when payment would be recovered, or indeed how much would be received. The group would now be focusing on shorter-term, and therefore more tightly specified, contracts.

Mr Anthony Rush, former chief operating officer of Lilley, the failed construction and property company, is being brought in as managing director of Shanks & McEwan Contractors. Mr Rush, who was on Lilley's construction side, will replace Mr John Mackenzie, who has retired.

Mr Hewitt said the group would be vigorously pursuing payment. Should payments be received in future years they would appear above the line in future year's earnings.

The provision relates to about 10 main contracts, five of them large road construction deals.

The Financial Times, 2 June 1993

Exhibit 13.0 **Contract work can be an extremely hazardous business as this article clearly demonstrates.**

In the last three chapters, we have concentrated on manufacturing companies producing specific identifiable units. We have done so because such entities are useful in demonstrating a wide range of cost accounting principles and procedures. However, many entities either do not make specific identifiable units, or they may not be involved in manufacturing. Thus, many of the procedures outlined in the earlier chapters will have to be adapted in order to allow for different manufacturing conditions, and for entities operating in different sectors of the economy. For example, unit costing is not used in the glass industry, or material pricing in hospices.

This chapter has two main aims:

1 to introduce you to different product costing systems;
2 to make you aware of some recent developments in management accounting.

You will be pleased to know that your cost accounting knowledge is now sufficient for you to be able to adapt it to most manufacturing and non-manufacturing situations. The chapter introduces you to management accounting systems that are somewhat different from the ones that we have described so far, and it also demonstrates that management accounting generally is undergoing a period of change and development.

In the first section of the chapter, we examine some product costing methods, and in the second section, we outline some recent developments in management accounting.

LEARNING OBJECTIVES

By the end of this chapter, you will be able to:
● distinguish between different basic costing methods;
● identify five product costing systems;
● recognize the importance of service costing;
● describe three recent developments in management accounting.

COSTING METHODS

Product costing systems can be analysed into two broad categories: specific order, and continuous operation. The formal CIMA definitions are as follows:

Specific order costing: the basic cost accounting method applicable where work consists of separate contracts, jobs or batches.
Continuous operation costing: the costing method applicable where goods or services result from a sequence of continuous or repetitive operations of processes. Costs are averaged over the units produced during the period.

This distinction might become clearer if you imagine a company producing milk. In one sense, it produces a specific identifiable unit, i.e. a bottle of milk, but it is usually only at a later stage in the production process that it is economic to identity each bottle separately. Thus, for costing purposes, the amount of milk transferred from the farm to the dairy will be treated as a bulk amount until the milk is ready to be bottled. It would clearly be difficult to try to cost each separate bottle of milk. This point also applies to the manufacture of glass. Glass is eventually sold in recognizable units, but it is not economic to cost each pane of glass separately. Instead, it is costed in bulk.

Three main types of specific order costing can be distinguished: job costing, contract costing, and batch costing, and there are two main types of continuous operation costing: process costing, and service costing. We will examine each of them briefly in the following sub-sections.

Job costing

Job costing is used when specific units are produced, such as parts produced in an engineering works, or in service jobs, e.g. a garage where jobs are done for particular customers. Most of the previous exhibits used so far in this book have, in fact, been based on job costing..

In the case of most service jobs (such as decorating, joinery, or plumbing), many of the cost accounting problems that we have outlined will not arise. For example, material pricing and overhead apportionment are not major issues in a small plumbing business.

In service costing, a separate account will be kept for each customer. In it will be recorded: the direct materials used, the direct labour hours spent on the job (perhaps the largest item), an addition for overheads (probably on a direct labour hour basis), and a percentage for profit.

Contract costing

Contract costing is particularly associated with the construction industry, such as building bridges, hospitals, power stations, roads, schools, and ships. In essence, it is very similar to job costing, except that the contract is usually a long-term one, perhaps stretching over many years. It does give rise, therefore, to some special accounting problems, such as the valuation of work done to date, and the recognition of profit on an ongoing basis.

A separate account would normally be opened for each contract. As a result of the size of most contract work, it is not usually too difficult to identify material and labour costs with individual contracts. Also, in construction companies, overheads tend to be relatively small in proportion to total costs, and so overhead absorption is not a major issue. Overheads would probably be absorbed on the basis of direct labour hours.

As many contracts are awarded on the basis of a tender, the company will have had to estimate the total cost of a particular contract, and then add a percentage for profit. It is most important, therefore, that the progress of the contract is monitored regularly in order to ensure that the actual costs are kept in line with the original estimates. Normally, a customer will not expect to pay more than the agreed tender price, unless certain events occur, e.g. because of exceptionally bad weather conditions.

If the contract is likely to take several years, there may come a time when its profitability is reasonably assured. It is then permissible to take some profit on account. You may find this surprising, as it seems to be in conflict with the prudence rule (outlined in Chapter 2). At any stage of a contract, it is very easy for some quite unforseen circumstances to arise, and a loss may then be incurred.

None the less, in certain circumstances, accountants have usually recommended taking *some* profit on account when, as SSAP 9 puts it . . . 'where it is considered that the outcome of a long-term contract can be assessed with reasonable certainty before its conclusion, the prudently calculated attributable profit should be recognized in the profit and loss account as the difference between the reported turnover and related costs for that contract'. To understand what this really means, we had better give you SSAP 9's definition of attributable profit. It is as follows:

> **Attributable profit:** that part of the total profit currently estimated to arise over the duration of the contract, after allowing for estimated remedial and maintenance costs, and increases in costs so far as not recoverable under the terms of the contract, that fairly reflects the profit attributable to that part of the work performed at the accounting date. (There can be no attributable profit until the profitable outcome of the contract can be assessed with reasonable certainty.)

Notice the word 'estimated' appears twice in the above definition, along with the phrase 'reasonable certainty'. Perhaps you really do not need reminding at this stage, but this confirms once again just how imprecise accounting information can be! A construction company could pay out a dividend on the basis of 'attributable profit', and then find that it eventually makes a loss on a number of contracts. It is obviously important not to be too imprudent!

In accordance with SSAP 9, your accountants will spend a lot of time 'estimating' what is reasonable. Their calculations may appear somewhat formidable, but there is nothing magic in what they do. It is important that, as a manager, you become involved in their discussions. Do not leave it to them: you also have a responsibility to ensure that the attributable profit is justified. The contract may make a loss, so be cautious. However, do not be unduly cautious (i.e. lacking in objectivity), as this could be unfair to your existing shareholders: you cannot expect them to wait (say) ten years before you decide to pay a dividend based on what appears to be a particularly lucrative contract.

Batch costing

Batch costing is used when specific physically identifiable units are uneconomic to cost individually. It may be used, for example, in manufacturing nuts and bolts, or boots and shoes.

In effect, each batch is treated as a separate job, with the result that all the material, labour, and other costs that it is economically viable to identify with the batch will be allocated to it. Overheads will then be absorbed into the batch on either a machine hour or a direct labour hour basis.

Process costing

Process costing is frequently found in those industries that use a continuous or repetitive operation in manufacturing products. Raw materials, for example, may be converted into a finished good state after undergoing some chemical change, and, by the time that the process has been completed, the raw materials may be completely unrecognizable (e.g. flour in cakemaking). Process costing can be found in a wide range of industries, such as cement, chemicals, glass, iron and steel, oil, paint, and textiles.

Process costing is very similar to job costing: an account will be opened for each process (instead of each unit). Direct materials, direct labour, and other direct expenses will be charged to the account, along with a share of overheads. The unit cost of each process will be, basically, the total process cost dividend by the number of completed units. However, a number of specific cost accounting problems arise with process costing that do not apply to job costing. We will deal briefly with each of them below.

Normal loss

In many process industries there is often an unavoidable loss of output during the production process. This sometimes arises because of the chemical change undergone by the raw materials in the process (perhaps through evaporation, or because of natural wastage caused by larger items being broken down into smaller ones). For example, for every 1000 kilograms of material fed into a production process, only 900 kilograms (say) of finished goods may be produced. The 100 kilograms lost in production is known as a *normal loss*. How should it be dealt with in the accounts?

The usual procedure is to charge the good production with its share of the normal loss. Suppose that the total process cost in the above example amounted to £900, then each kilogram would be costed at £1 per kilogram (i.e. £900/900). It is not possible, of course, to be certain that the loss will always be 'normal'. What happens if it is less or more than 100 kilograms? This would result in what is called an *abnormal gain* (if it is less than 100 kilograms), or an *abnormal loss* (if it is more than 100 kilograms). How should abnormal gains and losses be accounted for?

The rule is that they should be written off to the profit and loss account for the period in which they were incurred. They should not be charged as a current direct process cost, and they should not be carried forward to the next accounting period. Why? The short answer is that it would be unfair. Let us take an example from the service sector to illustrate the point.

Suppose a football supporters' club regularly hires a coach to take the members to a match 150 miles away. The coach company charges £300 for a day's hire of a 55-seater coach. The treasurer has estimated that normally 50 members will join each trip, so she decides to charge £6 (i.e. £300/50) per seat per trip (instead of £5.46, i.e. £300/55). In other words, five spare seats are the normal loss. What happens, therefore, if on one trip only 25 members attend? Should they be charged £12 (i.e. £300/25)? If not, an abnormal loss of £150 would be incurred (i.e. 25 × £6). However, it would be a bit unfair to charge the members who *did* go an extra amount, simply because of the poor attendance on that particular day. Instead, the £150 abnormal loss would have to be written off to the club's general funds. Of course, if the attendance sinks regularly to 25, then the 'normal' loss would have to be recalculated, or the club would have to hire a cheaper and smaller coach.

It is, of course, impossible to calculate precisely what is a 'normal' loss. The above example helps to make the point that: (a) it is essential to estimate a normal loss as accurately as possible: (b) the position should be monitored carefully; and (c) it will have to be adjusted if it appears that there has been a permanent change. The company should strive to minimize normal losses, and to eliminate material abnormal gains and losses. It would soon go into liquidation if it was always writing off the equivalent of the club's £150.

Work-in-process

Another accounting problem associated with process costing is the valuation of work-in-process, i.e. uncompleted work at the end of an accounting period. This information will be needed for incorporation into the financial accounts, so what value should be put on it?

Imagine the difficulty. Suppose you are making cakes. A number of ingredients have been fed into the mixing, and a certain amount of time has been spent in stirring them. At that stage, the ingredients are no longer raw materials, but they are still not recognizable as cakes. At the end of the financial year, suppose some cakes are still being prepared: what value should be placed on the mix? As is usual in accounting, you would have to estimate it! In process costing, this is normally done on the basis of *equivalent units*.

The procedure is as follows: Each element of cost is taken in turn, and the stage of completion is estimated, e.g. the raw material may be 100% completed, but only 50% of the labour time may have been spent on the process. How should the work-in-process be calculated? The procedure is illustrated in Exhibit 13.1.

Exhibit 13.1 Calculation of work-in-process using the equivalent units method

The following information relates to Process X:

Opening work-in-process	Nil
Units introduced into the process	100
Units transferred to Process Y	60
Closing work-in-process units	40
Material cost per unit added during the period	£10
Conversion cost per unit added during the period	£8

It is estimated that the closing work-in-process units are 90% complete as regards materials, and 30% complete as regards conversion costs.

Required:
Calculate the value of the closing work-in-process.

Answer to Exhibit 13.1

	WIP units	Degree of completion %	Equivalent units		Cost £	Amount £
Material	40	90	36	(40 x 90)	10	360
Conversion cost	40	30	12	(40 x 30)	8	96
Value of work-in-process						£456

Exhibit 13.1 is a very simple example, but it does highlight the point that we want to make. This method requires an estimate to be made of the degree of completion for each element of cost. This would be easy in the case of our cake example: we would know if all the ingredients had been included, and we could be fairly sure how much more mixing time it would need. In a more complex industrial process, however, estimating completeness is by no means easy.

By-products   A by-product is an output of some value arising out of a process that is incidental to the main product. Income arising from the sales of by-products (less any further conversion costs) would normally go to offset the total process cost. If a by-product requires any further processing before it can be sold, it can be regarded as a joint product, although one of the products may be relatively insignificant in relation to the others.

Joint products

Joint products are those recognizable products that arise out of a production process. There could be two or more joint products, and they may all have equal status. If one (or more) of the products requires further processing before it is eventually sold, the further conversion cost could be matched with the ultimate sales revenue. However, if the *total* cost of the product is required, how can the joint process costs arising before the point of separation be apportioned equitably?

The answer is that it cannot: if a general cake mix is used as the base for different varieties of cakes, how is it possible to measure the pre-separation cost attached to each cake? It is impossible and so, once again, it has to be estimated. There are several methods that could be adopted, viz.:

1 as a proportion of the number of units at the separation point;
2 as a proportion of the weight of products as at that point;
3 as a proportion of the total sales value of each product;
4 as a proportion of the total sales value less any further conversion costs.

It should be emphasized that all of these methods are highly questionable. We do not recommend that you should attempt to apportion joint costs for *control* purposes, since managers cannot be expected to control costs that have been apportioned on a purely arbitrary basis. You might want to apportion costs if you need to fix selling prices on a cost-plus basis, but you should still view the results fairly sceptically. It follows that you must not then be too rigid in adhering to your original estimates.

Service costing

There are many types of entities whose basic function is to provide a service, rather than to deliver a product. We are all familiar with service industries in our everyday lives (although we may not think of them as being industries). The local authority provides a service when it empties our dustbins and educates our children. The doctor provides a service when we are ill. If we have problems with our neighbours, we might turn to a solicitor for help. In describing a cost and management accounting system so far in this book, we have tended to assume that we were dealing largely with manufacturing industry, so the model we have used does need some modification to allow for those entities that do not deal in 'products'.

We have met the problem of accounting for services before, of course, even when dealing with manufacturing companies, since they also provide services within the entity itself. Then, we had to adopt some arbitrary apportionment method in charging the internal service cost to products. This might be understandable in the case of a manufacturing company, but why should we want to bother if we are dealing with a service industry?

The answer to this question is basically no different than if it were asked of manufacturing industry. Just to remind you, a cost and management accounting system offers the following benefits to management:

1 it aims to help the entity meet its objectives;
2 it lays down plans for future action;
3 it provides information to assist in monitoring those plans;
4 it assists in cost control;
5 it aids decision making;
6 it can be used in pricing.

In other words, irrespective of the type of entity, cost and management accounting is useful in planning and controlling the entity's activities. In essence, the only real difference between manufacturing and service industries is that in service industries we are not dealing with a physical product. As a result, labour costing is probably of greater significance than material pricing. However, overhead apportionment may be a problem in both sectors. For example, solicitors dealing with clients will incur few (if any) material costs, but there will probably be hefty costs for labour, something for overheads, and an addition for profit. The labour cost will normally be charged out on an hourly basis (it is even known for solicitors to charge by the minute!). Most overheads will probably be fixed, so it will be difficult to relate them to one particular client. The chances are, therefore, that the labour rate per hour includes an addition for fixed overheads, and a further addition for profit.

Non-profit making entities in the service sector (many accountants prefer the term *'not-for-profit'* entities) are not concerned with charge-out rates. Let us take a school as an example. It is likely that the local authority *allocates* a certain amount of money to each school for certain miscellaneous purposes, such as books, chalk, and school visits. It will then be up to the headteacher to use the allocation as effectively and as efficiently as possible in respect of the requirements of that particular school. Some headteachers may, for example, want to spend more on books, and less on visits to the zoo, while other heads want to buy a great deal of computer equipment. What then, is the benefit of a cost and management accounting system to a school?

The short answer to this question is that it will be as much use as the headteacher wants to make of it. Obviously, the system will not need to be as complicated as (say) that of ICI, but basically, the procedures are similar: decide on your objectives, lay down your plans, monitor them, and then take action if they are going wrong. To do of all this, headteachers need information, and they also need to ask a lot of questions, such as: What am I trying to do? How should I go about it? How much money have I got to spend? How much have I spent? Is there anything I can do to cut back to keep within my allocation?

This type of monitoring procedure is, of course, a relatively new experience for most headteachers (and, for that matter, doctors, nurses and surgeons). Many of them do not like being faced with such questions. They argue that they were appointed to teach (or heal the sick), and not to get involved in accounting. Medical staff also argue, that they must treat patients if they are ill, even if the hospital has exceeded its budget. They have a point, but there are some advantages in controlling costs at the individual school or hospital level. As with any system, however, there has to be some flexibility. This point about service costing is developed further in Exhibit 13.2

Exhibit 13.2 A mini-case study of cost control in a primary school – The case of Southbank Primary School

Background:
This mini-case study is based on an incident that happened in one particular school . . .

The Eastland Local Education Authority decided to install a cost and management accounting system at the school level. Each school was given what the Authority called a 'budget' (i.e. it was allocated a certain sum of money). This meant that each headteacher had complete discretion on how the various items within his/her budget should be spent. Every month, the heads were supplied with computerized information showing how much and on what they had spent their allocation.

It so happened that in one particular month at the Southbank Primary School, the Head noticed that she seemed to be spending far more than she had expected on telephone calls. Before the new system was introduced, telephone expenses were borne by the Education Authority's Central Administration Unit, so, until recently, the Head had no idea what the school spent on telephone calls.

Upon investigation, it was discovered that the school caretaker was telephoning his girlfriend in Australia during the evenings. Action was taken to stop this happening, but the Head found that for the rest of that year she had less money to spend on other activities.

The Head was still not convinced that the cost and management accounting system was useful. She believed that it was counter-productive, as she had to spend a lot of her time in deciding where and how she should spend her allocation. The actual expenditure had then to be monitored and any variances investigated. In her view, her time would be better spent doing what she was trained to do, i.e. dealing with the children, and talking to their parents.

While the new cost and management system was beginning to save money for the Local Authority, the Head argued that there were education costs attached to it, and these were not taken into account.

Required :
Discuss the above case, being careful to contrast the apparent financial savings against any possible educational disadvantages.

Exhibit 13.2 deals with an example where large sums of money were not at stake, but there is no doubt that, to some extent, the children at Southbank were deprived both of some school supplies and the Head's attention. Without a detailed information system operating at the school level, the excess telephone costs would never have come to light. Of course, as we have argued earlier, there is a financial cost attached to operating any cost and management accounting system, but in the case of a school, there is an educational cost: should the headteachers be spending their time 'book-keeping' instead of dealing with children and seeing parents? No doubt, you came to your own views about this question, and we will leave it to you to decide. Note that exactly the same arguments could be applied if cost and management accounting systems are installed in other service sectors, e.g. in the National Health Service.

The point being made in the case study is a serious one, and we have used it to demonstrate that cost and management accounting systems may have a part to play in the service sector, irrespective of whether we are dealing with profit- or non-for-profit making entities. Whether they are welcomed by heads, doctors, or nurses, is quite another matter!

We will now move on to have a look at some other issues and developments in management accounting that you might well hear about. We examine them in the next section.

SOME RECENT DEVELOPMENTS

Most of the above cost accounting techniques are used to some extent in both the public and private sectors, although cost accounting itself is still relatively uncommon. The techniques that are in use were developed many years ago at a time when the economy was very different from what it is now. Manufacturing industry was a much more significant, and direct labour costs formed a much greater part of total cost than they do in the 1990s.

The public sector has also changed. In local government, for example, the Local Authority Treasurer's Department used to be primarily responsible for providing information for rating purposes. Thereafter, it was largely a matter of keeping the books of account. Now, the accent is very much on obtaining value for money, i.e. in ensuring that, for every £1 spent, the community gets the maximum possible benefit. In addition, many local services are put out to tender, and the local authority no longer operates directly many of the services that it administers on behalf of the public.

In these changed circumstances, the practice of management accounting is also beginning to change. Progress has been slow because, unlike financial accounting, it is not subject to either statutory or mandatory professional accounting requirements. The need to adapt arises from two main sources: (a) the overall change in the national economic and financial climate; and (b) the need for British industry to begin to compete with the Japanese (and other emerging countries) in world markets.

There is now some discussion in management accounting circles of the

need to adopt new techniques to meet the changing operational circumstances of British industry, and many of the larger UK companies have, in
fact, adopted some of these newer techniques. We outline a few of them in
the following sub-sections, but we do so briefly because most of them are
still at an early stage of development.

Activity based costing

Activity based costing (ABC) was virtually unknown in the UK prior to
1988. Much interest is being taken in the technique, and it is now sometimes referred to as *activity based management* (ABM), as it is believed
that its basic ideas go well beyond cost accounting. The CIMA definition
of ABC is: 'Cost attribution to cost units on the basis of benefits received
from indirect activities, e.g. ordering, setting up, assuring quality'.

The technique came about as a result of the great unease arising from
the traditional way of absorbing overheads, i.e. on the basis of cost centre
activity measured usually in terms of direct labour hours or machine hours.
In Chapter 11, we were fairly critical of this method, and it now seems to
have been generally recognized that a new method is required.

As you might imagine, ABC is not an easy technique to understand.
Basically, it revolves around a recognition that specific activities cause
costs to arise. Thus, if it is possible to isolate the activities that cause the
costs, it would be possible to absorb overheads much more fairly on the
basis of those activities (instead of using the simple direct labour hour or
machine hour method).

This argument has given rise to use of the term 'cost drivers' to describe
a measure of the activities performed. CIMA simply define a cost driver as
'an activity which generates cost'. For example, in order to manufacture
certain products, a number of orders may have to be placed, the material
may have to be handled several times, and the machines may need re-set-
ting. All of these activities will have an effect on overheads, so it seems
only fair to charge some products less for overheads than others: for example, if less orders are placed, materials are only handled once, and the
machines do not have to be re-set. All of these activities can be described
as cost drivers, i.e. the number of orders, the number of times handled, and
the number of set-ups.

Do you get the basic idea? In effect, instead of charging overheads to
production by using just one factor, ABC adopts a considerable number,
depending upon how many activities can be isolated within a particular
entity.

It is obviously a much more involved and costly system of achieving
some control over overheads than the one that we described in Chapter 11.
The proponents of ABC claim that it avoids over-costing high volume
products, and under-costing low volume ones. This benefit arises because

the cost drivers reflect the activity generated by particular products. In traditional overhead absorption, units are charged with a share of the total cost centre overheads based on the total direct labour hours (or the total machine hours) worked in that cost centre. In an ABC system, if both products A and B require one set-up, but A consists of one unit and B 1000, they will both be charged the same amount of overhead.

ABC is still at an early stage of development in the UK, and so, for the time being we need not go into any further detail. As a non-accountant, it is sufficient for you to have heard of the technique, to understand what is meant by a cost driver, and to know that overheads are apportioned on the basis of cost drivers.

Just-in-time

In Chapter 10 we dealt with the problem of charging direct materials to production. A relatively new technique, known as just-in-time (JIT), may help us avoid this problem.

CIMA define JIT as follows: 'A technique for the organization of work flows, to allow rapid, high quality, flexible production whilst minimizing manufacturing waste and stock levels.' When applied to production, it is defined as: 'A system which is driven by demand for finished products whereby each component on a production line is produced only when needed for the next stage.'

To illustrate this technique, let us assume that you are having some construction work done at home. The contract supervisor has to schedule the work so that once the foundation and walls have been built, the joiner and glaziers are ready to fit the windows. They are then followed in turn by the plumber, the electrician, and the plasterer. All of these tradesmen will, of course, require materials to be delivered just when they need them. If there is a delay in one tradesman arriving, or in some materials not being to hand, the whole job could be stopped. In other words, it is vital that all of the various tasks are closely synchronized and timed.

In essence, this forms the basis of JIT. The technique is now becoming widespread in British industry (although it has been common in Japan for many years). It can also be applied to the *purchasing* function. Just-in-time purchasing is defined by CIMA as follows: 'Matching the receipt of material closely with usage so that raw material inventory is reduced to near-zero levels.'

JIT purchasing has some very important implications for cost accounting, especially in respect of material pricing, as it practically solves the problem for us! If materials are ordered for a specific job, and they are then delivered straight onto the production line, there should hardly be any difficulty in identifying their cost. Under a JIT system material pricing is not a major issue.

There are also additional benefits. Ordering straight to production reduces the cost of ordering, handling, storing, issuing, and the risk of stock deterioration or obsolescence. Of course, some problems may arise from following the principle. For example, if the supplier is late in delivering a particular order, or there is some interruption to supplies, the entire production staff might have to be laid off. None the less, JIT has some exciting possibilities, and its future looks well assured.

Total quality management

Total quality management (TQM) is another management technique that has begun to take off in the UK. It is now sometimes referred to as Quality Management (QM). TQM can be introduced into any entity irrespective of whether it is profit- or a non-profit making.

CIMA defines it as follows: 'The continuous improvement in quality, productivity and effectiveness obtained by establishing management responsibility for processes as well as outputs. In this every process has an identified process owner and every person in an entity operates within a process and contributes to its improvement.'

The definition 'quality' is elusive. For example, we can refer to a quality car (like a Rolls Royce), but in the context of TQM, we can also mean a small mass-produced car which is as high quality as it is possible to get in terms of its basic specification.

The concept of TQM can be summed up in the phrase 'getting it right first time'. In other words, it is less expensive to make sure that all tasks and duties are always completed correctly the first time that they are undertaken. Getting it right the first time means that there will be savings on internal failures (e.g. the cost of wastage, re-working, re-inspection, downgrading, and discounting), and also on external costs (e.g. field repairs, handling, legal, lost sales, and warranties). However, there could be some additional costs on prevention (planning, training, and operating the system), and on appraisal (administration, audit, and inspection).

TQM is a technique that involves every employee in an entity from the chairman downwards. Accountants are automatically included. In addition, the management accounting function will have some responsibility towards collecting and reporting on appraisal, prevention, and internal and external prevention costs. However, it is rather curious that accountants have not yet become heavily involved in the implementation and operation of TQM systems. In the past, they have tended to get involved in everything!

We do not know to what extent traditional management accounting practices may (or will) have to change in order to accommodate a TQM system. Thus, the quesion that accountants are probably going to have to answer is: 'Does a traditional cost and management accounting system become obsolete if a TQM system is installed?'

Other developments

A number of other developments are taking place in management accounting. We summarize some of these very briefly below.

Life-cycle costing

In an advanced manufacturing environment, planning and prototypes decisions taken in the early stages of a product's development have an important impact throughout its entire life. Management accounting has a role to play in providing information for planning and control at the design stage of a product, and thereafter, in plotting the product's life-time costs and revenues.

This technique is known as 'life-cycle costing', and CIMA define it as follows: 'The practice of obtaining, over their lifetimes, the best use of physical assets at the lowest total cost to the entity (terotechnology).' The definition then goes on to suggest that this can be achieved 'through a combination of management, financial, engineering and other disciplines.'

Target costing

Target costing is another technique imported from Japan. Before a product is designed, the marketing function sets a selling price that will capture a designated share of the market. The product will then have to be designed in such a way that the total unit cost plus an allowance for profit does not exceed the target market price. CIMA defines a target cost as follows: 'A product cost estimate derived from a competitive market price. Used to reduce costs through continuous improvement and replacement of technologies and processes.'

Strategic management accounting

Strategic management accounting (SMA) is a relatively new development arising out of traditional management accounting practices. Instead of just reporting to management details of the internal costs and incomes of the entity, a SMA approach would also involve reporting on similar information about the entity's competitors. CIMA puts it this way: 'The preparation and presentation of information for decision making, laying particular stress on external factors.' Thus, reports will be prepared on the external aspects of the entity's operations, e.g. information about competitors, customers, suppliers, the economy, miscellaneous governmental factors, and legal changes and requirements.

We should stress that some of the techniques that we have briefly outlined in this section of the chapter are not yet widely applied in British manufacturing or service industries, so you may not come across them. It may well be that some of the new techniques are little more than gimmicks, soon to be forgotten. However, there is no doubt that present management accounting practices are locked into an economic, financial, and political culture that has long ceased to exist, so there is a need to develop more effective planning and control mechanisms.

CONCLUSION

In previous chapters, we concentrated in looking at unit cost accounting in a manufacturing environment. In this chapter we have tried to demonstrate that the basic cost accounting principles and procedures outlined in those earlier chapters can be used in non-manufacturing and non-profit making entities. Some modifications may be needed, of course, depending upon the nature of the entity, and whether it is profit or non-profit making, but the essential requirements are remarkably similar.

We have also shown that management accounting has entered a period of great change. Many new developments are taking place. Two of them in particular, just-in-time purchasing and activity based costing, may help to solve two major drawbacks of traditional absorption costing, i.e. material pricing, and the relationship of overheads to production units.

We can now move on to look in more detail at another aspect of management accounting: the method of cost control. We do so in the next two chapters.

KEY POINTS

1 There are two main types of product costing systems: specific order costing and continuous operation costing.

2 Specific order costing contains three main methods of costing: job, contract, and batch; and continuous operation contains two main methods: process and service.

3 Irrespective of the costing method adopted, the basic cost accounting principles and procedures are still relevant to non-manufacturing and non-profit making entities, although they may require some slight modification to allow for the nature of the product or the service, e.g. in process costing, or in education.

4 In the non-profit making service sector, the control of costs is particularly important in order to ensure the most efficient use is made of existing resources, and that the customer benefits from a high quality service.

5 Some new developments are taking place in management accounting, such as activity based costing, just-in-time purchasing, and total quality management (although the latter has not yet been taken up to any great extent by the accountancy profession). Other possible developments include life-cycle costing, target costing, and strategic management accounting.

CHECK YOUR LEARNING

1 Name two broad categories into which product costing systems may be divided.

2 What type of costing system would you expect to find in the following entities?
(a) boot and shoe manufacturer
(b) road construction firm
(c) plumber
(d) chemical firm
(e) hospital

3 What do the following initials mean?
(a) ABC
(b) JIT
(c) TQM.

4 Give an example of a cost driver.

5 State whether each of the following assertions is true or false:
(a) Strategic management accounting incorporates external information into the reporting system.   True/False
(b) Abnormal gains should be absorbed into process costs.   True/False
(c) A contract must be completed before any profit can be taken.   True/False

ANSWERS

1 specific order; continuous operations
2 (a) batch (b) contract (c) job (d) process (e) service
3 (a) activity based costing (b) just-in-time (c) total quality management
4 number of set-ups
5 (a) true (b) false (c) false

QUESTIONS

13.1 Describe briefly each of the following product costing systems:
(a) batch costing
(b) contract costing
(c) process costing
(d) service costing

13.2 Explain why abnormal losses and gains should not be incorporated directly into product costs.

13.3 Should a hospital be required to operate a cost and management accounting system?

13.4 How does just-in-time purchasing help avoid the material pricing problem?

13.5 Examine and respond to the following assertion:
'There is nothing new about activity based costing: all it does is introduce a more complicated way of absorbing overheads into production.'

CHAPTER 14

Budgetary control

Trinity aims for further expansion

Trinity International Holdings yesterday took another step in its plan to expand its UK newspaper empire with the proposed takeover of Joseph Woodhead & Sons, the publisher of the Huddersfield *Daily Examiner*.

Last month the publisher of Liverpool's *Daily Post and Echo* announced an agreement to buy Argus Press for £23 million, marking its first move into the south of England.

A year ago the Chester-based group, which owns papers in Canada and the US, bought Scottish & Universal Newspapers from Lonrho for £45 million.

Joesph Woodhead, an independent private company, has accepted an offer of approximately £12.6 million from Trinity. The deal is subject to offical approval.

As well as the *Daily Examiner*, which has a circulation of around 40 000, the company publishes a number of paid-for and free weekly and monthly titles and owns a small stationers.

Trinity's finance director, Michael Masters, said: "We are clearly delighted to be able to acquire such strong and respected titles which have benefited from good operational management.

'Trinity will continue to operate the titles on an autonomous basis, protecting their editorial freedom.' – PA.

The Scotsman, 4 August 1993.

Exhibit 14.0 The acquisition of new companies will make the budgeting process an extremely unpredictable exercise.

In the last five chapters we have dealt with the basic principles of cost and management accounting. Throughout our analysis, there has been an underlying assumption that much of the information has been prepared *after* the event, i.e. on an historical basis. However, the managers of an entity are probably more concerned with looking to what might happen, rather than what did happen. If we are to get the best out of a cost and management accounting system, we ought to provide management with information about the future as well as the past. It is a relatively easy task to do so by incorporating a control method known as *budgetary control*. Budgetary control is the subject of this chapter.

The CIMA definition of budgetary control is as follows:

> **Budgetary control**: the establishment of budgets relating the responsibilities of executives to the requirements of a policy, and the continuous comparison of actual with budgeted results, either to secure by individual action the objectives of that policy or to provide a basis for its revision.

Budgetary control takes up a lot of time and managerial effort. The system is usually administered by a team of accountants specially employed for the purpose, although it is necessary for the team to be assisted by other personnel. Indeed, if budgetary control is to work effectively, most employees will need to be heavily involved in the entire exercise.

We could go into considerable detail about the system of budgetary control, but in this book we are only concerned with those aspects of it that are of particular relevance to the non-accountant. We shall, therefore, avoid too much detail. In the next section, we outline some of the background to budgeting and budgetary control. This is followed by an explanation of the budget procedure. A further section examines the preparation of functional budgets, while the final section deals with flexible budgets. We start by examining what is meant by the terms 'budget' and 'budgeting'.

LEARNING OBJECTIVES

> By the end of this chapter, you will be able to:
> - describe the nature and purpose of budgeting and budgetary control;
> - list the steps involved in operating a budgetary control system;
> - describe the difference between fixed and flexible budgets.

BUDGETING AND BUDGETARY CONTROL

The term 'budget' is usually well understood by the layman. Many people, for example, often prepare a quite sophisticated budget for their own household expenses. In fact, albeit in a very informal sense, everyone does some budgeting at some time or other, e.g. by making a rough comparison between the next month's salary and the next month's expenditure. Such a budget may not be very precise, and it may not be formally written down; none the less, it contains all the ingredients of what accountants mean by a budget.

The CIMA definition of a budget is as follows:

> **Budget**: a plan expressed in money. It is prepared and approved prior to the budget period and may show income, expenditure, and the capital to be employed. May be drawn up showing incremental effects on former budgeted or actual figures, or be compiled by zero-based budgeting.

The above definition uses the term 'zero-based budgeting'. The formal CIMA definition is as follows:

Zero-based budgeting: a method of budgeting whereby all activities are re-evaluated each time a budget is set. Discrete levels of each activity are valued and a combination chosen to match funds available.

In other words, we would prepare the budget as though it is the first time that we have ever prepared one, and without reference to previous budgets.

The essential features of a budget can summarized as follows:

1 it lays down policies that are expected to be pursued in order to meet the overall objectives of an entity;
2 it contains both quantitative and financial data;
3 the data are usually formally documented;
4 the budget covers a defined future period of time.

In practice, a considerable number of budgets will be prepared, e.g. for sales, production, and administration. These budgets will then be combined into an overall budget known as a *master budget*, comprising (a) a budgeted profit and loss account; (b) a budgeted balance sheet; and (c) a budgeted cash flow statement.

Once the master budget has been prepared, it will be closely examined to see whether the overall plan can be accommodated. It could be the case, for example, that the sales budget indicates a large increase in sales. This may require the production budgets to be prepared on the basis of this extra sales demand. However, the cash budget might suggest that the entity cannot meet the extra sales and production activity that will be required. In these circumstances, additional financing arrangements may have to be be made, because obviously no organization would normally turn down the opportunity of increasing its sales.

In practice, the preparation of individual budgets can be a useful exercise even if nothing further is then done about it, since it forces management to look ahead. It is a natural human tendency to be always looking back, but past experience is not always a guide for the future. If managers are asked to produce a budget, at least it does encourage them to examine what they have done in relation to what they could do. None the less, the full benefits of a budgeting system are only realized when it is also used for control purposes, i.e. by the constant comparison of actual results with the budgeted results, and then taking any necessary corrective action. This leads us on to consider in a little more detail what we mean by 'budgetary control'.

Budgetary control has several important features, and these may be summarized as follows:

1 managerial responsibilities have to be clearly defined;
2 individual budgets lay down a detailed plan of action for a particular sphere of responsibility;
3 managers have a responsibility to adhere to their budgets once the budgets have been approved;
4 the actual performance is constantly monitored and compared with their budgeted results;
5 corrective action is taken if the actual results differ from the budget;
6 departures from budget are only permitted if they have been approved by senior management;
7 variances (i.e. differences) that are unaccounted for will be subject to individual investigation.

Any variance that does occur should be carefully investigated. If it is considered necessary, then the current actual performance will be immediately brought back into line with the budget. Sometimes the budget itself will be changed, e.g. if there is an unexpected increase in sales. Such changes may, of course, have an effect on the other budgets, so it cannot be done in isolation.

Now that we have outlined the nature and purpose of budgeting and budgetary control, we are in a position to investigate how the system works. We do so in the next section.

BUDGET PROCEDURE

The budget procedure starts with an examination of the entity's objectives. These may be very simple. They may include, for example, an overall wish to maximize profits, to foster better relations with its customers, or to improve the working conditions of its employees. Once the entity has decided upon its overall objectives, it is in a position to formulate some detailed plans.

These will probably start with a forecast. Note that there is a technical difference between a forecast and a budget. A forecast is a prediction of what is *likely* to happen. CIMA defines it as follows:

> **Forecasting**: the identification of factors and quantification of their effect on an entity, as a basis for planning.

By comparison, a budget is a formal written statement of what *should* happen.

In order to make it easier for us to guide you through the budgeting process, we will examine each stage individually. We do so in the following sub-sections.

The budget period

The main budget period is usually based on a calendar year. It could be shorter or longer depending upon the nature of the product cycle, e.g. the fashion industry may adopt a short budget period of less than a year, while the construction industry may choose (say) a five-year period. Irrespective of the industry, however, a calendar year is usually a convenient period to choose as the base period, because it fits in with the financial accounting period.

Besides determining the main budget period, it is also necessary to prepare sub-period budgets. Sub-period budgets are required for budgetary control purposes, since the actual results have to be frequently compared with the budgeted results. The sub-budget periods for some activities may need to be very short if tight control is to be exercised over them. The cash budget, for example, may need to be prepared on a weekly basis, whereas the administration budget may only need to be prepared quarterly.

Administration

The budget procedure may be administered by a special budget committee, or it may supervised by the accounting function. It will be necessary for the budget committee to lay down general guidelines in accordance with the entity's objectives, and to ensure that individual departments do not operate completely independently. The production department, for example, needs to know what the entity is budgeting to sell, so that it can prepare its own budget on the basis of those sales. However, the detailed production budget must still remain the entire responsibility of the production manager.

This procedure is in line with the concept of responsibility accounting which we outlined in Chapter 9. If the control procedure is to work properly, managers must be given responsibilty for a clearly defined area of activity, such as a cost centre. Thereafter, they are fully answerable for all that goes on there. Unless managers are given complete authority to act within clearly defined guidelines, they cannot be expected to be answerable for something that is outside their control. This means that as far as budgets are concerned, managers must help prepare, amend and approve their own responsibility centre's budget, otherwise the budgetary control system will not work.

The budgeting process

The budgeting process is illustrated in Exhibit 14.1. Study the Exhibit very carefully, noting how the various budgets all fit together.

Later on in the chapter we shall be using a quantitative example to illustrate how the budgeting process works. For the moment, however, it will be sufficent to give a brief description.

Exhibit 14.1 The inter-relationship of budgets in a budgeting system

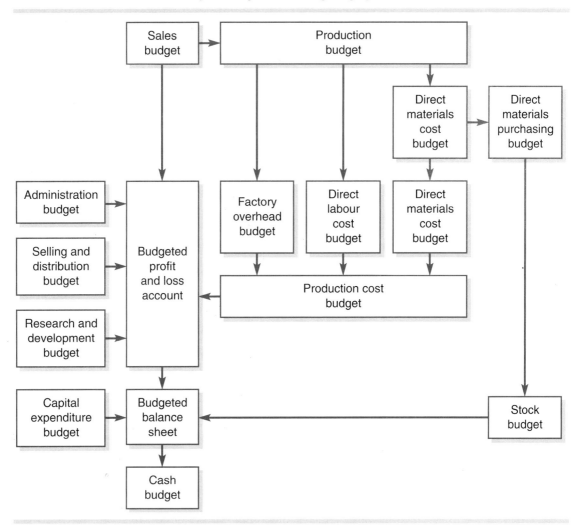

In commercial organizations, the first budget to be prepared is usually the sales budget. Once the sales for the budget period (and for each sub-budget period) have been determined, the next stage is to calculate the effect on production. This will then enable an agreed level of activity to be determined. The *level of activity* may be expressed in so many units, or as a percentage of the theoretical productive capacity of the entity. Once it has been established, departmental managers can be instructed to prepare their budgets on the basis of the required level of activity.

Let us assume, for example, that 1000 units can be sold for a particular budget period. The production department manager will need this information in order to prepare his budget. This does not necessarily mean that he will budget for a production level of 1000 units, because he will have to allow for the budgeted level of opening and closing stocks.

The budgeted production level will then be translated into how much material and labour will be required to meet that particular level. Similarly, it will be necessary to prepare overhead budgets. Much of the general overhead expenditure of the entity (such as factory administrative costs, head office costs, and research and development expenditure) will tend to be fixed, and such overheads will not be directly affected by production levels. However, in some instances, a marked change in activity may lead to a change in fixed costs.

The sales and distribution overhead budget may be the one overhead budget that will not be entirely fixed in nature. An increase in the number of units sold, for example, may involve more van delivery costs.

Not all entities start the budget process with sales. A local authority usu-ally prepares a budget on the basis of what it is likely to spend. The total budgeted expenditure is then compared with the total amount of council tax (after allowing for the income and grants) needed to cover it. The council tax is a new form of local authority taxation which has recently replaced the former community charge (or poll tax, as it was commonly known). If the political cost of an increase in the council tax appears too high, then the council will demand a reduction in the budgeted expendi-ture. Once the budget has been set, and the tax has been levied on that basis, departments have to work within the budgets laid down. However, since the budget will have been prepared on an estimate of the actual expenditure for the last two or three months of the old financial year, account has to be taken of any a surplus or short-fall expected in the cur-rent year. If the estimate eventually proves excessive, the local authority will have over-taxed. This means that it has got some additional funds available to cushion the current year's expenditure. Of course, if it is under-taxed for any balance carried forward, departments might have to start cutting back on what they thought they could spend.

This process is quite different from the private sector in which the bud-geted sales effectively determine all the other budgets. In a local authority, it is the expenditure budgets that determine what the council tax should be, and it is only the control exercised by central government and by the local authority itself that places a ceiling on what is spent.

FUNCTIONAL BUDGETS

A budget prepared for a particular department, cost centre, or other identi-fiable sphere of responsibility is known as a *functional budget*. All the functional budgets will then be combined into the *master budget*. As we described earlier in this chapter, the master budget is, in effect, a combined budgeted profit and loss account, budgeted balance sheet, and budgeted cash flow statement.

An initial draft of the master budget may well not be acceptable to the senior management of the entity. This may be because the entity cannot cope with that particular budgeted level of activity, e.g. as a result of production or cash constraints. Indeed, one of the most important budgets is the *cash budget*. The cash budget translates all the other functional budgets (including that for capital expenditure) into cash terms. It will show in detail the pattern of cash inputs and outputs for the main budget period, as well as for each sub-budget period. If it shows that the entity will have difficulty in financing a particular budgeted level of activity (or if there is going to be a period when cash is exceptionally tight), the management will have an opportunity to seek out alternative sources of finance.

This latter point illustrates the importance of being aware of future commitments, so that something can be done in advance if there are likely to be constraints (irrespective of their nature). The master budget usually takes so long to prepare, however, that by the time that it has been completed, it will be almost impossible to make major alterations to it. It is then tempting for senior management to make changes to the functional budgets without referencing them back to individual cost centre managers. It is most unwise to amend them in this way, because it is then difficult to use such budgets for control purposes. If managers have not agreed to the changes, they will argue that they can hardly take responsibility for budgets which have been imposed on them.

We appreciate that a descriptive analysis makes it difficult to see clearly how all the functional budgets fit together, so in the next section we will illustrate the procedures by using a quantitative example.

AN ILLUSTRATIVE EXAMPLE OF FUNCTIONAL BUDGETS

It would obviously be very difficult to observe the basic procedures involved in the preparation of the functional budgets if we used an extremely detailed example, so in Exhibit 14.2 we have cut out all the incidental information. As a result, the Exhibit only illustrates the main procedures, but at least you will get some idea of how the whole process works.

Exhibit 14.2

Sefton Limited manufactures one product known as EC2. The following information relates to the preparation of the budget for the year to 31 March 19X9:
1 Sales budget details for product EC2:
    Expected selling price per unit: £100.
    Expected sales in units: 10 000.
    All sales are on credit terms.

2 EC2 requires 5 units of raw material E and 10 units of raw material C. E is expected to cost £3 per unit, and C £4 per unit. All goods are purchased on credit terms.

3 Two departments are involved in producing EC2, machining and assembly. The following information is relevant:

	Direct labour per unit of product (hours)	Direct labour rate per hour £
Machining	1.00	6
Assembling	0.50	8

4 The finished production overhead costs are expected to amount to £100 000.

5 At 1 April 19X8, 800 units of EC2 are expected to be in stock at a value of £52 000, 4500 units of raw material E at a value of £13 500, and 12 000 units of raw materials are planned to be 10% above the expected opening stock levels as at 1 April 19X8.

6 Administration, selling and distribution overhead is expected to amount to £150 000.

7 Other relevant information:

  (a) Opening trade debtors are expected to be £80 000. Closing trade debtors are expected to amount to 15% of the total sales for the year.

  (b) Opening trade creditors are expected to be £28 000. Closing trade creditors are expected to amount to 10% of the purchases for the year.

  (c) All other expenses will be paid in cash during the year.

  (d) Other balances at 1 April 19X8 are expected to be as follows:

	£	£
(i) Share capital; ordinary shares		225 000
(ii) Retained profits		17 500
(iii) Proposed dividend		75 000
(iv) Fixed assets at cost	250 000	
Less: Accumulated depreciation	100 000	
		150 000
(v) Cash at bank and in hand		2 000

8 Capital expenditure will amount to £50 000 payable in cash on 1 April 19X8:

9 Fixed assets are depreciated on a straight-line basis at a rate of 20% per annum on cost.

Required:

As far as the information permits, prepare all the relevant budgets for Sefton Limited for the year to 31 March 19X9.

Answer to Exhibit 14.2

Even with a much simplified budgeting exercise, there is clearly a great deal of work involved in preparing the budgets. To make it easier for you to understand what is happening, the procedure will be outlined step by step.

Step 1: Prepare the sales budget

Units of EC2	Selling price per unit £	Total sales value £
10 000	100	1 000 000

Step 2: Prepare the production budget

	Units
Sales of EC2	10 000
Less: Opening stock	800
	9 200
Add: Desired closing stock (opening stock +10%)	880
Production required	10 080

Step 3: Prepare the direct materials usage budget

Direct material:
    E: 5 units x 10 080   50 400 units

    C: 10 units x 10 080   100 800 units

Step 4: Prepare the direct materials purchases budget

Direct material	E (Units)	C (Units)
Usage (as per Step 3)	50 400	100 800
Less: Opening stock	4 500	12 000
	45 900	88 800
Add: Desired closing stock (opening stock+10%)	4 950	13 200
	50 850	102 000
	x £3	x £4
∴ Total value of purchase	£152 550	£408 000

Step 5: Prepare the direct labour budget

	Machining	Assembling
Production units (as per Step 2)	10 080	10 080
x direct labour hours required	x 1 DLH	x 0.50 DLH
	10 080 DLH	5 040 DLH
x direct labour rate per hour	x £6	x £8
	£60 480	£40 320

Step 6: Prepare the fixed production overhead budget

Given   £100 000

Step 7: Calculate the value of the closing raw material stock

Raw material	Closing stock* (units)	Cost per unit £	Total value £
E	4 950	3	14 850
C	13 200	4	52 800
			£67 650

*Step 4

Step 8: calculate the value of the closing finished stock

	£	£
Unit cost:		
Direct materials: E – 5 units x £3 per unit	15	
C – 10 units x £4 per unit	40	55
Direct labour: Machining – 1 hour x £6 per DLH	6	
Assembling – 0.50 hours x £8 per DLH	4	10
Total direct cost		£65
x units in stock		x 880
		£57 200

Step 9: Prepare the administration, selling and distribution budget

Given   £150 000

Step 10: Prepare the capital expenditure budget

Given   £50 000

Step 11: Calculate the cost of goods sold

	£
Opening stock (given)	52 000
Manufacturing cost:	
Production units (Step 2) x total direct cost (Step 3)	
= 10 080 x £65	655 200
	707 200
Less: Closing stock (Step 8: 880 units x £65)	57 200
Cost of goods sold (10 000 units)	£650 000

Step 12: Prepare the cash budget

	£
Receipts	
Opening debtors	80 000
Sales (£1 000 000 x 85%)	850 000
	930 000

Payments

Opening creditors	28 000
Purchases [Step 4: (152 550 + 408 000) x 90%]	504 495
Wages (Step 5: 60 480 + 40 320)	100 800
Fixed production overhead	100 000
Administration, selling and distribution overhead	150 000
Capital expenditure	50 000
Proposed dividend (19X8)	75 000
	1 008 295
Net receipts	(78 295)
Add: Opening cash	2 000
Budgeted closing cash balance (overdrawn)	£(76 295)

Step 13: Prepare the budgeted profit and loss account

	£	£
Sales (Step 1)		1 000 000
Less: Variable cost of sales (Step 8: 10 000 x 65)		650 000
Gross margin		350 000
Less: Fixed production overhead (Step 6)	100 000	
Depreciation [(250 000 + 50 000) x 20%]	60 000	160 000
Production margin		190 000
Less: Administration, selling and distribution overhead (Step 9)		150 000
Budgeted net profit		£40 000

Step 14: Prepare the budgeted balance sheet

	£	£	£
Fixed assets (at cost)			300 000
Less: Accumulated depreciation			160 000
			140 000
Current assets			
Raw materials(Step 7)		67 650	
Finished stock (Step 8)		57 200	
Trade debtors (15% x 1 000 000)		150 000	
		274 850	
Less: Current liabilities			
Trade creditors [Step 4: 10% x (152 550 + 408 000)]	56 055		
Bank overdraft (Step 12)	76 295	132 350	142 500
			£282 500

Financed by:
Share capital
Ordinary shares   225 000
Retained profits (17 500 + 40 000)   57 500
                                                           ————————
                                                           £282 500
                                                           ════════

Exhibit 14.2 is a fairly complicated example, although we have tried to avoid too much detail, e.g. we have assumed that the company produces only one product, and that the value of the opening stocks at 1 April 19X8 will be the same as the budgeted costs of manufacture in the year to 31 March 19X9. It might be worth while, therefore, to go through the exhibit once again, and make sure that you understand how all the various budgets fit together. You can use, as your guide, the budgeting process shown in diagrammatic form in Exhibit 14.1. It would then be advisable to have yet another go at Exhibit 14.2, but this time without referring to the solution.

FIXED AND FLEXIBLE BUDGETS

Once the master budget has been agreed, it becomes the detailed plan for future action which everyone is expected to work towards. However, some entities only use the budgeting process as a *planning* exercise. Once the master budget has been agreed, there may be no attempt to use it as a control technique. Thus, the budget may be virtually ignored, and it may not be compared with the actual results. If this is the case, then the entity is not getting the best out of the budgeting system.

As we suggested earlier, budgets are particularly useful if they are also used as a means of control. The control is achieved if the actual performance is used to compare it with the budget. Significant variances should then be investigated, and any necessary corrective action taken.

The constant comparison of the actual results with the budgeted results may be done either on a *fixed* budget basis or a *flexible* budget basis. A fixed budget basis means that the actual results for a particular period are compared with the original budgets. This is as you would expect, for the budget is a measure. You would get some very misleading results, for example, if you used an elastic ruler to measure distances. Similarly, an elastic-type budget might also give some highly unreliable results. In some cases, however, a variable measure *is* used in budgeting in order to allow for certain circumstances which might have taken place since the budgets were prepared. Accountants call this *flexing* the budget. The CIMA definition of a flexible budget is as follows:

> **Flexible budget**: a budget which, by recognizing different cost behaviour patterns, is designed to change as volume of output changes.

It may seem a little contradictory to argue that the budget should be changed once it has been agreed, but a fixed budget (i.e. one that does not change) can also be misleading. We explained earlier that in order to prepare their budgets, managers (especialy those directly involved in production) will need to be given the budgeted level of activity. Consequently, their budgets will be based on that level of activity, but if the *actual* level of activity is greater (or less) than the budgeted level, managers will have to allow for more (or less) expenditure on materials, labour, and other expenses.

Suppose, for example, that a manager has prepared his budget on the basis of an anticipated level of activity of 70% of the maximum number of units that the plant is capable of producing. The company turns out to be much busier than it expected, and it achieves an actual level of activity level of 80%. The production manager is likely to have spent far more on materials, labour, and other expenses than he had originally budgeted. If the actual performance is then compared with the budget (i.e. on a fixed budget basis), it will appear as though he had greatly exceeded what he thought he would spend. No doubt, he would then argue that the differences had arisen as a result of a greatly increased level of activity (which may be outside his control). While this may be true, we cannot be certain that all of the differences were caused by the increased activity.

Hence, the need to flex the budget, i.e. we revise it on the basis of what it would have been if the manager had budgeted for an activity level of 80% instead of 70%. The other assumptions and calculations made at the time the budget was prepared (such as material prices and wage rates) will not be amended.

If the entity operates a flexible budget system, the original budgets may be prepared on the basis of a wide range of possible activity levels. This method, however, is very time consuming, and managers will be very lucky if they prepare one that is identical to the actual level of activity. The best method is to wait until the actual level of activity is known, and then flex the budget on that basis.

This procedure might appear fairly complicated, so it is best if we illustrate it with an example. We do so in in Exhibit 14.3.

Exhibit 14.3 Flexible budget procedure

The following information had been prepared for Carp Limited for the year to 30 June 19X6:

	Budget	Actual
Level of activity	50%	60%
	£	£
Costs:		
Direct materials	50 000	61 000
Direct labour	100 000	118 000
Variable overhead	10 000	14 000
Total variable cost	160 000	193 000
Fixed overhead	40 000	42 000
Total costs	£200 000	£235 000

Required :
Prepare a flexed budget operating statement for Carp Limited for the year to 30 June 19X6.

Answer to Exhibit 14.3

Carp Limited
Flexed budget operating statement for the year 30 June 19X6

	Flexed budget	Actual costs	Variance: favourable/ (adverse)
	£	£	£
Direct materials (1)	60 000	61 000	(1 000)
Direct labour (1)	120 000	118 000	2 000
Variable overhead (1)	12 000	14 000	(2 000)
Total variable costs	192 000	193 000	(1 000)
Fixed overhead (2)	40 000	42 000	(2 000)
Total costs (3)	£232 000	£235 000	£(3 000)

Tutorial notes

1 All the budgeted variable costs have been flexed by 20% because the actual activity was 60% compared with a budgeted level of 50% (i.e. a 20% increase).

2 The budgeted fixed costs are not flexed because by definition they ought not to change with activity.

3 Instead of using the total fixed budget cost of £200 000 (as per the question), the total flexed budget costs of £232 000 can be compared more fairly with the total actual cost of £235 000.

4 Note that the terms 'favourable' and 'adverse' (as applied to variances) mean favourable or adverse to profit. In other words, profit will be either greater or less than the budgeted profit.

5 The reasons for the variances between the actual costs and the flexed budget will need to be investigated. The flexed budget shows that even allowing for the increased activity, the actual costs were in excess of the budget allowance.

6 Similarly, it will be necessary to investigate why the actual activity was higher than the budgeted activity. It could have been caused by inefficient budgeting, or by quite an unexpected increase in sales activity. While this would normally be welcome, it might have place a strain on the productive and financial resources of the entity. If the increase is likely to be permanent, management will need to make immediate arrangements to accomodate the new level of activity.

It should be emphasized that the primary purpose of a budgetary control system is to control as closely as possible the activities of the entity. There will invariably be differences between the actual and the budgeted results, no matter how carefully the budgets are prepared. This does not matter unduly, as long as it is possible to find out why there were differences, and to take action before it is too late to do something about them.

CONCLUSION

We have suggested in this chapter that the full benefits of a cost and management accounting system can best be gained if it is combined with a budgetary control system. The preparation of budgets is a valuable exercise in itself for it forces management to look ahead to what might happen, rather than to look back to what did happen. However, it is even more valuable if it is also used as a form of control.

Budgetary control enables actual results to be measured frequently against an agreed budget (or plan). Departures from that budget can be quickly spotted, and steps taken to correct any unwelcome trends. However, the comparison of actual results with a fixed budget may not be particularly helpful if the actual level of activity is different from that budgeted. It is advisable, therefore, to compare actual results with a flexed budget.

Since so many of the functional budgets are based upon the budgeted level of activity, it is vital that it is calculated as accurately as possible, since an error in estimating the level of activity could affect all of the company's financial and operational activities. Thus, it is important that any difference between the actual and the budgeted level of activity is carefully investigated.

The next chapter deals with standard costing. Standard costing is another control method that is very similar to budgetary control, except it goes into very much more detail.

KEY POINTS

1 A budget is a plan.

2 Budgetary control is a cost control method that enables actual results to be compared with the budget, thereby enabling any necessary corrective action to be taken.

3 The preparation of budgets will be undertaken by a budget team.

4 Managers must be responsible for producing their own functional budgets.

5 Functional budgets are combined to form a master budget.

6 A fixed budget system compares actual results with the original budgets.

7 A flexible budget system compares actual results with the original budget, flexed (or amended) to allow for the actual activity level being different from that budgeted.

CHECK YOUR LEARNING

1 Fill in the missing words in each of the following sentences:
  (a) A budget is a _____ expressed in money.
  (b) The continuous comparison of actual with budgeted results is known as

  _____ _____.

  (c) A _____ budget is one which recognizes different cost behaviour patterns.

2 Over what period of time might a budget be normally prepared?
  (a) three months (b) a year (c) two years (d) five years (e) none of these

3 What is the term normally given to the overall budgeted profit and loss account, budgeted balance sheet, and budgeted cash flow statement?

4 (a) In a manufacturing entity, which budget will normally be prepared first?
  (b) What is the main determinant of a local authority's budget?

ANSWERS

1 (a) plan   (b) budgetary control   (c) flexible
2 (b) a year
3 master budget
4 (a) sales budget   (b) estimate of total expenditure

QUESTIONS

14.1 You are presented with the following information for Moray Limited.
Budgeted sales units for the six months to 30 June 19X1

January	200
February	250
March	370
April	400
May	500
June	550

Additional information:
1 Opening stock at 1 January 19X1 was expected to be 320 units.
2 Desired closing stock level at 30 June 19X1 was 450 units.

Required:
Calculate the minimum number of units to be produced each month if an even production flow is to be established.

14.2 You have been presented with following budgeted information relating to Jordan Limited for the six months to 31 December 19X2:

	July	August	September	October	November	December
Sales (units)	70	140	350	190	150	120
Closing stock (units)	230	370	200	190	180	100

Additional information:
Opening stock at 1 July 19X2 is expected to be 100 units.

Required:
Calculate the monthly production levels required to meet the above budgeted data.

14.3 The directors of Dalton Limited have been presented with the following budgeted information for the six months to 30 June 19X3:

	January	February	March	April	May	June
Sales (units)	90	150	450	150	130	120

Additional information:
1 The opening stock at 1 January 19X3 is expected to be 100 units.
2 Units are only available for sale in the period following the month in which they were manufactured.

Required:
Calculate the minimum number of units to be produced each month in order to meet the budgeted monthly sales figures assuming that the directors wish to adopt the minimum possible production flow.

14.4 The following information has been prepared for Tom Limited for the six months to 30 September 19X4:

Budgeted production levels Product X

	Units
April	140
May	280
June	700
July	380
August	300
September	240

Product X uses two units of component A6 and three units of component B9. At 1 April 19X4 there were expected to be 100 units of A6 in stock, and 200 units of B9. The desired closing stock levels of each component were as follows:

Month end 19X4	A6 (units)	B9 (units)
30 April	110	250
31 May	220	630
30 June	560	340
31 July	300	300
31 August	240	200
30 September	200	180

During the six months to 30 September 19X4, component A6 was expected to be purchased at a cost of £5 per unit and component B9 at a cost of £10 per unit.

Required:
Prepare the following budgets for each of the six months to 30 September 19X4:
1 direct materials usage budget; and
2 direct materials purchase budget.

14.5 Don Limited has one major product which requires two types of direct labour to produce it. The following data refer to certain budget proposals for the three months to 31 August 19X5:

Month	Production units
30.6.X5	600
31.7.X5	700
31.8.X5	650

Direct labour hours required per unit:

	Hours	Budgeted rate per hour £
Production	3	4
Finishing	2	8

Required:
Prepare the direct labour cost budget for each of the three months to 31 August 19X5.

14.6 Gorse Limited manufactures one product. The budgeted sales for period 6 are for 10 000 units at a selling price of £100 per unit. Other details are as follows:
1 Two components are used in the manufacture of each unit:

Component	Number	Unit cost of each component £
XY	5	1
WZ	3	0.50

2 Stocks at the beginning of the period are expected to be as follows:
   (a) 4000 units of finished goods at a unit cost of £52.50 per unit.
   (b) Component XY: 16 000 units at a cost of £1.
       Component WZ: 9600 units at a unit cost of £0.50.
3 Two grades of employees are used in the manufacture of each unit:

Employee	Hours per unit	Labour rate per hour £
Production	4	5
Finishing	2	7

4 Factory overhead is absorbed into units cost on the basis of direct labour hours. The budgeted factory overhead for the period is estimated to be £96 000.

5 The administration, selling and distribution overhead for the period has been budgeted at £275 000.

6 The company plans a reduction of 50% in the quantity of finished stock at the end of period 6, and an increase of 25% in the quantity of each component.

Required:
Prepare the following budgets for period 6:

1 sales;
2 production quantity;
3 materials usage;
4 materials purchase;
5 direct labour;
6 the budgeted profit and loss account.

14.7 The following budget information relates to Flossy Limited for the three months to 31 March 19X7.

1 Budgeted profit and loss accounts:

Month	31.1.X7	28.2.X7	31.3.X7
	£000	£000	£000
Sales (all on credit)	2000	3000	2500
Cost of sales	1200	1800	1500
Gross profit	800	1200	1000
Depreciation	(100)	(100)	(100)
Other expenses	(450)	(500)	(600)
	(550)	(600)	(700)
Net profit	£250	£600	£300

2 Budgeted balance sheets:

Budgeted balances	31.12.X6	31.1.X7	28.2.X7	31.3.X7
	£000	£000	£000	£000
Current assets:				
Stocks	100	120	150	150
Debtors	200	300	350	400
Short-term investments	60	–	40	30
Current liabilities:				
Trade creditors	110	180	160	150
Other creditors	50	50	50	50
Taxation	150	–	–	–
Dividends	200	–	–	–

3 Capital expenditure to be incurred on 20 February 19X7 was expected to amount to £470 000.

4 Sales of plan and equipment on 15 March 19X7 are expected to raise £30 000 in cash.

5 The cash at bank and in hand on 1 January 19X7 was expected to be £15 000.

Required:

Prepare Flossy Limited's cash budget for each of the three months during the quarter ending 31 March 19X7.

14.8 Chimes limited has prepared a flexible budget for one of its factories for the year to 30 June 19X8. The details are as follows;

Production capacity	30%	40%	50%	60%
	£000	£000	£000	£000
Direct materials	42	56	70	84
Direct labour	18	24	30	36
Factory overhead	22	26	30	34
Administration overhead	17	20	23	26
Selling and distribution overhead	12	14	16	18
	£111	£140	£169	£198

Additional information:

1 the company is only operating at 45% of its capacity, and an increase in capacity during the year to 30 June 19X8 is unlikely. At that capacity, the sales revenue has been budgeted at a level of £135 500.

2 it would be possible to close the factory down for 12 months, and then re-open it again on 1 July 19X8 when trading conditions were expected to improve. The costs of doing so are estimated to be as follows.

	£000
Redundancy and other closure costs	30
Property and plant maintenance during the year to 30 June 19X8	10
Re-opening costs	20

However, £30 000 would be saved as a result of a reduction in general company and factory fixed overheads.

Required :

Determine whether the factory should be closed during the year to 30 June 19X8.

ADDITIONAL QUESTIONS (WITHOUT ANSWERS)

14.9 Avsar limited has extracted the following budgeting details for the year to 30 September 19X9:

1 Sales: 4000 units of V at £500 per unit
7000 units of R at £300 per unit

2 Materials usage (units):

	Raw material		
	O1	I2	L3
V	11	9	12
R	15	1	10

3 Raw material costs (per unit)

	£
O1	8
I2	6
L3	3

4 Raw material stocks:

	Units		
	O1	I2	L3
At 1 October 19X8	1300	1400	400
At 30 September 19X9	1400	1000	200

5 Finished stocks

	Units	
	V	R
At 1 October 19X8	110	90
At 30 September 19X9	120	150

6 Direct labour

	Product	
	V	R
Budgeted hours per unit	10	8
Budgeted hourly rate (£)	12	6

7 Variable overhead

	Product	
	V	R
Budgeted hourly rate (£)	10	5

8 fixed overhead; £193 160 (to be absorbed on the basis of direct labour hours).

Required :
(a) Prepare the following budgets:
  (i)   sales:
  (ii) production units;
  (iii) materials usage;
  (v)   materials purchase; and
  (vi) production cost; and
(b) calculate the total budgeted profit for the year to 30 September 19X9.

14.10 The following budgeted trading, and profit and loss accounts, and balance sheets, relating to the three months to 31 March 19X4, have been prepared for Ramsay Limited:

	January	February	March
Trading, profit and loss accounts			
	£000	£000	£000
Sales	200	300	400
Opening stock	15	20	30
Purchases	145	220	330
	160	240	360
Less: Closing stock	20	30	80
	140	210	280

Gross profit	60	90	120	
Less: Expenses	20	30	40	
Profit	40	60	80	

Balance sheets	1.1.X4	31.1.X4	28.2.X4	31.3.X4
	£000	£000	£000	£000
Fixed assets at cost	390	400	410	420
Less: Accumulated depreciation	155	160	166	180
	235	240	244	240
Investments	18	50	35	60
Current assets				
Stocks	15	20	30	80
Trade debtors	20	25	45	100
Prepayments	2	2	3	10
Cash and bank	4	3	2	–
	41	50	80	190
Current liabilities				
Bank overdraft	–	–	–	(8)
Trade creditors	(35)	(40)	(50)	(90)
Accruals	(3)	(4)	(3)	(2)
Taxation	(30)	(30)	–	–
Dividends	(20)	(20)	–	–
	(88)	(94)	(53)	(100)
Debenture loans	–	–	–	(4)
	£206	£246	£306	£386
Capital and reserves				
Share capital	200	200	200	240
Profit and loss account	6	46	106	146
	£206	£246	£306	£386

Note:
It is not expected that there will be any disposal of fixed assets during the three months to 31 March 19X4.

Required:
Prepare Ramsay's cash budget for *each* of the three months to 31 March 19X4 respectively.

CHAPTER 15

Standard costing

SmithKline sells bodycare brands

**By Maggie Urry in London
and Nikki Tait in New York**

Brylcreem, the preparation which slicked back the hair of pre-war England cricketer Denis Compton, of 1950s teddy boys and the youth of today, is being sold.

SmithKline Beecham, the Anglo-American healthcare group, yesterday announced sales of a range of brands for about £260m. But it said there would be a £100m restructuring charge set off against the profit on the sales in this year's accounts.

SB has agreed to Brylcreem – which has expanded to a range of men's toiletries – and other bath and bodycare brands, such as Badedas and Body Mist, to Sara Lee, the Chicago-based consumer products group, for £211m.

It is also selling its hair care brands, including Silvikrin, Vosene and Bristows to Wella, the German hair care group, for an undisclosed sum. Analysts speculated this was between £50m and £60m.

SB said the deals almost completed its programme of disposals since it was formed through a merger four years ago. It would now concentrate on its prescription and over-the-counter drugs, oral care products such as toothpaste and mouthwashes, and drinks such as Ribena and Lucozade.

Mr Harry Groome, head of SB's consumer brands division, said: "Our goal is to become the world leader in consumer healthcare," although he admitted this was a 10-year aim. It claims to be fourth currently.

SB would pursue its goal through alliances and acquisitions, expanding existing brands and converting prescription drugs to over-the-counter medicines.

The business being sold to Sara Lee has assets of £55m, including five plants in continental Europe, and made trading profit of £36m on sales of £164m in 1992. Wella is buying a business with assets of £5m and sales of £46m.

Mr Hugh Collum, chief financial officer of SB, said the sales would be slightly dilutive in the short term but the payback from the restructuring would be rapid.

Sara Lee's household and personal care activity is the smallest of its four main divisions. It combines such brands as Kiwi shoe polish, Sanex skin care, Zendium toothpaste and the Zwitsal baby-care lines, all of which sell in continental Europe.

The former SB brands will significantly enlarge the division, where sales and operating profits fell to $1.23bn (£790m) and $107m respectively last year following the sale of an over-the-counter drugs business.

Sara Lee said the deal would take it into the German personal care market for the first time, and it expected manufacturing and marketing synergies.

Wella said the purchase would more than double its UK market share from 5 to 11.3 per cent. The deal also gives it a strong position in the Middle East.

The Financial Times, 10 June 1993

Exhibit 15.0 Of course, no matter what control you have over your costs, you may still wish to improve your profits by a vigorous programme of acquisitions and disposals.

S tandard costing is similar to budgetary control, except that in standard costing, a budget is prepared for each unit (or each process), instead of just for each particular department. The budgeted unit (or process) cost is referred to as the *standard* cost.

The technique is also similar to budgetary control in that the standard cost of each unit is compared with the actual unit cost. Immediate action is then taken to correct any adverse trends.

The chapter is divided into two main sections. In the first section we examine the background to standard costing and its administration, including the types of standards, their preparation, and performance measurement. The second section deals with variance analysis, including both cost and sales variances.

We start with the background to standard costing.

LEARNING OBJECTIVES

By the end of this chapter, you will be able to:
- describe the nature and purpose of standard costing;
- identify the main steps involved in implementing and operating a standard costing system;
- calculate three performance measures and four variances;
- describe the importance of standard costing and variance analysis.

BACKGROUND AND ADMINISTRATION

It will be helpful if we first give you two key definitions recommended by CIMA. They are as follows:

> **Standard cost**: a standard expressed in money. It is built up from an assessment of the value of cost elements. Its main uses are providing bases for performance measurement, control by exception reporting, valuing stock and establishing selling prices.
>
> **Standard**: a predetermined measurable quantity set in defined conditions.

We suggested in the opening paragraphs that there were close similarities between budgetary control and standard costing, the main difference being that in standard costing we go into much more detail. For example, we not only calculate a total variance between the actual cost of a particular unit and the standard cost, but we also analyse it into the elements of cost. The degree of analysis depends partly upon management requirements, and partly upon the type of product being produced. This type of detailed analysis is known as *variance analysis*. Variance analysis and variance are defined by CIMA as follows:

> **Variance analysis**: the analysis of performance by means of variances. Used to promote management action at the earliest possible stages.
> **Variance**: difference between planned, budgeted, or standard cost and actual cost; and similarly for revenue. Not to be confused with statistical variance which measures the dispersion of a statistical population.

The calculation of variances is largely a routine arithmetical exercise, and as a non-accountant you are unlikely to be involved in it. You are much more likely to be responsible for investigating why variances have arisen. It is much easier to investigate the possible causes, however, if you have some idea of where to look for them. If you know, for example, that a variance has been caused mainly because of over-spending on direct materials, then you can begin to investigate whether there was an increase in material prices or whether more materials were used.

It is unlikely that all entities need (or will want) a standard costing system. Standard costing is particularly suited to manufacturing industry producing identifiable products, although there is no reason why it cannot be adopted in non-manufacturing entities. All entities, however, are recommended to have a budgetary control system, and, in order to prepare standard costs, it is necessary to prepare a budget for each cost centre. It is, therefore, quite possible to have a budgetary control system without having a standard costing system, but it is impossible to have standard costing without budgetary control.

In the following sub-sections we outline some of the requirements of a standard costing system.

Administration

The responsibility for administering a standard costing system is normally that of a special budget committee or of the accounting function.

The standard costing period

The overall period for which the standards are prepared will usually conform with the main and sub-budget periods. It may also be necessary (as it sometimes is with budgeting) to adopt fairly short standard periods, e.g. where market and production conditions are subject to frequent changes, or where it is difficult to plan very far ahead. As the selling price charged to customers will usually be based on the standard cost of a particular unit, it would be unwise to fix the selling price on out-of-date information, so, in some circumstances, it may be subject to fairly frequent changes.

Types of standard

The preparation of standard costs requires great care and attention. As each element of cost is subject to detailed arithmetical analysis, it is important that the initial information is accurate. Indeed, the information produced by a standard costing system will be virtually worthless if subsequent analyses reveal that variances were caused by inefficient budgeting and standard setting.

In preparing standard costs, management will need to be informed of the level of activity to be used in preparing the standard costs (i.e. whether the entity will need to operate at say 80% or 90% of its theoretical capacity). An activity level should be chosen that is capable of being achieved. It would be possible to choose a standard that was *ideal*, i.e one that represented a performance that could be achieved only under the most favourable of conditions. Such a standard would, however, be unrealistic, because it is rare for ideal conditions to prevail. CIMA defines an ideal standard as follows:

Ideal standard: a standard which can be attained under the most favourable conditions, with no allowance for normal losses, waste and machine downtime. Also known as potential standard.

A much more realistic standard is called an *attainable* standard. An attainable standard is one that the entity can expect to attain in reasonably efficient working conditions. In other words, it accepts that some delays and inefficiencies will occur, but it assumes that management will attempt to minimize them. CIMA defines it as follows:

Attainable standard: a standard which can be obtained if a standard unit of work is carried out efficiently, a machine properly operated or a material properly used. Allowances are made for normal losses, waste and machine downtime.

You may also come across the term *basic cost standards*. These are standards that are left unchanged over long periods of time. This enables some consistency to be achieved in comparing actual results with the same standards over a substantial period of time, but the standards may become so out of date that meaningful comparisons are not possible.

Preparation and information required

Standard costing is a sophisticated means of planning and controlling a company's operations. Standard costings are time consuming to prepare, and costly to produce, and the entire system is expensive to operate. The technique requires so much detailed information that most employees need to be convinced of its value if it is to work properly, so it does call for considerable team work.

There is no point in having a standard costing system if those who are supposed to benefit do not want it. If standard costing is to operate effectively its purpose must be understood by the employees, because they will have to provide the basic information. If this is done ineffectively or inefficiently, then any decision based upon it will be questionable.

The types of information required to produce standard costs can be summarized as follows:

1 **Direct materials**: types, quantities and price.
2 **Direct labour**: grades, numbers and rates of pay.
3 **Variable overhead**: the total variable overhead cost analysed into various categories, such as employee and general support costs.
4 **Fixed overhead**: the total fixed overhead analysed into various categories such as employee costs, building costs and general administration expenses.

From the above information, it can be seen that the standard cost of a particular unit is comprised of four main elements: (a) direct materials; (b) direct labour; (c) variable overhead; and (d) fixed overhead. In turn, each element is comprised of two factors, viz. quantity and price. The total standard cost of a specific unit may be built up as shown in Exhibit 15.1. The exhibit is based on some fictitious data.

Exhibit 15.1 Calculation of the total standard cost of a specific unit using absorption costing

	£
1 Direct materials	
Quantity × price (2 units × 5)	10
2 Direct labour	
Hours × hourly rate (5 hours × 10)	50
3 Variable overhead	
Hours × variable overhead absorption rate per hour	
(5 hours × 6)	30
4 Fixed overhead	
Hours × fixed overhead absorption rate per hour	
(5 hours × 3)	15
TOTAL STANDARD COST PER UNIT	£105

Note: The exhibit assumes that the unit cost is calculated on the basis of standard *absorption* costing. This is the most common method of standard costing, although it is possible to adopt a system of standard *marginal* costing.

Standard hours and the absorption of overhead

Assuming that the standard costs are prepared on the basis of absorption costing, overhead will be absorbed on the basis of *standard* hours (you will recall that in a non-standard costing system, overhead is absorbed on the basis of actual hours). A standard hour represents the amount of work that should be performed in an hour, given that it is produced in standard conditions, i.e. in *planned* conditions. CIMA puts it as follows:

> **Standard hour or minute**: the quantity of work achievable at standard performance in an hour or minute.

Each unit is given a standard time of so many hours in which to produce it, and it is against that standard that the actual hours will be compared.

In order to calculate the standard overhead cost of a unit, remember that the standard overhead absorption rate for the period is multiplied by the number of standard (not actual) hours that the unit should have taken to produce. The absorption of overhead by multiplying the standard absorption rate by the standard hours is a significant departure from that adopted in a non-standard costing system. This is a most important point, and we shall be returning to it a little later on in the chapter.

Sales variances

Some companies also prepare standard costings for sales, although they are not as common as cost variances. If sales variances are required, the difference between the actual sales revenue and the standard revenue is analysed into a number of appropriate sales variances, such as price and quantity. A detailed analysis of the budgeted sales will be needed in order to obtain the following information:

1 the range and number of each product to be sold;
2 the selling price of each product;
3 the respective periods in which sales are to take place;
4 the geographical areas in which they are to be sold.

Performance measures

Management may find it useful if some performance measures are extracted from the standard costing data. There are three particularly important ones. They assist in informing managers about the level of efficiency of the entity, help them to spot unfavourable trends, and enable them to take immediate corrective action.

Before we examine these performance measures, we must emphasize once again that in standard costing, actual costs are compared with the standard cost of the *actual* level of activity. It is tempting to compare the actual costs with the budgeted cost, but it is not customary to do so in standard costing. By comparing the actual cost with the standard cost of the actual production, we are effectively flexing the budget. This means that any variances that do then arise can be more realistically assessed, as we are then using the same level of activity to measure the actual costs against the budgeted costs. You will find the relationship between actual, budgeted, and standard shown in diagrammatic form in Exhibit 15.2.

Exhibit 15.2 The constituent elements in three important capacity ratios

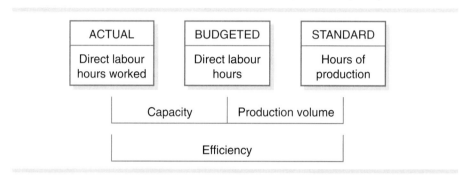

Bearing this point in mind, we can now introduce the performance measures. You will notice that they are all expressed as ratios. They are as follows:

The efficiency ratio

This ratio compares the total standard (or allowed) hours of units produced with the total actual hours taken to produce those units. It is calculated as follows:

$$\frac{\text{Standard hours produced}}{\text{Actual direct labour hours worked}} \times 100$$

The efficiency ratio enables management to check whether the company has produced the units in more or less time than had been allowed.

The capacity ratio

The capacity ratio compares the total actual hours worked with the total budgeted hours. It is calculated as follows:

$$\frac{\text{Actual direct labour hours worked}}{\text{Budgeted direct labour hours}} \times 100$$

This ratio enables management to ascertain whether all of the budgeted hours where used to produce actual units.

| The production volume ratio | This ratio compares the total allowed hours for the work actually produced with the total budgeted hours. It is calculated as follows: |

$$\frac{\text{Standard hours produced}}{\text{Budgeted direct labour hours}} \times 100$$

The production volume ratio enables management to compare the work produced (measured in terms of standard hours) with the budgeted hours of work. This ratio gives management some information about how effective the company has been in using the budgeted hours.

The efficiency, capacity, and production volume ratios are illustrated in Exhibit 15.3.

Exhibit 15.3

The following information relates to the Frost Production Company Limited for the year to 31 March 19X4:
1 Budgeted direct labour hours: 1000.
2 Budgeted units: 100.
3 Actual direct labour hours worked: 800.
4 Actual units produced: 90.

Required:
Calculate the following performance ratios:
(a) the efficiency ratio;
(b) the capacity ratio; and
(c) the production/volume ratio.

Answer to Exhibit 15.3

(a) The efficiency ratio:

$$\frac{\text{Standard hours produced}}{\text{Actual direct labour hours worked}} \times 100 = \frac{900^*}{800} \times 100 = 112.5\%$$

* Each unit is allowed 10 standard hours (1000 hours/100 units), and since 90 units were produced, the total standard hours of production = 900.

It would appear that the company has been more efficient in producing the goods than was expected. It was allowed 900 hours to do so, but it produced them in only 800 hours.

(b) The capacity ratio:

$$\frac{\text{Actual direct labour hours worked}}{\text{Budgeted hours}} \times 100 = \frac{800}{1000} \times 100 = 80\%$$

In this case, all of the time planned to be available (the capacity) was not utilized, either because it was not possible to work 1000 direct labour hours, or because the company did not undertake as much work as it could have done.

(c) The production volume ratio:

$$\frac{\text{Standard hours produced}}{\text{Budgeted hours}} \times 100 = \frac{900^*}{1000} \times 100 = \underline{\underline{90\%}}$$

* As calculated for the efficiency ratio.

It appears that if 90 units had been produced in standard conditions, another 100 hours would have been available (10 units × 10 hours). In fact, since the 90 units only took 800 hours to produce, at least another 20 units could have been produced in standard conditions.

$$\frac{1000 - 800}{10} = \underline{\underline{20 \text{ units}}}$$

Comments on the results
The budget allowed for 100 units to be produced and each unit was expected to take 10 direct labour hours to complete, a total budgeted activity of 1000 direct labour hours. However, only 90 units were actually produced. If these units had been produced in standard time, they should have taken 900 hours (90 units × 10 direct labour hours). These are the standard hours produced. In fact, the 90 units were completed in 800 actual hours. It appears, therefore, that the units were produced more efficiently than had been expected. The management will still need, of course, to investgate why only 90 units were produced and not the 100 budgeted units.

We have now covered the background to standard costing and its administration, so we can move on to look at what we mean by variance analysis. We do so in the next section.

VARIANCE ANALYSIS

As we have seen, the difference between actual costs and standard costs consists of two main variances: price and quantity. These variances may either be favourable (F) to profit, or adverse (A). This means that the actual prices paid or costs incurred can be more than was anticipated (adverse to profit), or less than anticipated (favourable to profit). Similarly, the quantities used in production can result in more being used (adverse to profit) or less than expected (favourable to profit).

Each element of cost can be analysed into price and quantity variances (although different terms may be used). The main sales and cost variances are shown in diagrammatic form in Exhibit 15.4. The main cost variances are also summarized below. We deal with sales variances later on in the chapter.

1 Direct material: Total = price + usage
2 Direct labour: Total = rate + efficiency
3 Variable production overhead: Total = expenditure + efficiency
4 Fixed production overhead: Total = expenditure + volume *

    * The fixed production overhead volume variance is usually sub-analysed as follows:
       Volume = capacity + productivity

Exhibit 15.4 Analysis of the main standard cost variances

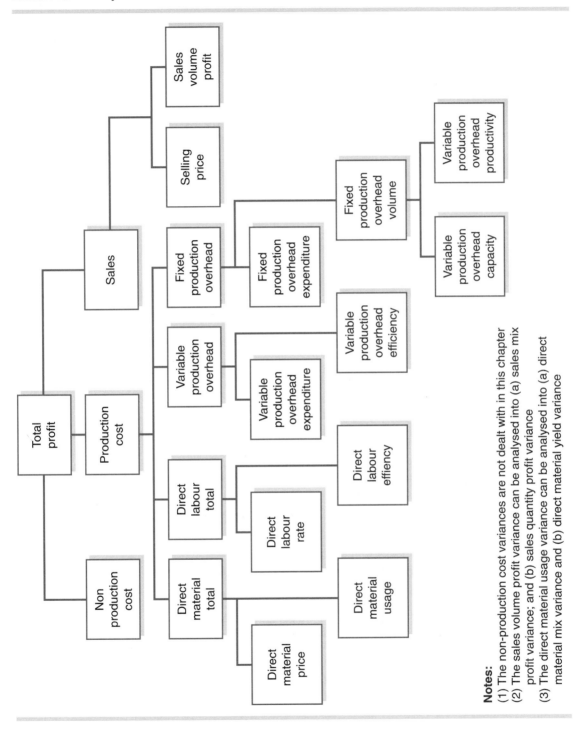

Notes:
(1) The non-production cost variances are not dealt with in this chapter
(2) The sales volume profit variance can be analysed into (a) sales mix profit variance; and (b) sales quantity profit variance
(3) The direct material usage variance can be analysed into (a) direct material mix variance and (b) direct material yield variance

Variance analysis formulae

Before we explain how to calculate cost variances, it would be useful if we summarize the basic formulae. You will then it convenient to refer back to this summary when examining later exhibits.

The formulae used in calculating the main standard cost variances are as follows:

Direct materials

1 Total = (actual price per unit × actual quantity used) − (standard price per unit × standard quantity for actual production)
2 Price = (actual price per unit − standard price per unit) × total actual used
3 Usage = (total actual quantity used − standard quantity for actual production) × standard price

These relationships are also shown in Exhibit 15.5.

Exhibit 15.5 Calculation of direct material variances

Direct labour

1 Total = (actual hourly rate × actual hours) − (standard hourly rate × standard hours for actual production)
2 Rate = (actual hourly rate − standard hourly rate) × actual hours worked
3 Efficiency = (actual hours worked − standard hours for actual production) × standard hourly rate

These relationships are also shown in Exhibit 15.6.

Exhibit 15.6 Calculation of direct labour variances

Variable production overhead

1 Total = actual overhead − (standard hours for actual production × variable production overhead absorption rate (V.OAR))
2 Expenditure = actual expenditure − (actual hours worked) × V.OAR
3 Efficiency = (standard hours of production − actual hours worked) × V.OAR

These relationships are also shown in Exhibit 15.7.

Exhibit 15.7 Calculation of variable production overhead variances

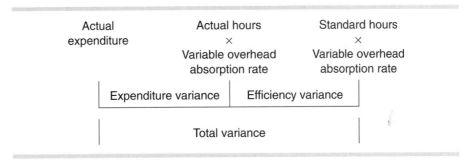

Fixed production overhead

1 Total = actual overhead − (standard hours of production × fixed overhead absorption rate (F.OAR))
2 Expenditure = actual expenditure − total budgeted expenditure
3 Capacity = budgeted − (actual hours worked × F.OAR)
4 Productivity = (actual hours worked − standard hours for actual production) × F.OAR
5 Volume = budgeted expenditure − (standard hours for actual production × F.OAR)

Note: Capacity = productivity + volume

These variances are also shown in Exhibit 15.8.

Exhibit 15.8 Calculation of fixed production overhead variances

Actual expenditure		Budgeted expenditure		Actual hours × Fixed overhead absorption rate		Standard hours × Fixed overhead absorption rate
	Expenditure variance		Capacity variance		Productivity variance	
	Expenditure variance		Volume variance			
	Total variance					

AN ILLUSTRATIVE EXAMPLE

We will now explain how to calculate the main cost variances by using an illustrative example. The details are contained in Exhibit 15.9.

Exhibit 15.9

The following information has been extracted from the records of the Frost Production Company Limited for the year to 31 March 19X4:

Budgeted costs per unit:	£
Direct materials (15 kilograms × £2 per kilogram)	30
Direct labour (10 hours × £4 per direct labour hour)	40
Variable overhead (10 hours × £1 per direct labour hour)	10
Fixed overhead (10 hours × £2 per direct labour hour)	20
Total budgeted cost per unit	£100

The following budgeted data are also relevant:
1 The budgeted production level was 100 units.
2 The total standard direct labour hours amounted to 1000.
3 The total budgeted variable overhead was estimated to be £1000.
4 The total budgeted fixed overhead was £2000.
5 The company absorbs both fixed and variable overhead on the basis of direct labour hours.

Actual costs:	£
Direct materials	2100
Direct labour	4000
Variable overhead	1000
Fixed overhead	1600
Total actual costs	£8700

Note: 90 units were produced in 800 actual hours, and the total actual quantity of direct materials consumed was 1400 kilograms.

Required:
Calculate the direct materials, direct labour, variable production overhead and fixed production overhead cost variances.

Answers to Exhibit 15.9

To begin the answer to this question, first summarize the total variance for each element of cost:

Actual units produced	Actual costs(1)	Total standard cost for actual production		Variance	
	£	£		£	
Direct materials	2100	2700	(1)	600	(F)
Direct labour	4000	3600	(2)	400	(A)
Variable production overhead	1000	900	(3)	100	(A)
Fixed production overhead	1600	1800	(4)	200	(F)
Total	£8700	£9000		£300	(F)

Notes:

(a) F= favourable to profit; A = adverse to profit.

(b) The numbers in brackets refer to the tutorial notes below.

Tutorial notes

1 The standard cost of direct labour for actual production = the actual units produced × the standard direct material cost per unit, i.e. 90 × 30 = £2700.

2 The standard cost of direct labour for actual production = the actual units produced × standard direct labour cost per unit, i.e. 90 × 40 = £3600.

3 The standard variable cost for actual performance = the actual units produced × variable overhead absorption rate per unit, i.e. 90 × 10 = £900.

4 The fixed overhead cost for the actual performance = the actual units produced × fixed overhead absorption rate, i.e. 90 × 20 = £1800.

As you can see from Exhibit 15.9, the total actual cost of producing the 90 units was £300 less than the budget allowance. An investigation would need to be held in order to find out why only 90 units were produced when the company had budgeted for 100. Furthermore, although the 90 units have cost £300 less than might have been expected, a number of other variances have contributed to the overall variance. Assuming that these variances are considered significant, they would need to be carefully investigated in order to find out what caused them. Both the direct materials and the fixed production overhead, for example, cost £600 and £200 respectively less than the budget allowance, while the direct labour cost £400 and the variable production overhead £100 more than might have been expected.

As a result of calculating variances for each element of cost, it would now be much easier for management to investigate why the actual production cost was £300 less than might have been expected. However, by analysing the variances into their major causes, the accountant can provide even greater guidance. We will explain how this is done by examining each element of cost. We do so by showing how we calculate the various variances, and then by giving a brief explanation of what might have caused them.

Direct materials

1 Price = (actual price per unit – standard price per unit) × total actual quantity used.

$$\text{The price variance} \therefore = (£1.50 - 2.00) \times 1400 \text{ kg} = \underline{\underline{£700 \text{ (F)}}}$$

The actual price per unit was £1.50 (£2100/1400) and the standard price was £2.00 per unit. There was, therefore, a total saving (as far as the price of the materials was concerned) of £700 (£0.50 × 1400). This was favourable (F) to profit.

2 Usage = (total actual quantity used – standard quantity for actual production) × standard price.

$$\text{The usage variance} \therefore = (1400 - 1350) \times £2.00 = \underline{\underline{£100 \text{ (A)}}}$$

In producing 90 units, Frost should have used 1350 kilograms (90 × 15 kg), instead of the 1400 kilograms actually used. If we value this extra usage at the standard price (the difference between the actual price and the standard price has already been allowed for), there is an adverse usage variance of £100 (50 kg × £2.00).

3 Total = price + usage:

$$= £700 \text{ (F)} + £100 \text{ (A)} = \underline{\underline{£600 \text{ (F)}}}$$

The £600 favourable total variance was shown earlier in the cost summary in Exhibit 15.9. This variance might have arisen because Frost purchased cheaper materials. If this was the case, then it probably resulted in a greater wastage of materials, perhaps because the materials were of an inferior quality.

Direct labour

1 Rate = (actual labour hourly rate – standard labour hourly rate) × actual hours worked.

$$\text{The rate variance} \therefore = (£5.00 - 4.00) \times 800 \text{ DLH} = \underline{\underline{£800 \text{ (A)}}}$$

The actual hourly rate is £5.00 per direct labour hours (DLH) (£4,000/800). Every extra actual hour worked, therefore, resulted in an adverse variance of £1.00, or £800 in total (£1.00 × 800).

2 Efficiency = (total actual hours worked – total standard hours for actual production) × standard hourly rate.

$$\text{The efficiency variance} \therefore = (800 - 900) \times £4.00 = \underline{\underline{£400 \text{ (F)}}}$$

The actual hours worked were 800. However, 900 hours would have been allowed for the 90 units actually produced (90 × 10 DLH). If these hours are valued at the standard hourly rate (differences between the actual rate and the standard rate have already been allowed for when calculating the rate variance), a favourable variance of £400 arises. The favourable efficiency variance has arisen because the 90 units took less time to produce than allowed for in the budget.

3 Total = rate + efficiency:

$$£800 \text{ (A)} + £400 \text{ (F)} = \underline{\underline{£400 \text{ (A)}}}$$

The £400 adverse variance was shown earlier in the cost summary in Exhibit 15.9. It arises because the company paid more per direct labour hour than had been budgeted, although this was offset to some extent by the units being produced in less time than the budgeted allowance. This variance could have been caused by using a higher grade of labour than had been intended. Unfortunately, the higher labour rate per hour was not completely offset by greater efficiency.

Variable production overhead

Not all accountants consider it necessary to analyse the variable production overhead total variance into sub-variances. The adverse variance of £100 (A) (as shown earlier in the summary of variances in Exhibit 15.9), arises because the variable overhead absorption rate was calculated on the basis of a budgeted cost off £10 per unit. In fact the absorption rate ought to have been £11.11 per unit (£1000/90), because the total actual variable cost was £1000. There would, of course, be no variable production overhead cost for the ten units that were not produced.

If the variable production overhead total variance is analysed into sub-variances, the result would be as follows:

1 Expenditure = actual variable overhead expenditure – (actual hours worked × variable production overhead absorption rate).

$$\therefore \text{ Expenditure variance} = £1000 - (800 \times £1.00) = \underline{\underline{£200 \text{ (A)}}}$$

2 Efficiency = (standard hours of production – actual hours worked) × variable production overhead absorption rate.

$$\therefore \text{ Efficiency variance} = (900 - 800) \times £1.00 = \underline{\underline{£100 \text{ (F)}}}$$

3 Total = expenditure + efficiency:

$$= £200 \text{ (A)} + £100 \text{ (F)} = \underline{\underline{£100 \text{ (A)}}}$$

Fixed production overhead

1 Expenditure = actual expenditure – budgeted expenditure.

$$\text{Expenditure variance} = £1600 – £2000 = \underline{\underline{£400 \text{ (F)}}}$$

The actual expenditure was £400 less than the budgeted expenditure. This means that the fixed production overhead absorption rate was £400 higher than it needed to have been if there had not been any other fixed overhead variances.

2 Volume = budgeted overhead – (standard hours of production × fixed production overhead absorption rate).

$$\text{Volume variance} \therefore = £2000 – (900 × £2.00) = \underline{\underline{£200 \text{ (A)}}}$$

As a result of producing fewer units than expected, £200 less overhead has been absorbed into production.

3 Capacity = budgeted overhead – (actual hours worked × fixed production overhead absorption rate).

$$\text{Capacity variance} \therefore = £2000 – (800 × £200) = \underline{\underline{£400 \text{ (A)}}}$$

The capacity variance shows that the actual hours worked were less than the budgeted hours. Other things being equal, therefore, not enough overhead would have been absorbed into production. It should be noted that the capacity variance will be favourable when the actual hours are in excess of the budgeted hours. This might seem odd, but it means that the company has been able to use more hours than it had originally budgeted. As a result, it should have been able to produce more units, thereby absorbing more overhead into production. This variance links with the capacity ratio calculated earlier in the chapter. The capacity ratio showed that only 80% of the budgeted capacity had been utilized, so probably not as much overhead was absorbed into production as had been originally expected.

4 Productivity = (total actual hours worked – total standard hours for actual production) × fixed production overhead absorption rate.

$$\text{Productivity variance} \therefore = (800 – 900) × £2.00 = \underline{\underline{£200 \text{ (F)}}}$$

This variance shows the difference between the 900 standard hours that the work is worth (90 × 10 = 900 hours), compared with the amount of time that it took to produce those units (i.e. 800 hours). As we emphasized earlier, in a standard costing system overhead is absorbed on the basis of standard hours. Assuming that the budgeted fixed overhead expenditure had been equal to the actual fixed overhead expenditure, production would have been charged with £200 of extra overhead, because the 90 units were produced in less time than the standard allowance. The factory has been more efficient in producing the goods than might have been expected. This variance complements the efficiency ratio of 112.5% which we illustrated earlier in the chapter in Exhibit 15.3.

Remember that the capacity variance + the productivity variance = the volume variance.

$$\text{Volume variance } \therefore = \text{£400 (A)} + \text{£200 (F)} = \text{£200 (A)}$$
$$\text{(see also 2 above).}$$

5 Fixed production overhead total variance.

We calculated this variance earlier (shown on the summary of variances in Exhibit 15.9). The simplified formula is as follows: Total = expenditure + volume:

$$= \text{£400 (F)} + \text{£200 (A)} = \underline{\underline{\text{£200 (F)}}}$$

The actual activity was less than the budgeted activity. Thus, less fixed overhead was absorbed into production. However, the overhead expenditure was budgeted at a level of £2000, but the actual expenditure was only £1600. The over-estimate of expenditure, therefore, compensated for the over-estimate of activity. This means that the 90 units actually produced were charged £200 more of overhead than was necessary. If the selling price is based on the standard cost, it is possible that this over-estimate could make their eventual selling price less competitive. In this example, the variance would appear to be very small.

We have now worked through a considerable number of variances. Using the formulae listed on pages 352–3, you are now recommended to attempt Exhibit 15.9 without reference to the solution.

SALES VARIANCES

Sales variances are not common in practice, but if they are adopted there is a choice between two different types:

1 variances bases on profit (using absorption costing);
2 variances based on contribution (using marginal costing).

Exhibit 15.10 shows sales variances based on absorption costing, while Exhibit 15.11 shows sales variances based on marginal costing.

Exhibit 15.10 Analysis of sales variance using absorption costing

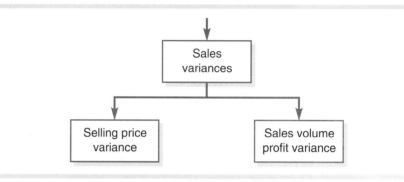

Exhibit 15.11 Analysis of sales variance using marginal costing

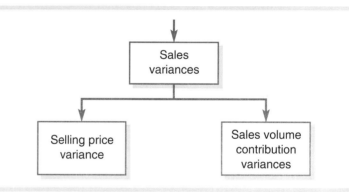

The formulae used in calculating sales variances are summarized below. The summary is divided in two parts. The first part shows the formulae for sales variances based on profit, and the second part shows the formulae for sales variances based on contribution.

1 Sales variances based on profit
  (a) sales variances

$$[\text{actual quantity} \times (\text{actual selling price per unit} - \text{standard cost per unit})] - (\text{budgeted quantity} \times \text{standard profit per unit})$$

  (b) selling price variance

$$\text{actual quantity} \times (\text{actual selling price per unit} - \text{budgeted selling price per unit})$$

(c) sales volume profit variance

$$(\text{actual quantity} - \text{budgeted quantity}) \times \text{standard profit}$$

(d) note that the sales variances = selling price + sales volume.

These relationships are also shown in Exhibit 15.12.

Exhibit 15.12 Calculation of sales variances based on profit

Note:
The selling price variance may also be calculated as follows:

Actual sales − (actual quantity × standard selling price)

2 Sales variance based on contribution
(a) sales variances

$$[\text{actual quantity} \times (\text{actual selling price per unit} - \text{standard variable cost})] - (\text{budgeted quantity} \times \text{standard contribution})$$

(b) selling price variance

$$[\text{actual quantity} \times (\text{actual selling price per unit} - \text{budgeted selling price per unit})]$$

(c) sales volume contribution variance

$$(\text{actual quantity} - \text{budgeted quantity}) \times \text{standard contribution}$$

(d) note that the sales variances = selling price + sales volume contribution.

These relationships are also shown in Exhibit 15.13.

You will note from the above formulae that apart from substituting 'contribution' for 'profit', the calculation of sales variances based on profit is identical to the calculation of sales variances based on contribution.

Exhibit 15.13 Calculation of sales variances based on contribution

Note:
The selling price variance may also be calculated as follows:

Actual sales − (actual quantity × standard selling price)

The use of these formulae is illustrated in Exhibit 15.14

Exhibit 15.14

The following data relate to Frozen Limited for the year to 31 July 19X9:

	Budget/standard	Actual
Sales (units)	100	90
Selling price per unit	£10	£10.50
Standard absorption cost per unit	£7	−

Required:
Calculate the sales variances (based on profit).

Answer to Exhibit 15.14

(a) selling price variance
    actual quantity × (actual selling price per unit − budgeted selling price per unit)
    = 90 × (10.50 − 10) = (90 × 0.5) = £45 (F)

The actual selling price per unit was £0.50 more than the standard selling price, so the variance is favourable. Other things being equal, the profit would be £45 higher.

(b) sales volume profit variance
    (actual quantity − budgeted quantity) × standard profit
    = (90 − 100) × 3 = £30 (A)

This variance arises because the number of units sold fell below the budgeted level. Other things being equal, this would result in less profit of £30.

(c) sales variances
    [actual quantity × (actual selling price per unit − standard cost per unit)] − (budgeted quantity × standard profit per unit)
    = [90 × (10.50 −7)] − (100 × 3)
    = 90 × 3.50 = 315 − 300 = £15 (F)

In Exhibit 15.14, the favourable selling price of £45 (or £0.50 per unit) helped to offset the adverse volume variance of £30 caused by selling ten fewer units. It should be noted that the standard cost is used in calculating sales variances based on profit. Any variance between actual costs and standard costs will be dealt with as part of the cost variance analysis. Also note that the Exhibit could have been applied to sales variances based on contribution simply be substituting the standard marginal cost for the standard absorption cost.

You are now recommended to work through Exhibit 15.14 without reference to the answer, although you will need to refer to the sales variance formulae listed on pages 360–1.

OPERATING STATEMENTS

As we have seen, the calculation of standard cost variances is a complex arithmetical process. The process can become more complicated if the variances outlined in the preceding sections are analysed into even more sub-variances (e.g. sales mix and sales quantity, and direct material mix and direct material yield). Fortunately as a non-accountants, it is unlikely that you will ever have to calculate such variances for yourself. However, it is important for you to have some knowledge of how variances are calculated so that you are in a better position to investigate how they may have occurred. Indeed, your main role will probably be to carry out a detailed investigation of the causes of variances, and then to take any necessary corrective action.

It is, however, very difficult to carry out a meaningful variance analysis if you have no idea what you are supposed to be investigating. Hence, you ought to be able to define the main variances, and to have some knowledge of how they have been calculated so that you know where to begin looking for any discrepancies.

Once all the variances have been calculated, they may usefully be summarized in the form of an operating statement. There is no standardized format for such statements, but the one shown in Exhibit 15.15 is reasonably representative.

Exhibit 15.15 Preparation of a standard cost operating statement

Exhibit 15.19 gave some information relating to the Frost Production Company Limited for the year to 31 March 19X4. The cost data used in that exhibit will now be used in Exhibit in 15.15, but some additional information is required.

Additional information
1 Assume that the budgeted sales were 100 units at a selling price of £150 per unit.
2 90 units were sold at £160 per unit.

3 Actual non-production overhead expenditure was as follows:

	£
Administration	750
Research and development	150
Selling and distribution	300

Required:
Prepare a standard cost operating statement for the year to 31 March 19X4.

Answer to Exhibit 15.15

Frost Manufacturing Company Limited standard cost operating statement for the year to 31 March 19X4:

			£
Budgeted profit [100 × (150 − 100)]			5000
Sales volume profit variance (1)			(500)
Standard margin of actual sales			4500
Selling price variance (2)			900
Actual margin of actual sales			5400

Cost variance: (3)	*Adverse*	*Favourable*	
	£	£	
Direct materials:			
Price		700	
Usage	100		
Direct labour:			
Rate	800		
Efficiency		400	
Variable production overhead			
Expenditure	200		
Efficiency		100	
Fixed production overhead			
Expenditure		400	
Capacity	400		
Productivity		200	
	1500	1800	300
Operating profit			5700
Less: Actual non-production overhead:			
Administration		750	
Research and development		150	
Selling and distribution		300	1200
Actual profit			£4500

Tutorial notes

1 Sales volume profit variance
= (Actual quantity − budgeted quantity) × standard profit
= (90 − 100) × 50 − £500 (A)

2 selling price variance
= Actual quantity × (actual selling price per unit − budgeted selling price per unit)
= 90 × (£160 − 150) = £900 (F)

3 Details of cost variances were shown in the answer to Exhibit 15.9 on pages 354–5.

The format used in Exhibit 15.15 is particularly helpful because it shows the link between the budgeted profit and the actual profit. Thus, management can trace the main causes of sales and cost variances. In practice, the statement would also show the details for each product.

The operating profit statement will help management decide where to begin an investigation into the causes of the respective variances. It is unlikely that they will all need to be investigated. It may be company policy, for example, to investigate only those variances that are particularly significant irrespective of whether they are favourable or adverse. In other words, only exceptional variances would be investigated, and a policy decision would have to be taken on what is meant by exceptional.

CONCLUSION

We have now come to the end of a long and complex chapter. You may have found that it has been extremely difficult to understand just how standard cost variances are calculated. Fortunately, it is unlikely that as a non-accountant you will ever have to calculate variances for yourself. It is sufficient, for your purposes, to understand their meaning, and to have some idea of the arithmetical foundation on which they are based.

Your job will largely be to investigate the causes of the variances, and to take necessary action. A standard costing system is supposed to help management plan and control the entity much more tightly than can be achieved in the absence of such a system. However, it can only be of real benefit if it is welcomed by those managers whom it is supposed to help. It can hardly be of help if it just produces a great deal of incomprehensible data. After reading this chapter, we hope that the data will now mean something to you.

In the next chapter we move on to deal with capital investment appraisal, but before doing so, you would be well advised to work your way through this chapter once again.

KEY POINTS

1 **A standard cost is the planned cost of a particular unit or process.**

2 **Standard costs are usually based on what is reasonably attainable.**

3 Actual costs are compared with standard costs.

4 Corrective action is taken if there are any unplanned trends.

5 Three performance measures used in standard costing are: the efficiency ratio, the capacity ratio, and the production volume ratio.

6 Variance analysis is an arithmetical exercise that enables differences between actual and standards costs to be broken down into the elements of cost.

7 The degree of analysis will vary, but usually a total cost variance will be analysed into direct material, direct labour, variable overhead and fixed overhead variances. In turn, these will be analysed into quantity and expenditure variances, although an even more detailed analysis is possible.

8 Sales variances may also be calculated, but they are not very common. There are two main types: sales variances based on profit, and sales variances based on contribution. Like cost variances, sales variances may also be analysed in greater detail, e.g. selling price, and sales volume.

9 The variances help in tracing the main causes of differences between actual and budgeted results, but they do not explain what has actually happened.

CHECK YOUR LEARNING

1 What is a standard?

2 List four main steps in setting up a standard costing system.

3 Name three performance measures used in standard costing.

4 Complete the following equations:
  (a) ——— = direct material price + direct material usage
  (b) Direct labour total = ——— + direct material efficiency
  (c) variable production overhead total = variable production expenditure + ———
  (d) Fixed production overhead total = fixed production expenditure + ——— + fixed productivity volume
  (e) Sales variances = ——— + sales volume profit

ANSWERS

1 A predetermined measurable quantity set in defined conditions.
2 (a) set up a unit responsible for implementing it;
  (b) select an appropriate a standard costing period;
  (c) determine the type of standard to be adopted;
  (d) obtain the information necessary to calculate the standards.
3 (a) efficiency (b) capacity (c) production volume
4 (a) direct material total (b) direct labour rate (c) variable production overhead efficiency (d) fixed production overhead capacity (e) selling price

15.1 You are presented with the following information for X Limited:
Standard price per unit: £10.
Standard quantity for actual production: 5 units.
Actual price per unit: £12.
Actual quantity: 6 units.

Required:
Calculate the following variances:
1 direct materials cost variance;
2 direct materials price variance; and
3 direct materials usage variance.

15.2 The following information relates to Malcolm Limited.
Budgeted production: 100 units.
Unit specification (direct materials): 50 kilograms × £5 per kilogram = £250.
Actual production: 120 units.
Direct materials used: 5400 kilograms at a total cost of £32 400.

Required:
Calculate the following variances:
1 direct materials cost;
2 direct materials price; and
3 direct materials usage.

15.3 The following information relates to Bruce Limited:
Actual hours: 1000
Actual wage rate per hour: £6.50.
Standard hours for actual production: 900.
Standard wage rate per hour: £6.00.

Required:
Calculate the following variances:
1 direct labour cost;
2 direct labour rate; and
3 direct labour efficiency.

15.4 You are presented with the following information for Duncan Limited:
Budgeted production: 1000 units.
Actual production: 1200 units.
Standard specification for one unit: 10 hours at £8 per direct labour hour.
Actual direct labour cost: £97 200 in 10 800 actual hours.

Required:
Calculate the following variances:
1 direct labour cost;
2 direct labour rate; and
3 direct labour efficiency.

15.5 The following overhead budget has been prepared for Anthea Limited:
Actual fixed overhead: £150 000.
Budgeted fixed overhead: £135 000.
Fixed overhead absorption rate per hour: £15.
Actual hours worked: 10 000.
Standard hours of production: 8000.

Required:
Calculate the following fixed overhead variances:
1 fixed production overhead variance;
2 expenditure variance;
3 volume variance;
4 capacity variance; and
5 productivity variance.

15.6 Using the data contained in the previous question, calculate the following performance measures:
1 efficiency ratio;
2 capacity ratio; and
3 production/volume ratio.

15.7 The following information relates to Osprey Limited:
Budgeted production: 500 units.
Standard hours per unit: 10.
Actual production: 600 units.
Budgeted fixed overhead: £125 000.
Actual fixed overhead: £120 000.
Actual hours worked: 4900.

Required:
Calculate the following fixed overhead variances:
1 fixed production overhead;
2 expenditure;
3 volume;
4 capacity; and
5 productivity.

15.8 Using the data from the previous question, calculate the following performance measures:
1 efficiency ratio;
2 capacity ratio; and
3 production/volume ratio.

15.9 Milton Limited has produced the following information:
Total actual sales: £99 000.
Actual quantity sold: 9000 units.
Budgeted selling price per unit: £10.
Standard variable cost per unit: £7.
Total budgeted units: 10 000 units.

Required:
Calculate the sales variances.

15.10 You are presented with the following information for Doe Limited:

Budget sales	100 units

Per unit:

Budget selling price	£30
Less: Budget variable cost	20
Contribution	10
Actual sales	120 units
Actual selling price per unit	£28

Required:
Calculate the sales variances.

15.11 The following data relate to Judith Limited:

Budget specification

Production at sales budget		2 000 units

Per unit	£	£
Selling price		150
Less: Variable costs:		
Direct materials (7 kilos × £10 per kilo)	70	
Direct wages (5 DJH × £5 per DLH)	25	
Fixed overhead (5 DLH × £6 F.OAR)	30	125
Budgeted profit per unit		£25

Actual production and sales		2 200 units
Actual selling price per unit		£145

Actual cost:

Direct material (8 kilos × £9 per kilo)	£72 per unit
Direct wages (4 DLH × £6 per DLH)	£24 per unit
Total actual fixed overhead	£65 000

Required:
(a) Calculate the following performance measures:
1 efficiency ratio;
2 capacity ratio; and
3 production/volume ratio.
(b) Calculate the following variances:
1 selling price;
2 sales volume contribution;
3 sales variances (in total);
4 direct materials cost;
5 direct materials price;
6 direct materials usage;
7 direct labour cost;
8 direct labour rate variance;

9 direct labour efficiency;
10 fixed production overhead;
11 fixed production overhead expenditure;
12 fixed production overhead volume;
13 fixed production overhead capacity; and
14 fixed production overhead productivity.
(c) Prepare the standard cost operating statement for the period.

ADDITIONAL QUESTIONS (WITHOUT ANSWERS)

15.12 The budgeted selling price and standard cost of a unit manufactured by Smillie Limited is as follows:

	£
Selling price	30
Direct materials (2.5 kilos)	5
Direct labour (2 hours)	12
Fixed production overhead	8
	25
Budgeted profit	5

Total budgeted sales: 400 units

During the period to 31 December 19X2, the actual sales and production details were as follows:

	£
Sales (400 units)	13 440
Direct materials (1260 kilos)	2 268
Direct labour (800 hours)	5 200
Fixed production overhead	3 300
	10 768
Profit	2 672

Required:
Prepare a standard cost operating statement for the period to 31 December 19X2.

15.13 Mean Limited manufactures a single product, and the following information relates to the actual selling price and actual cost of the product for the four weeks to 31 March 19X3:

	£000
Sales (50 000 units)	2250
Direct materials (240 000 hours)	528
Direct labour (250 000 hours)	1375
Variable production overhead	245
Fixed production overhead	650
	2798
Loss	(548)

The budgeted selling price and standard cost of each unit was as follows:

	£
Selling price	55
Direct materials (5 litres)	10
Direct labour (4 hours)	20
Variable production overhead	5
Fixed production overhead	15
	50
Budgeted profit	5

Total budgeted production: 40 000 units.

Required:
Prepare a standard cost operating statement for the four weeks to 31 March 19X3, utilizing as many variances as the data permit.

CHAPTER 16

Capital investment appraisal

Recharger electrifies Kleen-e-Ze

The launch of a "world first" device to recharge normal batteries electrified the shares of Kleen-e-Ze Holdings yesterday. They soared 44p to 226p, after gaining 28p on Monday, adding £10 million to the group's stock market value in two days.

The home-shopping and consumer-marketing group is selling its Battery Manager through its *Innovations* catalogue and the Leading Edge and Innovation shops.

It claims the new product, which took six years to develop, will extend the life of most ordinary general-purpose batteries by up to ten times.

Two models, at £29.95 and £39.95, will be sold and the group aims for worldwide sales of about 500 000 over the next year.

The Battery Manager will be made exclusively for Innovations in southern China by a leading Hong Kong electronics company.

Kleen-e-Ze's chief executive, Robin Klein, said the new product would yield considerable financial benefits to the group's mail-order, retail and wholesale businesses. – PA

The Scotsman, 4 August 1993

Exhibit 16.0 Clearly, the development of a new product will have a marked effect on a company's capital expenditure requirements.

As we saw in Chapter 14, the budgetary process usually starts with the preparation of the sales forecast. The forecast then enables the production manager to assess whether he is likely to have the productive capacity to meet it. If the capacity is not available, then the sales budgets will have to be prepared on what can be produced. In the long run, of course, the entity will want to maximize its sales. If the forecasts suggest a sustained growth in sales, therefore, additional capital expenditure may be required, such as for new factories, plant, and equipment. Expenditure on such proposals is known as *capital investment* (CI), and accountants refer to the process of investigating them as *capital investment appraisal*. CIMA define capital investment appraisal as follows:

Capital investment appraisal: the evaluation of benefits and costs of proposed investments in specific fixed assets.

Thus, capital investment may be considered to be part of the capital budgeting process. It involves both the selection of long-term investments and the financing of them, and these are the matters that we are going to consider in this chapter. We are only going to deal with them briefly, however, as the detailed considerations are well outside the scope of this book. The main purpose is to give you an overall appreciation of what is involved in capital investment appraisal, as it is unlikely that as a non-accountant you will have to deal with the involved arithmetical calculations used in CI appraisal. We intend to use only simple examples, but these should enable you to grasp the main principles behind the technique.

The chapter is divided into three main sections. In the first section, we outline the background to CI appraisal. The following section examines the main accounting techniques used in selecting individual projects, and the final section summarizes the main sources of finance available for capital investment.

LEARNING OBJECTIVES

By the end of this chapter, you will be able to:
- describe what is meant by capital investment appraisal;
- identify five capital investment appraisal techniques;
- recognize the significance of such techniques;
- list three main sources of financing capital investment projects.

THE BACKGROUND

We explained in an earlier chapter that accountants distinguish between capital expenditure and revenue expenditure (the same distinction also applies to income). The actual delineation between capital and revenue is somewhat imprecise. Generally, any expenditure that is likely to be of benefit in more than one accounting period is to be classed as capital expenditure. The more formal definition offered by CIMA is as follows:

Capital expenditure: the cost of acquiring, producing or enhancing fixed assets.

To understand this definition, it is necessary to know how CIMA defines a fixed asset. It is as follows:

Fixed asset: any asset, tangible or intangible, acquired for retention by an entity for the purpose of providing a service to the business, and not held for resale in the normal course of trading.

By contrast, revenue expenditure is expenditure that is of benefit in only one time period. CIMA define it as follows:

> **Revenue expenditure**: expenditure on the supply and manufacture of goods and provisions of services charged in the accounting period in which they are consumed. This includes repairs and depreciation of fixed assets as distinct from the provision of those assets.

In this chapter, we are primarily concerned with capital expenditure, and we can see from the above definitions that it is likely to have a number of important characteristics. These can be summarized as follows:

1 it will probably involve substantial expenditure;
2 the benefits may be spread over very many years;
3 it will be difficult to predict what the benefits will be;
4 it will help the company to achieve its organizational objectives;
5 it will have some impact on the company's employees.

Indeed, if the company is to survive, and especially if it wants to grow, it will need to invest continuously in capital projects. Existing fixed assets will begin to wear out, and more efficient ones will become available. Furthermore, capital expenditure may be required not just in the administration, production, and stores departments, but also on social and recreational facilities. Similarly in the public sector, universities and colleges may be faced with capital expenditure decisions that go beyond providing lecture halls and tutorial rooms, e.g. student accommodation and union facilities.

Irrespective of where the demand for capital expenditure arises, however, all entities face two common problems: (a) the priority to be given to individual projects; and (b) how they can be financed. Hence, competing projects will need to be ranked according to either their importance, or their potential profitability.

We examine the techniques involved in the selection of projects in the next section.

THE SELECTION OF PROJECTS

There is little point in investing in a project unless it is likely to make a profit. The exceptions are those projects that are necessary on health, social, and welfare grounds, and these are particularly difficult to assess. In other cases, there are five main techniques that accountants can use in CI appraisal. They are shown in diagrammatic form in Exhibit 16.1. We examine each of them in the following sub-sections.

Exhibit 16.1 Methods of capital investment appraisal

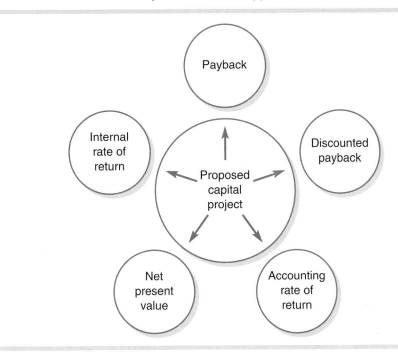

Payback

The payback method is an attempt to estimate how long it would take before a project begins to pay for itself. For example, if a company was going to spend £300 000 on purchasing some new plant, the accountant would calculate how many years it would take before £300 000 had been received back in cash. The recovery of an investment in a project is usually measured in terms of *net cash flow*. Net cash flow is the difference between cash received and cash paid during a defined period of time. In order to adopt this method, therefore, the following information is required:

1 the total cost of the investment;
2 the amount of cash instalments payable back on the investment;
3 the accounting periods in which the instalments will be paid;
4 the cash receipts and and any other cash payments connected with the project;
5 the accounting periods in which they fall.

As this method measures the rate of recovery of the original investment in terms of net cash flow, it follows that non-cash items (such as depreciation, and profits and losses on sales of fixed assets) are not taken into account.

The payback method is illustrated in Exhibit 16.2.

Exhibit 16.2 The payback method

Miln Limited is considering investing in some new machinery. The following information has been prepared to support the project:

	£000	£000
Cost of machinery		20
Expected net cash flow:		
Year 1	1	
2	4	
3	5	
4	10	
5	10	30
Net profitability		£10

Required:
Calculate the prospective investment's payback period.

Answer to Exhibit 16.2

The payback period is as follows:

	£000
Cumulative net cash flow:	
Year 1	1
2	5
3	10
4	20
5	30

Thus, the investment will have paid for itself at the end of the fourth year. At that stage £20 000 will have been received back from the project in terms of net cash flow, and that sum would be equal to the original cost of the project.

As can be seen from Exhibit 16.2, the payback method is a fairly straightforward technique, but it does have several disadvantages. These are as follows:

1 An estimate has to be made of the amount and the timing of cash instalments due to be paid on the original investment.
2 It is difficult to calculate the net cash flows and the period in which they will be received.

3 There is a danger that projects with the shortest payback periods may be chosen even if they are less profitable than projects that have a longer payback period (the method does not measure profitability, only cash flow).

4 The total amount of the overall investment is ignored, and comparisons made between different projects may result in a misleading conclusion. Thus, a project with an initial investment of £10 000 may have a shorter payback period than one with an initial investment of £100 000, although in the long run, the larger investment may prove more profitable.

5 The technique ignores any net cash flows received after the payback period.

6 The timing of the cash flows is not taken into account: £1 received now is clearly preferable to £1 received in five years' time. Thus, a project with a short payback period, may recover most of its investment towards the end of its payback period, while another project with a longer payback period may recover most of the original investment in the first few years. There is clearly less risk in accepting a project which recovers most of its cost very quickly than there is accepting one where the benefits are much more long term.

Notwithstanding these disadvantages, the payback method has something to be said for it. While it may appear to be rather simplistic, it does help managers to compare projects, and to think in terms of how long it takes before a project has recovered its original cost. The timing problem can also be overcome by adopting what is called the *discounted payback method*. We examine this method in the next sub-section.

Discounted payback

As we explained above, the simple payback method ignores the timing of net cash receipts. This problem can be overcome by *discounting* the net cash receipts. You will probably be familiar with discounting in your everyday life. You know, for example, that if you put £91 into the building society, and the rate of interest is 10% per annum, your original investment will be worth about £100 [£91 + 9 (10% × 91)] at the end of the year. We could look at this example from another point of view. Assuming a rate of interest of 10% per annum, what amount of money do you have to invest in the building society in order to have £100 at the end of the year? Ignoring the odd 10p, the answer is, of course, £91. In other words, £91 received now is the same as £100 received in a year's time. This is what is meant by *discounting*. The procedure is as follows:

1 we take future net cash flows;
2 we estimate an appropriate rate of interest;
3 we then reduce the net cash flows to their *present value* by multiplying them by a discount factor.

In the case of the building society example above, the discount factor is actually 0.9091 (i.e. £100 × 0.9091 = £90.91). To check: take the £90.91 and add the year's interest, i.e. (90.91 × 10% = 9.091) + 90.91 = 100.00). You will not have to calculate discount factors: these are available in readily available tables, and one is included in Appendix 2 on page 484.

To confirm that you understand the point about discounting, turn to Appendix 2. Look along the top line for the appropriate rate of interest: in this case it is 10%. Work down the 10% column until you come to the line opposite the year (shown in the left-hand column) in which the cash would be received. In this example, the cash is going to be received in one year's time, so it is not necessary to go further than the first line. The present value of £1 receivable in a year's time is, therefore, £0.9091, or £90.91 if £100 is to be received in a year's time.

In order to confirm that you follow the principle behind discounting, try the following example. Assuming a rate of interest of 15% per annum, what is the present value of £200 receivable in three years' time? Consult Appendix 2. The answer is £151.22 (£200 × 0.7561).

You can check this as follows:

	£
At the beginning of the year:	151.22
At the end of year 1, add 15% (151.22 × 15%):	22.69*
	173.91
At the end of year 2, add 15% (173.90 × 15%):	26.09
Total	200.00

* This should really be 22.68. The discount table used in Appendix 2 only goes to four places of decimals, and so some rounding up is usually necessary.

Do you feel reasonably confident that you now know what is meant by the net present value of future net cash flows, and what is involved in discounting? If so, we can move on to examine how discounting can be applied to the payback method. An example is shown in Exhibit 16.3.

Exhibit 16.3 An illustration of the discounted payback method

Newland District Council has investigated the possibility of investing in a new project, and the following information has been obtained:

	£000	£000
Total cost of project		500
Expected net cash flows:		
Year 1	20	
2	50	
3	100	
4	200	
5	300	
6	30	700
Net return		£200

Required:
Assuming a rate of interest of 8%, calculate the project's overall return using the following methods:
(a) payback; and
(b) discounted payback.

Answer to Exhibit 16.3

Year	Net cash flow	Cumulative net cash flow	Discount factors	Present value at 8%	Cumulative present value
	£000	£000		£000	£000
0	(500)	(500)	1.000 0	(500)	(500)
1	20	(480)	0.925 9	19	(481)
2	50	(430)	0.857 3	43	(438)
3	100	(330)	0.793 8	79	(359)
4	200	(130)	0.735 0	147	(212)
5	300	170	0.686 0	206	(6)
6	30	200	0.630 2	19	13

Using the payback method, the project will have paid for itself after 4 years. However, by discounting the net cash flows, the project will not have paid for itself until after the fifth year. Note also that by using this method, this particular project only just recovers the initial investment.

The discounted payback method has the following advantages:

1 it is relatively easy to understand;
2 it is not too difficult to compute;
3 it focuses on the cash recovery of an investment;

4 it does allow for the fact that cash received now may be worth more than cash receivable in the future;

5 it takes into account more of the net cash flows, since the discounted payback period is always longer than under the simple payback method;

6 it enables a clear-cut decision to be taken, since a project is acceptable if the discounted net cash flow throughout its life exceeds the cost of the original investment.

However, like the simple payback method, it has some disadvantages. These are as follows:

1 it is sometimes difficult to estimate the amount and timing of of instalments due to be paid on the original investment;

2 it is difficult to estimate the amount and timing of future net cash receipts and other payments;

3 it is not easy to determine an appropriate rate of interest;

4 in arriving at a decision, net cash flows received after the payback period are ignored.

Irrespective of these disadvantages, the discounted payback method can be usefully and readily adopted by those entities that do not employ staff specially trained in capital investment appraisal techniques.

Accounting rate of return

The accounting rate of return (ARR) method attempts to compare the *profit* of a project with the capital invested in it. It is usually expressed as a percentage, i.e.:

$$\text{ARR} = \frac{\text{Profit}}{\text{Capital employed}} \times 100$$

Two important problems arise from this definiton. These may be summarized as follows:

1 The definition of profit. Normally, we would use the average annual net profit earned by the project. However, as was explained in earlier chapters, accounting profit can be subject to a number of different assumptions and distortions (e.g. depreciation, taxation, and inflation), and so it is relatively easy to arrive at different profit levels depending upon the accounting policies adopted. The most common definition is to take profit before interest and taxation. The profit included in the equation would then be a simple average of the profit the project earns over its entire life.

2 The definition of capital employed. The capital employed could be either the initial capital employed in the project, or the average capital employed over its life.

Thus, depending upon the definitions adopted, the ARR may be calculated in one of two ways, as follows:

1 using the original capital employed:

$$\text{ARR} = \frac{\text{average annual net profit before interest and taxation}}{\text{initial capital employed on the project}} \times 100$$

2 using the average capital employed:

$$\text{ARR} = \frac{\text{average annual net profit before interest and taxation}}{\text{average annual capital employed on the project *}} \times 100$$

$$* = \frac{\text{initial capital employed} + \text{residual value}}{2}$$

The two methods are illustrated in Exhibit 16.4.

Exhibit 16.4 The accounting rate of return method

Bridge Limited is considering investing in a new project, the details of which are as follows:

Project life		5 years
	£000	£000
Project cost		50
Estimated net profit:		
Year 1	12	
2	18	
3	30	
4	25	
5	5	
Total net profit	£90	

The estimated residual value of the project at the end of year 5 is £10 000.

Required:
Calculate the accounting rate of return of the proposed new project.

Answer to Exhibit 16.4

The accounting rate of return would be calculated as follows:
(a) Using the initial capital employed.

$$\frac{\text{Average annual net profits}}{\text{Cost of the investment}} \times 100$$

Average annual net profits = 18 000 (90 000/5)

$$\therefore \text{Accounting rate of return} = \frac{18\ 000}{50\ 000} \times 100 = \underline{\underline{36\%}}$$

(b) Using the average capital employed

$$\frac{\text{Average annual net profits}}{\text{Average capital employed}} \times 100$$

$$= \frac{18\ 000}{2\ (50\ 000 + 10\ 000)} = \underline{\underline{60\%}}$$

Like the payback and discounted payback methods, the accounting rate of return method has several advantages and disadvantages. These may be summarized as follows:

Advantages

1 The method is compatible with a similar accounting ratio used in financial accounting.
2 It is relatively easy to understand.
3 It is not difficult to compute.
4 It draws attention to the notion of overall profit.

Disadvantages

1 Net profit can be subject to different definitions, e.g. it can mean net profit before or after allowing for depreciation on the project.
2 It is not always clear whether the original cost of the investment should be used, or whether it is more appropriate to substitute an average for the amount of capital invested in the project.
3 The use of a residual value in calculating the average amount of capital employed means that the higher the residual value, the lower the ARR, e.g. with no residual value, the ARR on a project costing £100 000 and an average net profit of £50 000 would be 100%, i.e.:

$$\frac{50\ 000}{2 \times (100\ 000 + 0)} \times 100 = 100\%$$

whereas with a residual value of (say) £10 000, the ARR would be 90.9%, i.e.:

$$\frac{50,000}{2 \times (100,000 + 10,000)} \times 100 = 90.9\%$$

Estimating residual values is very difficult, and so the assumption adopted can make all the difference between one project and another.

4 The method gives no guidance on what is an acceptable rate of return.
5 The benefit of earning a high proportion of the total profit in the early years of the project is not allowed for.
6 It does not take into account the time value of money.

With all of these disadvantages, you might wonder whether the ARR method can ever be used. However, it may be suitable where very similar short-term projects are being considered.

Net present value

One of the main disadvantages of both the payback and ARR methods of CI appraisal is that they ignore the time value of money. We have already explained what this concept means when we examined the discounted payback method. There are two other methods that also follow this concept: the net present value method, and the internal rate of return method. In this sub-section, we will examine the net present value (NPV) method.

The NPV method recognizes that cash received today is preferable to cash receivable sometime in the future. There is more risk in having to wait for future cash receipts and, while we might get a smaller sum now, at least we can do what we like with it. For example, it can be invested, and the subsequent rate of return may then compensate for the smaller amount received now (or at least be equal to it).

As we saw earlier in the chapter, £91 received now (assuming a rate of interest of 10%) is just as beneficial as receiving £100 in a year's time. This is the principle behind the NPV method of CI appraisal. Basically, it involves taking the following steps:

1 calculate the annual net cash flows expected to arise from the project;
2 select an appropriate rate of interest, or required rate of return;
3 obtain the discount factors appropriate to the chosen rate of interest or return;
4 in order to arrive at the present value for each annual net cash flow, multiply them by their appropriate discount factor;
5 add together the present values for each of the net cash flows;
6 compare the total net present value with the initial outlay;
7 if the total NPV is positive, consider accepting the project (a negative factor might suggest that the project should be rejected, but other factors would have to be taken into account).

This procedure is outlined in Exhibit 16.5.

Exhibit 16.5 The net present value method

Rage Limited is considering to capital investment projects. The details are outlined as follows.

Project	1	2
Estimated life	3 years	5 years
Commencement date	1.01.X1	1.01.X1
	£000	£000
Project cost at 1.01.X1	100	100

Estimated net cash flows:		
Year to: 31.12.X1	20	10
31.12.X2	80	40
31.12.X3	40	40
31.12.X4	–	40
31.12.X5	–	20

The company expects a rate of return of 10% per annum on its capital employed.

Required:
Using the net present value method of project appraisal, assess which project would be more profitable.

Answer to Exhibit 16.5

RAGE LIMITED

Project appraisal:

Year	Net cash flow	Project 1 Discount factor	Present value	Net cash flow	Project 2 Discount factor	Present vatue
	£	10%	£	£	10%	£
31.12.X1	20 000	0.909 1	18 182	10 000	0.909 1	9 091
31.12.X2	80 000	0.826 4	66 112	40 000	0.826 4	33 056
31.12.X3	40 000	0.751 3	30 052	40 000	0.751 3	30 052
31.12.X4	–	–	–	40 000	0.683 0	27 320
31.12.X5	–	–	–	20 000	0.620 9	12 418
Total present value			114 346			111 937
Less: Initial cost			100 000			100 000
Net present value			£14 346			£11 937

Tutorial note

The discount factors have been obtained from the discount table shown in Appendix 2.

Although both projects have a positive NPV, project 1 should be chosen in preference to project 2, because its NPV is higher.

The advantages and disadvantages of the NPV method are as follows:

Advantages

1 Using net cash flows emphasizes the importance of liquitity.
2 Different accounting policies are not of relevance, as they do not affect the calculation of net cash flows.
3 The time value of money is taken into account.
4 It is easy to compare the NPV of different projects, and to reject projects that do not have an acceptable NPV.

Disadvantages

1 Some difficulties may be incurred in estimating the initial cost of the project, and the time periods in which instalments must be paid back (this is a common problem in CI appraisal).
2 It is difficult to estimate accurately the net cash flow for each year during the life of the project (a difficulty which is again common to most other methods of project appraisal).
3 It is not easy to select an appropriate rate of interest: this is sometimes referred to as the *cost of capital*, i.e. the cost of financing an investment. One rate that could be chosen is that rate which the company could earn if it decided to invest the funds outside the business (the external rate of interest). Alternatively, an internal rate of interest could be chosen. This rate would be based on an estimate of what return the company expects to earn on its existing investments. In the long run, if its internal rate of return is lower than the external rate, then it would appear more profitable to liquidate the company and invest the funds elsewhere. A local authority, however, may not have the same difficulty, because it would probably use a rate of interest which is set by central government.

NPV is considered to be a highly acceptable method of CI appraisal. It does take into account the timing of the net cash flows, the project's profitability, and the return of the original investment. However, an entity would not necessary accept a project just because it had an acceptable NPV, as there are many non-financial factors that must be allowed for. Furthermore, other less profitable projects may go ahead, perhaps because they are concerned with employee safety or welfare.

Internal rate of return method

An alternative method of investment appraisal based on discounted net cash flow is known as the *internal rate of return* (IRR). This method is very similar to the NPV method. However, instead of discounting the expected net cash flows by a predetermined rate of return, the IRR method seeks to answer the following question:

> What rate of return would be required in order to ensure that the total NPV equals the total initial cost?

In theory, a rate of return that was lower than the entity's required rate of return would be rejected. In practice, however, the IRR would only be one factor to be taken into account in deciding whether to go ahead with the project. The method is illustrated in Exhibit 16.6.

Exhibit 16.6 The internal rate of return method

Bruce Limited is considering whether to invest £50 000 in a new project. The project's expected net cash flows would be as follows:

Year	£000
1	7
2	25
3	30
4	5

Required:
Calculate the internal rate of return for the proposed new project.

Answer to Exhibit 16.6

BRUCE LIMITED

Calculation of the internal rate of return:

Step 1: Select two discount rates
The first step is to select two discount rates, and then calculate the net present value of the project. The two rates usually have to be chosen quite arbitrarily, although they should preferably cover a narrow range. One of the rates should produce a positive rate of return, and the other rate a negative rate of return. As far as this question is concerned, rates of 10% and 15% will be chosen to illustrate the method.

Year	Net cash flow	Discount factors		Present value	
				10%	15%
	£	10%	15%	£	£
1	7 000	0.909 1	0.869 6	6 364	6 087
2	25 000	0.826 4	0.756 1	20 660	18 903
3	30 000	0.751 3	0.657 5	22 539	19 725
4	5 000	0.683 0	0.571 8	3 415	2 859
Total present values				52 978	47 574
Initial cost				50 000	50 000
Net present value				£2 978	£(2 426)

The project is expected to cost £50 000. If the company expects a rate of return of 10%, the project will be accepted, because the NPV is positive. However, if the required rate of return is 15% it will not be accepted, because its NPV is negative. The maximum rate of return that will ensure a positive rate of return must, therefore, lie somewhere between 10% and 15%, so the next step is to calculate the rate of return at which the project would just pay for itself.

Step 2: Calculate the rate of return
To do so, it is necessary to interpolate between the rates used in Step 1. This can be done by using the following formula:

$$\text{IRR} = \text{Positive rate} + \left\{ \frac{\text{Positive NPV}}{\text{Positive NPV} - \text{Negative NPV}^*} \times \text{Range of rates} \right\}$$

*The negative sign is ignored.

$$\begin{aligned}
\text{Thus: IRR} &= 10\% + \left\{ \frac{2978}{(2\,978 + 2426)} \times (15\% - 10\%) \right\} \\
&= 10\% + (0.5511 \times 5\%) \\
&= 10\% + 2.76\% \\
&= 12.76\%
\end{aligned}$$

The project will be profitable provided that the company does not require a rate of return in excess of about 13%. Note that the method of calculation used above does not give the precise rate of return (because the formula is only an approximation), but it is adequate enough for decision-making purposes.

Exhibit 16.6 demonstrates that the IRR method is similar to the NPV method: (a) the initial cost of the project has to be estimated, as well as the future net cash flows arising from the project; and (b) the net cash flows are then discounted to their net present value using discount tables.

The main difference between the two methods is that the IRR method requires a rate of return to be estimated in order to give a NPV equal to the initial cost of the investment. The main difficulty arises in deciding which two rates of return to use, one which will give a positive NPV or one which will give a negative NPV. The range between the two rates should be as narrow as possible. You will find that if you use a trial and error method, you may have to try many times before you arrive at two suitable rates!

The advantages and disadvantages of the IRR method may be summarized as follows:

Advantages
1 Care has to be taken in estimating the initial cost of a project.
2 Emphasis is placed on liquidity.
3 Attention is given to the timing of net cash flows.
4 An appropriate rate of return does not have to be calculated.
5 It gives a clear percentage return on an investment.

Disadvantages

1 It is not easy to understand.
2 It is difficult to determine which of two suitable rates to adopt unless a computer is used.
3 It gives only an approximate rate of return.
4 In complex CI situations, it can give some misleading results, e.g. where there are negative net cash flows in subsequent years, and where there are mutually exclusive projects.

As a non-accountant, you do not need to be too worried about the details of such rather technical considerations. All you need to know is that, in practice, the IRR method has to be used with some caution. This takes us on to the choice of method. We will consider this in the next sub-section.

Choice of method and other points

The description of CI appraisal techniques has been kept deliberately simple. Non-accountants will not normally be expected to involve themselves in the detailed calculations behind the various methods. You will, however, want to know which method your accountant is using, and the major disadvantages of each. For example, you should question him most carefully if he uses the ARR method. Why? Could he not at least try the discounted payback method? Why has the NPV method not been used?

We would suggest that unless there are very good reasons why your entity is unable to adopt it, you should adopt the NPV method. Otherwise, go for the discounted payback method. We do not recommend that ARR method, and we do not think that it is necessary for most entities to become involved in IRR calculations.

There are two other matters that we ought to mention before we leave this section: the effect of inflation and taxation on CI appraisal.

1 The effect of inflation (i.e. when prices go up, £1 now is worth less than £1 receivable in the future) can be taken into account in either of two ways:
   (a) by including an allowance for inflation in the calculation of net cash flows, i.e. you will need to allow for £1 in the future not purchasing as much as £1 now; it might be necessary (say) to assume that £1 will be the same as £1.20 in a year's time.
   (b) the expected rate of return can be amended to allow for inflation, i.e. the return will have to be higher; instead of (say) 8% per annum, it might have to be 10%.
2 The effect of taxation. Often there is a time-lag between when the profit is earned on a project, when cash is received for it, and when tax will be payable on the profits. Also, some tax allowances may be given on certain types of capital investment. Thus, the timing of taxation payments will have an important effect on the calculation of net cash flows.

Inflation and taxation are just two of the problems inherent in determining future net cash flows. No doubt you will have begun to see why in practice such an exercise is difficult and complex. Happily, as a manager, you can leave the details to your accountant, but at least you should now be in a position to ask him some searching questions to make sure that you know what he is doing – and why.

Once the entity has decided which projects to accept, it has then to find the funds to finance them. We consider this problem in the next section.

SOURCES OF FUNDS

As far as a company is concerned, there are basically five main sources of funds available for financing capital investments. They are as follows:

1 **From retained profits**. For most companies, this is probably the main source of funds.
2 **By issuing more shares for cash.** This can be an expensive administrative operation. If preference shares are issued the company is committing itself to paying preference dividends. If it issues ordinary shares, the total amount of ordinary dividends paid out is likely to increase, even if the same rate of dividend is maintained. Thus, if its profits do not match its expectations, the company may have difficulty in meeting a higher amount of dividend.
3 **By long-term borrowing**. The company could issue debentures to pay for its capital investment programme. The debenture interest would be allowable against corporation tax, but the company could become very high geared if it issued more long-term debt. This might cause a problem if profits began to decline, and it was committed to paying out a high proportion of its earnings in the form of debenture interest.
4 **By short-term borrowing**. This may be achieved by delaying payments to trade creditors, or by obtaining overdraft facilities at the bank. Capital investments financed by short-term borrowings are clearly very risky: loans may be called in at short notice, and they may not be renewable.
5 **By leasing and hire purchase contracts**. In the last 20 years or so, leasing has become a popular way of obtaining the use of fixed assets, probably because of the tax advantages which the method used to attract. These tax advantages have now been reduced, and leasing as a form of financing is not quite as popular as it used to be. Hire purchase is also a quite common form of financing, but it is an expensive method as a result of the high rate of interest usually charged on such arrangements.

Not-for-profit entities, such as local authorities and large charities, also have formidable problems in CI appraisal. A local authority, for example, will be severely constrained by central government in the amount that it is allowed to borrow for capital investment. It cannot issue shares in the same way that a company can, although it can borrow money from the general public on a long-term basis. In fact, a local authority may raise finance for capital expenditure from a number of sources: (a) by obtaining loans and grants from central government and other bodies (such as the EU); (b) by borrowing on the open market; (c) by providing for it out of revenue (i.e. through the council tax); and (d) by making leasing and hire purchase arrangements. A charity can similarly borrow, lease and hire, but it may also be able to depend on a substantial level of donations and legacies.

You will recall that in an earlier part of this chapter, we argued that CI appraisal forms part of the budgeting process. The budget will have identified what projects need to be undertaken. Usually there are so many competing ones that the entity has to rank them in some order of priority. Some priority has also to be given to those projects that do not necessarily contribute directly to profit, such as those that are perhaps necessary on health, social or welfare grounds. In the case of a local authority, there will be competing claims for the replacement of schools or the building of new social service centres. Such claims cannot really be based on 'profitability', and the calculation of 'net cash flow' is largely irrelevant, so it is difficult to use the techniques that we have outlined in this chapter.

In such instances, capital expenditure may have to based on an estimate of 'need', i.e. a concept that is difficult to define. Hence, a decision to build a school in a certain area may be determined by the projected growth in the child population in that area, or it may be related to the fact that the local primary school is over 100 years old. When it comes to a decision by the full council (instead of the education committee), such considerations may be overturned because of a perceived need to satisfy electors in entirely different part of the district. Indeed, if there are several high-ranking claims, the decision will inevitably be taken on political grounds.

In a commercial context, however, capital expenditure programmes will be determined partly by financial and non-financial considerations, and the results of a CI appraisal method (such as the ones outlined earlier in this chapter) will form only part of the overall decision. The projects that are given the go-ahead will need to be so scheduled that the implementation of them matches the availability of the finance (irrespective of its source). In most circumstances, companies finance their capital expenditure programmes out of retained earnings, but with large projects they may have to issue more shares or engage in long-term borrowing. If this is the case, there may well be a considerable time-lag before a project can go ahead.

CONCLUSION

CI appraisal is a complex and time-consuming exercise. It is not possible to be totally accurate in determining the viability of individual projects, but a reasoned comparison can be made between them.

Managers tend to be very enthusiastic about their own sphere of responsibility. Thus, the marketing manager may be sure that additional sales will be possible, the production director certain that a new machine will pay for itself, while the data processing manager convinced that a new computer is essential.

In choosing between such competing projects, the accountant's role is to try to assess their costs, and to compare them with the possible benefits. Once a choice has been made, he then has to ensure that the necessary finance will be available for them. CI appraisal should not be used as a means of blocking new projects. It is no different from all the other accounting techniques. It is meant to provide additional guidance to management, and, ultimately, it is the responsibility of management to ensure that other factors are taken into account.

Capital investment appraisal concludes this part of the book. We have now covered the two main branches of accounting: financial accounting, and cost and management accounting. In both branches, we have concentrated on examining accounting techniques for *internal* management purposes. In the final part of the book we shall be looking at information prepared largely for *external* reporting purposes.

KEY POINTS

1 **Capital investment appraisal forms part of the budgeting process.**

2 **There are five main methods of determining the viability of a project:**
   (a) payback;
   (b) discounted payback;
   (c) accounting rate of return;
   (d) net present value;
   (e) internal rate of return.

3 **All these methods have their advantages and disadvantages, but the recommended methods are discounted payback and net present value.**

4 **Capital expenditure may be financed out of variety of sources: by short-term and long-term borrowing, and by leasing and hire purchase. A company may also finance projects out of retained profits, and by issuing shares, while a not-for-profit entity may use revenue income, grants, special loans, and legacies.**

CHECK YOUR LEARNING

1 Insert the missing word or words in each of the following statements:
   (a) The evaluation of costs and benefits of proposed investments in specific fixed assets is known as _____ _____ _____.
   (b) The _____ of _____ is the cost of financing an investment, expressed as a percentage rate.
   (c) _____ _____ _____ refers to the discounting of the net cash flows of a capital project to ascertain present value.

   2 List five methods used in capital investment appraisal.

   3 Identify (a) three main sources of finance available to a limited liability company in financing a capital investment, and (b) two main sources for a local authority.

ANSWERS

1 (a) capital investment appraisal   (b) cost (of) capital   (c) discounted cash flow
2 (a) payback   (b) discounted payback   (c) accounting rate of return   (d) net present value   (e) internal rate of return
3 (a) (i) retained profits   (ii) issue of shares   (iii) leasing   (b) (i) long-term borrowing (ii) through the council tax.

QUESTIONS

16.1 Prospect limited is considering investing in a new project. The project would cost £100 000 to implement, it would last 5 years, and it would then be sold for £50 000. The relevant profit and loss accounts for each year during the life of the project are as follows:

Year to 31 March	19X1	19X2	19X3	19X4	19X5
	£000	£000	£000	£000	£000
Sales	2000	2400	2800	2900	2000
Less: Cost of goods sold					
Opening stock	–	200	300	450	350
Purchases	1600	1790	2220	1960	1110
	1600	1990	2520	2410	1460
Less: Closing stock	200	300	550	350	50
	1400	1690	1970	2060	1410
Gross profit	600	710	830	840	590
Less: Expenses	210	220	240	250	300
Depreciation	190	190	190	190	190
	400	410	430	440	490
Net profit	200	300	400	400	100
Taxation	40	70	100	100	10
Relained profits	£160	£230	£300	£300	£90

Additional information:
1 All sales are made and all purchases are obtained on credit terms.
2 Outstanding trade debtors and trade creditors at the end of each year are expected to be as follows:

Year	Trade debtors	Trade creditors
	£000	£000
19X1	200	250
19X2	240	270
19X3	300	330
19X4	320	300
19X5	400	150

3 Expenses would all be paid in cash during each year in question.
4 Taxation would be paid on 1 January following each year end.
5 Half the project would be paid for in cash on 1 April 19X0, and the remaining half (also in cash) on 1 January 19X1. The resale value of £50 000 will be received in cash on 31 March 19X6.

Required:
Calculate the annual net cash flow arising from this project.

16.2 Buchan Enterprises is considering investing in a new machine. The machine will be purchased on 1 January 19X1 and at a cost of £50 000. It is estimated that it would last for 5 years, and it will then be sold at the end of the year for £2000 in cash. The respective net cash flows estimated to be received by the company as a result of purchasing the machine during each year of its life are as follows:

Year	£	
1	8 000	(excluding the initial cost)
2	16 000	
3	40 000	
4	45 000	
5	35 000	(exclusive of the project's sale proceeds)

The company's cost of capital is 12%.

Required:
Calculate (a) the payback period for the project; and (b) its discounted payback period.

16.3 Lender Limited is considering investing in a new project. It is estimated that it will cost £100 000 to implement, and that the expected net profit after tax will be as follows:

Year	£
1	18 000
2	47 000
3	65 000
4	65 000
5	30 000

Required:
Calculate the accounting rate of return of the proposed project.

16.4 The following net cash flows relate to Lockhart Limited in connection with a certain project which has an initial cost of £2 500 000:

Year	Net cash flow
	£000
1	800 (excluding the initial cost)
2	850
3	830
4	1200
5	700

The company's required rate of return is 15%.

Required:
Calculate the net present value of the project.

16.5 Moffat District Council has calculated the following net cash flows for a proposed project costing £1 450 000:

Year	Net cash flow
	£000
1	230 (excluding the initial cost)
2	370
3	600
4	650
5	120

Required:
Calculate the internal rate of return generated by the project.

16.6 Marsh Limited has investigated the possibility of investing in a new machine. The following data have been extracted from the report relating to the project:

Cost of machine on 1 January 19X6: £500 000.
Life: 4 years to 31 December 19X9.
Estimated scrap value: Nil.
Depreciation method: Straight-line.

Year	Accounting profit after tax	Net cash flows
	£000	£000
1	100	50 (excluding the initial cost)
2	250	200
3	250	225
4	200	225
5	–	100

The company's required rate of return is 15%.

Required:
Calculate the return the machine would make using the following investment appraisal methods:

1 payback;
2 accounting rate of return;
3 net present value; and
4 internal rate of return.

ADDITIONAL QUESTIONS (WITHOUT ANSWERS)

16.7 Nicol Limited is considering investing in a new machine. The machine would cost £500 000. It would have a life of five years, and a nil residual value. The company uses the straight line method of depreciation.

It is expected that the machine will earn the following extra profits for the company during its expected life:

Year	Profits
	£000
1	200
2	120
3	120
4	100
5	60

The above profits also represent the extra net cash flows expected to be generated by the machine (i.e. they exclude the machine's initial cost and the annual depreciation charge).
The company's cost of capital is 18%.

Required:
(a) Calculate:
  (i) the machine's payback period; and
  (ii) its net present value; and
(b) advise management as to whether the new machine should be purchased.

16.8 Hewie Limited has some capital available for investment, and is considering two projects, only one of which can be financed. The details are as follows:

	Project	
	1	2
Expected life (years)	4	3
	£000	£000
Initial cost	600	500
Expected net cash flows (excluding		
the initial cost)		
Year		
1	10	250
2	200	250
3	400	50
4	50	–
Residential value	Nil	Nil

Required:
Advise management on which project to accept.

PART 4

Annual reports

CHAPTER 17

Disclosure of information

Extent of audit change deplored

By Andrew Jack

Companies are being bombarded with far too many demands for reform of accounting and auditing, the chairman of a group of leading finance directors said yesterday.

Mr Michael Lawrence, finance director of Prudential and chairman of the 100 Group of finance directors, told a Confederation of British Industry conference in London that there was a "huge labyrinth" through which people were struggling to find their way.

"We are concerned about the volume of material being produced and the numbers of bodies becoming involved," he said.

"Many chairmen and chief executives will begin to lose patience with all this," he continued. " They will see time and energy being spent by self interested bureaucracies producing sheaves of requirements. The good and the essential will be criticised along with the unnecessary and the unwieldly."

It is said he had received recent documents from bodies including the Institute of Chartered Accountants in England and Wales, the Association of Corporate Treasurers and the Institute of Investment Management Research.

Mr Lawrence said the Accounting Standards Board should be the primary forum for issuing standards, if balance and consistency were to be preserved.

He also criticised the proposals of the Auditing Practices Board to expand the role of auditing. He said most corporate failures were failures of financial reporting or basic auditing and did not require an expansion in the scope of auditing.

He said there was a need for greater focus on the point that accounts are primarily to communicate with shareholders, and not other potential audiences such as employees and creditors.

"Financial reporting is essentially an exercise in proactical communication, and as with all communication should be geared to its audience and its purpose," he said.

He said that companies' financial reporting had been too flexible and "innovative" in the past, and there was a need for less discretion in the future.

He said the goal of international harmonisation of accounting standards was well worth pursuing. But he added that there were many reporting differences between different countries which did not need to be harmonised but simply understood.

The Financial Times, 16 June 1993

Exhibit 17.0 The growth in corporate financial reporting requirements is causing concern among some observers, but there is no sign of it slowing down.

In Chapter 6, we explained how to construct a set of company accounts. Those accounts were prepared mainly for the benefit of management. All limited liability companies, however, have to supply a copy of their annual accounts to their shareholders. These accounts (they are often referred to as the *published* accounts) are an abbreviated version of those prepared for management purposes. The law only requires a certain minimum amount of information to be disclosed to the owners of the company, i.e. the shareholders. The details are contained within the Companies Act 1985 (as amended by the Companies Act 1989). In effect, the shareholders are only entitled to receive a *summary* of the annual accounts. In addition, there are a number of professional requirements which accountants are expected to follow.

In this chapter, we are going to review the legal and professional requirements governing the minimum amount of disclosure to shareholders. In later chapters we will be going into great detail about the way in which accountants report to their shareholders in an annual report.

LEARNING
OBJECTIVES

By the end of this chapter, you will be able to:
● describe the background to UK financial reporting practices;
● list the main contents of an annual report.

MINIMUM DISCLOSURE REQUIREMENTS

During the last 50 years, there has been a gradual increase in the minimum amount of information that companies have to disclose to their shareholders. This means that the accounts are now very complex, even if they just contain the minimum disclosure requirements. A distinct change became apparent about 25 years ago. In 1971, some mandatory professional accountancy requirements were introduced, and then in the Companies Act 1981, Parliament laid down some specific formats for the presentation of the profit and loss account and the balance sheet. Prior to 1981, the law had laid down only broad guidelines for the disclosure of information to shareholders, and it had been left largely to each individual company to decide how and in what format that information should be presented.

The Companies Act 1981 was eventually consolidated into the Companies Act 1985 (along with the Companies Acts of 1948, 1967, 1976 and 1980). The Companies Act 1985 has now been amended by the Companies Act 1989, and prescribed formats are still required. The Companies Act 1985 (as amended) is now the major source of company account legislation in the UK.

In addition to legal requirements, the six major professional accountancy bodies also insist upon certain additional information being included in published accounts. We outlined some of the background to these requirements in Chapter 2. Until 1990, these requirements were administered by the Accounting Standards Committee (ASC). The ASC was set up in 1970, primarily with the task of narrowing the areas of difference in accounting practice. The mandatory requirements were contained within what were called 'statements of standard accounting practice' (SSAPs). During its lifetime, the ASC issued 25 SSAPs, and professionally qualified accountants were expected to abide by them. Unfortunately, this did not always happen. The ASC was often slow in dealing with new or contentious issues, and many standards were clearly the result of some highly questionable compromises. This meant that some of them contained a number of loopholes which some companies were only too eager to exploit.

The ASC fell into such disrepute that it had to be disbanded. In August 1990, it was replaced by a body called the Financial Reporting Council (FRC). The FRC is financed and supported by the six major professional accountancy bodies, government and industry, and it is considered to have much more authority and independence than did the ASC. The FRC's main work is carried out be a committee called the Accounting Standards Board (ASB). The ASB has a full-time chairman and technical director, and the ASB is now responsible for issuing accounting standards. These are called Financial Reporting Standards (FRSs). Within three years, the ASB had issued three FRSs. The ASB also took over all the then existing SSAPs. Eventually, these will all be withdrawn, but, for the time being, the ASB is amending some and withdrawing others.

It remains to be seen whether the ASB is any more successful than was the ASC. The ASB does have one overwhelming advantage over its predecessor. The Companies Act 1989 made accounting standards (or their equivalent) semi-statutory. What this means is that if a company has appeared to ignore the requirements of a particular standard, its directors can be asked by the courts for an explanation. If the court is not satisfied, then the company can be forced into amending its accounts. However, it is debatable whether even this device will work. An overriding rule of the Companies Act is that accounts should present what is called 'a true and fair view'. This requirement is not capable of precise definition, and much depends upon individual interpretation. Consequently, if the directors of a company do not comply with a particular standard, they can always claim that they have not done so because otherwise the accounts would not give a true and fair view. In most circumstances, it is difficult to see how any court of law could disagree with the views of the directors, especially if they were supported by the auditors.

FRSs and SSAPs do not lay down precise guidelines. It is recognized that individual circumstances vary so considerably that it would be impossible to insist upon a rigid interpretation of most accounting matters. However, professionally qualified accountants are expected to do their best to ensure that companies follow the spirit, as well as the letter of the standards. It should also be noted that the standards do not apply exclusively to companies, and, wherever possible, they should be adopted by other entities, such as local authorities and the nationalized industries.

As well as supplying a copy of their annual accounts to shareholders, *all* public and private companies have to file a copy of their annual accounts with the Registrar of Companies at Companies House in either Cardiff or Edinburgh. This means that on payment of a small fee, the accounts of limited liability companies are open to public inspection. Thus, the same information that is available to shareholders is available to any member of the general public.

The 1985 Companies Act does, however, allow some concessions to *private companies*. This depends upon their size. All public companies must file the same set of accounts as the ones that they submit to their shareholders, but private companies may file abbreviated accounts if they meet two out of the three following criteria:

	Company	
Criteria	*Small*	*Medium*
	(not greater than)	*(not greater than)*
Turnover	£2.8 million	£11.2 million
Gross assets	£1.4 million	£5.6 million
Employees	50	250

Notwithstanding this concession, it should be noted that shareholders in small and medium-sized companies must still be supplied with a set of accounts that comply with the minimum disclosure requirements laid down in the Companies Act 1985.

The Companies Act does not require employees or other interested parties to be supplied with a copy of the annual accounts. Some large public companies may present their employees with a copy of the accounts supplied to shareholders, although they have no legal right to it. Employees of private companies may not have even this facility, and they may have to resort to inspecting a copy of their company's accounts at Companies House (there are various agencies that will do this for you), but if they are employed in small or medium-sized companies, they will only be able to inspect the abbreviated version.

In recent years, however, there has been a tendency for both private and public companies to prepare accounts specially for their employees. Although successive governments have prepared legislation which has encouraged this trend, most has never been enacted, and employees still do not have the same rights as shareholders. None the less, many companies do now supply some fairly detailed information to their employees. Sometimes, this may be in the form of a written report, but the practice is growing of presenting some details about the company's performance in an audio-visual format.

Although in this book, we are only concerned with the *minimum* disclosure requirements, it must be appreciated that an annual report is still a fairly long and complicated document. Shareholders who do not have a knowledge of accounting are probably quite mystified by the contents of such reports. However, students who have worked through this book should not have too much difficulty in understanding them!

CONTENTS OF AN ANNUAL REPORT

As can be seen in Exhibit 17.1, the contents of an annual report now contain much more than a summary of the internal profit and loss account and a balance sheet. They usually include some promotional material, as well as a considerable number of detailed notes, reports and statements required by FRSs and SSAPs (there may also be some extra Stock Exchange requirements). However, even though the contents of an annual report are quite complex, it is possible to break down a fairly typical report into four main sections. These may be summarized as follows:

Promotional material

Companies usually take the opportunity to include details of their products. Shareholders are consumers, of course, so it is beneficial to the company if it can persuade its shareholders to buy its products. As this type of information does not form part of the accounting function, we shall not be discussing it any further in this book.

Specialist reports

The annual report will usually include the following specialist reports:

1 a report from the chairman;
2 a report from the directors;
3 a report from the auditors.

In this book, we shall refer to such reports as the *principal* reports. The principal reports form the subject of the next chapter.

The main financial statements

The main financial statements comprise the following main reports:

1 a profit and loss account;
2 a balance sheet;
3 a cash flow statement (apart from small companies).

We shall be examining these statements in Chapter 19.

Supplementary report

A number of other reports are usually included in an annual report. The exact number and type depend upon the company, but in Chapter 20 we shall be examining some typical examples. Chapter 20 also includes a brief outline of some other current financial reporting issues.

Exhibit 17.1 The contents of a typical annual report

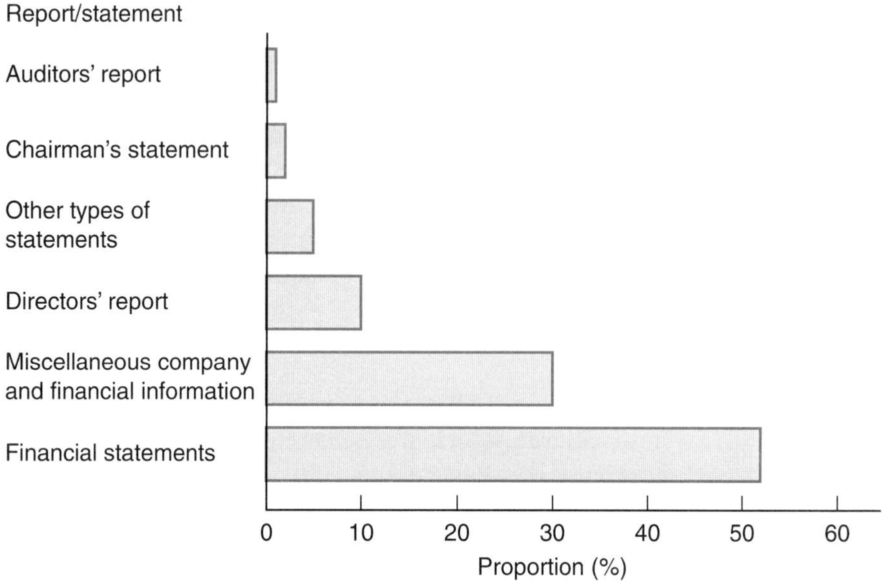

Report/statement

Note: The actual proportions will vary from company to company

CONCLUSION

As a non-accountant, it is unlikely that you will be involved in the detailed preparation of your company's annual report, although you may well have to provide information that will be included in it. Otherwise, you are only likely to see the entire published version of your company's accounts if it is issued to you as an employee, or if you happen to be a shareholder.

The annual report will probably not mean very much to you unless you have had some specialist training in financial accounting. We have attempted to provide that training in the earlier chapters of this book, and so you are now in a position to have a look at the structure of an annual report in more detail.

KEY POINTS

1 By law, companies have to disclose a minimum amount of information annually to their shareholders. The minimum amount required is supplemented by professional requirements.

2 The main statutory requirements are contained in an auditors' and a directors' report, a profit and loss account, and a balance sheet.

3 **The ASB also requires the publication of a cash flow statement (except for small companies).**

4 **Other statements may be found in a typical annual report, such as the chairman's statement.**

CHECK YOUR LEARNING

1 What are the two main sources of authority for the disclosure of information to shareholders?

2 List the three main types of reports contained within an annual report.

3 What do the following initials mean? (a) ASC (b) SSAP (c) FRC (d) ASB (e) FRS

ANSWERS

1 legislation; professional requirements
2 specialist reports; main financial statements; supplementary statements.
3 (a) Accounting Standards Committee (b) Statement of Standard Accounting Practice (c) Financial Reporting Council (d) Accounting Standards Board (e) Financial Reporting Statement

ASSIGNMENT

An assignment covering this chapter will be found at the end of Chapter 20.

CHAPTER 18

The principal reports

Auditors qualify annual report of ECH subsidiary

By Paul Taylor

Enterprise Computer Holdings' principal subsidiary, Enterprise Computer Services, has had its annual report qualified on a going concern basis by KPMG Peat Marwick, its auditors.

The accounts cover the 15 months to March 31 1992 when the group posted pre-tax losses of £8.33m on turnover of £157.9m.

However, the supplier of second user IBM computers said the boards of both the parent company and the subsidiary were satisfied that the group's bank facilities would continue to be available for a period "which will allow the auditors to report on the accounts to March 31 1993 without a going concern qualification."

In a statement yesterday the group said its confidence stemmed from the improved trading performance during the last quarter, and the pending merger of Teltronics and SRH, a company in which Enterprise has a 25 per cent equity stake, which is expected to be completed before June 30.

The merger is expected to result in the group receiving £5.3m in cash, property and securities over the next 12 months.

Since June last year Enterprise has undergone a substantial reorganisation and restructing under a new management team led by Mr Shaun Dowling, non-executive chairman.

The Financial Times, 5 May 1993

Exhibit 18.0 Auditors do not always let companies have it their own way.

S hareholders are required to receive a copy of the annual accounts of a company at least 21 days before they are to be considered at a general meeting of the company. This requirement also applies to both the auditors' report and the directors' report. It is also usual for the chairman to prepare a report for the shareholders. It seems convenient, therefore, to examine these three reports together (see Exhibit 18.1), and this is what we will do so in this chapter. We start with the chairman's report.

Exhibit 18.1 The inter-connection between the three principal reports and the main financial statements

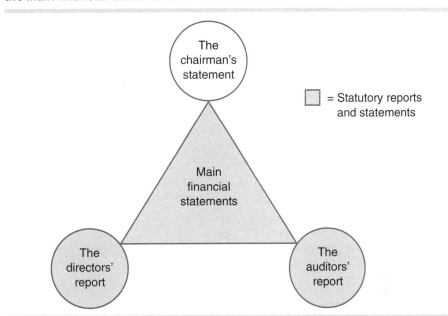

LEARNING
OBJECTIVES

By the end of this chapter, you will be able to:
● identify the three principal reports included in an annual report;
● describe the main contents of such reports.

THE CHAIRMAN'S REPORT

There are no statutory, professional, or Stock Exchange requirements for the chairman to report to the shareholders, although most chairmen do so. The report (or statement) is usually presented in an early part of the annual report, often following a list of the board of directors, and a brief summary of some key statistics.

The report may be a very long one, although most chairmen manage to limit their comments to one or two pages. As there are no requirements covering the contents of such a report, a chairman is quite free to include almost anything that he likes. However, the auditors now have a duty to review the report, and they may wish to express an opinion about its contents. However, the chairman will be mindful of the effects that his remarks are likely to have on the company's share price, and he will know that he could cause a great deal of embarrassment if his comments were eventually proved unjustified.

A chairman's report may include the following items:

1 A review of the company's overall results for the year, including some information on divisional, product, and sectional performance.
2 A very brief summary of the financial results for the year, especially a comment about the net profit for the year compared with the previous year.
3 A brief statement of the company's paid and proposed dividends for the year.
4 An explanation of what steps have been taken to improve the company's efficiency and productivity.
5 Details of major acquisitions and disposals of shares in which the company has a controlling interest.
6 Some information about the board of directors, e.g. about new members, resignations, retirements, achievements, and honours.
7 Details about employees, such as those retiring after exceptionally long service.
8 The chairman's thanks to fellow directors, employees, and other personnel involved in the company.
9 Some comments about the company's prospects.

THE DIRECTORS' REPORT

The directors' report usually follows the chairman's report. It is a statutory requirement that the directors should attach a copy of their report to the set of accounts that are sent to the shareholders. A directors' report now contains a great deal of information, so all we can do in this section is to summarize the main contents. We do so in the sub-sections below.

Activities

The directors' report may include details of the following activities:

1 principal activities of the company, and any changes in them during the year;
2 a review of developments during the year, and a statement of future ones;
3 research and development activities;
4 important events that have happened during the year;
5 the recommended dividend;
6 the amount set aside or withdrawn from reserves.

Auditors

The auditors have to be re-appointed annually by the shareholders, so it is necessary to state in the report that the auditors are seeking election (or otherwise).

Directors

All the names of those individuals who have been directors during the year should be stated. The directors who are still directors at the end of the year must have their share and loan capital holdings listed. Any director not having any shares or debentures must disclose that fact.

Subject to the company's articles (i.e. its rules), the directors of public companies who are over the age of 70 have to retire or be re-appointed annually. The names of such directors should be stated and the fact that they are offering themselves for re-election has also to be mentioned.

Donations

If the company has made certain charitable and political donations during the year which *together* exceed £200, then the separate total for both the charitable and the political donations must be stated. If a particular political donation exceeds £200, both the amount and the name of the recipient must be reported.

Employment policy

The company's employment policy towards disabled persons should be stated, along with their training and their career development.

Fixed assets

Any major changes in fixed assets or any significant difference between the market value and the book value of land and buildings should be noted.

Share capital

Information about changes in the company's share capital will be given in the accounts, but any such changes should be referred to in the directors' report.

The directors' report should end with the signature of the chairman (or one of the other directors) and stated as being signed 'on behalf of the board'. The signature should then be followed by the date when the report was agreed by the board. If the report is signed by anyone other than the chairman or one of the directors (such as the company secretary), he may sign it 'by order of the board'.

THE AUDITORS' REPORT

The auditors' report will normally be quite short (although it is now much longer than it used to be). Most auditors' reports will be fairly similar. The basic elements are summarized below:

1 Title. This identifies the person(s) to whom it is addressed.
2 Introductory paragraph. This will identify what financial statements have been audited.
3 Main contents:
  (a) a statement detailing the responsibilities of both the directors and the auditors;
  (b) the basis for the auditors' opinion;
  (c) the auditors' opinion about the financial statements.
4 Signature. The signature would either be the original hand-written signature or a printed version.
5 Date. The date when the auditors sign the report.

A typical auditors' report would read as in Exhibit 18.2.

Exhibit 18.2 An example of a typical auditors' report

AUDITORS' REPORT TO THE SHAREHOLDERS OF ENERGY PLC

We have audited the financial statements on pages 14 to 30 which have been prepared under the historical cost convention and the accounting policies set out on page 14.

Respective responsibilities of directors and auditors
As described on page 5, the company's directors are responsible for the preparation of financial statements. It is our responsibility to form an independent opinion, based on our audit, on those statements, and to report our opinion to you.

Basis of opinion
We conducted our audit in accordance with Auditing Standards issued by the Auditing Practices Board. An audit includes examination, on a test basis, of evidence relevant to the amounts and disclosures in the financial statements. It also includes an assessment of the statements, and of whether the accounting policies are appropriate to the company's circumstances, consistently applied, and adequately disclosed.

We planned and performed our audit so as to obtain all the information and explanations which we considered necessary in order to provide us with sufficient evidence to give reasonable assurance that the financial statements are free from material mis-statement, whether caused by fraud or other irregularity or error. In forming our opinion we also evaluated the overall adequacy of the presentation of information in the financial statements.

Opinion
In our opinion the financial statements give a true and fair view of the state of the company's affairs as at 31 March 19X5 and of its profit for the year then ended, and have been properly prepared in accordance with the Companies Act 1985.

Cope & Co
Registered auditors
31 May 19X5

Cope House
Trial Lane
Casterton
CA12 9PK

Source: Statement of Auditing Standards, Auditors' Report on Financial Statements, The Auditing
Practices Board, May 1993, page 28.

The type of auditors' report displayed in Exhibit 18.2 would be regarded
as an *unqualified* audit report. This means that in the opinion of the auditors, the accounts give a true and fair view, and that they have no
reservations about them. A *qualified* audit report is supposed to draw the
attention of the shareholders to certain aspects of the accounts which do
not appear to give a true and fair view, e.g. perhaps because of the method
used to value stocks. The qualification may arise only as a result of a
minor point, but even a minor qualification should be taken very seriously.

There is some uncertainty about the importance and relevance of a qualified audit report, particularly if the qualification appears to be relatively
insignificant. It used to be rare for audit reports to be qualified, but in
recent years it has become quite common. The effect of a qualified audit
report ought, at the very least, to result in some searching questions being
put to the directors at the general meeting. If the explanations appear quite
unsatisfactory, then the shareholders ought to consider dismissing the
directors, although such an event is not very common.

CONCLUSION

This chapter has outlined the contents of three main reports which are contained within a typical annual report. We first reviewed the chairman's
report. The chairman's report is not a report which is required either by
statute or by professional requirements. We then summarized the contents
of a directors's report, now a major source of much statutory and professional accounting information. Finally, we outlined the contents of a
typical auditors' report. The auditors' report is one of the shortest reports
to be found in the annual report.

KEY POINTS

1 **An annual report contains three main reports.**

2 **The chairman's report is not required by statute or by any professional
   requirement.**

3 The directors' report contains a great deal of statutory information.

4 The auditors' report is a statutory requirement normally containing very little information.

CHECK YOUR LEARNING

1 What are the three main principal reports contained within an annual report?

2 Which two principal reports are a statutory requirement?

3 In which principal report are you likely to find the following information?
(a) a statement about the historic cost convention;
(b) the policy towards disabled employees;
(c) future prospects for the company;
(d) thanks to retiring directors;
(e) political donations.

ANSWERS

1 chairman's; directors'; auditors'

2 directors'; auditors'

3 (a) auditors'   (b) directors'   (c) chairman's   (d) chairman's   (e) directors'

ASSIGNMENT

An assignment covering this chapter will be found at the end of Chapter 20.

CHAPTER 19

The main financial statements

Restructured Borthwicks £2m in the red

By Catherine Milton

Borthwicks, the flavourings maker, yesterday reported a swing from profits of £1.29m to losses of £1.99m pre-tax for the 12 months ended March 27 at the end of 13 years of restructuring.

The deficit mainly reflected the one-off cost of disposing of loss-making meat interests and concealed operating profits on continuing operations of £1.97m (£1.53m) after stripping out losses from businesses now sold.

Comparisons have been restated to comply with the FRS 3 accounting standard.

Losses per share emerged at 3.8p (earnings 1.8p) but a proposed final dividend of 0.7p lifts the total by 9 per cent to 1.2p (1.1p).

Mr John Thomson, chairman, said: "A serious profit haemorrhage has been staunched and Borthwicks is now moving forward unemcumbered in its chosen field of natural flavours."

Borthwicks said it now produced a range of flavours, some of which were popular with cave men in prehistory, while others were aimed at the new age community.

Recessionary conditions pushed turnover down to £43m (£44.4m). The figure included £17.4m from discontinued operations – Burton Son & Sanders, the bakery business, Consumer Products, the prepared meals maker and Ringer abattoir, which have all been sold.

The company reported net exceptional charges of £2.65m relating to the final stages of the restructuring. Interest payments fell to £614 000 (£707 000). Gearing declined to 44 per cent (67 per cent).

The Financial Times, 2 June 1993

Exhibit 19.0 Changes in accounting practice can sometimes have unfortunate consequences.

The main financial statements that we are going to consider in this chapter are the profit and loss account, the balance sheet, and the cash flow statement. The interrelationship between them is shown in diagrammatic form in Exhibit 19.1. Annual reports usually contain other types of statements, but we shall leave these to the next chapter.

Exhibit 19.1 The inter-linking of the main financial statements

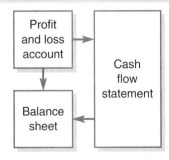

THE BACKGROUND TO PUBLISHED ACCOUNTS

We have already examined the structure and format of profit and loss accounts, balance sheets and cash flow statements in earlier chapters. In those chapters we were primarily concerned with preparing the accounts for internal management purposes. In practice, the contents of *internal* financial statements can be enormously detailed and extremely complex.

The Companies Act 1985 (amended by the Companies Act 1989) recognizes that it would be impracticable to expect a company to supply the same amount and type of information to all its shareholders, so it details what are considered to be the *minimum* requirements. Unfortunately, when additional professional requirements (there are also some Stock Exchange requirements) are incorporated into the accounts, shareholders still face a considerable burden in sorting out what it all means.

In this chapter, we will outline what you might expect to find in most published profit and loss accounts, balance sheets, and cash flow statements, and we will offer a brief explanation of each main item. However, companies do have slightly different ways of presenting their results, so you must not expect to find accounts that necessarily match our examples.

We start first with some items that that we have not dealt with in earlier chapters.

ADDITIONAL FEATURES

There are some features of published financial statements that are mainly relevant for external reporting purposes. In this section we summarize the main ones for you.

Group accounts

Most published annual accounts that you are likely to come across will contain the results for a *group* of companies. There are a few examples of large public companies that are not part of a group, but they are comparatively rare. If you manage to obtain an annual report for a small company, then you may well find that it is just a single company.

A group is like a family. One company (say Company A) may buy shares in another company (say Company B). When Company A owns more than 50% of the voting shares in Company B, B becomes a *sub-sidiary* of A. If A owned more than 20% of the voting shares in B but less than 50%, B would be known as an *associated* or *related* company of A. In effect, B is considered to be the offspring of A. In turn, B might have children of its own (say Company C and Company D). C and D then become part of the family, i.e. they become part of the group structure. This type of group structure is illustrated in Exhibit 19.2.

Exhibit 19.2 Example of a group of companies

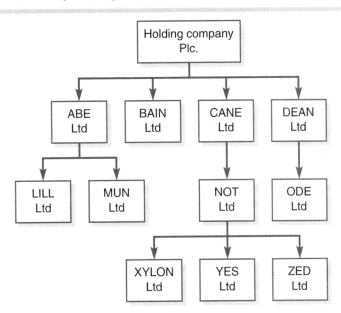

In fact, the Companies Act 1985 uses the terms *group undertaking* for a subsidiary company, and *undertakings in which the company has a participating interest* for an associated or related company. The reason for this difference in terminology is that the Companies Act 1989 requires other types of entities (and not just companies) to be included in the 'group' accounts.

The significance of these relationships is that the published accounts will be prepared for the group as a whole. Even though, for example, B, C and D are companies in their own right (and might therefore be expected to prepare accounts for themselves), the entity as a whole becomes the group. Thus, we ignore any inter-group relationships when preparing the *group* accounts.

When inspecting a set of published accounts you can normally expect to see a group profit and loss account, a group balance sheet, and a group cash flow statement. The 1985 Companies Act permits group accounts to be presented in several ways, but the most common method is to prepare a group profit and loss account, a group balance sheet, and a balance sheet for the *holding* company (Company A in our example). A cash flow statement (whether a group one, or otherwise) is not required by law, but it is a professional requirement for all companies (except small ones).

In order to prepare group accounts, it is necessary to add together, i.e. *consolidate* all of the company accounts that form part of the group. As a result, the subsidiary company and associated company results are absorbed into the holding company's accounts (although some specific information about such companies has still to be disclosed). The preparation of group accounts can be an enormous and highly specialized task, and it is somewhat of a specialism even among accountants.

Notes to the accounts

Another additional feature of group accounts is that they will almost certainly be accompanied by many pages of notes. These notes provide additional information about the items disclosed in the accounts, but they may also contain some quite new material. Such notes form an integral part of the accounts. Unfortunately, they usually contain so much information that it is difficult to find what you are looking for.

Comparative figures

The Companies Act 1985 also requires the previous year's accounts to be included alongside the current year's results. This adds to the amount of information given in the accounts, although there is some advantage in being able to make comparisons between the two years.

With this preliminary review of published accounts, it is now possible for us to begin our investigation of them in some detail. We start first with the group profit and loss account.

THE GROUP PROFIT AND LOSS ACCOUNT

In presenting the profit and loss account, the Companies Act 1985 permits a choice of two types of format, as follows:

1 **Horizontal format**. In the horizontal format, the expenditure is listed on the left-hand side of the page, and the income on the right-hand side.
2 **Vertical format**. The vertical format displays the income and expenditure on a line-by-line basis.

When we have been preparing accounts in the earlier part of this book, we have used the vertical format almost exclusively, so it should be familiar to you. We deliberately chose to use this format, because it is the one adopted by most UK companies, and so it is the one that you are most likely to come across.

Besides permitting a choice of structural formats, the Companies Act 1985 also permits the expenditure to be displayed according to *type*. There are again two formats permitted by the Act:

1 the operation format;
2 the type of expenditure format.

These formats are illustrated in Exhibit 19.3.

Exhibit 19.3 Examples of the vertical profit and loss account expenditure formats

1 Operational	£000	2 Type of expenditure	£000	£000
Turnover	9000	Turnover		9000
Cost of sales	(5500)	Changes in stocks of finished goods and work in-progress		200
Gross profit	3500	Own work capitalized		50
		Other operating income		100
				9350
Distribution costs	(1000)	Raw materials and consumables	(4000)	
Administrative expenses	(1600)	Other external charges	(400)	
Operating profit	900	Staff costs	(3000)	
		Depreciation and other amounts written off tangible and intangible fixed assets	(900)	
Other operating income	100	Other operating charges	(50)	(8350)
Operating profit	£1000	*Operating profit*		£1000

Notes:
1 The exhibit contains dummy information.
2 After the operating profit stage the two formats are identical.

As can be seen from Exhibit 19.3, the type of expenditure format is very much more detailed than the operational format. Both types are used in the UK, but the operational format is more popular, probably because it is a little easier to follow. It is, in fact, basically the same format that we have adopted in examples used in earlier chapters.

We can now examine a published profit and loss account in some detail. We do so in Exhibit 19.4.

Exhibit 19.4 Example of a published profit and loss account

Energy public limited company
Group profit and loss account for the year to 31 March 19X2

	19X2 £000	19X2 £000	19X1 £000
Turnover[1]			
Continuing operations	44 000		30 000
Acquisitions	2 000		
	46 000		
Discontinued operations	3 000	49 000	4 000
Cost of sales[2]		(40 000)	(26 000)
Gross profit [3]		9 000	8 000
Distribution costs[4]		(4 000)	(3 000)
Administrative expenses[5]		(2 000)	(1 480)
Other operating income[6]		20	20
Operating profit [7]			
Continuing operations	2 740		3 500
Acquisitions	250		
	2 990		
Discontinued operations	30		20
Profit on ordinary activities before interest		3 020	3 520
Other interest receivable and other income[8]		295	220
Interest payable and similar charges[9]		(260)	(90)
Profit on ordinary activities before taxation [10]		3 055	3 650
Tax on profit on ordinary activities[11]		(145)	(850)
Profit on ordinary activities after taxation [12]		2 910	2 800
Minority interests[13]		(110)	(200)
Profit for the financial year [14]		2 800	2 600
Dividends paid and proposed[15]		(2 400)	(2 300)
Retained profit for the year [16]		£400	£300
Earnings per share[17]		2.85p	2.85p

Note: In an actual profit and loss account, there would be a note number column to refer to the formal notes which you would find attached to the accounts. In order to simplify the Exhibit, we have not included the formal notes.

Tutorial notes

1 Turnover is usually defined as being sales to customers outside the group less returns by customers, exclusive of trade discounts and value added tax. You will notice that turnover has been analysed between continuing operations, acquisitions and discontinued operations. In other words, sales from activities that are on-going, sales arising from entities taken over during the year, and sales arising from activities prior to their disposal during the year. FRS 3 (Reporting Financial Performance) requires this breakdown of turnover.

2 The detailed calculation for the cost of sales does not have to be disclosed. The term is not defined in the Companies Act 1985.

3 The gross profit may not be identical to that shown in the internal accounts because of the definition used for the cost of sales.

4 The Companies Act 1985 does not define what is meant by distribution costs.

5 Similarly, administrative expenses are not defined in the Act.

6 Other operating income will include income from rentals and royalties.

7 Operating profit. This is the point at which the operational and type of expenditure formats become identical. Note that FRS 3 requires the operating profit to be broken down into operating profit from continuing operations, aquisitions, and discontinued operations.

8 Other interest receivable and similar income includes interest received on loans

9 Interest payable and similar charges will include interest payable on bank and other short-term borrowings.

10 The profit on ordinary activities before taxation will require a detailed formal note to the accounts. It will include such information as the auditors' remuneration, directors' emoluments (as they are called), details of wages and salaries (in total), depreciation charges (in total), and social security and pension costs.

11 The tax on the profit on ordinary activities will consist largely of the company's corporation tax, but it may also include a number of technical accounting adjustments affecting taxation.

12 The amount shown for profit on ordinary activities after taxation is simply a sub-total.

13 A proportion of the after-tax profits may be due to shareholders outside the group if the holding company has not purchased all of the shares in a subsidiary company.

14 The profit for the financial year is the total amount of net profit for the year that could be distributed to group members.

15 The dividends paid and proposed to be paid will include dividends paid or payable on all types of shares.

16 The retained profit for the year will be transferred to the revenue reserves shown in the balance sheet. It will be used to help finance the future expansion of the company.

17 The formal definition of earnings per share is quite complex, but basically it is calculated by taking the after-tax earnings less preference dividends, and dividing them by the number of issued ordinary shares.

Exhibit 19.4 demonstrates quite clearly that a profit and loss account showing even the *minimum* amount of information results in a fairly complex statement. It should also be remembered that we have not illustrated examples of the formal notes that would normally be attached to it. For a large company, such notes could easily extend to at least six pages of closely printed material.

Now that we have examined a published profit and loss account, we will move on to conduct a similar examination of a published balance sheet. We do so in the next section.

THE GROUP BALANCE SHEET

The Companies Act 1985 allows a choice to be made between different balance sheet formats. The choice is as follows:

1 **Horizontal format**. In the horizontal format, the assets are laid out on the left-hand side of the page, and the capital on the right-hand side.
2 **Vertical format.** The vertical format shows the assets listed before the liabilities on a line-by-line basis.

In this book we have adopted, almost exclusively, the vertical format, so at this stage it should not be unfamiliar to you. In the UK, vertical balance sheets are the most popular, although occasionally you may come across examples of the horizontal type.

Published balance sheets do not look very different from those prepared for internal purposes, although, as we noted earlier, they will probably be prepared for a group, comparative figures will be shown, and there will be many formal notes to attached to them.

A typical published balance sheet is shown in Exhibit 19.5. The exhibit is followed by tutorial notes which give an explanation of each item.

Exhibit 19.5 Example of a published balance sheet

Energy public limited company
Group balance sheet at 31 March 19X2

	Group 19X2 £000	Company 19X1 £000	Group 19X2 £000	Company 19X1 £000
Fixed assets [1]				
Intangible assets[2]	90	60	–	–
Tangible assets[3]	1 400	1 350	1 300	1 200
Investments[4]	70	50	1 300	1 200
[5]	1 560	1 460	2 600	2 400

Current assets [6]				
Stocks[7]	6 500	3 800	3 300	1 350
Debtors[8]	7 500	4 500	4 800	1 800
Investments[9]	60	50	–	–
Cash in bank and in hand[10]	700	130	20	10
[11]	14 760	8 480	8 120	3 160
Creditors: Amounts falling due within one year[12]	(8 500)	(3 800)	(7 000)	(2 900)
Net current assets [13]	6 260	4 680	1 120	260
Total assets less current liabilities[14]	7 820	6 140	3 720	2 660
Creditors: amounts falling due after more than one year[15]	(3 000)	(1 700)	–	–
Provisions for liabilities and charges [16]	(1 200)	(1 500)	–	–
[17]	£3 620	£2 940	£3 720	£2 660
Capital and reserves [18]				
Called up share capital [19]	1 000	1 000	1 000	1 000
Share premium account [20]	500	500	500	500
Revaluation reserve[21]	600	600	900	900
Other reserves[22]	360	100	300	60
Profit and loss account[23]	1 040	640	1 020	200
[24]	3 500	2 840	3 720	2 660
Minority interests [25]	120	100	–	–
[26]	£3 620	£2 940	£3 720	£2 660

Approved by the board on XX June 19X2

_____ Director[27]

Note: In an actual balance sheet, there would be a note number column to refer to the formal notes which you would find attached to the accounts. In order to simplify the Exhibit, we have not included the formal notes.

Tutorial notes

1 The net book value of the fixed assets must be shown under three headings: (a) intangible assets; (b) tangible assets; and (c) investments.
2 Intangible assets are those assets that are not of a physical nature, such as goodwill, patents, and development costs.
3 Tangible assets include land and buildings, plant and machinery, fixtures, fittings, tools, and equipment.
4 Fixed assets investments are those that are intended to be held for the long term, i.e. in excess of 12 months.
5 This line is the total of all the fixed assets.

6 Current assets have also to be analysed into a number of categories.

7 Stocks must be disclosed under a number of categories, e.g. raw materials and consumables, work-in-progress, finished goods and payments on account. The detail will be shown in a formal note.

8 Debtors have also to be analysed under headings such as trade debtors, other debtors, prepayments, and accrued income. These will be included in a formal note.

9 Current asset investments are those investments held for the short term, i.e. normally for less than 12 months.

10 Cash at bank and in hand. This will be the same amount that will be included in the balance sheet prepared for internal purposes.

11 This line represents the total of current assets.

12 Creditors have to be analysed between short-term creditors (i.e. those payable within the next 12 months), and long-term creditors (i.e. those that do not have to be paid for at least 12 months). Both short- and long-term creditors have to be analysed into a number of categories, such as trade creditors, other creditors, and accruals and deferred income. The details will be found in a formal note.

13 The net current assets line is a sub-total (current assets)[11] less creditors: amounts falling due within one year[12].

14 This is another sub-total fixed assets[6] plus net current assets[13].

15 See 12 above.

16 Provisions for liabilities and charges include provisions for pensions and similar obligations, taxation (including deferred taxation), as well as other provisions which are not specified in the Companies Act 1985.

17 This line represents the balance sheet total.

18 The capital and reserves section is the other main part of the balance sheet. It explains how the net assets[17] have been financed.

19 The called up share capital represents all of the shares that have been issued, details of which will be shown in a formal balance sheet note.

20 The share premium account records the extra amount on top of the nominal value of their shares which shareholders were willing to pay when they bought their shares. It does not attract a dividend, and the Companies Act permits only a few, highly selected uses.

21 Sometimes fixed assets, such as land and buildings, will be revalued. The difference between the revalued amount and the net book value will be credited to a revaluation reserve account. The balance cannot be distributed to shareholders.

22 Other reserves. This balance may include a number of other reserve accounts both of a capital nature (i.e. reserves that cannot be distributed to shareholders) and of a revenue nature (i.e. amounts that may be distributed to shareholders).

23 This the total of all the profits that have not been distributed to shareholders, less those that have been put into special reserve accounts.

24 This is the total of the capital and reserves' section of the balance sheet. It represents shareholders' funds.

25 The minority interests represent that proportion of the net assets of subsidiary companies which is owned by shareholders outside the group.

26 This line should balance with line 17.

27 The balance sheet should be signed by one director.

Study Exhibit 19.5 very carefully. Its basic layout should be reasonably familiar to you, although there is a lot more detail than you have been used to in previous examples. In the next section, we will look at published cash flow statements.

GROUP CASH FLOW STATEMENTS

We have already examined the construction of a cash flow statement (CFS) in some detail in Chapter 7. CFSs differ little from the format that we used in that chapter, apart from reflecting the activities of a group of companies, and the inclusion of comparative figures.

Unlike the profit and loss account and the balance sheet, CFSs do not have any statutory backing, although they are now considered so important that they are usually regarded as being one of the main financial statements. Indeed, FRS 1 (the very first financial reporting standard) requires most companies (except for small ones) to prepare a CFS, and it is most unlikely that you will now refer to a set of company accounts that does not include one.

Exhibit 19.6 is an example of a group cash flow statement. You will notice that, apart from some extra detail, its format is reasonably familiar to you.

Exhibit 19.6 Example of a group cash flow statement

	19X2 £000	19X2 £000	19X1 £000	19X1 £000
Energy public limited company				
Group cash flow statement for the year ended 31 March 19X2				
Operating activities				
Net cash inflow from operating activities		2 820		2 300
Returns on investments and servicing of finance				
Interest received	200		150	
Interest paid	(250)		(180)	
Dividend received from associated undertaking	30		20	
Dividends paid	(1660)		(1100)	
Net cash outflow from returns on investments and servicing of finance		(1 680)		(1 110)

Taxation				
UK corporation tax paid	(600)		(500)	
Overseas tax paid	(60)		(40)	
Tax paid		(660)		(540)
Investing activities				
Purchase of intangible fixed assets	(30)		–	
Purchase of tangible fixed assets	(400)		(830)	
Purchase of subsidiary undertakings	(250)		(60)	
Sale of plant and machinery	100		80	
Sale of business	70		90	
Sale of trade investment	20		10	
Net cash outflow from investing activities		(490)		(710)
Net cash outflow before financing		(10)		(60)
Financing				
Issue of ordinary share capital	100		–	
New loans	690		100	
Repayment of amounts borrowed	(200)		(60)	
Net cash inflow from financing		590		40
Increase/ (decrease) in cash and cash equivalents		£580		£(20)

Tutorial notes

1 The exhibit contains dummy information.
2 The formal notes that would normally be attached to the statement have not been included.
3 The above format is only a guide: it is not mandatory.
4 Apart from some items that relate only to a group, e.g. dividend received from associated undertakings, and purchase of subsidiary undertakings, the statement is very similar to the ones that we compiled in Chapter 7.

Exhibit 19.6 is based on the example given in FRS 1, but it is likely that you will come across other slightly different formats. Some can be a little confusing, especially when figures are shown in brackets. Remember that the basic idea of a CFS is to show where the cash has come from and where it has gone to, and that it can broken down into five main sections, viz.:

1 operating activities (supported by a reconciliation statement);
2 returns on investments and costs of financing the entity;
3 taxation;
4 investing activities (largely in operating investments);
5 sources of finance.

Most of these sections contain both cash received and cash paid out. It is usual to put brackets around amounts paid in cash, but sometimes the opposite is the case. For example, FRS 1 gives an illustrative example of a CFS for a group that shows the net cash received from financing in brackets. This is a most confusing example, and it is very difficult to follow. Be very careful, therefore, when examining figures that are bracketed.

CONCLUSION

You are now recommended to study most carefully the format of a published profit and loss account, a published balance sheet, and a published cash flow statement. In this chapter, we have given you the a basic outline of such statements but, in practice, you will find very many variations of them. Do not be put off by the vast amount of information given (see Exhibit 19.7, for an example). In their 1993 accounts, for example, Marks and Spencer used four pages for the three main statements, and nineteen pages for the formal notes. Fortunately, a very high proportion of the material will now be familiar to you, and you should have no difficulty in sorting out what is peculiar to individual companies.

Exhibit 19.7 Example of the breakdown of the financial statements contained in a typical annual report

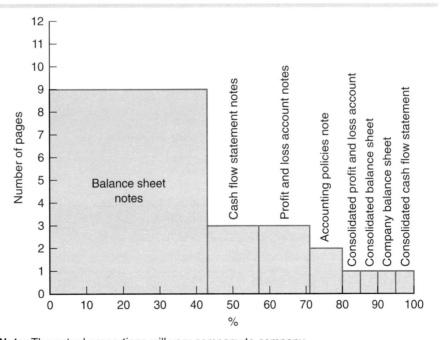

Note: The actual proportions will vary company to company

It would be advisable if you now obtain some copies of published accounts. Examine them carefully, and assess to what extent they conform to the structures that we have illustrated in this chapter.

KEY POINTS

1 The main financial statements comprise a profit and loss account, a balance sheet, and a cash flow statement.

2 Published accounts usually show the results for a *group* of companies.

3 In order to comply with the Companies Act 1985, groups will normally also include a balance sheet for the holding company, as well as one for the group as a whole.

4 In published accounts, comparative figures for the previous year are required.

5 The Companies Act 1985 permits a considerable amount of statutory information to be included in notes to the accounts, instead of showing it all on the face of the profit and loss account or the balance sheet.

6 A considerable amount of additional professional requirements will also be found in the formal notes.

CHECK YOUR LEARNING

1 What are the three main financial statements normally found in a company's annual report?

2 In which of the three main financial statements would you expect to find reference to each of the following items?
   (a) creditors: amounts falling due within one year
   (b) share premium account
   (c) distribution costs
   (d) directors' emoluments
   (e) cash from sale of trade investment
   (f) intangible assets
   (g) auditors' remuneration
   (h) movement on reserves
   (i) turnover on discontinued operations
   (j) cash and cash equivalents

ANSWERS

1 profit and loss account; balance sheet; cash flow statement

2 (a) balance sheet (b) balance sheet (c) profit and loss account (d) profit and loss account (e) cash flow statement (f) balance sheet (g) profit and loss account (h) balance sheet (i) profit and loss account (j) cash flow statement

ASSIGNMENT

An assignment covering the material in this chapter will be found at the end of Chapter 20.

Supplementary financial reports and other issues

Directors size up new rules

Norma Cohen on company compliance with the Cadbury code

The ink has barely dried on the final version of the Cadbury rules – the definitive rulebook on good corporate governance – and already corporations are keen to show their compliance.

From June 30 every company whose shares are traded on the London Stock Exchange will be required, as a condition of listing, to disclose in its annual report the extent to which it complies with the code drawn up by the Committee on the Financial Aspects of Corporate Governance, which bears the name of its chairman, Sir Adrian Cadbury.

The committee has made 19 recommendations intended to improve the functioning of corporate boards of directors. Although company annual reports for 1993 will most reflect the changes required, some companies are already expressing in their 1992 accounts their intention to follow best practice.

Ms Gina Cole, secretary to the committee, said "If there is mass non-compliance, the government may wish to step in." She said the committee would have to look behind published statements to see whether companies really were complying with the code.

Not surprisingly, one company which has stated its good intentions is Cadbury Schweppes, the company of which Sir Adrian was chairman. It says in its 1992 annual report: "The company complies with 17 of the 19 items of the code."

It says it will consider compliance with items covering the effectiveness of a company's systems of internal controls, and with directors reporting that a business is a going concern "when guidelines for those two items have been developed".

The annual report also describes the roles of the audit, remuneration and nominations committees, all of which are chaired – as recommended by the Cadbury committee – by a non-executive director.

Also making reference to best corporate governance practice is M&G Group, the UK's largest unit trust manager. M&G, as an institutional shareholder, has taken a vigorous line on corporate governance matters and its chief executive, Mr Paddy Linaker, had urged the Cadbury committee to take a tougher stance on some issues than it did.

M&G's 1992 accounts spell out the composition of the audit, remuneration and executive committees and their reporting functions and say the executive directors are employed under one-year rolling contracts of employment.

The committee had recommended a change in the Companies Act to cut to three years from five the maximum length of a director's contract.

Also announcing their compliance with the code in their 1992 annual reports are British Gas, the management consultants Holmes and Marchant Group, the freight group NFC, and Wellcome.

Grand Metropolitan, which violates one of the central recommendations of the Cadbury report – the separation of the roles of chairman and chief executive – also includes a compliance statement.

The committee had said that separation of the top roles was desirable but not absolutely necessary if the proper checks and balances were in place.

Grand Met's statement, from its non-executive deputy chairman, does not mention the combination of the roles. It does say though that the company complies with 16 of the 19 recommendations.

Continued

Directors size up new rules (cont'd)

Three corporations have amended their rules so that executive directors are periodically required to seek shareholder approval of their appointment.

Ms Anne Simpson, director of Pensions and Investments Research Consultants, a group which advises shareholders on corporate governance matters, said the three were TSB Plc, British Petroleum and Commercial Union. All three companies insulated executive directors from shareholder endorsement, although TSB required a quarter of its non-executive directors to stand for election each year.

The companies are now seeking changes to their articles which will provide for elections for executive directors.

Ms Simpson said: "This is a great step forward for shareholders. The spirit of the Cadbury report is accountability of directors, but these Insulation provisions render key executives unaccountable to shareholders."

Other shareholder groups, including the National Association of Pension Funds and the Association of British Insurers, have called for insulation rules to be abandoned.

The Financial Times, 10 April 1993

Exhibit 20.0 The corporate financial reporting world is gradually changing, but is it for the better?

Annual reports usually contain other reports as well as the ones that we have examined in the previous two chapters. In certain circumstances, for example, the Companies Act 1989 permits shareholders to be supplied with a *summary* of the annual report, while it is a Stock Exchange requirement that shareholders should receive an *interim* report. There are also many other supplementary reports which some companies include in their annual report. In addition, they may take the opportunity to comment on some current financial reporting issues.

In this chapter, we examine some of the supplementary reports that you might come across, and deal with some current financial reporting issues. The chapter is divided into three main sections. In the first section, we look at three fairly common supplementary reports. In the second section, we examine eight much less common statements. In the third section, we outline five current issues in financial reporting, including the phenomenon of inflation.

We start with the more common types of supplementary reports.

LEARNING OBJECTIVES

By the end of this chapter, you will be able to:
● describe three common supplementary financial reports;
● identify at least four other less common financial reports;
● recognize at least three current issues in financial reporting;
● state the effect of inflation on historic cost accounting.

COMMON SUPPLEMENTARY REPORTS

In this section we are going to examine three of the more common types of supplementary types of reports: interim reports, statistical summaries, and summarized financial statements. These are shown in diagrammatic form in Exhibit 20.1, and we outline them in the following sub-sections.

Exhibit 20.1 Common supplementary reports

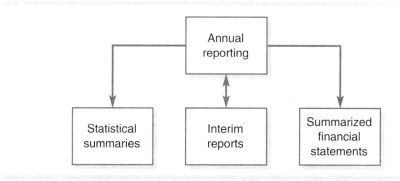

Interim reports

The Stock Exchange requires listed companies to issue interim reports. These are usually produced half-yearly. They are slimmer, and they contain much less information that does the annual report. In fact, some companies manage to produce the required information on no more than two sides of A4 paper. As an example, we will take Cadbury-Schweppes Interim Report for the 24 weeks to 19 June 1993.

The report is eight pages long, each page being approximately of A4 size. The report is bound in glossy covers. A summary of the coverage is as follows:

	Number of pages
Chairman's statement	1.0
Review of operations	1.0
Sales, trading profit and operating assets analysis	1.0
Group profit and loss account	0.6
Movements in shareholders' funds	0.4
Group balance sheet	1.0
Group cash flow statement	1.0
Notes (to the accounts)	1.0
Shareholder information	1.0
Total	8.0

Interim reports are a model of how it is possible to convey a limited amount of key information in just a few pages (although the annual report is, of course, a statutory requirement, and it has to disclose much more information). Unfortunately, even interim reports are still sometimes published in a format and in a language that is quite beyond most shareholders.

Statistical summaries

In Chapter 2 we dealt with the *periodicity* rule. We suggested that, in order to provide a regular report for the owners of the entity, it was necessary to establish an accounting period of some consistent length. Most entities have adopted a 12-months' accounting period, largely because this is a legal requirement. However, a calendar year can be quite an artificial period of time, especially if an entity has an unlimited life, e.g. an industrial company, or a local authority.

In recent years, many entities (especially companies) have begun to realize that it may be misleading to present their results purely in annual terms. As a result, it has become common for them to include periodic statistical summaries in their annual reports, even though there are no statutory or professional requirements obliging them to do so.

There is no general agreement on how long such a period should be. Some companies adopt a five-year period, while others go for ten years. The contents of statistical statements are also subject to much variety. The information may include summaries of sales, profit and dividends, assets employed and cash flow, and the basic financial information may be accompanied by key statistics and a number of selected accounting ratios. We illustrate an example of a five-year financial summary in Exhibit 20.2

Exhibit 20.2 Example of a five-year statistical summary

	Energy public limited company				
	19X1	19X2	19X3	19X4	19X5
	£m	£m	£m	£m	£m
Profit summary					
Turnover	9	14	28	52	85
Profit before taxation	1	2	5	8	9
Balance sheet items					
Tangible fixed assets	15	18	20	23	45
Net current assets	180	200	210	220	230
Called up share capital	5	15	15	30	30
Reserves	100	150	180	200	250

Statistics					
Earnings per ordinary share	20p	40p	60p	100p	125p
Dividends per ordinary share	5p	10p	15p	20p	25p
Dividend cover (times)	4	4	4	5	5

Statistical summaries covering an extended period of time are helpful in establishing trends, but it is important to ensure that each year's results have been applied consistently. In some years, the company may have changed its accounting policies, and both legal and professional requirements also change from time to time. Furthermore, if a fair comparison is to be made between respective periods, it essential that some allowance is to be made for inflation. Remember that at a rate of inflation of 5% per annum, prices double over a fifteen-year period, i.e. the equivalent of about 28% over a five-year period. Be cautious, therefore, if you are comparing (say) sales or profits in Year 1 with Year 5 if no allowance has been made for inflation.

Summarized financial statements

Instead of the detailed annual accounts, the Companies Act 1989 permits fully listed companies to supply (in certain circumstances), a *summarized financial statement* (SFS) to their shareholders. This move came about largely as a result of the privatization of some industries, such as British Telecom and the Trustee Savings Bank. In the ensuring privatization, literally millions of people took the opportunity of becoming shareholders in these new companies. Some companies then felt it would be too costly to send the traditional annual report to so many shareholders. The government agreed with this point of view, and it was then decided to make some allowance in the Act.

It is still to early to judge whether this move has been successful. There seems to be some evidence that it is very expensive both to issue a full report (if requested), and a summarized version of it. Similarly, there is little evidence to confirm that shareholders are better informed. This is not really surprising, because the format laid down in the regulations (the Department of Trade and Industry takes responsibility for this) is still far from easy for the lay-person to follow.

SFSs are certainly shorter than the full version. On average they are about four pages long, compared with an average of twenty-two pages for the full version. It is more likely, therefore, that they will be read. However, we believe that if they are to become readable, they will need to be even shorter, better designed, and absolutely free from jargon.

You might find that some companies attach an SFS to their annual report, whereas other companies will require you to let them know which report you want.

The three reports that we have covered in this section all have some authoritative backing behind them, and you are, therefore, likely to come across examples of them. In the next section we will consider other types of reports that are less common.

LESS COMMON SUPPLEMENTARY REPORTS

There are many other types of reports that companies might publish. In this section, we will have a brief look at some of the other reports you may come across occasionally. The ones that we are going to comment on are as follows:

1 statement of corporate objective;
2 disaggregated statements;
3 employee reports;
4 employment reports;
5 statement of future prospects;
6 statement of money exchanges with government;
7 statement of transactions in foreign currency;
8 value added statements.

These reports are also shown in diagrammatic form in Exhibit 20.3.

Exhibit 20.3 Less common supplementary reports

Statement of corporate objectives	Statement of future prospects
	Statement of money exchanges with government
Value added statements	
	Statement of transactions in foreign currency
Disaggregated statements	Employee reports
	Employment reports

Statement of corporate objectives

In this statement, some reference would be made to the company's objectives. However, many companies might prefer to include the details in the chairman's report, rather than in a seperate statement. If it forms a separate statement, it would probably include such matters as the company's policy over sales ('to increase them'), profits, investment, dividends, employment, and consumer issues.

Disaggregated statements

Disaggregated statements show the financial information broken down on a geographic location, or product basis. This is sometimes referred to as *segmental reporting*. Some segmental information has been both a statutory requirement and a requirement by the Stock Exchange for some time, and there is also an accounting standard that now covers the subject (SSAP 25: Segmental reporting). The requirements are not particularly onerous. Further developments in this area are, therefore, highly likely.

Employee reports

The Companies Act 1985 pays very little attention to the interests of employees. It has been left largely to employment protection legislation to encourage employee reporting. As a result, many companies now prepare reports specifically for their employees. Such information may be included either as a special section in the shareholders' annual report, or as a quite separate report.

There are no recommended guidelines for the presentation of employee reports, and they tend to be merely simplified and shortened versions of the shareholders' report. Employee reports sometimes use elaborate charts and diagrams, often in many different typefaces, styles, and colours of print. They may make no attempt to translate difficult accounting terminology into the sort of language that everyone understands, and their linguistic style is often highly condescending. There is still much work to do before the accountancy profession is in a position to produce an acceptable employee report.

As the content and style of employee reports varies so enormously, you are encouraged to collect your own examples. It would be useful for you to assess the impact that they have on you as a non-accountant.

Employment reports

Employment reports must not be confused with employee reports (although they may contain some similar information). They would include, *inter alia* details concerning the number of employees, their age and sex, employment costs and benefits, pension scheme arragements, training costs, and health and safety matters.

Statement of future prospects

This statement would include details of the company's expected future profit, employment, and investment levels. Instead of a separate statement, some companies now include this type of information in the chairman's report.

Statement of money exchanges with government

Included in such statements would be details outlining all the payments to the government (e.g. PAYE, VAT, corporation tax, local rates), along wtih details of any amounts received back from the government, such as grants and subsidies.

Statement of transactions in foreign currency

This type of statement would include all types of cash receipts and payments arising from the company's overseas operations.

Value added statements

In the late 1980s, many companies included in their annual report a statement of value added. They are much less common now, probably because they have never received any statutory or professional accountancy backing.

Value added was defined in *The Corporate Report* (published by the former Accounting Standards Steering Committee, now the ASC, in 1975) as 'the wealth created by the entity as a result of the collective efforts of capital, employees and management'. It was believed that the statement should show how the value was added (i.e. sales revenue less materials and purchased services), and how the value was used (i.e., to pay employees, shareholders and the government).

There is no generally recommended format, but you will find that those value added statements you do come across are split into two main sections. The first section usually explains where the value has come from, while the second section illustrates what has happened to it.

An example of a value added statement is shown in Exhibit 20.4. The exhibit is based on the example used in *The Corporate Report*.

The detail included in a value added statement is simply a re-arrangement of the information contained in the profit and loss account, although the value added cannot always be directly linked with specific balances contained within the profit and loss account.

Exhibit 20.4 Example of a value added statement

Energy public limited company
Group value added statement for the year to 31 March 19X2

	19X2		19X1	
	£000	%	£000	%
Turnover[1]	1500		1200	
Bought-in materials and services[2]	(1000)		(800)	
	500		400	
Other incomes[3]	50		40	
Value added[4]	550		440	
Applied the following ways:				
To pay employees[5]				
Wages, pensions, and fringe benefits	300	55	280	64
To pay providers of capital[5]				
Interest on loans	30		25	
Dividends to shareholders	60		55	
	90	16	80	18
To pay government[5]				
Corporation tax payable	45	8	40	9
To provide for maintenance and expansion of capital[5]				
Depreciation	40		35	
Retained profits	75		5	
	115	21	40	9
Value added[6]	£550	100%	£440	100%

Note: The exhibit contains dummy information.

Tutorial notes

1 Turnover represents sales to external customers, net of trade discounts, value added tax, and other sales taxes.
2 Bought-in materials and services includes, *inter alia*, the cost of sales, salaries, wages, and other employment costs.
3 Other incomes includes investment income.
4 Value added is the wealth created during the particular period in question.
5 The disposition of the wealth is shown under four main headings:
    (a) to pay employees; (b) to pay the providers of capital;
    (c) to pay the government; and (d) to provide for maintenance and expansion of the assets.
6 The total disposition should agree with the total value added (see note 4).

A value added statement has several uses. We summarize some of the main ones below:

1 It provides additional information about the company's performance.
2 It shows the increase in the company's resources.
3 It highlights the proportion of the value added paid to the employees.
4 It shows the sometimes large contribution paid to the government.
5 It may be helpful in implementing profit schemes, in encouraging employee participation, and in creating a more co-operative working environment.

In respect of the latter point, a value added statement is sometimes seen by employees as a political statement, and it has, therefore, sometimes proved to be some- what controversial.

General points

Before moving on to look at some current developments and issues in financial reporting, it might be useful if we gave you one or two hints about how to assess the value of the many types of financial reports you might come across. View such reports carefully, and assess their impact on you. Ask yourself the following questions:

1 What is the purpose of the report?
2 Is it clearly laid out, and easy to follow?
3 Is the language understandable?
4 Is the statistical information clear?
5 What is the statement really telling me?
6 Does it appear to have met its objectives?

With this brief look at other less common reports, we will now move on to examine some other controversal issues and topics in modern financial reporting. We do so in the next section.

CURRENT FINANCIAL REPORTING ISSUES

In this section, we are going to look at some current financial reporting issues and developments. This will be of benefit to you for three main reasons:

1 in this book, we have tended to concentrate on *traditional* accounting practices, but we also ought to take our own advice and look ahead as well;
2 some of these developments may already be major issues within your own entity;

3 important changes are taking place in financial reporting and if you are to have a balanced picture of the accounting world, you ought to know something about them.

We cannot possibly deal with all the emerging issues, so we will select just a few that are of particular interest. These are as follows:

1 corporate governance;
2 group accounting (especially goodwill and brand accounting);
3 inflation and its effect on historic cost accounting (we shall be looking as this in some detail);
4 international accounting;
5 social and environmental accounting.

Corporate governance

You will no doubt be well aware now that the accountancy profession is very worried about its future. Like many professions e.g. the church and teaching, its members were once very highly regarded. To some extent, that is now changing as the public realize that even accountants have faults. A number of well-publicized audit failures (usually referred to as 'scandals') have resulted in the profession receiving some well-deserved criticism.

Of course, not all of these alleged 'scandals' have been entirely the fault of the accountancy profession, but it does not help when the profession appears incapable of dealing with some fundamental accounting issues (such as inflation accounting). To be fair, it is not just the role accountants and auditors play in the company affairs that is in question, but also of directors and senior managers. They too have not helped to present their affairs in the best possible light. For example, some directors have awarded themselves large increase in pay at a time when inflation and taxation rates are low, and increases for other employees have been severely limited.

It was partly to have a look at all these problems that a committee was set up in May 1991 by the Financial Reporting Council, the Stock Exchange and the accountancy profession. It was called the Committee on the Financial Aspects of Corporate Governance, and it became known as the Cadbury Committee. Its main purpose was to have a look at the financial aspects of how companies are directed. It reported in 1992, and the main recommendations that are relevant to this book are as follows:

1 The directors should explain their responsibility for preparing the accounts, and this should be presented next to a statement outlining the auditors' reporting responsibilities.
2 The directors should state that the business is a going concern.
3 The directors should report on the effectiveness of their internal control systems, and the auditors should comment on what they say.

4 All listed companies should establish an audit committee.

5 Interim statements issued by the company should include balance sheet information, and such statements should be reviewed by the auditors before they are issued.

It is too soon to know whether the Cadbury Committee's proposals will help companies to be more accountable. The results of its recommendations are due to be reviewed in 1995. Unless there is some statutory intervention, on past experience there is unlikely to be much improvement.

Group accounting

In Chapter 19, we examined the format of group accounts. As we mentioned in what chapter, the consolidation (i.e. the adding together) of the accounts of different entities is a formidable task, particularly if some of te entities are based overseas. The old ASC issued four accounting standards dealing with group accounting although the ASCs standards will all eventually be withdrawn. The new ASB has already issued one of its own (FRS 2: Accounting for subidiary undertakings), and there are more to come.

Many of the issues with which these standards deal are highly technical, and as a non-acountant you do not need to be too concerned with the fine details. However, accounting information does have an impact on how your company is perceived, so you must be very careful how you present your accounts to the world. You must be prepared to question your accoutants what they are doing and why. We will illustrate the problem of group accounting by examining just two deceptively simple issues: goodwill and brands.

Goodwill and brands

Let us assume that Company A buys a controlling interest in Company B (i.e. it buys more than 50% of the voting shares). Company A may pay more for the net tangible (i.e. physical) assets of B than they are worth. The difference between what A pays and what the assets are worth is called *goodwill*. In other words, A pays a premium. It may be willing to do so because B is a long-established company with ready markets, a good product, reliable customers, and an efficient work-force.

If A and B's accounts are consolidated, the consolidated balance sheet will show an item for goodwill: after all, the company has bought something that it considers valuable in just the same way that it does for land and buildings. However, goodwill is referred to as an *intangible* fixed asset, because it does not have a physical presence. Returning to our example, A may not be confident that it can retain the goodwill: customers may go elsewhere, for example, and employees may leave. It seems prudent, therefore, to write it off (i.e. eliminate it from the group accounts) as soon as possible.

This is exactly what SSAP 22 (Accounting for goodwill) requires: goodwill should be written off immediately when acquired. But how? SSAP 22 prefers that it should be immediately written off against reserves (it does not specify which reserves), but it may be amortized. This means that it will be depreciated (like tangible fixed assets), and an amount will be charged against each year's profit and loss account.

This procedure might be seen as a rather routine accounting adjustment, but think of the consequences! The goodwill may reduce the reserves to such a level that it might affect the company's ability to distribute its profits (there are some highly technical legal conditions affecting distribution of profits), but what happens if the goodwill is in excess of all the reserves? The company might then have to amortize the goodwill, and this will reduce the net profit for the year. This means that it could affect the company's ability to pay a dividend, but it would decrease its earnings per share, and possibly reduce its share price on the Stock Exchange.

Thus, an apparent minor book-keeping adjustment may result in some unwelcome consequences for the company. Indeed, as a result of this problem, some companies have tried to inflate their balance sheet figures by inserting a value for their 'brands', such as well-known chocolate bars, or for popular beers. Unless the brand name is purchased, such procedures are purely a book exercise, i.e. they are entirely an internal arrangement, since they do not involve any outside parties. Thus, the value of the fixed assets is automatically increased, and a corresponding figure has to be included in the reserves in order to get the balance sheet to balance. This means that goodwill can then be written off against the reserves without any adverse effects either on the reserves themselves, or on the annual profit and loss account.

The problem is that no one knows how to put an objective value on brands for balance sheet purposes, and so it is anybody's guess as to what should be. As yet, the issue is unresolved. The recommendation of the ASB is that brand values should not be separated from goodwill, since it is argued that the goodwill figure will include something for any brand value.

Inflation and historic cost accounts

In recent years, the accountancy profession has produced a number of proposals which would require financial reports to reflect the effects of inflation. In this book so far, we have assumed that the monetary unit remains stable, and that we can ignore inflation.

As yet, all of the proposals that have been put forward for producing inflation adjusted reports have got nowhere, and current financial reporting in the UK is still based on the notion of price stability. This means that it is assumed that the original price (i.e. the historic cost) at which goods and services are exchanged retains its original value, but as you will know from your own experience, you need more pounds sterling to buy your weekly groceries today than you did last month.

Inflation and its effects

There is no satisfactory definition of inflation, but for our purposes we can regard it as either an upward movement in prices, or a downwards movement in the purchasing power of the monetary unit. This means that, during a period of inflation, £100 available in cash in 19X1 will purchase fewer goods in 19X2 than it did in 19X1. Thus, in order to purchase the same amount of goods in 19X2 as we did in 19X1, we will have to pay more than £100. You can see the effect of real price changes between 1951 and 1992 in Exhibit 20.5. Prices are anything but stable, and in 1975, for example, the increase over the previous year reached the unprecedented level of 24.4%.

As far as accounting is concerned, the effect of inflation on traditional historic cost accounts can be stated quite simply: it tends to overstate the amount of profit. By over-stating profit, the proprietors may withdraw more cash from the business, and this may adversely effect the entity's liquid resources. Eventually, the entity may find that it does not have enough cash to replace its fixed assets or its stocks, and it may have to cut back on what it is doing, or even go out of business. The main effects can be summarized as follows:

1 The closing stock tends to have a higher value than goods purchased in earlier periods, thereby overstating the gross profit (because the closing stock is *deducted* from the opening stock + purchases). However, when the stock is eventually sold it will probably cost more to replace than it did when it was purchased.

2 Depreciation is under-stated as it is usually based on the historic cost of the fixed assets. The fixed assets will eventually have to be replaced at a greater cost than was originally paid, so not enough cash may have been set aside to replace them if the depreciation charge is based on the historic cost.

3 There is a loss on loans. If the entity has put some of its funds into short- or long-term loans (such as in a bank deposit account or into debenture stock), such loans will lose value in a period of inflation. The entity might have invested (say) £10 000 in debenture stock in 19X1 which will be repaid in 19X5. In 19X5 it will be repaid the £10 000, but £10 000 received in 19X5 will not purchase the same amount of goods as £10 000 did in 19X1. Thus the entity loses by putting its cash into investments which are fixed in monetary terms. It also loses by allowing credit to its customers. Such debts will be fixed in money terms, so when the cash is eventually received (even if it is only a few months later), it will purchase fewer goods.

Exhibit 20.5 Percentage increases in the UK retail price index (yearly average) for the period 1950–1992

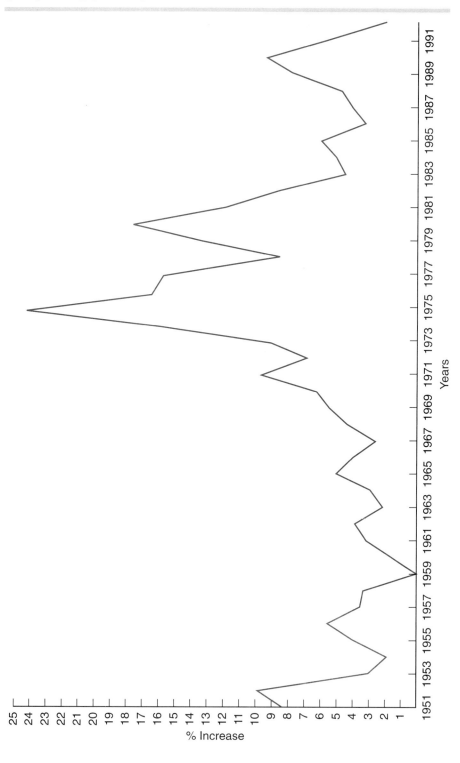

4 Gains on borrowings. An entity does not always lose during a period of inflation. If it borrows money on a short- or a long-term basis it will benefit. Goods purchased on credit terms, for example, will be settled in *money* terms, but the monetary payment will not be worth as much as it was when the goods were purchased. An entity gains similarly by borrowing on a long-term basis. By borrowing money through issuing debentures, for example, it will eventually have to pay back less money in purchasing power (or *real*) terms than it actually borrowed.

So what has the accountancy profession done to help overcome these problems? We try to answer this question below.

The accountancy profession's answer

In trying to cope with with the effects of inflation on historic cost accounts, two main schools of thought have evolved (see Exhibit 20.6).

Exhibit 20.6 Accounting for changing prices: the two schools of thought

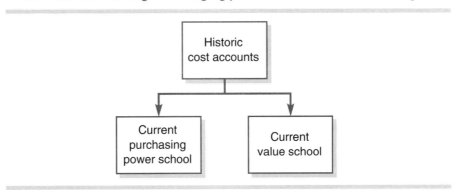

The purchasing power school

This school of thought recommends that the historic cost accounts should be adjusted by adopting some suitable inflation index. In the UK, the index that is usually adopted is the *retail price index* (RPI). This index is generally well known and understood. While this is an advantage, the RPI suffers from two main disadvantages:

1 it measures the effect of inflation on retail consumption;
2 it does not necessarily measure the effect of inflation on specific entities.

However, this method of allowing for inflation is relatively easy to adopt. The procedure is as follows:

1 take the historic cost (HC) accounts;
2 measure each transaction (or collection of transactions) in the HC accounts against the index at the time that it took place, and compare it with the index at the end of the relevant accounting period;

3 adjust the historic cost of the transaction by multiplying it by the closing index and dividing it by the opening index.

An example should help to make this procedure a little clearer. Suppose that we are presented with the following information:

	£	RPI
Fixed asset purchased on 1.01.X1:	1000	100
Historic cost accounts prepared on		
31.12.X1		120

$\therefore$ in the 'current purchasing power' accounts, the fixed asset would be shown as £1200 (£1000 × 120)/100).

You may find that some tables and charts in an annual report have been adjusted on to a current purchasing power (CPP) basis. In presenting the main financial statements, however, most companies adopt the historic cost principle.

The current value school

The current purchasing power (CPP) school of thought was much in favour until about 1975, but since then it has lost ground to the current value school. There are several versions of current value accounting. Basically, the current value school (of whatever dimension) requires fixed assets and stocks to be included in the accounts at their *current* value, rather than at their historic cost. In the vast majority of cases, current cost is the same as the *replacement* cost, i.e. what it would now cost to purchase an asset identical to one purchased in the past.

The main version of current value accounting used in the UK is known as *current cost accounting* (CCA). CCA became the subject of an accounting standard in 1980 (SSAP 16). Like all standards, it was supposed to be mandatory, but it became so unpopular that it was abandoned in 1985.

SSAP 16 was a very complicated statement (probably one reason for its unpopularity). In essence, what it tried to do was to reduce the level of the historic cost profit so that some allowance was made for the effects of inflation. Thus, the entity would always be able to retain sufficient cash in the business in order to continue operating at the same level that it had done in the past. In the jargon of accounting, this is known as 'maintaining an entity's operating capability'.

The statement required four main adjustments to be made to the historic cost profit and loss account, and two to the balance sheet (see Exhibit 20.7).

We will describe each of these adjustments separately, so that you can judge for yourself whether you think they cope with the inflation accounting problems we outlined earlier. We will start with the profit and loss account adjustments.

Exhibit 20.7 Current cost accounting: adjustments to the profit and loss account and the balance sheet

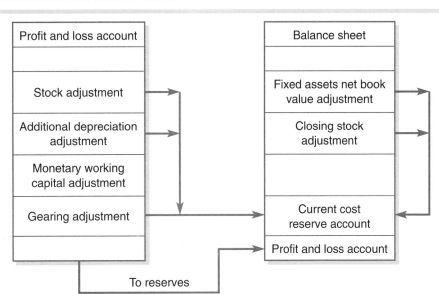

1 **A cost of sales adjustment (COSA).** This adjustment required both the opening and closing stock to be adjusted (normally by choosing a suitable index, and applying it to the historic cost of the stocks) to a value which represented the average value of stock for the period. Hence, both the opening and the closing stocks were put on the same price basis as any purchases made during the period.

2 **An additional depreciation adjustment (ADA).** This adjustment meant that the depreciation charge for the year was normally based on the *replacement* cost of the asset, rather than on its historic cost.

3 **A monetary working capital adjustment (MWCA).** Monetary working capital was defined basically as the difference between trade debtors and trade creditors. SSAP 16 required an adjustment to made to monetary working capital, the reasons being very similar to the ones that we outlined earlier, viz. in times of inflation, entities gain by borrowing, and lose by lending. The MWCA, therefore, makes an allowance for short-term borrowing and lending. The adjustment could be made by indexing both the opening net monetary working capital and closing net monetary capital so that they were measured on the same price basis. The opening and closing values are usually indexed in such a way that they both represent the average value for the year. The calculation is very similar to that adopted for the cost of sales adjustment.

4 **A gearing adjustment (GA).** It is quite customary for a company to finance some of its operations from long-term borrowings. As we have

indicated earlier, if it has borrowed money during a period of inflation, it will benefit by being able to repay the loan in monetary terms, although, by the time that it does so, the purchasing power of the original loan will have declined. The cost of sales adjustment, the additional depreciation adjustment, and the monetary working capital adjustment will all normally reduce the profit available for distribution to the shareholders. It seems only fair, therefore, that an adjustment should also be made if shareholders *benefit* from inflation (as they do if the company finances itself through borrowings).

This is what the gearing adjustment is about. It tries to measure the extent of the shareholders' gain through borrowing. The method advocated by SSAP 16 was highly complex and very controversial, but basically it was calculated by taking the total of the three other profit and loss adjustments (COSA, ADA, and MWCA) and reducing it by an amount based on the extent of the company's borrowings.

Suppose, for example, the total of COSA + ADA + MWCA = £10 000, and that the *gearing proportion* was estimated to be 20% (i.e. 20% of the company was financed out of borrowings), then £2000 (£10 000 × 20%) would be *credited* to the profit and loss account. The net extra cost charged to the profit and loss account to allow for inflation would be £8000 (£10 000 – £2000).

It is only necessary for non-accountants to understand the reasoning behind the gearing adjustment, and there is no need for you to know how to calculate it.

We move on now to look at the two balance sheet adjustments required under SSAP 16. These were as follows:

1 **Fixed assets.** Fixed assets would normally be included at their net *replacement* cost, i.e. their gross replacement cost less the accumulated depreciation based on that replacement cost. In effect, the gross replacement cost would be what the company would have to pay for similar fixed assets if the original fixed assets were to be replaced as at the date of the balance sheet.
2 **Closing stocks.** The closing stocks were also to be included in the balance sheet at their replacement cost. This would be based on their value as at the balance sheet date.

It will be appreciated, of course, that these six adjustments (four in the profit and loss account, and two in the balance sheet) alter the balancing of the accounts, and some sub-totals and totals also need to be changed. SSAP 16 allowed for the double-entry effect of the changes in an account called the *current cost reserve account*. This account was simply a balancing account, e.g. debit the profit and loss account, credit the current cost reserve account, or debit the current cost reserve account, credit the profit and loss account.

The current position

As a result of the abandonment of SSAP 16, most companies do not now publish current cost accounts, or even make any sort of adjustment to their historic cost accounts in order to allow for inflation. However, some companies do produce summaries of their historic cost accounts that have been adjusted. They do this usually in one of two ways:

1 **A CPP appoach**. Some of the historic cost inflation is indexed, using the RPI or some other suitable index.
2 **A CCA approach.** The fixed assets and stocks may be included at their replacement cost, and in the case of the fixed assets, depreciated on that basis.

Such price adjusted information may be included in the formal notes, or in a separate statement.

As a non-accountant, you need not be unduly concerned with the technicalities of accounting for inflation, although you should be aware of the misleading impression gained by referring to accounting reports that have not been adjusted. As we have stated before, with inflation at a rate of only 5% per annum, prices double over something like a 15-year period. Thus, accounting information is significantly distorted even if it covers only a five-year period. If you are presented with only historic cost information, you ought to make some allowance for inflation. We would suggest that the retail price index can be used as a rough guide to the effects of inflation.

We have dealt with inflation and its effect of historic cost accounts at some length, because we believe that it is still one of the major problem areas in financial reporting.

International accounting

Accountants in the UK do not work entirely in a vacuum. They are influenced by what is happening in other countries, not least because many entities now operate on a global basis. Although we have concentrated almost exclusively on UK statutory and professional requirements, it is a fact that what is happening in the UK has been (and is being) strongly influenced by the experiences of other countries. The necessity to adapt UK requirements is coming from two main sources. We discuss each of them briefly below:

European Union (EU)

As a member of the EU, the UK is subject to directives approved by the Council of Ministers. A directive has to be incorporated into the national law of each member state. There have been three directives so far that influence UK accounting practice:

1 **The Fourth Directive**. The UK built this directive into the Companies Act 1981, the most notable feature being the introduction of standardized formats for presenting accounts.

2 **The Seventh Directive**. This was incorporated into the Companies Act 1989, and it basically tightened up the accounting requirements relating to group accounts.

3 **The Eighth Directive**. This directive dealt with the qualifications of auditors. It has not had the same impact in the UK as in some other countries, because the UK auditing profession was already strongly organized and highly trained.

International
Accounting
Standards
Committee
(IASC)

Besides national accounting standards, financial reports are supposed to incorporate international standards. The IASC was formed in 1973, and the UK was a founder member. It is a private body, financed largely by its members. The IASC aims to make financial statements more comparable on a world-wide basis. Its method of working is similar to that of the ASB. To date, it has issued over 30 accounting standards, some on issues not dealt with by UK standards. As economic, financial, legal, and political conditions differ so markedly in various countries, IASC requirements tend to be much more general than are UK standards. This usually means that where UK FRS/SSAPs cover similar topics as do the international accounting standards, observance of the UK ones normally ensure compliance with the IASC's requirements.

As countries become more inter-dependent. and as they operate more and more on a global basis, international accounting is becoming an important branch of accounting in its own right. There are enormous accounting problems to be solved in this area, covering such matters as accounting for groups, foreign currency translation methods, the treatment of taxation in accounts, the prices to charge between different segments operating in different parts of the world (known as *transfer pricing*), and the reporting of segmental activities.

Social and environmental accounting

Many accountants believe that traditional accounting is too narrowly based. They argue that accountants should concern themselves with a wider definition of profit, and that they should go beyond just reporting to shareholders. This type of accounting is sometimes referred to as *social and environmental accounting*. More recently it has been dubbed *green accounting*. No doubt it is possible to argue that social accounting, environmental accounting, and green accounting should all be treated as separate issues, but for our purposes it is convenient to consider them collectively.

The main idea behind this type of accounting is that entities should report on the costs and benefits of their social and environmental activities, e.g. on matters affecting conservation, energy use, and pollution control. As we suggested in Chapter 2, accountants have long argued that if some information is difficult to quantify, then it should be ignored. But why ignore costs and benefits that you might have a duty to report, simply because they are too difficult to do so? The same argument could equally be applied to traditional financial reporting: it is not easy, but we do, it notwithstanding all its imperfections. So why not, for example, tell the world that your company finds it cost effective not to pollute rivers or tear down trees to print newspapers?

In other words, we should drop the entity rule, and report on the effect that the company is having on the community, both the benefits it provides and the costs that it causes.

You will appreciate such reporting would considerably widen the scope of traditional accounting, not just in method and content, but also the parties to whom reports would be addressed.

The whole notion of social and environmental accounting has not yet got very far, although it has been given a boost as the environmental or 'green' movement has begun to take off. Indeed, there is some evidence that some companies do now include some social and environmental matters in their annual reports, although the development of the subject is still at a very early stage.

CONCLUSION

This chapter has examined a considerable number of supplementary reports, and financial reporting issues. Some issues are clearly of more importance that others. For example, the effects of inflation on accounts is a world-wide issue. By contrast, some reports (e.g. value added statements, and employment reports) are hardly of major importance.

As yet, some companies are content to produce annual reports that contain the absolute minimum amount of statutory and professional accountancy information, while other reports contain so much information that it is difficult to take it all in. In some cases, there appears to be a tendency to include an enormous amount of promotional material, and this makes it difficult to pick out the vital financial information. However, we are confident that if you have worked your way through this book, you should now be in an excellent position to make the most of any such annual report, regardless of what it looks like and what it contains!

KEY POINTS

1 Annual reports may contain a wide variety of other types of reports. The main ones that you are likely to come across are: interim reports, statistical summaries, and summarized financial statements.

2 Other reports that you might come across include reports on corporate objectives, disaggregation, employees, employment, transactions in foreign currency, future prospects, money exchanges with government, and value added statements.

3 Financial reporting is going through an intense period of reappraisal, and there are a number of issues that are in a state of flux, e.g. the way that companies are governed, the way that group accounts are consolidated, the problem of inflation in accounts, international aspects, and social and environmental matters.

4 The UK accountancy profession has no mandatory requirements governing the treatment of inflation in historic cost accounts. In the absence of any other information, HC accounts should be converted on to a current purchasing power basis, using an appropriate index (like the RPI)

CHECK YOUR LEARNING

1 List three common supplementary financial reports.

2 List four less common financial reports.

3 Name three current issues in financial reporting.

4 State whether each of the following statements is true or false:
(a) Interim reports are required by law.   True/False
(b) Goodwill must be amortized.   True/False
(c) The costs of brands should be shown separately in the
  balance sheet.   True/False
(d) EU directives must be incorporated into British law.   True/False
(e) The Companies Act 1989 requires companies to follow
  international accounting standards.   True/False
(f) The law does not allow companies to disclose details about
  their social policies in their annual report .   True/False

5 Identify two items in the profit and loss accounting that are required when adjusting for inflation.

ANSWERS

1 interim reports; statistical summaries; summarized financial statements
2 disaggregated statements; employee reports; employment reports; value added statements
3 corporate governance; accounting for goodwill; social and environmental accounting
4 (a) false (b) false (c) false (d) true (e) false (f) false
5 stocks; depreciation

ASSIGNMENT ON COMPANY FINANCIAL REPORTING

Objectives
1 To enable you to familiarize yourself with what is contained in a company's annual report; and

2 to know where to look for information within it.

Required:

1 Obtain a copy of the annual report of a public limited liability company.

Note: You are encouraged to choose a manufacturing company or a retail company, and to avoid banks, insurance companies, and investment trusts, as they produce somewhat specialist reports.

2 Using the report that you have obtained, complete the following schedule:

NAME OF COMPANY

YEAR END

MAIN OPERATING ACTIVITIES

CHAIRMAN'S NAME

CHIEF EXECUTIVE'S NAME

CHAIRMAN'S STATEMENT
   Tone of the Chairman's statement in respect of the company's future:
      highly optimistic ☐ optimistic ☐ neutral ☐ pessimistic ☐
      highly pessimistic ☐

DIRECTOR'S REPORT
   Amount of the recommended final dividend
   Charitable donations
   Political donations
   Job title of officer signing the report

ACCOUNTING POLICIES
   Accounting convention
   Depreciation rates for each major class of fixed assets

CONSOLIDATED PROFIT AND LOSS ACCOUNT
   Turnover
   Gross profit
   Net profit before taxation
   Net profit after taxation
   Dividends paid and proposed
   Retained profits
   Earnings per share

CONSOLIDATED BALANCE SHEET
   Total of all fixed assets
   Cash at bank and in hand
   Current assets total
   Creditors: amounts falling due within one year total

Net current assets/(liabilities) total
Creditors: amounts falling due after more than one year total
Provisions for liabilities total
Shareholders' funds total

CONSOLIDATED CASH FLOW STATEMENT
Opening balance of cash and cash equivalents
Increase/(decrease) in cash and cash equivalents
Closing balance of cash and cash equivalents

NOTES TO THE ACCOUNTS
Geographical analysis of turnover:

Total operating profit
Geographical analysis of operating profit:

Total of tangible fixed assets' depreciation
Auditors' remuneration
Total of directors' emoluments
Average number of employees during the year
Debtors receivable after more than one year
Bank loans and overdrafts:
    in one year or less
    between one and two years
    between two and five years
    after five years
Total of the issued share capital
Profit and loss account balance

AUDITORS' REPORT
List any qualifications:

OTHER REPORTS AND STATEMENTS
List:

ACCOUNTING RATIOS
Calculate the following accounting ratios for the current year and (if possible) the previous year:
    Current ratio
    Acid test ratio
    Gearing
    Gross profit ratio
    Net profit before tax
    Net profit after tax
    Return on capital employed

Stock turnover
Trade debtor collection period
Trade creditor payment period
Fixed assets ratio

OVERALL ASSESSMENT

Liquidity
very strong ☐ strong ☐ neutral ☐ weak ☐ very weak ☐

Profitability
very healthy ☐ healthy ☐ neutral ☐ sick ☐ very sick ☐

Efficiency
very efficient ☐ efficient ☐ neutral ☐ inefficient ☐
highly inefficient ☐

CONCLUSION

Insert below your conclusions on the overall financial strength of the company:

QUESTIONS (WITHOUT SOLUTIONS)

20.1 The following trial balance has been extracted from the books of Grieve Public Limited Company as at 31 Decenber 19X1:

	Dr £000	Cr £000
Accruals		1 800
Administrative expenses	4 200	
Called up share capital (£1 ordinary shares)		5 600
Cash and bank	200	
Distribution costs	1 800	
Fixed assets: at cost	5 500	
Accumulated depreciation (at 31 December 19X1)		2 000
Prepayments	300	
Profit and loss account		900
Purchases	11 000	
Sales		18 100
Stock (at 1 January 19X1)	2 000	
Trade creditors		1 600
Trade debtors	5 000	
	£30 000	£30 000

Additional information:
1 Stocks at 31 December 19X1: £3 000 000.
2 Corporation tax based on the profit for the year at a rate of 33% is estimated to be £1 025 000.
3 The company proposes to pay an ordinary divided of 10p per share.
4 Ignore advance corporation tax.

Required:
Insofar as the information permits, prepare Grieve's profit and loss account for the year to 31 December 19X1 and a balance sheet as at that date in accordance with the Companies Act 1985 and related statements of standard accounting pratice.

20.2 On 1 April 19X2, Duff Limited purchased an 80% holding in Ruff Limited.The following extracts relate to the financial year ending 31 March 19X3:

	Duff Ltd £000	Ruff Ltd £000
Profit and loss accounts		
Sales	1400	400
Cost of sales	(640)	(280)
Gross profit	760	120
Distribution costs	(50)	(20)
Administrative expenses	(550)	(40)
Profit before taxation	160	60
Taxation	(20)	(30)
Profit after taxation	140	30
Dividends	(120)	(10)
Retained profits	£20	£20
Balance sheets		
Fixed assets at net book value	450	150
Investment		
Ruff Limited	150	–
Current assets		
Stocks	160	30
Debtors	1000	60
Cash and bank	30	10
	1190	100
Current liabilities		
Creditors	(430)	(50)
Taxation	(20)	(30)
Dividend	(120)	(10)
	(570)	(90)
	£1220	£160

Capital and reserves		
Called up share capital (£1 ordinary shares)	800	100
Profit and loss account	420	60
	£1220	£160

Additional information:

1 Ruff's profit and loss account at 1 April 19X2 was £40 000.
2 Ignore advance corporation tax.
3 Any goodwill arising on acquisition should be written off immediately at the time of acquisition.

Required:

Prepare the Duff Group of Companies consolidated profit and loss account for the year to 31 March 19X3, and a consolidated balance sheet as at that date. (Ignore the detailed disclosure provisions of the Companies Act 1985.)

PART 5

Case studies

1 THE REALIZATION CONCEPT

LEARNING OBJECTIVES

After preparing this case study, you will be able to:
- outline the nature of cash flow accounting;
- describe what accountants mean by the realization rule;
- state the legal and professional requirements governing the realization of profit;
- use the realization rule in contract accounting.

FIDDLING THE BOOKS

LOCATION   Gibson Products Limited: the Managing Director's office.

PERSONNEL   Frances Morton: Chief Accountant
Norman Gibson: Managing Director
Pam Kershaw: Secretary to the Managing Director

SYNOPSIS

Frances Morton popped her head round the door of Pam Kershaw's office. 'Pam, could I have a word with Mr Gibson?', she enquired. Frances was the recently appointed Chief Accountant of Gibson Products Limited. 'Sure, Frances,' Pam responded, 'he's free now. I'll buzz through, but just walk in.'

Frances did as she was requested. She was warmly greeted by the Managing Director, Norman Gibson. 'Come in, Frances. Glad to see you. It's been a few days since we met. What's the problem?'

Norman was noted for not wasting any time on pleasantries.

'Well, as you know Norman, I was appointed near the end of the financial year, and so my top priority up until now has been to get to grips with the accounting system. My next task is to get on with preparing the annual accounts.'

'That's fine by me, Frances, but where do I come in?'

'The main problem seems to be in calculating the sales figure for the year,' replied Frances. 'I've traced last year's sales and sales returns through the books, but I've found it difficult to check the turnover shown in the annual accounts.'

Norman laughed. 'Funnily enough, I had the same problem when I started the business. In those days the business was very small, and I did the accounts myself. But when I got an accountant to help me, he said that I had been doing it all wrong. You see, I had just been including the cash that we had received during a financial year as the sales for that year. Apparently, that's not right.'

'Not necessarily,' murmured Frances, 'But it's one way of doing it. That type of accounting is known as 'cash flow accounting'. It tends to be used by very small businesses and voluntary organizations like clubs and societies.'

'I must admit I never really understood what was wrong with it,' said Norman. 'It seemed a very accurate method to me. After all, we could always check that we had made those sales for the year, as we could see the cash had gone into the bank.'

'Yes,' parried Frances, 'that's true, but the receipt of cash may be a bit haphazard. Your sales for a particular year may be affected by cash being received a day or two before or after the year end. It follows that the sales you record in your accounts may not necessarily be a fair reflection of your sales' activity for that period.'

'Yes, yes, the last accountant said all that,' interrupted Norman somewhat testily, 'so I told him to go ahead and do what he thought was right.'

'Well,' said Frances, 'he seems to have taken you at your word. As far as I can tell, he appears to have built up the turnover figure using a very complicated formula.'

'You don't say,' prompted the now somewhat chastened Managing Director without a trace of irony in his voice. 'What has he done?'

'Mmmm,' hesitated Frances. 'Our basic business is, of course, constructing ventilation systems in accordance with specifications laid down by the customers. What the previous accountant seems to have done is to define turnover as a combination of a number of factors, such as orders placed, deliveries made, installations completed, systems commissioned, and contracts at the end of their warranty period.'

The Managing Director went white. 'Good g-g-g-racious,' he stammered, 'You mean he's classed *orders* as part of turnover? Is that allowed?'

Frances hesitated. 'Probably, she replied, 'but it certainly seems to be an unusual, and perhaps quite a questionable practice.'

'But how much of a particular contract has he taken into each bit? And what happens if a contract goes horribly wrong?'

By this time Norman looked and sounded a very worried man. 'It's so easy for a contract to go sour, and we could have been over-stating our profit for years. What happens if it all catches up with us?'

'I don't really know the answer to those questions at this stage,' said Frances, 'but take some comfort in one fact: it's quite normal to take credit for sales made, even if the cash for them is still to be received. That can be risky, but the risk can be reduced by building in what is known as a 'provision for bad and doubtful debts'. Your previous accountant will almost certainly have done something similar.'

'Let's hope he has,' said Norman. 'For goodness' sake, find out as soon as you can what he has done, and let me have a full and detailed report on it. I had no idea that I had been a party to fiddling the books.'

'Oh! I shouldn't think that there has been any fiddle, Norman,' said Frances, as she picked up her papers. 'I'm sure that it's probably not as bad as that. I'll report back, probably in a day or so. Is that OK?'

Norman nodded, but he did not say anything until Frances had left his office. Then he exploded. And as was usual, it was left to Pam Kershaw to pick up the pieces.

Required:

1 Examine the advantages and disadvantages of cash flow accounting.

2 (a) Outline the legal and professional requirements governing the realization of profits; and

 (b) explain what an accountant means by the term 'realization'.

3 Assume that the practice adopted by the previous accountant of Gibson Products Limited was not in conflict with best accounting practice:

 (a) advise Norman Gibson how it might be possible to include some profit in the profit and loss account for a contract that has not yet been completed; and

 (b) state what action you would take if previous estimates about profitability appeared somewhat over-optimistic.

2 INTERPRETATION OF ACCOUNTS

LEARNING
OBJECTIVES

At the end of this case study, you will be able to:
- analyse financial statements;
- extract additional information from a set of financial statements;
- summarize information contained within them;
- prepare a report based on your observations.

NOT SO SECURE

LOCATION   Security Systems Limited: the Head Office

PERSONNEL   Alan Pymn: Joint Managing Director
Frank Lynch: Joint Managing Director

SYNOPSIS

Some years ago, Alan Pymn and Frank Lynch went into partnership marketing and installing security alarm systems. Both Alan and Frank had previously worked at the local brewery, Alan in plant maintenance, and Frank in the sales office.

They lived in Stutfield, a quiet north country town of about 80 000 inhabitants. Stutfield was within easy travelling distance of several major cities. At that time, the town was suffering from an increasing amount of crime and vandalism, and house owners were extremely worried by the number of houses being burgled.

The two partners were neighbours. They were also both keen members of the local squash club. Talking at the bar one night about the latest burglary, they had the idea of forming their own security system business. The idea appealed to them, especially as neither of them wanted to work for someone else for the rest of their lives.

They thought about the idea for a little while. In the meantime, by working for a friend at the weekend, Alan was able to gain some experience of installing security systems, and Frank learned something about the administrative and marketing side of the security business. Financial backing was promised from various friends and relatives, and within just a few months, they were able to set up their business.

The business was an instant success as everyone in the town seemed to want some form of protection. After a few years of rapid growth they decided to convert the partnership into a limited liability company called 'Security Systems Limited'.

The charge for installing a security system was based partly on the size of the property and partly on the complexity of the installation. The policy of the company was to invoice customers 30 days after a job had been satisfactorily completed.

After the first year, a fixed annual maintenance charge became payable. This charge covered all further inspections and repairs. Customers were contracted to pay this charge for five years, but after that time only a nominal annual charge was made. All contracts had a maximum life of ten years.

Following the formation of the company, the business continued to grow, although at a slower rate than had previously been experienced. By the time that Security Systems was formed, most householders in Stutfield had obtained a burglar alarm, so the company began to conduct more of its business in the nearby cities.

It proved to be much more difficult to operate outside Stutfield. Although there was quite a demand for such services, the competition was extremely tough. Furthermore, city customers always argued about the effectiveness of the system, and both operative and office staff spent a great deal of time persuading customers to settle their accounts.

An additional worrying feature first became apparent in 19X4. Contrary to expectations, those security systems installed in the earlier years of the business proved increasingly expensive to maintain, and the operative staff spent more and more of their time repairing old systems instead of installing new ones. Under the terms of the contract, it was not possible to increase the annual maintenance charge.

The company's accounting policy had always been to claim any profit made on the installation of a system in the year of installation, and to credit maintenance fees receivable to each year's profit and loss account. Separate records were not kept of installation expenses and maintenance costs, and no provision had been made for maintenance and repairs.

Required:

1 Inspect the summarized accounts for Security Systems Limited for the five-year period 1 April 19X3 to 31 March 19X8 (Appendix A). Make a note of any obvious changes or features that become apparent as you read through the accounts.

2 Confirm your initial impressions by preparing the following analyses:
   (a) cash flow statement in columnar format for each of the four years 31 March 19X5 to 31 March 19X8 inclusive;
   (b) using *selected* data for the five-year period 1 April 19X3 to 31 March 19X8, prepare the following analyses on both a historical cost account (HCA) basis, and where appropriate, on a current purchasing power (CPP) basis:

- a horizontal analysis;
- a trend analysis;
- a vertical analysis:
- a ratio analysis.

3 Using the information obtained in completing 1 and 2 above, and including the information contained in Appendix B and Appendix C, prepare a report for the Board of Directors of Security Systems Limited examining the company's efficiency, liquidity and profitability during the five-year period 1 April 19X3 to 31 March 19X8 inclusive.

Note: Be careful to state what recommendations you would make to the Board of Directors in order to enable the company to continue in business.

Appendix A

PROFIT AND LOSS ACCOUNTS (EXTRACTS) FOR THE YEAR
TO 31 MARCH

	19X4 £000	19X5 £000	19X6 £000	19X7 £000	19X8 £000
INCOME					
Installation fees	1250	1500	2100	2400	2500
Maintenance fees	1000	1500	1920	2340	2600
	2250	3000	4020	4740	5100
EXPENDITURE					
Direct materials	250	306	437	528	575
Direct labour	795	1254	1753	2182	3060
Direct expenditure	40	40	70	90	120
Operational overheads	140	200	280	370	470
	1225	1800	2540	3170	4225
OPERATING PROFIT	1025	1200	1480	1570	875
Directors'emoluments	80	100	130	150	150
Loan interest	–	–	–	75	75
Office expenses	675	780	995	1040	1085
Office salaries	120	140	155	180	210
	875	1020	1280	1445	1520
NET PROFIT (LOSS)	150	180	200	125	(645)
Taxation	45	60	65	70	–
	105	120	135	55	(645)
Dividends	100	115	115	120	–
RETAINED PROFIT/(LOSS)	£5	£5	£20	£(65)	£(645)

BALANCE SHEET (EXTRACTS) AT 31 MARCH

	19X4 £000	19X5 £000	19X6 £000	19X7 £000	19X8 £000
FIXED ASSETS					
At cost	1400	1450	1500	1550	1900
Less: Accumulated depreciation	275	355	440	530	695
	1125	1095	1060	1020	1205
CURRENT ASSETS					
Stocks at cost (19X3 £15,000)	20	25	40	50	80
Trade debtors	200	240	363	434	806
Other debtors	25	25	30	40	50
Cash and bank	–	–	–	278	–
	245	290	433	802	936
	£1370	£1385	£1493	£1822	£2141
CAPITAL AND RESERVES					
Ordinary shares of £1 each	1000	1000	1000	1000	1000
Retained profits/(losses)	55	60	80	15	(630)
	1055	1060	1080	1015	370
DEBENTURE LOANS (15%)	–	–	–	500	500
CURRENT LIABILITIES					
Trade creditors	26	31	43	52	66
Other creditors	40	50	60	65	80
Bank overdraft	104	69	130	–	1125
Taxation	45	60	65	70	–
Proposed dividend	100	115	115	120	–
	315	325	413	307	1271
	£1370	£1385	£1493	£1822	£2141

Notes:

1 There were no sales of fixed assets during the period 1 April 19X3 to 31 March 19X8 inclusive.

2 Advance corporation tax may be ignored.

Appendix B

CURRENT PURCHASING POWER INDEX FOR
SECURITY SYSTEMS LIMITED
Average for the year to 31 March

19X3	72
19X4	76
19X5	81
19X6	87
19X7	96
19X8	110

Appendix C

SECURITY SYSTEMS LIMITED: AVERAGE WAGE AND
SALARY INCREASES

Year to 31 March

	Operatives	*Office staff*
	%	%
19X4	10	8
19X5	12	10
19X6	15	12
19X7	20	15
19X8	20	15

3 THE USEFULNESS OF FINANCIAL REPORTS

LEARNING OBJECTIVES

After preparing this case study, you will be able to:
- state the desirable characteristics of financial reports;
- design a questionnaire;
- interview the users of accounts;
- write up the results of your survey.

ELIZABETH LO AND FRIENDS

LOCATION   The University of East Cheshire: The Main Lecture Theatre

PERSONNEL   Dale Galloway: Accounting Lecturer
Heather Watt: Student
Elizabeth Lo: Student

SYNOPSIS

Elizabeth Lo was a first year student in business studies at the University of East Cheshire. She had been born and brought up in Lighton, a small market town in the Midlands. Elizabeth was an attractive, bright and popular girl, and she had many sports and activities in which she was involved. She had been hoping to go to one of the ancient universities to read philosophy, but her 'A' level results had been disappointing. In desperation, and somewhat at the last minute, her father had managed to get her a place at East Cheshire.

To begin with, Elizabeth had no more interest in business studies than she had in going to the moon, but the course was quite a varied one and she got on well with her fellow students. While there were one or two subjects that some of the class hated, everyone found accounting to be the most boring.

Dale Galloway, their accounting lecturer, did his best, but it was hard going for all of them. During the first term, they ploughed through the mechanics of double entry book-keeping, and it took a long time before it began to make sense. The one golden rule in accounting seemed to be that the answer to any question was the opposite of whatever you first thought.

In the spring term, the class began to study the format and structure of published financial statements. There were lots of rules to learn that were based partly on the Companies Act and partly on what were called 'financial reporting standards'.

As it was a degree class, Dale was very keen to be critical of such procedures. Elizabeth was not alone in finding it very difficult to understand what he was talking about. It was not easy to remember all that they were supposed to learn, and it was almost impossible to criticize something that was not very clear to you in the first place.

As the term went by, Elizabeth began to realize that accounting was not like simple arithmetic. She came to appreciate that, although you were supposed to follow a lot of accounting rules, it was possible to interpret them in any way you wished. It was quite a shock to find out that accountants were just as fallible as anybody else. You could, in fact, *fix* accounting statements so that they showed what you wanted, and yet you could still be following the rules! It was all very confusing.

Dale was even more scathing about the contents of an annual report. 'Just get hold of an annual report,' he invited the class. 'You have now done some accounting. Tell me honestly: does it mean anything to you?' Heather Watt, one of Elizabeth's friends, *did* get hold of an annual report, and they both had a good look at it. They quite agreed with Dale: it did appear to be meaningless.

By this time the class was thoroughly disillusioned. Although the students found the subject boring, they had understood that accountancy was a highly regarded profession, and yet it now appeared to be nothing more than a gigantic confidence trick.

Fortunately, Dale was a very experienced lecturer. He realized that some of the class did not understand him, while the remainder had been put off accounting for life. He tried to argue that while the current method of reporting financial results was open to question, neither the accountancy profession nor anyone else had anything better to put in its place. In other words, he stated, 'It's better to be vaguely right, than precisely wrong.'

'Well, why doesn't your profession try to do something about making it precisely *right*?', asked Heather (who was one of more bolder elements in the class). 'Why, for example, don't you ask people, such as shareholders, what they want, instead of supplying all this information that you say is rubbish?'

'Now that's a very good question,' replied Dale without a trace of sarcasm in his voice. 'Perhaps we *should* be able to design financial reports that will be useful to those who want to use them.' A thought struck him.

'I tell you what, we'll make this the subject of a tutorial exercise. I think it would be a lot more interesting for you, and it might either prove or disprove my point. How about it?' The class agreed, and Dale began preparing a suitable assignment.

By the next week he had come up with a few ideas. 'I want you to work in your respective tutorial groups,' he said. Elizabeth was pleased, because she was in a good tutorial group of only eight students. 'As part of a group exercise I want you to do two things: first, find out from looking at books in the library what are the desirable characteristics of financial reports. Now, I think you will find that, while it is relatively easy to put them down on paper, it is less easy to apply them in practice.'

'And that takes me on to the second part of the exercise. I want you to do a survey of what use shareholders make of their annual reports. I want each group to prepare a report on its findings, and then to present it to the rest of the class. There are one or two suggestions on how you should go about doing this exercise in the hand-out I circulated at the beginning of the lecture. Now, I think that four weeks should be long enough for the project, particularly as we shall not be holding any accounting lectures or tutorials during that time.'

The class cheered, and Elizabeth became quite excited. This seemed a lot more interesting than sitting in an uncomfortable lecture theatre taking notes from dozens of overhead slides.

Required:
1 Desirable characteristics of financial reports:
   (a) Consult a number of books on financial reporting in your library. List the desirable characteristics of financial reports as outlined in such books.
   (b) Obtain a number of annual reports of limited liability companies. Most companies will let you have a copy of their latest report if you write to the Company Secretary.

   Examine such reports, and then assess them to see how far in your view they appear to contain the desirable characteristics of financial reports as outlined in the textbooks.

2 Shareholders' information needs and requirements:
   It would be interesting to find out what use shareholders make of a company's annual report, and what improvements they would like to see in its presentation.
   (a) Prepare a questionnaire suitable for surveying a number of shareholders in limited liability companies. You may need to consult a book on question- naire design, but some idea of the type of questions that you might ask are listed in Appendix D.
   Note: Be careful that you do not ask questions that suggest a particular answer.
   (b) The next stage of the exercise is even more difficult. It perhaps would not be wise to stop people in the street and ask them if they would be prepared to answer some questions about their shareholdings! But you could ask family and friends who are shareholders in public limited liability compa- nies whether they would be prepared to answer your questions. You will not have the time to survey a totally representative group of shareholders, but try and survey about ten people.
   (c) Prepare a written report on your findings, and present it to your tutorial group. In your conclusions, try to answer the following questions:

   - To what extent do shareholders use their annual reports?
   - What particular items are they interested in?
   - Can they follow the structure of them?
   - Do they understand the terminology used in the report?
   - Would they like a different type of annual report, and if so what?

Appendix

SHAREHOLDERS' QUESTIONNAIRE: THE TYPE OF QUESTIONS TO ASK

1 Would you mind answering a few questions?
2 Do you have any shares in a company?
3 Did you buy the shares on the Stock Exchange?
4 Have you received an annual report from the company?
5 Can you tell from the envelope that it is an annual report?
6 Do you take it out of the envelope?
7 Do you look at the report at all?
8 Do you flick through it?
9 Do you look at the pictures?
10 Do you look at the advertising material?
11 Do you look at the other pages?
12 Do you read through the Chairman's report?
13 Do you read through the Director's report?
14 Do you have a look at the profit and loss account?
15 Do you go through the profit and loss account notes?
16 Do you have a look at the balance sheet?
17 Do you go through the balance sheet notes?
18 Do you go through the cash flow statement?
19 Do you look at anything else in the report?
20 Is there anything else you would like to see given in the report?
21 Have you any knowledge of book-keeping or accounting?

4 COST AND MANAGEMENT ACCOUNTING SYSTEMS

LEARNING OBJECTIVES

After preparing this case study, you will be able to:
- describe the nature and purpose of a cost and management accounting system;
- list the benefits of such a system;
- state the problems inherent in quantifying the benefits;
- prepare a report for management on cost and management accounting systems.

NO PROBLEM

LOCATION   Yewtree Limited: the Managing Director's office.

PERSONNEL   Mark Pope: Managing Director
Alison Webster: Senior Auditor, Simey and Simey,
Chartered Accountants

SYNOPSIS

Following the completion of the audit for the year to 30 June 19X1, a meeting had been arranged between Mark Pope, the Managing Director of Yewtree Limited, and Alison Webster, a Senior Auditor in Simey and Simey, the company's auditors.

After the usual pleasantries, Mark got down to business. As befitted his Army training, he did not believe in wasting time. 'Now, what was it you wanted to see me about, Alison?' he enquired.

'Well, as you will recall, Mark, we usually hold a post-audit meeting. The audit has gone very well this year, and we're quite happy with the accounts. This time, what we really wanted to do was to have a close look at the future of the company.'

Mark immediately pricked up his ears. 'You mean you think we've got problems?' he queried, the alarm registering in his voice.

'Not in the immediate future,' responded Alison, 'but there are one or two matters that we would like to advise you about.'

Mark was not easily placated. 'What on earth do you mean?' he asked somewhat aggressively. 'We seem to be doing all right. Surely there can't be a problem?'

'No real problem,' replied Alison. 'I agree that everything seems fine, but be honest now. We did an interim audit towards the end of the financial year, and you were having some problems then, weren't you?'

'Yes,' admitted a somewhat reluctant Managing Director, 'but once you pointed them out, we took immediate action.'

Alison smiled to herself. Mark had walked right into a fairly obvious trap. 'Oh yes,' she said, 'but only when the year was almost over. It's probably only because you had good results up until December that the overall results for the year appear satisfactory.'

'I don't see how you can say that,' muttered Mark. 'You can't be sure.'

'That's exactly the point I am making,' said Alison. 'You don't really know, and neither, for that matter, do we.'

'Well, we pay you to tell us these things,' Mark snapped back. 'And if I may say so, we pay you rather a lot.'

'Actually, you don't,' replied Alison. 'I mean, you don't pay us to advise on such matters. Your shareholders pay us to do the audit. Advice about the management of the company is outside the audit, and it is not strictly part of our function.'

Mark backtracked a little. 'Be that as it may, what are you trying to tell me?'

Alison consulted her notes. 'Basically, Mark, we think that you and your senior staff have found it more and more difficult in the last few years to control the company. The company has grown considerably, and now you all spend most of your time at your desks, and less time on the shop floor seeing what's going on.'

'Yes, I know,' Mark murmured. 'It certainly wasn't like that in the old days, still less so in the Army, but I do my best.' He had a feeling that he was not going to like what he was about to hear.

'Of course, Mark. I appreciate that. But it does mean that you don't *really* know what's gone on until the annual accounts are ready. When the company was small, you were always wandering around the place. You knew everybody. Everybody knew you, and you could tell if something was not quite right.'

'I must admit, I preferred the old days. But what are we to do? We can't turn the clock back.'

'I'm not suggesting you should, Mark. What I think you should do now, is to install what we call a "cost and management accounting system".'

'What! Even more book-keeping,' glared a somewhat revitalised Managing Director. 'More staff. More office space. More paper work. I thought that you had always warned us against too much administration.'

'Well, there would be an extra cost,' admitted Alison, 'although I would expect the benefits to outweigh the costs.'

'What benefits?' queried Mark.

'I should think substantial,' parried Alison. 'At the moment you get most information from the annual accounts. That's a long time since some of the events took place. That means you have little idea anything's gone wrong until it's too late. And even worse, you just guess when you are asked to quote a price for an order.'

'I've always been very good at that,' replied Mark, very much on his dignity.

'Yes, but you've less time for that now, and, frankly, your staff are not as good at it as you were.'

Mark noted the past tense and, in his heart of hearts, he knew that Alison was right. It was not easy to take such criticism about yourself and the company that you had founded. After his Army service, the company became Mark's only love, and now here was this jumped up book-keeper daring to criticize the only thing that mattered to him.

Mark broke the silence. 'I suppose this company has prospered because I've always been willing to consider new ideas, and I'm not going to stop now. I will think about this "cost and management accounting system" you've mentioned, but I'm not having more administration just for the sake of it. I know that there are fashions in accounting, just as there are in anything else. If I buy it, it will have to pay for itself.'

'I agree with you Mark, although frankly it is difficult to prove on paper that such a system pays for itself.'

'Well, there you are,' said Mark. 'But I've said I would consider it, and I will. Can you look into it for me?'

'Actually, Mark, that's a bit difficult for my firm to do. You see, we are your company's auditors, and we cannot get too involved in such work. But I tell you what I can do in the meantime. I will get one of my colleagues to prepare a report for you. If you like it, maybe our Management Consultancy firm could take over. Would that arrangement suit you?'

Mark said that it suited him fine, and at that point, the meeting was concluded.

Required:

Yewtree's problem is probably not unique. There is a great deal of evidence that many British companies still depend almost entirely on their financial accounting system for management control purposes. Check this assertion by undertaking the following tasks:

(a) refer to a number of articles in your library that report on studies undertaken into the use made of management accounting systems;

(b) undertake a survey of local industry into the use made of such systems.
   Note: You may be able to do this task either by personal contact with some firms that you know, or by circulating a questionnaire.

2 Many accounting texts list the benefits of installing a cost and management accounting system, but they do not say much about what such systems cost to install and to operate. Consult a number of articles and textbooks in your library. Note whether they make any attempt to quantify in monetary terms the benefits of such systems.

3 Assume that you are employed by Alison Webster's firm and that you have been asked to draw up a preliminary report suitable for presentation to Mark Pope. Prepare such a report, and then present it to your tutorial group.

5 PRODUCT PRICING

LEARNING OBJECTIVES

After preparing this case study, you will be able to:
- describe the circumstances in which total absorption costing may be used as a means of pricing products;
- outline the technique of marginal costing;
- prepare a report suitable for presentation to management containing data based on the marginal costing technique.

A special order

LOCATION   Fast Clean Products Limited: the Managing Director's office

PERSONNEL   Stanley Newton: Managing Director
Omar Khan: Mini-supermarket owner
Ralph Timmins: Production Manager
Su Yamamoto: Distribution Manager
Gerald White: Chief Accountant

SYNOPSIS

Fast Clean Products Limited manufactures household cleaning products, operating from a small factory on the outskirts of Leeds. The company has always been reasonably profitable, although for the last two years it has been producing well under capacity, largely as a result of a general reduction in consumer spending.

Stanley Newton, the Managing Director of the company, has been assiduously reading the financial press, and he has come to the conclusion that there is not likely to be an upturn in the market for at least the next 12 months. He assumes, therefore, that Fast Clean Products is also unlikely to see a revival in its fortunes for at least that time.

Stanley spends a lot of time playing golf. Some months ago he had got talking to a new member of the golf club, Omar Khan, who told him that he owned a chain of mini-supermarkets. The other day, Stanley was going through his morning mail and, rather to his surprise, he found a letter from Omar asking him to quote for a special order.

'Who said that golf was a waste of time?' Stanley asked himself.

He immediately called in his team of senior managers to tell them about the request. 'Can we do it?' he asked each one of them in turn.

Ralph Timmins, the Production Manager, was the first to be asked. 'Well, Stanley, we have the capacity at the moment, although we might have to take on more staff. But what happens if trade revives? We certainly could not do this order and satisfy our ordinary trade outlets.'

'As far as I can gather, Ralph, this is a one-off request,' replied Stanley. 'Omar has been let down by his ordinary supplier, and he cannot promise us anything beyond this order.'

He then turned to his Distribution Manager, 'I take it that you will not have any problems in dealing with this order if we take it on?' he queried.

'None whatsoever, Stanley,' replied Su. 'As you know, we have not laid-off any of the distribution staff. And, to be quite honest, most of them have forgotten what it's like to work hard.'

Stanley made a mental note that order or no order, he must take up this point with Su. 'What on earth are we doing with under-employed staff?' he asked himself.

Su continued. 'And it's also highly unlikely that we would need any more vehicles, although some of the present ones are getting very old.'

''Yes, yes,' intervened Stanley hastily. 'We won't go into that this morning.'

For some time Su had been campaigning for a greater allocation of the capital expenditure budget for the replacement of distribution vehicles.

'So, it seems that we don't anticipate any great problems if we take on this order,' stated Stanley.

'Excuse me, Stanley,' interjected a quiet voice. 'You haven't asked about the costings.' The voice belonged to Gerald White, the company's Chief Accountant.

Gerald was a highly self-effacing member of the management team. He was precise and pedantic, but he was usually right.

'Oh! I don't think that there is any problem there, Gerald,' he replied. 'We shall just cost the job as we normally do, and then charge accordingly.'

Some time ago, Gerald had persuaded Stanley to introduce a cost and management accounting system into the company. Stanley was largely a marketing man, and he was not really interested in accounting. However, like most converts, he was all for an idea once he had accepted it.

'I shall expect you to cost the product on the normal absorption costing lines. I will have a word with you about the precise profit percentage to be added once you have got the details,' said Stanley firmly.

'That may not be wise, Stanley,' responded Gerald.

The others laughed, but Gerald did not see the joke. He carried on regardless.

'These chains of supermarkets are very competitive. You can, I beg your pardon, *one* can guarantee that Mr Khan will have asked other companies to tender and, unless Fast Clean Products is competitive, the order will go elsewhere.'

The room went quiet. Some of the excitement and elation felt by all members of the management team began to evaporate.

'That's just like all you accountants,' interposed Su, who besides looking after distribution, also had an interest in sales. 'Gloom, gloom and yet more gloom. You're always looking on the black side. Here we are: for the first time for months we've got the chance of a large new order, and you want to put the brake on it.'

'I am afraid that you have misunderstood me, Susan,' Gerald replied quietly. 'Far from wanting to reject the order, I want to ensure that the company is successful. All I meant was that the company's normal accounting procedures may not be appropriate in the case of a 'one-off' order, as some people call it. A total absorbed cost may not, in fact, be the most suitable one to adopt in the case of a special order.'

'But you've always been going on at me,' interjected Su, rather angrily, 'that it's no use making sales if we don't make a profit on them.'

'That is quite correct, Susan, but only in the long run. Over a period of time, the company must, of course, cover all of its costs. For a special order, however, it may be profitable to accept that order, provided that the extra costs incurred by undertaking it are less than the amount received from the customer.'

By now, everyone at the meeting had gone unusually quiet. 'I'm not quite sure that I understand you,' said Stanley. 'You seem to be suggesting that we undercut our normal prices, and I don't like the idea of that. But in any case, how do you work out, the "extra" costs of an order?'

'Ah, Stanley, that is an accounting problem of some complexity,' responded Gerald with some satisfaction. 'But I shall be glad to discuss it with you when the accounting team has derived some appropriate costings.'

'Please do,' said Stanley with heavy irony. 'I would like the costings in the morning, *if* you please.'

'Certainly, Stanley. I shall arrange for that. You will have them on your desk at eight o'clock tomorrow morning.'

Stanley realized that he should have known better. Nothing seemed to ruffle the calm of his Chief Accountant. 'Suppose I had asked for them at eight o'clock this evening 'he thought, 'would he have replied,"Certainly, Stanley. I shall arrange for that"?' He answered his own question. 'Probably,' he muttered rather gloomily. 'One of these days I shall put that to the test.'

Required:

1 Prepare a critical appraisal of the marginal cost technique, and then be prepared to defend your arguments in your tutorial group. Be careful to explain why the total absorbed cost of a product may not be an appropriate method of determining the selling price of a special order.

2 Assume that you are Gerald White. Using the information listed in Appendix E, prepare a report suitable for presentation to Stanley Newton.

Appendix

MISCELLANEOUS DATA FOR THE YEAR TO 30 JUNE 19X5

1 Abridged profit and loss account

	£000	£000	£000
Sales			3260
Less: Cost of goods sold			
Direct materials	560		
Direct labour	1660	2220	
Factory overhead		400	
FACTORY COST OF PRODUCTION		2620	
Administration overhead		250	
Selling and distribution overhead		300	
TOTAL OPERATING COST			3170
OPERATING PROFIT			£90

2 The company uses a total absorption costing system. The selling price of it goods is determined on a cost-plus price basis. A 20% loading for non-manufacturing overhead is added to the total factory cost, to which is added a further 10% for profit. Factory overheads are absorbed into product costs on the basis of machine hours. The machine hour absorption rate for the year to 30 June 19X5 was £2 per hour.

3 Gerald White's team had available to them the following breakdown of overheads for the year to 30 June 19X5:

	Factory	*Administration*	*Selling and Distribution*
	%	%	%
Fixed	80	90	60
Variable	20	10	40
Total	100	100	100

4 From the preliminary investigation made, it is expected that Omar Khan's special order would require £75 000 of direct materials. The direct labour cost would be £200 000, and the variable overhead cost, £25 000. The order would involve 40 000 machine hours.

5 Although it is anticipated that prices will rise during the year to 30 June 19X6, Gerald White decided to base his initial costings on the financial results for the year to 30 June 19X5.

6 BUDGETARY CONTROL

LEARNING OBJECTIVES

After preparing this case study, you will be able to:
- describe the nature and purpose of budgetary control;
- outline the acounting treatment of research and development expenditure in financial accounts;
- assess the behavioural implications of implementing and operating a budetary control system.

IT CAN'T BE DONE

LOCATION   Glass Products Plc: the Managing Director's office.

PERSONNEL   Ken Whalley: Managing Director
Philippa Morgan: Public Relations Manager
Dr Ross Hunt: Director of Research and Development

SYNOPSIS

Ken Whalley, the Managing Director of Glass Public Limited Company, had called a meeting of the senior management. Rumours had been rife in the company for some months that a big new initiative was afoot, but nobody had any real idea what was going on. Now all had been revealed.

Ken had reminded his audience that the company once had a near monopoly in its supply of glass products to the home market. In more recent years, however, international trade barriers had broken down, and the company was now finding it increasingly difficult to maintain the scale of operations that was needed to support its high level of fixed costs. Indeed, all employees had become aware last year that the situation was extremely serious when no annual bonus was paid.

'We are going to have to look at all our operations, Ken explained to the senior managers. 'We might have to cut out unprofitable products, reduce costs, and, wherever possible, go for a big increase in our sales. That's going to mean a big change for everyone.'

'Do you exclude redundancies?' Philippa Morgan, the Public Relations Manager asked immediately.

'No,' Ken replied, 'but what we aim to do is to expand. Any surplus labour we have we would hope to absorb into other activities. If we can't, then of course some staff would have to be laid off.'

There was an immediate murmur from his audience.

Ken hastily spoke again. 'I repeat, we shall only make someone redundant if all the other things we are going to do don't work. Now I have asked you here today to talk about those other things.'

Ken then went into some detail about what the Board had in mind, including the introduction of a sophisticated budgetary control system. 'At the moment,' he explained, 'our management reporting procedures are little better than a back of an envelope exercise. That's got to change. It's going to mean creating responsibility centres. It's going to mean managers doing some serious budgeting. And it's going to mean those same managers answering for what goes wrong.'

'Would this system be introduced into the research and development department?' asked Dr Ross Hunt, the Director of Research and Development activities.

'Yes,' replied Ken. 'No department will be excluded, and in the case of R and D, you will become a function. Within that function you will have a number of cost centres, or if you like, smaller departments.'

'Each one working towards a separate budget?' queried Ross.

'That is so,' responded Ken, who was now answering Ross's questions somewhat warily.

'That's impossible,' retorted Ross. 'You can't budget for R and D. You don't know where an experiment is going to take you, and so you don't know what it's going to cost.'

'Dr Hunt …'

Ross broke in again. 'Look at our opaque products!' he explained triumphantly.

Ross was, in fact, referring to one of the company's most successful product ranges. For years, millions of pounds had been spent on researching into opaque products. It was just about to be abandoned, when the technical problems were overcome. The products had been sold widely, and the company had made a fortune.

'Dr Hunt,' Ken began again, 'if you don't mind, I don't want to go into too much detail at this stage. Perhaps we could have a chat sometime?'

Ross nodded his head, but he decided to say nothing further.

Ken got through his agenda without further interruption, and the meeting was eventually concluded at 4.55 pm, just in time for everyone to go home no later than the usual time of 5 o'clock.

The next day, Ken sent for Ross Hunt. He tried to explain to him the benefits of a budgetary control system. It was hard going. Eventually, Ken realized that Ross's main objection was that he thought that he would never be allowed to spend more than a fixed amount of cash, and he was particularly worried because he knew that he would have to agree to this months ahead of when he planned to spend it.

Ken explained that Ross had misunderstood the purpose of budgeting control. In response, Ross came back on an earlier point: it would be difficult for him to work out in advance what he was going to spend. He tried to explain to Ken. 'You just don't know where an experiment is going to take you. It would be madness to stop just when a breakthrough might be round the corner.'

Ken was getting a little weary. 'Yes, but ... Ross. That would mean that once you start on a project you never stop it, just because eventually it *might* pay off. The company can't go on supporting all your projects because one day they may be successful.'

Ross counterattacked by remarking that this was not his problem: he just looked after R and D.

Ken's retort was crushing. 'Ah, but that's just where you are wrong: it *is* your responsibility. You might not have thought so up to now, but it's certainly going to be so in the future.'

The meeting ended at that point, because Ken had to rush off to Brussels. But he did so a very worried man. Research and development expenditure was an important element in total cost, and Dr Ross Hunt could cause a lot of trouble. In any case, Ken knew that a budgetary control system would not work unless it had the support of everyone in the company.

Required:

1 Consult a number of management accounting textbooks in your library, and then write a brief description of each of the following terms:

(a) responsibility accounting;

(b) division;

(c) function;

(d) profit centre;

(e) investment centre;

(f) cost centre;

(g) pure (or basic) research;

(h) applied research;

(i) development;

(j) budget;

(k) budgetary control.

2 Explain how you think (a) research expenditure, and (b) development expenditure should be dealt with in preparing a company's financial accounts.

3 Obtain a number of company annual reports and accounts covering a particular sector of the economy, for example, chemicals, electronics, pharmaceuticals. Assess the treatment of research and development expenditure, and its importance in relation to the company's other costs.

4 Assume that the directors of Glass Products Plc intend to introduce a budgetary control system throughout the company. Outline the arguments that you would use in convincing the Director of Research and Development that it was possible to introduce such a system into his area of responsibility, and that it would be of benefit to him and everyone in the company.

Further reading

This book contains sufficient material for most first-year courses in accounting for non-accounting students. Some courses may require additional information, however, and most students may find it necessary to consult other books when attempting some exercises and case studies.

There are many very good acounting books available for *accounting* students, but they usually go into considerable technical detail. Non-accounting students must use them with caution, otherwise they will be completely lost. In any case, non-accounting students do not need to process vast amounts of highly specialist data. It is sufficient for their purpose if they have an understanding of where accounting information comes from, why it is prepared in that way, what it means, and what reliance can be placed on it.

Bearing these points in mind, the following books are worth considering:

Financial accounting

Elliott, B. and Elliott J.: *Financial Accounting and Reporting,* Prentice Hall, Hemel Hempstead, 1993
This is a recently published book which has been well received. It should be a very useful reference book for non-accounting students.

Holmes, G. and Sugden, A.: *Interpreting Company Reports and Accounts*, 4th e. revised, Woodhead-Faulkner, Cambridge, 1993.
A well-established text that deals with company financial reporting in some detail.

Wood, F.: *Business Accounting*, Volumes 1 and 2, 6th e., Pitman, London, 1993.
Wood is the master accounting textbook writer. His books can be recommended with absolute confidence.

Management accounting

Arnold, J. and Hope, T.: *Accounting*, 2nd e., Prentice Hall, Hemel Hempstead, 1990.
This book is aimed at first- and second-year undergraduate and professional courses. Non-accounting students should be able to follow it without too much difficulty.

Drury, C.: *Management and Cost Accounting*, 3rd e., Chapman and Hall, London, 1992.
This book has become the established British text on management accounting. It is a big book in every sense of the word. Non-accounting students should only use it for reference.

Wilson, R.M.S. and Chua, W.F.: *Managerial Accounting – method and meaning*, 2nd e., Chapman and Hall, London, 1993.
This book is another first- and second-year undergraduate text. It has much more of a behavioural approach than most other management accounting books. It is a bit heavy going, but it is useful to see how management accounting can be approached from a completely different angle.

Discount table

Present value of £1 received after n years discounted at $i\%$

i	1	2	3	4	5	6	7	8	9	10
n										
1	0.9901	0.9804	0.9709	0.9615	0.9524	0.9434	0.9346	0.9259	0.9174	0.9091
2	0.9803	0.9612	0.9426	0.9246	0.9070	0.8900	0.8734	0.8573	0.8417	0.8264
3	0.9706	0.9423	0.9151	0.8890	0.8638	0.8396	0.8163	0.7938	0.7722	0.7513
4	0.9610	0.9238	0.8885	0.8548	0.8227	0.7921	0.7629	0.7350	0.7084	0.6830
5	0.9515	0.9057	0.8626	0.8219	0.7835	0.7473	0.7130	0.6806	0.6499	0.6209
6	0.9420	0.8880	0.8375	0.7903	0.7462	0.7050	0.6663	0.6302	0.5963	0.5645

i	11	12	13	14	15	16	17	18	19	20
n										
1	0.9009	0.8929	0.8850	0.8772	0.8696	0.8621	0.8547	0.8475	0.8403	0.8333
2	0.8116	0.7929	0.7831	0.7695	0.7561	0.7432	0.7305	0.7182	0.7062	0.6944
3	0.7312	0.7118	0.6931	0.6750	0.6575	0.6407	0.6244	0.6086	0.5934	0.5787
4	0.6587	0.6355	0.6133	0.5921	0.5718	0.5523	0.5337	0.5158	0.4987	0.4823
5	0.5935	0.5674	0.5428	0.5194	0.4972	0.4761	0.4561	0.4371	0.4190	0.4019
6	0.5346	0.5066	0.4803	0.4556	0.4323	0.4104	0.3910	0.3704	0.3521	0.3349

APPENDIX 3

Answers to end-of-chapter questions

Chapter 1

1.1 (a) To keep a record of the company's day-to-day progress.
(b) To prepare the company's annual financial accounts.
(c) To supply information to the management for decision making and control.
(d) To operate a system of internal auditing.
(e) To minimize the company's tax liailities.

1.2 It is required by law. External auditors report to the shareholders on whether the accounts represent a true and fair view (the discovery of fraud is only incidental to this purpose).

1.3 Accountants collect a great deal of information about an entity's activities and then translate it into monetary terms – a language that everyone understands. The information that is collected can help non-accountants do their job more effectively because it provides them with better guidance upon which to take decisions, but the decision is still theirs. Futhermore, all managers must be aware of the statutory accounting obligations to which their organization has to adhere if they are to avoid taking part in unlawful acts.

1.4 None. The preparation of management accounts is for the entity to decide if it believes that they serve a useful purpose.

1.5 Yes. These are contained in the Companies Act 1985. In addition, listed companies have to abide by certain Stock Exchange requirements, and qualified accountants are also bound by a great many mandatory professional requirements.

1.6 To collect and store detailed information about an entity's activities, and then to abstract it and summarize it in the most effective way for whatever purpose it is intended to be used.

Chapter 2

2.1 1 Matching.
2 Historic cost.
3 Quantitative.
4 Periodicity.
5 Prudence.
6 Going-concern.

2.2 1 Relevance.
2 Entity.
3 Consistency.
4 Materiality.
5 Historic cost.
6 Realization.

2.3 1 Entity.
2 Objectivity.
3 Periodicity.
4 Prudence.
5 Dual aspect.
6 Realization.

2.4 1 (a) Prudence.
(b) The long-term services obtained from a professional footballer are highly unpredictable.
2 (a) Realization.
(b) Although it may appear somewhat imprudent to do so, in general the risk is usually small in taking profit prior to the receipt of cash.
3 (a) Entity.
(b) The company does not have a legal title to the house.
4 (a) Prudence.
(b) The profit cannot be known for some time (although in some cases a proportion may be claimed if the final outcome is reasonably certain).
5 (a) Materiality.
(b) It would be unduly pedantic to insist on matching the cost of small stocks of stationery purchased in an earlier period with the revenue of a future period.
6 (a) Prudence.
(b) The improvement work may never result in a more successful revenue earning drug. (*Note:* In certain specific instances, earlier period costs on development work may be matched with revenues earned after the work has been completed.)

Chapter 3

3.1 Adam's books of account:

Account

Debit	*Credit*
1 Cash	Capital
2 Purchases	Cash
3 Van	Cash
4 Rent	Cash
5 Cash	Sales
6 Office machinery	Cash

3.2 Brown's books of account:

Account

Debit	Credit
1 Bank	Cash
2 Cash	Sales
3 Purchases	Bank
4 Office expenses	Cash
5 Bank	Sales
6 Motor car	Bank

3.3 Corby's books of account:

Account

Debit	Credit
1 Purchases	Smith
2 Cash	Capital
3 Cash	Sales
4 Purchases	Cash
5 Bank	Cash
6 Machinery	Cash

3.4 Davies' books of account:

Account

Debit	Credit
1 Bank	Capital
2 Purchases	Swallow
3 Cash	Sales
4 Purchases	Cash
5 Dale	Sales
6 Motoring expenses	Bank

3.5 Edgar's books of account:

Account

Debit	Credit
1 Purchases	Gill
2 Ash	Sales
3 Cash	Sales
4 Purchases	Cash
5 Gill	Bank
6 Cash	Ash

3.6 Ford's books of account:

Account

Debit	Credit
1 Cash	Sales
2 Purchases	Carter
3 Holly	Sales
4 Purchases	Cash
5 Sales returns	Holly
6 Carter	Purchases returned

3.7 Gordon's books of account:

Account

Debit	Credit
1 Purchases	Watson
2 Cash	Sales
3 Moon	Sales
4 Watson	Bank
5 Watson	Discounts received
6 Cash	Moon
7 Discounts allowed	Moon
8 Purchases	Cash

3.8 Harry's books of account:

Account

Debit	Credit
1 Cash	Capital
2 Bank	Cash
3 Rent	Bank
4 Purchases	Paul
5 Van	Bank
6 Cash	Sales
7 Purchases	Nancy
8 Motoring expenses	Cash
9 Nancy	Purchases returned
10 Mavis	Sales
11 Drawings	Cash
12 Purchases	Cash
13 Sales return	Mavis
14 Nancy	Bank
15 Cash	Mavis
16 Nancy	Discount received
17 Discounts allowed	Mavis
18 Petty cash	Bank

3.9 Ivan's ledger accounts:

Cash Account

	£			£
1.09.X9 Capital	10 000	2.09.X9	Bank	8 000
12.09.X9 Cash	3 000	3.09.X9	Purchases	1 000

Capital Account

	£		£
		1.09.X9 Cash	10 000

Bank Account

	£		£
2.09.X9 Cash	8 000	20.09.X9 Roy	6 000
30.09.X9 Norman	2 000		

Purchases Account

	£		£
3.09.X9 Cash	1 000		
10.09.X9 Roy	6 000		

Roy's Account

		£			£
20.09.X9	Bank	6 000	10.09.X9	Purchases	6 000

Sales Account

	£			£
		12.09.X9	Cash	3 000
		15.09.X9	Norman	4 000

Norman

		£			£
15.09.X9	Sales	4 000	30.09.X9	Bank	2 000

3.10 Jones' ledger accounts

Bank Account

		£			£
1.10.X1	Capital	20 000	10.10.X1	Petty cash	1 000
			25.10.X1	Lang	5 000
			29.10.X1	Green	10 000

Capital Account

	£			£
		1.10.X1	Bank	20 000

Van Account

		£	£
2.10.X1	Lang	5 000	

Lang's Account

		£			£
25.10.X1	Bank	5 000	2.10.X1	Van	5 000

Purchases Account

		£	£
6.10.X1	Green	15 000	
20.10.X1	Cash	3 000	

Green's Account

		£			£
28.10.X1	Discounts received	500	6.10.X1	Purchases	15 000
29.10.X1	Bank	10 000			

Petty Cash Account

		£			£
10.10.X1	Bank	1 000	22.10.X1	Miscellaneous expenses	500

Sales

	£			£
		14.10.X1	Haddock	6 000
		18.10.X1	Cash	5 000

Haddock

		£			£
14.10.X1	Sales	6 000	20.10.X1	Discounts allowed	600
			31.10.X1	Cash	5 400

Cash Account

		£			£
18.10.X1	Sales	5 000	20.10.X1	Purchases	3 000
31.10.X1	Haddock	5 400			

Miscellaneous Expenses

		£		£
22.10.X1	Petty cash	500		

Discounts Received Account

	£			£
		28.10.X1	Green	500

Discounts Allowed Account

		£		£
30.10.X1	Haddock	600		

3.11 Ken's ledger accounts:

Cash Account

		£			£
1.11.X2	Capital	15 000	2.11.X2	Bank	14 000
27.11.X2	Sales	5 000	28.11.X2	Purchases	4 000
			30.11.X2	Bank	1 000

Capital Account

	£			£
		10.11.X2	Cash	15 000

Bank Account

		£			£
2.11.X2	Cash	14 000	3.11.X2	Rent	1 000
30.11.X2	Main	1 000	26.11.X2	Office expenses	2 000
30.11.X2	Pain	2 000	29.11.X2	Ace	4 000
30.11.X2	Vain	3 000	29.11.X2	Mace	5 000
30.11.X2	Cash	1 000	29.11.X2	Pace	6 000

Rent Account

		£		£
3.11.X2	Bank	1 000		

Purchases Account

		£		£
4.11.X2	Ace	5 000		
4.11.X2	Mace	6 000		
4.11.X2	Pace	7 000		
25.11.X2	Ace	3 000		
25.11.X2	Mace	4 000		
25.11.X2	Pace	5 000		
28.11.X2	Cash	4 000		

Ace's Account

		£			£
29.11.X2	Bank	4 000	4.11.X2	Purchases	5 000
30.11.X2	Discounts		25.11.X2	Purchases	3 000
	received	200			

Mace's Accounts

		£			£
29.11.X2	Bank	5 000	4.11.X2	Purchases	6 000
30.11.X2	Discounts		25.11.X2	Purchases	4 000
	received	250			

Pace's Account

		£			£
15.11.X2	Purchases				
	returned	1 000	4.11.X2	Purchases	7 000
29.11.X2	Bank	6 000	25.11.X2	Purchases	5 000
30.11.X2	Discounts				
	received	300			

Sales Account

	£			£
		10.11.X2	Main	2 000
		10.11.X2	Pain	3 000
		10.11.X2	Vain	4 000
		27.11.X2	Cash	5 000

Main's Account

		£			£
10.11.X2	Sales	2 000	30.11.X2	Bank	1 000
			30.11.X2	Discounts	
				allowed	100

Pain's Account

		£			£
10.11.X2	Sales	3 000	22.11.X2	Sales return	2 000
			30.11.X2	Bank	2 000
			30.11.X2	Discounts	
				allowed	200

Vain's Account

		£			£
10.11.X2	Sales	4 000	30.11.X2	Bank	3 000
			30.11.X2	Discounts	
				allowed	400

Purchases Returned Account

	£			£
		15.11.X2	Pace	1 000

Sales Returns Account

		£		£
22.11.X2	Pain	2 000		

Office Expenses Account

		£			£
26.11.X2	Bank	2 000			

Discounts Received Account

		£			£
			30.11.X2	Ace	200
			30.11.X2	Mace	250
			30.11.X2	Pace	300

Discounts Allowed Account

		£			£
30.11.X2	Main	100			
30.11.X2	Pain	200			
30.11.X2	Vain	400			

3.12 (a), (b) and (c) Pat's ledger accounts:

Cash Account

		£			£
1.12.X3	Capital	10 000	24.12.X3	Office expenses	5 000
29.12.X3	Fog	4 000	31.12.X3	Grass	6 000
29.12.X3	Mist	6 000	31.12.X3	Seed	8 000
			31.12.X3	Balance c/d	1 000
		£20 000			£20 000
1.01.X4	Balance b/d	1 000			

Capital Account

		£			£
			1.12.X3	Cash	10 000

Purchases Account

		£			£
2.12.X3	Grass	6 000			
2.12.X3	Seed	7 000			
15.12.X3	Grass	3 000			
15.12.X3	Seed	4 000	31.12.X3	Balance c/d	20 000
		£20 000			£20 000
1.01.X4	Balance b/d	20 000			

Grass's Account

		£			£
12.12.X3	Purchases returned	1 000	2.12.X3	Purchases	6 000
31.12.X3	Cash	6 000	15.12.X3	Purchases	3 000
31.12.X3	Balance c/d	2 000			
		£9 000			£9 000
			1.01.X4	Balance b/d	2 000

Seed's Account

	£		£
12.12.X3 Purchases returned	2 000	2.12.X3 Purchases	7 000
31.12.X3 Cash	8 000	15.12.X3 Purchases	4 000
31.12.X3 Balance c/d	1 000		
	£11 000		£11 000
		0.01.X4 Balance b/d	1000

Sales Account

	£		£
		10.12.X3 Fog	3 000
		10.12.X3 Mist	4 000
		20.12.X3 Fog	2 000
31.12.X3 Balance c/d	12 000	20.12.X3 Mist	3 000
	£12 000		£12 000
		1.01.X4 Balance b/d	12 000

Fog's Account

	£		£
10.12.X3 Sales	3 000	29.12.X3 Cash	4 000
20.12.X3 Sales	2 000	31.12.X3 Balance c/d	1 000
	£5 000		£5 000
1.01.X4 Balance b/d	1 000		

Mist's Account

	£		£
10.12.X3 Sales	4 000	29.12.X3 Cash	6 000
20.12.X3 Sales	3 000	31.12.X3 Balance c/d	1 000
	£7 000		£7 000
1.01.X4 Balance b/d	1 000		

Purchases Returned Account

	£		£
		12.12.X3 Grass	1 000
31.12.X3 Balance c/d	3 000	12.12.X3 Seed	2 000
	£3 000		£3 000
		1.01.X4 Balance b/d	3 000

Office Expenses Account

	£		£
24.12.X3 Cash	5 000		

Tutorial note

It is unnecessary to balance off an account and bring down the balance if there is only a single entry in it.

(d)

PAT
Trial Balance at 31 December 19X3

	£	£
	Dr	Cr
Cash	1 000	
Capital		10 000
Purchases	20 000	
Grass		2 000
Seed		1 000
Sales		12 000
Fog	1 000	
Mist	1 000	
Purchases returned		3 000
Office expenses	5 000	
	£28 000	£28 000

3.13 (a) Vale's books of account:

Bank Account

		£			£
1.01.X3	Balance b/d	5 000	31.12.X3	Dodd	29 000
31.12.X3	Fish	45 000	31.12.X3	Delivery van	12 000
31.12.X3	Cash	3 000	31.12.X3	Balance c/d	12 000
		£53 000			£53 000
1.01.X4	Balance b/d	12 000			

Capital Account

		£			£
			1.01.X3	Balance b/d	20 000

Cash Account

		£			£
1.01.X3	Balance b/d	1 000	31.12.X3	Purchases	15 000
31.12.X3	Sales	20 000	31.12.X3	Office expenses	9 000
31.12.X3	Fish	7 000	31.12.X3	Bank	3 000
			31.12.X3	Balance c/d	1 000
		£28 000			£28 000
1.01.X4	Balance b/d	1000			

Dodd's account

		£			£
31.12.X3	Bank	29 000	1.01.X3	Balance b/d	2 000
31.12.X3	Balance c/d	3 000	31.12.X3	Purchases	30 000
		£32 000			£32 000
			1.01.X4	Balance b/d	3000

Fish's Account

		£				£
1.01.X3	Balance b/d	6 000	31.12.X3	Bank		45 000
31.12.X3	Sales	50 000	31.12.X3	Cash		7 000
			31.12.X3	Balance c/d		4 000
		£56 000				£56 000
1.01.X4	Balance b/d	4000				

Furniture Account

		£		£
1.01.X3	Balance b/d	10 000		

Purchases Account

		£			£
31.12.X3	Cash	15 000			
31.12.X3	Dodd	30 000	31.12.X3 Balance c/d		45 000
		£45 000			£45 000
1.01.X4	Balance b/d	45 000			

Sales Account

		£			£
			31.12.X3 Cash		20 000
31.12.X3	Balance c/d	70 000	31.12.X3 Fish		50 000
		£70 000			£70 000
			1.01.X4 Balance b/d		70 000

Office Expenses Account

		£		£
31.12.X3	Cash	9 000		

Delivery Van Account

		£		£
31.12.X3	Bank	12 000		

(b)

VALE
Trial balance at 31 December 19X3

	Dr	Cr
	£	£
Bank	12 000	
Capital		20 000
Cash	1 000	
Dodd		3 000
Fish	4 000	
Furniture	10 000	
Purchases	45 000	
Sales		70 000
Office expenses	9 000	
Delivery van	12 000	
	£93 000	£93 000

3.14 (a) Brian's ledger accounts:

Bank Account

		£			£
1.01.X4	Capital	25 000	2.01.X4	Rent	2 000
23.01.X4	Cash	6 000	25.01.X4	Petty cash	500
26.01.X4	Ann	5 500	29.01.X4	Savoy Motors	4 000
31.01.X4	Capital	5 000	30.01.X4	Linda	8 000
			30.01.X4	Sydney	2 000
			31.01.X4	Rent	2 000
			31.01.X4	Balance c/d	23 000
		£41 500			£41 500
1.02.X4	Balance b/d	23 000			

Capital Account

		£			£
			1.01.X4	Bank	25 000
31.01.X4	Balance c/d	30 000	31.01.X4	Bank	5 000
		£30 000			£30 000
			1.02.X4	Balance b/d	30 000

Rent Account

		£			£
2.01.X4	Bank	2 000			
31.01.X4	Bank	2 000	31.01.X4	Balance c/d	4 000
		£4 000			£4 000
1.02.X4	Balance b/d	4 000			

Purchases Account

		£			£
3.01.X4	Linda	5 000			
5.01.X4	Sydney	3 000			
15.01.X4	Linda	10 000	31.01.X4	Balance c/d	18 000
		£18 000			£18 000
1.02.X4	Balance b/d	18 000			

Linda's Account

		£			£
22.01.X4	Purchases returned	2 000	3.01.X4	Purchases	5 000
30.01.X4	Bank	8 000	15.01.X4	Purchases	10 000
30.01.X4	Discounts received	700			
31.01.X4	Balance c/d	4 300			
		£15 000			£15 000
			1.02.X4	Balance b/d	4 300

Motor Car Account

		£			£
4.01.X4	Savoy Motors	4 000			

Savoy Motors Account

		£			£
29.01.X4	Bank	£4 000	4.01.X4	Motor car	£4 000

Sydney's Account

		£			£
30.01.X4	Bank	2 000	5.01.X4	Purchases	3 000
30.01.X4	Discounts received	100			
31.01.X4	Balance c/d	900			
		£3 000			£3 000
			1.02.X4	Balance b/d	900

Cash Account

		£			£
10.01.X4	Sales	£6 000	23.01.X4	Bank	£6 000

Sales Account

		£			£
			10.01.X4	Cash	6 000
31.01.X4	Balance c/d	14 000	20.01.X4	Ann	8 000
		£14 000			£14 000
			1.02.X4	Balance b/d	14 000

Ann's Account

		£			£
20.01.X4	Sales	8 000	24.01.X4	Sales return	1 000
			26.01.X4	Bank	5 500
			26.01.X4	Discounts allowed	500
			31.01.X4	Balance c/d	1 000
		£8 000			£8 000
1.02.X4	Balance b/d	1 000			

Purchases Returned Account

		£			£
			22.01.X4	Linda	2000

Sales Returns Account

		£			£
24.01.X4	Ann	1000			

Petty Cash Account

	£			£
25.01.X4 Bank	500	28.01.X4 Office expenses		250
		31.01.X4 Balance c/d		250
	£500			£500
1.01.X4 Balance b/d	250			

Discounts Allowed Account

	£		£
26.01.X4 Ann	500		

Office Expenses Account

	£		£
28.01.X4 Petty cash	250		

Discounts Received Account

	£			£
		30.01.X4 Linda		700
31.01.X4 Balance c/d	800	30.01.X4 Sydney		100
	£800			£800
		1.02.X4 Balance b/d		800

(b)

BRIAN
Trial balance at 31 January 19X4

	Dr	Cr
	£	£
Bank	23 000	
Capital		30 000
Rent	4 000	
Purchases	18 000	
Linda		4 300
Motor car	4 000	
Sydney		900
Sales		14 000
Ann	1 000	
Purchases returned		2 000
Sales return	1 000	
Petty cash	250	
Discounts allowed	500	
Office expenses	250	
Discounts received		800
	£52 000	£52 000

3.15

FIELD
Trial balance at 28 February 19X5

	Dr £	Cr £
Bank	13 000	
Cash	2 000	
Capital		15 000
Creditors		4 000
Debtors	10 000	
Drawings	5 000	
Electricity	4 000	
Furniture	7 000	
Office expenses	3 000	
Purchases	50 000	
Sales		100 000
Wages	25 000	
	£119 000	£119 000

3.16

TRENT
Corrected trial balance at 31 March 19X4

	Dr £	Cr £
Bank (overdrawn)		2 000
Capital		50 000
Discounts allowed	5 000	
Discounts received		3 000
Dividends received		2 000
Drawings	23 000	
Investments	14 000	
Land and buildings	60 000	
Office expenses	18 000	
Purchases	75 000	
Sales		250 000
Rates	7 000	
Vans	20 000	
Van expenses	5 000	
Wages and salaries	80 000	
	£307 000	£307 000

3.17

SEVERN
Trial balance at 30 April 19X7

	Dr £000	Cr £000
Advertising	14	
Bank (current)	5	
Bank (deposit)	50	
Bank interest received		1
Capital		100
Cash	8	
Creditors		12
Debtors	30	
Discounts allowed	5	
Discounts received		2
Drawings	45	
Fees received		10
Furniture and fittings	18	
Land and buildings	40	
Motor cars	22	
Motor car expenses	4	
Plant and equipment	37	
Purchases	300	
Purchases returned		15
Rents received		5
Sales		500
Sales returns	20	
Telephone	3	
Wages	44	
	£645	£645

Chapter 4

4.1

ETHEL
Trading, profit and loss account for the year to 31 January 19X1

	£
Sales	35 000
Less: Purchases	20 000
Gross profit	15 000
Less: Expenses;	
Office expenses	11 000
Net profit	£4 000

ETHEL
Balance sheet at 31 January 19X1

	£	£
Fixed assets		
Premises		8000
Current assets		
Debtors	6000	
Cash	3000	
	9000	
Less: Current liabilities		
Creditors	3000	6000
		£14 000

Financed by:		
Capital		
Balance at 1 February 19X0		10 000
Net profit for the year		4000
		£14 000

4.2

MARION
Trading, profit and loss account for the year to 28 February 19X2

	£000	£000
Sales		400
Less: Purchases		200
Gross profit		200
Less: Expenses;		
Heat and light	10	
Miscellaneous expenses	25	
Wages and salaries	98	133
Net profit		£67

MARION
Balance sheet at 28 February 19X2

	£000	£000
Fixed assets		
Buildings		50
Current assets		
Debtors	30	
Bank	4	
Cash	2	
	36	
Less: Current liabilities		
Creditors	24	12
		£62
Financed by:		
Captial		50
Balance at 1 March 19X2		
Net profit for the year	67	
Less: Drawings	55	12
		£62

4.3

GARSWOOD

Trading, profit and loss account for the year to 31 March 19X3

	£	£
Sales (63 000 – 3000)		60 000
Less: Purchases (21 400 – 1 400)		20 000
Gross profit		40 000
Add: Other incomes:		
Discounts received	600	
Investment income received	400	1000
		41 000
Less: Expenses:		
Advertising	2 300	
Discounts allowed	100	
Electricity	1 300	
Stationery	900	
Wages	38 700	43 300
		£(2 300)

GARSWOOD

Balance sheet at 31 March 19X3

	£	£	£
Fixed assets			
Machinery			20 000
Office equipment			10 000
			30 000
Investments			4 000
Current assets			
Trade debtors		6 500	
Other debtors		1 500	
Bank		300	
Cash		100	
		8 400	
Less: Current liabilities			
Trade creditors	5 200		
Other creditors	800	6 000	2 400
			£36 400
Financed by:			
Capital			
Balance at 1 April 19X2			55 700
Less: Net loss for the year		(2 300)	
Add: Drawings		(17 000)	(19 300)
			£36 400

4.4 (a)

LATHOM
Trading account for the year to 30 April 19X4

	£	£
Sales		60 000
Less: Cost of goods sold:		
Opening stock	3 000	
Purchases	45 000	
	48 000	
Less: Closing stock	4 000	44 000
		£16 000

(b) Under current assets as the first item.

4.5 (a)

RUFFORD
Trading account for the year to 31 March 19X5

Stock method	1		2		3	
	£	£	£	£	£	£
Sales (82 000 – 4 000)		78 000		78 000		78 000
Less: Cost of goods sold						
Opening stock	4 000		4 000		4 000	
Purchases (48 000 – 3 000)	45 000		45 000		45 000	
	49 000		49 000		49 000	
Less: Closing stock	8 000	41 000	16 000	33 000	4 000	45 000
Gross profit		£37 000		£45 000		£33 000

(b) For the year to 31 March 19X6, other things being equal, using method 1 would result in a *higher* gross profit than using method 2 (whereas the reverse would be true for the year to 31 March 19X5).

4.6

STANDISH
Trading, profit and loss account for the year to 31 May 19X6

	£	£
Sales		79 000
Less: Cost of goods sold:		
Opening stock	7 000	
Purchases	52 000	
	59 000	
Less: Closing stock	12 000	47 000
Gross profit		32 000
Less: Expenses:		
Heating/light	1 500	
Miscellaneous	6 700	
Wages and salaries	17 800	26 000
Net profit		£6 000

STANDISH
Balance sheet at 31 May 19X6

	£	£
Fixed assets		
Furniture and fittings		8 000
Current assets		
Stock	12 000	
Debtors	6 000	
Cash	1 200	
	19 200	
Less: Current liabilities		
Creditors	4 300	14 900
		£22 900
Financed by:		
Capital		
Balance at 1 June 19X5		22 400
Net profit for the year	6 000	
Less: Drawings	5 500	500
		£22 900

4.7

WITTON
Trading, profit and loss account for the year to 30 June 19X7

	£	£
Sales		30 000
Less: Cost of goods sold:		
Purchases	14 000	
Less: Closing stock	2 000	12 000
Gross profit		18 000
Less: Expenses:		
Office expenses	8 000	
Motor car: depreciation (20% × 5 000)	1 000	9 000
Net profit		£9 000

WITTON
Balance sheet at 30 June 19X7

	£	£
Fixed assets		
Motor car		5 000
Less: Depreciation		1 000
		4 000
Current assets		
Stocks	2 000	
Debtors	3 000	
Cash	500	
	5 500	
Less: Current liabilities		
Creditors	1 500	4 000
		£8 000

Financed by:
Capital
At 1 July 19X6 | | | 3 000
Net profit for the year | | 9 000 |
Less: Drawings | | 4 000 | 5 000
| | | £8 000

4.8

CROXTETH
Trading, profit and loss account for the year to 31 July 19X8

	£	£	£
Sales			85 000
Less: Cost of goods sold:			
Opening stock		4000	
Purchases		70 000	
		74 000	
Less: Closing stock		14 000	60 000
Gross profit			25 000
Less: Expenses:			
Depreciation: delivery vans (30% × 40 000)	12 000		
shop equipment (10% × 8 000)	800	12 800	
Shop expenses		7 200	20 000
Net profit			£5 000

CROXTETH
Balance sheet at 31 July 19X8

	£	£	£
Fixed assets	Cost	*Accumulated depreciation*	*Net book value*
Delivery vans	40 000	24 000	16 000
Shop equipment	8 000	3 200	4 800
	48 000	27 200	20 800
Current assets			
Stock		14 000	
Bank		2 000	
		16 000	
Less: Current liabilities			
Creditors		4 800	11 200
			32 000
Financed by:			
Capital			
Balance at 1 August 19X7			35 000
Net proft for the year		5 000	
Less: Drawings		8 000	(3 000)
			£32 000

Tutorial note
Accumulated depreciation:
Delivery vans: 12 000 (b/f) + 12 000 = 24 000.
Shop equipment: 2 400 (b/f) + 800 = 3 200.

4.9 (a) Calculation of the depreciation charge for the year to 31 August 19X9:

	£	£	£	£
1 Land				–
2 Buildings: 2% × 150 000			=	3 000
3 Plant at cost	55 000			
Less: Residual value	5 000			
	50 000 × 5%		=	2 500
4 Vehicles at cost		45 000		
Less: Accumulated depreciation at				
31 August 19X8		28 800		
		16 200 × 40%	=	6 480
5 Furniture at cost		20 000		
Less: Residual value		2 000		
		18 000 × 10% = 1 800		
Additions at cost		3 000		
Less: Residual value		300		
		2 700 × 10% =	270	2 070
Total amount of depreciation (charged to the profit and loss account				£14 050
for the year to 31 August 19X9)				

(b)

BARROW
Balance sheet (extract) at 31 August 19X9

Fixed assets	_Cost_	_Accumulated depreciation_	_Net book value_
	£	£	£
Land	200 000	–	200 000
Buildings	150 000	63 000	87 000
Plant	55 000	40 000	15 000
Vehicles	45 000	35 280	9 720
Furniture	23 000	14 670	8 330
	£473 000	£152 950	320 050

4.10

PINE
Trading, profit and loss account for the year to 30 September 19X2

	£	£
Sales		40 000
Less: Cost of goods sold:		
Purchases	21 000	
Less: Closing stock	3 000	18 000
Gross profit	c/f	22 000

		b/f	22 000
Less: Expenses:			
Depreciation: furniture (15% × 8 000)		1 200	
General expenses		14 000	
Insurance (2 000 – 200)		1 800	
Telephone (1 500 + 500)		2 000	19 000
			£3 000

PINE
Balance sheet at 30 September 19X2

	£	£	£
Fixed assets			
Furniture			8 000
Less: Depreciation			1 200
			6 800
Current assets			
Stock		3 000	
Debtors		5 000	
Prepayments		200	
Cash		400	
		8 600	
Less: Current liabilites			
Creditors	5 900		
Accrual	500	6 400	2 200
			£9 000
Financed by:			
Capital			
At 1 October 19X1			6 000
Net profit for the year			3 000
			£9 000

4.11

DALE
Trading, profit and loss account for the year to 31 October 19X3

	£	£	£
Sales			350 000
Less: Cost of goods sold:			
Opening stock		20 000	
Purchases		240 000	
		260 000	
Less: Closing stock		26 000	234 000
Gross profit			116 000
Less: Expenses:			
Depreciation: office equipment	7 000		
vehicles	4 000	11 000	
Heating and lighting (3 000 + 1 500)		4 500	
Office expenses		27 000	
Rates (12 000 – 2 000)		10 000	
Wages and salaries		47 000	99 500
Net profit			£16 500

DALE
Balance sheet at 31 October 19X3

	£ Cost	£ Accumulated depreciation	£ Net book value
Fixed assets			
Office equipment	35 000	21 000	14 000
Vehicles	16 000	8 000	8 000
	51 000	29 000	22 000
Current assets			
Stocks		26 000	
Trade debtors		61 000	
Prepayments		2 000	
Bank		700	
		89 700	
Less: Current liabilities			
Trade creditors	21 000		
Accruals	1 500	22 500	67 200
			£89 200
Financed by;			
Capital			
At 1 November 19X2			85 000
Net profit for the year		16 500	
Less: Drawings		12 300	4 200
			£89 200

4.12 (a)

ASTLEY
Adjustments for accruals and prepayments for the year to 30 November 19X4

	Electricity £	Gas £	Insurance £	Rates £	Telephone £	Wages £
Cash paid during the year	26 400	40 100	25 000	16 000	3 000	66 800
Add: Prepayments at 1 December 19X3	–	–	12 000	4 000	–	–
	26 400	40 100	37 000	20 000	3 000	66 800
Less: Accruals at 1 December 19X3	5 200	–	–	–	1 500	1 800
Add: Accruals at 30 November 19X4	21 200	40 100	37 000	20 000	1 500	65 000
	8 300	–	–	6 000	–	–
	29 500	40 100	37 000	26 000	1 500	65 000
Less: Prepayments at 30 November 19X4	–	4 900	14 000	–	200	–
Charge to the profit and loss account for the year to 30 November 19X4	£29 500	£35 200	£23 000	£26 000	£1 300	£65 000

(b)

Balance sheet at 30 November 19X4

	£
Current assets	
Prepayments (4 900 + 14 000 + 200)	19 100
Current liabilities	
Accruals (8 300 + 6 000)	14 300

4.13

DUXBURY

Trading, profit and loss account for the year to 31 December 19X3

	£	£
Sales		95 000
Less: Cost of goods sold:		
Purchases	65 000	
Less: Closing stock	10 000	55 000
Gross profit		40 000
Less: Expenses:		
Depreciation: delivery van (20% × 20 000)	4 000	
Office expenses (12 100 + 400 − 500)	12 000	
Provision for doubtful debts (5% × 32 000)	1 600	17 600
Net profit		£22 400

DUXBURY

Balance sheet at 31 December 19X3

	£	£	£
Fixed assets			
Delivery van at cost			20 000
Less: Depreciation			4 000
			16 000
Current assets			
Stocks		10 000	
Trade debtors	32 000		
Less: Provision for doubtful debts	1 600	30 400	
Prepayment		500	
Cash		300	
		41 200	
Current liabilities			
Trade creditors	5 000		
Accrual	400	5 400	35 800
			£51 800
Financed by:			
Capital			
Balance at 1 January 19X3			40 000
Net profit		22 400	
Less: Drawings		10 600	11 800
			£51 800

4.14 (a)

BEECH

Balance sheet (extracts) at	19X4	19X5	19X6	19X7
	£	£	£	£
Current assets				
Trade debtors	60 000	55 000	65 000	70 000
Less: Provision for doubtful debts (10%)	6 000	5 500	6 500	7 000
	54 000	49 500	58 500	63 000

(b) Profit and loss accounts: increase/decrease in provision for doubtful debts:

	£	£
Year to:		
31 January 19X4		6 000 (New)
31 January 19X5	5 500	
Less: Provision at 31 January 19X4	6 000	500 (Decrease)
31 January 19X6	6 500	
Less: Provision at 31 January 19X5	5 500	1 000 (Increase)
31 January 19X7	7 000	
Less: Provision at 31 January 19X6	6 500	500 (Increase)

4.15

ASH

Trading, profit and loss account for the year to 31 March 19X5

	£	£
Sales		150 000
Less: Cost of goods sold:		
Opening stock	10 000	
Purchases	80 000	
Less: Closing stock	15 000	75 000
Gross profit		75 000
Less: Expenses:		
Bad debt	6 000	
Depreciation: furniture (10% × 9 000)	900	
Electricity (2 000 + 600)	2 600	
Increase in provision for doubtful debts		
(21 000 − 6 000 = 15 000 × 10%) − 1 200)	300	
Insurance (1 500 − 100)	1 400	
Miscellaneous expenses	65 800	77 000
Net loss		£(2 000)

ASH

Balance sheet at 31 March 19X5

	£	£	£
Fixed assets			
Furniture at cost			9 000
Less: Accumulated depreciation (3 600 + 900)			4 500
c/f			4 500

		£	£	£
	b/f			4 500
Current assets				
Stocks			15 000	
Trade debtors (21 000 – 6 000)		15 000		
Less: Provision for doubtful debts		1 500	13 500	
Prepayment			100	
			28 600	
Less: Current liabilities				
Trade creditors		20 000		
Accrual		600		
Bank overdraft		4 000	24 600	4 000
				£8 500
Financed by:				
Capital				
Balance at 1 April 19X4				20 500
Less: Net loss for the year			(2 000)	
Add: Drawings			(10 000)	(12 000)
				£8 500

4.16

ELM

Trading, profit and loss account for the year to 30 June 19X6

	£	£	£
Sales (820 000 – 4 000)			816 000
Less: Cost of goods sold:			
Opening stock		47 000	
Purchases (645 000 – 2 000)		643 000	
		690 000	
Less: Closing stock		50 000	640 000
Gross profit			176 000
Add: Other incomes:			
Discounts received		500	
Interest on investments		800	
Decrease in provision for doubtful			
debts (42 000 × 5% – 2 300)		200	1 500
			177 500
Less: Expenses:			
Advertising		3 000	
Depreciation: Furniture (15% × 12 000)	1 800		
Vehicles (35 000 – 7 000 × 20%)	5 600	7 400	
Discounts allowed		400	
Electricity (3 200 + 300)		3 500	
General expenses		28 900	
Rates (6 000 – 1 000)		5 000	
Telephone		1 300	
Wages and salaries		77 600	127 100
Net profit			£50 400

ELM
Balance sheet at 30 June 19X6

	£ Cost	£ Accumulated depreciation	£ Net book value
Fixed assets			
Furniture	12 000	3 600	8 400
Vehicles	35 000	12 600	22 400
	47 000	16 200	30 800
Investments at cost			5 000
Current assets			
Stocks		50 000	
Trade debtors	42 000		
Less: Provision for doubtful debts	2 100	39 900	
Prepayment		1 000	
Bank		400	
Cash		100	
		91 400	
Less: Current liabilities			
Trade creditors	13 000		
Accrual	300	13 300	78 100
			£113 900
Financed by;			
Capital			
Balance at 1 July 19X6			73 500
Net profit for the year		50 400	
Less: Drawings		10 000	40 400
			£113 900

4.17

LIME
Trading, profit and loss account for the year to 30 September 19X7

	£	£
Sales		372 000
Less: Cost of goods sold:		
Opening stock	36 000	
Purchases	320 000	
	356 000	
Less: Closing stock	68 000	288 000
Gross profit		84 000
Less: Expenses:		
Bad debts	13 000	
Depreciation: office equipment $(44\,000 - 4\,000 \times 25\%)$	10 000	
Insurance $(1\,800 - 200)$	1 600	
Loan interest	7 500	
Loss on disposal of office equipment $(4\,000 - 3\,000 - 500)$	500	
Miscellaneous expenses	57 700	
Provision for doubtful debts		
$(10\% \times (93\,000 - 13\,000) - 2\,000)$	6 000	
Rates $(10\,000 + 2000)$	12 000	108 300
Net loss		£(24 300)

LIME
Balance sheet at 30 September 19X7

	£	£	£
Fixed assets			
Office equipment at cost (44 000 – 4 000)			40 000
Less: Accumulated depreciation			
(22 000 – 3 000 + 10 000)			29 000
			11 000
Current assets			
Stocks		68 000	
Trade debtors (93 000 – 13 000)	80 000		
Less: Provision for doubtful debts	8 000	72 000	
Prepayment		200	
		140 200	
Less: Current liabilities			
Trade creditors	105 000		
Accrual	2 000		
Bank overdraft	15 200	122 200	18 000
			£29 000
Financed by:			
Capital			
Balance at 10 October 19X6			19 300
Less: Net loss for the year		(24 300)	
Add: Drawings		(16 000)	(40 300)
			(21 000)
Loan (from Cedar)			50 000
			£29 000

4.18

TEAK
Trading, profit and loss account for the year to 31 December 19X8

	£	£
Sales		164 000
Less: Cost of goods sold:		
Opening stock	2 800	
Purchases (83 000 – 6 000)	77 000	
	79 800	
Less: Closing stock	15 800	64 000
Gross profit		100 000
Add: Incomes:		
Building society interest (700 + 800)	1 500	
Dividends (100 + 600)	700	
Interest from Gray	500	2 700
		102 700
Less: Expenses:		
Depreciation: Plant and equipment (30 % × 50 000)	15 000	
Vehicles (64 000 – 16 000) × 25%)	12 000	
Office expenses (39 000 + 1 200 – 9 000)	31 200	
Vehicle expenses	12 600	70 800
Net profit		£31 900

TEAK
Balance sheet at 31 December 19X8

	£ Cost	£ Accumulated depreciation	£ Net book value
Fixed assets			
Plant and equipment	50 000	45 000	5 000
Vehicles	64 000	28 000	36 000
	114 000	73 000	41 000
Investments at cost			5 000
Current assets			
Stocks		15 800	
Short-term loan		10 000	
Trade debtors		13 200	
Debtors (800 + 600)		1 400	
Building society deposit		20 000	
Cash at bank and in hand		400	
		60 800	
Less: Current liabilities			
Trade creditors	22 200		
Accrual	1 200	23 400	37 400
			£83 400
Financed by:			
Capital			
Balance at 1 January 19X8			66 500
Net profit for the year		31 900	
Less: Drawings (6 000 + 9 000)		15 000	16 900
			£83 400

Chapter 5

5.1

MEGG
Manufacturing account for the year to 31 January 19X1

	£000	£000
Direct material:		
Stock at 1 February 19X0	10	
Purchases	34	
	44	
Less: Stock at 31 January 19X1	12	
Materials consumed		32
Direct wages		65
Prime cost		97
Factory overhead expenses:		
Administration	27	
Heat and light	9	
Indirect wages	13	49
c/f		146

b/f	146
Add: Work-in-progress at 1 February 19X0	17
Less: Work-in-progress at 31 January 19X1	14
Manufacturing cost of goods produced	£149

5.2

MOOR

Manufacturing, trading, and profit and loss account for the year to 28 February 19X2

	£	£	£
Sales			250 000
Cost of sales:			
Direct materials consumed:			
Stock at 1 March 19X1	13 000		
Purchases	127 500		
	140 500		
Less: Stock at 28 February 19X2	15 500	125 000	
Direct labour		50 000	
Prime cost		175 000	
Factory overheads		27 700	
		202 700	
Add: Work-in-progress at 1 March 19X1		8 400	
		211 100	
Less: Work-in-progress at 28 February 19X2		6 300	
Manufacturing cost		204 800	
Add: Stock of finished goods at			
1 March 19X1		24 000	
		228 000	
Less: Stock of finished goods at			
28 February 19X2		30 000	198 800
Gross profit			51 200
Administration expenses		33 000	
Selling and distribution expenses		10 200	43 200
Net profit			£8 000

5.3

STUART

Manufacturing, trading, and profit and loss account for the year to 31 March 19X3

		£000	£000	£000
Sales				1932
Cost of sales:				
Direct materials consumed:				
Stock at 1 April 19X2		38		
Purchases		1123		
		1161		
Less: Stock at 31 March 19X3		44	1117	
Direct labour			330	
Prime cost	c/f		1447	1932

	b/f		1447	1932
Factory overheads			230	
			1677	
Work-in-progress: at 1 April 19X2		29		
at 31 March 19X3		42	(13)	
Manufacturing cost			1664	
Finished stock: at 1 April 19X2		67		
at 31 March 19X3		65	2	1666
Gross profit				266
Administration expenses			112	
Miscellaneous expenses			16	128
Net profit for the year				£138

STUART

Balance sheet at 31 March 19X3

	£000	£000	£000
Fixed assets			
Plant and machinery at cost			594
Less: Accumulated depreciation			199
			395
Current assets			
Stocks: raw materials	44		
work-in-progress	42		
finished goods	65	151	
Debtors		184	
Bank		7	
		342	
Less: Current liabilities			
Creditors		335	7
			£402
Financed by:			
Capital			
At 1 April 19X2			264
Add: Net profit for the year			138
			£402

5.4

THE DAVID AND PETER MANUFACTURING COMPANY

Manufacturing, trading, and profit and loss account for the year to 30 April 19X4

	£000	£000	£000
Sales			420
Cost of sales:			
Direct materials consumed:			
Stock at 1 May 19X3	12		
Purchases	100		
	112		
Less: Stock at 30 April 19X4	14	98	
Direct labour		70	
Prime cost c/f		168	420

	b/f		168	420
Factory overhead expenses:				
General factory expenses		13		
Heat and light ($\frac{3}{4} \times 52\ 000$)		39		
Rent and rates ($\frac{2}{3} \times 42\ 000$)		28		
Depreciation of equipment ($15\% \times 360\ 000$)		54	134	
			302	
Work-in-progress: at 1 May 19X3		18		
at 30 April 19X4		16	2	
Manufacturing cost			304	
Finished goods: at 1 May 19X3		8		
at 30 April 19X4		22	(14)	290
Gross profit				130
Administration salaries			76	
General office expenses			9	
Heat and light ($\frac{1}{4} \times 52\ 000$)			13	
Rent and rates ($\frac{1}{3} \times 42\ 000$)			14	112
Net profit for the year				£18

THE DAVID AND PETER MANUFACTURING COMPANY
Balance sheet at 30 April 19X4

	£000	£000	£000
Fixed assets			
Equipment at cost			360
Less: Accumulated depreciation ($180 + 54$)			234
			126
Current assets			
Stocks:			
Raw materials	14		
Work-in-progress	16		
Finished goods	22	52	
Debtors		116	
Cash		18	
		186	
Current liabilities			
Creditors		102	84
			£210
Financed by:			
Capital			
At 1 May 19X3			218
Net profit for the year		18	
Less: Drawings		26	(8)
			£210

5.5

JEFFREY

Manufacturing, trading, and profit and loss account for the year to 31 May 19X5

	£000	£000	£000
Sales			693
Cost of sales:			
Direct materials:			
Stock at 1 June 19X4		17	
Purchases		180	
		197	
Less: Stock at 31 May 19X5		20	
		177	
Direct labour		200	
Prime cost		377	
Factory overhead expenses:			
General expenses	60		
Plant depreciation (20% × 160 000)	32	92	
		469	
Work-in-progress: at 1 June 19X4	21		
at 31 May 19X5	30	(9)	
Manufacturing cost		460	
Manufacturing profit (20%)		92	
Market value of goods produced		552	
Purchases of finished goods		55	
		607	
Finished goods stock: at 1 June 19X4	26		
at 31 May 19X5	29	(3)	604
Gross profit on trading			89
Gross profit on manufacture			92
			181
Office expenses		127	
Office equipment depreciation (10% × 30 000)		3	130
Net profit for the year			£51

JEFFREY

Balance sheet at 31 May 19X5

	£000	£000	£000
	Cost	*Depreciation*	*Net book value*
Fixed assets			
Plant	160	102	58
Office equipment	30	12	18
	190	114	c/f 76

	b/f			76
Current assets				
Stocks:				
Raw materials		20		
Work-in-progress		30		
Finished goods		29	79	
Debtors			89	
Bank			6	
			174	
Less: Current liabilities				
Creditors			156	18
				£94
Financed by:				
Capital				
At 1 June 19X4				58
Add: Net profit for the year			51	
Less: Drawings			15	36
				£94

5.6

CLARICO

Manufacturing, trading, and profit and loss account for the year to 30 June 19X6

	£000	£000	£000
Sales			1570
Cost of sales:			
Direct materials consumed:			
Stock at 1 July 19X5		120	
Purchases	450		
Carriage inwards	22	472	
		592	
Less: Stock at 30 June 19X6		102	
		490	
Direct labour		142	
Prime cost		632	
Factory overhead expenses:			
Electricity [(16 + 4) × 80%]	16		
Plant depreciation (20% × 110)	22		
Rent and rates [(70 + 15 − 25) × 60%]	36		
Indirect wages	48	122	
		754	
Work-in-progress: at 1 July 19X5	40		
at 30 June 19X6	74	(34)	
Manufacturing cost		720	
Manufacturing profit (10%)		72	
Market value of goods produced		792	
Purchases of finished goods		30	
c/f		822	1570

	b/f		822	1570
Finished goods stock: at 1 July 19X5		48		
at 30 June 19X6		76	(28)	794
Gross profit on trading				776
Gross profit on manufacture				72
				848
Administration expenses:				
General		39		
Electricity $[(16 + 4) \times 20\%]$		4		
Rent and rates $[(70 + 15 - 25) \times 40\%]$		24		
Wages		26	93	
Selling and distribution expenses:				
Sales expenses		56		
Wages		18		
Delivery van expenses $(12 + 3 - 2)$		13		
Delivery van depreciation $(25\% \times 36)$		9	96	
Other expenses				
Increase in provision for doubtful debts				
$[(10\% \times 800) - 55]$			25	214
Net profit for the year				£634

CLARICO
Balance sheet at 30 June 19X6

	£000	£000	£000
	Cost	*Depreciation*	*Net book value*
Fixed assets			
Plant	110	62	48
Delivery vans	36	27	9
	146	89	57
Current assets			
Stocks:			
Raw materials	102		
Work-in-progress	74		
Finished goods	76	252	
Trade debtors	800		
Less: Provision for doubtful			
debts (10%)	80	720	
Prepayments $(25 + 2)$		27	
Cash		7	
		1006	
Less: Current liabilities			
Trade creditors	265		
Accruals $(4 + 15 + 3)$	22	287	719
			£776
Financed by:			
Capital			
At 1 July 19X5			252
Add: Net profit for the year		634	
Less: Drawings		110	524
			£776

Chapter 6

6.1

MARGO LIMITED
Profit and loss account for the year to 31 January 19X1

	£000
Profit for the financial year	10
Tax on profit	3
	7
Proposed dividend (10p × 50)	5
Retained profit for the year	£2

MARGO LIMITED
Balance sheet at 31 January 19X1

	£000	£000	£000
Fixed assets			
Plant and equipment at cost			70
Less: Accumulated depreciation			25
			45
Current assets			
Stocks		17	
Trade debtors		20	
Cash at bank and in hand		5	
		42	
Less: Current liabilities			
Trade creditors	12		
Taxation	3		
Proposed dividend	5	20	22
			£67

Capital and reserves	*Authorized*	*Issued and fully paid*
	£000	£000
Share capital (ordinary shares of £1 each)	75	50
Profit and loss account (15 + 2)		17
		£67

6.2

HARRY LIMITED
Profit and loss account for the year to 28 February 19X2

	£000	£000
Gross profit for the year		150
Adminitsration expenses [65 + (10% × 60)]	71	
Distribution costs	15	86
Profit for the year		64
Taxation		24
Dividends: Ordinary proposed	20	40
Preference paid	6	26
Retained profit for the year		£14

HARRY LIMITED
Balance sheet at 28 February 19X2

	£000	£000	£000
Fixed assets			
Furniture and equipment at cost			60
Less: Accumulated depreciation			42
			18
Current assets			
Stocks		130	
Trade debtors		135	
Cash at bank and in hand		10	
		275	
Less: Current liabilities			
Trade creditors	25		
Taxation	24		
Proposed dividend	20	69	206
			£224

	Authorized, issued and fully paid £000
Capital and reserves	
Ordinary shares of £1 each	100
Cumulative 15% preference shares of £1 each	40
	140
Share premium account	20
Profit and loss account (50 + 14)	64
	£224

6.3

JIM LIMITED
Trading and profit and loss account for the year to 31 March 19X3

	£000	£000	£000
Sales			270
Less: Cost of goods sold:			
Opening stock		16	
Purchases		124	
		140	
Less: Closing stock		14	126
Gross profit			144
Less: Expenses:			
Advertising		3	
Depreciation: Furniture and fittings (15% × 20)	3		
Vehicles (25% × 40)	10	13	
Directors' fees		6	
Rent and rates		10	
Telephone and stationery		5	
Travelling		2	
Wages and salaries		24	63
Net profit c/f			81

	b/f	81
Corporation tax		25
		56
Proposed dividend		28
Retained profit for the year		£28

JIM LIMITED
Balance sheet at 31 March 19X3

	Cost £000	*Depreciation* £000	*Net book value* £000
Fixed assets			
Vehicles	40	20	20
Furniture and fittings	20	12	8
	60	32	28
Current assets			
Stocks		14	
Debtors		118	
Bank		11	
		143	
Less: Current liabilities			
Creditors	12		
Taxation	25		
Proposed dividend	28	65	78
			£106

	Authorized £000	*Issued and fully paid* £000
Capital and reserves		
Ordinary shares of £1 each	100	70
Profit and loss account (8 + 28)		36
		£106

6.4

CYRIL LIMITED
Trading, profit and loss account for the year to 39 April 19X4

	£000	£000	£000
Sales			900
Less: Cost of goods sold:			
Opening stock		120	
Purchases		480	
		600	
Less: Closing stock		140	460
Gross profit			440
Add: Income:			
Investment income			5
		c/f	445

	£000	£000	£000
			b/f 445
Less: Expenses:			
Advertising		2	
Auditors' remuneration		6	
Bank interest		4	
Directors' remuneration		30	
Depreciation: Buildings	28		
Vehicles	9	37	
General expenses	—	15	
Repairs and renewals (4 – 2)		2	
Wages and salaries		221	317
Net profit			128
Corporation tax			60
			68
Dividends: Proposed ordinary			
(10p per share)		50	
Preference paid		15	65
Retained profit for the year			£3

CYRIL LIMITED
Balance sheet at 30 April 19X4

	Cost £000	Accumulated Depreciation £000	Net book value £000
Fixed assets			
Freehold land and buildings	800	130	670
Motor vehicles	36	27	9
	836	157	679
Investments at cost (Market value £35 000)			30
Current assets			
Stocks		140	
Debtors		143	
Prepayment		2	
		285	
Less: Current liabilities			
Bank overdraft	20		
Creditors	80		
Accrual	6		
Taxation	60		
Proposed dividend	50	216	69
			£778

	Authorized, issued and fully paid £000
Capital and reserves	
Ordinary shares of £1 each	500
Cumulative 10% preference shares of £1 each	150
	650
Share premium account	25
Profit and loss account (100 + 3)	103
	£778

6.5

NELSON LIMITED

Trading, profit and loss account for the year to 31 May 19X5

	£000	£000
Sales		800
Less: Cost of goods sold:		
Opening stock	155	
Purchases	400	
	555	
Less: Closing stock	195	360
Gross profit		440
Add: Income:		
Investment income		22
		462
Less: Expenses:		
Administrative expenses (257 +13)	270	
Auditors' fees	10	
Debenture interest (12% × 100)	12	
Directors' remuneration	60	
Depreciation: Furniture and fittings		
(12.5% × 200)	25	
Wages and salaries (44 − 4)	40	417
Net profit		45
Corporation tax		8
		37
Dividends: Ordinary – interim	20	
– proposed	5	
Preference (paid and payable)	10	35
Retained profit for the year		£2

NELSON LIMITED
Balance sheet at 31 May 19X5

	£000	£000	£000
Fixed assets			
Furniture and fittings at cost			200
Less: Accumulated depreciation			
(48 + 25)			73
			127
Investments at cost (Market value £340 000)			335
Current assets			
Stock		195	
Debtors		225	
Prepayment		4	
Cash at bank and in hand		5	
		429	
Less: Current liabilities			
Creditors	85		
Accruals (13 + 6)	19		
Corporation tax	8		
Proposed dividends: Ordinary	5		
Preference	5	122	307
			£769

Capital and reserves	Authorized	Issued and fully paid
	£000	£000
Ordinary shares of £1 each	500	400
Cumulative 5% preference shares of £1 each	200	200
	700	600
Share premium account		50
Profit and loss account (17 + 2)		19
Shareholders' funds		669
Loans:		
12% Debentures		100
		£769

6.6

KEITH LIMITED
Trading, profit and loss account for the year to 30 June 19X6

	£000	£000
Sales		2100
Less: Cost of goods sold:		
Opening stock	134	
Purchases	1240	
c/f	1374	2100

		£000	£000
	b/f	1374	2100
Less: Closing stock		155	1219
			881
Add: Income:			
Investment income			4
			885
Less: Expenses:			
Advertising		30	
Auditors' remuneration		12	
Debenture interest (10% × 70)		7	
Directors' remuneration		55	
Electricity		28	
Insurance (17 − 3)		14	
Depreciation: Machinery (20% × 420)		84	
Vehicles (25% × 80)		20	
Increase in provision for doubtful debts			
[(5% × 300) − 8]		7	
Office expenses		49	
Rent and rates		75	
Wages and salaries		358	739
Net profit			146
Corporation tax			60
			86
Dividends: Proposed ordinary			
(400 000 × 10p)		40	
Preference		4	44
Retained profit for the year			£42

KEITH LIMITED
Balance sheet at 30 June 19X6

	Cost £000	Accumulated depreciation £000	Net book value £000
Fixed assets			
Machinery	420	236	184
Vehicles	80	60	20
	500	296	204
Investments (Market value £30 000)			28
Current assets			
Stock		155	
Trade debtors	300		
Less: Provision for doubtful			
debts (5%)	15	285	
Prepayment		3	
Bank		7	
	c/f	450	232

	£000	£000	£000
b/f		450	232
Less: Current liabilities			
Creditors	69		
Accruals (7 + 12)	19		
Corporation tax	60		
Proposed dividend	40	188	262
			£494

	Authorized £000	Issued and fully paid £000
Capital and reserves		
Ordinary shares of 50p each	300	200
Cumulative 8% preference shares of £1 each	50	50
	350	250
Profit and loss account (132 + 42)		174
Shareholders' funds		424
Loans:		
10% Debentures		70
		£494

Chapter 7

7.1

DENNIS LIMITED
Cash flow statement for the year ended 31 January 19X2

	£000	£000
Net cash inflow from operating activities		4
Investing activities		
Payments to acquire tangible fixed assets	(100)	
Net cash outflow from investing activities		(100)
Net cash outflow before financing		(96)
Financing		
Issue of ordinary share capital	100	
Net cash inflow from investments		100
Increase in cash and cash equivalents		£4

Notes to the cash flow statement:

1 Reconciliation of operating profit to net cash inflow from operating activities

	£000
Operating profit (60 – 26)	34
Increase in stocks	(20)
Increase in debtors	(50)
Increase in creditors	40
Net cash inflow from operating activities	4

2 Analysis of changes in cash and cash equivalents during the year

	£000
Balance at 1 February 19X1	6
Net cash inflow	4
Balance at 31 January 19X2	10

3 Analysis of the balances of cash equivalents as shown in the balance sheet

	19X2 £000	19X1 £000	Change in year £000
Cash at bank and in hand	10	6	4

4 Analysis of changes in financing during the year

	Share Capital £000
Balance at 1 February 19X1	700
Cash inflow from financing	100
Balance at 31 January 19X2	800

7.2

FRANK LIMITED
Cash flow statement for the year ended 28 February 19X2

	£000	£000
Net cash inflow from operating activities		70
Investing activities		
Purchase of investments	(100)	
Net cash outflow from investing activities		(100)
Net cash outflow before financing		(30)
Financing		
Issue of debenture loan	60	
Net cash inflow from investments		60
Increase in cash and cash equivalents		£30

Notes to the cash flow statement:

1 Reconciliation of operating profit to net cash inflow from operating activities

	£000
Operating profit (40 − 30)	10
Depreciation charges	20
Increase in stocks	(30)
Decrease in debtors	110
Decrease in creditors	(40)
Net cash inflow from operating activities	70

2 Analysis of changes in cash and cash equivalents during the year

	£000
Balance at 1 March 19X1	(20)
Net cash inflow	30
Balance at 28 February 19X2	10

3 Analysis of the balances of cash equivalents as shown in the balance sheet

	19X2 £000	19X1 £000	Change in year £000
Cash at bank and in hand	10		10
Bank overdraft		(20)	20
	10	(20)	30

4 Analysis of changes in financing during the year

	Debenture loan £000
Balance at 1 March 19X1	
Cash inflow from financing	60
Balance at 28 February 19X2	60

Note: No details of debenture interest were given in the question.

7.3

STARTER

Cash flow statement for the year ended 31 March 19X3

	£	£
Net cash in flow from operating activities		2 500
Investing activities		
Payments to acquire tangible fixed assets	(10 000)	
Net cash outflow from investing activities		(10 000)
Net cash outflow before financing		(7 500)
Financing		
Capital introduced	20 000	
Net cash inflow from investments		20 000
Increase in cash and cash equivalents		£12 500

Notes to the cash flow statements:

1 Reconciliation of operating profit to net cash inflow from operating activities

	£
Operating profit	4 000
Depreciation charges	2 000
Increase in stocks	(1 000)
Increase in trade debtors	(5 000)
Increase in trade creditors	2 500
Net cash inflow from operating activities	2 500

2 Analysis of chages in cash and cash equivalents during the year
   Balance at 1 April 19X2

	£
Net cash inflow	12 500
Balance at 31 March 19X3	12 500

3 Analysis of the balances of cash equivalents as shown in the balance sheet

	19X3 £	19X2 £	Change in year £
Cash at bank and in hand	12 500	–	12 500

4 Analysis of changes in financing during the year

	Capital £
Balance at 1 April 19X2	–
Cash inflow from financing	20 000
Balance at 31 March 19X3	20 000

7.4

GREGORY LIMITED
Cash flow statement for the year ended 30 April 19X4

	£000	£000
Net cash inflow from operating activities		145
Return on investments and servicing of finance		
Dividends paid	(35)	
Net cash outflow from servicing of finance		(35)
Taxation		
Corporation tax paid	(18)	
Tax paid		(18)
Investing activities		
Payments to acquire tangible fixed assets	(150)	
Net cash outflow from investing activities		(150)
Net cash outflow before financing		(58)
Financing		
Issue of debenture loan	50	
Net cash inflow from financing		50
Decrease in cash and cash equivalents		£(8)

Notes to the cash flow statement:

1 Reconciliation of operating profit to net cash inflow from operating activities

	£000
Operating profit	75
Depreciation charges	80
Increase in stocks	(40)
Decrease in debtors	20
Increase in creditors	10
Net cash inflow from operating activities	145

2 Analysis of changes in cash and cash equivalents during the year

	£000
Balance at 1 May 19X3	10
Net cash outflow	(8)
Balance at 30 April 19X4	2

3 Analysis of the balances of cash equivalents as shown in the balance sheet

	19X4 £000	19X3 £000	Change in year £000
Cash at bank and in hand	2	10	(8)

4 Analysis of changes in financing during the year

	Debenture loan £000
Balance at 1 May 19X3	–
Cash inflow from financing	50
Balance at 30 April 19X4	50

7.5

PILL LIMITED
Cash flow statement for the year ended 31 May 19X5

	£000	£000
Net cash inflow from operating activities		554
Return on investments and servicing of finance		
Interest paid (10% × 40)	(4)	
Dividends paid (150 + 250 – 100)	(300)	
Net cash outflow from servicing of finance		(304)
Taxation		
Corporation tax paid (170 + 150 – 220)	(100)	
Tax paid		(100)
Investing activities		
Payments to acquire tangible fixed assets		
[(800 – 600) + 250 – 200]	(250)	
Net cash outflow from investing activities		(250)
Net cash outflow before financing		(100)
Financing		
Issue of ordinary share capital (550 – 500)	50	
Repurchase of debenture loan (190 – 40)	(150)	
Net cash outflow from financing		(100)
Decrease in cash and cash equivalents		£(200)

Notes to the cash flow statement:

1 Reconciliation of operating profit to net cash inflow from operating activities

	£000
Operating profit [580 + (10% × 40)]	584
Depreciation charges	100
Increase in stocks	(140)
Increase in debtors	(20)
Increase in creditors	30
Net cash inflow from operating activities	554

2 Analysis of changes in cash and cash equivalents during the year

	£000
Balance at 1 June 19X4	320
Net cash outflow	(200)
Balance at 31 May 19X5	120

3 Analysis of the balances of cash equivalents as shown in the balance sheet

	19X5	19X4	Change in year
	£000	£000	£000
Cash at bank and in hand	120	320	(200)

4 Analysis of changes in financing during the year

	Share capital	Debenture loan
	£000	£000
Balance at 1 June 19X4	500	190
Cash inflow from financing	50	(150)
Balance at 31 May 19X5	550	40

7.6

BRIAN LIMITED
Cash flow statement for the year ended 30 June 19X6

	£000	£000
Net cash inflow from operating activities		137
Return on investments and servicing of finance		
Dividends paid	(20)	
Net cash outflow from servicing of finance	—	(20)
Taxation		
Corporation tax paid	(52)	
Tax paid	—	(52)
Investing activities		
Payments to acquire tangible fixed assets	(75)	
Receipts from sales of tangible fixed assets	12	
Net cash outflow from investing activities		(63)
Increase in cash and cash equivalents		£2

Notes to the cash flow statement:

1 Reconciliation of operating profit to net cash inflow from operating activities

	£000
Operating profit	115
Depreciation charges	35
Loss on sale of vehicle	3
Increase in provision for doubtful debts	1
Decrease in stocks	10
Increase in trade debtors	(20)
Decrease in trade creditors	(7)
Net cash inflow from operating activities	137

2 Analysis of changes in cash and cash equivalents during the year

	£000
Balance at 1 July 19X5	6
Net cash inflow	2
Balance at 30 June 19X6	8

3 Analysis of the balances of cash equivalents as shown in the balance sheet

	19X6 £000	19X5 £000	Change in year £000
Cash at bank and in hand	8	6	2

Chapter 8

8.1 BETTY

Accounting ratios year to 31 January 19X1:

1 Gross profit ratio:

$$\frac{\text{Gross profit}}{\text{Total sales revenue}} \times 100 = \frac{30}{100} \times 100 = 30\%$$

2 Net profit ratio:

$$\frac{\text{Net profit}}{\text{Sales}} \times 100 = \frac{14}{100} \times 100 = 14\%$$

3 Return on captial employed:

$$\frac{\text{Net profit}}{\text{Average capital}} \times 100 = \frac{14}{\frac{1}{2}(40 + 48)} \times 100 = 31.8\%$$

$$or \ \frac{\text{Net profit}}{\text{Capital}} \times 100 = \frac{14}{48} \times 100 = 29.2\%$$

4 Current ratio:

$$\frac{\text{Current assets}}{\text{Current liabilities}} = \frac{25}{6} = 4.2 \text{ to } 1$$

5 Acid test:

$$\frac{\text{Current assets} - \text{stock}}{\text{Current liabilities}} = \frac{25 - 10}{6} = 2.5 \text{ to } 1$$

6 Stock turnover:

$$\frac{\text{Cost of goods sold}}{\text{Average stock}} = \frac{70}{\frac{1}{2}(15 + 10)} = 5.6 \text{ times}$$

7 Debtor collection period:

$$\frac{\text{Trade debtors}}{\text{Credit sales}} \times 365 = \frac{12}{100} \times 365 = 43.8 \text{ days}$$

8.2 **JAMES LIMITED**

Accounting ratios year to 28 February 19X2:

1 Return on capital employed:

$$\frac{\text{Net profit before taxation and dividends}}{\text{Average shareholders' funds}} \times 100 = \frac{90}{\frac{1}{2}(600 + 620)} \times 100 = 14.8\%$$

$$or \quad \frac{\text{Net profit before taxation and dividends}}{\text{Shareholders' funds}} \times 100 = \frac{90}{620} \times 100 = 14.5\%$$

2 Gross profit:

$$\frac{\text{Gross profit}}{\text{Sales}} \times 100 = \frac{600}{1200} \times 100 = 50\%$$

3 Mark-up:

$$\frac{\text{Gross profit}}{\text{Cost of goods sold}} \times 100 = \frac{600}{600} \times 100 = 100\%$$

4 Net profit:

$$\frac{\text{Net profit before taxation and dividends}}{\text{Sales}} \times 100 = \frac{90}{1200} \times 100 = 7.5\%$$

5 Acid test:

$$\frac{\text{Current assets} - \text{stock}}{\text{Current liabilities}} = \frac{275 - 75}{240} = 0.83 \text{ to } 1$$

6 Fixed assets turnover:

$$\frac{\text{Sales}}{\text{Fixed assets (NBV)}} = \frac{1200}{685} = 1.75 \text{ times}$$

7 Debtor collection period:

$$\frac{\text{Trade debtors}}{\text{Credit sales}} \times 365 = \frac{200}{1200} \times 365 = 60.8 \text{ days}$$

8 Capital gearing:

$$\frac{\text{Long-term loans}}{\text{Shareholders' funds and long-term loans}} \times 100 = \frac{100}{720} \times 100 = \underline{\underline{13.9\%}}$$

8.3 Accounting ratios year to 31 March 19X3

	Mark Limited	Luke Limited	John Limited
1 Return on capital employed:			
$\dfrac{\text{Net profit before taxation and dividends}}{\text{Shareholders' funds}} \times 100$	$\dfrac{64}{250} \times 100$ $= \underline{\underline{25.6\%}}$	$\dfrac{22}{327} \times 100$ $= \underline{\underline{6.7\%}}$	$\dfrac{55}{290} \times 100$ $= \underline{\underline{19.0\%}}$
2 Capital gearing:			
$\dfrac{\text{Preference shares + Long-term loans}}{\text{Shareholders' funds + Long-term loans}} \times 100$	No preference shares or long-term loans	$\dfrac{20}{327} \times 100$ $= \underline{\underline{6.1\%}}$	$\dfrac{10 + 100}{390} \times 100$ $= \underline{\underline{28.2\%}}$

8.4 HELENA LIMITED
Accounting ratios 19X2 to 19X6

	19X2	19X3	19X4	19X5	19X6
1 Gross profit: $\dfrac{\text{Gross profit}}{\text{Sales}} \times 100$	$\dfrac{30}{130} \times 100$ $= 23.1\%$	$\dfrac{40}{150} \times 100$ $= 26.7\%$	$\dfrac{60}{190} \times 100$ $= 31.6\%$	$\dfrac{70}{210} \times 100$ $= 33.3\%$	$\dfrac{75}{320} \times 100$ $= 23.4\%$
2 Mark up: $\dfrac{\text{Gross profit} \times 100}{\text{Cost of goods sold}}$	$\dfrac{30}{100} \times 100$ $= 30\%$	$\dfrac{40}{110} \times 100$ $= 36.4\%$	$\dfrac{60}{130} \times 100$ $= 46.2\%$	$\dfrac{70}{140} \times 100$ $= 50\%$	$\dfrac{75}{245} \times 100$ $= 30.6\%$
3 Stock turnover: $\dfrac{\text{Cost of goods sold}}{\text{Average stock}}$	$\dfrac{100}{\frac{1}{2}(20+30)}$ $= 4 \text{ times}$	$\dfrac{110}{\frac{1}{2}(30+30)}$ $= 3.7 \text{ times}$	$\dfrac{130}{\frac{1}{2}(30+35)}$ $= 4 \text{ times}$	$\dfrac{140}{\frac{1}{2}(35+40)}$ $= 3.7 \text{ times}$	$\dfrac{245}{\frac{1}{2}(40+100)}$ $= 3.5 \text{ times}$
4 Trade debtor collection period: $\dfrac{\text{Average trade debtors}}{\text{Credit sales}} \times 365$	$\dfrac{\frac{1}{2}(45+40)}{130} \times 365$ $= 119.3 \text{ days}$	$\dfrac{\frac{1}{2}(40+45)}{150} \times 365$ $= 103.4 \text{ days}$	$\dfrac{\frac{1}{2}(70+40)}{190} \times 365$ $= 105.7 \text{ days}$	$\dfrac{\frac{1}{2}(100+70)}{210} \times 365$ $= 147.7 \text{ days}$	$\dfrac{\frac{1}{2}(150+100)}{320} \times 365$ $= 142.6 \text{ days}$
5 Trade creditor payment period: $\dfrac{\text{Average trade creditors}}{\text{Credit purchases}} \times 365$	$\dfrac{\frac{1}{2}(20+20)}{110} \times 365$ $= 66.4 \text{ days}$	$\dfrac{\frac{1}{2}(25+20)}{110} \times 365$ $= 74.7 \text{ days}$	$\dfrac{\frac{1}{2}(25+25)}{135} \times 365$ $= 67.6 \text{ days}$	$\dfrac{\frac{1}{2}(30+25)}{145} \times 365$ $= 69.2 \text{ days}$	$\dfrac{\frac{1}{2}(60+30)}{305} \times 365$ $= 53.9 \text{ days}$

8.5 HEDGE PLC
Accounting ratios:

1 Dividend yield:

$$\frac{\text{Dividend per share}}{\text{Market price per share}} \times 100 = \frac{7}{350} \times 100 = 2\%$$

2 Dividend cover:

$$\frac{\text{Net profit after taxation}}{\text{Ordinary dividends}} = \frac{70\,000}{35\,000} = 2 \text{ times}$$

3 Earnings per share:

$$\frac{\text{Net profit after taxation}}{\text{Number of ordinary shares in issue}} = \frac{70\,000}{500\,000} = 14\text{p}$$

4 Price/earnings ratio:

$$\frac{\text{Market price per share}}{\text{Earnings per share}} = \frac{3.50}{0.14} = 25$$

8.6 (a)
STYLE LIMITED
Accounting ratios:

1 Gross profit:

	19X5	19X6
$\dfrac{\text{Gross profit}}{\text{Sales}} \times 100$	$\dfrac{525}{1500} \times 100 = 35\%$	$\dfrac{600}{1900} \times 100 = 31.6\%$

2 Mark-up:

$$\frac{\text{Gross profit}}{\text{Cost of goods sold}} \times 100 \qquad \frac{525}{975} \times 100 = 53.8\% \qquad \frac{600}{1300} \times 100 = 46.2\%$$

3 Net profit:

$$\frac{\text{Net profit}}{\text{Sales}} \times 100 \qquad \frac{275}{1500} \times 100 = 18.3\% \qquad \frac{250}{1900} \times 100 = 13.2\%$$

4 Return on capital employed:

$$\frac{\text{Net profit}}{\text{Shareholders' funds}} \times 100 \qquad \frac{275 \times 100}{\frac{1}{2}(900 + 1000)} \qquad \frac{250 \times 100}{\frac{1}{2}(900 + 1250)}$$

$$= 28.9\% \qquad\qquad = 23.3\%$$

or

$$\frac{\text{Net profit}}{\text{Shareholders' funds}} \times 100 \qquad \frac{275 \times 100}{1000} \times 100 \qquad \frac{250}{1250} \times 100$$

$$= 27.5\% \qquad\qquad = 20.0\%$$

5 Stock turnover:

$$\frac{\text{Cost of goods sold}}{\text{Average stock}} \qquad \frac{975}{\frac{1}{2}(£80 + 100)} = 10.8 \text{ times} \qquad \frac{1300}{\frac{1}{2}(£100 + 200)} = 8.7 \text{ times}$$

6 Current ratio:

$$\frac{\text{Current assets}}{\text{Current liablilities}} \qquad \frac{500}{80} = 6.3 \text{ to } 1 \qquad \frac{1000}{210} = 4.8 \text{ to } 1$$

7 Acid test:

$$\frac{\text{Current assets} - \text{stock}}{\text{Current liabilities}} \qquad \frac{500 - 100}{80} = 5 \text{ to } 1 \qquad \frac{1000 - 200}{210} = 3.8 \text{ to } 1$$

8 Trade debtor collection period:

$$\frac{\text{Trade debtors}}{\text{Credit sales}} \times 365 \qquad \frac{375}{1500} \times 365 = 92 \text{ days} \qquad \frac{800}{1900} \times 365 = 154 \text{ days}$$

9 Trade creditor payment period:

$$\frac{\text{Trade creditors}}{\text{Purchases}} \times 365 \qquad \frac{80}{995} \times 365 = 30 \text{ days} \qquad \frac{200}{1400} \times 365 = 53 \text{ days}$$

(b) *Brief comments*

The company increased its sales in 19X6 by £400 000 (26.7%). It appeared to achieve this by reducing its profit on goods sold, but the increased activity probably resulted in additional expenses. As a result, even in absolute terms, its net profit was down from £275 000 to £250 000. It should also be noted there is no explanation why an amount was not set aside for taxation or dividends either in 19X5 or 19X6.

Its liquidity position is still healthy, even if its debtor collection period (based on year-end figures) has increased substantially (as has the time taken to pay the creditors). This may be a deliberate policy to stimulate sales or it may be that it has been too busy to encourage its customers to settle their debts.

Not surprisingly, the cash position has deteriorated and at the end of 19X6 the company was in overdraft.

Increased trading activity does not always guarantee survival if the company cannot settle its debts as they fall due. Unless it becomes more efficient in this respect, the company's long-term future could be uncertain.

Chapter 9

9.1 *Financial accounting* is mainly concerned with supplying information to the external users of an entity.

Management accounting is concerned with producing information for use within an entity.

9.2 1 Elements
2 Units
3 Direct and indirect
4 Fixed and variable
5 Controllable and non-controllable
6 Relevant and irrelevant
7 Responsibility
8 Normal and abnormal

9.3 1 Board of directors
2 Divisions
3 Factories or works

    4 Functions
    5 Cost centres

9.4 A clearly defined area of responsibility that is charged with its own indentified operating costs. A cost centre may take the form of a department, an area, a machine or an individual (such as a salesperson).

9.5 In *absorption costing*, all production costs (including fixed production overheads) are charged out to individual units or processes.

In *marginal costing*, fixed production overheads are not charged out to individual units or processes.

Chapter 10

10.1 1 FIFO:

		£
1000 units	@ £20 =	20 000
250 units	@ £25 =	6 250
Charge to production		£26 250

2 LIFO:

		£
500 units	@ £25 =	12 500
750 units	@ £20 =	15 000
Charge to production		£27 500

3 Periodic weighted average:

Units		Value £
1 000	@ £20	20 000
500	@ £25	12 500
1 500		£32 500

$$\text{Average} = \frac{32\ 500}{1\ 500} = £21.67$$

Charge to production = 1 250 × 21.67 = £27 088

10.2 MATERIAL ST 2

	Stock	Units	Total stock value £	Average unit price £
1.02.X2	Opening	500	500	1.00
10.02.X2	Receipts	200	220	
		700	720	1.03
12.02.X2	Receipts	100	112	
		800	832	1.04
17.02.X2	Issues	(400)	(416)	
	c/f	400	416	

			£	£
	b/f	400	416	
25.02.X2	Receipts	300	345	
		700	761	1.09
27.02.X2	Issues	(250)	(273)	
28.02.X2	*Closing stock*	£450	£488	

10.3 Closing stock calculations:

1 FIFO:

800 units		@ £12 =	£9 600

2 LIFO:

			£
600 units		@ £12 =	7 200
200 units		@ £10 =	2 000
800			£9 200

3 Continuous weighted average:

		Units	Total stock Value £	Average unit price £
	Stock	*Units*		
1.01.X3	Purchases	2 000	20 000	10.00
31.03.X3	Issues	(1 600)	(16 000)	
		400	4 000	
1.02.X3	Purchases	2 400	26 400	
		2 800	30 400	10.86
28.02.X3	Issues	(2 600)	(28 236)	
		200	2 164	
1.03.X3	Purchases	1 600	19 200	
		1 800	21 364	11.87
31.03.X3	Issues	(1 000)	(11 870)	
		800	£9 494	

10.4 Calculation of closing stock:

	Units	*Value* £
Total receipts:	240	1692

Periodic weighted average price: $\dfrac{1692}{240} = £7.05$

Total issues: 195 units – all issued at £7.05 = £1375

	£	*Units*
In stock at 30.04.X4 *Less:* Issues		
1,692 – 1,375 =	317	45 (240 – 195)
Add: Stock at 1.04.X4	120	20
Closing stock at 30.04.X4	£437	65

10.5

STEED LIMITED
Trading Account for the year to 31 May 19X5

	FIFO	LIFO	Periodic weighted average	Continuous weighted average
	£	£	£	£
Sales	500 000	500 000	500 000	500 000
Less: Cost of goods sold:				
Opening stock	40 000	40 000	40 000	40 000
Purchases	440 000	440 000	440 000	440 000
	480 000	480 000	480 000	480 000
Less: Closing stock	90 000	65 000	67 500	79 950
	390 000	415 000	412 500	400 050
Gross profit	£110 000	£85 000	£87 500	£99 950

10.6   IRON LIMITED

(a) Pricing the issue of materials to production

    1 *First in, first out (FIFO):*

       Total receipts   = 2 400 litres

       Total issues   = 2 200 litres

       Therefore closing stock = 200 litres @ £5 per litre = £1 000

    2 *Last in, first out (LIFO):*

       Closing stock position at 31 December 19X4:

		£
October receipts	All issued in December	
June receipts:	400 litres issued in July	
	400 litres issued in December	
April receipts:	300 litres issued in May	
	leaving	
	100 litres in stock @ £3.00	
	per litre =	300
January receipts:	100 litres issued in February	
	leaving	
	100 litres in stock @ £2.00	
	per litre =	200
Closing stock value:		£500

    3 *Periodic weighted average:*

       Total vaue of receipts = £9 600

       Total receipts = 2 400 litres

       Therefore periodic weighted average price per litre = £4.00.

       Value of stock = £4 × 200 litres = £800

4 *Continuous weighted average:*

Month	Quantity	Stock balance Value	Average price per litre in stock	Issued at per litre
	(litres)	£	£	£
January	200	400	2.00	
February	(100)	(200)		2.00
	100	200		
April	500	1 500		
	600	1 700	2.83	
May	(300)	(849)		2.83
	300	851		
June	800	3 200		
	1 100	4 051	3.68	
July	(400)	(1 472)		3.68
	700	2 579		
October	900	4 500		
	1 600	7 079	4.42	
December	(1 400)	(6 188)		4.42
	200	£891		

(b) Calculation of gross profit
Method

	1 FIFO	2 LIFO	3 Periodic weighted average	4 Continuous weighted average
	£	£	£	£
Sales	20 000	20 000	20 000	20 000
Less: Cost of goods sold:				
Purchases	9 600	9 600	9 600	9 600
Less: Closing stock	1 000	500	800	891
	8 600	9 100	8 800	8 709
Conversion costs	7 000	7 000	7 000	7 000
Manufacturing cost	15 600	16 100	15 800	15 709
Gross profit	£4 400	£3 900	£4 200	£4 291

Chapter 11

11.1 SCAR LIMITED

Overhead apportionment January 19X1:

	Production Department A £000	Production Department B £000	Service Department £000
Allocated expenses	65	35	50
Apportionment of services department's expenses in the ratio 60:40	30	20	(50)
Overhead to be charged	£95	£55	–

11.2 BANK LIMITED

Assembly department – overhead absorption methods:

1 Specific units:

$$\frac{\text{Total cost centre overhead}}{\text{Number of units}} = \frac{250\ 000}{50\ 000} = £5 \text{ per unit}$$

2 Direct materials:

$$\frac{\text{Total cost centre overhead}}{\text{Direct materials}} \times 100 = \frac{250\ 000}{500\ 000} \times 100 = 50\%$$

Therefore 50% of £8 = £4 per unit

3 Direct labour:

$$\frac{\text{Total cost centre overhead}}{\text{Direct labour}} \times 100 = \frac{250\ 000}{1\ 000\ 000} \times 100 = 25\%$$

Therefore 25% of £30 = £7.50 per unit

4 Prime cost:

$$\frac{\text{Total cost centre overhead}}{\text{Prime cost}} \times 100 = \frac{250\ 000}{1\ 530\ 000} \times 100 = 16.34\%$$

Therefore 16.34% of £40 = £6.54 per unit

5 Direct labour hours:

$$\frac{\text{Total cost centre overhead}}{\text{Direct labour hours}} = \frac{250\ 000}{100\ 000} = £2.50 \text{ per direct labour hour}$$

Therefore £2.50 of 3.5 DLH = £8.75 per unit

6 Machine hours:

$$\frac{\text{Total cost centre overhead}}{\text{Machine hours}} - \frac{250\ 000}{25\ 000} = £10 \text{ per machinc hour}$$

Therefore £10 of 0.75 = £7.50 per unit

11.3 CLOUGH LIMITED

(a) Overhead absorption for March 19X3 – Production department:

1 Direct labour hours:

$$\frac{\text{Total cost centre overhead}}{\text{Direct labour hours}} = \frac{150\,000}{30\,000} = £5 \text{ per DLH}$$

Therefore for order number 123: £5 × 5 = £25

2 Machine hours:

$$\frac{\text{Total cost centre overheads}}{\text{Machine hours}} = \frac{150\,000}{10\,000} = £15 \text{ per MH}$$

Therefore for order number 123 : £15 × 2 = £30

Selling price of order number 123	*Direct labour hours* £	*Machine hours* £
Direct materials	20	20
Direct wages	25	25
Prime costs	45	45
Overhead	25	30
Total cost	70	75
Administration + profit (50%)	35	37.50
Selling price	£105	£112.50

(b) As the department appears more labour intensive than machine intensive, use the direct labour hour method.

11.4 BURNS LIMITED

Overhead absorption schedule – April 19X4

	Processing £	Assembling £	Finishing £	Administration £	Work study £
			Departments		
Direct labour	–	–	–	65 000	33 000
Allocated costs	15 000	20 000	10 000	35 000	12 000
				100 000	
Apportion: Administration (50:30:15:5)	50 000	30 000	15 000	(100 000)	5 000
					50 000
Work study (70:20:10)	35 000	10 000	5 000	–	(50 000)
Overhead to be absorbed	£100 000	£60 000	£30 000	–	–

Calculation of absorbtion rates:

Processing department: $\dfrac{\text{TCCO}}{\text{Machine hours}} = \dfrac{100\,000}{25\,000} = £4 \text{ per MH}$

Assembling department: $\dfrac{\text{TCCO}}{\text{Direct labour hours}} = \dfrac{60\,000}{30\,000} = £2 \text{ per DLH}$

Finishing department: $\dfrac{\text{TCCO}}{\text{Direct labour cost}} \times 100 = \dfrac{30\ 000}{120\ 000} \times 100 = \underline{\underline{25\%}}$

Total cost of producing unit XP6:

	£	£
Prime cost		47
Overhead:		
Processing (4×6 MH)	24	
Assembling (2×1)	2	
Finishing ($25\% \times 12$)	3	29
Total cost		£76

11.3 OUTLANE LIMITED

(a) *Overhead charge – direct labour cost method:*

	Contract 1	Contract 2
Direct labour cost:		
DLH × rate per hour = $100 \times £3.00$	£300	£300
Therefore overhead to be absorbed		
(100%) =	£300	£300

(b) *Overhead charge – machine hour rate method:*

Overhead absorption schedule

	Apportionment method	L £000	M £000	N £000	O £000
Administration	Total number of employees	40	30	20	10
Depreciation of machinery	Depreciation rate	22	8	10	40
Employer's National Insurance	Total number of employees	4	3	2	1
Heating and light	Cubic capacity	6	3	1	5
Holiday pay	Total number of employees	8	6	4	2
Indirect labour cost	Number of indirect employees	4	3	2	1
Insurance: machinery	Capital cost	11	4	5	20
property	Floor space	4	3	2	2
Machine maintenance	Maintenance hours	15	12	9	6
Power	Kilowatt hours	30	50	90	60
Rent and rates	Floor space	20	15	10	10
Supervision	Total number of employees	20	15	10	5
Overhead to be absorbed		184	152	165	162
÷ Machine hours		92	38	165	27
= Overhead absorption rate		£2	£4	£1	£6

Department	Contract 1			Contract 2		
	Machine hours	Absorption rate	Total	Machine hours	Absorption rate	Total
		£	£		£	£
L	60	2	120	20	2	40
M	30	4	120	10	4	40
N	10	1	10	10	1	10
O	–	–	–	60	6	360
Total overhead to be absorbed			£250			£450

11.6 SARAH LIMITED

Overhead absorption schedule for June 19X6:

Cost centre	Production		Service		
	D	P	1	2	3
	£000	£000	£000	£000	£000
Method 1: specified order of closure					
Allocated costs	45	35	160	71	34
Apportion the service cost centre costs in the following order (different orders are possible):					
1 (55 : 20 : 15 : 10)	88	32	(160)	24	16
				95	
2 (45 : 40 : – : 10)	45	40	–	(95)	10
3 (50 : 10)	50	10	–	–	(60)
Overhead to be absorbed	£228	£117	–	–	–
Method 2: Ignore inter-department servicing					
Allocated costs	45	35	160	71	34
Apportion the service cost centre costs as follows:					
1 (55 : 20)	117	43	(160)	–	–
2 (45 : 40)	38	33	–	(71)	–
3 (50 : 10)	28	6	–	–	(34)
Overhead to be absorbed	£228	£117	–	–	–

Chapter 12

12.1

POLE LIMITED

Marginal cost statement for the year to 31 January 19X2

	£000	£000
Sales		450
Less: Variable costs:		
Direct materials	60	
Direct wages	26	
Administration expenses: variable (7 + 4)	11	
Research and development expenditure:		
variable (15 + 5)	20	
Selling and distribution expenditure:		
variable (4 + 9)	13	
		130
		320
Contribution		
Less: Fixed costs:		
Administration expenses (30 + 16)	46	
Materials: indirect	5	
Production overhead	40	
Research and development expenditure		
(60 + 5)	65	
Selling and distribution expenditure		
(80 + 21)	101	
Wages: indirect	13	270
Profit		£50

12.2 GILES LIMITED

(a) (i) *Break-even point*

In value terms:

$$\frac{\text{Fixed costs} \times \text{sales}}{\text{Contribution}} = \frac{150}{(500 - 300)} \times 500 = £375\,000$$

In units:

	£
Selling price per unit (500 ÷ 50)	10
Less: Variable cost per unit (300 ÷ 50)	6
Contribution per unit	£4

$$\frac{\text{Fixed costs}}{\text{Contribution per unit}} = \frac{150\,000}{4} = 37\,500 \text{ units}$$

(ii) Margin of safety

In value terms:

$$\frac{\text{Profit} \times \text{sales}}{\text{Contribution}} = \frac{50 \times 500}{200} = £125\,000$$

In units:

$$\frac{\text{Profit}}{\text{Contribution per unit}} = \frac{50\,000}{4} = 12\,500 \text{ units}$$

12.2 (b) *Break-even chart*

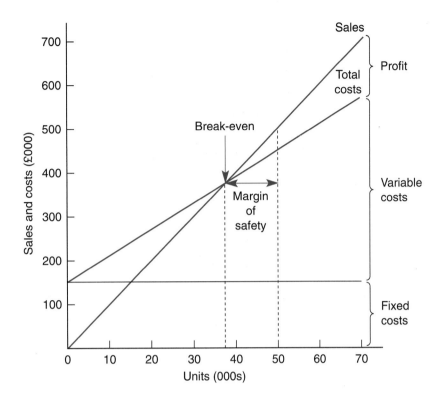

12.3 AYRE LIMITED

Since the company makes a profit of £100 000 on sales of £750 000, all the fixed costs must have been covered. A rise in sales, therefore, of £250 000 (1 000 000 – 750 000) giving an increase in profit of £150 000 (250 000 – 100 000) means that the increased variable cost was £100 000. Therefore the profit/volume ratio is 60% (150/250 × 100) and the variable cost of sales must be 40%.

Year to 31 March 19X3	*Budget*	*Actual*
	£000	*£000*
Budget sales	1200	1000
Less: Variable costs (40%)	480	400
Contribution	720	600
Less: Fixed costs (60% × 1 000 – profit of 250)	350	350
Budget profit	£370	£250

12.4

CARTER LIMITED
Marginal cost statement year to 30 April 19X3

	Per unit	Total
		(50 000 units)
	£	£000
Selling price	40	2000
Variable cost	24	1200
Contribution	16	800
Less: Fixed costs		350
Profit		£450

Budgeted marginal cost statement year to 30 April 19X4

	Per unit	Total
		£000
Selling price (40 – 20%)	32	
Variable costs	24	
Contribution	8	830*
Fixed costs		380
Profit required		£450

*Contribution required.

$$\text{Therefore number of units to be sold} = \frac{830\,000}{8} = 103\,750 \text{ units.}$$

103 750 units will have to be sold in 19X4 to make the same amount of profit as in 19X3 if the company reduces its selling price per unit by 20% and increases its fixed costs by £30 000 per annum.

12.5 PUZZLED LIMITED
Option 1 – Reduce the selling price by 15%:

	£
New selling price per unit	8.50
Variable cost per unit	7.50
Contribution per unit	£1.00

$$\text{Therefore break-even} = \frac{\text{Fixed costs}}{\text{Contribution per unit}} = \frac{40\,000}{1.00} = 40\,000 \text{ units}$$

Option 2 – Improve the product:

	£
Selling price per unit	10.00
New variable cost per unit	8.80
Contribution per unit	£1.20

$$\text{Therefore break-even} = \frac{\text{Fixed costs}}{\text{Contribution per unit}} = \frac{40\,000}{1.20} = 33\,333 \text{ units}$$

Option 3 – Advertising campaign:

	£
Selling price per unit	10.00
Variable cost per unit	7.50
Contribution per unit	£2.50

$$\text{Therefore break-even} = \frac{\text{Fixed costs}}{\text{Contribution per unit}} = \frac{40\ 000 + 15\ 000}{2.50}$$

$$= 22\ 000 \text{ units}$$

Option 4 – Improve factory efficiency:

$$\text{Break-even} = \frac{\text{Fixed costs}}{\text{Contribution per unit}} = \frac{40\ 000 + 22\ 500}{2.50}$$

$$= 25\ 000 \text{ units}$$

Conclusion

The advertising campaign would require fewer extra units to be sold in 19X5 compared with 19X4 in order to break even: 22 000 units compared with 16 000 (40 000 ÷ 2.50).

This would require an increase of 10% on the current year's sales just to break even, although it is fewer than the other options. To make the same profit as in 19X4, 30 000 units would have to be sold (30 000 × 2.50 = 75 000, to cover the fixed costs of £55 000 + the profit of £20 000). Would the campaign also have to be repeated in future years? Has the company got the immediate cash resources in order to carry out the campaign? Can the sales be increased by the required amount simply by advertising?

12.6 MICRO LIMITED

Budgeted contribution per unit of limiting factor for the year:

$$\frac{250\ 000}{50\ 000} = £5 \text{ per direct labour hour}$$

Contribution per unit of limiting factor for the special contract:

	£	£
Contract price		50 000
Less: Variable costs:		
Direct materials	10 000	
Direct labour	30 000	40 000
Contribution		£10 000

Therefore contribution per unit of limiting factor:

$$\frac{10\ 000}{4000} = £2.50 \text{ per direct labour hour}$$

Conclusion

The special contract earns less contribution per unit of limiting factor than does the *average* of ordinary budgeted work. It may be profitable to accept the contract if either it displaces less profitable work or surplus direct labour hours are available. A careful assessment should be undertaken to ascertain whether much more profitable work would be found than is the case with the contract if it will displace other more profitable contracts that could arise in the near future.

Chapter 13

13.1 (a) *batch costing*: a form of cost accounting whereby relatively small identifiable units are treated collectively
   (b) *contract costing*: a form of cost accounting usually found in the construction industry whereby individual contracts are treated separately
   (c) *process costing*: a form of cost accounting where individual inputs into a production process become indistinguishable, and thereby requiring the total input to be treated as a whole
   (d) *service costing*: a form of cost accounting in which there is no physical or tangible product, and so the service provided becomes the chargeable unit.

13.2 It is a conventional rule of process costing that abnormal gains and losses should not be charged directly to production, but should be written off to the profit and loss account for the period in which they arose.

This treatment is recommended because (a) it is considered unfair to burden current production costs that by definition, are not expected to occur frequently or regularly; and (b) if such gains and losses were charged directly to the process, the total cost thereby derived may become somewhat erratic, and this would make it difficult to keep track of normal costs.

Note also that abnormal gains or losses should not be carried forward into the next costing period, as this would add an extra benefit or burden that was unrelated to that period.

13.3 The answer to this question could become somewhat emotive. The argument for introducing a cost and management accounting system into a hospital is no different than it would be if it were asked of manufacturing industry, i.e. to help plan and control what is going on.

Unfortunately, when accounting systems are introduced into an area like the Health Service it is often assumed that the only reason is to cut expenditure. It is then easy to argue that if departments are to be limited to what is sometimes called a 'budget', some sick patients may go untreated if the budget limit has been reached.

It is a misuse of a budgetary control system if a budget is being used in this way. It is important for a department to know in advance that it appears likely that it is now going to spend more than it had budgeted for (and that it is not just wasting money). The overspend may arise because of an unexpected demand for its services, but if it is known that this is happening, further resources can be looked for elsewhere. In other words, as some of the accounting textbooks put it, a budget should not be a strait-jacket.

Chapter 14

14.1 MORAY LIMITED

	Units
Total budgeted sales: January – June 19X1	2270
Add: Desired stock at 30 June 19X1	450
	2720
Less: Opening stock at 1 January 19X1	320
∴ Required production units	2400

$$\text{Monthly average production} = \frac{2400}{6} = 400 \text{ units}$$

14.2 JORDAN LIMITED

Budgeted production for the six months to 31 December 19X1:

19X2		Sales (units)	Production (units)	Balance (units)
1.07	Balance b/f	–	–	100
31.07	Sales	70	–	30
	Production	–	200	230
31.08	Sales	140	–	90
	Production	–	280	370
30.09	Sales	350	–	20
	Production	–	180	200
31.10	Sales	190	–	10
	Production	–	180	190
30.11	Sales	150	–	40
	Production	–	140	180
31.11	Sales	120	–	60
	Production	–	40	100

14.3 DALTON LIMITED

	Units
Total budgeted sales: January to June 19X3	1090
Less: Expected opening stock at 1 January 19X3	100
	990

Average monthly production required ∴ = 165 (990/6)

Note that: Opening stock – sales = stock remaining + monthly production
= closing stock.

19X3	O/stock	–	sales	=	stock remaining	+	monthly production	=	c/stock
January	100	–	90	=	10	+	165	=	175
February	175	–	150	=	25	+	165	=	190
March	190	–	450	=	(260)				

165 units produced in both January and February will not enable the company to meet its monthly budgeted sales figure for March 19X3. In order to do so, it could produce 295 units (165 + 260/2) in both January and February, and produce 150 units per month in March, April, May and June. This would enable the company to meet its budgeted April sales figure and to achieve a reasonably smooth production flow. However, it would mean that by the end of June 19X3, the budgeted closing stock will be 200 units compared with 100 units at 1 January 19X3.

The calculations are as follows:

19X3	O/stock	–	sales	=	stock remaining	+	monthly production	=	c/stock
January	100	–	90	=	10	+	295	=	305
February	305	–	150	=	155	+	295	=	450
March	450	–	450	=	0	+	150	=	150
April	150	–	150	=	0	+	150	=	150
May	150	–	130	=	20	+	150	=	170
June	170	–	120	=	50	+	150	=	200

Whether the company would wish to adopt this policy is debatable. It might wish, for example, to keep a minimum number of units in stock (perhaps 100 units) at any one time. This would mean increasing the number of units produced in 19X2, because according to the above figures, the company would be left with only 10 units ready for sale at the end of January 19X3. Another 295 units would, however, be immediately ready for sale in February 19X3.

14.4 TOM LIMITED

1 *Direct materials usage budget:*

Month	30.04.X4	31.05.X4	30.06.X4	31.07.X4	31.08.X4	30.09.X4	*Six months to 30.09.X4*
Component:							
A6 (2 units for X)	280	560	1 400	760	600	480	4 080
B9 (3 units for X)	420	840	2 100	1 140	900	720	6 120

2 *Direct materials purchase budget:*

	30.04.X4	31.05.X4	30.06.X4	31.07.X4	31.08.X4	30.09.X4	Six months to 30.09.X4
Component A6							
Material usage (as above)	280	560	1 400	760	600	480	4 080
Add: Desired closing stock	110	220	560	300	240	200	200
	390	780	1 960	1 060	840	680	4 280
Less: Opening stock	100	110	220	560	300	240	100
Purchases (units)	290	670	1 740	500	540	440	4 180
Price per unit	£5	£5	£5	£5	£5	£5	£5
Total purchases	£1 450	£3 350	£8 700	£2 500	£2 700	£2 200	£20 900
Component B9							
Material usage (as above0	420	840	2 100	1 140	900	720	6 120
Add: Desired closing stock	250	630	340	300	200	180	180
	670	1 470	2 440	1 440	1 100	900	6 300
Less: Opening stock	200	250	630	340	300	200	200
Purchases (units)	470	1 220	1 810	1 100	800	700	6 100
Price per unit	£10	£10	£10	£10	£10	£10	£10
Total purchases	£4 700	£12 200	£18 100	£11 000	£8 000	£7 000	£61 000

14.5 DON LIMITED

Direct labour cost budget:

Grade:	30.06.X5	*Quarter* 31.07.X5	31.08.X5	*Three months to 31.08.X5*
Production (units)	600	700	650	1 950
Direct labour hours per unit	3	3	3	3
Total direct labour hours	1 800	2 100	1 950	5 850
Budgeted rate per hour (£)	4	4	4	4
Production cost (£)	7 200	8 400	7 800	23 400
Finishing (units)	600	700	650	1 950
Direct labour hours per unit	2	2	2	2
Total direct labour hours	1 200	1 400	1 300	3 900
Budgeted rate per hour (£)	8	8	8	8
Finishing cost (£)	9 600	11 200	10 400	31 200
Total budgeted direct labour cost	£16 800	£19 600	£18 200	£54 600

14.6 GORSE LIMITED

1 *Sales budget:*

Quantity	*Selling price* £	*Sales volume* £
10 000	100	1 000 000

2 *Production quantity budget:*

Sales budget (units)	*Closing stock (units)*	*Opening stock (units)*	*Production required (units)*
10 000	2 000	(4 000)	8 000

3 *Materials usage budget:*

Component	*Component usage*	*Production (units)*	*Total component usage (units)*
XY	5	8 000	40 000
WZ	3	8 000	24 000

4 *Materials purchase budget:*

	XY	*Component* WZ	*Total* £
Budget usage	40 000	24 000	
Stock increase (25%)	4 000	2 400	
Purchase quantities	44 000	26 400	
Cost price per unit	£1	£0.50	£0.50
Purchase values	£44 000	£13 200	£57 200

5 *Direct labour budget:*

Grade	Production budget	Budgeted hours per unit	Total budgeted hours	Budget labour rate per hour £	Total direct labour cost £
Production	8 000	4	32 000	5	160 000
Finishing	8 000	2	16 000	7	112 000
			48 000		£272 000

6 *Budgeted profit and loss account:*

		Per unit £	Total £
Sales units			10 000
Sales revenue		100.00	1 000 000
Less: costs:			
Production (see workings)		52.50	525 000
Total factory cost		47.50	475 000
Administration, selling and distribution			275 000
Budgeted profit for period 6			£200 000

Workings:	£	£
Unit cost:		
Direct materials;		
Component XY:5 × £1	5.00	
WZ:3 × £0.50	1.50	6.50
Direct labour:		
Production: 4 × £5	20.00	
Finishing: 2 × £7	14.00	34.00
		40.50

Production overhead:
$$\frac{96\ 000}{48\ 000} = £2 \text{ per DLH} \times 6$$

		12.00
		£52.50

14.7

FLOSSY LIMITED
Cash budget for the three months to 31 March 19X7

	January £000	February £000	March £000
Receipts:			
Debtors (Workings 1)	1 900	2 950	2 450
Sales of plant and equipment	–	–	30
Sales of short-term investments	60	–	10
	£1 960	£2 950	£2 490

	January £000	February £000	March £000
Payments:			
Trade creditors (Workings 2)	1150	1850	1510
Other creditors	450	500	600
Capital expenditure	–	470	–
Short-term investments	–	40	–
Tax	150	–	–
Dividends	200	–	–
	£1950	£2860	£2110
Monthly net cash flow	10	90	380
Opening balance	15	25	115
Closing balance	£25	£115	£495
Workings:			
1 *Trade debtors*			
Sales	2000	3000	2500
Add: Opening debtors	200	300	350
	2200	3300	2850
Less: Closing debtors	300	350	400
Cash from trade debtors	£1900	£2950	£2450
2 *Purchases*			
Cost of goods sold	1200	1800	1500
Add: Closing stock	120	150	150
	1320	1950	1650
Less: Opening stock	100	120	150
Purchases for each quarter	1220	1830	1500
Add: Opening trade creditors	110	180	160
	1330	2010	1660
Less: Closing trade creditors	180	160	150
Cash to trade creditors	£1150	£1850	£1510

14.8 CHIMES LIMITED

Option 1 – Keep the factory open

		£000	45% £000
Production capacity			
Sales revenue			135.5
Less: Variable cost of sales:			
Direct materials		63	
Direct labour		27	
Variable overhead:			
Factory		18	
Administration		13.5	
Selling and distribution		9	130.5
Contribution	c/f		5

	b/f		5
Contribution			
Less: Fixed costs:			
Factory		10	
Administration		8	
Selling and distribution		6	24
Budgeted loss			£(19)

Option 2 – Close the factory

	£000
Costs:	
Redundancy and other clsoure costs	(30)
Property and plant maintenance	(10)
Re-opening costs	(20)
	(60)
Less: Saving in fixed overheads	30
Net cost of closure	£(30)

Decision
As the factory will still make a contribution during the year to 30 June 19X8, it should be kept open. However, there may be other non-cost factors to take into account.

Chapter 15

15.1 X LIMITED

1 Direct materials cost variance: £

Actual price per unit × actual quantity = 12 × 6: 72

Less: Standard price per unit × standard quantity
for actual production = 10 × 5: 50

£22 (A)

2 Direct materials price variance:

(Actual price – standard price) × actual quantity
= (12 – 10) × 6: £12 (A)

3 Direct materials usage variance;

(Actual quantity – standard quantity) × standard
price = (6 – 5) × 10: £10 (A)

15.2 MALCOLM LIMITED

1 Direct materials cost variance: £

Total actual cost 32 400

Less: Standard quantity for actual production ×
standard price = (50 × 120) × £5: 30 000

£2 400 (A)

2 Direct materials price variance:

(Actual price – standard price) × actual quantity =
(6* – 5) × 5400: £5 400 (A)

*$\dfrac{32\,400}{5400}$

3 Direct materials usage variance:
(Actual quantity – standard quantity) × standard
    price = (5400 – 6000*) × £5:   £3 000 (F)

*(120 units × 50 kilograms)

15.3 BRUCE LIMITED

	£
1 Direct labour cost variance:	
Actual hours × actual hourly rate = 1000 × £6.50:	6 500
Less: Standard hours for actual production ×	
standard hourly rate = 900 × £6.00:	5 400
	£1 100 (A)

2 Direct labour rate variance:
(Actual hourly – standard hourly rate)
    × actual hours = (6.50 – 6.00) × 1000:   £500 (A)

3 Direct labour efficiency variance:
(Actual hours – standard hours for actual production)
    × standard hourly rate = (1000 – 900) × 6.00:   £600 (A)

15.4 DUNCAN LIMITED

	£
1 Direct labour cost variance:	
Actual direct labour cost	97 200
Less: Standard hours for actual production ×	
Standard hourly rate = (10 × 1200) × 8:	96 000
	£1 200 (A)

2 Direct labour rate variance:
(Actual hourly rate – standard hourly rate) × actual
    hours = (*9 – 8) × 10 800:   £10 800 (A)

$$*\frac{97\ 200}{10\ 800}$$

3 Direct labour efficiency variance:
(Actual hours – standard hours for actual
    production) × standard hourly rate
    = (10 800 –12 000*) × 8:   £9 600 (F)

*1200 × 10 DLH = 12 000

15.5 ANTHEA LIMITED

	£
1 Fixed production overhead variance:	
Actual fixed overhead	150 000
Less: Standard hours of production × fixed	
production overhead absoption rate = 8000 × 15	120 000
	£30 000 (A)

2 Fixed overhead expenditure variance:
Actual fixed overhead – budgeted fixed overhead =
  150 000 – 135 000:   £15 000 (A)

3 Fixed overhead volume variance:
Budgeted fixed overhead – (standard hours of
  production × fixed production overhead
  absorption rate) = 135 000 – (8000 × 15):   £15 000 (A)

4 Fixed overhead capacity variance:
Budgeted fixed overhead – (actual hours worked
  × fixed production overhead absorption rate
  = 135 000 – (10 000 × 15):   £15 000 (F)

5 Fixed overhead productivity variance:
Actual hours worked – standard hours of production
  × fixed production overhead absorption rate
  = (10 000 – 8000) × 15 000:   £30 000 (A)

15.6 ANTHEA LIMITED

Performance measures:

1 Efficiency ratio:
$$\frac{SHP}{Actual\ hours} \times 100 = \frac{8\ 000}{10\ 000} \times 100 = 80\%$$

2 Capacity ratio:
$$\frac{Actual\ hours}{Budgeted\ hours^*} \times 100 = \frac{10\ 000}{9000} \times 100 = 111.1\%$$
$$^*\frac{135\ 000}{15}$$

3 Production volume ratio:
$$\frac{SHP}{Budgeted\ hours} \times 100 = \frac{8000}{9000} \times 100 = 88.9\%$$

15.7 OSPREY LIMITED

1 Fixed production overhead variance: £
Actual fixed overhead   120 000
Less: Standard hours of production × fixed
  production overhead absorption rate =
  $$(600 \times 10) \times \left(\frac{125\ 000}{500 \times 10}\right)$$ 150 000
                                                                   £30 000 (F)

2 Fixed overhead expenditure variance:
Actual fixed overhead – budgeted fixed overhead =
  120 000 – 125 000:   £5 000 (F)

3 Fixed overhead volume variance;
   Budgeted fixed overhead – (standard hours of
      production × fixed production overhead absorption rate)
      = 125 000 – (6000* × 25) :   £25 000 (F)

4 Fixed overhead capacity variance;
   Budgeted fixed overhead – (actual hours worked ×
      fixed production overhead absorption rate)
      = 125 000 – (4900 × 25):   £2 500 (A)

5 Fixed overhead productivity variance:
   (Actual hours worked – standard hours of
      production) × fixed production overhead absorption rate
      = (4900 – 6000*) × 25 :   £27 500 (F)

   *600 units × 10 standard hours

15.8 OSPREY LIMITED
Performance measures:
1 Efficiency ratio:
$$\frac{SHP}{Actual\ hours} \times 100 = \frac{6000}{4900} \times 100 = 122.4\%$$

2 Capacity ratio:
$$\frac{Actual\ hours}{Budgeted\ hours^*} \times 100 = \frac{4900}{5000} \times 100 = 98\%$$

3 Production volume ratio:
$$\frac{SHP}{Budgeted\ hours} \times 100 = \frac{6000}{5000} \times 100 = 120\%$$

15.9 MILTON LIMITED
1 Selling price variance:
   Actual quantity × (actual selling price per unit – budgeted
   selling price percentage) = 9000 × (11* – 10) =   £9000 (F)

   $$*\frac{99\ 000}{9\ 000}$$

2 Sales volume contribution variance:
   (Actual quantity – budgeted quantity) × standard
   contribution = (9000 – 10 000) × 3:   £3000 (A)

3 Sales variances ∴ = 9000 (F) + 3000 (A) =   £6000 (F)

15.10 DOE LIMTED
1 Selling price variance:
   Actual quantity × (actual selling price – budgeted
   selling price) = 120 × (28 – 30) =   £240 (A)

2 Sales volume contribution variance:
(Actual quantity − budgeted units) × standard
contribution $(120 − 100) × 10$:   £200 (F)

3 Sales variance ∴ = 240 (A) + 200 (F) =   £40 (A)

15.11 JUDITH LIMITED

(a) 1 Efficiency ratio:
$$\frac{\text{SHP}}{\text{Actual hours}} \times 100 = \frac{5 \times 2200}{4 \times 2200} \times 100 = 125\%$$

2 Capacity ratio:
$$\frac{\text{Actual hours}}{\text{Budgeted hours*}} \times 100 = \frac{8800}{5 \times 2000} \times 100 = 88\%$$

3 Production volume ratio:
$$\frac{\text{SHP}}{\text{Budgeted hours}} \times 100 = \frac{11\,000}{10\,000} \times 100 = 110\%$$

(b) 1 Selling price variance:
(Actual selling price − budgeted selling price)
× actual units = $(145 − 150) × 2200$:   £11 000 (A)

2 Sales volume contribution variance:
(Actual quantity − budgeted units) × standard
margin = $(2200 − 2000) × 25$:   £5 000 (F)

3 Sales variance = 11 000 (A) + 5000 (F) =   £6 000 (A)

4 Direct materials cost variance:
Actual quantity × actual price = $2200 × 72$:   158 400
Less: Standard quantity for actual production
× standard price = $(7 × 2200) × 10$:   154 000

                                                     £4 400 (A)

5 Direct materials price variance:
(Actual price − standard price) × actual
quantity = $(9 − 10) × (2200 × 8)$:   £17 600 (F)

6 Direct materials usage variance:
(Actual quantity − standard quantity)
× standard price = $(8 × 2200) −$
$(7 × 2200) × 10$:   £22 000 (A)

7 Direct labour cost variance:
Actual hours × actual hourly rate =
 (4 × 2200) × 6:   52 800
Less: Standard hours for actual production
 × standard hourly rate = (2200 × 5)
 × 5:   55 000
               £2 200 (F)

8 Direct labour rate variance:
(Actual hourly rate − standard hourly rate)
 × actual hours = (6 − 5) × (4 × 2200):   £8 800 (A)

9 Direct labour efficiency variance:
(Actual hours − standard hours for actual
 production) × standard hourly rate =
 (8800 − 11 000) × 5:   £11 000 (F)

10 Fixed production overhead variance:
Actual fixed overhead: 65 000
Less: Standard hours of production × fixed
 production overhead absorption rate =
 (2200 × 5) × 6:   66 000
               £1 000 (F)

11 Fixed production overhead expenditure variance:
Actual fixed overhead − budgeted fixed
 overhead = 65 000 − (30 × 2000):   £5 000 (A)

12 Fixed production overhead volume variance:
Budgeted fixed overhead − (standard hours of
 production × fixed production overhead
 absorption rate = 60 000 − (11 000 × 6):   £6 000 (F)

13 Fixed production overhead capacity variance:
Budgeted fixed overhead − (actual hours worked ×
 fixed production overhead absorption rate) =
 £60 000 − (8800 × 6):   £7 200 (A)

14 Fixed production overhead productivity variance:
(Actual hours worked − standard hours of
 production) × fixed production overhead
 absorption rate = (8800 − 11 000) × 6:   £13 200 (F)

(c) Standard cost operating statement for the period   £
  Budgeted profit (25 × 2000)   50 000
  Sales volume contribution variance (25 × 200)   5 000

  Standard margin of actual sales   55 000
  Selling price variance (5 × 2200)   (11 000)

  Actual margin of actual sales   c/f   44 000

	b/f			44 000
Cost variances:		*Adverse*	*Favourable*	
		£	£	
Direct materials:				
Price			17 600	
Usage		22 000		
Direct labour:				
Rate		8 800		
Efficiency			11 000	
Fixed production overhead;				
Expenditure		5 000		
Capacity		7 200		
Productivity			13 200	
		£43 000	£41 800	(1 200)
Actual profit				£42 800

Chapter 16

16.1 PROSPECT LIMITED
Calculation of net cash flows:

Year to 31 March	19X1	19X2	19X3	19X4	19X5	19X6
	£000	£000	£000	£000	£000	£000
Cash receipts						
Trade debtors (Working 1)	1800	2360	2740	2880	1920	400
Sale of project	–	–	–	–	–	50
	1800	2360	2740	2880	1920	450
Cash payments						
Purchase of project	1000	–	–	–	–	–
Trade creditors						
(Working 2)	1350	1770	2160	1990	1260	150
Expenses	210	220	240	250	300	–
Taxation	–	40	70	100	100	10
	2560	2030	2470	2340	1660	160
Net cash flows	£(760)	£330	£270	£540	£260	£290

	19X1	19X2	19X3	19X4	19X5	19X6
	£000	£000	£000	£000	£000	£000
Workings:						
Year to 31 March						
1 *Trade debtors*						
Sales	2000	2400	2800	2900	2000	–
Less: Closing trade						
debtors	200	240	300	320	400	–
	1800	2160	2500	2580	1600	–
Add: Opening trade						
debtors	–	200	240	300	320	400
Cash received	£1800	£2360	£2740	£2880	£1920	£400

	19X1 £000	19X2 £000	19X3 £000	19X4 £000	19X5 £000	19X6 £000
Trade creditors						
Purchases	1600	1790	2220	1960	1110	–
Less: Closing trade creditors	250	270	330	300	150	–
	1350	1520	1890	1660	960	–
Add: Opening trade creditors	–	250	270	330	300	150
Cash purchases	£1350	£1770	£2160	£1990	£1260	£150

16.2 BUCHAN ENTERPRISES

1 Payback period:

Year	Investment outlay	Cash inflow	Net cash flow	Cumulative cash flow
	£	£	£	£
1	(50 000)	8 000	(42 000)	(42 000)
2	–	16 000	16 000	(26 000)
3	–	40 000	40 000	14 000
4	–	45 000	45 000	59 000
5	–	37 000	37 000	96 000

Payback period therefore = 2 years, 7.8 months*

*Net cash flow becomes positive in Year 3. Assuming the net cash flow accrues evenly it becomes positive during August: $(26/40 \times 12) = 7.8$ months (i.e. 2 years and 7.8 months).

2 Discounted payback period:

Year	Net cash flow	Discount factor at 12%	Discounted net cash flow	Cumulative net cash flow
	£		£	£
0	(50 000)	1.0000	(50 000)	(50 000)
1	8 000	0.8929	7 143	(42 857)
2	16 000	0.7929	12 686	(30 171)
3	40 000	0.7118	28 472	(1 699)
4	45 000	0.6355	28 598	26 899
5	37 000	0.5674	20 994	47 893

Discounted payback period therefore = 4 years, 1 month*

*Discounted net cash flow becomes positive in Year 4. Assuming the net cash flow accrues evenly throughout the year, it becomes positive in January (1699/28 598 × 12 = 0.7). This is in contrast with the payback method where the net cash flow becomes positive in August of Year 3.

16.3 LENDER LIMITED

$$\text{Accounting rate of return} = \frac{\text{Average annual net profit after tax}}{\text{Cost of the investment}} \times 100$$

$$= \frac{\frac{1}{5}(18\ 000 + 47\ 000 + 65\ 000 + 30\ 000)}{100\ 000} \times 100$$

$$= \frac{45\ 000}{100\ 000} \times 100$$

$$= \underline{\underline{45\%}}$$

Note: Based on the average investment, the ARR

$$= \frac{45\ 000}{\frac{1}{2}(0 + 100\ 000)} \times 100$$

$$= \underline{\underline{90\%}}$$

16.4 LOCKHART LIMITED

Net present value:

Year	Net cash flow £000	Discount factor @15%	Present value £000
1	800	0.8696	696
2	850	0.7561	643
3	830	0.6575	546
4	1200	0.5718	686
5	700	0.4972	348
Total present value			2919
Initial cost			2500
Net present value			£419

16.5 MOFFAT DISTRICT COUNCIL

Internal rate of return:

Year	Net cash flow £000	5%	7%	Present value £000 @5%	Present value £000 @7%
1	230	0.9524	0.9346	219	215
2	370	0.9070	0.8734	336	323
3	600	0.8638	0.8163	518	490
4	420	0.8227	0.7629	346	320
5	110	0.7835	0.7130	86	78
Total present value				1505	1426
Initial cost				1450	1450
Net present value				£55	£(24)

Internal rate of return

$$= \text{Positive rate} + \frac{\text{Positive NPV}}{\text{Positive NPV} + \text{Negative NPV}} \times \text{Range}$$

$$= 5\% + \frac{55}{55 + 24} \times 2\%$$

$$= 5\% + 1.4\%$$

$$= \underline{\underline{6.4\%}}$$

16.6 MARSH LIMITED

1 Payback

Year	Investment outlay £000	Cash inflow £000	Net cash flow £000	Cumulative cash flow £000
1	(500)	50	(450)	(450)
2	–	200	200	(250)
3	–	225	225	(25)
4	–	225	225	200
5	–	100	100	300

Therefore payback $= 3$ years $+ \dfrac{(25 \times 12)}{225} = 3$ years, 1.3 months

2 Accounting rate of return:

$$\frac{\text{Average annual net profit after tax}}{\text{Cost of the investment}} \times 100$$

$$= \frac{(100 + 250 + 250 + 200)}{4}$$

$$= \frac{200}{500} \times 100$$

$$= 40\%$$

Note: If the average cost of the investment is used:

$$= \frac{200}{\frac{1}{2}(£0 + 500)} = \frac{200}{250} \times 100 = 80\%$$

3 Net present value:

Year	Net cash flow £000	Discount factors @15%	Present value £000
1	50	0.8696	43
2	200	0.7561	151
3	225	0.6575	148
4	225	0.5718	129
5	100	0.4972	50
Total present value			521
Initial cost			500
Net present value			£21

3 Internal rate of return:

Year	Net cash flow £000	Discount factor 15%	Discount factor 17%	Present value @15% £000	Present value @17% £000
1	50	0.8696	0.8547	43	43
2	200	0.7561	0.7305	151	146
3	225	0.6575	0.6244	148	140
4	225	0.5718	0.5337	129	120
5	100	0.4972	0.4561	50	46
Total present value				521	495
Initial cost				500	500
Net present value				£21	£(5)

$$\text{IRR} = \text{Positive rate} + \frac{\text{Positive NPV}}{\text{Positive NPV} + \text{Negative NPV}} \times \text{Range}$$

$$= 15\% + \frac{22}{21 + 5} \times 2\%$$

$$= 15\% + 1.7\%$$

$$= \underline{\underline{16.7\%}}$$

INDEX

absorption 262
account 4, 9, 19, 44–5, 60
  abbreviated 137, 402
  annual 26, 147, 222, 399, 401, 406
  balancing the 53–5
  bank 47, 50
  book of 44–5
  budgeted profit and loss 321, 326
  capital 46, 132, 134
  cash 47, 50
  choice of 45–8
  company 130–47
  creditor 47
  current 132, 134
  current cost reserve 446
  debtor 47
  discounts allowed 47
  discounts received 47
  drawings 47
  entering transactions in 48–51
  final 79
  financial 26, 59
  finished goods stock 113
  format of 78–9
  group 414–16, 448, 450
  group profit and loss 416–20
  historic cost 440–7
  interpretation of 180–207, 208–9
  ledger 45, 59, 80
  management 26
  manufacturing 110–121, 138, 157
  notes to 416
  partnership 130–4, 147
  petty cash 47
  profit and loss 11–12, 71–2, 74–5, 95,
    111, 116, 132, 138, 140, 157,
    158, 161, 403, 404, 425, 426
  profit and loss appropriation 132,
    134, 138, 147
  published 399, 414, 415, 426
  purchases 47, 111, 117
  sales 48, 50
  sole trader 72, 147
  statement 180
  stock 48
  stores ledger 244
  trade creditor 48
  trade debtor 48
  trade discount 48
  trading 71–2, 74–5, 95, 111, 116,
    138, 157
accountancy 10–11, 23

chartered 14
  profession 3, 11, 14–16
accountant 5, 7, 9, 10, 13, 14, 16, 19,
  72, 131
  financial 13
  management 13, 19
  non-qualified 14
  qualified 14
  services 14
accounting 3–11, 12, 13, 18–19
  accrual 71, 85, 161
  accrual and prepayment system 29
  adjustments 80, 85–7
  branches 3, 10–14
  brand 438
  cash flow (CFA) 28
  cost 12, 13, 19, 121, 206, 219–392
  current cost (CCA) 444–7
  entering transactions 48–51
  financial 6, 7, 8, 12, 13, 19, 26,
    39–216, 219, 221, 222, 224, 391,
    404
  green 448
  group 438, 439, 448
  historic cost (HCA) 27, 28, 94, 429
  historical development 219–20,
    222–3
  implementation 220
  international 438, 447–8, 450
  management 7, 8, 13, 19, 121, 206,
    219–392
  nature and purpose 3, 4–7, 219,
    220–2
  partnership 18
  period 26
  policies 32
  profit 73–4, 93–5
  ratios 162, 163–207, 208–9
  recording information 41–60
  responsibility 228–9, 237
  rules 19, 22–36
  segmental 448
  social and environmental 438,
    448–49, 450
  sole trader 72
  standards *see* Statements of Standard
    Accounting Practice
  Standards Board (ASB) 32, 34, 36,
    169, 401, 405, 439, 440, 448
  Standards Committee (ASC) 32, 400,
    435, 439
  Standards Steering Committee

    (ASSC), see Accounting
    Standards Committee
  strategic management 315, 316
  system 4
  technician 16
  theory 34–6
  world 3–19
accrual 28–9, 85–6, 94, 95, 161, 162
acquisition 342
activity 259, 281, 286, 295, 324–5, 332,
  334, 335, 345, 348, 408
adjustments
  accruals and prepayments 80, 85–7,
    95
  additional depreciation (ADA) 445–6
  bad and doubtful debts 80, 87–90, 95
  closing stocks 446
  cost of sales (COSA) 445–6
  depreciation 80, 82–5, 95
  fixed assets 446
  gearing (GA) 445–6
  monetary working capital (MWCA)
    445–6
  post-trial balance 79–90
  stock 80–2, 95
administrator 14
adverse 271, 272, 350
allocate 256, 258, 272, 273, 309
amortize 440
analysis
  horizontal 183, 206
  ratio 183, 184–6, 206–7, 208–9
  trend 183, 206
  variance 343–4, 350–3, 366
  vertical 183, 206
analyst 7, 181
annual report *see* report, annual
apportion 258, 260, 272, 273
appraisal, capital investment 365,
  372–92
  background 373–4
  selection of projects 374–89
  source of funds 389–91
area, floor 259
asset 12
  fixed 73, 373, 409
  intangible fixed 439
Association, Football 23
  of Accounting Technicians (AAT) 16
  of Authorized Public Accountants 15
  of Cost and Executive Accountants 15
  of International Accountants 15

assumption 23
audit
  internal 221
  management 221
auditing 11, 13, 15, 19
auditor 11, 407, 408, 448
authority, local 16, 25, 308, 309, 401, 431
  treasurer's department 311
average
  continuous weighted 243, 244–5,
    247, 248, 249, 250
  periodic weighted 243–4, 247
  weighted 243, 245, 247, 248, 250,
    251
avoidance, tax 13
axiom 23

balance sheet 11–12, 71–2, 75, 95, 116,
    141–2, 157, 312, 326, 403, 404,
    413, 414, 425, 426
  accruals and prepayments 80, 85–7, 95
  bad and doubtful debts 80, 87–90, 95
  depreciation 80, 82–5, 95
  group 416, 420–3
  stock 80–2, 95
bankruptcy 14
bodies, secondary 15–16, 19
book-keeping 4, 5, 11–12, 19, 29,
    41–60
  cost 12, 13
  double-entry 4, 29, 41–60, 111, 112,
    121
borrowing 196–8, 389, 391
brand 440
budget 320–2, 334, 375
  administration 326
  cash 326
  fixed 331–4, 335
  functional 325–31, 335
  flexible 331–4, 335, 348
  master 321, 325, 326, 331, 335
  period 323
  procedure 322, 325
  process 323–5
  zero-based 321
business 25
by-product 307

capability, operating 444
capital 46, 72, 94, 95, 147, 187
  authorized 136
  cost of 385
  employed 223, 380
  issued 136
  investment appraisal *see* appraisal,
    capital investment
  share 135–6, 409
  working 163
Cardiff 137, 401
cash 157–70

equivalents 168–9, 170
flow 158–9
flow statements *see* statements, cash
  flow centre
cost 226, 227, 228, 238
  production 256, 272, 273
  profit 228
  responsibility 228
  service 256, 258–9, 272, 273
charity 25, 390
chart
  break-even 286, 287, 290
  profit/volume 286, 288, 290
charter, royal 15
Chartered Association of Certified
    Accountants (ACCA) 14, 15, 19
Chartered Institute of Management
    Accountants (CIMA) 14, 15, 19
Chartered Institute of Public Finance
    and Accountancy (CIPFA) 14,
    15, 19
closure, specified order of 259–60
coding 225, 229–30, 234, 235
commerce 15
committee
  Cadbury 438, 439
  education 390
  International Accounting Standards
    see International Accounting
    Standards Committee
company 14
  accounts, 137–8
  Act 1948 400
  Act 1967 400
  Act 1976 400
  Act 1980 400
  Act 1981 400, 447
  Act 1985 18, 32, 147, 399, 400, 402,
    414, 415, 416, 417, 420, 426,
    434
  Act 1989 18, 399, 410, 414, 415, 429,
    432, 448
  articles 409
  associated 415, 416
  disclosure of information 147
  group 426
  holding 416
  house 401, 402
  industrial 431
  limited liability 11, 14, 18, 19, 26,
    131, 134–47
  loans 137
  manufacturing 226, 227
  medium 402
  private 136, 402
  registrar of 137
  public 136, 181
  related 415
  small 164, 402, 403
  subsidiary 415, 416

types 136
component 113
concept 23
  entity 135
consolidate 416, 439
contribution 286, 293, 295, 296, 359
control 6, 12, 220, 223–4, 237, 251,
    268, 316, 345–6
  budgetary 234, 319–35, 343
  cost 225, 234, 235, 251
  financial 221
  managerial 222
  method 225, 234, 235
  operational 224
  standard 234
convention 23
Corporate Report, The 435
cost
  direct 111, 112, 121, 237–51, 256, 272
  elements of 112, 231, 232, 350, 355
  fixed 231, 282, 295
  historic 24, 27, 33, 36
  indirect 112, 113, 121, 238, 248,
    256–73
    labour 113
    material 113
  interdepartmental 259
  manufacturing 111
    of goods produced
      113, 114
  material 239–48
  other direct 250
  original 27
  prime 113
  product 231, 234, 235
  reciprocal service 259–60
  replacement 444, 445, 446, 447
  standard 246, 251, 343, 365
  total manufacturing incurred 113
  variable 281, 295
costing 12
  absorption 232–3, 256–73, 280, 281,
    282, 283
  activity based (ABC) 272, 312–13,
    316
  batch 305, 317
  control 303–4, 316
  job 303, 316
  life-cycle 315, 316
  marginal 232, 233, 280–96
  process 305–8, 316
  service 308–11, 316
  specific order 302, 316
  standard 12, 220, 334, 342–66
    absorption 346
    marginal 346
    system 282–4
  target 315, 316
  unit 251, 259, 316
cost-plus 195

counting 4
credit 44, 48, 55, 59, 60
creditor 7, 12, 14, 59, 116, 162, 181
current (definition) 190
cycle, agrarian 26

data
   accounting 41
   financial 10, 12, 18
   non-financial 12
debenture 136, 137
debit 44, 48, 55, 59, 60, 196, 389
debt
   bad 28, 87–90, 95, 161
   bad, adjustment for 80, 87–90, 95
   doubtful 80, 87–90, 94, 95
   doubtful, adjustment for 80, 87–90, 95
   provision for doubtful 88–9
debtor 59
   other 116
   trade 116
department 226, 227
depreciation 32, 82, 161
   adjustments 80, 82–5, 95
   reducing balance 83–4
   straight-line 82–3
developments, some recent 311–16
Directive 447
   Fourth 447
   Seventh 447
   Eight 447
director 11, 138–9, 409
   board of, 407
disclosure, minimum 402, 404
discounting 377–8
disposal 342
dividend 136, 139, 140, 147, 163
   cumulative 136
   final 139
   proposed 139, 147
division 226, 227
donation 390, 409
drawings 134, 139
driver, cost 312

economics 13
Edinburgh 137, 401
effective 8
efficient 8
elements
   direct 283
   fixed 283
   indirect 283
   variable 283
employee 4, 7, 11, 12, 138–9, 181, 205, 259, 402
employer 4
employment policy 409
entity 3, 5, 19
   manufacturing 16–17

non-profit making 25, 309, 314, 316
not-for-profit making 19, 25, 309, 314, 316, 389–90, 391
partnership 135, 139, 146
profit making 19, 25
service 16–17
sole trader 131, 135, 139, 147
trading 111
types 16–18
equivalents, cash 168–9, 170
Europe, Western 26
evasion, tax 13
exchange, stock *see* stock exchange
expenditure 28, 73
   annual 73
   capital 73, 75, 82, 373. 374
   revenue 73, 75, 373, 374
expenses 113, 231, 232
   direct 113
   indirect 113
   manufacturing 121
explanation 4

factor 4
   discount 378
   feel good 205
   key 293
   limiting 293–5
   non-financial 282
factory 113, 226, 227
favourable 271, 272, 350
figures, comparative 416
finance, servicing 163
Financial Reporting Council (FRC) 40, 438
Financial Reporting Standards (FRSs) 23, 32, 401, 403, 448
   FRS 1: Cash flow statements 164, 169, 170, 423, 424, 425
   FRS 2: Accounting for subsidiary undertakings 439
first-in, first-out (FIFO) 240–1, 242, 243, 246, 248, 250, 251
flow, net cash 375, 378, 390
folio 44, 60
forecast 322
   sales 372
format 447
   horizontal 78, 111, 121, 416, 420
   operation 417, 418
   pyramid 226
   type of expenditure 417, 418
   vertical 78–9, 111, 112, 416, 417, 420
framework, conceptual 34–6
function 226, 227
   purchasing 313
funds
   shareholder 187, 197–8
   source of 389–90

gain, abnormal 305–6
gearing
   high 198, 389
   low 198
goods, finished 111
goodwill 438, 439–40
governance, corporate 438–9, 450
government 7, 390
   grant 391
   central 15, 389, 390
   local 15, 389, 390

hire purchase 389, 390, 391
hospice 301
hour, standard 347

income 28, 73
   capital 73
   revenue 73, 391
index, retail price (RPI) 183, 443, 447, 450
industry 13, 15
   cement 305
   chemicals 305
   construction 26, 303
   fashion 26
   glass 301, 302–3, 305
   iron and steel 305
   manufacturing 308, 311, 344
   nationalized 40
   oil 305
   paint 305
   service 231, 308–11
   textiles 305
inflation 27, 183, 388, 389, 429, 432, 440–7, 449, 450
information
   accounting disclosure 94, 95, 137, 399–405
   financial 221
   obtaining 182
   operating 221
   management 223
   minimum 420
   statutory 412
insolvency 14
   practitioner 14
insolvent 157
Institute of Chartered Accountants in England and Wales (ICAEW) 14, 15, 19
Institute of Chartered Accountants in Ireland (ICAI) 14, 15, 16, 19
Institute of Chartered Accountants of Scotland (ICAS) 14, 15, 19
integral system 223
interest 385
interlocking system 223
International Accounting Standards Committee (IASC) 448

interpretation 205–6
investment 168, 170
   capital 205, 372–92
   return 163
issues, current financial reporting 429, 437–49, 450
items, trading 28

Japan 311, 313
Joint Stock Companies Act 1856, 135
journalist 181
just-in-time 248, 313–14, 316

labour 112, 231
   direct 113, 121, 248–50, 346
last-in, first-out (LIFO) 241–2, 247, 248, 250–1
leasing 389, 390, 391
ledger 45
legacy 390, 391
lender 7
level of activity 271
liability 12
limited liability 134–5
   Act 1855 134–5
liquidation 14
liquidity 157, 158, 159
loan 73, 136–7
   debenture 137
   partnership 134
      interest on 134
loss
   abnormal 306
   net 75
   normal 305–6

management 9, 13, 138, 181, 205
   activity based 312
   external 391
   financial 13, 19, 221, 222
   internal 391
   total quality (TQM) 314, 316
   quality 314
manager 4, 5, 6, 7, 9, 391
manufacture 111
manufacturing 16–17, 19
market 205
   researchers 10
material 29, 112, 113, 121, 238, 239–48, 250, 251
   component 239
   consumed 113
   direct 346
   promotional 403
   raw 111, 113, 239
measures, performance 343, 347–50
meeting, general 139
method
   direct, of preparing cash flow
      statements 169, 170

indirect, of preparing cash flow
   statements 169, 170
   other pricing 245–6
   pricing, choice of 246–8
   pricing material 239–48, 250, 251
   specific identification 239, 251
Ministers, Council of 447
minute, standard 347
monetary system 4

need 390
non-accountant 3, 7–9, 18–19, 42, 59
note, goods received 244
number, stores requisition 244

objective 32, 223–4, 237, 322
   company 434
   financial 13
office, practising 15
operational analyst 10
organization 3
   manufacturing 26
overhead 256, 273
   administrative 269–70
   fixed 346
   fixed production 225, 231–3, 234, 235
   manufacturing 113
   non-production 233, 268–70, 272, 273
   non-production, absorption methods 269–70
   production 258–65, 282
   production, absorption of 262–5
   research and development 270
   selling and distribution 270
   total manufacturing incurred 113
   variable 346
over-trading 158
owner 5, 6, 7, 19

Pacioli 4, 5
part, component 239
partnership 17, 18, 19, 131–4, 137, 139, 147
   accounts 132–4
   loan 134
   management 131–2
Partnership Act 1890 18, 132
pay-as-you-earn (PAYE) 435
payback 375–7, 383, 391
   discounted 377–80, 391
plan 6, 12, 13, 224, 345–6
   strategic 221, 224
   tactical 224
planning 220, 221, 223, 224, 256
point, break-even 280
postulate 23
prepayment 28–9, 86–7, 94, 95, 161, 162
price 346, 350
   selling 268
pricing

material 301
   transfer 448
principle 23, 30
procedure 23
   double-entry 112
proces, budgeting 372, 390
product 308
   joint 308
profession, accountancy 434, 438, 440, 443
profit 5, 10, 12, 71, 140, 147, 187, 205, 221, 359, 380, 382, 391
   accounting 158–9
   attributable 304
   estimating accounting 93–5
   gross 75
   making entity 25
   measurement 72–4
   net 75
      before interest and taxation 187
      after taxation 187
      after taxation and preference dividend 187
      before taxation 187
   operating 161, 163, 187
   retained 389
public 7, 13
   general 181
purchases 28, 47

qualification, accountancy 15
quantity 346, 350

rates
   business 229
   historical 270
   local 435
   pre-determined 270–2
ratio 182, 184–6
   accounting 207
   acid test 189, 190–91, 208
   capacity 349
   capital gearing 195–7, 207, 209
   current assets 189, 190, 208
   dividend cover 194–5, 209
   dividend yield 194, 209
   earning per share 195, 209
   efficiency 191–4, 208–9
   efficiency (in standard costing) 348
   fixed assets turnover 192, 208
   gross profit 188, 208
   investment ratios 194–8, 208
   liquidity 189–91, 208
   mark-up 188–9, 208
   net profit 189, 208
   price/earnings (P/E) 195, 209
   production volume 349
   profitability 186–9, 208
   profit/volume (P/V) 286
   quick 190
   return on capital employed (ROCE) 186–8, 195, 207, 208

stock turnover 191–2, 208
trade creditor payment period 193–4, 209
trade debtor collection period 192–3, 209
receiver 14
record, cost accounting 282
recording, accounting information 41–60
relations, industrial 205
report 4
  annual 137, 182, 399–450
  auditors 403, 404, 406, 409–11, 412
  cash 26
  chairman 403, 406, 407–8, 411, 434, 435
  common supplementary 430–3
  contents 403–4
  directors 403, 404, 406, 408–9, 411, 412
  employee 433, 434, 450
  employment 433, 434–5, 449, 450
  interim 429, 430–1, 449
  minimum 414
  principal 406–12
  specialist 403
  statutory 407, 408, 412
  Stock Exchange 414
  supplementary 403–4
    financial 428–50
    less common 433–7
  system 4
reporting
  external 222
  internal 222
  segmental 434
requirement
  legal 9, 19, 135, 147
  professional 400–1, 404, 407, 414
retail price index (RPI) 183
return
  accounting rate of 380–3, 391
  internal rate of 383, 385–8, 391
revenue 94, 95
rules
  accounting 19, 22–36, 41, 72, 157
  boundary 24, 25–7, 33, 36
  conservatism 31
  consistency 24, 31, 33, 36
  dual aspect 24, 29, 33, 36, 41, 42–5
  entity 24, 25, 33, 36, 449
  ethical 24, 30–2, 33, 36
  going concern 24, 26, 33, 36
  historic cost 24, 27, 33, 36
  matching 24, 28–9, 30, 33, 36, 73
  materiality 24, 29–30, 33, 36
  measurement 24, 27–30, 33, 36
  money measurement 24, 27, 33, 36
  objectivity 24, 31, 33, 36
  periodicity 24, 25–6, 33, 36, 431

prudence 24, 31–2, 33, 36, 74, 304
  quantitative 24, 26–7, 33, 36
  realization 24, 27–8, 33, 36, 73
  relevance 24, 32, 33, 36

sales 205
school
  current purchasing power 443–4, 447
  current value 443, 444–7
secondary bodies 15–16, 19
sector
  manufacturing 19, 206
  public 13
  service 19, 206
Service, National Health 311
servicing 16–17
share 389, 391
  cumulative 136
  fully paid 136
  issued 136
  ordinary 136, 389
  preference 136, 389
shareholder 11, 138–9, 181
  company 222
sheet, balance see balance sheet
Society of Company and Commercial Accountants 15
sole trader 17–18, 51, 131, 132, 134, 137
solicitor 13, 15, 131
standard 343
  attainable 345
  basic cost 345
  Financial Reporting see Financial Reporting Standard
  ideal 345
statements
  accounting 180
  basic financial 71–95, 121
  basic financial, summary 111
  basic financial, cash flow 157–70
  budgeted cash flow 321, 326
  cash flow 157–70, 403, 405, 413, 414, 423, 425, 426
  corporate objectives 433, 434, 450
  disaggregated 433, 434
  financial accounting 26
  future prospects 433, 435, 450
  group-flow 164, 423–25
  internal financial 414
  of standard accounting practice (SSAPs) 23, 32, 400–1, 403, 448
    SSAP 9: Stocks and long-term contracts 282, 304
    SSAP 16: Current cost accounting 444, 445, 446, 447
    SSAP 22: Accounting for goodwill 440
    SSAP 25: Segmental reporting 434
  main financial 403, 413–26
  money exchanges with government 433, 435, 450

operating 363–5
  published financial 414
  statistical summaries 430, 431–2, 449
  summarized financial (SFSs) 430, 432–3
  transactions in foreign currency 433, 435, 450
  value added 433, 435, 437, 449, 450
stock 162
  adjustment 80–2, 95
  exchange 136, 137, 403, 407, 414, 429, 430, 434, 438, 440
structure,
  group 164
  organizational 225, 226–9, 234, 235, 237
subsidiary 415
system
  accounting 4, 12
  coding 225, 229, 230, 234, 235
  cost accounting 121, 280
  documentary 4
  double-entry 111, 121
  integral 223
  interlocking 223
  ledger 232
  management accounting 13, 121, 280, 302
  monetary 4
  non-monetary 4
  product costing 225, 230–1, 234, 235, 280, 301–11, 316
  recording 5
  reporting 4

tax 13–14, 26, 137, 140, 147, 389
  advance corporation (ACT) 139–40, 147
  avoidance 13
  corporation 139, 147
  corporation, mainstream 140
  council 390
  demands 26
  evasion 13
taxation 13, 14, 15, 19, 32, 139–40, 163, 388–9, 448
  corporation 435
  local authority 229
techniques, accounting 17
trade 17
trader, sole 17–18, 19, 131, 132, 137, 139
translation, foreign currency 448
trial balance 55–9, 60, 71, 74, 79
  errors 58–9
true and fair 32

undertaking
  group 415
  participating company interest in 415

unions
  economic (EU) 390, 447
  trade 181
unit 301
  costing 301
  strategic business 228
users, external 10

valuations, stock 268–9
value
  added tax (VAT) 435
  current 444
  market, of goods produced 114
  net present 383–5, 391
  present 378
variance 271, 272, 343

direct labour efficiency 352, 366
direct labour rate 352, 366
direct material expenditure 352, 366
direct material usage 352, 366
exceptional 365
fixed production overhead capacity 353
fixed production overhead expenditure 353, 366
fixed production overhead productivity 353
fixed production overhead volume 353, 366
profit 360–1, 366
sales 347, 359–65
sales volume 360–1, 366

sales volume contribution 360–2, 366
selling price 360–1, 366
variable production overhead efficiency 353, 366
variable production overhead expenditure 353, 366
Venice 4
view, true and fair 401, 411

work-in-process 306–7
work-in-progress 113, 422
works 113, 226, 227
world
  accounting 438
  War, First 223
  War, Second 223